W9-DDL-465

WHERE
WOMEN
STAND

An International Report
on the Status of Women
in 140 Countries
1997–1998

NAOMI NEFT and
ANN D. LEVINE

RANDOM HOUSE
NEW YORK

To our families,

especially our husbands,

for their enthusiastic support,

encouragement,

and patience.

*Where Women Stand: An International Report on the Status of Women
in 140 Countries 1997–1998*

Copyright © 1997 by Naomi Neft and Ann D. Levine

Library of Congress Cataloging-in-Publication Data
Neft, Naomi.
    Where women stand : an international report on the status of women
in 140 countries, 1997–1998 / by Naomi Neft and Ann D. Levine.
      p.   cm.
    Includes bibliographical references and index.
    ISBN 0-679-78015-7
      1. Women—Social conditions. 2. Women—Economic conditions.
    3. Women's rights—Cross cultural studies. I. Levine, Ann D.
    II. Title.
    HQ1154.N39 1997
    305.42—dc21   97-1728
                                                                  CIP

Typeset and printed in the United States of America.

Visit the Random House Web site at http://www.randomhouse.com/

First Edition
0 9 8 7 6 5 4 3 2 1
ISBN 0-679-78015-7

New York Toronto London Sydney Auckland

Contents

Foreword   vii
Acknowledgments   viii

WOMEN IN TODAY'S WORLD   1

Global Gender Gaps   1
Where Today's Women Live   6
Women's Rights   8
Women in Politics   19
For Additional Information   27

WOMEN'S EDUCATION   28

Literacy   29
Education   32
For Additional Information   47

WOMEN'S EMPLOYMENT 48

Women's Share of the Work Force	50
Women's Participation in the Work Force	54
Discrimination in the Workplace	54
Areas of Employment	62
Pay Differences	70
Working Hours	71
Maternity Leave and Benefits	74
Child Care	74
Unemployment	75
For Additional Information	81

MARRIAGE AND DIVORCE 83

Marriage	86
Divorce	98
For Additional Information	101

FAMILY PLANNING 102

Fertility Rates	102
Contraception	109
Abortion	121
For Additional Information	127

WOMEN'S HEALTH 128

Life Expectancy	129
Maternal Mortality	136
Leading Causes of Death	142
Women and AIDS	143
For Additional Information	150

VIOLENCE AGAINST WOMEN 151

Domestic Violence	153
Rape	156
Prostitution	160
Female Genital Mutilation	162
For Additional Information	164

COUNTRY PROFILES 165

Argentina	166
Australia	177
Bangladesh	192
Brazil	210
Canada	221
China	236
Egypt	252
France	267
Germany	281
India	295
Israel	310
Italy	325
Japan	338
Mexico	353
Nigeria	363
Philippines	374
Russia	387
South Africa	400
Sweden	414
United Kingdom	428
United States	443

COUNTRY TABLES 481

Population
    Total population and sex ratios
       (women per 100 men)   482

Women in Politics
Women in national legislatures, cabinets
Year of women's voting rights 485
Women's Education
Literacy rates: women's and men's
Female enrollment in primary, secondary,
and higher education 488
Women's Employment
Women's share of the workforce
Labor force participation rate: women's
and men's 492
Employment: Occupational Groups
Women per 100 men 495
Marriage and Divorce
Average age at first marriage: women
and men
Births to unmarried women 499
Family Planning
Fertility rate
Contraceptive use
Births to teens
Abortion policies 502
Women's Health
Life expectancy: women and men
Maternal mortality
Lifetime chances of dying from
pregnancy-related causes 506

Significant Signposts on the Road to Equality 510
Glossary 519
Bibliography 522
Index 530

Foreword

The 20th century has delivered dizzying progress for women in many countries. Only 100 years ago, women in the United States had a life expectancy of 48 years. They could not vote, most higher educational institutions excluded them, and opportunities for work outside the home were limited. Ending the 20th century, American women have a life expectancy of almost 80 years, they have flown in space, are winning gold medals in the Olympics, are serving in the military, and are recognized leaders almost everywhere in government and industry except the White House. But we know that this commendable record of advancement is still marred by domestic violence and abuse, unequal pay scales, and many vestiges of the old order. Although full equity and equality have not occurred, there's no denying that serious progress has been made.

Unfortunately, in many other countries, women have not had the chance to prosper as well. This book reminds us not to forget them. *Where Women Stand* does an outstanding job of giving us the information we need to work effectively toward a better future for all of us.

Onward!

Pat Schroeder
Former Congresswoman
Princeton, New Jersey

Acknowledgments

The compilation of *Where Women Stand: An International Report on the Status of Women in 140 Countries 1997–1998* required an enormous number of sources. Much of the statistical information was obtained from the United Nations and its affiliated organizations. Especially valuable were recent editions of the *Demographic Yearbook* and the *Statistical Yearbook,* along with many of the journals, data sheets, and other publications of the World Health Organization, the International Labor Organization, the United Nations Development Program, the United Nations Children's Fund, the United Nations Development Fund for Women, the United Nations International Research and Training Institute for the Advancement of Women, and the United Nations Population Fund. Also extremely helpful were the individual national and status reports submitted by member nations to the Division for the Advancement of Women and the Committee for the Elimination of Discrimination Against Women.

The World Bank, the Population Reference Bureau, the Alan Guttmacher Institute, the Population Council, and the International Women's Tribune Centre were also valuable resources, as were the U.S. Department of Labor, the U.S. Department of State, the U.S. Department of the Army, the North Atlantic Treaty Organization, Population Action International, Human Rights Watch, the European Parliament and the Inter-Parliamentary Union. The

International Olympic Committee, the U.S. Olympic Committee, and the Atlanta Committee for the Olympic Games also provided significant data. The New York City Public Library proved an especially useful resource, as did the New York Medical Society Library and the New York Society Library. A large number of professional journals, newspapers, and periodicals were also helpful.

For information on women in the United States, the U.S. Bureau of the Census and the U.S. Centers for Disease Control were particularly helpful, as were the American Society for Reproductive Medicine, the Center for Research on Women and Politics of the Eagleton Institute of Politics at Rutgers University, the Lamda Legal Defense Fund, and the National Victim Center.

We would also like to acknowledge the assistance of many individual national representatives and agencies in providing a wealth of information concerning the status of women in their countries:

Permanent Missions to the United Nations:

Argentina	Greece	Poland
Australia	Haiti	Portugal
Austria	Hungary	Russia
Bangladesh	Indonesia	Sierra Leone
Belgium	Iran	South Africa
Brazil	Iraq	South Korea
China	Ireland	Sri Lanka
Denmark	Israel	Sudan
Egypt	Italy	Sweden
Ethiopia	Japan	Turkey
Finland	Mexico	United Kingdom
France	Netherlands	Yugoslavia
Germany	Norway	Zimbabwe

Embassies:

Argentina	India	South Africa
Bangladesh	Italy	Sudan
Brazil	Japan	Sweden
Chile	Philippines	Yugoslavia
China	Romania	
Greece	Russia	

Consulates General:

Argentina	Brazil	Chile
Australia	Canada	China

Egypt	Italy	Philippines
France	Japan	Romania
Germany	Mexico	South Africa
India	New Zealand	Spain
Israel	Nigeria	Sweden

Ministries and Other Government Agencies:

Ministry of Health, Brazil

Chinese Information and Cultural Center, New York

Ministry of Women's Affairs and Social Development, Nigeria

Sex Equality Branch, United Kingdom Department of Education and Employment

A dedicated team of hardworking researchers contributed much of the information for the individual country profiles:

Danielle Cione	Melvin Maskin	David Reiss
Cassie Ehrenberg	Maureen McSherry	Peter Rider
Jesse Goichman	Michael Neft	Lori Rothstein
Danielle Levine	Marsha Pauker	Melissa Waiser

Cynthia Levine and Debbie Neft also provided skilled research assistance, and we owe a very special thanks to Ida Silver for her many hours on the telephone tracking down those elusive details. We are also greatly indebted to Ann and Lonnie Morin for their expert tutelage in the art of manuscript preparation.

We want to express our deep appreciation to Robert Markel, our literary agent, for his inspiration, confidence, and patience. We also owe a great debt of gratitude to David Neft for his expertise in statistics, and to David Levine for guiding us through the world of computer technology. Special thanks also to Deborah Fogel for a superb editing job.

A number of people also gave us valuable information, assistance, and advice: Mona Angel, formerly of the Committee for the Elimination of Discrimination Against Women; Janice Ballou, Eagleton Institute of Politics, Rutgers University; Gene Bovis, U.S. State Department; Richard Gelles, director, Family Violence Research Program, University of Rhode Island; Marilyn Greene, *USA Today;* Daniel Kolaj, United Nations Public Inquiry Office; Larry Lancaster, Fox Sports; John Macisco, Jr., Fordham University; Melvin Maskin, Bronx High School of Science; Kathy Townsend, Office of the Status of Women, Australia; and Siddhida Trevedi, of Bombay, India.

Cynthia Rothstein is a special friend who inspired us with her unflagging support, enthusiasm, and good humor. Additional thanks to Deena Cloud, Barbara Feinberg, Cornelia Szekely, and Janett Velez for their assistance and advice.

WOMEN IN TODAY'S WORLD

Women throughout the world today live longer, healthier lives, are better educated, enjoy more job opportunities, and earn higher salaries than ever before. In many countries around the globe there are more women than men in college and more women than ever in top-level leadership roles, both in business and in public life. The past several decades have witnessed tremendous improvements in women's literacy, longevity, education and employment opportunities, and general standard of living. And as women's lives have gotten better, their families have become better educated, better nourished, healthier, and more productive. Where women thrive, communities and nations thrive.

GLOBAL GENDER GAPS

Yet progress has not always been even, and some parts of the world have suffered recent reversals. There are many places in the world where women's average life expectancy is less than 50 years and where the great majority of women can neither read nor write. And in country after country, women constitute the majority of the poor, accounting for more than 70% of the world's 1.3 billion people living in poverty.

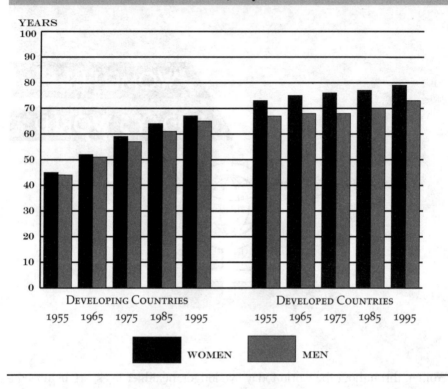

LIFE EXPECTANCY RATES, 1955–1995
At birth, in years

Despite having made many great strides in attaining women's rights and improving their lives, all too often girls and women find that their access to education, employment, health care, political influence, and sometimes even food or life itself is limited solely because of their gender. In some parts of the world, it is not uncommon for a fetus to be aborted or a baby killed for no other reason than because she is female. Around the world, millions of women live in societies where centuries-old social and religious laws, customs, and traditions have created insurmountable barriers to education, jobs, and health care, as well as depriving women of most of their political and civil rights. And where women have limited access to schooling, health care, and economic opportunities, their families tend to be larger, poorer, less educated, and debilitated by malnutrition and disease.

Although Female Enrollment in School Is Higher Than Ever and Literacy Rates Are Rising:

▲ Women make up nearly two-thirds of the world's 960 million illiterates.

WOMEN'S SHARE OF THE LABOR FORCE, 1955–1995
Women's and men's percentages of total labor force

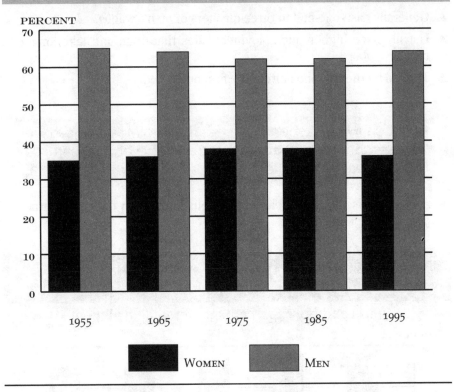

▲ In primary school, enrollment rates for girls are about equal to boys', yet girls' dropout rates are higher and girls account for two-thirds of the 100 million children who drop out of primary school in the first four years.

▲ Female students are still enrolled mostly in the courses traditionally regarded as suitable for women: home economics, humanities, education, and the arts.

▲ Women teachers predominate in preschools and primary schools, are a minority in colleges and universities, and rarely attain the rank of full professor.

Although More Women Than Ever Are Working Outside the Home and Make up One-Third of the World's Labor Force, They:

▲ Are concentrated in the least skilled and the lowest paying jobs.

▲ Occupy less than 6% of top management positions.

▲ Work overwhelmingly more in part-time jobs than men and are thus often not eligible for maternity, health insurance, and other benefits.

▲ Generally earn one-half to three-quarters of men's wages.

▲ Usually have higher unemployment rates than men and take longer to find new jobs.

▲ Tend to be the last ones hired, the first ones fired.

Although Most Women Have the Right to Marry Whom They Choose and Have Legal Access to Divorce and Inheritance Rights, There Are Still Parts of the World Where:

▲ A husband is the legal head of the household, with complete authority over his wife and children.

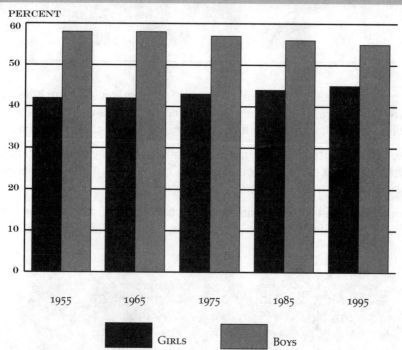

PRIMARY AND SECONDARY SCHOOL ENROLLMENT, 1955–1995

Girls and boys, percentage of total enrollment

PERCENT

1955   1965   1975   1985   1995

GIRLS   BOYS

▲ A married woman cannot work, obtain a passport, buy or sell property, secure a bank loan, or open a bank account without her husband's permission.

▲ A widow is entitled to only a small fraction of her husband's estate, and customary law may even award the entire estate to the husband's family, leaving her destitute.

▲ Adultery is defined differently for women and men (a woman may be guilty if she has been unfaithful only once, a man only if he keeps a mistress).

Although Women Throughout the World Are Healthier Than Ever and Their Life Expectancy Rates Are Rising:

▲ There are 17 countries where women's average life expectancy is less than 50 years.

▲ In some countries, particularly where sons are favored over daughters, it is not unusual for baby girls to die of neglect or even to be killed by their parents.

▲ Over half a million women around the world die from pregnancy-related causes every year, while another 15 million suffer serious long-term complications.

▲ 70,000 to 200,000 women, including teenage girls, die every year as a result of unsafe, illegal abortions.

▲ Women now account for nearly half of all new cases of HIV infection.

Although Many Countries Have Enacted Laws Specifically Aimed at Prohibiting Acts of Violence Against Women:

▲ In some societies, physical abuse of wives is an accepted part of marriage.

▲ In most countries, marital rape is not considered a crime.

▲ The great majority of rapes and other assaults are never reported, let alone prosecuted, and when convictions do occur, sentences are often light.

▲ In some Islamic countries, women are beaten and sometimes even killed for not wearing the traditional Muslim head covering.

▲ In war-torn countries around the globe, thousands of women and girls are victims of mass rape and torture.

Although Women Make Up About Half the World's Electorate:

▲ Only five countries, all in Europe, have national legislatures with 30% or more female members.

▲ Sweden is the only country with more women than men in its cabinet.

▲ Only five countries currently have women leaders.

▲ There is still one country—Kuwait—where only men can vote.

WHERE TODAY'S WOMEN LIVE

There are slightly more than 2.8 billion females in the world today, and about half of them live in just six countries: China, India, the United States, Indonesia, Brazil, and Russia. Women constitute just under half the global population—there are 98.6 females for every 100 males.

While women outlive men almost everywhere, there are 39 countries where males outnumber females. Countries with larger female populations tend to be the developed ones, such as Canada, the United States, and many European nations, where people live longer and more women than men survive to old age.

The relatively few countries where men outnumber women tend to be those where life expectancy for both sexes is fairly short. Nature dictates that more boys are born than girls—about 105 boys for every 100 girls—but because survival rates are usually greater for girls, females generally soon equal and eventually outnumber the males. Thus, countries where overall life expectancy is short—such as Afghanistan, Bangladesh, China, India, Pakistan,

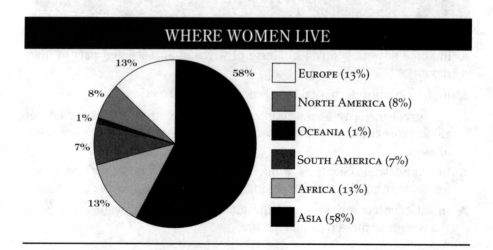

WHERE WOMEN LIVE

- 13%
- 8%
- 1%
- 7%
- 13%
- 58%

☐ EUROPE (13%)

▨ NORTH AMERICA (8%)

■ OCEANIA (1%)

▨ SOUTH AMERICA (7%)

▨ AFRICA (13%)

■ ASIA (58%)

SEX RATIOS WORLDWIDE
Number of females per 100 males

FEMALES	COUNTRY	FEMALES	COUNTRY
117	Ukraine	102	Argentina
114	Belarus	102	Benin
114	Latvia	102	Bolivia
113	Russia	102	Burkina Faso
112	Estonia	102	Chile
111	Georgia	102	Colombia
111	Lithuania	102	Denmark
110	Moldova	102	Israel
108	Cambodia	102	Madagascar
107	Austria	102	Malawi
107	Hungary	102	Mauritania
107	Portugal	102	Mozambique
106	Central African Republic	102	Netherlands
106	Croatia	102	New Zealand
106	Czech Republic	102	Niger
106	Finland	102	Nigeria
106	Germany	102	Norway
106	Italy	102	Romania
106	Kazakhstan	102	Rwanda
106	Slovenia	102	Somalia
105	Azerbaijan	102	Tanzania
105	France	102	Thailand
105	Kyrgyzstan	102	Togo
105	Lebanon	102	Trinidad and Tobago
105	Nicaragua	102	Uzbekistan
105	Poland	102	Yemen
105	Puerto Rico	102	Yugoslavia
105	United States	102	Zaire
105	Uruguay	102	Zambia
104	Armenia	101	Bosnia-Herzegovina
104	Belgium	101	Brazil
104	Bulgaria	101	Cameroon
104	Burundi	101	Ghana
104	Congo	101	Indonesia
104	El Salvador	101	Mexico
104	Haiti	101	Myanmar
104	Slovakia	101	South Africa
104	Switzerland	101	Sri Lanka
104	United Kingdom	101	Tajikistan
103	Angola	101	Uganda
103	Canada	101	Zimbabwe
103	Chad	100	Algeria
103	Greece	100	Australia
103	Japan	100	Ethiopia
103	Korea, North	100	Ireland
103	Laos	100	Jamaica
103	Mali	100	Kenya
103	Sierra Leone	100	Morocco
103	Spain	100	Senegal
103	Sweden	99	Cuba
103	Turkmenistan	99	Ecuador
103	Vietnam	99	Eritrea

(continued)

SEX RATIOS WORLDWIDE *(cont.)* Number of females per 100 males			
FEMALES	**COUNTRY**	**FEMALES**	**COUNTRY**
99	Guinea	97	Kuwait
99	Peru	97	Panama
99	Sudan	97	Philippines
99	Venezuela	97	Singapore
98	Costa Rica	96	Iraq
98	Guatemala	96	Turkey
98	Honduras	95	Afghanistan
98	Korea, South	95	Albania
98	Liberia	95	China
98	Macedonia	95	Jordan
98	Malaysia	95	Nepal
98	Paraguay	94	Bangladesh
98	Syria	94	Taiwan
98	Tunisia	93	India
97	Dominican Republic	92	Libya
97	Egypt	92	Pakistan
97	Iran	81	Saudi Arabia
97	Ivory Coast	52	United Arab Emirates

and many Middle Eastern countries—have larger male populations. (In some oil-producing countries of the Middle East, such as Saudi Arabia and the United Arab Emirates, the sex ratio is further affected by the large numbers of male immigrant workers.) And in those countries that also favor sons over daughters, this natural sex imbalance is skewed even further by the abortion of a disproportionate number of female fetuses and higher death rates among female infants and young girls. Among the countries with such "missing" girls are Bangladesh, China, India, Pakistan, and to a lesser extent Egypt, Nepal, South Korea, and Turkey.

WOMEN'S RIGHTS

Throughout history there has never been a time or place where women enjoyed complete equality with men. Since ancient times women have been considered men's inferiors—physically, morally, and intellectually. In most parts of the world women have traditionally been considered men's property, to be handed over from fathers to husbands. Over the years laws and customs concerning women's rights have been shaped by a variety of Greek, Roman, and other ancient legal systems, as well as by Christian, Jewish, Hindu, Islamic, and other religious laws and traditions.

Women in the Ancient World

In most ancient societies women were considered legal minors, under the

SEX RATIOS BY REGION
Number of females per 100 males

FEMALES	COUNTRY	FEMALES	COUNTRY
101	**Africa**	103	Korea, North
	(average of countries)	103	Laos
106	Central African Republic	103	Turkmenistan
104	Burundi	103	Vietnam
104	Congo	102	Israel
103	Angola	102	Thailand
103	Chad	102	Uzbekistan
103	Mali	102	Yemen
103	Sierra Leone	101	Indonesia
102	Benin	101	Myanmar
102	Burkina Faso	101	Sri Lanka
102	Madagascar	101	Tajikistan
102	Malawi	98	Malaysia
102	Mauritania	98	Syria
102	Mozambique	97	Iran
102	Niger	97	Kuwait
102	Nigeria	97	Philippines
102	Rwanda	97	Singapore
102	Somalia	96	Iraq
102	Tanzania	96	Turkey
102	Togo	95	Afghanistan
102	Zaire	95	China
102	Zambia	95	Jordan
101	Cameroon	95	Nepal
101	Ghana	94	Bangladesh
101	South Africa	94	Taiwan
101	Uganda	93	India
101	Zimbabwe	92	Pakistan
100	Algeria	81	Saudi Arabia
100	Ethiopia	52	United Arab Emirates
100	Kenya		
100	Morocco	**105**	**Europe**
100	Senegal		**(average of countries)**
99	Eritrea	117	Ukraine
99	Guinea	114	Belarus
99	Sudan	114	Latvia
98	Liberia	113	Russia
98	Tunisia	112	Estonia
97	Egypt	111	Lithuania
97	Ivory Coast	110	Moldova
92	Libya	107	Austria
		107	Hungary
98	**Asia**	107	Portugal
	(average of countries)	106	Croatia
111	Georgia	106	Czech Republic
108	Cambodia	106	Finland
106	Kazakhstan	106	Germany
105	Azerbaijan	106	Italy
105	Kyrgyzstan	106	Slovenia
105	Lebanon	105	France
104	Armenia	105	Poland
103	Japan	104	Belgium

(continued)

SEX RATIOS BY REGION *(cont.)*
Number of females per 100 males

FEMALES	COUNTRY	FEMALES	COUNTRY
104	Bulgaria	101	Mexico
104	Slovakia	100	Jamaica
104	Switzerland	99	Cuba
104	United Kingdom	99	Costa Rica
103	Greece	99	Guatemala
103	Spain	99	Honduras
103	Sweden	97	Dominican Republic
102	Denmark	97	Panama
102	Netherlands		
102	Norway	**101**	**Oceania**
102	Romania		**(average of countries)**
102	Yugoslavia	102	New Zealand
101	Bosnia-Herzegovina	100	Australia
100	Ireland		
98	Macedonia	**101**	**South America**
95	Albania		**(average of countries)**
		105	Uruguay
101	**North America**	102	Argentina
	(average of countries)	102	Bolivia
105	Nicaragua	102	Chile
105	Puerto Rico	102	Colombia
105	United States	101	Brazil
104	El Salvador	99	Ecuador
104	Haiti	99	Peru
103	Canada	99	Venezuela
102	Trinidad and Tobago	98	Paraguay

control of either their fathers or husbands. They were seldom allowed to own property or manage their own finances. Yet the earliest known code of law, the 18th-century B.C. Babylonian Code of Hammurabi, afforded women some measure of economic independence. They were entitled to dowries, could pass land and other possessions down to their children, and shared equal authority with their husbands over their children. In ancient Egypt women were considered equal to their husbands in law and business, and they could dispose of their own property.

Throughout most of ancient Greece and Rome, women enjoyed very few rights. Marriages were arranged; usually the bride was in her early teens and the groom was 15 years or more her senior. A wife had no control over her property or children, and if the family produced no male heirs, an adult male might be adopted to marry one of the daughters. The Greek colony of Sparta was the exception: women enjoyed great freedom, and girls were entitled to the same education as boys.

In ancient China the yin and yang philosophy of nature reinforced the notion of women's inferiority; the yang (male) principle always dominated the yin (female). China also devised one of the most repressive and painful customs for women—foot binding—which arose in the 10th century. Limited at first to the wealthy upper class, by the 14th century the practice had become widespread. A young girl, between the ages of four and seven, would have all four little toes bent under and bound to make her foot narrower. At the same time, her big toe was pulled toward the heel so that the arch rose and broke, ideally shortening the foot to about three inches. Only the heel could bear any weight, and she could not walk unassisted. For the rest of her life she was generally confined to her chambers, totally dependent on family and servants.

Under ancient Hebrew law a woman could inherit property, but her contracts could be invalidated by her father or husband. If a widow had no children, she was required to marry her husband's brother to continue the dead husband's lineage. In both Hebrew and Islamic law, polygamy was allowed and divorce was legal, but according to Islam, divorce was the sole prerogative of the husband. In Jewish law, a woman could not be divorced against her will, but neither could she obtain a divorce decree without her husband's consent. Islamic women were expected to remain secluded in the home, and when going out had to covered from head to toe.

Among some North American Indian tribes, too, a girl was kept secluded in the company of other females, rarely seeing even her brothers, and it was not unusual for a man to have more than one wife. Among the Aztecs of ancient Mexico, daughters could inherit their parents' property, and women gained honor and respect by bearing children. A woman who died in childbirth was revered as a goddess.

Although Christian doctrine preached equality of all souls before God, it held that women were inferior to men and taught women to be obedient to their husbands. According to the Hindu laws of Manu, women were subservient to all male relatives. Only a husband could initiate a divorce, and disobedience was just cause. In addition, a widow could not remarry, and the law sanctioned *sati,* the burning alive of a widow on her husband's funeral pyre.

Women in the Middle Ages

Over the centuries, as traditional patriarchal customs and laws became more deeply entrenched, women's lives became more restricted and their rights more limited. During the Middle Ages most women were still denied an education, and their lives generally revolved around managing their homes and caring for their families. Women in rural areas often worked alongside their husbands in the fields, while those in towns and cities sometimes assisted their husbands in a trade or craft.

Beginning in the 15th century, women in Europe slowly started gaining some rights and freedoms. During the Renaissance, learning was considered a virtue, and many girls as well as boys were taught to read. The invention of the printing press in Germany in the mid-15th century, made books and other printed materials readily available, and the burgeoning Protestant sects encouraged women to read the Bible and conduct religious services at home. However, church leaders were still preaching that the subjugation of women was God's law and that because women were weaker than men, they were subject to male control. In 1533 the Protestant Reformation leader Martin Luther explained, "Girls begin to talk and to stand on their feet sooner than boys because weeds always grow up more quickly than good crops."

Emergence of Modern Feminism

By the 17th century a few women had started speaking out for women's rights, especially for educational opportunities, but it was not until the 18th century that the seeds of modern feminism were sown. With the intellectual movement known as the Enlightenment came many democratic ideas and values, including the rights of the individual. Yet most women were untouched by the social, political, and economic rights that the Enlightenment conferred on men. Even as feudalism disintegrated as a social system, feudal relations of power persisted in marriage: wives were still regarded as the property of their husbands.

The first major feminist work was Mary Wollstonecraft's *A Vindication of the Rights of Woman,* published in Britain 1792. It argued for increased educational opportunities for women as well as political equality with men. Gradually, women in many countries started to organize to advance their own concerns, which usually included such issues as educational opportunities, the right to work, and laws pertaining to divorce and child custody.

The Struggle to Vote

Over the next two centuries women made tremendous strides toward equality with men. The single most important and most arduous struggle during this period was the fight for women's suffrage, which originated in western Europe and spread, ironically, largely through colonization, around the globe.

In many countries, women attained the right to vote only after years of difficult struggle. In most Western countries, the women's suffrage movement grew out of decades of women's increasing public involvement in social issues, such as the abolition of slavery and the temperance movement. By the mid-1800s many of the women who had been active in these movements started banding together in a campaign for women's rights, especially the right to vote. In Britain and the United States, as the movement for suffrage gained momentum, it sometimes grew militant and even violent.

Despite these efforts, by the dawn of the 20th century only one country had granted its female citizens the right to vote. In 1893 New Zealand granted women equal voting rights with men. It took nearly a decade for the next country to follow suit: in 1902 Australia granted women the right to vote in federal elections, even though some states still barred them from voting in local elections. Finland (1906), Norway (1913), Denmark (1915), and a host of other European countries followed in quick succession.

In 1918 Canada became the first North American country to extend the franchise to women, followed by the United States in 1920. Ecuador, in 1928, was the first South American country to grant women's suffrage, and in 1931 Sri Lanka became the first Asian country to do so, followed by Thailand in 1932. The first African country to grant women the right to vote was Senegal in 1945. Cameroon and Liberia followed in 1946.

Following World War II the process greatly accelerated, and today practically every woman in the world has the right to vote. In only a small handful of countries—Bahrain, Brunei, Kuwait, Oman, Qatar, Saudi Arabia, and United Arab Emirates—are women still denied access to the ballot box. However, it should be noted that in all of these countries except Kuwait, men cannot vote either. And in Kuwait, for many years voting was strictly limited to literate, native-born males whose families had lived in the country since 1920. It was not until the mid-1990s, that the government extended voting rights to naturalized male citizens and their sons. Although a separate law granting women the right to vote was under consideration at the same time, it was never adopted.

In a few countries, including Russia and China, women's suffrage was adopted practically overnight as part of a national revolution that granted equal political rights to women and men. Elsewhere, suffrage was often achieved only after many years of struggle, and sometimes it came in stages. In several countries women were first allowed to vote in local elections, later on a national level. In Chile, for example, women could vote in municipal elections as early as 1931 but had to wait until 1949 to cast their ballots in legislative and presidential elections.

In other countries, voting rights were first limited to certain groups of women, defined by age, education, or other criteria. The United Kingdom, for example, first extended voting rights to women in 1918, but only to women over the age of 30. It was not until 1928 that the franchise was extended to all women over 21, finally giving them complete voting equality with men. In Belgium a 1919 law granted national voting rights to widows or mothers of servicemen and civilians killed during World War I, as well as to women who had been political prisoners. Only in 1948 was the franchise extended to all women. In Portugal a 1931 law gave voting rights to women who had completed secondary or higher education, whereas men were required only to know how to read and write. It was not until 1976 that full equality was achieved. In South Africa voting rights were granted to white women in 1930,

WOMEN'S VOTING RIGHTS*

YEAR	COUNTRY	YEAR	COUNTRY
1893	New Zealand		Senegal
1902	Australia		Slovenia
1906	Finland	1946	Cameroon
1913	Norway		Guatemala
1915	Denmark		Korea, North
1918	Austria		Liberia
	Canada		Macedonia
	Estonia		Panama (1941)
	Georgia		Romania (1929)
	Kyrgyzstan		Taiwan
	Latvia		Trinidad and Tobago
	Poland		Venezuela
	Russia		Vietnam
1919	Belarus	1947	Argentina
	Germany		Bangladesh
	Netherlands		Mexico
	Sweden		Pakistan
	Ukraine		Singapore
1920	Albania	1948	Belgium
	Czech Republic		Israel
	Slovakia		Korea, South
	United States		Niger
1921	Armenia	1949	Bosnia-Herzegovina
	Azerbaijan		China
	Lithuania		Costa Rica
1924	Kazakhstan		Greece
	Tajikistan	1950	Haiti
1927	Turkmenistan		India
1928	Ecuador	1951	Nepal
	Ireland (1918)	1952	Bolivia
	United Kingdom (1918)		Lebanon
1930	Turkey	1953	Syria (1949)
1931	Chile	1954	Ghana
	Spain	1955	Cambodia
	Sri Lanka		Eritrea
1932	Brazil		Ethiopia
	Thailand		Nicaragua
	Uruguay		Peru
1934	Cuba	1956	Benin
1935	Myanmar		Egypt
	Puerto Rico (1929)		Ivory Coast
1937	Philippines		Mali
1938	Uzbekistan		Somalia
1939	El Salvador		Togo
1942	Dominican Republic		Tunisia
1943	Yugoslavia	1957	Colombia
1944	Bulgaria		Honduras
	France		Malaysia
	Jamaica		Zimbabwe
1945	Croatia	1958	Burkina Faso
	Hungary		Chad
	Indonesia		Guinea
	Italy		Laos
	Japan	1959	Madagascar

(continued)

WOMEN'S VOTING RIGHTS* *(cont.)*			
YEAR	COUNTRY	YEAR	COUNTRY
	Morocco	1964	Afghanistan
	Tanzania		Libya
1960	Zaire	1965	Sudan (1953)
1961	Burundi	1970	Yemen (1967)
	Malawi	1971	Switzerland
	Mauritania	1974	Jordan
	Rwanda	1975	Angola
	Sierra Leone		Mozambique
1962	Algeria	1976	Portugal (1931)
	Paraguay	1978	Moldova
	Uganda		Nigeria (1957)
	Zambia	1980	Iraq
1963	Congo	1986	Central African Republic
	Iran	1994	South Africa (1930, 1983)
1963	Kenya (1956)		

* The date given indicates when all adult women won the right to vote in any major election, local or national. An additional date in parentheses indicates when the vote was first granted to a large group of women, but not all.

to Indian and colored women and men in 1983, and to African women and men in 1994.

New Wave of Feminism

In many countries, once suffrage was attained, women's movements began diminishing in strength as well as size, and it was not until the 1960s that a new wave of feminism emerged. By this time several factors—lower infant mortality rates, rising life expectancy, and the introduction of modern contraceptives—had given women more control over their lives and greater freedom from childbearing responsibilities.

At the same time, rising inflation was propelling more women into the labor force, and by 1970 women constituted 40% or more of the work force in more than a dozen developed countries, among them Canada, Denmark, France, the United Kingdom, and the United States. The blatant discrimination these women encountered reinvigorated the older feminist organizations; it also inspired a new generation of women's groups that were concerned largely with women's rights in general and employment discrimination in particular. In the United States and parts of Europe, this resurgence became known as the women's liberation movement, and much attention was given to consciousness raising, that is, making women more aware of their common problems.

Today's Issues

As the feminist movement gained momentum in many countries, it grew stronger, earned greater acceptance, and broadened its scope to encompass a wider range of issues. Today almost every country has a wide array of women's organizations—some dealing with the broad issue of women's rights, others focusing on specific concerns such as abortion, sexual harassment, violence against women, or the problems of immigrant or minority women. In poorer countries women's groups concentrate more on obtaining adequate food and health care; gaining legal rights and educational opportunities; and improving their economic status, for example through gaining easier access to credit.

Although progress on many fronts has been fairly steady over the past several decades, the recent marked growth of religious fundamentalism has begun to pose a serious threat to women's rights in many countries. While fundamentalist movements within Catholicism, evangelical Protestantism, Judaism, and Hinduism have had serious repercussions in some parts of the world, none has had such a far-reaching effect on women as the worldwide resurgence of the various forms of Islamic fundamentalism. One of the most militant and repressive of these movements has taken hold in Afghanistan, where a fundamentalist force known as Taliban has imposed strict Islamic law. Afghani women, who once enjoyed a number of rights and freedoms, are now being forced to observe *purdah,* the practice of keeping women in seclusion and prohibiting them from seeing any men other than their relatives. In public they must be accompanied by a male relative and must always be swathed in the traditional *burqua,* a head-to-toe covering with only a netted opening for the wearer's eyes. In addition, girls can no longer attend school and women may not work outside the home except in hospitals or clinics—and even then only with female patients. By late 1996 the Taliban force had captured over two-thirds of the country. Militant Islamic groups have also emerged in Algeria, Egypt, Iran, Somalia, and Turkey, where they have attacked and even killed women who were not wearing the traditional head covering. They have also closed shelters for battered women and revised schoolbooks to emphasize their interpretation of Islamic teachings, including those aspects that restrict women.

In some of the Eastern European countries that have recently undergone a transition from communism to democracy, a resurgence of the Roman Catholic Church has been a critical factor in curtailing women's access to abortion. In Poland in 1993, the church lobbied successfully to greatly restrict the country's liberal abortion law and keep sex education out of the classroom. Three years later a revised law reinstated sex education and somewhat liberalized the country's abortion rules although it was still far from the abortion-on-demand policy that existed under communism.

Other setbacks for women, especially in the area of employment, are evident in those parts of the world currently suffering drastic economic down-turns. Women are bearing the brunt of these crises, suffering high levels of unemployment coupled with cutbacks in child care and other government services. And in the many war-torn nations of the world, such as Bosnia, Cambodia, Croatia, Liberia, Peru, Rwanda, Somalia, and Uganda, it is estimated that women and children account for about 70% of all civilian fatalities. Whether a conflict is with another country or an internal ethnic, religious, or civil war, women and girls are often prime targets, and those who survive suffer the many devastating effects of armed conflict: torture, mass rape, broken families, and the loss of homes and property.

International Organizations

At the international level, a number of nongovernmental women's groups support research on women's issues and coordinate and disseminate information among women of different countries. These groups include such organizations as Women's Studies International, Human Rights Watch, the International Center for Research on Women, and the International Women's Health Coalition. In recent years the Asia Foundation founded the Asia-Pacific Women in Politics network, which conducts workshops, study groups and training programs aimed at encouraging women to vote, speak out on issues, and become political leaders. Similar efforts are in the planning stages for Latin America, Africa, and the Middle East.

Undoubtedly the single most important international organization concerned with women's issues and committed to promoting equal rights for women throughout the world is the United Nations, which in 1975, launched its Decade for Women program and since then has sponsored four major international women's conferences: Mexico City (1975), Copenhagen (1980), Nairobi (1985), and Beijing (1995). In addition, several U.N. agencies and affiliated organizations are concerned primarily with women's issues: International Research and Training Institute for the Advancement of Women (INSTRAW), the United Nation's Development Fund for Women (UNIFEM), and the United Nation's Division for the Advancement of Women (DAW), which services the Commission on the Status of Women, the main U.N. body responsible for all policies concerning gender issues.

One of the most important ways in which the United Nations has had an impact on the status of women has been through its sponsorship of several major international agreements or conventions. The most recent of these is the Convention on the Elimination of All Forms of Discrimination Against Women (CEDAW), an international bill of rights for women that also includes guidelines for implementing the policies and laws required to guarantee those rights.

WOMEN IN THE UNITED NATIONS

The United Nations Charter, adopted in 1945, was the first international document to prohibit specifically "restrictions on the eligibility of men and women to participate in any capacity" in the United Nations or any of its subsidiary organs. Yet despite this commitment, women are far from equally-represented.

In its 50-year history, the United Nations has never had a woman secretary-general, and only two women have ever been elected to preside over the U.N. General Assembly: India's Vijaya Lakshmi Pandit in 1953, and Liberia's Angie Brooks in 1969. The year 1948 was the first in which a delegation was led by a woman ambassador: Minerva Bernardino from the Dominican Republic. Almost 50 years later, however, only 6 countries were represented by women ambassadors, and approximately 40% of delegations still had no women of professional diplomatic status.

WOMEN AMBASSADORS TO THE UNITED NATIONS (1997)

COUNTRY	AMBASSADOR
Guinea	Mahawa Bangoura Camara
Jamaica	Patricia Durrant
Kazakhstan	Akmaral Kh. Arystanbekova
Liechtenstein	Claudia Fritsche
Trinidad and Tobago	Annette Des Iles
Turkmenistan	Aksoltan T. Ataeve

In 1949 only 4% of all of the delegates to the General Assembly were women. By 1994 this proportion had reached 20%, the largest representations from Latin America and the Caribbean and the smallest from eastern Europe and southern and western Asia and Oceania. Among U.N. professional staff, women make up about 30% of all employees, but they tend to be concentrated in entry-level positions, accounting for less than 15% of senior management.

One of the highest-ranking women in the United Nations today is Carol Bellamy, who was named executive director of the United Nations Children's Fund (UNICEF) in 1996. Other top-level women include Catherine Bertini, who heads the World Food Program (WFP), Elizabeth Dowdeswell, who heads the U.N. Environment Program (UNED), Noeleen Heyzer, director of the U.N. Development Fund for Women (UNIFEM), Sadako Ogata, High Commissioner for Refugees; and Nafis Sadik, executive director of the U.N. Population Fund (UNFPA). The highest-ranking woman in the Secretariat is Rosario Green, who serves as assistant secretary general for political affairs as well as coordinator of all women's issues throughout the entire U.N. system.

CEDAW was adopted by the U.N. General Assembly in 1979 and by the mid-1990s had been ratified or signed by 156 member nations. Upon ratifying the convention, a country makes a commitment to enact legislation and promote policies in accordance with the treaty's conditions. In addition, each country agrees to submit a periodic progress report on the status of women in that country and the way in which the convention is being implemented. By 1996 only a few countries, including Afghanistan, Switzerland, and the United States had not ratified the convention but had simply signed it; about 30 others had ratified it while declaring substantive reservations, some based on religious or customary laws, concerning certain provisions.

WOMEN IN POLITICS

Despite the fact that women make up half or sometimes more than half of the electorates in most countries, there are only a handful of women who serve as heads of states throughout the world and there is not a single country where women enjoy the same political status, access, or influence as men do. In no country do women even come close to constituting half the national legislature or other major elected political body.

Women Political Leaders

The first woman ever elected to lead a country was Sirimavo Bandaranaike, who became prime minister of Sri Lanka (then called Ceylon) in 1960. By 1970 two other countries, India and Israel, were led by women, and in 1988, Benazir Bhutto became the first woman to head a Muslim country when she was elected Pakistan's prime minister. By 1997 five countries were headed by women. One of these women was Sirimavo Bandaranaike, serving her third term as prime minister of Sri Lanka, this time appointed by her daughter, Chandrika Kumaratunga, Sri Lanka's president.

Women in National Legislatures

Overall, the percentage of women in national legislatures has been declining somewhat in recent years, largely because the quotas formerly allotted to women in the former Soviet Union and socialist states of Eastern Europe were abolished when these governments turned to democracy. Elsewhere the proportion of women legislators has been rising. In fact, some countries have adopted quotas to ensure a minimum representation of women.

Five countries—all in Europe—have now crossed the 30% threshold, the minimum proportion of women in national legislatures recommended in 1990

WOMEN POLITICAL LEADERS

NAME	TITLE	COUNTRY	YEARS
Sirimavo Bandaranaike	Prime Minister	Sri Lanka	1960–1965, 1970–1977, 1994–
Indira Gandhi	Prime Minister	India	1966–1977, 1980–1984
Golda Meir	Prime Minister	Israel	1969–1974
Isabel Perón	President	Argentina	1974–1976
Elizabeth Domitien	Prime Minister	Central African Republic	1975–1976
Maria de Lourdes Pintassilgo	Prime Minister	Portugal	1979
Lidia Gueiler	President	Bolivia	1979–1980
Margaret Thatcher	Prime Minister	United Kingdom	1979–1990
Vigdis Finnbogadottir	President	Iceland	1980–
Mary Eugenia Charles	Prime Minister	Dominica	1980–1995
Gro Brundtland	Prime Minister	Norway	1981, 1986–1989, 1990–1996
Milka Planinc	President	Yugoslavia	1982–1986
Agatha Barbara	President	Malta	1982–1987
Maria Liberia-Peters	Prime Minister	Netherlands Antilles	1984–1986, 1988–1994
Corazon Aquino	President	Philippines	1986–1992
Benazir Bhutto	Prime Minister	Pakistan	1988–1990, 1993–1996
Ertha Pascal-Trouillot	President	Haiti	1990
Kazimiera Prunskiene	Prime Minister	Lithuania	1990–1991
Violeta Chamorro	President	Nicaragua	1990–1996
Mary Robinson	President	Ireland	1990–
Edith Cresson	Prime Minister	France	1991–1992
Khaleda Zia	Prime Minister	Bangladesh	1991–1996
Hanna Suchocka	Prime Minister	Poland	1992–1993
Kim Campbell	Prime Minister	Canada	1993
Sylvie Kinigi	Prime Minister	Bolivia	1993
Tansu Ciller	Prime Minister	Turkey	1993–1996
Agathe Uwilingiyimana	Prime Minister	Rwanda	1993–1994
Chandrika Kumaratunga	Prime Minister President	Sri Lanka	1994 1994–
Claudette Werleigh	Prime Minister	Haiti	1995–1996
Hasina Wazed	Prime Minister	Bangladesh	1996–
Ruth Perry	President	Liberia	1996–

Countries with Quota Systems Promoting Women's Representation in National Legislatures Include:

▲ Argentina   ▲ France   ▲ Spain

▲ Austria   ▲ Germany   ▲ Sweden

▲ Bangladesh   ▲ Greece   ▲ Tanzania

▲ Belgium   ▲ Netherlands   ▲ Venezuela

▲ Denmark   ▲ Norway

WOMEN IN NATIONAL LEGISLATURES WORLDWIDE
Percentage of total legislature and cabinet

LEGISLATURE	CABINET	COUNTRY
41%	52%	Sweden
39%	39%	Norway
34%	39%	Finland
33%	35%	Denmark
30%	31%	Netherlands
29%	4%	New Zealand
26%	12%	Germany
25%	5%	Mozambique
25%	11%	South Africa
23%	30%	Austria
23%	12%	Cuba
22%	0%	Argentina
21%	8%	China
21%	4%	Eritrea
20%	4%	Korea, North
19%	23%	Canada
19%	6%	Vietnam
18%	13%	Australia
18%	27%	Spain
18%	14%	Trinidad and Tobago
17%	5%	Rwanda
17%	14%	Switzerland
17%	13%	Tanzania
17%	13%	Uganda
16%	8%	Costa Rica
16%	6%	Nicaragua
15%	7%	Angola
15%	13%	Belgium
15%	0%	Latvia
15%	13%	Slovakia
14%	6%	Bulgaria
14%	13%	Guatemala
14%	12%	Mexico
14%	13%	Slovenia
13%	13%	Ireland
13%	14%	Philippines
13%	6%	Poland
12%	5%	Cameroon
12%	13%	Jamaica
12%	9%	Senegal
11%	10%	Bangladesh
11%	9%	Burundi
11%	8%	El Salvador
11%	0%	Estonia
11%	7%	Honduras
11%	7%	Hungary
11%	5%	Indonesia
11%	0%	Iraq
11%	3%	Kazakhstan
11%	8%	Malaysia
11%	8%	Taiwan
11%	29%	United States

(continued)

WOMEN IN NATIONAL LEGISLATURES WORLDWIDE *(cont.)*
Percentage of total legislature and cabinet

LEGISLATURE	CABINET	COUNTRY
11%	12%	Zimbabwe
10%	18%	Colombia
10%	0%	Czech Republic
10%	38%	Dominican Republic
10%	13%	Ethiopia
10%	6%	Syria
10%	8%	United Kingdom
9%	4%	India
9%	15%	Italy
9%	0%	Laos
9%	14%	Peru
9%	13%	Portugal
8%	10%	Chad
8%	12%	Ghana
8%	6%	Israel
8%	10%	Ivory Coast
8%	0%	Japan
8%	5%	Sierra Leone
7%	0%	Algeria
7%	20%	Benin
7%	5%	Brazil
7%	14%	Chile
7%	4%	Croatia
7%	6%	Georgia
7%	0%	Lithuania
7%	27%	Panama
7%	3%	Russia
7%	4%	Tunisia
7%	9%	Zambia
6%	7%	Albania
6%	0%	Armenia
6%	0%	Bolivia
6%	13%	Burkina Faso
6%	0%	Cambodia
6%	7%	Greece
6%	12%	Kyrgyzstan
6%	17%	Liberia
6%	5%	Madagascar
6%	4%	Malawi
6%	5%	Thailand
6%	8%	Uruguay
6%	7%	Venezuela
6%	4%	Zaire
5%	8%	Belarus
5%	0%	Bosnia-Herzegovina
5%	6%	Ecuador
5%	13%	France
5%	0%	Moldova
5%	0%	Romania
5%	0%	Singapore
5%	21%	Sri Lanka
5%	0%	Turkmenistan

(continued)

WOMEN IN NATIONAL LEGISLATURES WORLDWIDE *(cont.)*
Percentage of total legislature and cabinet

LEGISLATURE	CABINET	COUNTRY
5%	5%	Uzbekistan
4%	8%	Central African Republic
4%	0%	Iran
4%	5%	Kenya
4%	13%	Niger
4%	9%	Paraguay
4%	4%	Ukraine
3%	15%	Haiti
3%	7%	Jordan
3%	5%	Korea, South
3%	10%	Macedonia
3%	25%	Mali
3%	0%	Nepal
3%	13%	Tajikistan
3%	7%	Yugoslavia
2%	15%	Azerbaijan
2%	9%	Egypt
2%	0%	Lebanon
2%	7%	Pakistan
2%	5%	Turkey
1%	14%	Congo
1%	0%	Morocco
1%	5%	Togo
1%	0%	Yemen
0%	15%	Guinea
0%	0%	Kuwait
0%	4%	Mauritania
0%	0%	Somalia

WOMEN IN NATIONAL LEGISLATURES BY REGION
Percentage of total legislature

PERCENT	COUNTRY	PERCENT	COUNTRY
8%	**Africa**	8%	Ghana
	(average of countries)	8%	Ivory Coast
25%	Mozambique	8%	Sierra Leone
25%	South Africa	7%	Algeria
21%	Eritrea	7%	Benin
17%	Rwanda	7%	Tunisia
17%	Tanzania	7%	Zambia
17%	Uganda	6%	Burkina Faso
15%	Angola	6%	Liberia
12%	Cameroon	6%	Madagascar
12%	Senegal	6%	Malawi
11%	Burundi	6%	Zaire
11%	Zimbabwe	4%	Central African Republic
10%	Ethiopia	4%	Kenya
8%	Chad	4%	Niger

(continued)

WOMEN IN NATIONAL LEGISLATURES BY REGION *(cont.)*
Percentage of total legislature

PERCENT	COUNTRY	PERCENT	COUNTRY
4%	Sudan	39%	Norway
3%	Mali	34%	Finland
2%	Egypt	33%	Denmark
1%	Congo	30%	Netherlands
1%	Morocco	26%	Germany
1%	Togo	23%	Austria
0%	Guinea	19%	Spain
0%	Mauritania	17%	Switzerland
0%	Somalia	15%	Belgium
		15%	Latvia
		15%	Slovakia
7%	**Asia**	14%	Bulgaria
	(average of countries)	14%	Slovenia
21%	China	13%	Ireland
20%	Korea, North	13%	Poland
19%	Vietnam	11%	Estonia
13%	Philippines	11%	Hungary
11%	Bangladesh	10%	Czech Republic
11%	Indonesia	10%	United Kingdom
11%	Iraq	9%	Italy
11%	Kazakhstan	9%	Portugal
11%	Malaysia	7%	Croatia
11%	Taiwan	7%	Lithuania
10%	Syria	7%	Russia
9%	India	6%	Albania
9%	Israel	6%	Greece
9%	Laos	5%	Belarus
8%	Japan	5%	Bosnia-Herzegovina
7%	Georgia	5%	France
6%	Armenia	5%	Moldova
6%	Cambodia	5%	Romania
6%	Kyrgyzstan	4%	Ukraine
6%	Thailand	3%	Macedonia
5%	Singapore	3%	Yugoslavia
5%	Sri Lanka		
5%	Turkmenistan		
5%	Uzbekistan	**13%**	**North America**
4%	Iran		**(average of countries)**
3%	Jordan	23%	Cuba
3%	Korea, South	19%	Canada
3%	Nepal	18%	Trinidad and Tobago
3%	Tajikistan	16%	Costa Rica
2%	Azerbaijan	16%	Nicaragua
2%	Lebanon	14%	Guatemala
2%	Pakistan	14%	Mexico
2%	Turkey	12%	Jamaica
1%	Yemen	11%	El Salvador
0%	Kuwait	11%	Honduras
		11%	United States
		10%	Dominican Republic
14%	**Europe**	7%	Panama
	(average of countries)	3%	Haiti
41%	Sweden		

(continued)

WOMEN IN NATIONAL LEGISLATURES BY REGION *(cont.)*
Percentage of total legislature

PERCENT	COUNTRY	PERCENT	COUNTRY
24%	**Oceania**	9%	Peru
	(average of countries)	7%	Brazil
29%	New Zealand	7%	Chile
18%	Australia	6%	Bolivia
		6%	Uruguay
8%	**South America**	6%	Venezuela
	(average of countries)	5%	Ecuador
22%	Argentina	4%	Paraguay
10%	Colombia		

by the United Nations Commission on the Status of Women. Sweden, with 41%, has the world's largest proportion of women legislators as well as the highest percentage of women in the cabinet, 52%. Other countries that have crossed the critical 30% threshold of women in their national legislatures include Norway, with 39%; Finland, with 34%; Denmark, with 33%; and the Netherlands, with 30%.

Women in International Parliaments

Among some European countries, women are better represented in delegations to the European Parliament than in their national legislatures. The European Parliament is the only body of the European Union whose mem-

WOMEN IN THE EUROPEAN PARLIAMENT
Percentage and number of female delegates elected in 1994

PERCENT	NUMBER	COUNTRY
63%	16	Finland
45%	22	Sweden
44%	16	Denmark
35%	99	Germany
33%	21	Austria
33%	6	Luxembourg
33%	64	Spain
32%	25	Belgium
32%	31	Netherlands
30%	87	France
27%	15	Ireland
18%	87	United Kingdom
16%	25	Greece
13%	87	Italy
8%	25	Portugal

A WOMAN'S DAY OR A MAN'S DAY?

According to the Swedish International Development Agency, the following is a typical day for a poor, rural African couple who grows their own food as well as some cash crops:

The Woman's Day begins with kindling the fire, breast-feeding the baby, making breakfast, eating, and washing and dressing the children. She then walks about one kilometer to fetch water, which she carries home, she then feeds and waters the livestock and washes her cooking utensils. Next she fetches more water, washes clothing, breast-feeds the baby, and brings food to a field a kilometer away where her husband is working. After returning home, she walks another kilometer to another field, which she weeds; on the way home, she breast-feeds the baby and gathers firewood. At home she pounds maize into flour, fetches more water, kindles the fire, prepares the evening meal, serves and eats it, breast-feeds the baby, washes up, puts the house in order, and is the last one in bed.

The Man's Day begins when breakfast is ready. After eating, he walks one kilometer to the field where he works until his wife arrives with his food. After eating, he resumes working in the field and later returns home, rests, eats dinner, and walks to the village to visit with other men before going to bed.

bers are directly elected by the citizens of its 15 member states. Of the Parliament's total 626 members, 173 (28%) are women. Finland has by far the largest female representation, followed by Sweden and Denmark. The countries with the smallest percentages of female delegates are the United Kingdom, Greece, Italy, and Portugal. Only one woman has ever been elected president of the European Parliament: Simone Veil of France, who served from 1979 to 1982.

The Central American Parliament, or Parlacen, created in 1987, consists of representatives of its six member nations: Costa Rica, El Salvador, Guatemala, Honduras, Nicaragua, and Panama. As of 1996, only El Salvador, Honduras, and Panama had elected representatives to this body, and approximately 10% of them were women. Only one woman has ever served as president of the Parlacen: Ilsa Diaz Zelaya of Honduras, who was elected in 1993.

FOR ADDITIONAL INFORMATION

Committee for the Elimination of Discrimination Against Women (CEDAW)
Two United Nations Plaza
New York, NY 10017, United States
Telephone: 212-963-3153
Fax: 212-963-3463
Web site: gopher://gopher.undp.org/ 1/ecosocdocs/edaw/

European Parliament Commission for Women in Decision-Making
Rue Mercelisstraat 33A
B-1050 Brussels, Belgium
Telephone: 2-512-77-23
Fax: 2-514-40-28

International Center for Research on Women
1717 Massachusetts Avenue, NW
Washington, DC 20036, United States
Telephone: 202-797-0007
Fax: 202-797-0020
E-mail: icrw@igc.apc.org

International Women's Tribune Center
777 United Nations Plaza
New York, NY 10017, United States
Telephone: 212-687-8633
Fax: 212-661-2704
E-mail: iwtc@igc.apc.org

Inter-Parliamentary Union
Place du Petit-Saconnex
Case Postale 438
CH-1211 Geneva 19, Switzerland
Telephone: 22-734-4150
Fax: 22-733-3141
Web site: http://www.ipu.org

Population Reference Bureau (PRB)
1875 Connecticut Avenue, NW
Washington, DC 20009, United States
Telephone: 202-483-1100
Fax: 202-328-3937
E-mail: popref@prb.org
Web site: http://www.igc.apc.org/prb

U.N. Department of Public Information
Room S-1040, United Nations
New York, NY 10017, United States
Telephone: 212-963-1262
Fax: 212-963-4361

U.N. Division for the Advancement of Women (DAW)
P.O. Box 20, United Nations
New York, NY 10017, United States
Telephone: 212-963-5086
Fax: 212-963-3463
*Web site:*http://www.un.org/DPCSD/ daw

U.N. International Research and Training Institute for the Advancement of Women (INSTRAW)
P.O. Box 21747
Santo Domingo, D.N., Dominican Rep.
Telephone: 809-685-2111
Fax: 809-685-2117

U.N. Population Fund (UNFPA) Women, Population, and Development Branch
220 East 42nd Street
New York, NY 10017, United States
Telephone: 212-297-5141
Fax: 212-297-5145
Web site: http://www.unfpa.org

WOMEN'S EDUCATION

Although women throughout the world have made tremendous progress in many areas, advances in literacy and education are perhaps the most striking and most auspicious. While literacy rates around the globe are climbing for both women and men, they are rising faster for women. The past few decades have seen a marked increase in the number of women who have learned to read and write; since 1960, the number of literate women in the world has grown by more than 600 million.

Worldwide, girls are still outnumbered by boys in primary and secondary school. Yet girls' enrollment is rising steadily, though slowly, and over the past two decades the gap in enrollment has been cut by more than 50%. In higher education women students outnumber men in more than 40 countries, and more and more of them are enrolling in the traditionally male-dominated courses. Women now constitute nearly half of all students in advanced degree law classes and the majority in medical studies.

Education is probably the single most important factor in improving a woman's life; the more schooling she has, the brighter her future, for herself and her family. Throughout the world, an education opens the door to a higher-paying job, a better standard of living, and a healthier, more productive life. Compared with a young woman who has had at least some secondary schooling, one with little or no education is much more likely to get married in her teens, have a large family, and—even if she finds work—is destined to live in poverty.

Although it is true that boys as well as girls benefit from an education, it seems that educating girls actually produces a greater return; in many parts of the world it is the woman's schooling that is the crucial factor in lifting her family out of poverty. Not only does an education enable her to find a higher-paying job and increase the family income, it also makes her more likely to take better care of herself and her family. A woman will be better nourished and healthier, and her children will be better educated. And a woman usually shares her knowledge with friends and family members, especially daughters, thus greatly multiplying the effects of her education.

Yet despite the long-term benefits of educating girls, parents in many parts of the world prefer to invest in educating their sons, keeping their daughters home to help with household chores and care for younger siblings. In many countries schools charge tuition, even at the primary level, and often there are additional fees for uniforms, textbooks, and transportation. Sending a daughter to school is often too costly for a poor family, especially since she will soon marry into another family and take the advantages of her education with her. Religious laws and customs also affect girls' schooling. In some Muslim societies girls are kept at home because their parents refuse to have them taught by male teachers or sit in classrooms with boys.

LITERACY

Of the estimated 960 million illiterates in the world, about two-thirds are women. In some places, especially poor rural communities, more than half the female population aged 15 and over can neither read nor write. Yet female literacy is rising in all regions of the world and is increasing faster than men's. The past few decades have witnessed significant progress toward both reducing female illiteracy and closing the literacy gap between women and men.

While literacy rates are climbing worldwide, there are still tremendous differences among regions. In Latin America and the Caribbean overall female literacy reached 85% in 1995, an increase of about 10 percentage points from 1980. In sub-Saharan Africa women's literacy rates rose from about 29% to nearly 49% during this period. Northern Africa and western Asia also saw dramatic increases, from 25% to 45%, while in southern Asia female literacy rose from 25% to about 38%.

Just as literacy rates vary from one region to the next, they also vary greatly within regions and within countries. In the Arab world overall female literacy is slightly over 50%, but it ranges from lows of 20% in Yemen and 22% in Morocco to highs of 89% in Lebanon and 73% in Jordan and Kuwait. And even within a country there are often wide gaps between rural and urban

COUNTRIES WHERE WOMEN'S LITERACY HAS INCREASED BY 30 PERCENTAGE POINTS OR MORE SINCE 1970

COUNTRY	1970	MOST RECENT YEAR (1990–1995)	INCREASE (% POINTS)
Kenya	19%	65%	46
Jordan	29%	73%	44
Libya	13%	57%	44
Saudi Arabia	2%	46%	44
Zaire	22%	64%	43
Indonesia	42%	79%	37
Turkey	34%	69%	35
Algeria	11%	44%	33
Tunisia	17%	50%	33
Syria	20%	52%	32
Ghana	18%	49%	31

LITERACY RATES WORLDWIDE*

WOMEN	MEN	COUNTRY	WOMEN	MEN	COUNTRY
99%	99%	Australia	97%	99%	Bulgaria
99%	99%	Austria	97%	99%	Tajikistan
99%	99%	Belgium	97%	99%	Turkmenistan
99%	99%	Canada	97%	99%	Ukraine
99%	99%	Czech Republic	97%	97%	Uruguay
99%	99%	Denmark	96%	96%	Argentina
99%	99%	Estonia	96%	99%	Azerbaijan
99%	99%	Finland	96%	99%	Kazakhstan
99%	99%	France	96%	99%	Korea, South
99%	99%	Germany	96%	99%	Kyrgyzstan
99%	99%	Hungary	96%	99%	Trinidad and
99%	99%	Ireland			Tobago
99%	99%	Italy	96%	98%	Uzbekistan
99%	99%	Japan	95%	99%	Croatia
99%	99%	Korea, North	95%	99%	Romania
99%	99%	Latvia	94%	95%	Chile
99%	99%	Netherlands	94%	94%	Costa Rica
99%	99%	New Zealand	94%	96%	Cuba
99%	99%	Norway	94%	99%	Moldova
99%	99%	Poland	93%	94%	Philippines
99%	99%	Russia	91%	96%	Thailand
99%	99%	Slovakia	90%	90%	Colombia
99%	99%	Sweden	90%	93%	Paraguay
99%	99%	Switzerland	90%	91%	Venezuela
99%	99%	United Kingdom	89%	97%	Greece
99%	99%	United States	89%	95%	Israel
98%	99%	Armenia	89%	94%	Lebanon
98%	99%	Georgia	89%	90%	Panama
98%	98%	Lithuania	89%	96%	Vietnam
98%	98%	Spain	88%	97%	Bosnia-
97%	99%	Belarus			Herzegovina

(continued)

LITERACY RATES WORLDWIDE* *(cont.)*

WOMEN	MEN	COUNTRY	WOMEN	MEN	COUNTRY
88%	79%	Jamaica	48%	72%	Cameroon
88%	97%	Macedonia	47%	61%	Guatemala
88%	90%	Puerto Rico	46%	63%	Central African
88%	97%	Slovenia			Republic
88%	97%	Yugoslavia	46%	70%	Saudi Arabia
87%	91%	Ecuador	46%	71%	Uganda
86%	91%	Mexico	44%	71%	Algeria
86%	93%	Sri Lanka	44%	65%	Rwanda
84%	95%	Singapore	42%	63%	Nigeria
81%	81%	Dominican Rep.	41%	65%	Egypt
81%	94%	Peru	41%	68%	Iraq
81%	89%	Portugal	41%	67%	Laos
79%	89%	Indonesia	40%	46%	Haiti
79%	93%	Taiwan	39%	64%	India
78%	89%	Zimbabwe	39%	70%	Malawi
77%	76%	Brazil	33%	64%	Togo
77%	78%	United Arab	31%	60%	Chad
		Emirates	31%	55%	Sudan
76%	88%	Myanmar	28%	56%	Angola
75%	88%	Malaysia	26%	43%	Ethiopia
73%	89%	Bolivia	26%	47%	Ivory Coast
73%	91%	Jordan	25%	48%	Mauritania
73%	80%	Kuwait	24%	48%	Bangladesh
73%	87%	Madagascar	22%	48%	Cambodia
70%	71%	Honduras	22%	49%	Morocco
70%	70%	South Africa	22%	48%	Pakistan
69%	90%	Turkey	20%	47%	Burundi
68%	87%	China	20%	35%	Mali
68%	72%	El Salvador	20%	54%	Mozambique
67%	84%	Zambia	20%	65%	Yemen
66%	64%	Nicaragua	19%	47%	Guinea
65%	84%	Kenya	19%	37%	Senegal
64%	84%	Zaire	18%	49%	Liberia
63%	80%	Albania	16%	32%	Benin
59%	78%	Congo	16%	42%	Sierra Leone
57%	86%	Libya	14%	36%	Somalia
55%	75%	Iran	13%	44%	Afghanistan
52%	84%	Syria	13%	39%	Nepal
52%	77%	Tanzania	10%	20%	Eritrea
50%	75%	Tunisia	8%	27%	Burkina Faso
49%	73%	Ghana	7%	18%	Niger

* Percentage of population aged 15 and over who can read and write a simple statement about their everyday life.

women. In India female literacy is only 30% in rural regions, compared with 64% in urban areas.

Age is also a major factor. Not surprisingly, illiteracy is much more prevalent among older women. In Egypt more than half the women under 45 are

RANGES IN FEMALE LITERACY
Percentage of women aged 15 and over

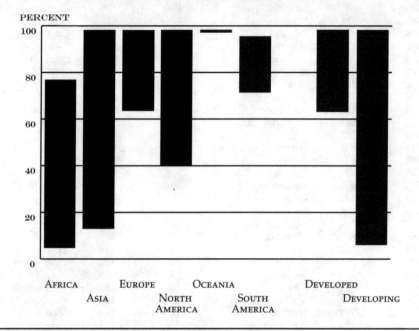

PERCENT

AFRICA   EUROPE   OCEANIA   DEVELOPED
    ASIA   NORTH   SOUTH   DEVELOPING
         AMERICA   AMERICA

literate, while only 15% of those aged between 45 and 64 can read and write. For women aged 65 and over, the literacy rate drops to 6%.

In the world's poorest countries, where literacy rates are among the lowest, the gender gap tends to be widest. This is especially evident in parts of Africa and Asia.

Literacy and Fertility

As one might expect, women's literacy and fertility rates are often closely related. Women with at least several years of primary school education are more likely to use birth control measures and have smaller families with children spaced further apart. They are also generally healthier and suffer fewer complications of pregnancy.

EDUCATION

Throughout the world, about 100 million children enter primary school each year. Of the estimated 130 million children who are not in school, a sizable majority, about 60%, are girls. In almost every region of the world, there are fewer girls in school than boys.

Even where girls and boys enter primary school in equal or nearly equal numbers, as they get older, more girls tend to drop out. About two-thirds of all children who leave school before completing the first four years are girls. This disparity is most evident in the developing countries. In Ghana, for example, almost as many girls as boys enter primary school, but by secondary school, they are outnumbered three to two. At the university level, the male-female ratio is about five to one. Similarly, in Uganda only 5% of girls reach secondary school, and in rural India, where approximately 60% of children attend primary school, only about 15% of girls remain after five years, compared with 35% of boys.

Innovative programs designed to keep girls in school have been developed in many countries, often by local communities and parents working together with various international, governmental, and nongovernmental organizations. In the countryside these programs often offer special nontraditional village schools that encourage girls' enrollment by providing conve-

COUNTRIES WHERE MORE THAN HALF OF THE WOMEN ARE ILLITERATE
Africa

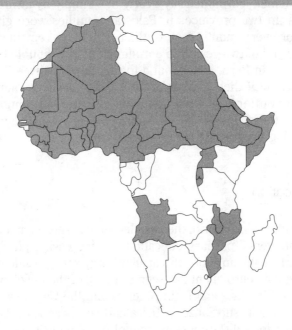

COUNTRIES WHERE MORE THAN
HALF THE WOMEN ARE ILLITERATE

COUNTRIES WHERE MORE THAN HALF OF THE WOMEN ARE ILLITERATE

Asia

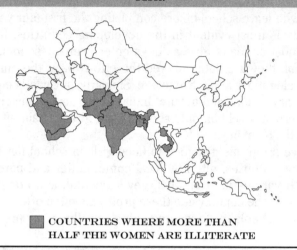

COUNTRIES WHERE MORE THAN
HALF THE WOMEN ARE ILLITERATE

nient locations, a greater number of female teachers, flexible schedules, and sometimes monetary incentives. In Bangladesh one program succeeded in raising female enrollment by nearly 50% simply by awarding scholarships to girls. In two provinces in Pakistan, families were given a can of cooking oil for every month each of their daughters remained in primary school. At the end of two years the enrollment of girls doubled. In an experimental program in Peru, it was found that girls were three times as likely to enroll in school if their textbooks were free. (Boys' enrollment was not affected by this offer.) In some countries private and nongovernmental organizations offer scholarships and similar incentives for young women to enroll in training programs that will enable them to upgrade their employment skills.

Primary Education

Throughout much of the world, the past decade has seen significant progress in providing universal primary education and increasing girls' enrollment. Worldwide, girls make up about 45% of all primary school students. The highest levels of female enrollment are seen in many of the developed countries as well as in eastern Asia and Latin America and the Caribbean. The lowest rates occur mostly in sub-Saharan Africa and southern Asia. Usually, there are also tremendous differences in school enrollment between rural and urban areas in the same country. For example, in the Central African Repub-

COUNTRIES WITH A LITERACY GENDER GAP OF 20 POINTS OR MORE

COUNTRY	WOMEN	MEN	LITERACY GAP (% POINTS)
Africa			
Mozambique	20%	54%	34
Liberia	18%	49%	31
Malawi	39%	70%	31
Togo	33%	64%	31
Chad	31%	60%	29
Libya	57%	86%	29
Angola	28%	56%	28
Guinea	19%	47%	28
Morocco	22%	49%	27
Algeria	44%	71%	27
Burundi	20%	47%	27
Sierra Leone	16%	42%	26
Tanzania	52%	77%	25
Tunisia	50%	75%	25
Uganda	46%	71%	25
Cameroon	48%	72%	24
Egypt	41%	65%	24
Ghana	49%	73%	24
Sudan	31%	55%	24
Mauritania	25%	48%	23
Somalia	14%	36%	22
Ivory Coast	26%	47%	21
Nigeria	42%	63%	21
Rwanda	44%	65%	21
Zaire	64%	84%	20
Asia			
Yemen	20%	65%	45
Syria	52%	84%	32
Afghanistan	13%	44%	31
Iraq	41%	68%	27
Cambodia	22%	48%	26
Laos	41%	67%	26
Nepal	13%	39%	26
Pakistan	22%	48%	26
India	39%	64%	25
Bangladesh	24%	48%	24
Saudi Arabia	46%	70%	24
Turkey	69%	90%	21
Iran	55%	75%	20

lic 60% to 70% of urban girls attend primary school, compared with only 10% to 20% of their rural counterparts.

Even though there are many countries where large numbers of girls do not attend primary school, boys' enrollment in these countries is also usually low. There are only about a dozen countries with a substantial percentage

FEMALE ILLITERACY AND FERTILITY: FERTILITY RATES
Average of countries in regions

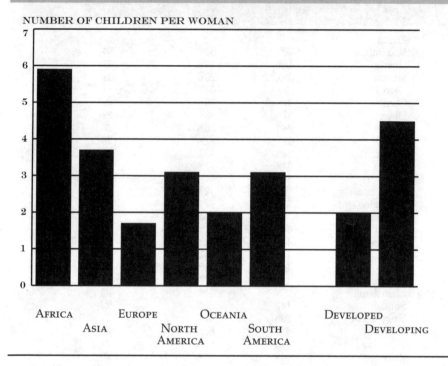

NUMBER OF CHILDREN PER WOMAN

AFRICA   EUROPE   OCEANIA   DEVELOPED
       ASIA   NORTH   SOUTH   DEVELOPING
                    AMERICA   AMERICA

point gap between girls' and boys' enrollment. They include Yemen, with a 37-point gap; Benin, with 36 points; Afghanistan, Chad, and Nepal, with 28 points; Central African Republic, with 25 points; and Togo, with 22 points.

In the majority of countries, girls' primary school enrollment has reached or nearly reached parity with boys'; in more than 80 countries female students make up 48% or more of the total student body.

Secondary Education

Female enrollment in secondary education is sometimes considered the best indication of a country's educational progress. In this area girls outnumber boys in many developed nations as well as in many Latin American and Caribbean countries, where girls tend to stay in school longer than their male classmates. As with primary school enrollment, girls lag farthest behind in sub-Saharan Africa and parts of Asia.

Over the past few decades some countries have witnessed dramatic

FEMALE ILLITERACY AND FERTILITY: ILLITERACY RATES
Average of countries in regions

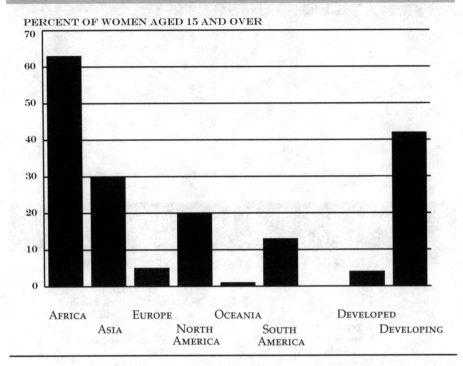

PERCENT OF WOMEN AGED 15 AND OVER

increases in the number of girls remaining in school through the secondary level. In Australia the number of girls completing secondary school was 81% in 1993, more than double the 37% in 1980. A similar increase has taken place in the United States, where 75% of girls now complete high school, up from 53% in 1970.

Higher Education

The number of women enrolled in institutions of higher education is often used as a measure of women's current and future status in that country. In many of the developed countries women already outnumber their male classmates in colleges and universities. Two notable exceptions are Switzerland and Japan, where women students account for only 36% and 40% of the student body, respectively.

Large parts of Latin America and the Caribbean also have high proportions of women students in higher education: Bolivia (74%), Cuba (58%),

COUNTRIES WHERE MORE THAN HALF OF PRIMARY SCHOOL-AGE GIRLS ARE NOT IN SCHOOL

COUNTRY	PERCENT	COUNTRY	PERCENT
Somalia	94%	Mozambique	65%
Afghanistan	86%	Benin	65%
Mali	86%	Yemen	64%
Niger	86%	Morocco	55%
Ethiopia	84%	Pakistan	55%
Eritrea	76%	Central African Rep.	54%
Burkina Faso	75%	Burundi	53%
Haiti	74%	Zaire	53%
Chad	73%	Nigeria	51%
Senegal	70%		

FEMALE PRIMARY SCHOOL ENROLLMENT WORLDWIDE
Percentage of student body

PERCENT	COUNTRY	PERCENT	COUNTRY
54%	Germany	49%	Kenya
51%	Brazil	49%	Korea, North
51%	Nicaragua	49%	Kuwait
50%	Argentina	49%	Latvia
50%	Colombia	49%	Madagascar
50%	El Salvador	49%	Malaysia
50%	Honduras	49%	Moldova
50%	Jamaica	49%	New Zealand
50%	Netherlands	49%	Norway
50%	Russia	49%	Philippines
50%	Rwanda	49%	Poland
50%	Venezuela	49%	Romania
50%	Zimbabwe	49%	Slovakia
49%	Australia	49%	Slovenia
49%	Austria	49%	Sweden
49%	Belgium	49%	Switzerland
49%	Chile	49%	Tajikistan
49%	Costa Rica	49%	Tanzania
49%	Croatia	49%	Thailand
49%	Czech Republic	49%	Trinidad and Tobago
49%	Denmark	49%	Ukraine
49%	Dominican Republic	49%	United Kingdom
49%	Ecuador	49%	Uruguay
49%	Estonia	49%	Yugoslavia
49%	Finland	48%	Albania
49%	Hungary	48%	Angola
49%	Ireland	48%	Bulgaria
49%	Israel	48%	Canada
49%	Italy	48%	Cuba
49%	Japan	48%	France
49%	Jordan	48%	Greece
49%	Kazakhstan	48%	Haiti

(continued)

FEMALE PRIMARY SCHOOL ENROLLMENT WORLDWIDE
(cont.)
Percentage of student body

PERCENT	COUNTRY	PERCENT	COUNTRY
48%	Indonesia	45%	Egypt
48%	Korea, South	45%	Eritrea
48%	Lebanon	45%	Ghana
48%	Libya	45%	Malawi
48%	Lithuania	44%	Iraq
48%	Macedonia	44%	Laos
48%	Mexico	44%	Nigeria
48%	Myanmar	43%	India
48%	Panama	43%	Mauritania
48%	Paraguay	43%	Sudan
48%	Peru	43%	Uganda
48%	Portugal	42%	Ivory Coast
48%	Spain	42%	Mozambique
48%	Sri Lanka	42%	Zaire
48%	United Arab Emirates	41%	Sierra Leone
48%	United States	40%	Ethiopia
48%	Vietnam	40%	Morocco
47%	Bolivia	40%	Senegal
47%	China	39%	Burkina Faso
47%	Iran	39%	Central African Republic
47%	Singapore	39%	Togo
47%	South Africa	37%	Mali
47%	Syria	36%	Niger
47%	Turkey	35%	Liberia
47%	Zambia	34%	Benin
46%	Cameroon	34%	Pakistan
46%	Congo	34%	Somalia
46%	Guatemala	33%	Afghanistan
46%	Saudi Arabia	32%	Chad
46%	Tunisia	32%	Guinea
45%	Algeria	32%	Nepal
45%	Bangladesh	24%	Yemen
45%	Burundi		

Panama (58%), Jamaica (57%), Dominican Republic (55%), Argentina (53%), Uruguay (53%), Brazil (52%), and Colombia (51%). Not surprisingly, nearly all the countries where female students constitute less than 20% of the student body are in sub-Saharan Africa.

Although female enrollment is rising, women in higher education still tend to predominate in what are traditionally regarded as women's fields—home economics, education, arts, literature, and languages—and rarely study engineering, mathematics, and technical subjects. However, increasing numbers of women are entering the fields of law, medicine, and business administration, especially in Latin American and Caribbean countries. In science and technology courses women are starting to catch up with men in every region except Africa. Some countries have programs actively encourag-

FEMALE SECONDARY SCHOOL ENROLLMENT WORLDWIDE
Percentage of student body

PERCENT	COUNTRY	PERCENT	COUNTRY
61%	Russia	49%	Kuwait
59%	Puerto Rico	49%	Macedonia
58%	Nicaragua	49%	Madagascar
57%	Brazil	49%	Mexico
57%	Venezuela	49%	New Zealand
56%	Libya	49%	Romania
55%	Honduras	49%	Slovenia
55%	Nigeria	49%	Sweden
54%	Colombia	49%	United States
54%	Finland	48%	Greece
54%	Germany	48%	Korea, South
53%	Bosnia-Herzegovina	48%	Netherlands
53%	El Salvador	48%	Norway
53%	Portugal	48%	Thailand
53%	South Africa	47%	Austria
53%	Uruguay	47%	Peru
52%	Argentina	47%	Switzerland
52%	Cuba	47%	Tajikistan
52%	Jamaica	46%	Bolivia
51%	Chile	46%	Paraguay
51%	Costa Rica	45%	Albania
51%	Croatia	45%	Algeria
51%	Estonia	45%	Ethiopia
51%	Ireland	45%	Guatemala
51%	Israel	45%	Indonesia
51%	Latvia	45%	Tunisia
51%	Malaysia	44%	Egypt
51%	Panama	44%	Rwanda
51%	Spain	44%	Saudi Arabia
51%	Sri Lanka	44%	Sudan
51%	United Arab Emirates	44%	Syria
50%	Bulgaria	44%	Tanzania
50%	Czech Republic	44%	Zimbabwe
50%	Ecuador	43%	China
50%	France	43%	Iran
50%	Jordan	42%	Congo
50%	Lithuania	41%	Cameroon
50%	Philippines	41%	Kenya
50%	Poland	41%	Morocco
50%	Singapore	39%	Burundi
50%	Slovakia	39%	Ghana
50%	Trinidad and Tobago	39%	Laos
50%	United Kingdom	39%	Myanmar
50%	Vietnam	38%	Iraq
50%	Yugoslavia	38%	Mozambique
49%	Australia	38%	Turkey
49%	Belgium	37%	Zambia
49%	Canada	35%	Burkina Faso
49%	Denmark	35%	Senegal
49%	Hungary	35%	Somalia
49%	Italy	34%	India
49%	Japan	34%	Malawi

(continued)

FEMALE SECONDARY SCHOOL ENROLLMENT WORLDWIDE
(cont.)
Percentage of student body

PERCENT	COUNTRY	PERCENT	COUNTRY
34%	Uganda	29%	Eritrea
33%	Bangladesh	29%	Niger
33%	Mauritania	29%	Pakistan
32%	Mali	28%	Liberia
32%	Nepal	25%	Guinea
32%	Zaire	25%	Togo
30%	Ivory Coast	18%	Chad
29%	Benin	17%	Sierra Leone
29%	Central African Republic	12%	Yemen

ing women to enter these traditionally male fields. Yet progress is slow. In the United States, female students in technical fields are still far outnumbered by their male classmates, earning only one out of every six engineering degrees and one out of every three computer science degrees.

Women's Studies and Gender Bias

A relatively recent development in many countries has been the introduction of women's studies courses in higher education. In addition, as many as 30 countries have well-established women's studies centers both inside and outside the formal educational system. These centers generally conduct research on women's issues; publish books, fact sheets and other informational materials; and organize workshops, seminars, and training programs.

With the emergence of women's studies programs, many countries have started focusing on the problem of gender bias in schools, in the curriculum as well as in textbooks and other educational materials. In addition, some countries are taking measures to ensure that girls and boys are afforded equal opportunities to enroll in the same courses and training programs. In the United Kingdom, after the national curriculum was redesigned in 1989 to offer a more balanced, less gender-stereotyped range of courses, the proportion of girls taking science, technology, and computing courses rose significantly. In Sweden the government recently established special gender-related programs and projects, such as summer technology classes for girls and nursing for boys. A new nationwide curriculum introduced in 1994 stressed equality between women and men, and one of the government's primary goals is to ensure that no educational program contains less than 40% of either sex.

FEMALE ENROLLMENT IN HIGHER EDUCATION WORLDWIDE
Percentage of student body

PERCENT	COUNTRY	PERCENT	COUNTRY
75%	United Arab Emirates	48%	Croatia
74%	Bolivia	48%	Korea, North
61%	Kuwait	48%	Slovakia
60%	Portugal	48%	South Africa
59%	Philippines	47%	Austria
58%	Cuba	47%	Guatemala
58%	Panama	47%	Ireland
57%	Bulgaria	47%	Myanmar
57%	Jamaica	47%	Peru
56%	Poland	47%	Romania
56%	Sweden	47%	Venezuela
56%	United States	46%	Libya
55%	Dominican Republic	45%	Egypt
54%	Canada	45%	Madagascar
54%	New Zealand	45%	Mexico
54%	Norway	45%	Netherlands
54%	Slovenia	44%	Chile
53%	Argentina	44%	Czech Republic
53%	Australia	43%	Germany
53%	Denmark	42%	Singapore
53%	Finland	41%	Sri Lanka
53%	Israel	41%	Tunisia
53%	Latvia	40%	Japan
53%	Lebanon	40%	Saudi Arabia
53%	Thailand	40%	Sudan
53%	Uruguay	39%	Ecuador
53%	Yugoslavia	39%	Honduras
52%	Albania	38%	Iraq
52%	Brazil	38%	Syria
52%	France	38%	Trinidad and Tobago
52%	Macedonia	36%	Morocco
52%	Russia	35%	Switzerland
52%	Ukraine	35%	Turkey
51%	Belarus	34%	China
51%	Colombia	34%	Korea, South
51%	Estonia	33%	Afghanistan
51%	Hungary	33%	El Salvador
51%	Italy	33%	India
51%	Kazakhstan	33%	Uganda
51%	Moldova	32%	Laos
51%	Spain	31%	Algeria
50%	Bosnia-Herzegovina	30%	Iran
50%	Greece	30%	Ivory Coast
50%	Malaysia	29%	Benin
50%	Vietnam	28%	Kenya
49%	Azerbaijan	28%	Liberia
49%	Haiti	28%	Malawi
49%	Jordan	28%	Pakistan
49%	Nicaragua	28%	Zambia
49%	United Kingdom	27%	Zimbabwe
48%	Belgium	26%	Burundi

(continued)

FEMALE ENROLLMENT IN HIGHER EDUCATION WORLDWIDE *(cont.)*
Percentage of student body

PERCENT	COUNTRY	PERCENT	COUNTRY
26%	Mozambique	16%	Central African Republic
24%	Eritrea	16%	Yemen
24%	Nepal	15%	Mauritania
24%	Nigeria	15%	Niger
24%	Senegal	14%	Indonesia
23%	Burkina Faso	14%	Mali
20%	Somalia	13%	Tanzania
19%	Congo	13%	Togo
19%	Rwanda	12%	Guinea
17%	Angola	9%	Chad
17%	Ghana	8%	Ethiopia
16%	Bangladesh		

One of the lengthiest and most contentious battles over a gender-biased curriculum was waged in Japan. Following World War II women's groups successfully lobbied to make home economics compulsory for boys as well as girls, but in a resurgence of traditional attitudes several years later, the curriculum was revised and boys were forced to take industrial arts while girls still had to take home economics. In the early 1990s women's groups mobilized once more, and home economics again became mandatory for both boys and girls.

In addition to the numerous women's groups and government programs in various countries that are focusing on eliminating gender bias in schools, many nongovernmental organizations have been sponsoring public campaigns to combat sex stereotyping and encourage girls to consider a wide range of career choices. In the United States an annual "Take Our Daughters to Work Day" coordinates parents, schools, and employers in a massive campaign to encourage young girls to explore a variety of careers.

Nonformal Educational Opportunities

In many rural regions where large numbers of children, especially girls, are not enrolled in formal educational systems, experimental programs have been created to provide special, nontraditional learning centers. Bangladesh, Chad, the Dominican Republic, India, Nepal, Pakistan, Tanzania, and Thailand, are among the many countries that have developed innovative educational programs primarily for girls. The most effective programs are generally those that offer free tuition, flexible hours, local female teachers, day care for younger siblings, a convenient location, and a school calendar that takes the girls' agricultural chores into account.

WOMEN AND THE NOBEL PRIZE

Since its inception in 1901, the Nobel Prize—the world's most prestigious international award—has been bestowed upon more than 650 prominent scientists,
writers, peace activists, and economists around the globe. By 1996 only 28 women,
about 4% of the total number of laureates, had been selected to join this elite group.

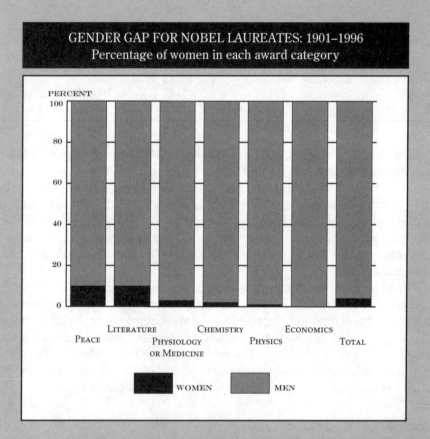

GENDER GAP FOR NOBEL LAUREATES: 1901–1996
Percentage of women in each award category

Why so few? Traditionally, women have been discouraged from studying math and
science, and tremendous social pressures forced many to abandon thoughts of a
career in a male-dominated field. For most girls these obstacles proved insurmountable. One of the exceptions was Gerty Cori, who grew up in Czechoslovakia around
the turn of the century and could not attend medical school because her girls'
school did not teach the subjects required for admission. On her own, she had to
master the necessary Latin, math, and science before she could be admitted. In
1947 she and her husband were awarded a share of the Nobel Prize in physiology
or medicine for their research on carbohydrate metabolism and the role enzymes

(continued)

WOMEN AND THE NOBEL PRIZE *(cont.)*

play in this process. A few months earlier, at the age of 50, she had received—and accepted—her first offer of a job as a full professor.

Another exception was Gertrude Elion who, despite her graduation honors and Phi Beta Kappa key, was denied financial aid for graduate school and spent years working part-time to earn money for her education. She worked as a secretary, receptionist, and substitute teacher before getting a job in scientific research, never actually earning a Ph.D. But in 1988, she shared the Nobel Prize in physiology or medicine for discovering the first antiviral drug and for her groundbreaking research that paved the way for the development of the anti-AIDS drug AZT.

And for every woman who has been awarded a Nobel Prize, there is probably at least one other who has conducted valuable research or played a major role in an outstanding discovery but was overlooked by the Nobel Committee in favor of her male supervisor or co-workers. One such woman was the British researcher Rosalind Franklin. Using X-rays to help decipher the structure of the cell's genetic material, she provided James Watson, Francis Crick, and Maurice Wilkins with valuable information about the structure of DNA, a discovery for which they received the 1962 Nobel Prize in physiology or medicine. Ironically, four years earlier, at the age of 37, Franklin had died of cancer, most likely caused by exposure to the X-rays in her lab.

Another woman scientist overlooked by the Nobel Committee was Jocelyn Bell Burnell. As a graduate student in astronomy at Cambridge University, she helped construct and operate a huge radio telescope; and while studying the charts produced by the telescope, she discovered the existence of pulsars. Although she was listed as the second author of the paper announcing the finding, when the 1974 Nobel Prize in physics was awarded for the discovery, it went to her supervisor.

WOMEN NOBEL LAUREATES			
YEAR	NAME	COUNTRY	CATEGORY
1903	Marie Curie	France	Physics
1905	Bertha von Suttner	Austria	Peace
1909	Selma Lagerlöf	Sweden	Literature
1911	Marie Curie	France	Chemistry
1926	Grazia Deledda	Italy	Literature
1928	Ingrid Undset	Norway	Literature

(continued)

WOMEN AND THE NOBEL PRIZE *(cont.)*

WOMEN NOBEL LAUREATES *(cont.)*

YEAR	NAME	COUNTRY	CATEGORY
1931	Jane Addams	USA	Peace
1935	Irène Joliet-Curie	France	Chemistry
1938	Pearl Buck	USA	Literature
1945	Gabriela Mistral	Chile	Literature
1946	Emily Balch	USA	Peace
1947	Gerty Cori	USA	Physiology or Medicine
1963	Maria Goeppert-Mayer	USA	Physics
1964	Dorothy Hodgkin	UK	Chemistry
1966	Nellie Sachs	Sweden	Literature
1976	Mairead Corrigan	Ireland	Peace
1976	Betty Williams	Ireland	Peace
1977	Rosalyn Yallow	USA	Physiology or Medicine
1979	Mother Teresa	India	Peace
1982	Alva Myrdal	Sweden	Peace
1983	Barbara McClintock	USA	Physiology or Medicine
1986	Rita Levi-Montalcini	Italy/USA	Physiology or Medicine
1988	Gertrude Elion	USA	Physiology or Medicine
1991	Daw Aung San Suu Kyi	Myanmar	Peace
1991	Nadine Gordimer	South Africa	Literature
1992	Rigoberta Menchu	Guatemala	Peace
1993	Toni Morrison	USA	Literature
1995	Christiane Nüsslein-Volhard	Germany	Physiology or Medicine
1996	Wislawa Szymborska	Poland	Literature

Yet despite the meager representation of women among Nobel laureates, the outlook is not quite as bleak as it appears. Over the past few decades, as more and more women have entered the sciences and chosen professional careers, the number of female Nobel Prize winners has slowly increased. More important, the percentage of women recipients has been rising. In the two decades from 1976 to 1996, nearly 8% of the prize winners were women, a jump from 3% over the previous 75 years.

One of the most successful of these programs is in Bangladesh, where nonformal community schools were started in 1985, now number more than 35,000, and have an enrollment of nearly a million children, 70% of whom are girls. Created by the Bangladesh Rural Advancement Committee (BRAC), each school hires women teachers from the community and is run by a village committee that relies heavily on input from parents. A similar project has been started in some regions of India, where special courtyard schools have been opened just for girls. Older women in the community escort the girls to and from school and also care for the girls' younger siblings while they are in class. In Nepal approximately 70,000 girls have enrolled in similar nonformal classes that meet two hours a day six days a week for nine months of the year. The government provides an additional incentive: small subsidies for poor families whose daughters remain in school.

FOR ADDITIONAL INFORMATION

**International Programs Center
International Data Base**
Bureau of the Census
Washington Plaza II, Room 207
Washington, DC 20233–8860
United States
Telephone: 301-457-1403
Fax: 301-457-3034

Nobel Foundation
Box 5232
S–10245 Stockholm, Sweden
Telephone: 8-663-0920
Fax: 8-660-3847
Web site: http://www.nobel.se

**United Nations Children's Fund
(UNICEF)**
Three United Nations Plaza
New York, NY 10017, United States
Telephone: 212-326-7000
Fax: 212-326-7518
Web site: http://www.unicef.org

**United Nations Educational,
Scientific, and Cultural
Organization (UNESCO)**
7, Place de Fontenoy
F-75700 Paris, France
Telephone: 15-68-38-24/23
Fax: 15-67-71-57
Web site: http://www.unesco.org

WOMEN'S EMPLOYMENT

Throughout history, women have been laborers. Even in ancient civilizations, women in towns and cities worked as laundresses, seamstresses, hairdressers, domestics, shopkeepers, and midwives while rural women were involved in all aspects of farming, from raising crops and livestock to spinning yarn and preserving food. Through the centuries, though, it was the household that remained the center of production; all basic needs were produced by family members, adults and children alike. Children who were not needed to help at home were sent to work; girls were hired out as domestics, boys were enrolled as apprentices. Although wives were responsible for caring for the household and small children, they also often assisted their husbands in the fields or workshops. Sometimes, by selling extra produce or fabric, they earned extra money for their families.

In many countries dramatic changes in this pattern occurred as the Industrial Revolution transformed agricultural economies into ones dominated by industry. Family members increasingly worked in the factories, but they continued to function as a unit, pooling their wages to support the family. As more goods were manufactured, more money was needed to purchase them. Fathers and children over the age of 10 made up the ranks of the wage earners. Mothers remained at home, still responsible for domestic chores and rearing the younger children. A wife tended to work outside the home only if necessary, for example, when her husband lost his job or died. Because of their household duties, these women required jobs with shorter hours or that could be performed at home, such as piecework. Occasionally, they took in boarders to earn extra money.

Some women worked in the factories, but generally not in the same industries as men. They worked mostly in the lower-paying light industries, such as textile production, while men labored in the higher-paying heavy industries, such as iron and steel manufacturing. Even in their own factories, women were rarely promoted to supervisory positions.

As the standard of living for many families increased with industrialization, the more educated young single women of the emerging middle class were attracted to the more prestigious white-collar jobs—such as secretary or sales clerk—which educated men had deserted for better paying supervisory positions in industry. These women started joining the labor force in large numbers around the turn of the 20th century, filling many of the new teaching positions as well as clerical jobs in the civil service and in new areas such as the expanding telephone and telegraph industries. But they were still expected to retire upon marriage so that they could stay home and raise their families.

With the advent of World War I, scores of women, even married women with children, started joining the labor force to fill the positions of men who had gone off to fight. But for the most part they returned to their homes when the war was over. During World War II women again became a vital part of the work force, especially as factory and clerical workers in war-related industries. However, when the soldiers returned home this time, large numbers of women remained in the labor force, taking many of the service and clerical jobs that were opening up in the postwar economy.

Since the mid-1900s, women's participation in the labor force has continued to rise just about everywhere in the world, not just in the highly industrialized nations. As their educational opportunities have improved, women have made tremendous strides in all areas of employment. Growing numbers are entering previously male-dominated professions, others are attaining high-level positions in management and administration, and many more are starting their own businesses.

Yet these are the minority. In country after country, in the developed as well as the developing world, most women workers still tend to be segregated into low-level jobs in low-paying industries. Even when they perform the same tasks as men, they rarely receive the same wages. And all over the globe, especially in times of economic crisis, women tend to be the last ones hired, the first ones fired. Despite the fact that many countries, particularly in developed regions, have enacted antidiscrimination legislation aimed specifically at protecting working women, these laws are often poorly enforced or too weak to be effective, and blatant discrimination remains rampant.

WOMEN'S SHARE OF THE WORK FORCE

Women have been entering the world's labor force in steadily increasing numbers over the past few decades. By 1995 they made up about 36% of the total global work force. The countries with the sharpest growth rates during this period were the highly industrialized nations (except Eastern Europe). The areas with the lowest rates of growth were those regions that already had large proportions of working women—eastern and central Asia and Eastern Europe. Sub-Saharan Africa recorded a slight decline.

Today there are only 33 countries in which women constitute 45% or more of the total labor force. Nearly half of them are Eastern Europe's formerly communist countries, where women have long been viewed as the "great army of labor." At the other end of the spectrum, there are 30 countries where women make up 25% or less of the work force. Nearly two-thirds of these countries are the predominantly Muslim nations of the Middle East, sub-Saharan Africa, and southern Asia.

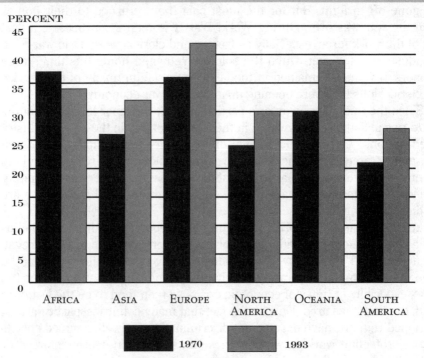

WOMEN'S SHARE OF THE WORK FORCE, 1970–1993
Percentage of total work force

PERCENT

Legend: ■ 1970 ▨ 1993

Regions: AFRICA, ASIA, EUROPE, NORTH AMERICA, OCEANIA, SOUTH AMERICA

WOMEN'S PARTICIPATION IN THE WORK FORCE WORLDWIDE
Percentage of women aged 15–64

PERCENT	COUNTRY	PERCENT	COUNTRY
80%	China	55%	Austria
80%	Niger	55%	Madagascar
80%	Rwanda	55%	Somalia
80%	Sweden	55%	Yugoslavia
79%	Burundi	54%	Angola
78%	Mozambique	53%	Congo
77%	Benin	53%	Eritrea
77%	Burkina Faso	53%	Ethiopia
77%	Vietnam	53%	Macedonia
76%	Laos	53%	Singapore
75%	Denmark	53%	Switzerland
75%	Jamaica	52%	Malaysia
74%	Czech Republic	52%	Senegal
73%	Belarus	51%	Haiti
73%	Finland	51%	Ivory Coast
73%	Tanzania	51%	Kenya
72%	Russia	51%	Myanmar
72%	Estonia	50%	Cambodia
71%	Latvia	50%	Japan
71%	Poland	49%	Ghana
71%	Slovakia	49%	New Zealand
71%	United Kingdom	48%	Portugal
70%	Central African Republic	48%	Turkey
70%	Lithuania	47%	Bosnia-Herzegovina
70%	Moldova	47%	Korea, South
70%	Ukraine	47%	Netherlands
69%	Armenia	47%	Zaire
69%	Romania	46%	Indonesia
68%	Bulgaria	46%	Togo
68%	Kazakhstan	45%	Taiwan
68%	Norway	43%	Israel
68%	United States	43%	Nepal
67%	Hungary	43%	Nigeria
67%	Thailand	42%	Belgium
65%	Korea, North	42%	Cuba
65%	Kyrgyzstan	42%	South Africa
65%	Slovenia	41%	Cameroon
64%	Georgia	41%	Zimbabwe
64%	Turkmenistan	40%	Brazil
64%	Uzbekistan	40%	Sierra Leone
63%	Albania	39%	Trinidad and Tobago
63%	Australia	39%	Uruguay
62%	Bangladesh	38%	Philippines
62%	Germany	37%	Italy
60%	Uganda	36%	Ireland
59%	Guinea	36%	Liberia
58%	Canada	36%	Zambia
57%	France	34%	Panama
57%	Malawi	33%	Chile
56%	Azerbaijan	33%	Mexico
56%	Croatia	33%	Venezuela
56%	Tajikistan	32%	Argentina

(continued)

WOMEN'S PARTICIPATION IN THE WORK FORCE WORLDWIDE *(cont.)*
Percentage of women aged 15–64

PERCENT	COUNTRY	PERCENT	COUNTRY
32%	Nicaragua	23%	Chad
31%	India	23%	Colombia
30%	Greece	23%	Iran
30%	Sri Lanka	23%	Morocco
29%	El Salvador	22%	Egypt
29%	Puerto Rico	20%	Ecuador
28%	Tunisia	19%	Guatemala
27%	Lebanon	19%	United Arab Emirates
27%	Sudan	18%	Dominican Republic
26%	Costa Rica	17%	Syria
26%	Mauritania	16%	Mali
26%	Peru	16%	Pakistan
26%	Spain	12%	Yemen
25%	Bolivia	10%	Jordan
25%	Kuwait	10%	Libya
24%	Honduras	10%	Saudi Arabia
24%	Iraq	9%	Afghanistan
24%	Paraguay	8%	Algeria

WOMEN'S PARTICIPATION IN WORK FORCE BY REGION
Percentage of women aged 15–64

PERCENT	COUNTRY	PERCENT	COUNTRY
48%	**Africa**	43%	Nigeria
	(average of countries)	42%	South Africa
80%	Niger	41%	Cameroon
80%	Rwanda	41%	Zimbabwe
79%	Burundi	40%	Sierra Leone
78%	Mozambique	36%	Liberia
77%	Benin	36%	Zambia
77%	Burkina Faso	28%	Tunisia
73%	Tanzania	27%	Sudan
70%	Central African Republic	26%	Mauritania
60%	Uganda	23%	Chad
59%	Guinea	23%	Morocco
57%	Malawi	22%	Egypt
55%	Madagascar	16%	Mali
55%	Somalia	10%	Libya
54%	Angola	8%	Algeria
53%	Congo		
53%	Eritrea	**45%**	**Asia**
53%	Ethiopia		**(average of countries)**
52%	Senegal	80%	China
51%	Ivory Coast	77%	Vietnam
51%	Kenya	76%	Laos
49%	Ghana	69%	Armenia
47%	Zaire	68%	Kazakhstan
46%	Togo	67%	Thailand

(continued)

PERCENT	COUNTRY	PERCENT	COUNTRY
65%	Korea, North	65%	Slovenia
65%	Kyrgyzstan	63%	Albania
64%	Georgia	62%	Germany
64%	Turkmenistan	57%	France
64%	Uzbekistan	56%	Croatia
62%	Bangladesh	55%	Austria
56%	Azerbaijan	55%	Yugoslavia
56%	Tajikistan	53%	Macedonia
53%	Singapore	53%	Switzerland
52%	Malaysia	48%	Portugal
51%	Myanmar	47%	Bosnia-Herzegovina
50%	Cambodia	47%	Netherlands
50%	Japan	42%	Belgium
48%	Turkey	37%	Italy
47%	Korea, South	36%	Ireland
46%	Indonesia	30%	Greece
45%	Taiwan	26%	Spain
43%	Israel		
43%	Nepal	**38%**	**North America**
38%	Philippines		**(average of countries)**
31%	India	75%	Jamaica
30%	Sri Lanka	68%	United States
27%	Lebanon	58%	Canada
25%	Kuwait	51%	Haiti
24%	Iraq	42%	Cuba
23%	Iran	39%	Trinidad and Tobago
19%	United Arab Emirates	34%	Panama
17%	Syria	33%	Mexico
16%	Pakistan	32%	Nicaragua
12%	Yemen	29%	El Salvador
10%	Jordan	29%	Puerto Rico
10%	Saudi Arabia	26%	Costa Rica
9%	Afghanistan	24%	Honduras
		19%	Guatemala
60%	**Europe**	18%	Dominican Republic
	(average of countries)		
80%	Sweden	**56%**	**Oceania**
75%	Denmark		**(average of countries)**
74%	Czech Republic	63%	Australia
73%	Belarus	49%	New Zealand
73%	Finland		
72%	Russia	**30%**	**South America**
71%	Estonia		**(average of countries)**
71%	Latvia	40%	Brazil
71%	Poland	39%	Uruguay
71%	Slovakia	33%	Chile
71%	United Kingdom	33%	Venezuela
70%	Lithuania	32%	Argentina
70%	Moldova	26%	Peru
70%	Ukraine	25%	Bolivia
69%	Romania	24%	Paraguay
68%	Bulgaria	23%	Colombia
68%	Norway	20%	Ecuador
67%	Hungary		

RANGE OF WOMEN'S PARTICIPATION RATES
Percentage of women aged 15–64

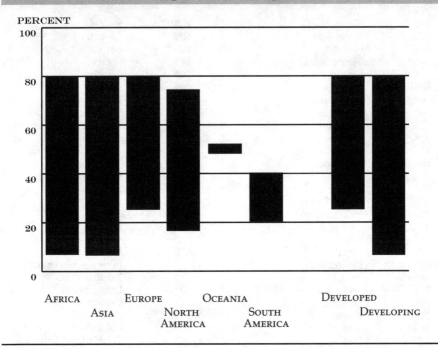

advancement opportunities, or outright exclusion from certain fields. In Egypt, for example, women are barred from serving in the judiciary, the police force, and the army.

Working mothers are especially disadvantaged. Often, because of inadequate child-care facilities, they are forced to accept lower-paying jobs with shorter or more flexible hours. These are usually part-time, temporary, or seasonal jobs, that provide few, if any, of the maternity, health care, pension, or other benefits afforded full-time workers.

Early Employment Laws

The earliest laws concerning women workers date back to mid-19th century Europe, when the Industrial Revolution was bringing more women into the work force and women's rights movements were gaining momentum. These early laws were concerned primarily with working conditions and occupational opportunities. Denmark, in 1857, became one of the first countries to grant women occupational freedom, allowing them to work in trades, crafts, and professions formerly closed to them. Similar laws were passed in Sweden in 1864, and in Norway in 1866.

In Russia the first woman physician received her medical degree in 1869, and in Britain women were first granted permission to practice medicine in 1877. In 1919 Britain's Sex Disqualification (Removal) Act opened the legal profession and higher grades of the civil service to women. In the United States, Iowa admitted a woman to the bar for the first time in 1869, although in that same year, Illinois denied another woman admission to its bar. It was not until 1920 that every state allowed women to engage in the practice of law.

International Labor Agreements

On an international level, laws protecting women workers date back to the early 1900s. In 1919 at a conference of the newly established International Labor Organization (ILO), members adopted an international agreement, the Maternity Protection Convention, specifying a minimum maternity leave and other rights for pregnant women. By the mid-1990s, however, this convention had been ratified by only 32 countries.

Later ILO conventions included provisions prohibiting women from performing heavy labor, working in an unhealthy environment, or doing jobs in industries considered dangerous. Women were also barred from working overtime or at night. Although these provisions were adopted by many countries, in later years they had to be revised or abolished on the grounds that they actually discriminated against women by barring them from certain occupations and industries.

In 1951 the ILO adopted the Equal Remuneration Convention, which mandated equal pay for work of equal value. This principle replaced the earlier concept of equal pay for equal work, which was difficult to apply in industries where there were no male equivalents to women's jobs and men's and women's positions could not be easily compared. In 1958 the ILO adopted the Discrimination (Employment and Occupation) Convention, which prohibited sex discrimination in hiring, training, and terms of employment. Both of these conventions have been ratified by more than 120 countries.

One of the most recent ILO agreements concerning women is the 1981 Workers with Family Responsibilities Convention, which set forth guidelines for child care, working hours, and assistance for women entering and reentering the work force. By the mid-1990s, this convention had been ratified by only 24 countries.

Antidiscrimination Laws

Beginning in the 1960s and 1970s, many countries, especially industrial nations with large numbers of women workers, began drafting legislation specifically aimed at prohibiting discrimination against women in the workplace. Many of these laws were based on ILO guidelines and were actively supported by women's movements demanding increased employment opportunities and an end to discrimination. Most of these laws, such as the U.S. Civil Rights Act of 1964, made it illegal for an employer to discriminate on the basis of sex in hiring, training, promotion, benefits, pay, or other working conditions. Later laws or amendments have addressed related issues, such as equal pay for work of equal value, affirmative action, and sexual harassment.

All too often, however, these and other antidiscrimination laws lack stringent penalties or are not adequately enforced. Some laws impose no sanctions on employers and are largely ignored. In Japan an equal opportunity employment law does not actually prohibit discrimination against women; it simply advises employers to "endeavor" to avoid it. Sometimes antidiscrimination laws apply only to certain groups of workers. In Canada, for example, federal equal value legislation covers only about 10% of the work force since it pertains only to federal employees and workers in federally regulated industries. Some Canadian provinces have enacted similar laws, though, so that about a third of the total work force is now covered by some form of equal value legislation.

Affirmative Action

In many countries one of the most contentious issues in recent years has been that of affirmative action, a policy that favors the preferential treatment of women in hiring, training, promotion, and other areas where they have traditionally suffered discrimination. A number of countries—among them Australia, Germany, Israel, Italy, the Netherlands, Norway, and the United States—have launched successful affirmative action programs but lately some of these policies have been attacked as violating equal opportunity laws and discriminating against men.

A major blow to affirmative action came in 1995, when the European Court of Justice issued a landmark ruling in which it found Germany's affirmative action legislation to be in violation of the equal opportunities law of the European Union (EU). Although the court's ruling is not binding on EU member nations, some women's groups have started calling for the EU's equal opportunities law to be amended.

Sexual Harassment

Sexual harassment is generally defined as a form of discrimination in which sexual advances or requests for sexual favors either constitute a condition of a person's employment or advancement or create a work environment that is hostile, intimidating, or offensive. It was not until the mid-1970s that public attention began focusing on the problem, and there is still very little reliable information about its extent.

From the few countries that have conducted surveys, sexual harassment seems to be a serious problem. The Netherlands, for example, reports that as many as a third of working women have experienced it in some form or another. In 1995, in a survey of 3,000 women in the United States, 76% reported at least some degree of sexual harassment in their workplace.

Although a number of countries—including Argentina, Australia, Canada, France, Germany, Israel, Mexico, the Netherlands, the United Kingdom, and the United States—have enacted laws specifically prohibiting sexual harassment, many others are still in the process of studying the problem or are just beginning to draft legislation. In Bolivia and other countries where sexual harassment is not illegal, employees must file charges under other provisions of the penal code.

Economies in Transition

Although antidiscrimination laws and policies are gradually making a difference in many parts of the world, women's employment rights have recently suffered serious setbacks in the formerly communist countries of Eastern Europe. With the transition to a market economy, many of these countries suffered dramatic economic reversals that resulted in rising prices, falling wages, and high unemployment. Women were especially hard hit. They had traditionally been concentrated in public sector jobs, and because these were among the first to be eliminated, large numbers of women suddenly lost their livelihood. Further, women working in the private sector found themselves unprotected by antidiscrimination laws, which were now largely ignored. For example, job advertisements placed by private employers were allowed to specify the desired sex of a prospective employee. In addition, many of the generous maternal benefits that women had enjoyed under communism were reduced or eliminated. Those benefits that remained had to be funded by individual employers, who then became reluctant to hire women.

Islamic Countries

Another form of economic discrimination is seen in some Muslim countries, where religious laws play an important role in defining women's employment. In some communities even highly educated women are not allowed to work; Saudi Arabian women, for example, constitute 55% of college graduates yet only 8% of the labor force. And those Muslim women who do work outside the home may be severely limited in their choice of occupations. In communities where Islamic law is strictly enforced, women are allowed to work only in schools and hospitals, and only with female students or patients.

AREAS OF EMPLOYMENT

Women are found in nearly every occupational category and in every industry. Approximately 50% of the world's working women are employed in the service sector: wholesale and retail trades, restaurants, hotels, communications, insurance, real estate, business services, and social and personal services. About 37% of women work in agriculture. The highest proportion is found in sub-Saharan Africa, where about three out of four female workers are agricultural laborers. The remaining 13% of the world's working women are found in manufacturing.

Women Make Up 97% or More of:

▲ Nurses in Japan, Bulgaria, and Poland.

▲ Kindergarten teachers in France and the United States.

▲ Secretaries in Sweden.

▲ Cashiers in Finland.

▲ Building cleaners in Australia.

▲ Child-care workers in China.

Job segregation is a serious problem for women throughout much of the world. Women are not only concentrated in fewer occupations than men, they are generally found at the very lowest levels within an occupational group, receiving the lowest pay and having the least opportunity for advancement. For example, throughout most of the world women predominate overwhelmingly in the teaching profession, but they tend to be concentrated at the less prestigious, lower-paying preschool and primary levels. Similarly, in the area of health care women constitute the great majority of nurses, midwives, social workers, and hospital aides but only a minority of physicians or hospital administrators.

Women in Administrative and Managerial Positions

In all regions of the world women are greatly underrepresented in administrative and managerial positions: chief executives and other corporate managers, senior government administrators, legislators, heads of villages, and others. Worldwide, they occupy only about 14% of these positions.

The developed countries, along with Latin America and the Caribbean, have the largest percentages of women in administrative and management posts. The lowest proportions are found mostly among the Islamic countries of the Middle East and southern and western Asia, although some of the

WOMEN IN ADMINISTRATIVE AND MANAGERIAL POSITIONS WORLDWIDE

WOMEN PER 100 MEN	COUNTRY	WOMEN PER 100 MEN	COUNTRY
139	Hungary	15	Iraq
91	Kazakhstan	14	Eritrea
68	Canada	14	Nicaragua
67	United States	13	China
64	Sweden	13	Ethiopia
49	United Kingdom	13	Mozambique
48	Guatemala	13	Myanmar
48	Haiti	12	Egypt
48	New Zealand	12	Liberia
44	Bulgaria	11	Cameroon
40	Puerto Rico	11	Greece
38	Honduras	10	Central African Republic
38	Philippines	10	France
37	Colombia	10	Ghana
36	Romania	10	Spain
35	Ecuador	10	Tunisia
34	Australia	10	Zaire
34	Morocco	9	Japan
34	Norway	9	Malawi
33	Sri Lanka	9	Rwanda
31	Croatia	9	Sierra Leone
31	Finland	9	Togo
30	Costa Rica	8	Mauritania
30	Nepal	7	Angola
30	Slovakia	7	Argentina
29	Slovenia	7	Benin
29	Thailand	7	Indonesia
29	Trinidad and Tobago	6	Algeria
28	Peru	6	Congo
27	Dominican Republic	6	Jordan
26	Uruguay	6	Nigeria
25	Mali	6	Switzerland
24	Chile	6	Zambia
24	Mexico	5	Bangladesh
24	South Africa	5	Kuwait
23	Cuba	4	Iran
23	Portugal	4	Italy
23	Venezuela	4	Korea, North
22	El Salvador	4	Korea, South
22	Israel	4	Senegal
21	Brazil	4	Turkey
20	Austria	3	Pakistan
20	Bolivia	3	Syria
19	Paraguay	2	India
19	Singapore	2	Lebanon
18	Ireland	2	Sudan
18	Poland	2	United Arab Emirates
18	Zimbabwe	2	Yemen
17	Denmark	1	Afghanistan
16	Burkina Faso	1	Malaysia
16	Burundi	1	Panama
16	Netherlands	0	Saudi Arabia
15	Belgium		

WOMEN IN ADMINISTRATIVE AND MANAGERIAL POSITIONS BY REGION

WOMEN PER 100 MEN	COUNTRY	WOMEN PER 100 MEN	COUNTRY
12	**Africa** (average of countries)	4	Iran
34	Morocco	4	Korea, North
25	Mali	4	Korea, South
24	South Africa	4	Turkey
18	Zimbabwe	3	Pakistan
16	Burkina Faso	3	Syria
16	Burundi	2	India
14	Eritrea	2	Lebanon
13	Ethiopia	2	United Arab Emirates
13	Mozambique	2	Yemen
12	Egypt	1	Afghanistan
12	Liberia	1	Malaysia
11	Cameroon	0	Saudi Arabia
10	Central African Republic		
10	Ghana	30	**Europe** (average of countries)
10	Tunisia	139	Hungary
10	Zaire	64	Sweden
9	Malawi	49	United Kingdom
9	Rwanda	44	Bulgaria
9	Sierra Leone	36	Romania
9	Togo	34	Norway
8	Mauritania	31	Croatia
7	Angola	31	Finland
7	Benin	30	Slovakia
6	Algeria	29	Slovenia
6	Congo	23	Portugal
6	Nigeria	20	Austria
6	Zambia	18	Ireland
4	Senegal	18	Poland
2	Sudan	17	Denmark
		16	Netherlands
13	**Asia** (average of countries)	15	Belgium
91	Kazakhstan	11	Greece
38	Philippines	10	France
33	Sri Lanka	10	Spain
30	Nepal	6	Switzerland
29	Thailand	4	Italy
22	Israel		
19	Singapore	34	**North America** (average of countries)
15	Iraq	68	Canada
13	China	67	United States
13	Myanmar	48	Guatemala
9	Japan	48	Haiti
7	Indonesia	40	Puerto Rico
6	Jordan	38	Honduras
5	Bangladesh	30	Costa Rica
5	Kuwait	29	Trinidad and Tobago

(continued)

WOMEN IN ADMINISTRATIVE AND MANAGERIAL POSITIONS BY REGION *(cont.)*

WOMEN PER 100 MEN	COUNTRY	WOMEN PER 100 MEN	COUNTRY
27	Dominican Republic	**24**	**South America**
24	Mexico		**(average of countries)**
23	Cuba	37	Colombia
22	El Salvador	35	Ecuador
14	Nicaragua	28	Peru
1	Panama	26	Uruguay
		24	Chile
		23	Venezuela
41	**Oceania**	21	Brazil
	(average of countries)	20	Bolivia
48	New Zealand	19	Paraguay
34	Australia	7	Argentina

RANGE OF WOMEN IN ADMINISTRATIVE AND MANAGERIAL POSITIONS

Number of women per 100 men

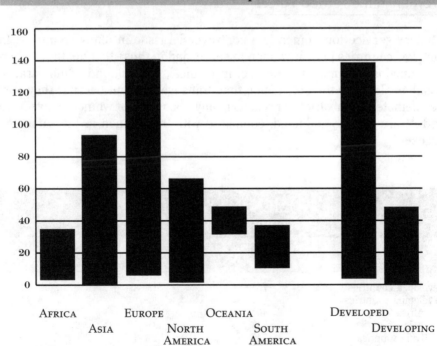

AFRICA ASIA EUROPE NORTH AMERICA OCEANIA SOUTH AMERICA DEVELOPED DEVELOPING

world's most industrialized countries are also ranked toward the bottom of the list: Italy has 4 women for every 100 men; Switzerland has 6; Japan, 9; and Spain and France 10 each.

Women in Professional and Technical Positions

Women are generally better represented in this category than in administrative and managerial positions. Professional and technical workers include teachers, medical and dental technicians, nurses, scientists, laboratory workers, artists, writers, and others. Women make up 42% of this category worldwide, with the largest concentrations being in the developed nations and countries of Latin America and the Caribbean. In 28 countries women in this occupational category outnumber men.

Teaching at the preschool and primary levels is a female-dominated profession throughout most of the world. However, the percentage of female teachers generally decreases in secondary school, and at the university level, most of the higher-paid, tenured positions are occupied by men. At all educational levels, women are seldom seen as principals or other top-level administrators.

Women in the Armed Forces

Military service for women is a controversial issue in many countries. In fact, few countries permit women to serve, and in those that do, they generally function as support personnel in medical, clerical, and administrative positions. Israel is the only nation that drafts women, but because they may be exempted for a variety of reasons, only about 60% of women between 18 and 21 are actually inducted, compared with 90% of men in the same age bracket.

WOMEN IN EDUCATION Percentage of total, by level			
	PRIMARY SCHOOL	SECONDARY SCHOOL	HIGHER EDUCATION
Developed countries	75%	51%	26%
Developing countries			
Africa	40%	25%	16%
Asia	54%	43%	24%
Latin America	74%	51%	27%
Caribbean	72%	54%	35%

WOMEN IN PROFESSIONAL AND TECHNICAL POSITIONS WORLDWIDE

WOMEN PER 100 MEN	COUNTRY	WOMEN PER 100 MEN	COUNTRY
194	Kazakhstan	72	Bolivia
172	Philippines	72	Colombia
170	Denmark	72	Japan
159	Finland	72	Myanmar
157	Uruguay	71	France
152	Poland	69	Indonesia
147	Jamaica	69	Peru
137	Slovakia	68	Singapore
133	Brazil	67	Zimbabwe
130	Norway	65	Haiti
127	Bulgaria	61	Lebanon
127	Canada	61	Switzerland
127	Sweden	59	Syria
124	Slovenia	58	Kuwait
123	Croatia	57	Nepal
123	Venezuela	55	Ghana
121	Argentina	51	Jordan
121	Trinidad and Tobago	48	Iran
119	Portugal	47	Rwanda
117	Israel	47	Sierra Leone
115	Puerto Rico	47	Turkey
111	Romania	47	Zambia
111	Thailand	44	Burundi
108	Chile	44	Tunisia
105	Paraguay	43	Benin
103	Panama	40	Congo
103	South Africa	40	Sudan
103	United States	39	Egypt
100	Honduras	39	Malawi
98	Dominican Republic	38	Algeria
96	Hungary	35	Burkina Faso
92	Austria	35	Nigeria
92	New Zealand	34	United Arab Emirates
91	Cuba	33	Korea, North
89	Belgium	33	Liberia
89	Spain	32	Cameroon
88	Ireland	32	Morocco
87	Malaysia	31	Ethiopia
86	Italy	30	Bangladesh
82	China	27	Togo
82	Guatemala	26	India
82	Sri Lanka	26	Mauritania
81	Costa Rica	26	Mozambique
79	Ecuador	23	Central African Republic
78	Iraq	23	Mali
78	United Kingdom	22	Pakistan
76	El Salvador	20	Senegal
76	Greece	20	Zaire
76	Mexico	18	Ivory Coast
75	Nicaragua	16	Afghanistan
74	Australia	13	Yemen
74	Korea, South	11	Saudi Arabia
74	Netherlands	7	Angola

WOMEN IN PROFESSIONAL AND TECHNICAL POSITIONS BY REGION

WOMEN PER 100 MEN	COUNTRY	WOMEN PER 100 MEN	COUNTRY
31	**Africa** (average of countries)	57	Nepal
103	South Africa	51	Jordan
67	Zimbabwe	48	Iran
55	Ghana	47	Turkey
47	Rwanda	34	United Arab Emirates
47	Sierra Leone	33	Korea, North
47	Zambia	30	Bangladesh
44	Burundi	26	India
44	Tunisia	22	Pakistan
43	Benin	16	Afghanistan
40	Congo	13	Yemen
40	Sudan	11	Saudi Arabia
39	Egypt		
39	Malawi	**108**	**Europe** (average of countries)
38	Algeria	170	Denmark
35	Burkina Faso	159	Finland
35	Nigeria	152	Poland
33	Liberia	137	Slovakia
32	Cameroon	130	Norway
32	Morocco	127	Bulgaria
31	Ethiopia	127	Sweden
27	Togo	124	Slovenia
26	Mauritania	123	Croatia
26	Mozambique	119	Portugal
23	Central African Republic	111	Romania
23	Mali	96	Hungary
20	Senegal	92	Austria
20	Zaire	89	Belgium
18	Ivory Coast	89	Spain
7	Angola	88	Ireland
		86	Italy
66	**Asia** (average of countries)	78	United Kingdom
194	Kazakhstan	76	Greece
172	Philippines	74	Netherlands
117	Israel	71	France
111	Thailand	61	Switzerland
87	Malaysia		
82	China	**97**	**North America** (average of countries)
82	Sri Lanka	147	Jamaica
78	Iraq	127	Canada
74	Korea, South	121	Trinidad and Tobago
72	Japan	115	Puerto Rico
72	Myanmar	103	Panama
69	Indonesia	103	United States
68	Singapore	100	Honduras
66	Lebanon	98	Dominican Republic
59	Syria	91	Cuba
58	Kuwait		

(continued)

WOMEN IN PROFESSIONAL AND TECHNICAL POSITIONS BY REGION *(cont.)*

WOMEN PER 100 MEN	COUNTRY	WOMEN PER 100 MEN	COUNTRY
82	Guatemala	**104**	**South America (average of countries)**
81	Costa Rica		
76	El Salvador	157	Uruguay
76	Mexico	133	Brazil
75	Nicaragua	123	Venezuela
65	Haiti	121	Argentina
		108	Chile
		105	Paraguay
83	**Oceania (average of countries)**	79	Ecuador
		72	Bolivia
92	New Zealand	72	Colombia
74	Australia	69	Peru

RANGE OF WOMEN IN PROFESSIONAL AND TECHNICAL POSITIONS

Number of women per 100 men

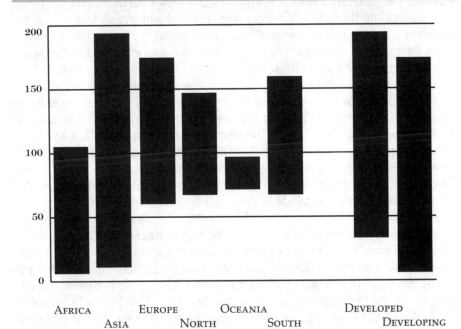

AFRICA ASIA EUROPE NORTH AMERICA OCEANIA SOUTH AMERICA DEVELOPED DEVELOPING

Very few nations allow women to serve in combat positions; these include Australia, Belgium, Canada, Eritrea, Ethiopia, Israel, the Netherlands, Norway, the United States, Venezuela, and Zambia. Barring women from combat duty often excludes them from certain training and career opportunities and makes them ineligible for promotion to the highest military ranks.

Self-Employment

One of the fastest-growing job categories for women in both the developed and the developing regions of the world is that of self-employment. In 1990 women accounted for 29% of all self-employed workers, up from 21% in 1970. Increasing numbers of women are becoming entrepreneurs; the number of new businesses owned by women is rising faster than the number owned by men. In Canada, for example, women comprise almost a third of all self-employed workers, and they have been starting their own businesses at three times the rate of men.

PAY DIFFERENCES

Although the difference between women's and men's earnings has gradually been narrowing, there is still no country in the world where women's average earnings are equal to those of men. The size of the wage gap, however, varies enormously from one country to the next, and even within the same country there may be vast differences between urban and rural areas.

One of the difficulties in comparing wage gaps among different countries is that much of the available data are based on different criteria and are thus difficult to compare. The figures most commonly reported are those of nonagricultural workers. Among the developed nations, this is not a serious problem, since a very small percentage of the labor force—both women and men—are engaged in agriculture. However, among the developing countries, where the majority of working women are engaged in agriculture, the fact that the statistics exclude these workers makes the data much less meaningful.

Among the 50 or so countries reporting nonagricultural wages for women and men, the average wage for women is about 75% of men's. In only 4 countries—Tanzania, Vietnam, Australia, and Sri Lanka—do women earn 90% or more of men's wages, and in five—China, South Korea, Japan, Bangladesh, and Russia—the proportion is less than 60%. It should be noted that in Russia the wage gap widened tremendously after the 1991 dissolution of the Soviet Union and the transition from communism to a market economy. In 1991 women were earning 75% of men's wages, but this proportion plummeted to 40% in 1994.

PAY DIFFERENCES WORLDWIDE
Women's (nonagricultural) wages as a percentage of men's

PERCENT	COUNTRY	PERCENT	COUNTRY
92%	Tanzania	76%	Portugal
92%	Vietnam	75%	Belgium
91%	Australia	75%	Israel
90%	Sri Lanka	75%	Mexico
89%	Sweden	75%	United States
86%	Colombia	75%	Uruguay
85%	Kenya	73%	Central African Republic
85%	Norway	71%	Singapore
85%	Turkey	70%	Spain
84%	Jordan	70%	United Kingdom
83%	Costa Rica	69%	Ireland
83%	Denmark	68%	Thailand
82%	Hungary	68%	Switzerland
81%	France	65%	Argentina
81%	New Zealand	64%	Ecuador
80%	Egypt	63%	Canada
80%	Italy	62%	Bolivia
78%	Austria	61%	Philippines
78%	Greece	61%	Chile
78%	Poland	60%	Syria
78%	Zambia	59%	China
77%	Finland	54%	Korea, South
77%	Netherlands	51%	Japan
76%	Brazil	42%	Bangladesh
76%	Germany	40%	Russia
76%	Paraguay		

A number of factors are important in determining the wage gap between women and men. In every country, compared with men, women work in lower-level, less skilled jobs in lower-paying industries. And despite the many equal pay laws, in practice women performing the same jobs as men generally receive lower salaries. In addition, women are much more likely than men to take temporary, seasonal, or part-time jobs, often because of child-care or other family obligations, or because they cannot find full-time work. Also, women usually have shorter careers than men because their work lives are typically interrupted for pregnancy and childbearing.

WORKING HOURS

Although women have been entering the work force in increasing numbers, permanent full-time jobs have not been increasing at the same pace, and the majority of new jobs are temporary or part-time positions. Between 1983 and 1987, 70% of all new jobs created in the European Community (now called the European Union) were part-time positions. Some women, especially

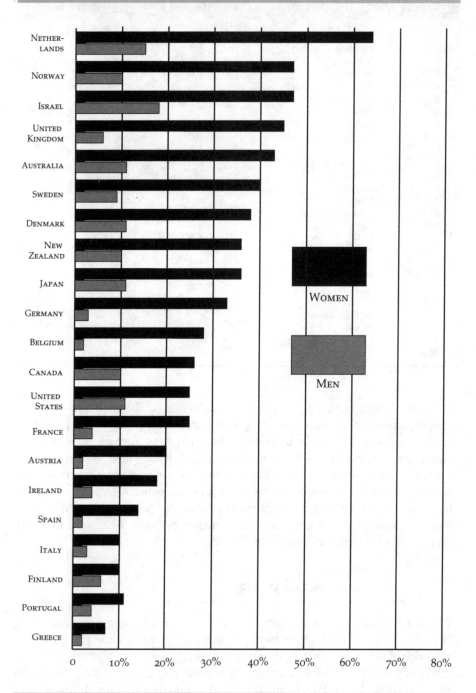

PART-TIME WORKERS
Percentage of total workers, selected countries

NETHER-LANDS

NORWAY

ISRAEL

UNITED KINGDOM

AUSTRALIA

SWEDEN

DENMARK

NEW ZEALAND

JAPAN

WOMEN

GERMANY

BELGIUM

MEN

CANADA

UNITED STATES

FRANCE

AUSTRIA

IRELAND

SPAIN

ITALY

FINLAND

PORTUGAL

GREECE

0   10%   20%   30%   40%   50%   60%   70%   80%

BANKING ON WOMEN ENTREPRENEURS

Obtaining start-up capital can be a major obstacle for any entrepreneur, but it is an especially difficult hurdle for poor women, who tend to have little collateral and in some countries cannot get a bank loan or sign a legal document without their husband's consent.

In recent years, however, women in some of the world's poorest nations have been helped to overcome this problem by the creation of a number of small banks and lending programs—called "micro banks"—that offer long-term, low-interest loans requiring little collateral. In rural India, where very few women own property or have bank accounts, the Self-Employed Women's Association (SEWA) Cooperative Bank even accepts pieces of jewelry as collateral and allows illiterate women to sign documents with a thumbprint.

Women who wish to expand or start their own businesses—as small-scale farmers, food vendors, clothing makers, or in other crafts or home-based trades—can borrow as little as $10 or $15 from these micro banks and repay it at low interest rates over extended periods, sometimes as long as five years. In Bolivia the average loan to a woman entrepreneur amounts to $400, compared with $200,000 for the average business loan.

Since their inception in the 1980s, these specialized lending programs have been enormously successful, and now more than 50 of them provide credit and other financial services to women in countries such as Chile, the Dominican Republic, Ghana, Indonesia, Ivory Coast, Kenya, Nepal, Niger, and Thailand. One reason for their success is that women borrowers have been found to be good business risks, with extremely high rates of repayment. The Banco Solidario in Bolivia reports a repayment rate of over 98% by its women customers, while the Grameen Bank and other banks report 97% repayment rates in Bangladesh and China.

When a women's bank moves in, the entire community benefits. After repaying their loans, women borrowers generally use their increased business profits to educate their children and provide better nutrition and health care for their families. They are also more likely than men to invest in improvements for their village, bringing in electricity, clean water, and sanitation, and building schools and medical facilities.

mothers of small children, prefer these jobs for their limited hours and flexibility, and in fact the Italian government is actively promoting the creation of part-time positions so that more mothers with young children can enter the labor force.

MATERNITY LEAVE AND BENEFITS

Paid maternity leave is an important benefit for working mothers. Most countries provide a maternity leave extending from before the birth of the child to at least several weeks after. During this period, which ranges from one to six months, the mother's job and health care benefits are guaranteed and some portion of her salary is paid by a government social security or health insurance system, the mother's employer, or a combination of both. In some countries she may be paid only 25% of her usual wages; elsewhere she may receive her entire salary. Two major industrialized countries that do not mandate paid maternity leave are New Zealand and the United States, which guarantee only unpaid leave.

In addition to paid leave time, other benefits to working mothers sometimes include cash payments for each child. In France the government pays every family a monthly sum for each child under the age of 18. Some countries also offer additional parental leave, with or without pay, shorter working hours for mothers, and time off during the day for child care.

Although maternity benefits are widely available, they are usually limited to full-time employees. As a result, many women—especially those working in agriculture, family-based enterprises, temporary or seasonal positions, or part-time jobs—are not eligible. Some countries place other restrictions on maternity benefits. In the Philippine civil service, for example, only married women are eligible for benefits.

RANGES IN MATERNITY LEAVE

Africa	30–105 days
Asia	40–180 days
Europe	56–168 days
North America	80–126 days
Oceania	84–98 days
South America	56–126 days

In other countries employers try to ensure that their female employees do not become pregnant. For instance, in Mexican factories employers routinely require female job applicants to submit to a pregnancy test. In Dominican Republic factories employers are known to distribute birth control pills, and in Brazil it is not unusual for an employer to require a woman to present a sterilization certificate before she can be hired.

CHILD CARE

Finding adequate child care is a major problem for working mothers around the globe. In most of the world, the scarcity of adequate and affordable child care remains a serious obstacle to women entering and remaining in the labor force.

Very few countries provide high-quality, subsidized child care. One of the most successful programs is in France, where parents can enroll their children in a variety of child-care centers, preschools, and special day-care homes run by the government. Tuition is free or minimal, adjusted according to the family income. Similar systems have been established in Denmark, Sweden, and other European countries, while in Australia a 1994 law provides a cash rebate to families to help defray child care costs.

In some of the formerly communist countries state-subsidized child care centers were available at a nominal fee, but since the transition to a market economy, many have closed, and those that remain have had to raise their tuition fees. In Poland a working mother may now have to spend nearly one-quarter of her salary to enroll her child in one of these facilities.

Single mothers and women who work nonstandard or erratic hours have an especially difficult time finding child care. In the United States a recent government study found that as many as 20% of full-time employees work nonstandard hours but that only about a dozen child care centers nationwide operate 24 hours a day.

UNEMPLOYMENT

Although in actual numbers more men than women worldwide are unemployed, the percentage of jobless women in the workforce is higher than that of jobless men. Of the 67 countries reporting unemployment rates for both sexes, about two-thirds list women's rates as greater than men's. Within Europe twice as many countries—including Austria, Belgium, Denmark, France, Germany, Italy, Russia, Spain, and Switzerland—have higher jobless rates for women. One reason women and men may have dissimilar rates of unemployment is that they tend to work in different industries and occupational categories and are therefore affected in different ways by changes in the economy and other conditions.

It should be noted that unemployment is difficult to measure, since many countries do not collect nationwide data on a regular basis. Even in countries

NUMBER OF COUNTRIES REPORTING DIFFERENCES IN MEN'S AND WOMEN'S UNEMPLOYMENT RATES

REGION	HIGHER FOR WOMEN	HIGHER FOR MEN
Africa	4	1
Asia	8	4
Europe	20	9
North America	6	4
Oceania	0	2
South America	6	3
Total	**44**	**23**

UNEMPLOYMENT RATES WORLDWIDE
Percentage of total work force

WOMEN	MEN	COUNTRY	WOMEN	MEN	COUNTRY
0.1%	0.8%	Ghana	10.1%	14.2%	Hungary
1.1%	0.8%	China	10.6%	11.8%	Canada
1.1%	0.4%	Russia	10.7%	6.0%	Peru
1.5%	2.1%	India	10.8%	12.1%	Slovenia
2.1%	1.7%	Estonia	11.2%	8.3%	Germany
2.1%	2.6%	Korea, South	11.5%	8.2%	Philippines
2.4%	2.1%	Thailand	11.6%	7.2%	Uruguay
2.6%	2.4%	Japan	11.7%	12.7%	Slovakia
2.6%	2.7%	Singapore	12.1%	8.5%	Israel
3.1%	2.1%	Mexico	12.6%	8.1%	Romania
3.3%	3.8%	Lithuania	12.9%	19.0%	Puerto Rico
3.4%	3.6%	Brazil	13.7%	11.3%	Denmark
4.6%	3.1%	Czech Republic	13.7%	10.0%	France
4.7%	5.4%	Paraguay	14.0%	5.2%	Syria
4.7%	4.4%	Switzerland	15.2%	6.4%	Greece
5.1%	7.5%	Sweden	15.7%	19.5%	Finland
5.2%	6.6%	Norway	15.8%	9.0%	Italy
5.4%	3.5%	Costa Rica	16.8%	4.5%	Pakistan
5.6%	4.1%	Chile	.17.4%	9.7%	Belgium
6.0%	6.2%	United States	17.9%	15.0%	Poland
6.0%	7.3%	Netherlands	17.9%	14.7%	Tunisia
6.4%	5.2%	Latvia	18.0%	12.0%	Croatia
6.5%	4.6%	Portugal	19.0%	18.7%	Bulgaria
6.9%	6.7%	Austria	19.4%	11.3%	Nicaragua
7.2%	8.4%	El Salvador	19.5%	18.8%	Ireland
7.2%	8.1%	Turkey	21.0%	16.0%	South Africa
7.5%	12.4%	United Kingdom	21.0%	10.6%	Sri Lanka
7.7%	6.6%	Argentina	21.2%	10.0%	Panama
7.8%	6.9%	Bolivia	21.3%	5.9%	Egypt
8.5%	4.1%	Ecuador	23.1%	9.3%	Jamaica
8.8%	9.4%	Australia	23.4%	15.7%	Trinidad and
8.9%	10.0%	New Zealand			Tobago
9.0%	5.0%	Belarus	23.8%	9.9%	Spain
9.4%	9.6%	Venezuela	35.1%	14.8%	Angola

where unemployment is carefully measured, the use of different definitions and sources of information can vary enough to make it difficult to compare one country with another. In countries where large numbers of people depend on subsistence farming, it is especially difficult to measure unemployment, and minimal data are available from many of the developing countries, particularly in Asia and Africa.

Countries with the widest gaps between women's and men's unemployment include Pakistan, where women's unemployment is more than 3.5 times that of men's; Greece and Syria, where women's unemployment rates are almost 3 times those of men; and Angola, Spain, Panama and Sri Lanka, where women's unemployment rates are about double those of men. Countries where women's jobless rates are substantially lower than men's include Finland, Hungary, and the United Kingdom.

WOMEN IN SPORTS

Professional sports have long been dominated by men. Yet in many countries more and more women are participating in high school and college sports, and increasing numbers of them are choosing careers in athletics. For most top women athletes, their ultimate goal is competing in the Olympics. While the best male competitors in many sports can often pursue careers as professional players, it is the Olympics that offer most female athletes their greatest chances for fame and financial reward. (The two major exceptions are tennis and golf, where the top women players can sign lucrative endorsement contracts and earn substantial special performance fees as well as large prize winnings.)

Since the modern Olympics began a century ago, the number of women competitors has mushroomed, from only 19 in 1900, the first year women were allowed to participate, to slightly more than 3,600 in 1996. Even though women's representation has grown from 1.6% of the total participants in 1900 to 34% in 1996, men still outnumbered women by nearly two to one at the 1996 games in Atlanta. In all, 170 countries sent women to the 1996 competitions, with the largest contingents coming from the United States (282), China (199), Germany (193), Australia (171), Russia (161), Canada (155), and Japan (150). Ten countries—including Albania, Denmark, Norway, Peru, and Zaire—sent more women than men to the 1996 games; but nearly 30—including Haiti, Kuwait, Saudi Arabia, and Venezuela—sent only male athletes.

As in the ancient Olympic Games, women were barred from competing in the first modern Olympics in 1896. According to Baron Pierre de Coubertin, the organizer of the games and a founding member of the International Olympic Committee (IOC), women were not meant to compete but had only one task, "that of crowning the winner with garlands." But in the next Olympiad, women were allowed to participate in a few events, including golf and tennis. The first woman to become a gold medalist was the English tennis player Charlotte Cooper, who won both the singles and mixed doubles titles. The women's golf championship went to the American Margaret Abbott.

Other events for women were gradually added to the games; by 1908 women were competing in archery, figure skating, and yachting; and in 1912 women swimmers made their debut. Women became eligible for high jump, discus, and other track and field events in the 1928 games, but because many of the runners were so exhausted after running the 800 meters, that event was eliminated and not reinstated until 1960. One newspaper at that time reported that after the race, "the cinder track was strewn with wretched damsels in agonized distress." Only the women's 100 meters remained, until in 1948 the women's 200 meters, long jump, and shot put were added, along with slalom, Alpine combined, and downhill skiing in the winter games. From 1948 through 1960 the number of women's events continued to grow: basketball, bobsledding, canoeing, cross-country skiing, handball, hockey, luge, pentathlon, rowing, speed skating, and volleyball.

(continued)

WOMEN IN SPORTS *(cont.)*

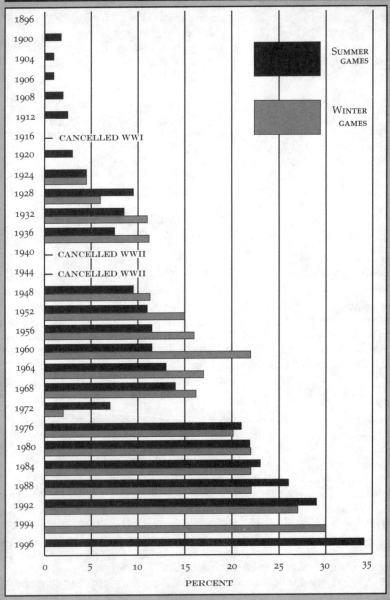

WOMEN IN THE OLYMPICS

Percentage of total participants, by year

(continued)

WOMEN IN SPORTS *(cont.)*

In 1984 the first women's 400-meter hurdles event was won by Nawal El Moutawake, the first Moroccan woman to win an Olympic gold medal. The women's marathon and heptathlon were also introduced that year, as were cycling, shooting, and synchronized swimming. Tennis, eliminated after the 1924 games, was reinstated in 1988, with West Germany's Steffi Graf winning the individual title.

The 1996 Olympiad, which added two new sports for women—soccer and softball—had a total of 271 events: 165 for men, 95 for women. Women competed directly against men in 11 events: mixed doubles badminton, some yachting events, and all equestrian events. Only four sports were still limited to male athletes: boxing, modern pentathlon, weightlifting, and wrestling.

It is interesting to note that while women's participation in the games was growing, their representation on the International Olympic Committee was lagging far behind. Founded in 1894, the IOC did not admit its first woman member until 1981, and by 1996 it had only 10 female members out of a total of 128, or just under 8%. But even with its own low proportion of women, the IOC has expressed concern about the poor representation of women on the 197 individual Olympic committees and has mandated that 10% of their decision-making positions be filled by women by the year 2000, increasing to 20% by 2005.

SOME OUTSTANDING WOMEN OLYMPIC MEDALISTS

Bonnie Blair, American speed skater, took home a total of five gold medals in individual events from three Olympic competitions (1988, 1992, and 1994), making her the only U.S. female Olympian ever to do so.

Fanny Blankers-Koen, a 30-year-old Dutch sprinter and mother of two, nicknamed the "flying housewife," took home four gold medals, making her the most successful female competitor in the 1948 games.

Valerie Brisco-Hooks, American runner, in 1984 became the first Olympic athlete—female or male—to win gold medals in both the 200-meter and the 400-meter races the same year. She won a third gold in the 4 × 400 meter relay.

Vera Cáslavská, Czech gymnast, won three gold and one silver medal in 1964, adding four more gold and two silver medals to her collection in 1968.

Nadia Comaneci, elfin 14-year-old gymnast from Romania, captured three golds, one silver, and one bronze medal in the 1976 games; her first exercise on the uneven bars won her the first perfect score in Olympic history.

Betty Cuthbert, Australian sprinter, captured three gold medals in 1956 and became the first winner of the women's 400-meter race when it was introduced in 1964.

(continued)

WOMEN IN SPORTS *(cont.)*

Mildred "Babe" Didrikson, outstanding all-round American athlete, won two gold medals and one silver medal in track and field in 1932 before turning to professional golf and becoming one of the leading women golfers in the United States.

Dawn Fraser, Australian swimmer, started her Olympic career in 1956 and by 1964, had captured four gold and two silver medals; her most outstanding achievement was winning the 100-meter freestyle three times in a row, a record that still stands.

Florence "Flo-Jo" Griffith-Joyner, American sprinter and sister-in-law of Jackie Joyner-Kersee, in 1988 captured three golds and one silver, setting a new world record in the 200 meters. In 1984, she took home the silver medal in the 200 meters.

Sonja Henie, 15-year-old skater from Norway, became the youngest athlete to win the figure skating championship, the first of three consecutive titles in that event: 1928, 1932, and 1936.

Jackie Joyner-Kersee, American sprinter and long jumper, often considered one of the world's greatest athletes, won a silver medal in the 1984 heptathlon, and in 1988 she became the first American to win the gold medal in this event. She also won a gold in the long jump in 1988 and won the heptathlon again in 1992. Recovering from an injury, she ended her Olympics career in 1996, taking home only one medal, the bronze in the long jump.

Olga Korbut, diminutive 17-year-old Soviet gymnast, the smallest on the team, took home three gold medals and one silver from the 1972 Olympic games.

Larissa Latynina, Soviet gymnast, won four gold medals in 1956 to become the most successful woman competitor that year. She went on to win a staggering total of 18 medals in her three-Olympic career—9 gold, 5 silver, 4 bronze—and remains the most successful Olympic athlete ever.

Debbie Meyer, 16-year-old American swimmer in 1968, became the first swimmer to win three gold medals in individual events in one Olympiad.

Ulrike Meyfarth, 16-year-old West German athlete, won the high jump title in 1972, becoming the youngest gold medalist in an individual track and field event.

Shannon Miller, American gymnast, won one silver and four bronze medals at age 15 in 1992 and two gold medals in 1996—one for team competition, the other in the individual beam event.

Marie-José Perec, French runner, in 1992 captured the gold in the 400-meter. In 1996 she became the first woman in a nonboycotted Olympiad to win gold medals in both the 200-meter and 400-meter races.

(continued)

WOMEN IN SPORTS *(cont.)*

Tamara Press, Soviet track and field athlete, won the shot put in 1960 and again in 1964, when she also won the discus; with every gold medal, she set an Olympic record. Tamara, along with her sister **Irena,** who won the 1964 pentathlon and hurdles championships, dropped out of Olympic competition when sex testing for women competitors was about to start in 1968, raising some suspicion as to their true gender.

Mary Lou Retton, 16-year-old American gymnast took home one gold, two silver, and two bronze medals from the 1984 games, becoming the first American gymnast to win the all-around title, the gold medal for individual combined exercises.

Wilma Rudolph, 20-year-old American sprinter, overcame childhood polio, to capture three gold medals in the 1960 games.

Michelle Smith, the first Irish woman to win an Olympic gold medal, took home no fewer than three swimming titles in 1996.

Aileen Soule, American swimmer, in 1924 became the first woman to win medals in two sports: a silver in springboard diving and a bronze in the 100-meter backstroke.

Ecaterina Szabó, Romanian gymnast was the most successful competitor at the 1984 games, winning four golds and one silver, and scoring a perfect ten in one round of floor exercises.

Amy Van Dyken, American swimmer, in 1996 became the first U.S. woman to take home four gold medals in one Olympiad: two in individual events and two in relays.

Katerina Witt, East German figure skater, won her first gold medal in 1984 and four years later became the first female skater since Sonja Henie to successfully defend her title.

FOR ADDITIONAL INFORMATION

International Labor Organization (ILO)
220 East 42nd Street
New York, NY 10017, United States
Telephone: 212-697-0150

International Labor Organization (ILO)
4, route des Morillons
CH-1211 Geneva 22, Switzerland
Telephone: 22-799-61-11

Fax: 22-798-86-85
Web site: http://www.unicc.org/ilo

International Olympic Committee (IOC)
Chateau de Vidy
CH-1007 Lausanne, Switzerland
Telephone: 21-621-61-11
Fax: 21-621-63-54
Web site: http://www.olympic.org

International Programs Center
  International Data Base
Bureau of the Census
Washington Plaza II, Room 207
Washington, DC 20233, United States
Telephone: 301-457-1403
Fax: 301-457-3034

United Nations Development Fund
  for Women (UNIFEM)
304 East 45th Street, 6th floor
New York, NY 10017, United States
Telephone: 212-906-6400
Fax: 212-906-6705
Web site: http://unifem.ingenia.com

United Nations Industrial
  Development Organization
  (UNIDO)
P.O. Box 300
Vienna International Center
A-1400 Vienna, Austria
Telephone: 1-211-310
Fax: 1-323-156
Web site: http://www.unido.org

World Bank
  Gender Analysis and Policy Unit
Washington, DC 20433, United States
Telephone: 202-473-5105
Fax: 202-522-3237
Web site: http://www.worldbank.org

MARRIAGE
AND DIVORCE

Throughout the world, laws pertaining to marriage and divorce have been shaped by centuries-old religious, ethnic, and regional customs and traditions. In many predominantly Roman Catholic countries, the church has played a crucial role in prohibiting divorce and remarriage. In Muslim countries Islamic law has permitted polygamy as well as denying women rights of inheritance and child custody. Hinduism has fostered the tradition of the dowry and arranged marriages, while Confucianism has granted fathers automatic custody of children after divorce and has favored sons over daughters in inheritance.

Because religious and customary laws are so deeply ingrained in many communities, some countries have more than one legal system, with religious and tribal as well as civil laws and courts. In South Africa, many Muslims and some Africans tribal members are not subject to civil courts but are allowed to live under their own religious or tribal customary laws, which permit polygamy, arranged marriages, and dowries. In Israel, nearly all matters relating to marriage and divorce come under the jurisdiction of religious courts. Thus, Jewish citizens are under the jurisdiction of the Orthodox rabbinical courts, while non-Jews defer to their own religious courts, either

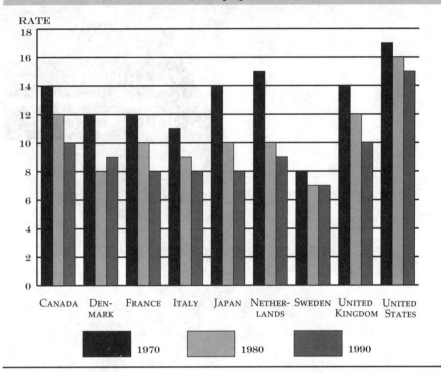

MARRIAGE RATES
Per 1,000 population

RATE

1970   1980   1990

Christian or Muslim. Israeli civil law prohibits polygamy, sets a minimum legal age for marriage, and exercises some control over such matters as guardianship of children and inheritance rights of widows.

Over the past several decades, several striking trends have emerged concerning marriage, divorce, and family structure. In country after country, marriage rates are declining, divorces are rising, and the traditional two-parent family structure, though still prevalent, is gradually eroding.

Recent decades have also seen a dramatic increase in cohabitation, that is, couples living together as husband and wife without being officially married. Partly as a result of this trend, there has also been a sharp rise in the number of births to unmarried women. In the United States 31% of all births in 1993 were to unwed mothers, a dramatic increase from 11% in 1970 and only 4% in 1950.

Around the globe, approximately one-third of households are headed by women, often with dependent children. The highest rates are found in sub-Saharan Africa, where in some nations women head as many as half the households; the lowest rates are found in Asia. Death of a husband, divorce,

DIVORCE RATES
Per 1,000 married women

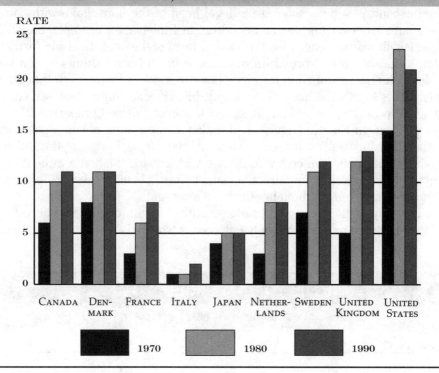

RATE

| | 1970 | 1980 | 1990 |

and separation are the most common reasons for a woman becoming head of a household; other reasons include disability of the husband, abandonment, migration, war, and out-of-wedlock births. In some cases a household is headed by a single woman living alone who never married.

Another recent trend affecting families worldwide is the increased number of married women in the labor force. In the developed countries, working men's wages have become less and less adequate to support a family, and more wives have had to work outside the home. In the United States, for example, nearly half of all employed women contribute at least half of their family's income. In the developing countries, as economies begin to modernize, families increasingly require cash for their basic needs as well as for new expenses, such as education fees for their children. Again, women have entered the labor market—often in the informal sector—to supplement their husbands' incomes. Interestingly, it has been found that working women tend to contribute a larger proportion of their wages to their family than their husbands, who often keep more of their earnings for their own personal use.

MARRIAGE

The concept of equality in marriage is far from universal. In many countries the husband is still considered the legal head of the household, with complete authority over his wife and children. In Ethiopia, for example, the civil code legally acknowledges the husband as head of the household and further states that his wife "owes him obedience in all lawful things which he orders." It also permits him to "guide her conduct." In Brazil, even though a husband is legally the head of the family, his wife can control her own earnings and property; yet he can dispose of any jointly owned property without her consent. In Kuwait, Nigeria, and Sudan a wife cannot obtain a passport without her husband's consent; in Mozambique, Nepal, Paraguay, the United Arab Emirates, and Yemen a wife cannot work outside the home without her husband's permission. In Zaire she cannot work, obtain a passport, or even open a bank account without her husband's consent.

In many of the nearly 40 predominantly Muslim countries where the Islamic law of *shari'a* is commonly enforced, a woman is regarded as a minor,

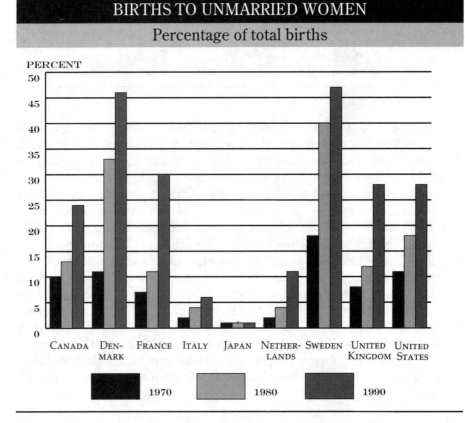

BIRTHS TO UNMARRIED WOMEN
Percentage of total births

PERCENT

CANADA   DEN-   FRANCE   ITALY   JAPAN   NETHER- SWEDEN   UNITED   UNITED
         MARK   LANDS   KINGDOM   STATES

■ 1970   ■ 1980   ■ 1990

under the legal guardianship of her father or husband. A married woman has no authority over her children, and only the husband can sign official documents regarding the family. Also according to *shari'a,* a man may have as many as four wives, while a woman may have only one husband.

Even in some developed countries, the idea of equality in marriage is a very recent legal concept. In Italy wives did not attain legal equality with their husbands until 1975, and in France it was not until 1985 that women were officially given autonomy in fiscal matters and granted equality with their husbands in managing joint assets.

Age at First Marriage

Nearly every country has a set minimum legal age for marriage, usually ranging from 18 to 21 for both the bride and groom. With parental consent, the minimum age for girls generally drops a few years. In some Latin American countries—including Cuba, Guatemala, El Salvador, Mexico, Paraguay, and Peru—it is as low as 14, while in Chile it drops to age 12.

AGE AT MARRIAGE AND FERTILITY RATE
Average age at first marriage; average number of children per woman

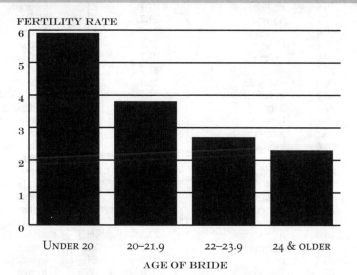

FERTILITY RATE

AGE OF BRIDE

AGE OF BRIDE AND FERTILITY RATE

Average Age at Marriage	Number of Countries	Average Country Fertility Rate
Under 20	25	5.9
20–21.9	46	3.9
22–23.9	44	2.8
24 and older	22	2.3

AVERAGE AGE AT FIRST MARRIAGE WORLDWIDE*

BRIDE	GROOM	COUNTRY	BRIDE	GROOM	COUNTRY
30.4	32.9	Sweden	22.4	24.6	Myanmar
29.7	30.8	Jamaica	22.3	26.3	Iraq
27.3	29.8	France	22.3	27.2	Morocco
27.0	29.8	Singapore	22.3	24.1	Puerto Rico
26.9	30.3	Japan	22.3	27.9	Trinidad and
26.7	28.8	New Zealand			Tobago
26.2	28.2	Canada	22.2	26.1	Bosnia-Herze-
26.1	28.5	Finland			govina
26.1	28.5	Germany	22.2	25.1	Costa Rica
25.8	29.0	Taiwan	22.2	26.1	Macedonia
25.8	28.1	United States	22.2	—	Mozambique
25.7	27.8	South Africa	22.2	25.4	Slovakia
25.6	28.4	Denmark	22.2	26.1	Yugoslavia
25.0	27.9	Switzerland	22.1	24.5	Bolivia
25.0	28.1	Tunisia	22.1	24.7	Portugal
24.7	27.8	Jordan	21.9	25.2	Burundi
24.7	27.8	Korea, South	21.9	27.0	Congo
24.5	26.7	Australia	21.9	25.4	Panama
24.4	27.9	Sri Lanka	21.8	24.5	Belarus
24.1	28.4	Slovenia	21.8	26.0	Paraguay
24.1	—	Sudan	21.7	24.7	Armenia
24.0	26.3	Norway	21.7	24.4	Azerbaijan
23.9	26.7	Israel	21.7	24.7	Czech Republic
23.8	27.3	Haiti	21.7	24.4	Estonia
23.8	26.3	Philippines	21.7	24.2	Georgia
23.7	27.7	Algeria	21.7	24.4	Kazakhstan
23.7	30.4	Senegal	21.7	24.4	Kyrgyzstan
23.6	25.7	Chile	21.7	24.4	Lithuania
23.6	26.6	Croatia	21.7	24.4	Moldova
23.5	27.0	Austria	21.7	26.5	Pakistan
23.5	26.6	Malaysia	21.7	24.4	Russia
23.4	24.4	Ireland	21.7	25.6	Saudi Arabia
23.2	27.1	Italy	21.7	24.4	Tajikistan
23.2	—	Lebanon	21.7	24.4	Turkmenistan
23.2	26.2	Netherlands	21.7	24.4	Ukraine
23.2	24.5	Vietnam	21.7	24.4	Uzbekistan
23.1	29.8	Mauritania	21.5	25.7	Syria
23.1	26.0	Spain	21.5	24.6	Turkey
23.1	25.6	United Arab	21.3	24.3	Cambodia
		Emirates	21.2	—	Rwanda
23.1	25.4	United Kingdom	21.2	24.8	Venezuela
23.0	26.2	Poland	21.1	24.9	Bulgaria
22.9	25.3	Argentina	21.1	24.3	Ecuador
22.9	25.2	Uruguay	21.1	26.9	Ghana
22.7	25.7	Peru	21.1	24.8	Indonesia
22.7	24.7	Thailand	21.1	25.5	Kenya
22.6	25.3	Brazil	21.1	24.9	Romania
22.6	25.9	Colombia	21.0	24.8	Hungary
22.5	27.6	Greece	20.7	25.4	Zimbabwe
22.4	24.8	Belgium	20.6	24.1	Mexico
22.4	25.1	China	20.6	24.9	Tanzania
22.4	26.7	Egypt	20.5	26.1	Dominican
22.4	25.2	Kuwait			Republic
22.4	24.0	Latvia	20.5	23.5	Guatemala

(continued)

AVERAGE AGE AT FIRST MARRIAGE WORLDWIDE* *(cont.)*

BRIDE	GROOM	COUNTRY	BRIDE	GROOM	COUNTRY
20.4	25.1	Albania	18.9	27.1	Ivory Coast
20.3	23.5	Madagascar	18.7	24.6	Libya
20.3	26.5	Togo	18.7	—	Nigeria
20.2	24.6	Nicaragua	18.3	24.9	Benin
20.1	26.5	Somalia	18.0	25.5	Bangladesh
20.0	24.4	Honduras	18.0	27.4	Sierra Leone
20.0	24.9	Zaire	17.9	23.8	Angola
20.0	25.1	Zambia	17.9	21.5	Nepal
19.9	23.5	Cuba	17.8	25.3	Afghanistan
19.7	26.2	Cameroon	17.8	22.9	Malawi
19.7	24.2	Iran	17.4	27.0	Burkina Faso
19.7	26.6	Liberia	17.1	23.3	Ethiopia
19.5	23.4	India	16.5	23.0	Chad
19.4	24.7	El Salvador	16.4	—	Mali
19.0	23.9	Uganda	16.3	23.7	Niger
18.9	24.1	Central African	16.0	26.8	Guinea
		Republic	15.0	22.9	Yemen

*Average age of bride and groom, in years.

AVERAGE AGE AT FIRST MARRIAGE BY REGION*

AGE OF BRIDE	COUNTRY	AGE OF BRIDE	COUNTRY
20.1	**Africa**	18.9	Central African Republic
	(average of countries)	18.9	Ivory Coast
25.7	South Africa	18.7	Libya
25.0	Tunisia	18.7	Nigeria
24.1	Sudan	18.3	Benin
23.7	Algeria	18.0	Sierra Leone
23.7	Senegal	17.9	Angola
23.1	Mauritania	17.8	Malawi
22.4	Egypt	17.4	Burkina Faso
22.3	Morocco	17.1	Ethiopia
22.2	Mozambique	16.5	Chad
21.9	Burundi	16.4	Mali
21.9	Congo	16.3	Niger
21.2	Rwanda	16.0	Guinea
21.1	Ghana		
21.1	Kenya	**22.1**	**Asia**
20.7	Zimbabwe		**(average of countries)**
20.6	Tanzania	27.0	Singapore
20.3	Madagascar	26.9	Japan
20.3	Togo	25.8	Taiwan
20.1	Somalia	24.7	Jordan
20.0	Zaire	24.7	Korea, South
20.0	Zambia	24.4	Sri Lanka
19.7	Cameroon	23.9	Israel
19.7	Liberia	23.8	Philippines
19.0	Uganda	23.5	Malaysia

(continued)

AVERAGE AGE AT FIRST MARRIAGE BY REGION* *(cont.)*

AGE OF BRIDE	COUNTRY	AGE OF BRIDE	COUNTRY
23.2	Lebanon	22.2	Macedonia
23.2	Vietnam	22.2	Slovakia
23.1	United Arab Emirates	22.2	Yugoslavia
22.7	Thailand	22.1	Portugal
22.4	China	21.8	Belarus
22.4	Kuwait	21.7	Czech Republic
22.4	Myanmar	21.7	Estonia
22.3	Iraq	21.7	Lithuania
21.7	Armenia	21.7	Moldova
21.7	Azerbaijan	21.7	Russia
21.7	Georgia	21.7	Ukraine
21.7	Kazakhstan	21.1	Bulgaria
21.7	Kyrgyzstan	21.1	Romania
21.7	Pakistan	21.0	Hungary
21.7	Saudi Arabia	20.4	Albania
21.7	Tajikistan		
21.7	Turkmenistan	**22.3**	**North America**
21.7	Uzbekistan		**(average of countries)**
21.5	Syria	29.7	Jamaica
21.5	Turkey	26.2	Canada
21.3	Cambodia	25.8	United States
21.1	Indonesia	23.8	Haiti
19.7	Iran	22.3	Puerto Rico
19.5	India	22.3	Trinidad and Tobago
18.0	Bangladesh	22.2	Costa Rica
17.9	Nepal	21.9	Panama
17.8	Afghanistan	20.6	Mexico
15.0	Yemen	20.5	Dominican Republic
		20.5	Guatemala
23.1	**Europe**	20.2	Nicaragua
	(average of countries)	20.0	Honduras
30.4	Sweden	19.9	Cuba
27.3	France	19.4	El Salvador
26.1	Finland		
26.1	Germany	**25.6**	**Oceania**
25.6	Denmark		**(average of countries)**
25.0	Switzerland	26.7	New Zealand
24.1	Slovenia	24.5	Australia
24.0	Norway		
23.6	Croatia	**22.4**	**South America**
23.5	Austria		**(average of countries)**
23.4	Ireland	23.6	Chile
23.2	Italy	22.9	Argentina
23.2	Netherlands	22.9	Uruguay
23.1	Spain	22.7	Peru
23.1	United Kingdom	22.6	Brazil
23.0	Poland	22.6	Colombia
22.5	Greece	22.1	Bolivia
22.4	Belgium	21.8	Paraguay
22.4	Latvia	21.2	Venezuela
22.2	Bosnia-Herzegovina	21.1	Ecuador

*Average age of bride, in years.

AFRICAN COUNTRIES WHERE THE AVERAGE AGE AT MARRIAGE IS LESS THAN 20 YEARS

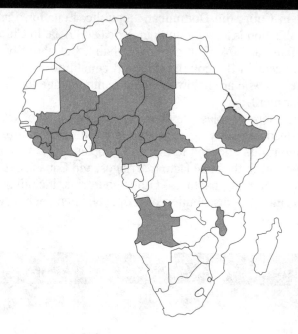

■ COUNTRIES WHERE AVERAGE AGE AT MARRIAGE
IS LESS THAN 20 YEARS

The average age at which women first marry varies tremendously from one country to another, and within each country there is often a wide age gap between the bride and groom. The developed nations tend to have the oldest brides, with the average age in Sweden heading the list at 30.4 years. The world's youngest brides are found chiefly in the Muslim world and in some non-Muslim countries of sub-Saharan Africa.

As one might expect, the age at which a woman marries is often directly related to the eventual size of her family. The younger the bride, the earlier her childbearing begins and the longer her reproductive life. Thus, countries with lower marriage ages tend to have higher fertility rates.

Cohabitation and Births to Unmarried Women

Cohabitation is rising almost everywhere but has been climbing most rapidly and is most prevalent among the industrialized countries. In Sweden as many as one in four couples are not legally married. Other European countries with high rates of cohabitation include Austria, France, Germany, and the

Netherlands. It is less common among the countries of southern Europe and in Australia, Canada, and the United States.

In Latin America and the Caribbean, where cohabitation is common, it is most prevalent in Cuba, the Dominican Republic, Ecuador, Panama, and Venezuela. Cohabitation is less common in Africa and Asia. In China it is estimated that as many as 30% of all couples cohabit, but about two-thirds of these instances occur in the countryside and constitute "early marriages" between adolescents who are below the legal minimum age for marriage (20 for women, 22 for men).

As more and more couples are choosing to live together either before marrying or instead of marrying, governments are beginning to extend to them some of the rights afforded to married couples. Argentina grants pension rights to spouses in these de facto marriages, and Canada extends insurance benefits to cohabiting partners. Other countries, including Australia, have laws concerning the distribution of property when such a relationship breaks up.

RANGE OF WOMEN'S AVERAGE AGE AT MARRIAGE

In years

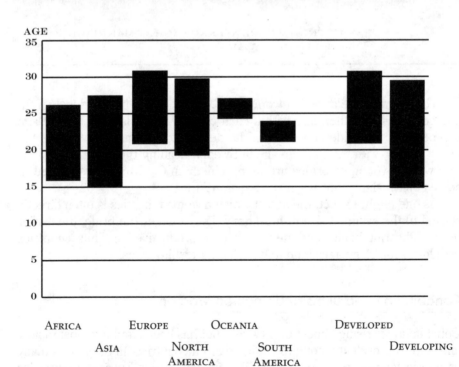

BIRTHS TO UNMARRIED WOMEN
Percentage of total births

PERCENT	COUNTRY	PERCENT	COUNTRY
1%	Egypt	16%	Hungary
1%	Japan	16%	Portugal
1%	Korea, South	18%	Ireland
2%	Israel	18%	Russia
3%	Greece	19%	Bulgaria
4%	Azerbaijan	19%	Georgia
4%	Romania	20%	Latvia
4%	Turkmenistan	23%	Afghanistan
4%	Uzbekistan	25%	Australia
5%	Armenia	25%	Austria
6%	Philippines	26%	Uruguay
6%	Sri Lanka	27%	Finland
6%	Switzerland	27%	Puerto Rico
7%	Bosnia-Herzegovina	28%	Mexico
7%	Italy	28%	Slovenia
7%	Macedonia	30%	Argentina
7%	Poland	31%	Estonia
8%	Croatia	31%	Paraguay
8%	Lithuania	31%	United Kingdom
8%	Slovakia	31%	United States
8%	Tajikistan	32%	France
9%	Belarus	34%	Canada
10%	Czech Republic	34%	Chile
10%	Spain	36%	New Zealand
11%	Moldova	41%	Costa Rica
12%	Belgium	43%	Norway
12%	Kyrgyzstan	47%	Denmark
12%	Ukraine	50%	Sweden
13%	Kazakhstan	67%	El Salvador
13%	Netherlands	75%	Panama
15%	Germany	84%	Jamaica

While many women may choose to postpone marriage, they do not always postpone childbearing. Not surprisingly, some of the countries with the oldest brides also have the highest rates of births to unmarried women. Jamaica, which has the world's second highest marriage age (after Sweden), has the highest rate of out-of-wedlock births: 84%. Panama and El Salvador also report high rates of births to single women, as do Sweden and the other Scandinavian countries. Countries with rates under 10% include Greece, Israel, Italy, Sri Lanka, and Switzerland. At the very top of the list, Egypt, Japan, and South Korea have rates of only 1%.

In many countries the rate of out-of-wedlock births is also closely related to the prevalence of cohabitation. Thus, countries that have seen a dramatic rise in cohabitation have also experienced an increase in births to unmarried women. In Australia, for example, the number of couples living together before marrying more than doubled in less than a decade, from 27% in 1983 to 56% in 1992. During the same period, births to unmarried women rose from 22% of all births to 30%. Similarly, in the United Kingdom 62% of couples marrying in 1992 reported living together prior to marriage, compared with 36% of couples in 1980. During roughly the same period of time, the incidence of out-of-wedlock births rose from 19% of all births to 31%.

Same-Sex Marriages

Same-sex marriages are not officially considered marriages but registered partnerships. They were first legalized in Denmark in 1989. Norway followed in 1993, and Sweden in 1994. Although the partners in these relationships are accorded many of the rights granted to married partners, they cannot adopt a child, serve as foster parents, or be married in church. In addition, these marriages are not recognized in other countries.

In 1994 the European Parliament passed a resolution declaring that same-sex marriages should be permitted and that the couples in these relationships should be allowed the right of adoption. The Netherlands is currently studying a bill giving full legal status to same-sex couples, including rights of adoption.

Although neither same-sex marriages nor registered partnerships are legal anywhere in the United States, some states have granted gay and lesbian couples certain rights, such as adoption; and some states, cities, other government entities, and major corporations have started extending medical and other benefits to the partners of gay and lesbian employees. In Canada, despite federal legislation prohibiting discrimination on the basis of sexual orientation, same-sex couples do not have the same rights as heterosexual cohabiting couples.

Polgyamy

Polygamy is legal in most Muslim countries. In Togo it is estimated that slightly more than half of all married women are in a polygamous relationship; in Mali, Nigeria, and Senegal this figure is over 40%. In most other Muslim countries, however, polygamy is practiced by a much smaller proportion of the population, and although Islamic law permits as many as four wives, it is extremely rare for a man to have more than two. In general, polygamy tends to prevail most in rural regions and among those with the least education. A 1992 study conducted in Nigeria found that nearly half of all women who had no schooling at all were in polygamous marriages, compared with only about 17% of women with secondary or higher education.

Only two Muslim countries—Tunisia and Turkey—have outlawed polygamy, but others have taken steps to curtail it by imposing various conditions under which a man may take more than one wife. In Egypt, for example, a 1995 law allows a wife to prohibit her husband from taking a second wife by so stipulating in her marriage contract.

Polygamy is also prevalent among many non-Muslim ethnic groups in Africa and Asia; the practice is common in Cameroon, Central African Republic, the Congo, Malaysia, and Singapore, among others. It is interesting to note that in the past the cost of supporting more than one family was a major factor in keeping the number of polygamous marriages low. Today, however, with more women in the developing countries entering the work force, it is becoming an advantage for a man to have two or more working wives.

Polygamy has recently become a problem in some European countries where large numbers of immigrants come from those parts of the world where it is commonly practiced. France, in particular, has received tens of thousands of immigrants from Mali, Mauritania, Senegal, and other Muslim countries where polygamy is widespread, and it is estimated that in the Paris metropolitan area alone more than 200,000 people live in polygamous marriages. Although the French government initially tolerated these relationships, it recently announced that it will officially recognize only one wife and consider any other marriages annulled.

Blood Relationships

There are a large number of civil, religious, and customary laws pertaining to the blood relationship between a prospective bride and groom. In many countries marriages between close blood relations, such as siblings or cousins, are prohibited by law. In northern India some groups observe a traditional rule of avoiding marriage with someone who is removed by less than seven degrees from the father and five degrees from the mother. Yet in parts of southern India a man often prefers to marry a maternal first cousin, his mother's brother's daughter.

In South Korea blood relationships were defined by a centuries-old ban on marriages between descendants of the same forefather, yet because many Koreans share the same dozen or so last names, it was not easy for a bride and groom with the same surname to prove that they were unrelated. Thus, thousands of couples chose to live out of wedlock or wait for one of the year-long suspensions of the ban that occur every ten years or so. In 1995, however, the country's highest court created a loophole in the law, saying that unrelated couples with the same last name could legally wed provided they first get married outside the country.

RELIGIOUS AND ETHNIC MARRIAGE CUSTOMS

In large parts of the world many of today's customs governing marriage and family matters have been derived from deeply ingrained ethnic and religious laws and traditions. Many of these practices are prohibited by law yet so deeply rooted, especially in rural areas, that the laws banning them are difficult to enforce and largely ignored.

DOWRIES

One of the most prevalent ancient marriage customs still widely practiced in many parts of the world is the giving of a dowry by a bride or her family to her husband. Although they are generally prohibited by law, dowries are commonly given in many countries—including Bangladesh, India, Kenya, Kuwait, Lebanon, Pakistan, Senegal, South Africa, and Sri Lanka—and among different ethnic and religious groups.

Originally, a dowry was granted to a daughter to compensate her for not being able to inherit her parents' property. In India gold jewelry, fine silk saris, and other precious gifts were bestowed on the bride by her family, and she in turn gave them to her husband. Today a dowry often involves large sums of money as well as extravagant gifts. A family often starts saving for a daughter's dowry from the time she is born, and it is believed that the high cost of dowries and lavish weddings is a major cause of indebtedness among India's poor. Another serious problem related to dowries is the growing number of dowry deaths, the killing of brides by husbands or in-laws dissatisfied with their dowries. Officials in India estimate that more than 7,000 of these dowry deaths occur every year, despite the fact that since 1986 the penal code has declared that if a woman dies within seven years of marriage, and there is sufficient evidence of cruelty or harassment, it will be presumed that she was driven to commit suicide or murdered by her husband or in-laws. Bangladesh is another country where dowry deaths are becoming a serious problem.

BRIDE PRICE

In some societies it is customary for the groom's family to pay a bride price, or bride wealth, to the woman's family, whether or not a dowry is also given. This practice is most common in the Central African Republic, Chad, and other parts of Africa. In addition to compensating the bride's family for her loss, the payment also transfers to the husband all rights to her sexuality, labor, and future children.

The bride price may consist of livestock, food, clothing, valuables, or money, and it is sometimes paid in installments: when the agreement is first made, at the time the bride moves into her husband's home, and when the first child is born. If the marriage breaks up, the bride price must be returned.

ARRANGED MARRIAGES

In large areas of the world arranged marriages are not unusual and sometimes involve young girls or even infants. In Ethiopia marriages are sometimes arranged

(continued)

RELIGIOUS AND ETHNIC MARRIAGE CUSTOMS *(cont.)*

among girls as young as nine years old, and in some rural parts of India half the girls between 10 and 14 are married. Usually, the young brides remain at home until the age of 16 or 17, at which time there may be a second wedding ceremony when the bride moves into her in-laws' home.

Other countries where arranged marriages are common include China, Japan, Pakistan, and South Korea. In some places, even marriages among the wealthy upper class may be arranged by the parents of the bride and groom. In India these marriages are sometimes said to be "semi-arranged," since the bride's family may conduct the search for likely candidates but the bride has the final say in the matter.

ABUSE OF YOUNG BRIDES

The custom of a young bride moving in with her husband's family is common in many cultures, and often also dictates that she become a virtual handmaiden to her in-laws as well as her husband. In some societies these young brides may be so maltreated that they are driven to suicide. One study in Uzbekistan estimated that in 1990 300 young women committed self-immolation because of abuse and harassment from their husbands' families.

Another abusive marriage custom seen among some ethnic groups in Sudan is the practice of taking a wife on a trial basis that may last as long as four years. If the husband finds his wife unsatisfactory during that time, he may return her to her family as long as he pays them a certain sum for each child she has borne.

INHERITANCE LAWS

Religious or customary laws in many regions prohibit wives from owning or inheriting property, even though the country's legal code may permit them to do so. As a result, widows are often left destitute, stripped of their possessions and sometimes even their children.

Zambian civil law dictates that children inherit 50% of a man's property, his widow inherits 20%, his parents receive 20%, and his other relatives are entitled to 10%. However, the local courts do not uphold this law, and in practice the husband's family usually gets everything. In Kenya a widow is often excluded from the inheritance settlement, and she cannot be the sole administrator of her husband's estate without the consent of her children. In Zimbabwe, according to local custom, the widow herself may be considered her husband's property and inherited by her husband's brother, whom she is forced to marry. Other countries where widows' inheritance rights are commonly restricted or completely nullified include Burundi, the Congo, Ghana, Kenya, Togo, Uganda, and Zaire.

DIVORCE

Divorce is now legal in nearly every country, and as marriage rates have been declining, divorce rates have been rising, even in some predominantly Roman Catholic countries where divorce has long been a contentious political issue. In Spain divorce was not legalized until 1981. In Brazil, although divorce became legal in 1977, each person was allowed only one divorce during his or her lifetime, a stipulation that was not removed until 1988. In 1995 Ireland became the last major European country to legalize divorce. By a narrow margin, Irish voters in a nationwide referendum lifted the country's constitutional ban on divorce and remarriage. In 1996 a last-minute effort to overturn the results of the referendum failed when the Supreme Court rejected a claim that the government's advertising campaign had unfairly influenced the vote. This ruling paved the way for divorce legislation, which, once enacted, permits divorce in cases where the couple have been separated for four of the last five years.

The Philippines, also predominantly Roman Catholic, is one of the few countries where divorce is still prohibited. Yet a 1987 law greatly extended the grounds for legal separation and allowed marriages to be easily annulled on psychological grounds. Chile, too, permits legal separation and annulment but not divorce. In both these countries, people who wish to remarry must seek an annulment, and since an annulled marriage never legally existed, the wives in these situations are not legally entitled to alimony or child support from their husbands.

Divorce Rates

Among developed countries, Russia has the highest divorce rate, for every 100 couples who get married each year, 60 couples get divorced. Other developed countries with high divorce rates include the United States, the Scandinavian countries, and the United Kingdom.

Mutual Consent and No-Fault Divorce

One of the reasons divorce rates are rising around the world is that since the 1970s many countries—among them Argentina, Australia, Canada, India, and Japan—have liberalized their divorce laws to provide divorce by mutual consent or on a no-fault basis. In both these situations the concept of blame is removed and the divorce process is less adversarial than when one partner sues the other. In divorce by mutual consent, the divorce is automatically granted after a mandatory separation period if both partners agree that the marriage has irretrievably broken down. A no-fault divorce is also sometimes called unilateral divorce because either partner can obtain the divorce without stating a reason and without the other partner's consent.

DEVELOPED COUNTRIES WITH DIVORCE RATES OVER 25*

RATE	COUNTRY	RATE	COUNTRY
60	Russia	37	Ukraine
51	United States	36	Switzerland
48	Sweden	34	Austria
46	Estonia	34	Moldova
44	Norway	33	Czech Republic
42	United Kingdom	33	France
41	Denmark	31	Belgium
41	Finland	30	Germany
38	Canada	28	Hungary
37	Belarus	28	Netherlands
37	Lithuania		

*Rate equals number of couples getting divorced each year per 100 couples getting married.

In recent years the alarming rise in divorce rates in countries with mutual consent and no-fault legislation has prompted some governments to consider revising or abolishing these laws. In the United States, where every state has some form of no-fault divorce legislation, some states have recently begun to consider rewriting their laws to require a waiting period or manda-

EUROPEAN COUNTRIES WITH DIVORCE RATES OVER 25

■ DIVORCE RATE OVER 25

tory marriage counseling. Some states are also considering limiting no-fault divorce to couples without children.

Adultery as Grounds for Divorce

In many countries, including those with mutual consent or no-fault divorce laws, spouses still have the option of suing each other for divorce. Acceptable grounds for divorce often include abandonment, cruelty, drunkenness, physical abuse, and adultery. The definition of adultery, however, is sometimes very different for women and men. Where this double standard prevails, it was supposedly adopted to protect a husband from the possibility of his wife bearing another man's child whom he would then have to support and who could inherit his property.

In Argentina a woman is guilty of adultery if she commits a single sexual act with another man, whereas a husband may be found guilty of adultery only if he keeps a mistress. In Cameroon a woman is guilty of adultery if she has sexual relations with a man anywhere, but a man cannot be found guilty unless he has had sexual relations with another woman in his own home. In Thailand a recent government decision amended the regulations concerning infidelity as grounds for annulling a marriage. Until 1996 a wife had to prove her husband's guilt, while the husband simply had to accuse his wife of being unfaithful. Under the changed regulation, the husband also has to prove his spouse's guilt. In the Ivory Coast, a law proposed in 1996 grants a husband the right to divorce his wife on grounds of adultery for little more than finding her in intimate conversation with another man. For a wife to obtain a divorce on the grounds of adultery, her husband must be found having sexual relations with the same woman inside the family home on more than two occasions.

Child Custody and Support

Child custody in many countries is usually granted to the mother, but both parents are expected to support the children. Joint custody, an arrangement whereby the children divide their time between each parent, has become increasingly common in recent years. Russia is one of the few developed countries where joint custody is not permitted.

In many cases, especially where the mother has little or no income, the court may require the father to pay child support—regular payments toward the children's maintenance and education. One of the greatest problems facing divorced mothers is the nonpayment of child support. In Japan about three-quarters of divorced fathers fail to make these payments; in Argentina the proportion is about two-thirds; in Malaysia, about half; and in the United States, about two-fifths.

Collecting payments from delinquent parents is often a difficult task. In the United States nonpayment of child support was made a federal crime under the 1992 Child Support Recovery Act. Under this law, a first offense is punishable by a maximum sentence of six months in prison and a fine of $5,000. The federal government has also been successful in collecting support payments by garnisheeing the federal tax refunds of nonpayers. At the state level, measures aimed at pressuring delinquent parents include suspending their driver's licenses and distributing their names and photographs on "wanted" posters. There are also plans to install a nationwide database capable of checking the records of all new employees to locate parents who try to avoid payment by moving across state lines.

Divorce Under Islamic Law

Divorce is rare in the Muslim world, but the husband may obtain one unilaterally merely by repeating the phrase, "I divorce thee" to his wife three times in front of witnesses. On the other hand, if a wife wishes to divorce her husband, she must usually take the matter to a religious court and prove that her husband has had a harmful moral effect on the family or that he has failed to support her. Some Islamic countries have started enacting laws affording wives some protection against arbitrary divorce. In Bangladesh, however, the protective law applies only to registered marriages, and because most couples in rural communities cannot afford the high marriage fees, the majority of marriages are not registered.

Following divorce, a Muslim man may remarry immediately, but a woman often has to wait three months, to determine if she is pregnant. If she is, she cannot remarry until the child has been born and raised, during which time her former husband must support her.

Official custody of the children is granted to the father under Islamic law, though the mother is usually expected to raise the children, who remain with her—a son until he reaches age 13 and a daughter until she is married. During this time the father is required to maintain the children as well as their mother.

FOR ADDITIONAL INFORMATION

International Programs Center
International Data Base
Bureau of the Census
Washington Plaza II, Room 207
Washington, DC 20233, United States
Telephone: 301-457-1403
Fax: 301-457-3034

United Nations Department for
Economic and Social Information
and Policy Analysis
Population Division (Statistics)
United Nations Secretariat
New York, NY 10017, United States
Telephone: 212-963-4970

FAMILY PLANNING

Soaring population growth has been a serious global problem for many years. Over the past several decades, the world population has more than doubled, from about 2.6 billion in 1950 to 5.6 billion in the mid-1990s, and it is expected to reach nearly 8 billion by the year 2020. Most of this population growth has occurred, and is expected to continue, in the developing countries of Africa, Asia, and Latin America.

But even though populations are getting larger, the annual rate of growth is declining just about everywhere. Among the most important factors determining a population's growth rate are the number of women of childbearing age and the fertility rate, that is, the average number of children born to each woman. Countries with the lowest fertility rates tend to have the slowest rates of population growth. China, for example, with a fertility rate of 2.0, has an annual population growth rate of 1.0%, while India, with a fertility rate of 3.6, has a growth rate of 1.8%.

FERTILITY RATES

Worldwide, the average fertility rate is 3.0 children for every woman, down from 3.7 in 1980. In the developed world the average fertility rate is 2.0,

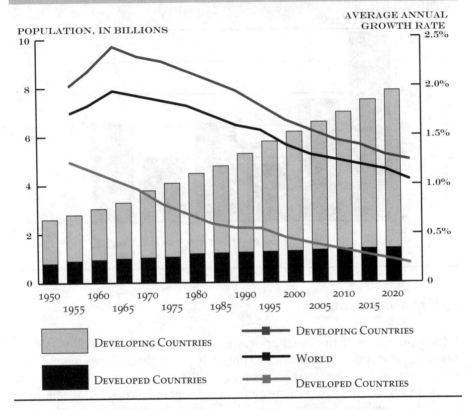

WORLD POPULATION GROWTH
Population totals; average annual growth rates

POPULATION, IN BILLIONS

AVERAGE ANNUAL GROWTH RATE

DEVELOPING COUNTRIES

DEVELOPING COUNTRIES

DEVELOPED COUNTRIES

WORLD

DEVELOPED COUNTRIES

slightly below the 2.1 generally considered necessary for a population to maintain itself. In developing countries the average fertility rate is 4.5, well above the replacement rate.

Changes in Fertility Rates

In both the developed and developing worlds, today's fertility rates represent substantial declines over the past several decades. The most dramatic decreases have occurred in countries with strong family planning programs, such as Bangladesh, Brazil, China, Indonesia, Peru, and Thailand. The only region that has not experienced a widespread reduction in fertility is sub-Saharan Africa, where significant declines in fertility rates are reported in only three countries: Botswana, Kenya, and Zimbabwe. Niger and Uganda have even reported slight increases.

FERTILITY RATES

Average number of children per woman; average of countries

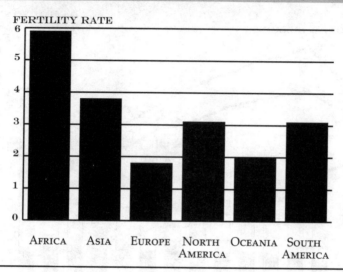

FERTILITY RATE

Fertility and Education

Education is one of the most critical factors affecting the fertility rate. In Senegal, for example, the overall fertility rate is 5.8 children per woman. Yet for women with no formal education at all, the rate jumps to 7.0, while for women who have had 10 or more years of schooling, it drops to 3.6. Similarly, in Peru the national fertility rate is 3.3 children; for women with little or no education it is 6.2, and for women with some college education it drops to 1.7. Often, women in urban areas have much lower fertility rates than their rural counterparts. Not only do urban woman tend to be better educated, but they often have greater access to family planning services.

Fertility and Infant Mortality Rates

Because family planning allows a woman to limit the number and spacing of her children, it improves her general well-being and the health of her babies. Poor health among women is often related to early childbearing, especially during the teenage years; having children less than two years apart; and having more than four children. And the babies born under these conditions are at increased risk of being underweight and sickly, often dying before the age of one. Not surprisingly, those parts of the world with the highest fertility rates are also those with the highest rates of infant mortality.

FERTILITY RATES WORLDWIDE
Average number of children per woman

RATE	COUNTRY	RATE	COUNTRY
1.2	Spain	2.4	Kazakhstan
1.3	Germany	2.4	Sri Lanka
1.3	Italy	2.5	Armenia
1.4	Greece	2.5	Chile
1.5	Bulgaria	2.6	Colombia
1.5	Japan	2.7	Argentina
1.5	Romania	2.8	Albania
1.5	Russia	2.8	Brazil
1.5	Slovenia	2.8	Indonesia
1.6	Austria	2.8	Israel
1.6	Bosnia-Herzegovina	2.8	Panama
1.6	Estonia	2.9	Dominican Republic
1.6	Latvia	2.9	Lebanon
1.6	Netherlands	3.0	Costa Rica
1.6	Portugal	3.0	Kuwait
1.6	Switzerland	3.0	Mexico
1.6	Ukraine	3.0	Tunisia
1.7	Belarus	3.1	Venezuela
1.7	Belgium	3.2	Turkey
1.7	Croatia	3.3	Ecuador
1.7	Denmark	3.3	Peru
1.7	France	3.4	Malaysia
1.7	Hungary	3.4	Morocco
1.7	Singapore	3.5	Kyrgyzstan
1.7	Taiwan	3.6	Algeria
1.8	Cuba	3.6	India
1.8	Czech Republic	3.7	Egypt
1.8	Korea, South	3.7	Uzbekistan
1.8	Lithuania	3.7	Vietnam
1.8	United Kingdom	3.8	El Salvador
1.9	Australia	3.8	Philippines
1.9	Canada	3.8	Turkmenistan
1.9	Finland	4.0	Myanmar
1.9	Poland	4.0	South Africa
1.9	Slovakia	4.1	Bangladesh
1.9	Yugoslavia	4.1	Paraguay
2.0	China	4.1	United Arab Emirates
2.0	Macedonia	4.6	Bolivia
2.0	Norway	4.6	Honduras
2.1	Georgia	4.7	Haiti
2.1	Ireland	4.7	Tajikistan
2.1	Moldova	4.8	Iran
2.1	New Zealand	4.8	Nicaragua
2.1	Sweden	4.8	Zimbabwe
2.1	Thailand	5.1	Cambodia
2.1	United States	5.1	Guatemala
2.2	Jamaica	5.2	Mauritania
2.2	Puerto Rico	5.2	Nepal
2.3	Korea, North	5.4	Jordan
2.3	Trinidad and Tobago	5.5	Cameroon
2.3	Uruguay	5.5	Central African Republic
2.4	Azerbaijan	5.5	Iraq

(continued)

FERTILITY RATES WORLDWIDE *(cont.)*
Average number of children per woman

RATE	COUNTRY	RATE	COUNTRY
5.6	Eritrea	6.3	Sierra Leone
5.6	Sudan	6.3	Togo
5.6	Syria	6.4	Laos
5.7	Chad	6.5	Burundi
5.7	Ghana	6.5	Zaire
5.7	Tanzania	6.6	Afghanistan
5.7	Zambia	6.6	Liberia
5.8	Senegal	6.8	Ethiopia
5.9	Madagascar	6.8	Guinea
5.9	Pakistan	6.8	Somalia
6.0	Kenya	6.9	Angola
6.1	Congo	6.9	Benin
6.2	Libya	6.9	Malawi
6.2	Nigeria	6.9	Mali
6.2	Saudi Arabia	7.0	Uganda
6.3	Burkina Faso	7.1	Ivory Coast
6.3	Mozambique	7.3	Niger
6.3	Rwanda	7.4	Yemen

FERTILITY RATES BY REGION
Average number of children per woman

RATE	COUNTRY	RATE	COUNTRY
5.9	**Africa**	6.3	Sierra Leone
	(average of countries)	6.3	Togo
3.0	Tunisia	6.5	Burundi
3.4	Morocco	6.5	Zaire
3.6	Algeria	6.6	Liberia
3.7	Egypt	6.8	Ethiopia
4.0	South Africa	6.8	Guinea
4.8	Zimbabwe	6.8	Somalia
5.2	Mauritania	6.9	Angola
5.5	Cameroon	6.9	Benin
5.5	Central African Republic	6.9	Malawi
5.6	Eritrea	6.9	Mali
5.6	Sudan	7.0	Uganda
5.7	Chad	7.1	Ivory Coast
5.7	Ghana	7.3	Niger
5.7	Tanzania		
5.7	Zambia	**3.7**	**Asia**
5.8	Senegal		**(average of countries)**
5.9	Madagascar	1.5	Japan
6.0	Kenya	1.7	Singapore
6.1	Congo	1.7	Taiwan
6.2	Libya	1.8	Korea, South
6.2	Nigeria	2.0	China
6.3	Burkina Faso	2.1	Georgia
6.3	Mozambique	2.1	Thailand
6.3	Rwanda	2.3	Korea, North

(continued)

FERTILITY RATES BY REGION *(cont.)*
Average number of children per woman

RATE	COUNTRY	RATE	COUNTRY
2.4	Azerbaijan	1.7	Croatia
2.4	Kazakhstan	1.7	Denmark
2.4	Sri Lanka	1.7	France
2.5	Armenia	1.7	Hungary
2.8	Indonesia	1.8	Czech Republic
2.8	Israel	1.8	Lithuania
2.9	Lebanon	1.8	United Kingdom
3.0	Kuwait	1.9	Finland
3.2	Turkey	1.9	Poland
3.4	Malaysia	1.9	Slovakia
3.5	Kyrgyzstan	1.9	Yugoslavia
3.6	India	2.0	Macedonia
3.7	Uzbekistan	2.0	Norway
3.7	Vietnam	2.1	Ireland
3.8	Philippines	2.1	Moldova
3.8	Turkmenistan	2.1	Sweden
4.0	Myanmar	2.8	Albania
4.1	Bangladesh		
4.1	United Arab Emirates	**3.1**	**North America**
4.7	Tajikistan		**(average of countries)**
4.8	Iran	1.8	Cuba
5.1	Cambodia	1.9	Canada
5.2	Nepal	2.1	United States
5.4	Jordan	2.2	Jamaica
5.5	Iraq	2.2	Puerto Rico
5.6	Syria	2.3	Trinidad and Tobago
5.9	Pakistan	2.8	Panama
6.2	Saudi Arabia	2.9	Dominican Republic
6.4	Laos	3.0	Costa Rica
6.6	Afghanistan	3.0	Mexico
7.4	Yemen	3.8	El Salvador
		4.6	Honduras
1.7	**Europe**	4.7	Haiti
	(average of countries)	4.8	Nicaragua
1.2	Spain	5.1	Guatemala
1.3	Germany		
1.3	Italy	**2.0**	**Oceania**
1.4	Greece		**(average of countries)**
1.5	Bulgaria	1.9	Australia
1.5	Romania	2.1	New Zealand
1.5	Russia		
1.5	Slovenia	**3.1**	**South America**
1.6	Austria		**(average of countries)**
1.6	Bosnia-Herzegovina	2.3	Uruguay
1.6	Estonia	2.5	Chile
1.6	Latvia	2.6	Colombia
1.6	Netherlands	2.7	Argentina
1.6	Portugal	2.8	Brazil
1.6	Switzerland	3.1	Venezuela
1.6	Ukraine	3.3	Ecuador
1.7	Belarus	3.3	Peru
1.7	Belgium	4.1	Paraguay
		4.6	Bolivia

CHANGES IN FERTILITY RATES, 1960–1995
Average number of children per woman

COUNTRY	1960	1995	CHANGE
Dominican Republic	7.4	2.9	−4.5
Thailand	6.4	2.1	−4.3
Colombia	6.8	2.6	−4.2
Tunisia	7.1	3.0	−4.1
China	5.9	2.0	−3.9
Mexico	6.8	3.0	−3.8
Morocco	7.2	3.4	−3.8
Ecuador	6.9	3.3	−3.6
Peru	6.8	3.3	−3.5
Brazil	6.2	2.8	−3.4
Egypt	7.0	3.7	−3.3
El Salvador	6.8	3.8	−3.0
Sri Lanka	5.3	2.4	−2.9
Trinidad and Tobago	5.2	2.3	−2.9
Zimbabwe	7.5	4.8	−2.7
Indonesia	5.5	2.8	−2.7
Paraguay	6.8	4.1	−2.7
India	5.9	3.6	−2.3
Jordan	7.7	5.4	−2.3
Bolivia	6.7	4.6	−2.1
Botswana	6.8	4.7	−2.1
Kenya	8.0	6.0	−2.0
Guatemala	6.9	5.1	−1.8
Ghana	6.9	5.7	−1.2
Senegal	7.0	5.8	−1.2
Tanzania	6.8	5.7	−1.1
Sudan	6.7	5.6	−1.1
Pakistan	6.9	5.9	−1.0
Zambia	6.6	5.7	−0.9
Nigeria	6.8	6.2	−0.6
Burundi	6.8	6.5	−0.3
Togo	6.6	6.3	−0.3
Cameroon	5.8	5.5	−0.3
Mali	7.1	6.9	−0.2
Liberia	6.6	6.6	—
Uganda	6.9	7.0	+0.1
Niger	7.1	7.3	+0.2

Births to Teenagers

Worldwide, approximately 15 million infants a year are born to teenage mothers, accounting for about 10% of all births. However, rates of teenage pregnancy vary tremendously from one region to the next. Africa leads the world, with births to teenagers accounting for 18% of all live births. Latin America is next, with 8%, followed by North America, with 5%, and Europe, with 3%. Although a number of factors are related to teenage birthrates, education

FERTILITY AND INFANT MORTALITY RATES
Average number of children per woman; number of deaths before age one per 1,000 live births

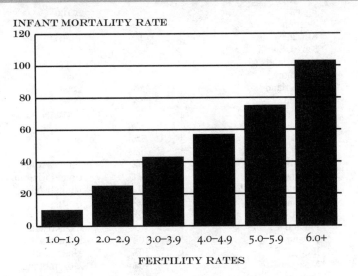

INFANT MORTALITY RATE

FERTILITY RATES

FERTILITY AND INFANT MORTALITY RATES

Fertility Rates	Number of Countries	Average of Country Infant Mortality Rate
1.0–1.9	36	10
2.0–2.9	29	24
3.0–3.9	19	43
4.0–4.9	12	57
5.0–5.9	18	74
6.0+	26	103

seems to be one of the most significant. Other factors include age at marriage and religious and cultural prohibitions against contraception and abortion.

CONTRACEPTION

One of the most significant developments affecting women in recent decades has been the introduction of new forms of contraception. Birth control pills, intrauterine devices (IUDs), and safe, simple sterilization techniques have revolutionized women's ability to determine the number and spacing of their children. And by giving women the means to more fully regulate their child-

BIRTHS TO TEENAGERS WORLDWIDE
Percentage of total births

PERCENT	COUNTRY	PERCENT	COUNTRY
1%	Japan	8%	Syria
1%	Sweden	9%	Angola
2%	Korea, North	9%	Bolivia
2%	Korea, South	9%	Croatia
2%	Netherlands	9%	Egypt
2%	Singapore	9%	Iran
2%	Switzerland	9%	Laos
3%	Albania	9%	Peru
3%	Denmark	9%	Portugal
3%	France	9%	Slovenia
3%	Germany	9%	Sudan
3%	Israel	9%	Turkey
3%	Turkmenistan	9%	United Arab Emirates
3%	Vietnam	9%	United Kingdom
4%	Belgium	9%	Zimbabwe
4%	Burundi	10%	Brazil
4%	China	10%	Ghana
4%	Finland	10%	Kazakhstan
4%	Ireland	10%	Lithuania
4%	Italy	10%	Madagascar
4%	Malaysia	10%	Mozambique
4%	Somalia	10%	Nepal
4%	Tajikistan	10%	Paraguay
5%	Australia	10%	Venezuela
5%	Azerbaijan	10%	Yemen
5%	Jordan	11%	Benin
5%	Norway	11%	Bosnia-Herzegovina
5%	Pakistan	11%	Burkina Faso
5%	Rwanda	11%	Cameroon
5%	Spain	11%	Colombia
5%	Taiwan	11%	Congo
5%	Uzbekistan	11%	Ecuador
6%	Algeria	11%	Guatemala
6%	Cambodia	11%	Honduras
6%	Kyrgyzstan	11%	India
6%	Morocco	11%	Indonesia
6%	Philippines	11%	Kenya
6%	Tunisia	11%	Libya
7%	Canada	11%	Macedonia
7%	Haiti	11%	Malawi
7%	Kuwait	11%	Mexico
7%	Lebanon	11%	Puerto Rico
7%	Myanmar	11%	Slovakia
7%	Poland	11%	Thailand
8%	Afghanistan	11%	Togo
8%	Austria	11%	Trinidad and Tobago
8%	Ethiopia	11%	Uruguay
8%	Greece	12%	Belarus
8%	Iraq	12%	Chile
8%	New Zealand	12%	Czech Republic
8%	Saudi Arabia	12%	Hungary
8%	Sri Lanka	12%	Latvia

(continued)

BIRTHS TO TEENAGERS WORLDWIDE *(cont.)*
Percentage of total births

PERCENT	COUNTRY	PERCENT	COUNTRY
12%	Mauritania	14%	Liberia
12%	Moldova	14%	Nicaragua
12%	Senegal	14%	Nigeria
12%	Zambia	14%	Romania
13%	Argentina	15%	El Salvador
13%	Estonia	15%	Panama
13%	Tanzania	15%	Russia
13%	Uganda	15%	South Africa
13%	United States	16%	Guinea
13%	Zaire	16%	Ukraine
14%	Armenia	17%	Ivory Coast
14%	Bangladesh	17%	Mali
14%	Central African Republic	18%	Chad
14%	Costa Rica	18%	Niger
14%	Dominican Republic	19%	Sierra Leone
14%	Georgia	20%	Bulgaria
14%	Jamaica	25%	Cuba

bearing, these measures have enabled them to better control and shape their own lives.

Over the past several decades, as contraceptives have become more widely available in many countries, fertility rates have dropped substantially. Even countries with limited economic resources have organized highly successful birth control programs. But not all countries promote the use of birth control. In places where strong traditional religious and ethnic laws prohibit the use of contraceptives, family planning programs are practically nonexistent or remain inaccessible to large numbers of women. Sometimes government-sponsored programs and services are available only to married women, so that single women and teenagers— those who may need these services the most—are excluded. In some countries even a married woman must have her husband's consent before receiving contraceptives. In Ethiopia, as soon as it was no longer necessary to obtain a spouse's permission, contraceptive use rose 26% in a matter of months.

Worldwide, it is estimated that about 57% of all married and other monogamous couples of childbearing age practice some form of family planning. Among the world's most highly industrialized nations, this percentage jumps to about 70%, but in the developing world it drops to 51%, and if China were excluded, it would plummet to 38%.

Government support for family planning has been increasing steadily over the last two decades in many developing countries, and contraceptive

BIRTHS TO TEENAGERS BY REGION
Percentage of total births

PERCENT	COUNTRY	PERCENT	COUNTRY
11%	**Africa**	4%	Tajikistan
	(average of countries)	5%	Azerbaijan
4%	Burundi	5%	Jordan
4%	Somalia	5%	Pakistan
5%	Rwanda	5%	Taiwan
6%	Algeria	5%	Uzbekistan
6%	Morocco	6%	Cambodia
6%	Tunisia	6%	Kyrgyzstan
8%	Ethiopia	6%	Philippines
9%	Angola	7%	Kuwait
9%	Egypt	7%	Lebanon
9%	Sudan	7%	Myanmar
9%	Zimbabwe	8%	Afghanistan
10%	Ghana	8%	Iraq
10%	Madagascar	8%	Saudi Arabia
10%	Mozambique	8%	Sri Lanka
11%	Benin	8%	Syria
11%	Burkina Faso	9%	Iran
11%	Cameroon	9%	Laos
11%	Congo	9%	Turkey
11%	Kenya	9%	United Arab Emirates
11%	Libya	10%	Kazakhstan
11%	Malawi	10%	Nepal
11%	Togo	10%	Yemen
12%	Mauritania	11%	India
12%	Senegal	11%	Indonesia
12%	Zambia	11%	Thailand
13%	Tanzania	14%	Armenia
13%	Uganda	14%	Bangladesh
13%	Zaire	14%	Georgia
14%	Central African Republic		
14%	Liberia	**8%**	**Europe**
14%	Nigeria		**(average of countries)**
15%	South Africa	1%	Sweden
16%	Guinea	2%	Netherlands
17%	Ivory Coast	2%	Switzerland
17%	Mali	3%	Albania
18%	Chad	3%	Denmark
18%	Niger	3%	France
19%	Sierra Leone	3%	Germany
		4%	Belgium
7%	**Asia**	4%	Finland
	(average of countries)	4%	Ireland
1%	Japan	4%	Italy
2%	Korea, North	5%	Norway
2%	Korea, South	5%	Spain
2%	Singapore	7%	Poland
3%	Israel	8%	Austria
3%	Turkmenistan	8%	Greece
3%	Vietnam	9%	Croatia
4%	China	9%	Portugal
4%	Malaysia	9%	Slovenia

(continued)

BIRTHS TO TEENAGERS BY REGION *(cont.)*
Percentage of total births

PERCENT	COUNTRY	PERCENT	COUNTRY
9%	United Kingdom	14%	Costa Rica
10%	Lithuania	14%	Dominican Republic
11%	Bosnia-Herzegovina	14%	Jamaica
11%	Macedonia	14%	Nicaragua
11%	Slovakia	15%	El Salvador
12%	Belarus	15%	Panama
12%	Czech Republic	25%	Cuba
12%	Hungary		
12%	Latvia	**7%**	**Oceania**
12%	Moldova		**(average of countries)**
13%	Estonia	5%	Australia
14%	Romania	8%	New Zealand
15%	Russia		
16%	Ukraine	**11%**	**South America**
20%	Bulgaria		**(average of countries)**
		9%	Bolivia
13%	**North America**	9%	Peru
	(average of countries)	10%	Brazil
7%	Canada	10%	Paraguay
7%	Haiti	10%	Venezuela
11%	Guatemala	11%	Colombia
11%	Honduras	11%	Ecuador
11%	Mexico	11%	Uruguay
11%	Puerto Rico	12%	Chile
11%	Trinidad and Tobago	13%	Argentina
13%	United States		

services and supplies are becoming more widely available. In Bangladesh a large-scale family planning campaign succeeded in substantially increasing the proportion of couples using contraceptives from 3% in 1970 to 40% in the mid-1990s, resulting in a corresponding drop in the fertility rate from 7.0 to 4.1 during this same period. As part of its campaign, the government promoted sterilization, offering cash payments to women and men agreeing to undergo the procedure. The government also distributed a variety of modern contraceptives, including birth control pills and IUDs.

Yet while Bangladesh's campaign has been successful in reducing the country's soaring rate of population growth, some experts have argued that any approach that promotes massive sterilization is demeaning and coercive. Instead, they propose that the government emphasize upgrading family health services (including prenatal care and AIDS education), improving women's education, and initiating a variety of other measures to promote women's equality. They point out that as women become better educated and have greater access to health care, more of their children will survive to adulthood and as a result the birthrate will drop.

CONTRACEPTIVE USE WORLDWIDE
Percentage of couples of childbearing age

PERCENT	COUNTRY	PERCENT	COUNTRY
83%	China	53%	Trinidad and Tobago
81%	France	53%	Vietnam
81%	United Kingdom	50%	Indonesia
80%	Finland	50%	South Africa
79%	Belgium	50%	Tunisia
79%	Korea, South	49%	Nicaragua
78%	Brazil	49%	Venezuela
78%	Denmark	48%	Malaysia
78%	Italy	48%	Paraguay
78%	Sweden	47%	Algeria
76%	Australia	47%	Egypt
76%	Bulgaria	47%	Honduras
76%	Netherlands	45%	India
76%	Norway	44%	Cambodia
75%	Costa Rica	43%	Chile
75%	Germany	43%	Zimbabwe
75%	Poland	42%	Morocco
75%	Taiwan	41%	United Arab Emirates
74%	Argentina	40%	Bangladesh
74%	Singapore	40%	Philippines
74%	Slovakia	35%	Jordan
74%	United States	35%	Kuwait
73%	Canada	33%	Kenya
73%	Hungary	32%	Russia
72%	Uruguay	31%	Kyrgyzstan
71%	Austria	30%	Bolivia
71%	Switzerland	30%	Kazakhstan
70%	Cuba	28%	Uzbekistan
70%	Puerto Rico	23%	Belarus
70%	New Zealand	23%	Guatemala
69%	Czech Republic	23%	Nepal
67%	Jamaica	23%	Ukraine
67%	Korea, North	22%	Armenia
66%	Colombia	22%	Moldova
66%	Portugal	21%	Rwanda
66%	Thailand	21%	Tajikistan
65%	Iran	20%	Chad
65%	Israel	20%	Syria
64%	Japan	20%	Turkmenistan
63%	Turkey	19%	Latvia
62%	Sri Lanka	18%	Laos
60%	Ireland	17%	Azerbaijan
59%	Peru	17%	Georgia
59%	Spain	17%	Madagascar
58%	Panama	16%	Cameroon
57%	Romania	16%	Central African Republic
56%	Dominican Republic	15%	Congo
55%	Lebanon	15%	Zambia
55%	Yugoslavia	14%	Iraq
53%	Ecuador	14%	Libya
53%	El Salvador	14%	Saudi Arabia
53%	Mexico	13%	Ghana

(continued)

CONTRACEPTIVE USE WORLDWIDE *(cont.)*
Percentage of couples of childbearing age

PERCENT	COUNTRY	PERCENT	COUNTRY
13%	Malawi	6%	Liberia
13%	Myanmar	6%	Nigeria
12%	Lithuania	5%	Guinea
12%	Pakistan	5%	Mali
12%	Togo	5%	Uganda
10%	Albania	4%	Ethiopia
10%	Haiti	4%	Mozambique
10%	Tanzania	4%	Niger
9%	Benin	4%	Sierra Leone
9%	Burundi	3%	Ivory Coast
9%	Sudan	3%	Eritrea
9%	Zaire	3%	Mauritania
8%	Burkina Faso	2%	Afghanistan
7%	Senegal	2%	Angola
7%	Yemen	1%	Somalia

Methods of Contraception

Popular methods of contraception vary widely from one country to the next. Female sterilization is rarely performed in African countries but is common in eastern Asia, Latin America, and among developed nations. The countries with the highest rates of female sterilization include Australia, Brazil, Canada, China, Cuba, the Dominican Republic, Panama, Singapore, South Korea, Sri Lanka, the United Kingdom, and the United States. IUDs, less common than sterilization, are most popular in China, Cuba, Egypt, Finland, France, Norway, Sweden, Tunisia, and Vietnam.

Birth control pills are widely used in a great many countries, including Algeria, Australia, Brazil, Iran, Jamaica, Kuwait, Morocco, New Zealand, Zimbabwe, and most Eastern European nations. Condoms are used mostly among the developed nations, with Japan heading the list. More than three-quarters of Japanese couples rely on condoms as their main method of birth control. In many of the developing countries, condoms are slowly gaining wider acceptance, especially among adolescents, as a means of curbing the spread of AIDS. Traditional methods of birth control, such as rhythm or withdrawal, are used mostly in African countries, where there is very little use of any type of birth control.

The predominant method of contraception in a country is not necessarily a major factor in determining its overall fertility rate. Italy and Spain, for example, have among the world's lowest fertility rates even though the main forms of birth control used in both countries are traditional methods, which are generally considered to be much less effective than modern methods.

CONTRACEPTIVE USE BY REGION
Percentage of couples of childbearing age

PERCENT	COUNTRY	PERCENT	COUNTRY
15%	**Africa**	64%	Japan
	(average of countries)	63%	Turkey
50%	South Africa	62%	Sri Lanka
50%	Tunisia	55%	Lebanon
47%	Algeria	53%	Vietnam
47%	Egypt	50%	Indonesia
43%	Zimbabwe	48%	Malaysia
42%	Morocco	45%	India
33%	Kenya	44%	Cambodia
21%	Rwanda	41%	United Arab Emirates
20%	Chad	40%	Bangladesh
17%	Madagascar	40%	Philippines
16%	Cameroon	35%	Jordan
16%	Central African Republic	35%	Kuwait
15%	Congo	31%	Kyrgyzstan
15%	Zambia	30%	Kazakhstan
14%	Libya	28%	Uzbekistan
13%	Ghana	23%	Nepal
13%	Malawi	22%	Armenia
12%	Togo	21%	Tajikistan
10%	Tanzania	20%	Syria
9%	Benin	20%	Turkmenistan
9%	Burundi	18%	Laos
9%	Sudan	17%	Azerbaijan
9%	Zaire	17%	Georgia
8%	Burkina Faso	14%	Iraq
7%	Senegal	14%	Saudi Arabia
6%	Liberia	13%	Myanmar
6%	Nigeria	12%	Pakistan
5%	Guinea	7%	Yemen
5%	Mali	2%	Afghanistan
5%	Uganda		
4%	Ethiopia	**59%**	**Europe**
4%	Mozambique		**(average of countries)**
4%	Niger	81%	France
4%	Sierra Leone	81%	United Kingdom
3%	Eritrea	80%	Finland
3%	Ivory Coast	79%	Belgium
3%	Mauritania	78%	Denmark
2%	Angola	78%	Italy
1%	Somalia	78%	Sweden
		76%	Bulgaria
40%	**Asia**	76%	Netherlands
	(average of countries)	76%	Norway
83%	China	75%	Germany
79%	Korea, South	75%	Poland
75%	Taiwan	74%	Slovakia
74%	Singapore	73%	Hungary
67%	Korea, North	71%	Austria
66%	Thailand	71%	Switzerland
65%	Iran	69%	Czech Republic
65%	Israel	66%	Portugal '

(continued)

CONTRACEPTIVE USE BY REGION *(cont.)*
Percentage of couples of childbearing age

PERCENT	COUNTRY	PERCENT	COUNTRY
60%	Ireland	53%	Trinidad and Tobago
59%	Spain	49%	Nicaragua
57%	Romania	47%	Honduras
55%	Yugoslavia	23%	Guatemala
32%	Russia	10%	Haiti
23%	Belarus		
23%	Ukraine	**73%**	**Oceania**
22%	Moldova		**(average of countries)**
19%	Latvia	76%	Australia
12%	Lithuania	70%	New Zealand
10%	Albania		
		57%	**South America**
55%	**North America**		**(average of countries)**
	(average of countries)	78%	Brazil
75%	Costa Rica	74%	Argentina
74%	United States	72%	Uruguay
73%	Canada	66%	Colombia
70%	Cuba	59%	Peru
70%	Puerto Rico	53%	Ecuador
67%	Jamaica	49%	Venezuela
58%	Panama	48%	Paraguay
56%	Dominican Republic	43%	Chile
53%	El Salvador	30%	Bolivia
53%	Mexico		

Contraception and Religious Attitudes

Prevailing religious attitudes play a crucial role in determining the availability and use of different contraceptive methods in some countries. Yet in other parts of the world, religious dictates are largely ignored. While the Roman Catholic Church is vehemently opposed to all nontraditional methods of birth control, in some predominantly Catholic countries the use of modern contraceptives is widespread. Brazil, for example, has the world's largest Roman Catholic population; yet despite opposition from the church, the government has organized one of the world's most successful family planning programs and ranks first in contraceptive use in South America. The great majority of Brazilian couples—78%—practice family planning, with 71% using modern methods; and the national fertility rate is 2.8. Similarly, in Argentina, where the Roman Catholic Church is so influential that it managed to keep the word *condom* out of the government's anti-AIDS advertisements, contraceptive use is high—74%—and the country's fertility rate is 2.7.

In Islamic countries large families are favored. Birth control is quietly tolerated, but not encouraged; sterilization is the only method specifically for-

CONTRACEPTIVE USE:
MODERN VS. TRADITIONAL METHODS*

REGION/COUNTRY	TRADITIONAL METHODS 1980	1990	MODERN METHODS 1980	1990
Africa				
Cameroon	2%	12%	1%	4%
Egypt	1%	2%	23%	45%
Ghana	8%	8%	4%	5%
Kenya	3%	5%	4%	28%
Malawi	6%	6%	1%	7%
Mauritania	1%	3%	0%	1%
Morocco	1%	6%	14%	36%
Nigeria	6%	3%	1%	4%
Rwanda	9%	8%	1%	13%
Senegal	3%	9%	1%	2%
South Africa	14%	1%	37%	48%
Sudan	1%	3%	4%	6%
Tunisia	7%	9%	25%	40%
Zimbabwe	9%	7%	5%	36%
Asia				
Bangladesh	4%	9%	8%	31%
India	7%	5%	26%	40%
Indonesia	2%	3%	7%	47%
Iraq	2%	3%	13%	11%
Japan	19%	14%	44%	44%
Jordan	7%	8%	18%	27%
Pakistan	4%	3%	2%	9%
Philippines	30%	15%	16%	25%
South Korea	11%	7%	43%	70%
Sri Lanka	23%	21%	18%	41%
Thailand	3%	2%	31%	64%
Yemen	0%	1%	1%	6%
North and South America				
Colombia	7%	12%	41%	55%
Costa Rica	11%	11%	57%	57%
Dominican Rep	6%	5%	36%	52%
Ecuador	7%	11%	28%	42%
El Salvador	2%	3%	33%	44%
Haiti	10%	1%	5%	9%
Jamaica	1%	3%	54%	51%
Mexico	9%	8%	20%	45%
Paraguay	6%	13%	26%	35%
Peru	21%	26%	20%	33%
Trinidad and Tobago	13%	8%	41%	45%
United States	7%	5%	61%	70%
Europe				
France	31%	16%	48%	64%
Hungary	21%	11%	52%	62%
Netherlands	8%	4%	65%	72%
Norway	7%	11%	64%	65%
United Kingdom	7%	8%	70%	78%

* Percentage of couples of childbearing age, based on an average 10-year span, approximately from 1980–1990.

METHODS OF CONTRACEPTION

TRADITIONAL METHODS

Traditional (Natural) Methods—75% Effective

The best-known traditional method, called *rhythm,* requires abstinence from sexual relations on days when fertilization is most likely to occur, that is, when the woman is about to or has just ovulated. To keep track of her ovulation cycle, or rhythm, a woman may record her menstrual cycle on a calendar, take her temperature daily, or note changes in her cervical mucus. Other traditional or natural methods include *withdrawal* and *douching.*

MODERN METHODS

Barrier Methods—85% to 97% Effective

Diaphragms and *cervical caps* are small rubber pouches that cover the opening of the cervix. They are used in conjunction with spermicidal creams or jellies and prevent conception by preventing the sperm from entering the uterus. The *vaginal sponge* is a disposable polyurethane sponge that is effective for about 24 hours after its insertion and prevents the sperm from reaching the uterus. It also contains a spermicide, which is slowly released. *Condoms* are thin rubber sheaths that cover the man's penis and prevent the sperm from entering the uterus. Some contain a spermicide.

Hormone Methods—99%+ Effective

Birth control pills, or *oral contraceptives,* are female hormones, usually a combination of estrogen and progesterone, which are taken regularly to prevent ovulation. They are also effective as a "morning after" contraceptive, if taken in large doses within 72 hours of unprotected sex. *Norplant* is a set of six small hormone-filled capsules that look somewhat like matches. Implanted under the skin of the woman's upper arm, they slowly release the hormone that inhibits ovulation and they are usually effective for about five years. *DepoProvera* is the trade name for a long-acting injectable synthetic hormone that prevents ovulation. At the present time it is used in over 90 countries throughout the world although it is not yet approved as a safe method of contraception in the United States. The injection usually has to be administered about every three months.

Intrauterine Devices (IUDs)—97% Effective

These devices are small molded pieces of plastic, usually coiled or T-shaped, and sometimes containing copper wire. They prevent pregnancy by keeping a fertilized egg from implanting in the uterus wall. Some IUDs release small amounts of progesterone, which also prevents conception. Once an IUD has been inserted in the uterus, it may remain there for as long as six years.

(continued)

METHODS OF CONTRACEPTION *(cont.)*

Sterilization—99%+ Effective
Female sterilization, or *tubal ligation,* is a surgical procedure in which the woman's fallopian tubes are severed and then tied. Sometimes the ends of the tubes are closed by electrocautery or by tiny metal or plastic rings or clips. Most often, the procedure is performed right after childbirth. Once the tubes are closed, egg cells cannot be fertilized. In recent years studies have indicated that sterilization may not be as effective for women under the age of 28 as for older women.

Male sterilization, or *vasectomy,* is a short, safe procedure in which the vas deferens, the two ducts that normally carry the sperm from the testes, are severed or removed. As a result, the man's semen no longer contains sperm cells.

METHODS UNDER DEVELOPMENT OR TESTING

An *antipregnancy vaccine* is currently undergoing testing in India. It prevents a fertilized egg from implanting in the uterus wall by temporarily causing the body to produce an antibody against a hormone necessary to maintain pregnancy. Another new type of contraceptive under study is the *male hormone injection,* which interferes with the pituitary gland's stimulation of sperm cell production. Researchers have found that weekly injections of testosterone decrease most men's sperm counts enough to make them infertile, but because the injections are painful, scientists are looking for other ways of delivering the hormone—perhaps through skin patches or implanted pellets. Similar research is being undertaken into the use of *male hormone pills* containing a combination of testosterone and progestogen to suppress sperm production. Other researchers are investigating ways of blocking fertilization by attacking the protein that a sperm cell needs in order to penetrate the outer layer of an egg cell.

CONTRACEPTIVE USE BY METHOD WORLDWIDE
Percentage of couples of childbearing age

METHOD	1983	1990
All Methods	51%	57%
Traditional Methods	9%	8%
Modern Methods	42%	49%
Female sterilization	13%	17%
Intrauterine devices (IUDs)	10%	12%
Birth control pill	7%	8%
Male sterilization	5%	5%
Condom	5%	5%
Injectable hormones	1%	1%
Diaphragm, similar methods	1%	1%

bidden, but is allowed to protect the woman's life or health. Nevertheless, use of modern contraceptives is high in several Muslim countries: Indonesia (47%), Iran (45%), Egypt (45%), Algeria (43%), Tunisia (40%), Turkey (35%), and Bangladesh (31%). Iran's family planning program, one of the world's most successful, includes free condoms, birth control pills, and sterilization for both women and men. In addition, before marrying, couples must attend an hour-long class on birth control methods.

ABORTION

Reliable statistics on the number of abortions performed annually are not available. However, a recent estimate by Population Action International put the number of total abortions at about 50 million, with illegal procedures accounting for about 20 million of these. In some countries, especially those with highly restrictive abortion laws, illegal abortions may terminate as many as one-quarter of all pregnancies.

Although abortion was widely practiced as a means of birth control in ancient times, it was later banned or restricted by most of the world's religions, and by the late 19th century the procedure was generally prohibited by secular law as well. One of the earliest civil laws, passed by the British Parliament in 1803, prohibited abortion after quickening of the fetus, that is, around the third or fourth month of pregnancy, when the fetus's movements are first felt by the mother. In 1837 this law was extended to prohibiting abortions before quickening, and in 1861 it was further revised to make abortion a criminal act in all circumstances. Other countries—including Belgium, Denmark, France, Germany, and Italy—enacted similar legislation during

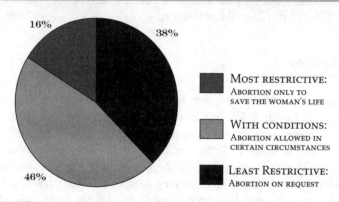

ABORTION POLICIES
Percentage of total world population

16%

38%

46%

MOST RESTRICTIVE:
ABORTION ONLY TO
SAVE THE WOMAN'S LIFE

WITH CONDITIONS:
ABORTION ALLOWED IN
CERTAIN CIRCUMSTANCES

LEAST RESTRICTIVE:
ABORTION ON REQUEST

this period. In the United States, by the close of the 19th century every state had a law restricting or banning abortion.

In addition to religious considerations, the main reason for outlawing abortion was to reduce the high death rate among women undergoing these unsafe procedures. In many countries, an abortion could be performed only to save the woman's life or, in some cases, to preserve her health. By the 1900s abortions were sometimes permitted for other reasons, including the woman's mental health.

The first time in modern history that women could obtain abortions on request was in 1920 in postrevolutionary Russia. (This policy, however, was rescinded by Stalin in 1936 but reinstated by Khrushchev in 1955.) In the aftermath of World War II, other countries, including Japan and the nations of Eastern Europe began following the Soviet Union's lead.

The late 1960s witnessed women's groups in many countries organizing vigorous campaigns for legalized abortion. Their primary goals were to reduce the high maternal mortality rates caused by unsafe illegal abortions and to curb the world's soaring population growth. At the same time, the expanding feminist movement was promoting the notion that women, as economically and socially independent individuals, should be entitled to control their own health and reproductive lives.

Today the battle over the legality of abortion is still being bitterly fought. In the United States, where abortion has been legal since the 1973 *Roe v. Wade* Supreme Court ruling, antiabortion groups are still actively trying to reverse that decision and are also lobbying for individual states to impose certain restrictions, such as mandatory waiting periods. Other countries where abortion is still a contentious issue include Canada, France, Germany, and Ireland.

A relatively recent development affecting the abortion debate was the introduction of an abortion pill, RU 486, which was developed in France in 1980. Because it allows abortions to take place at home or in a doctor's office, patients do not have to visit special abortion clinics where they can be targeted by antiabortion protesters. In addition, many physicians who may have stopped performing surgical abortions because of threats of violence can prescribe the pills without fear of harassment.

Abortion Policies

About 38% of the world's population live in countries where abortion is available on request. Another 46% live in countries where abortion is available in certain situations, ranging from preserving the woman's mental health to cases where the fetus is physically impaired, or the pregnancy resulted from rape or incest. The remaining 16% of the population live in countries where abortion is legal only when it is necessary to save the woman's life. Not unexpectedly, since Islam and Roman Catholicism strictly forbid abortion, the

GROUNDS FOR ABORTION WORLDWIDE*

Least Restrictive

Albania	Czech Republic	Moldova	Tajikistan
Armenia	Denmark	Netherlands	Tunisia
Austria	Estonia	Norway	Turkey
Azerbaijan	Georgia	Puerto Rico	Turkmenistan
Belarus	Greece	Romania	Ukraine
Bosnia-Herzegovina	Kazakhstan	Russia	United States
Bulgaria	Korea, North	Singapore	Uzbekistan
Canada	Kyrgyzstan	Slovakia	Vietnam
China	Latvia	Slovenia	Yugoslavia
Croatia	Lithuania	South Africa	
Cuba	Macedonia	Sweden	

With Conditions

Argentina	(1)	Guinea	(2)	India	(4)
Brazil	(1)	Jamaica	(2)	Iraq	(4)
Burkina Faso	(1)	Jordan	(2)	Israel	(4)
Burundi	(1)	Pakistan	(2)	Japan	(4)
Congo	(1)	Panama	(2)	Korea, South	(4)
Costa Rica	(1)	Sierra Leone	(2)	Liberia	(4)
Egypt	(1)	Switzerland	(2)	New Zealand	(4)
Eritrea	(1)	Thailand	(2)	Portugal	(4)
Ethiopia	(1)	Trinidad and Tobago	(2)	Spain	(4)
Malawi	(1)	Uganda	(2)	Taiwan	(4)
Mexico	(1)	Zaire	(2)	Togo	(4)
Morocco	(1)	Algeria	(3)	United Kingdom	(4)
Peru	(1)	Haiti	(3)	Zambia	(4)
Rwanda	(1)	Kenya	(3)	Australia	(5)
Saudi Arabia	(1)	Kuwait	(3)	Belgium	(5)
Sudan	(1)	Malaysia	(3)	Finland	(5)
Uruguay	(1)	Nepal	(3)	France	(5)
Bolivia	(2)	Zimbabwe	(3)	Hungary	(5)
Cameroon	(2)	Angola	(4)	Italy	(5)
Ecuador	(2)	Germany	(4)	Poland	(5)
El Salvador	(2)	Ghana	(4)		

Most Restrictive

Afghanistan	Honduras	Mauritania	Sri Lanka
Bangladesh	Indonesia	Mozambique	Syria
Benin	Iran	Myanmar	Tanzania
Cambodia	Ireland	Nicaragua	United Arab
Central African	Ivory Coast	Niger	Emirates
Republic	Laos	Nigeria	Venezuela
Chad	Lebanon	Paraguay	Yemen
Colombia	Libya	Philippines	
Dominican Republic	Madagascar	Senegal	
Guatemala	Mali	Somalia	

* Least restrictive = abortion on request; With Conditions = abortion allowed on various grounds, numbers in parentheses indicate number of grounds permitted in addition to saving the woman's life; Most restrictive = abortion only to save the woman's life.

RU 486: A SAFE ALTERNATIVE TO SURGICAL ABORTION

The abortion pill, commonly known as RU 486, is a recent development so dramatic that its introduction has virtually reshaped the whole abortion debate. Since its discovery in 1980, it has been used by more than 250,000 women throughout Europe and China. In 1996, despite strong opposition from antiabortion advocates, it was conditionally approved for use in the United States.

Developed by Roussel Uclaf, a French subsidiary of a German pharmaceutical company, RU 486 was originally tested as a contraceptive but was found to be effective in inducing abortion. There are some indications that it may also be useful in treating other conditions, including breast and cervical cancer.

RU 486, also known as mifepristone, causes an abortion by blocking the action of progesterone, a hormone essential for sustaining pregnancy. In the earliest stages of gestation, before the embryo has become attached to the uterine wall, the drug prevents its implantation. Although RU 486 by itself causes a miscarriage in about 80% of women, it is usually given in combination with another drug, misoprostol, a prostaglandin that causes the uterus to contract and shed its lining. The two drugs used in combination are effective in about 95% of women.

RU 486 is generally used only during the first seven weeks of pregnancy, counting from the first day of the woman's last normal menstrual period. It can be taken as soon as the woman knows she is pregnant, as early as the first day of her missed period.

On the woman's first visit to her doctor, she is given three tablets of RU 486. Two days later she returns to the doctor's office and is given two pills of misoprostol. She then waits about four hours in the office or clinic, during which time most women (about 70%) experience bleeding and cramping, soon followed by a miscarriage. Those women whose fetuses are not aborted during this time are sent home, and nearly all expel the fetus within 24 hours. A third visit to the doctor is recommended about two weeks later to ensure that the abortion is complete and that the bleeding is under control.

In about 4% to 5% of cases RU 486 does not terminate the pregnancy, and it is necessary for the woman to undergo a surgical abortion. If she decides to continue the pregnancy after having taken RU 486, there is a chance that her baby will be born with some deformities.

A major advantage of the abortion pill over surgical abortion is that it does not require anesthesia and eliminates the danger of perforating the uterus or damaging the cervix, two possible—though rare—complications of surgical abortion. Another advantage of RU 486 is that it may be administered much earlier in pregnancy than a surgical abortion, which is generally not performed before the sixth or seventh week.

(continued)

RU 486: A SAFE ALTERNATIVE TO SURGICAL ABORTION (cont.)

The most serious medical risk of RU 486 is severe bleeding. But there are also other disadvantages to using the pill. For example, the entire process may take several days, whereas a surgical abortion is accomplished in one visit to the clinic and one follow-up visit. In addition, surgery is effective in nearly 100% of women; the pill is effective in about 95%. Another advantage of surgery for some women is that they do not see the bloody tissue that is removed from the uterus.

Although RU 486 is widely known as the abortion pill, it is not the only drug that can be used to induce abortion. In 1996 it was reported that a cancer-fighting drug, methotrexate, is also safe and effective in inducing abortion. Like RU 486, it can be used during the earliest stages of pregnancy and is given in combination with misoprostol. One difference between the two drugs is the way in which they work: methotrexate terminates pregnancy by interfering with the growth of the embryo and placenta by blocking the action of the B vitamin folic acid. Another difference is that methotrexate is most successful during the first five weeks of pregnancy, counting from the first day of the woman's last menstrual period, while RU 486 is also very effective up to the seventh, and sometimes the ninth week.

great majority of these countries are overwhelmingly Islamic or Roman Catholic. Only a few countries do not allow abortion for any reason at all. The largest, Chile, abolished a law permitting abortion to save the life of the woman in 1989. Other countries that do not allow abortion are Andorra, Djibouti, and Malta.

Within the group of countries that allow abortion under certain conditions, some laws are highly restrictive, while others are much more liberal. In nearly 20 countries—including Argentina, Burundi, Costa Rica, Ethiopia, and Saudi Arabia—the only ground permitted, besides saving the woman's life, is preserving her physical health. Preserving her mental health is an additional ground for abortion in Jamaica, Pakistan, Sierra Leone, Trinidad and Tobago, and about a dozen other countries. In Algeria, Bolivia, Ecuador, Zimbabwe and several other countries, abortion is permitted if the pregnancy was caused by rape or incest. Fetal impairment constitutes another ground for abortion in more than 15 countries, including Ghana, India, Israel, Liberia, South Africa, and South Korea. The most liberal basis for abortion, short of availability on request, consists of a category called social or economic reasons; Australia, Belgium, Finland, France, Hungary, Italy, and Poland are among the few countries that include this condition.

More than half of all countries that permit abortion on request are in the developed world. The only industrialized nation where abortion is permitted only to save the woman's life is Ireland. Recently, though, Ireland's abortion law was liberalized very slightly, despite strong opposition from the Roman Catholic Church. In a 1992 national referendum Irish voters narrowly approved a measure revising two aspects of the abortion law: the right to travel out of the country for the specific purpose of having an abortion and the right to receive information about overseas abortion clinics. Every year an estimated 5,000 Irish women travel abroad to have abortions, and until 1995 these trips had been illegal.

Although Ireland has recently liberalized its abortion law, a trend toward stricter laws has recently been seen in some of the formerly communist countries of Eastern Europe. In 1993, after decades of allowing easy access to abortion, the Polish government enacted a law permitting a pregnancy to be terminated only if the fetus was a danger to the life or health of the woman, was the product of rape or incest, or had serious and irreversible abnormalities. Late in 1996 however, the law was eased considerably to allow first-trimester abortions for women with personal or financial difficulties. It also allowed abortions to be performed in private clinics in addition to state-run facilities.

Illegal Abortion

Every year an estimated 20 million women resort to unsafe, illegal abortions. The vast majority live in the developing countries, especially those with strict abortion laws and strong cultural and religious prohibitions against the use of contraceptives. The highest incidence of illegal abortion is in South America, where an estimated 41 out of every 1,000 women of childbearing age undergo this procedure each year. Eastern and western Africa also have a high incidence of illegal abortion: about 30 women per 1,000. The lowest incidence in the developing world is in Asia, where only 12 women per 1,000 undergo illegal abortions each year.

When abortions are performed by trained medical personnel under legal, sanitary conditions they are extremely safe procedures; less than 1 in every 100,000 result in maternal death. Illegal abortions, on the other hand, are usually performed by unskilled practitioners—sometimes the pregnant woman herself—under insanitary conditions without medical equipment or antibiotics or other drugs. Some estimates put the global death toll from these clandestine procedures at 70,000 to 200,000 a year. And for every woman who dies as a result of an illegal abortion, it is believed that another 30 suffer such serious complications that they are left with a wide range of painful, crippling, and lifelong disabilities. It is estimated that in many developing countries, complications from illegal abortions may account for as many as 70% of all gynecological hospital admissions.

Abortion for Sex Selection

In some parts of the world, especially in countries where sons are greatly favored over daughters, abortion is frequently used for the purpose of sex selection. In China, where the government has mandated a policy of one child per family, many couples try to ensure that their one child will be a boy by aborting female fetuses. Although abortions for this purpose have been prohibited by law, they are still common. Similarly in India, despite laws specifically prohibiting abortion for sex selection, the practice is nevertheless widespread and is believed to be a factor in the recent decline in the country's sex ratio to 93 women for every 100 men.

FOR ADDITIONAL INFORMATION

Alan Guttmacher Institute
120 Wall Street
New York, NY 10005, United States
Telephone: 212-248-1111
Fax: 212-248-1951

or

1120 Connecticut Avenue, NW
Washington, DC 20036, United States
Telephone: 202-296-4012
Fax: 202-223-5756

**International Planned Parenthood
  Federation**
810 Seventh Avenue
New York, NY 10019, United States
Telephone: 212-541-7800
Web site: http://www.oneworld.org/ippf

**International Programs Center
  International Data Base**
Bureau of the Census
Washington Plaza II, Room 207
Washington, DC 20233, United States
Telephone: 301-457-1403
Fax: 301-457-3034

Population Action International
1120 19th Street, NW
Washington, DC 20036, United States
Telephone: 202-659-1833
Fax: 202-293-1795

**Population Communications
  International**
777 United Nations Plaza
New York, NY 10017, United States
Telephone: 212-687-3366
Fax: 212-661-4188
Web site: http://www.charity.org/pci.html

WOMEN'S HEALTH

Women around the world are living longer, healthier lives than ever before. Over the past few decades, birthrates have declined, many infectious diseases have been brought under control, water supplies and sanitation methods have improved, and more women than ever have gained access to health care and family planning services, including safe, legal abortions. Yet millions of women—mostly in the developing world—still live under the most abysmal conditions, where access to health care is practically nonexistent, food and clean water are scarce, and the burden of large families coupled with early childbearing take an especially heavy toll. Many of these women are further debilitated by the painful, lifelong, and crippling complications of unsafe, illegal abortions and the dangerous consequences of female genital mutilation.

AIDS, once thought to be a man's disease, has recently become a serious threat to women. Around the globe women now account for nearly half of all new cases of HIV infection, and it is estimated that by the year 2000, about 13 million of the 30 to 40 million people expected to be infected with the deadly virus will be women.

LIFE EXPECTANCY

Life expectancy for women throughout the world has been increasing steadily, rising 20% faster than men's over the past two decades. In 11 countries, a baby girl born in the mid-1990s could expect to reach the age of 80 and beyond. Not a single country has a male life expectancy rate even close to 80; the highest, 76.6 years, is in Japan.

The greatest gains for women in recent decades—increases of 10 to 11 years—have occurred in northern Africa, large portions of Asia, and in Central America. In western Europe and other developed regions—including Australia, Canada, Japan, and the United States—women's longevity has generally risen by three to six years. The smallest gains, of only one or two years, have been among the nations of Eastern Europe.

Increases in women's longevity are related to several factors, including greater access to health care and family planning services; improved nutri-

COUNTRIES WHERE WOMEN'S LIFE EXPECTANCY IS OVER 80*

LIFE EXPECTANCY	COUNTRY	LIFE EXPECTANCY	COUNTRY
83.0	Japan	80.5	Italy
82.0	France	80.5	Spain
81.7	Switzerland	80.4	Netherlands
81.0	Canada	80.3	Norway
80.9	Australia	80.1	Greece
80.8	Sweden		

*At birth, in years.

COUNTRIES WHERE WOMEN'S LIFE EXPECTANCY IS UNDER 50*

LIFE EXPECTANCY	COUNTRY	LIFE EXPECTANCY	COUNTRY
42.0	Afghanistan	47.1	Chad
42.6	Sierra Leone	47.6	Mauritania
43.0	Guinea	47.7	Malawi
44.1	Central African Rep.	48.1	Mozambique
45.6	Ethiopia	48.3	Senegal
45.6	Mali	48.9	Burkina Faso
46.1	Angola	49.2	Burundi
46.1	Niger	49.9	Cambodia
46.6	Somalia		

*At birth, in years.

LIFE EXPECTANCY WORLDWIDE*

WOMEN	MEN	COUNTRY	WOMEN	MEN	COUNTRY
83.0	76.6	Japan	74.7	69.0	Armenia
82.0	73.5	France	74.2	66.6	Azerbaijan
81.7	74.6	Switzerland	74.1	70.1	Panama
81.0	74.6	Canada	74.0	67.4	Korea, South
80.9	75.0	Australia	73.8	64.5	Hungary
80.8	75.3	Sweden	73.5	68.5	Trinidad and
80.5	73.7	Italy			Tobago
80.5	73.4	Spain	73.4	68.6	Turkey
80.4	74.1	Netherlands	73.3	66.0	Romania
80.3	74.1	Norway	73.1	63.9	Kazakhstan
80.1	74.7	Greece	73.0	66.7	Korea, North
79.7	72.8	United States	72.9	68.6	United Arab
79.6	71.7	Finland			Emirates
79.5	72.9	Austria	72.5	68.3	Sri Lanka
79.1	72.3	Belgium	72.4	64.3	Kyrgyzstan
79.1	72.7	Germany	72.3	65.5	Moldova
79.0	73.6	United Kingdom	72.1	66.0	Uzbekistan
78.9	72.4	Bosnia-	71.9	65.0	Thailand
		Herzegovina	71.7	66.8	Tajikistan
78.6	72.0	Taiwan	71.6	67.5	Malaysia
78.5	75.1	Israel	71.0	57.3	Russia
78.4	70.5	Slovenia	70.2	64.9	Philippines
78.2	70.7	Portugal	70.2	67.4	Tunisia
78.1	72.7	Denmark	69.2	67.1	China
78.0	71.9	New Zealand	69.1	64.8	Paraguay
77.9	72.2	Ireland	68.4	61.8	Turkmenistan
77.9	68.8	Puerto Rico	68.1	63.9	Dominican Rep.
77.3	70.1	Croatia	67.9	63.4	Peru
77.2	68.7	Slovakia	67.9	62.4	South Africa
77.0	72.4	Costa Rica	67.8	64.2	Jordan
76.5	69.4	Chile	67.6	63.4	Ecuador
76.4	66.8	Belarus	67.6	63.4	Vietnam
76.4	70.8	Singapore	67.3	56.6	Brazil
76.3	72.7	Cuba	67.0	63.1	Lebanon
76.3	68.5	Czech Republic	66.9	63.2	Syria
76.2	66.5	Lithuania	66.5	58.0	El Salvador
76.0	71.0	Yugoslavia	66.1	61.9	Honduras
75.9	71.5	Macedonia	65.5	65.0	Iran
75.8	66.7	Poland	65.4	59.0	Bolivia
75.7	68.9	Argentina	65.2	61.7	Saudi Arabia
75.7	68.1	Georgia	65.0	63.0	Algeria
75.5	69.6	Albania	64.8	63.0	Iraq
75.4	71.2	Kuwait	64.6	62.0	Nicaragua
75.3	68.9	Uruguay	64.4	59.7	Guatemala
75.2	65.3	Latvia	64.0	60.0	Indonesia
75.2	69.3	Mexico	62.8	58.9	Egypt
75.2	69.4	Venezuela	62.5	59.1	Libya
74.9	69.3	Colombia	62.5	59.1	Morocco
74.9	64.7	Estonia	62.2	57.9	Myanmar
74.8	67.8	Bulgaria	60.5	56.5	Kenya
74.8	70.4	Jamaica	60.1	56.5	Zimbabwe
74.8	65.5	Ukraine	59.1	58.1	India

(continued)

LIFE EXPECTANCY WORLDWIDE* *(cont.)*

WOMEN	MEN	COUNTRY	WOMEN	MEN	COUNTRY
58.1	56.8	Pakistan	50.0	47.0	Laos
56.6	54.1	Nigeria	50.0	47.0	Tanzania
56.4	53.1	Haiti	49.9	47.0	Cambodia
55.8	52.2	Ghana	49.2	45.9	Burundi
55.6	55.6	Bangladesh	48.9	45.6	Burkina Faso
55.3	50.1	Congo	48.3	46.3	Senegal
55.0	52.0	Madagascar	48.1	44.9	Mozambique
54.8	51.3	Togo	47.7	46.3	Malawi
54.5	52.4	Zambia	47.6	44.4	Mauritania
54.2	50.8	Ivory Coast	47.1	43.9	Chad
54.0	51.0	Cameroon	46.6	43.4	Somalia
54.0	52.0	Liberia	46.1	42.9	Angola
53.7	49.9	Benin	46.1	42.9	Niger
53.7	50.3	Zaire	45.6	42.4	Ethiopia
52.7	49.4	Uganda	45.6	42.4	Mali
52.4	49.4	Yemen	44.1	41.0	Central African
51.8	48.3	Eritrea			Republic
51.0	48.6	Sudan	43.0	42.0	Guinea
50.3	51.5	Nepal	42.6	39.4	Sierra Leone
50.2	46.9	Rwanda	42.0	41.0	Afghanistan

*At birth, in years.

tion; and in many countries access to safe, legal abortion. Unfortunately, in some sub-Saharan countries, particularly Uganda and Zambia, the unremitting spread of AIDS over the past decade may be slowing or even starting to reverse the recent gains in women's longevity.

Despite the fact that women's longevity rates worldwide are climbing, there are still 17 countries where the average life expectancy for women is 50 years or less. Not surprisingly, they are among the world's poorest nations; 15 are in sub-Saharan Africa, 2 are in Asia.

Life Expectancy Gender Gap

Women outlive men in almost every country of the world. The largest gender gaps are seen in Eastern Europe and the countries of the former Soviet Union. In Russia the difference is a staggering 13.7 years, due less to a tremendous increase in women's life expectancy than to declining longevity among Russian men. Although the specific reasons for this trend are not fully understood, it is believed that rampant alcoholism among men coupled with increasing environmental pollution, deteriorating living conditions, and

WOMEN'S LIFE EXPECTANCY BY REGION*

LIFE EXPECTANCY	COUNTRY	LIFE EXPECTANCY	COUNTRY
53.0	**Africa** (average of countries)	74.0	Korea, South
70.2	Tunisia	73.4	Turkey
67.9	South Africa	73.1	Kazakhstan
65.0	Algeria	73.0	Korea, North
62.8	Egypt	72.9	United Arab Emirates
62.5	Libya	72.5	Sri Lanka
62.5	Morocco	72.4	Kyrgyzstan
60.5	Kenya	72.1	Uzbekistan
60.1	Zimbabwe	71.9	Thailand
56.6	Nigeria	71.7	Tajikistan
55.8	Ghana	71.6	Malaysia
55.3	Congo	70.2	Philippines
55.0	Madagascar	69.2	China
54.8	Togo	68.4	Turkmenistan
54.5	Zambia	67.8	Jordan
54.2	Ivory Coast	67.6	Vietnam
54.0	Liberia	67.0	Lebanon
54.0	Cameroon	66.9	Syria
53.7	Zaire	65.5	Iran
53.7	Benin	65.2	Saudi Arabia
52.7	Uganda	64.8	Iraq
51.8	Eritrea	64.0	Indonesia
51.0	Sudan	62.2	Myanmar
50.2	Rwanda	59.1	India
50.0	Tanzania	58.1	Pakistan
49.2	Burundi	55.6	Bangladesh
48.9	Burkina Faso	52.4	Yemen
48.3	Senegal	50.3	Nepal
48.1	Mozambique	50.0	Laos
47.7	Malawi	49.9	Cambodia
47.6	Mauritania	42.0	Afghanistan
47.1	Chad		
46.6	Somalia	**77.4**	**Europe** (average of countries)
46.1	Angola	82.0	France
46.1	Niger	81.7	Switzerland
45.6	Ethiopia	80.8	Sweden
45.6	Mali	80.5	Spain
44.1	Central African Republic	80.5	Italy
43.0	Guinea	80.4	Netherlands
42.6	Sierra Leone	80.3	Norway
		80.1	Greece
67.5	**Asia** (average of countries)	79.6	Finland
83.0	Japan	79.5	Austria
78.6	Taiwan	79.1	Belgium
78.5	Israel	79.1	Germany
76.4	Singapore	79.0	United Kingdom
75.7	Georgia	78.9	Bosnia-Herzegovina
75.4	Kuwait	78.4	Slovenia
74.7	Armenia	78.2	Portugal
74.2	Azerbaijan	78.1	Denmark
		77.9	Ireland

(continued)

WOMEN'S LIFE EXPECTANCY BY REGION* *(cont.)*

LIFE EXPECTANCY	COUNTRY	LIFE EXPECTANCY	COUNTRY
77.3	Croatia	74.1	Panama
77.2	Slovakia	73.5	Trinidad and Tobago
76.4	Belarus	68.1	Dominican Republic
76.3	Czech Republic	66.5	El Salvador
76.2	Lithuania	66.1	Honduras
76.0	Yugoslavia	64.6	Nicaragua
75.9	Macedonia	64.4	Guatemala
75.8	Poland	56.4	Haiti
75.5	Albania		
75.2	Latvia	**79.5**	**Oceania**
74.9	Estonia		**(average of countries)**
74.8	Bulgaria	80.9	Australia
74.8	Ukraine	78.0	New Zealand
73.8	Hungary		
73.3	Romania	**71.5**	**South America**
72.3	Moldova		**(average of countries)**
71.0	Russia	76.5	Chile
		75.7	Argentina
71.7	**North America**	75.3	Uruguay
	(average of countries)	75.2	Venezuela
81.0	Canada	74.9	Colombia
79.7	United States	69.1	Paraguay
77.9	Puerto Rico	67.9	Peru
77.0	Costa Rica	67.6	Ecuador
76.3	Cuba	67.3	Brazil
75.2	Mexico	65.4	Bolivia
74.8	Jamaica		

*At birth, in years.

health services are major factors contributing to this decline. Men in Egypt, India, and Iraq have a greater life expectancy than Russian men.

In many of the developed countries outside Eastern Europe—including Canada, Japan, New Zealand, Spain, Switzerland, and the United States—the longevity gap is somewhat smaller, generally between six and seven years. The narrowest gaps are seen in some of the developing countries, especially in Africa and southern Asia. In seven countries—Afghanistan, Guinea, India, Iran, Iraq, Malawi, and Pakistan—the gap is less than two years.

In Bangladesh women and men have the same life expectancy rates, and in one country, Nepal, the life expectancy for women is about a year less than that for men. Nepal is one of the world's poorest countries, where women suffer high rates of malnutrition, anemia, and other debilitating disorders and have practically no access to medical care. In addition, they have one of the world's highest rates of pregnancy-related deaths; the chance of a Nepalese woman dying as a result of pregnancy or childbirth is 1 in 13.

LIFE EXPECTANCY GENDER GAP*

GAP	COUNTRY	GAP	COUNTRY
13.7	Russia	5.7	Ireland
10.7	Brazil	5.6	Colombia
10.2	Estonia	5.6	Singapore
9.9	Latvia	5.5	South Africa
9.7	Lithuania	5.5	Sweden
9.6	Belarus	5.4	Denmark
9.3	Hungary	5.4	Greece
9.3	Ukraine	5.4	United Kingdom
9.2	Kazakhstan	5.3	Philippines
9.1	Poland	5.2	Congo
9.1	Puerto Rico	5.0	Trinidad and Tobago
8.5	El Salvador	5.0	Yugoslavia
8.5	France	4.9	Tajikistan
8.5	Slovakia	4.8	Turkey
8.1	Kyrgyzstan	4.7	Guatemala
7.9	Finland	4.6	Costa Rica
7.9	Slovenia	4.5	Peru
7.8	Czech Republic	4.4	Jamaica
7.6	Azerbaijan	4.4	Macedonia
7.6	Georgia	4.3	Myanmar
7.5	Portugal	4.3	Paraguay
7.3	Romania	4.3	United Arab Emirates
7.2	Croatia	4.2	Dominican Republic
7.1	Chile	4.2	Ecuador
7.1	Spain	4.2	Honduras
7.1	Switzerland	4.2	Kuwait
7.0	Bulgaria	4.2	Sri Lanka
6.9	Thailand	4.2	Vietnam
6.9	United States	4.1	Malaysia
6.8	Argentina	4.0	Indonesia
6.8	Belgium	4.0	Kenya
6.8	Italy	4.0	Panama
6.8	Moldova	3.9	Egypt
6.6	Austria	3.9	Lebanon
6.6	Korea, South	3.8	Benin
6.6	Taiwan	3.7	Syria
6.6	Turkmenistan	3.6	Cuba
6.5	Bosnia-Herzegovina	3.6	Ghana
6.4	Bolivia	3.6	Jordan
6.4	Canada	3.6	Zimbabwe
6.4	Germany	3.5	Eritrea
6.4	Japan	3.5	Saudi Arabia
6.4	Uruguay	3.5	Togo
6.3	Korea, North	3.4	Israel
6.3	Netherlands	3.4	Ivory Coast
6.2	Norway	3.4	Libya
6.1	New Zealand	3.4	Morocco
6.1	Uzbekistan	3.4	Zaire
5.9	Albania	3.3	Burkina Faso
5.9	Australia	3.3	Burundi
5.9	Mexico	3.3	Haiti
5.8	Venezuela	3.3	Rwanda
5.7	Armenia	3.3	Uganda

(continued)

LIFE EXPECTANCY GENDER GAP* *(cont.)*

GAP	COUNTRY	GAP	COUNTRY
3.2	Angola	2.6	Nicaragua
3.2	Chad	2.5	Nigeria
3.2	Ethiopia	2.4	Sudan
3.2	Mali	2.1	China
3.2	Mauritania	2.1	Zambia
3.2	Mozambique	2.0	Algeria
3.2	Niger	2.0	Liberia
3.2	Sierra Leone	2.0	Senegal
3.2	Somalia	1.8	Iraq
3.1	Central African Republic	1.4	Malawi
3.0	Cameroon	1.3	Pakistan
3.0	Laos	1.0	Afghanistan
3.0	Madagascar	1.0	Guinea
3.0	Tanzania	1.0	India
3.0	Yemen	0.5	Iran
2.9	Cambodia	0.0	Bangladesh
2.8	Tunisia	−1.2	Nepal

*Difference in women's and men's average life expectancy, in years.

RANGES IN WOMEN'S LIFE EXPECTANCY

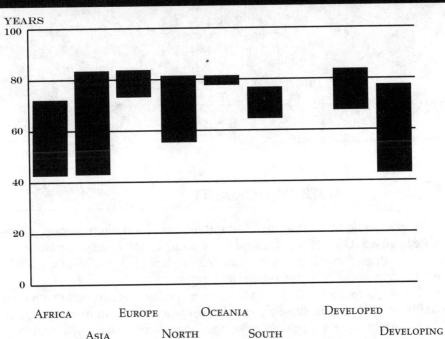

WOMEN'S LIFE EXPECTANCY IN THE ARAB WORLD

Longevity among Arab women ranges from extremely high to extremely low. In Israel Arab women have an average life expectancy three years shorter than that of the Jewish women living there; yet compared with women in Arab countries, they have the longest life span. Their life expectancy of 75.7 years puts them among the world's top 40 countries

LIFE EXPECTANCY RATES FOR ARAB WOMEN*

WOMEN	MEN	COUNTRY
75.7	74.2	Israel (Arab population only)
75.4	71.2	Kuwait
72.9	68.6	United Arab Emirates
67.8	64.2	Jordan
67.0	63.1	Lebanon
66.9	63.2	Syria
66.4	64.9	Tunisia
65.2	61.7	Saudi Arabia
65.0	63.0	Algeria
64.8	63.0	Iraq
62.8	58.9	Egypt
62.5	59.1	Libya
26.5	59.1	Morocco
52.4	49.4	Yemen
51.0	48.6	Sudan

*At birth, in years.

MATERNAL MORTALITY

Every year some 585,000 women throughout the world die from pregnancy-related causes. Over 99% of these deaths occur in the developing world; in some countries it is estimated that a quarter to half of all deaths of women of childbearing age are directly related to pregnancy.

The region with the highest maternal mortality average, 980 deaths per 100,000 live births, is sub-Saharan Africa, where six countries—Angola, Chad, Mozambique, Guinea, Somalia, and Sierra Leone—have maternal mortality rates of 1,500 or more. The lowest regional average is in Europe, where only one country, Romania, has a maternal mortality rate over 100.

DISTRIBUTION OF MATERNAL DEATHS

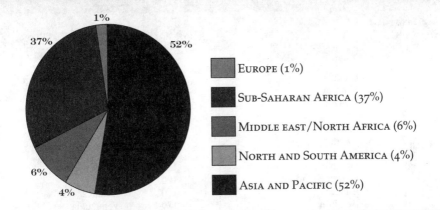

- ▮ Europe (1%)
- ▮ Sub-Saharan Africa (37%)
- ▮ Middle east/North Africa (6%)
- ▮ North and South America (4%)
- ▮ Asia and Pacific (52%)

A Woman's Lifetime Chances of Dying as a Result of Pregnancy or Childbirth Are ONE in

- ▲ 11,904 in Spain
- ▲ 10,417 in Switzerland
- ▲ 8,772 in Canada
- ▲ 8,333 in Norway
- ▲ 6,803 in Sweden
- ▲ 6,410 in Italy
- ▲ 6,173 in the United Kingdom
- ▲ 5,848 in Australia
- ▲ 5,102 in Israel
- ▲ 3,968 in the United States
- ▲ 3,922 in France
- ▲ 3,704 in Japan
- ▲ 3,497 in Germany

- ▲ 889 in Russia
- ▲ 526 in China
- ▲ 370 in Argentina
- ▲ 303 in Mexico
- ▲ 159 in Egypt
- ▲ 109 in South Africa
- ▲ 94 in the Philippines
- ▲ 49 in India
- ▲ 37 in Zimbabwe
- ▲ 12 in Mali
- ▲ 10 in Yemen
- ▲ 9 in Sierra Leone

Causes of Maternal Mortality

Of the more than 150 million women worldwide who become pregnant each year, about 23 million develop infections, severe bleeding, and other life-threatening complications, while another 12.5 million are physically compromised by other serious disorders such as malaria, tuberculosis, anemia, or

MATERNAL MORTALITY WORLDWIDE
Deaths per 100,000 live births

MATERNAL MORTALITY RATE	COUNTRY	MATERNAL MORTALITY RATE	COUNTRY
6	Canada	90	Trinidad and Tobago
6	Norway	95	China
6	Switzerland	95	Cuba
7	Israel	100	Argentina
7	Spain	100	Colombia
7	Sweden	110	Dominican Republic
9	Australia	110	Kyrgyzstan
9	Denmark	110	Mexico
9	United Kingdom	120	Iran
10	Austria	120	Jamaica
10	Belgium	120	Venezuela
10	Greece	130	Korea, South
10	Ireland	130	Romania
10	Singapore	130	Saudi Arabia
11	Finland	130	Tajikistan
12	Italy	140	Sri Lanka
12	Netherlands	150	Ecuador
12	United States	150	Jordan
13	Slovenia	160	Algeria
15	Czech Republic	160	Nicaragua
15	France	160	Paraguay
15	Portugal	160	Vietnam
18	Japan	170	Egypt
19	Poland	170	Tunisia
22	Azerbaijan	180	Syria
22	Germany	180	Turkey
25	New Zealand	200	Guatemala
26	United Arab Emirates	200	Thailand
27	Bulgaria	220	Brazil
29	Kuwait	220	Honduras
30	Hungary	220	Libya
33	Georgia	230	South Africa
36	Lithuania	280	Peru
37	Belarus	280	Philippines
40	Latvia	300	El Salvador
41	Estonia	300	Lebanon
50	Armenia	310	Iraq
50	Ukraine	340	Pakistan
55	Costa Rica	490	Madagascar
55	Panama	550	Cameroon
55	Turkmenistan	560	Liberia
55	Uzbekistan	560	Malawi
60	Moldova	570	India
65	Albania	570	Zimbabwe
65	Chile	580	Myanmar
70	Korea, North	610	Morocco
75	Russia	640	Togo
80	Kazakhstan	650	Bolivia
80	Malaysia	650	Indonesia
85	Uruguay	650	Kenya

(continued)

MATERNAL MORTALITY WORLDWIDE *(cont.)*
Deaths per 100,000 live births

MATERNAL MORTALITY RATE	COUNTRY	MATERNAL MORTALITY RATE	COUNTRY
650	Laos	1,200	Niger
660	Sudan	1,200	Senegal
700	Central African Republic	1,200	Uganda
740	Ghana	1,300	Burundi
770	Tanzania	1,300	Rwanda
810	Ivory Coast	1,400	Eritrea
850	Bangladesh	1,400	Ethiopia
870	Zaire	1,400	Yemen
890	Congo	1,500	Angola
900	Cambodia	1,500	Chad
930	Burkina Faso	1,500	Mozambique
930	Mauritania	1,500	Nepal
940	Zambia	1,600	Guinea
990	Benin	1,600	Somalia
1,000	Haiti	1,700	Afghanistan
1,000	Nigeria	1,800	Sierra Leone
1,200	Mali		

MATERNAL MORTALITY BY REGION
Deaths per 100,000 live births

MATERNAL MORTALITY RATE	COUNTRY	MATERNAL MORTALITY RATE	COUNTRY
911	**Africa (average of countries)**	890	Congo
		930	Burkina Faso
160	Algeria	930	Mauritania
170	Egypt	940	Zambia
170	Tunisia	990	Benin
220	Libya	1,000	Nigeria
230	South Africa	1,200	Mali
490	Madagascar	1,200	Niger
550	Cameroon	1,200	Senegal
560	Liberia	1,200	Uganda
560	Malawi	1,300	Burundi
570	Zimbabwe	1,300	Rwanda
610	Morocco	1,400	Eritrea
640	Togo	1,400	Ethiopia
650	Kenya	1,500	Angola
660	Sudan	1,500	Chad
700	Central African Republic	1,500	Mozambique
740	Ghana	1,600	Guinea
770	Tanzania	1,600	Somalia
810	Ivory Coast	1,800	Sierra Leone
870	Zaire		

(continued)

MATERNAL MORTALITY BY REGION *(cont.)*
Deaths per 100,000 live births

MATERNAL MORTALITY RATE	COUNTRY	MATERNAL MORTALITY RATE	COUNTRY
323	**Asia** **(average of countries)**	10	Belgium
		10	Greece
7	Israel	10	Ireland
10	Singapore	11	Finland
18	Japan	12	Italy
22	Azerbaijan	12	Netherlands
26	United Arab Emirates	13	Slovenia
29	Kuwait	15	Czech Republic
33	Georgia	15	France
50	Armenia	15	Portugal
55	Turkmenistan	19	Poland
55	Uzbekistan	22	Germany
70	Korea, North	27	Bulgaria
80	Kazakhstan	30	Hungary
80	Malaysia	36	Lithuania
95	China	37	Belarus
110	Kyrgyzstan	40	Latvia
120	Iran	41	Estonia
130	Korea, South	50	Ukraine
130	Saudi Arabia	60	Moldova
130	Tajikistan	65	Albania
140	Sri Lanka	75	Russia
150	Jordan	130	Romania
160	Vietnam		
180	Syria		
180	Turkey	**181**	**North America**
200	Thailand		**(average of countries)**
280	Philippines	6	Canada
300	Lebanon	12	United States
310	Iraq	55	Costa Rica
340	Pakistan	55	Panama
570	India	90	Trinidad and Tobago
580	Myanmar	95	Cuba
650	Indonesia	110	Dominican Republic
650	Laos	110	Mexico
850	Bangladesh	120	Jamaica
900	Cambodia	160	Nicaragua
1,400	Yemen	200	Guatemala
1,500	Nepal	220	Honduras
1,700	Afghanistan	300	El Salvador
		1,000	Haiti
27	**Europe** **(average of countries)**		
6	Norway	17	**Oceania**
6	Switzerland		**(average of countries)**
7	Spain	9	Australia
7	Sweden	25	New Zealand
9	Denmark		
9	United Kingdom	193	**South America**
10	Austria		**(average of countries)**
		65	Chile

(continued)

MATERNAL MORTALITY BY REGION *(cont.)* Deaths per 100,000 live births			
MATERNAL MORTALITY RATE	COUNTRY	MATERNAL MORTALITY RATE	COUNTRY
85	Uruguay	160	Paraguay
100	Argentina	220	Brazil
100	Colombia	280	Peru
120	Venezuela	650	Bolivia
150	Ecuador		

diabetes. Together these conditions kill more than half a million pregnant women every year and leave another 15 million with serious long-term complications, including infections of the reproductive tract, infertility, and neurological conditions so severe they make walking difficult.

The most common cause of pregnancy-related death is severe bleeding, which is responsible for about a quarter of all maternal deaths. Other serious health conditions—especially anemia, heart disease, diabetes, hepatitis, and malaria—account for an additional 20% of all maternal deaths, while infections cause about 15%. Complications arising from unsafe abortions are responsible for about 13% of all maternal deaths; other common causes include eclampsia (12%) and obstructed labor (8%), a frequent complication of infibulation, the most severe form of female genital mutilation.

Malnutrition is a serious debilitating condition affecting large numbers of women of childbearing age. In some Asian and African countries it is common for girls and women to eat only what is left over after the men have eaten, and some societies have cultural taboos against the eating of eggs, milk, beans, and other high protein foods during pregnancy.

Teenage Pregnancy and Maternal Mortality

Pregnant teenagers are especially at risk. It is estimated that about 15 million adolescent girls throughout the world become pregnant each year, and approximately 125,000 die as a result, accounting for about one-quarter of all maternal deaths.

Adolescent girls face much greater health hazards during pregnancy and childbirth than older women do. Young teenagers (those under the age of 15) are five times more likely to die during pregnancy or labor than women aged 20 to 24. Older teenagers (those between 15 and 19) are up to three times more likely to die. And not only is a young mother's health endangered by pregnancy, her baby is more likely to be born prematurely or with a low birth weight, both leading causes of infant death.

LEADING CAUSES OF DEATH

The leading causes of death are much the same for both women and men throughout the world. In many of the world's poorer nations, where health facilities and services are scarce, large numbers of women receive no medical care at all and their illnesses are never diagnosed, let alone treated. In South Africa, for example, the single largest official category of women's deaths is simply called "ill-defined" causes.

Although pregnancy-related deaths account for only about 2% of total women's deaths worldwide, they are responsible for 19% of all deaths of women aged 15 to 29. In the developed countries maternal deaths in this age bracket constitute only 2% of the total; in developing countries they make up 20% of these deaths.

LEADING CAUSES OF DEATH WORLDWIDE
Percentage of total deaths

CAUSE	WOMEN	MEN
Cardiovascular diseases	32%	26%
Infectious, parasitic diseases	19%	19%
Cancer	11%	13%
Injuries	5%	6%
Respiratory diseases	5%	6%
Pregnancy-related disorders	2%	—
Diabetes	2%	1%

Cardiovascular diseases, primarily strokes and heart attacks, are the leading killers of both women and men in developed as well as developing countries. Although communicable diseases are rarely fatal in the developed world, they are major causes of death elsewhere. Tuberculosis heads the list, especially as a killer of young women and men. AIDS, malaria, diarrheal diseases, and syphilis are also leading causes of death.

Cancers of all types are becoming more common among women throughout the world, though different kinds are prevalent in different regions.

LEADING CAUSES OF DEATH BY REGION
Percentage of total deaths

CAUSE	DEVELOPED WORLD		DEVELOPING WORLD	
	WOMEN	MEN	WOMEN	MEN
Cardiovascular diseases	55%	43%	25%	22%
Infectious, parasitic diseases	1%	2%	24%	24%
Cancer	20%	24%	8%	10%
Injuries	4%	10%	6%	11%
Respiratory diseases	4%	6%	6%	6%
Pregnancy-related disorders	<1%	—	2%	—
Diabetes	2%	1%	2%	1%

CANCER DEATHS
In order of frequency

	DEVELOPED WORLD	DEVELOPING WORLD	WORLDWIDE
Women	Breast	Stomach	Breast
	Colorectal	Cervix	Stomach
	Lung	Breast	Colorectal
	Stomach	Liver	Lung
Men	Lung	Stomach	Lung
	Stomach	Lung	Stomach
	Colorectal	Liver	Liver
	Prostate	Esophagus	Esophagus

WOMEN AND AIDS

AIDS first emerged as a major health problem in the mid-1980s and was initially thought to be primarily a man's disease. It was often referred to as the "gay plague" because a great many of the early victims were homosexual men and it was believed that women were not at risk. But by the mid-1990s the number of women contracting HIV, the virus that causes AIDS, was growing faster than the number of men, and women accounted for nearly half of all new cases.

Today more than 90% of all cases of HIV infection are found in the developing world. The largest concentration, nearly 70%, is found in the countries of sub-Saharan Africa, where the vast majority of cases are transmitted through heterosexual contact and where more women than men are infected. In Uganda, one of the hardest hit countries, among teenagers 15 to 19 years old the ratio of infected girls to boys is six to one; in Malawi and Zambia the ratio is five to one.

AIDS AND HIV INFECTION BY REGION*

REGION	NUMBER		RATIOS
	WOMEN	MEN	
Sub-Saharan Africa	5,447	4,952	110
South and Southeast Asia	1,374	2,748	50
Latin America	197	791	25
Caribbean	133	198	67
North America	129	773	17
Europe	107	552	19
Northeast Asia	21	107	20
Middle East	10	50	20

*Number in thousands; women per 100 men, 1994.

In 1996, scientists began noting the first signs that the spread of AIDS in Africa may be slowing. Studies showed that rates of infection among teenagers in some parts of Uganda had dropped sharply over the previous five years, most likely due to the increased use of condoms and other safe sex practices. Another hopeful sign was the decrease in the number of women who tested HIV-positive at

AIDS DEATHS BY REGION
Percentage of total AIDS deaths, 1994

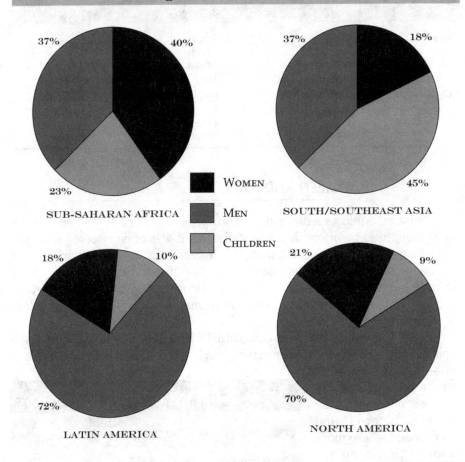

37% 40%

23%

SUB-SAHARAN AFRICA

37% 18%

45%

SOUTH/SOUTHEAST ASIA

■ WOMEN
■ MEN
■ CHILDREN

18% 10%

72%

LATIN AMERICA

21% 9%

70%

NORTH AMERICA

prenatal clinics. In some urban areas, the percentage of infected women dropped from 30% to between 15% and 20%.

Although Africa may have the largest concentration of AIDS cases, the area with the fastest-growing rate of infection is Asia, especially the southeastern portion of the continent, where the disease did not take hold until the late 1980s. Because of its long incubation period—usually ranging from seven to ten years—tremendous numbers of HIV-infected people are just now getting sick and dying. By 1996, just a decade after the virus had first been detected there, India had the world's largest number of people infected with HIV. Scientists fear that some of the world's most populous countries—China, Indonesia, and India—are now facing severe epidemics and that by the year 2000, more people will be infected in Asia than in the whole of the rest of the world.

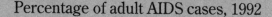

MAJOR MODES OF TRANSMISSION
Percentage of adult AIDS cases, 1992

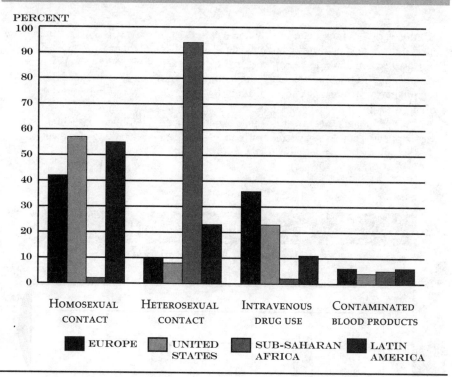

EUROPE   UNITED STATES   SUB-SAHARAN AFRICA   LATIN AMERICA

Women tend to have the highest rates of infection in countries where HIV transmission occurs mostly through heterosexual relations. Young women are especially vulnerable; the lining of their vaginal tract is more fragile, and young women often receive blood transfusions during pregnancy and childbirth because of anemia or severe bleeding. Although the use of condoms during intercourse can be an effective method of preventing transmission of the virus, there are many regions where prevailing religious laws or cultural customs prohibit their use. In Argentina, which has the second highest concentration of AIDS cases in South America, after Brazil, pressure from the Roman Catholic Church prevented a recent government anti-AIDS campaign from using the word *condom* in its advertisements. And in many parts of the world condoms are not readily available or men are reluctant to use them.

Some evidence has recently suggested that women infected with the AIDS virus die faster than infected men. Although the reason is not clear, a study conducted in the United States seemed to indicate that women may wait longer to seek treatment or may receive different medical care.

WOMEN AND SMOKING

Of the world's approximately 1.1 billion smokers, the great majority, 800 million, live in the developing world; but only about 100 million of them are women. There are also 100 million women smokers in the developed world, but there they make up one-third of the total smoking population, and lung cancer is the third most common cause of female cancer deaths. However, women's smoking rates are rising steadily in the developing countries, where lung cancer now ranks sixth as a cause of female cancer deaths. And as smoking rates continue to rise, lung cancer deaths are also expected to climb, especially since smoking is growing fastest among teenagers and young adults.

SMOKERS IN SELECTED COUNTRIES

Percentage of Adult Population

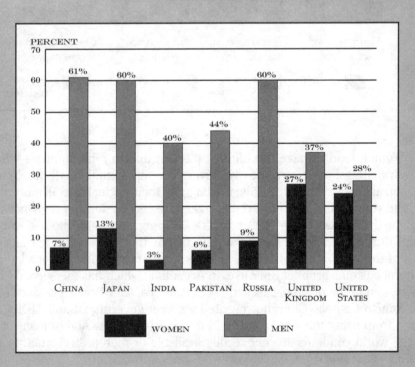

(continued)

WOMEN AND SMOKING *(cont.)*

SMOKING RATES WORLDWIDE: PERCENTAGE OF POPULATION AGED 15 AND OVER

WOMEN	MEN	COUNTRY	WOMEN	MEN	COUNTRY
1%	50%	Ghana	13%	48%	Romania
1%	—	Guinea	13%	59%	Thailand
1%	24%	Ivory Coast	14%	—	Dominican
1%	27%	Turkmenistan			Republic
1%	40%	Uzbekistan	15%	60%	Bangladesh
2%	33%	Egypt	16%	—	Ecuador
2%	48%	Sri Lanka	16%	84%	Philippines
2%	38%	Vietnam	17%	49%	Bulgaria
3%	28%	Ethiopia	17%	35%	Finland
3%	40%	India	18%	61%	Chile
3%	53%	Nigeria	19%	—	Sudan
3%	35%	Singapore	20%	—	Costa Rica
4%	41%	Malaysia	20%	49%	Estonia
5%	75%	Indonesia	20%	—	Panama
5%	35%	Trinidad and	21%	35%	Belgium
		Tobago	22%	33%	Austria
6%	45%	Iraq	23%	40%	Argentina
6%	44%	Pakistan	24%	28%	United States
6%	60%	Tunisia	25%	63%	Hungary
7%	62%	China	25%	38%	Israel
7%	69%	Korea, South	26%	28%	Canada
7%	34%	Peru	26%	—	Cuba
7%	39%	Zambia	26%	46%	Italy
8%	50%	Albania	27%	42%	Germany
9%	—	Morocco	27%	—	Jamaica
9%	60%	Russia	27%	58%	Spain
10%	36%	Guatemala	27%	37%	United
10%	52%	Lithuania			Kingdom
10%	37%	Portugal	28%	49%	Czech
10%	57%	Yugoslavia			Republic
11%	—	Honduras	28%	55%	Poland
12%	—	El Salvador	29%	—	Myanmar
12%	52%	Kuwait	29%	35%	New Zealand
12%	48%	Tanzania	29%	46%	Switzerland
13%	54%	Greece	30%	37%	Australia
13%	60%	Japan	30%	40%	Slovenia

(continued)

WOMEN AND SMOKING *(cont.)*

SMOKING RATES WORLDWIDE: *(cont.)*
PERCENTAGE OF POPULATION AGED 15 AND OVER

WOMEN	MEN	COUNTRY	WOMEN	MEN	COUNTRY
30%	26%	Sweden	35%	43%	Senegal
31%	57%	Colombia	38%	49%	Denmark
32%	39%	Ireland	44%	47%	Mexico
32%	42%	Norway	45%	45%	Uruguay
33%	63%	Brazil	50%	50%	Turkey
33%	49%	France	58%	79%	Nepal
33%	41%	Netherlands	61%	84%	Bolivia
33%	16%	Slovakia	67%	69%	Venezuela

In nearly every country, smoking is much more prevalent among men than among women; rates for men are often double or triple those for women. However, in a few countries smoking rates are about the same for both sexes, and in at least two countries—Sweden and Slovakia—more women than men smoke. In only four countries do more than half of all adult women smoke: Bolivia, Nepal, Turkey, and Venezuela.

For women as well as men, smoking is a life-threatening habit; it is estimated that for a regular smoker, every cigarette shortens his or her life span by about 5.5 minutes. Compared with nonsmokers, smokers are twice as likely to die from heart attacks and 14 times as likely to die from cancer of the lung, throat, or mouth. And according to a 1996 study conducted in the United States, women's lungs seem to be damaged more by cigarette smoking than men's, primarily because their lungs are smaller, with narrower air passages. Researchers also found that after quitting smoking, women do not recover as much lung capacity as men do. Another health risk is that women who smoke during pregnancy endanger the health of their babies. A pregnant woman who smokes 15 to 20 cigarettes a day doubles her chances of having a miscarriage, as well as increasing the likelihood of giving birth prematurely.

(continued)

WOMEN AND SMOKING *(cont.)*

OF THE WORLD'S 1.1 BILLION SMOKERS

300 MILLION LIVE IN DEVELOPED COUNTRIES

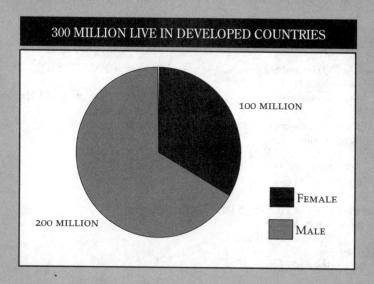

100 MILLION

200 MILLION

■ FEMALE

■ MALE

800 MILLION LIVE IN DEVELOPING COUNTRIES

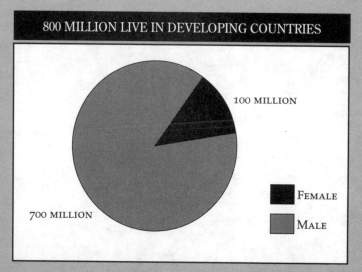

100 MILLION

700 MILLION

■ FEMALE

■ MALE

FOR ADDITIONAL INFORMATION

American Cancer Society
1599 Clifton Road, NE
Atlanta, GA 30329, United States
Telephone: 404-329-7963
Web site: http://www.cancer .org

**Centers for Disease Control and
   Prevention (CDC)**
1600 Clifton Road, NE
Atlanta, GA 30333, United States
Telephone: 404-639-3311
Web site: http://www.cdc.gov

Imperial Cancer Research Fund
44 Lincoln's Inn Fields
London WC2A 3PX, United Kingdom
Telephone: 171-242-0200
Web site: http://www.lif.icnet.uk

National Institutes of Health (NIH)
9101 Old Georgetown Road
Bethesda, MD 20892, United States
Telephone: 301-530-0567
Web site: http://www.nih.gov

World Health Organization (WHO)
1211 Geneva 27, Switzerland
Telephone: 22-791-3364
Fax: 22-791-0746
Web site: http://www.who.ch

WHO Global Program on AIDS
Telephone: 22-791-4652
Fax: 22-791-4652
E-mail: GPAINFO@WHO-CH

**WHO Office of World Health
   Reporting**
Fax: 22-791-4870

VIOLENCE AGAINST WOMEN

For millions of women around the globe, life is shadowed by the threat of violence. Wife battering, rape, and other forms of assault are universal problems that cut across all geographic, cultural, religious, racial, ethnic, and class boundaries. Although they are still grossly underreported, violent acts against women have assumed alarming proportions and are still growing.

Throughout history women have been perceived as the property of men, who were thus free to discipline or punish them at will with physical force. This prerogative of a man to beat his wife has been claimed at one time or another throughout most of the world, often sanctioned by law. In the United States wife beating was widely permitted until, in 1871, an Alabama court was the first to tell an abusive husband that "the privilege, ancient though it be, to beat her with a stick, to pull her hair, choke her, spit in her face or kick her about the floor or to inflict upon her other like indignities, is not now acknowledged by our law."

Today, in country after country, violent acts against women are often ignored or tolerated and sometimes still sanctioned by law or custom. The centuries-old patriarchal perception of women as men's property has shaped many modern laws that offer only limited protection to women while absolving or only lightly punishing their abusers. In a great many countries police, prosecutors, judges, and other officials turn a blind eye to the problem of domestic violence, reluctant to interfere in what they consider a private family matter. It is not surprising that so many incidents go unreported. Not only is the victim overcome with shame, embarrassment, and fear of reprisal; she knows that in all probability, very little, if anything, will be done to punish her abuser.

Because the vast majority of cases are never officially reported, there is very little reliable information on the incidence of violent acts against women. Although some countries have undertaken national or regional surveys, accurate measurement techniques are still being developed, and most data are only rough estimates. Statistics on sexual assault—rape, sodomy, or any other form of forced penetration—are especially limited.

Nevertheless, Recent Studies Have Found That:

▲ Among the more than 600 families surveyed in southern Asia, 51% reported having killed a baby girl during her first week of life.

▲ In the United States an estimated 42% of female homicide victims are killed by a current or former partner; in Bangladesh, Brazil, Kenya, and Thailand this figure reaches over 50%.

▲ In Chile and Pakistan as many as 80% of women are abused by their husbands.

▲ In South Africa a woman is raped every 83 seconds; in the United States, every three minutes.

▲ The Bolivian government estimates that 100,000 acts of violence against women are committed every year, 95% of which go unpunished.

Acts of violence against females are perpetrated not just against adults. Female infanticide and the abortion of female fetuses are not uncommon in China, India, South Korea, and other countries where sons are greatly valued over daughters. In India as many as 10,000 baby girls are murdered every year.

During childhood and adolescence, girls throughout the world are helpless victims of sexual assault. Even among some of the most highly industrialized nations—for example, Canada, the Netherlands, New Zealand, Norway, and the United States—surveys find that as many as one-third of women report sexual abuse during childhood or adolescence. In Myanmar, Thailand, and other parts of Asia, every year hundreds of thousands of girls are forced into prostitution, often lured by promises of legitimate jobs but sometimes kidnapped off the streets or sold to brothel owners by their parents.

Among some tribes in Benin, Ghana, Nigeria, and Togo an especially severe form of abuse is the practice of *tro-kosi,* in which a young girl is given as a slave to a fetish priest to atone for an offense committed by a family member. When she is released or if she dies, her family is expected to replace her with another young girl. It is estimated that there are several thousand of these young fetish slaves in southeastern Ghana alone.

Marriage in many countries affords no protection against violence. In certain cultures and religions, a husband can treat his wife as he pleases. Wife beating is therefore an accepted part of marriage, and large numbers of women throughout the world are not just assaulted by their partners but are killed or driven to suicide by them.

But despite this widespread pattern of violence, some changes are taking place and the outlook is beginning to appear less bleak. In many countries with active feminist movements, reducing violence has become a top priority among women's groups. Governments are under pressure to enact legislation prohibiting or increasing penalties for spousal abuse, rape (including marital rape), and other acts of violence against women. In a great many countries, women's groups, nongovernmental organizations, and government agencies are establishing shelters, telephone hotlines, and counseling services for victims. There are also many educational programs aimed at changing community attitudes. The women's groups most actively focusing on violence are scattered throughout Asia and the Pacific, western Europe, Latin America and the Caribbean, and North America.

DOMESTIC VIOLENCE

Domestic violence is widespread throughout the world and is one of the leading causes of female injuries in nearly every country. In the United States wife battering is believed to be the most common cause of women's injuries, accounting for more trauma than all rapes, muggings, and automobile accidents combined.

Many countries have no specific laws against spousal abuse, and where laws do exist, they are seldom enforced or are too weak to be effective. In the small percentage of cases where abusers are brought to trial, convictions are rare. Countries with strong patriarchal traditions often have laws that tend to favor the batterers, not the victims. Yet in some countries—among them the Ivory Coast, Laos, Madagascar, Myanmar, Singapore, and Yemen—wife abuse is not so common; it is not socially acceptable and carries harsh penalties. In other countries abusive husbands are vigorously prosecuted and convicted. In the Netherlands, for example, the penalty for battery is one-third more severe when the victim is a spouse.

But in the great majority of countries spousal abuse is pervasive, largely ignored by the police and the courts, who consider it a private family matter. In Eritrea, for example, an abused wife is urged not to press charges against her husband but to return to her family, while her husband is simply advised either to be discreet or offer her an apology.

In some countries a husband has the right to "discipline" or "correct" a disobedient wife, or even kill her if he suspects she has committed adultery. In Morocco the penal code states that if a husband catches his wife having sexual relations with another man, "murder, injuries, and blows are excusable" against the woman and her lover. (On the other hand, a Moroccan wife who kills an unfaithful husband is charged with murder.) Similarly, in Brazil and much of Latin America a man may be excused for killing his wife if he catches her in the act of having sexual relations with another man. This is commonly called a defense of honor, and it is often successful in cases where the husband can prove that he acted spontaneously in order to defend his honor. In some cases the husband may only have to suspect his wife's infidelity to qualify for a defense of honor. (The law does not provide such exoneration of a wife who kills her husband under the same circumstances.)

In Nigeria local customs and laws permit a husband to "correct" his wife as long as "the correction" does not leave a scar or require a stay of more than 21 days in a hospital. In Mexico an abusive husband may be pardoned or sentenced to no more than a very light prison term if his victim's wounds heal within 15 days. In Honduras courts take no action in domestic abuse cases unless the victim is so badly injured that she is incapacitated for more than 10 days. In Turkey wife beating is a crime only if the victim files a formal complaint, which is very rare since the wife must provide corroborating witnesses as well as a medical report supporting her claim. In parts of Somalia, according to local tradition, anyone found guilty of killing a woman pays only half as much compensation to her family (50 camels) as he would if the victim were a man (100 camels).

DOMESTIC VIOLENCE SURVEYS
Percentage of women reporting physical abuse by a male partner, 1986–1993

PERCENT	COUNTRY	PERCENT	COUNTRY
60%	Chile	41%	Belgium
60%	Ecuador	40%	Zambia
60%	Sri Lanka	39%	Malaysia
60%	Tanzania	27%–36%	Canada
59%	Japan	28%	United States
49%	Guatemala	25%	Norway
46%	Uganda	21%	Netherlands
42%	Kenya		

Dowry Deaths

Perhaps the most dramatic and flagrant form of domestic violence is the dowry death. This phenomenon is most common in Bangladesh, India, and other countries where a bride is expected to bring large amounts of money, gifts, and other valuables to a marriage. If a husband or his family are not satisfied with the bride's dowry, they may physically harass her, kill her, or drive her to suicide. In 1986, in an attempt to curb the growing number of these deaths, the government of India enacted a special amendment to the penal code stating that the husband or in-laws will be presumed responsible for a wife's unnatural death during the first seven years of marriage if there is sufficient evidence of cruelty or harassment. Yet despite this law, the number of dowry deaths has continued to climb. In 1995 the government reported over 7,000 of these fatalities, up from 5,400 in 1993.

Laws Against Domestic Violence

Over the past few decades many countries have implemented a wide range of measures to prevent spousal abuse, punish offenders, and support victims. Domestic violence laws have been enacted in a number of countries, including Australia, Ecuador, Jamaica, New Zealand, Trinidad and Tobago, the United Kingdom, and the United States. These laws specifically define domestic violence, facilitate the prompt arrest of wife batterers, and empower the courts to protect victims by such measures as restraining orders against abusive husbands. In the United States many states have passed laws in defiance of the traditional principle of spousal immunity, which prevents spouses from being forced to testify against each other. In cases of domestic violence, a wife can now be made to testify against her husband.

But there are also places where domestic violence laws are strongly opposed, particularly in countries with strong traditions of male domination. The Parliament in Malaysia, a predominantly Muslim nation, passed a Domestic Violence Act in 1994 but never implemented it because religious leaders feared that it would erode the power of the Islamic family court, which has jurisdiction over the country's 18.5 million Muslims. Under the new act, wife beating would become a criminal offense and a Malaysian wife would be able to obtain an order of protection against an abusive husband. Under the previous law, which is still in effect, a woman must first file for divorce before the police will issue such an order. The new law would also mandate counseling for the abusive spouse.

Services for Victims

In some countries residential shelters, free legal counseling, and other spe-

COUNTRIES WITH RESIDENTIAL SHELTERS OR SIMILAR REFUGES FOR BATTERED WIVES

Argentina	France	Netherlands	Thailand
Australia	Germany	New Zealand	Trinidad and
Austria	Honduras	Pakistan	Tobago
Bangladesh	Ireland	Peru	Turkey
Bolivia	Israel	Philippines	United Kingdom
Canada	Italy	South Korea	United States
Costa Rica	Japan	Sri Lanka	
Ecuador	Malaysia	Sweden	

cial services are available for victims of domestic violence. Often, these services are operated by women's groups or nongovernmental organizations, sometimes in cooperation with government agencies, which may provide some funding.

Another measure that has been adopted by some countries to aid victims of spousal abuse is a special women's desk at a local police station, which is staffed by trained officers, usually women, to investigate charges of domestic violence and provide support to victims. Brazil created eight of these desks in 1985, and five years later there were 74 scattered throughout the country. Similar police desks have been established in Bolivia, Nicaragua, Pakistan, Peru, the Philippines, and Spain.

In 1993 South Africa became one of the first countries to establish special courts solely for sex crimes. In 1994 India set up special women's courts, employing only women judges and prosecutors, exclusively to handle crimes of violence against women. Introduced as a one-year experiment in New Delhi, they became so successful that they were soon extended to other cities. The vast majority of countries, however, have no special training programs for police or other officials involved in domestic violence.

RAPE

Rape and other forms of sexual assault are probably the world's most underreported crimes; some countries estimate that only 5% to 25% of all incidences are ever reported. Most often, the victim is so overcome with feelings of shame and humiliation that she cannot bear to tell her family or friends, let alone report the crime to the authorities, who are likely to be insensitive to her feelings and treat her with disdain. In some communities a daughter who is raped brings shame on her entire family and she may be ostracized or abandoned. In Pakistan it is not unusual for a woman who reports being raped to find herself charged with adultery, and the penal code, heavily influenced by Islamic law, imposes harsh sentences, such as death by stoning, for

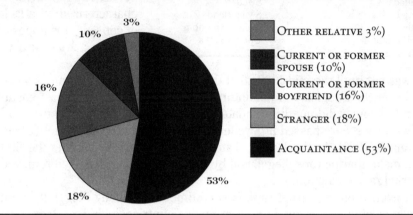

RAPE IN THE UNITED STATES: RELATIONSHIP OF OFFENDER TO VICTIM
Percentage of total rapes, 1992–1993

- OTHER RELATIVE 3%)
- CURRENT OR FORMER SPOUSE (10%)
- CURRENT OR FORMER BOYFRIEND (16%)
- STRANGER (18%)
- ACQUAINTANCE (53%)

unlawful sexual relations. For this reason it is estimated that 80% of rape cases in Pakistan are never brought to trial.

Because sexual assault is so greatly underreported, there are few reliable statistics regarding its incidence. What is known is that many of the victims are children and adolescents. In surveys in Canada, the Netherlands, Norway, New Zealand, and the United States, from a quarter to a third of women interviewed reported having been sexually abused during childhood. In India about 25% of the 10,000 cases of rape reported each year involve girls under the age of 16. In Belgium up to 40% of all reported rapes involve children.

Another common characteristic of rape is that in the majority of cases, the rapist is not a stranger but someone known to the victim, generally an acquaintance or relative. A recent study in the United States found that about 82% of rapes are committed by someone known to the victim. In Peru one survey of pregnant teenagers found that 90% of them had been raped by their father, stepfather, or other close relative.

Marital Rape

Marital rape is probably as ancient as the institution of marriage itself. In 17th century England Chief Justice Matthew Hale declared that a husband "cannot be guilty of rape committed by himself upon his lawful wife, for by their mutual matrimonial consent and contract the wife hath given up herself in this kind unto the husband, which she cannot retract." Many countries adopted this same policy, assuming that a wife who enters into a marriage contract

COUNTRIES WHERE MARITAL RAPE LAWS ARE ENFORCED

Australia	New Zealand
Canada	Sweden
Israel	Switzerland
Italy	United Kingdom
Netherlands	United States

gives her irrevocable consent to all sexual relations with her husband and that since the act of rape is always characterized by a lack of consent, it is impossible for a husband to rape his wife.

It was not until the mid-1900s that this attitude started changing as some countries enacted legislation making marital rape a crime, or at least ensuring that the courts did not differentiate between spousal rape and nonspousal rape. Such laws were passed in Sweden (1965), Canada (1982), Israel (1988), and France (1990). In the United States, Oregon, in 1977, became the first state to make marital rape illegal, and by 1996 every other state had removed the marital rape exception.

Yet even though marital rape is sometimes technically illegal, it is not generally treated as a crime in a great many countries, including Argentina, Brazil, Colombia, Egypt, Germany, Nigeria, the Philippines, and Thailand.

Mass Rape During Armed Conflicts

Throughout history, mass rape of women during periods of internal strife or armed conflicts have been documented in war-torn countries around the globe. Often, such incidents are part of an intentional strategy to conquer, punish, or terrorize large segments of the civilian population. Especially in countries where any act of violence against a woman is considered a serious attack against her family's honor, in times of conflict women become prime targets of violence.

In recent years mass rapes and other sexual assaults have been reported in Bangladesh, Burundi, Cambodia, Liberia, Peru, Rwanda, Somalia, and Uganda. Perhaps the most shocking reports of large-scale organized rape in recent years have come from the countries that made up the former Yugoslavia, where 20,000 or more women and girls were raped during the first few months of the war that followed the country's dissolution in 1992. Although all three parties to the conflict—Muslims, Croats, and Bosnian Serbs—were guilty of committing sexual assaults, the main abusers were the Bosnian Serbs, who were ordered to rape Muslim women as part of a brutal ethnic cleansing campaign as well as a deliberate attempt to terrorize civilians and drive them from their homes. In 1996 an International Criminal Tribunal, in an unprecedented action, indicted several Bosnian Serb military, paramilitary, and police officers for raping Muslim women. This was the first time in history that organized rape and other sexual assaults had been recognized as war crimes in international law.

Late in 1996 the United Nations, together with the International Federation of Red Cross and Red Crescent Societies, announced a new approach to the problem of mass rape during times of conflict—"morning after" contraceptive pills for women who had been raped by their attackers. Treatment services would also be available for complications of unsafe abortions, sexually-transmitted diseases, and injuries resulting from sexual assault.

Laws Against Rape

Laws concerning rape vary tremendously from one country to another. Many of the developed countries have strict laws that impose stiff penalties for convicted rapists. Usually, the punishment entails a fine and imprisonment for several years, with penalties increasing sharply in cases where the victim was under age or gang-raped, or where a gun or other weapon was involved. In Israel a 1990 amendment to the penal code deemed all sexual crimes more serious if committed within the family.

Some countries have enacted rape laws aimed at preserving the victim's privacy. In the United Kingdom rape victims are afforded anonymity by the 1976 Sexual Offences Act, which was expanded in 1992 to include victims of other kinds of sexual assault. In the United States so-called shield laws prohibit testimony about the victim's lifestyle, conduct, or sexual history. Other laws include provisions requiring automatic prosecution of rape, without the victim having to initiate it. Recently the U.S. Congress enacted new rules for federal courts, allowing the introduction of evidence relating to the offender's previous history of sexual assault.

Generally, though, in many parts of the world rape laws are often weak and rarely enforced. Accused rapists are seldom brought to trial, and convictions are rare. In many countries, including Romania and Russia, the burden of proof is on the victim, who must present a mass of evidence, including medical records and proof of resistance. A witness is also necessary to corroborate the victim's testimony. Among some ethnic groups in Sudan, there are no penalties for rape, but the rapist must pay the victim's family if she becomes pregnant. In several countries—including Argentina, Brazil, Chile, Egypt, Guatemala, and Morocco—a rapist may be allowed to preserve his victim's family's honor and even avoid prosecution if he marries her.

Services for Victims

Social, legal, and other services for rape victims vary greatly from country to country. Some provide a wide range of services, including shelters or treatment facilities and free legal counseling for victims. In Denmark, France, Germany, the Netherlands, and the United Kingdom, criminal compensation programs entitle sexual assault victims to financial compensation by the government. Most countries, however, provide few, if any, social services to rape victims. Those services that do exist are generally operated and maintained by private, nonprofit volunteer organizations.

PROSTITUTION

Prostitution has existed since earliest times and is deeply entrenched almost everywhere in the world. Although accurate statistics are not available, it is estimated that India alone has 2 million prostitutes, of whom 400,000 are under the age of 18. Thailand is another country with a thriving commerce in sex. Its 100,000 to 250,000 prostitutes support a flourishing industry whose brothels, massage parlors, and nightclubs attract tremendous numbers of male tourists every year.

Bangkok and other sex capitals throughout Asia—in Cambodia, China, the Philippines, South Korea, Taiwan, and Vietnam, among others—are supplied by tens of thousands of girls and young women, mostly from poor rural villages in neighboring countries, who are often tricked by unscrupulous recruiters promising them legitimate city jobs as domestics or waitresses. But after being smuggled across the border, they find that they have been sold to brothel owners who keep them as virtual slaves, forcing them to stay long enough to earn the money to repay their recruiters. Sometimes it is the girl's own parents who have sold her to the recruiter or brothel owner in return for a large cash advance against her future earnings. Because the young prostitutes often cannot speak the local language and are illegal immigrants, they are in no position to seek help from the local authorities. In Thailand alone there are more than 20,000 young women and girls from Myanmar working under such conditions in local brothels.

Asia is not the only region where sex is a thriving business. Brazil has a flourishing sex tourism industry that includes an estimated 500,000 girls under the age of 14. Large numbers of Brazilian girls are also taken to remote mining camps and villages, where they are kept as virtual sex slaves while they try to pay off the costs of their transportation and upkeep. In some Middle Eastern countries, including Kuwait and Saudi Arabia, thriving sex industries are fed by a steady supply of young women mostly from Bangladesh, India, the Philippines, Sri Lanka, and other poor countries where they cannot find employment. Often, the unsuspecting women are led to believe that they are accepting overseas jobs as maids or other domestic laborers, only to find that they have been duped into working as prostitutes. Even when they are employed as domestics, they are often subjected to harsh physical and sexual abuse by their employers, who keep them virtual captives by withholding their salaries and confiscating their passports and other travel documents.

During the last decade the appearance of AIDS has created a sharp increase in the demand for younger and younger prostitutes—even girls as

JAPAN'S COMFORT WOMEN: A SHAMEFUL LEGACY FROM WORLD WAR II

For more than three decades after the end of World War II, thousands of Asian women—Japan's comfort women—lived with a terrible secret.

It was only in the 1970s that reports started surfacing of huge numbers of mostly Korean but also Japanese, Philippine, Dutch, Indonesian, Chinese, and other young women who had been held captive by the Japanese army and compelled to provide sex for Japanese soldiers during World War II. From 80,000 to 200,000 women were enslaved for this purpose in brothels throughout the vast Japanese empire. The first of these military-run brothels were established in Shanghai in 1932 as a way of reducing the high number of rapes committed by the Japanese servicemen occupying the city.

During the course of the war many of the women died from venereal disease or physical abuse. Those who survived, overcome by feelings of shame and guilt, kept their ordeal a secret for decades, often not even telling their families. But starting around the mid-1970s, some of the comfort women began coming forward and demanding an apology and reparation from the Japanese government, which had long denied any involvement in the forced prostitution. In 1995, however, the Japanese government did establish the Asian Women's Fund to collect voluntary private donations that would eventually compensate the many women who had been victimized. The following year, Japan's prime minister offered a formal apology and started making the first payments, although many of the women refused to accept them on the grounds that the money came from private contributions, not government funds.

An interesting footnote to this story is that immediately following the war—no more than two weeks after surrendering—the Japanese government, through a specially created organization called the Recreation and Amusement Association, opened special brothels for the occupying American forces. Japanese officials were afraid that the American soldiers would behave as the Japanese soldiers had when occupying overseas territories. Young Japanese women, mostly between the ages of 18 and 25, were recruited to work in the brothels and asked to sacrifice themselves for the higher good of preserving the chastity of Japanese women as a whole and maintaining the purity of Japanese blood. About 55,000 women are believed to have been involved in this massive, government-run prostitution ring. Many of them did not survive, succumbing to venereal disease and maltreatment.

young as eight or nine years old. Many men mistakenly believe that younger girls are less likely to be infected with the AIDS virus. But in fact, they are more susceptible to HIV infection because their skin and tissues lining the vagina and anus are more fragile and likely to be torn during intercourse.

Prostitution and the Law

In a great many countries—including Argentina, Australia, Brazil, Germany, India, Italy, Nigeria, Russia, and the United Kingdom—prostitution itself is not against the law but pimping, soliciting, operating a brothel, and other activities related to prostitution are prohibited. Some countries set a legal age limit for prostitutes. In Bangladesh, for example, prostitution is legal for women over the age of 18. However, even in countries where prostitution or its related activities are prohibited, the laws are generally not strictly enforced and commercial sex remains widespread.

Only a few countries, among them the Netherlands and Sweden, have a legalized sex industry, strictly regulated by the government. In Australia one state—Victoria—has legal, licensed brothels, as does the state of Nevada in the United States. Legal brothels are generally limited to specified areas, and the prostitutes must undergo regular medical checkups that include testing for AIDS and other sexually transmitted diseases.

FEMALE GENITAL MUTILATION

Female genital mutilation (FGM) is an ancient custom in which a young girl's clitoris is cut off, sometimes along with the labia, and the remaining outer edges stitched together so that only a small opening remains. It is usually performed on girls between the ages of 4 and 10, but in some areas it may be performed shortly after birth or delayed until just after the young woman is married. Sometimes FGM is erroneously referred to as female circumcision, but a comparable procedure performed on a man would actually entail removing most or all of the penis, sometimes with its surrounding tissue.

Proponents of the practice, including women who have undergone the procedure themselves, claim that the reason for destroying a young woman's sexual sensation is to preserve her virginity until marriage and prevent her from succumbing to sexual temptation after marriage. There are also claims that it prevents homosexuality and "beautifies" the woman. In some societies a young woman is not considered socially acceptable or marriageable unless she has been subjected to the procedure.

It is estimated that 90 million women worldwide have undergone FGM, and more than 2 million girls are forced to submit to it every year. FGM is most commonly practiced in Africa, where Egypt, Ethiopia, Kenya, Nigeria, Somalia, and the Sudan account for about three-quarters of all cases. It is also practiced in a few Asian countries and in North America, Europe, and other parts of the world with large numbers of immigrants from those countries where it is a common custom.

Australia, Canada, France, Ghana, the Netherlands, Norway, Sweden, Switzerland, the United Kingdom, and the United States are among the

FEMALE GENITAL MUTILATION IN AFRICA
Estimated percentage of female population

PERCENT	COUNTRY	PERCENT	COUNTRY
98%	Somalia*	50%	Guinea
90%	Eritrea*	50%	Kenya
90%	Ethiopia*	50%	Nigeria
90%	Sierra Leone	50%	Togo
89%	Sudan*	30%	Ghana
80%	Mali	25%	Mauritania
70%	Burkina Faso	20%	Cameroon
60%	Chad	20%	Niger
60%	Ivory Coast	20%	Senegal
60%	Liberia	10%	Tanzania
50%	Benin	5%	Uganda
50%	Central African Republic	5%	Zaire
50%	Egypt		

*These countries practice infibulation, the most severe form of FGM.

countries that either have special laws to prohibit FGM or apply existing laws to prosecute those who practice it. In 1993 France became the first country to bring criminal charges against immigrants who were performing the procedure. That same year, Canada became the first country to include FGM as a form of abuse that could be used as grounds for granting political asylum to women and girls who would be forced to undergo the procedure if they were returned to their homelands. The United States followed suit in 1996, and that year also passed a federal law banning FGM.

There are two basic forms of female genital mutilation. Both are generally performed by traditional practitioners, usually older women, using unsterilized razor blades, knives, glass shards or other crude instruments and without benefit of anesthesia. In a clitoridectomy, the most common and mildest form of FGM, the clitoris is removed, sometimes along with part of the labia. In the most severe form, infibulation, the clitoris and labia are removed and the outer edges stitched together, sometimes with catgut or thorns, leaving only a tiny opening for the passage of urine and menstrual fluid. When the woman is about to give birth, the opening is enlarged to enable the baby to pass through, and after giving birth the sides are sewn back together. This process is repeated after every pregnancy.

The health hazards of female genital mutilation are numerous. Short-term complications include pain, severe bleeding, and sometimes death from tetanus or other infections. Long-term complications, especially of infibulation, include damage to the urethra or anus, chronic reproductive tract infections, infertility, massive scars that hinder walking, and the likelihood of obstructed labor, which is not only intensely painful but is a frequent cause of maternal death.

Although some countries where FGM is practiced have laws or government policies banning it, they are rarely enforced. A movement to prohibit the practice emerged in Africa in the 1960s, and many women's groups around the world are now supporting it. In Nigeria a national association of nurses and midwives has created an educational program aimed at eliminating FGM and has succeeded in having the program incorporated into nursing and medical school courses.

FOR ADDITIONAL INFORMATION

Center for Human Rights
Palais des Nations
1211 Geneva 10, Switzerland
Telephone: 22-917-3401
Fax: 22-917-0118

Human Rights Watch
1522 K Street, NW
Washington, DC 20005, United States
Telephone: 202-371-6592
Fax: 202-371-0124
E-mail: hrwdc@hrw.org
Web site: http://www.hrw.org

U.S. State Department
Human Rights Reports
Web site: http://www.hri.org/docs/
USSD-Rights/

The following section presents individual profiles of the following 21 countries:

Argentina	France	Nigeria
Australia	Germany	Philippines
Bangladesh	India	Russia
Brazil	Israel	South Africa
Canada	Italy	Sweden
China	Japan	United Kingdom
Egypt	Mexico	United States

Each country profile provides detailed information about the particular country for all of the categories covered in the previous sections. In addition, it includes a brief history of the women's movement in that country and a description of the role its women play in politics today.

Introducing each profile is a short list of some of the more important indicators of women's status. For some countries one or more of these items is marked with an up arrowhead (▲) or a down arrowhead (▼). The arrowhead (▲) indicates that the country ranks in the top 10% of that particular category; the down arrowhead (▼) indicates a ranking in the bottom 10%.

ARGENTINA

Population: *34.2 million*
Women per 100 men: *102*
Women's voting rights: *1947*
▲ Women in legislature: *22%*
Women's share of work force: *29%*
Literacy rates: women—*96%;* men—*96%*
Life expectancy: women—*75.7 years;* men—*68.9 years*
Average number of children: *2.7*
Maternal mortality rate: *100*

Argentina is the second largest country in South America (after Brazil), and it occupies much of that continent's southern portion. It is a major agricultural producer, but is also highly industrialized, with the vast majority of its people (86%) living in urban centers. More than 90% of the popula-tion are Roman Catholic, and the church plays a major role in shaping the country's laws and policies, especially those concerning contraception and abortion.

HISTORY OF THE WOMEN'S MOVEMENT

The emergence of women's groups began shortly after Argentina won its independence from Spain in 1816. By the early 1900s, these groups were actively campaigning for equal rights, maternity benefits, legalized divorce, and the right to vote. During the popular but repressive dictatorship of Juan Perón, which began with his election as president in 1946, Argentine women found a great ally in his second wife Eva, popularly known as Evita, who championed women's rights and advocated women's suffrage. Largely due to her efforts, in 1947 women were granted the right to vote. Eva Perón is also credited as the motivating force behind her husband's naming 30 women to the legislature, initiating divorce reform, and relaxing the government's official opposition to contraception.

Three years after Eva Perón died in 1952, at the age of 33, Juan Perón was ousted by a military regime. During the next two decades, women's rights were suppressed and feminist groups forced underground. It was not until the 1970s that feminist activists started resurfacing. In 1973 Juan Perón was reelected president, with his third wife, Isabel, as vice president. When he died the following year, she succeeded him and became the first woman to head a South American nation. However, her presidency ended abruptly in 1976, when she was ousted by a military junta that quickly imposed a virtual reign of terror throughout the country. During this period thousands of political activists, mostly young women and men, "disappeared"—kidnapped, tortured, and presumed killed by the military.

The first public opposition to the military junta was a small band of women, the *Madres de Plaza de Mayo,* who started holding weekly vigils in the main government square of Buenos Aires on behalf of their "disappeared" children and grandchildren. These small, peaceful demonstrations quickly garnered public support as the mothers were joined by thousands of other Argentine women. Although the military regime ended in 1983, the *Madres* have remained a vocal group, holding their weekly protests and still wearing their trademark white headscarfs bearing the names of missing children. They are still fighting to learn the fate of their children and demanding punishment for their abusers. The *Madres* have also been active in helping to locate and identify children who were born to those women who were pregnant when captured. Through genetic testing, more than 30 such children have been united with their biological families.

With the return to democracy in 1983, attention again focused on a variety of women's issues, including sex discrimination, employment opportunities, reproductive rights, and women's representation in government. The federal government responded by enacting legislation and creating several agencies aimed at eliminating discrimination against women and promoting their participation in society. The National Women's Council was established in 1992 and has since been actively involved in all executive branch projects dealing with women's affairs. In 1993 the Cabinet of Women Advisers to the President was created to encourage and monitor the implementation of government policies aimed at achieving equal opportunities for women.

WOMEN IN POLITICS

With the notable exceptions of Eva and Isabel Perón, Argentine women have historically been underrepresented at high levels of government. In 1993, however, a decree implementing a 1991 law required that at least 30% of all political party candidates must be women. As a result, in 1995 women were elected to 22% of the seats in the National Congress, by far the highest percentage in any South American legislature and one of the highest in the world. Previously, women had held only 10% of the seats. In the 257-seat Chamber of Deputies, the number of women nearly doubled, from 34 to 65, accounting for 25% of the total. Only 2 women were named to the 48-member Senate (4%), a chamber consisting of 2 representatives from each province and 2 from the Federal District.

Although Argentine women are fairly well represented in their national legislature, they remain grossly underrepresented in other high-level government positions. By 1996 there were no women cabinet members, no women governors, and 12 women ambassadors out of a total of 75 (16%). Even in the civil service, where more than half the employees were women, every top-level post was occupied by a man.

WOMEN'S EDUCATION

The Argentine constitution mandates seven years of free, compulsory primary school education for all girls and boys until the age of 14. On average, girls spend slightly more time in school than boys, 9.5 years as compared with 9.0 years. At the primary level, about 95% of all girls are enrolled in school, with girls equaling the number of boys. However, as these students progress through the educational system, more boys tend to drop out, most likely to enter the job market.

Literacy rates for adults tend to be lower in rural areas, where only about 10% of girls attend secondary school and only 2% go on to college. Nevertheless, average literacy rates for the country as a whole are 96% for both women and men.

In higher education women account for about 80% of the students in education, humanities, and philosophy courses. In architecture, law, and medical classes they make up 50% of the students, and in natural and applied sci-

FEMALE ENROLLMENT Percentage of student body, 1986	
LEVEL	PERCENT
Primary school	50%
Secondary school	52%
Higher education	53%

ences, they constitute 35%. In agriculture courses 21% of students are women; and in engineering, only 9%.

In 1987 the University of Buenos Aires established a postgraduate women's studies program to conduct research, training programs, and other activities to improve the status of women throughout Argentina. Other universities with similar programs include the National University of Comahue and the University of Cuyo. In 1991 the government created the National Program for the Promotion of Equal Opportunities for Women in the Educational Area. Its main goals include revising the national curriculum to make it less gender-biased and ensuring equal educational opportunities for women.

WOMEN'S EMPLOYMENT

Argentina's women have been entering the labor force in steadily increasing numbers over the past three decades. In the mid-1960s many of these women were from the middle class, working to improve their economic and social status. Since the economic crisis of the 1970s, however, many working-class wives have had to enter the job market to supplement their family income, and in some cases they have become the main breadwinner. According to official records, by the mid-1990s, about 32% of working-age women were in the labor force, and they made up about 29% of the total, up from 22% in 1960. Argentine men, in comparison, had an 80% participation rate in the work force.

Discrimination in the Workplace

Argentine law contains a number of rules and guidelines prohibiting sex discrimination and harassment in employment. However, the law does not impose sanctions for violating these policies; as a result, they are largely ignored and discrimination is widespread. For example, a recent study of public sector employees showed that in order for women to reach middle- and senior-level posts, they had to be either better educated or more experienced than their male counterparts. It was estimated that professional women required more than 16 years of seniority over male candidates to qualify for the same job.

Areas of Employment

Many Argentine women, because they lack proper training or need to work fewer or more flexible hours to take care of their families, cannot find suitable jobs in the formal sector. Instead they take jobs as maids, cooks, waitresses, and other unskilled daily laborers, which do not provide the health care or other benefits enjoyed by those working in the formal sector. It is estimated that the informal sector accounts for 40% of the country's economy and that women make up 60% of this labor force.

Those women employed in the formal sector of the economy tend to work in clerical, sales, and service occupations. They are rarely seen in high-level positions; for every 100 men in administrative or managerial posts, only 7 women occupy similar positions. However, for every 100 men in professional or technical jobs, there are 121 women. One reason for this high ratio is that teaching is a popular profession among Argentine women, who make up 91% of primary school and 67% of secondary school teachers. In higher education, however, only 35% of university teaching staff are women.

In recent years there has been a growing movement to recognize and remunerate housewives for their domestic chores. A Housewives Union, over 80,000 strong, provides medical services to its members and has launched a campaign calling for wages, pension benefits, and social security for housewives.

WOMEN IN THE JUDICIARY
Percentage of judges, 1993

COURT	NUMBER	PERCENT
Federal Justice (federal capital)	4	9%
Federal Justice (interior)	8	13%
Magistrate's Courts (Buenos Aires)	98	28%
Collegiate Courts	54	20%

Pay Differences

A 1994 government study reported that a disproportionately high number of Argentine women are concentrated in the lowest-paying occupations and that even when women perform the same work as men, they receive lower salaries. In addition, more women than men work in seasonal, temporary, and part-time jobs. As a result, women's average nonagricultural earnings are about 65% of men's.

Maternity Leave and Benefits

According to Argentine law, women are entitled to a 90-day maternity leave, extending from 45 days before the due date to 45 days after delivery. During this period the woman cannot be fired and receives social security payments equivalent to her full salary. Once she returns to work, she is entitled to two half-hour breaks a day for child care until her baby reaches the age of one.

Special leave is available to women who have worked at least a year and need to stay home to care for children or other family members. This type of leave ranges from six months to a year, during which the woman receives 25% of her regular salary.

Child Care

Argentine law stipulates that all businesses with more than 50 employees furnish child-care facilities. However, this law is difficult to enforce and is largely ignored.

Unemployment

Unemployment in Argentina is highest in urban areas, where in the mid-1990s it was 7.7% for women and 6.6% for men. Youngest workers were hardest hit, with women from 15 to 24 years old having a jobless rate of 15.6%. The comparable rate for young men was 11.5%.

MARRIAGE AND DIVORCE

A deeply ingrained patriarchal tradition has played a crucial role in shaping Argentina's laws and policies concerning marriage and the family. Until 1985, for example, parental authority over minor children was the sole prerogative of the father, and until 1987 a wife had to assume her husband's surname.

Recent years have seen a growth in the number of female-headed households in Argentina. National statistics are not available, but in the Buenos Aires metropolitan area, which contains nearly 40% of the total population, more than one-fifth of all households are headed by women.

Marriage

The legal minimum age for marriage is 21 for both women and men, but with parental consent, it drops to 16 and 18 respectively. On average, however, Argentine women marry at 22.9 years, men at 25.3 years.

There are no available statistics on the number of cohabiting couples, but 30% of all births are to unmarried women, indicating a fairly high incidence of cohabitation. In addition, the government has officially acknowledged cohabiting couples by granting pension rights to partners in these de facto marriages.

Divorce

The year 1985 witnessed a milestone in Argentine family law: the introduction of divorce by mutual consent. Previously, divorces had been nearly impossible to obtain, and many couples traveled to other countries to get divorced. (Juan Perón's legalized "dissolution of marriage" in 1954 was suspended by the succeeding regime.)

In divorces where one partner sues the other, adultery is an acceptable ground for divorce. However, Argentine law imposes different definitions of adultery for women and men. A husband is guilty of adultery only if he has a mistress. For a wife, a single sexual act with another man is sufficient. Presumably, this double standard protected a husband from the possibility of his wife having another man's child whom he would have to support and who would inherit his property.

The 1985 divorce law also specifically addressed the issue of alimony, awarding it on the basis of need as well as "guilt." However, it is estimated that nearly two-thirds of divorced fathers do not meet their payments. In 1995 the legislature was considering a law that would imprison delinquent spouses for a term of three to six years.

FAMILY PLANNING

Argentina is overwhelmingly Roman Catholic, and the church exerts a powerful influence in the country's policies regarding family planning. In a recent government campaign to curb the spread of AIDS, pressure from the church prevented the use of the word *condom* in posters and other advertisements. However, the government does acknowledge a need for family planning centers throughout the country.

Fertility Rate

The average number of children born to Argentine women in their lifetime is 2.7. The rate of births to teenagers, averaging about 13% of all births, is the highest on the continent and

BIRTHS BY AGE OF MOTHER Percentage of total births, 1993	
AGE	PERCENT
15–19	13%
20–24	28%
25–29	28%
30–34	19%
35–39	10%
40–44	3%
45–49	<1%

is of great concern to the government. In some rural provinces —such as Chaco, Chubut, Misiones, and Neuquén—births to teenagers account for more than 18% of all births.

Contraception

Although a 1974 decree banned the public distribution of contraceptives, this law was revoked in 1986. Today it is estimated that the proportion of married women of childbearing age who use some form of birth control is nearly 75%, the second highest rate of contraceptive use in South America (after Brazil). Yet in remote areas many women have no access at all to contraceptives or family planning information.

Abortion

Abortion is illegal in Argentina except to save the life or health of the woman or to terminate a pregnancy caused by rape or incest. As a crime, it is punishable by one to four years in prison for the woman and one to 10 years for the practitioner. Prosecution is rare, however, and a large number of illegal abortions are performed each year. Unofficial sources estimate that the number may be as high as 325,000, and it is believed that complications following these unsafe procedures are responsible for a large percentage of maternal deaths.

Sex Education

Sex education is not available in Argentina's schools. However, the government does acknowledge that schools should offer pupils over the age of 13 classes dealing with birth control, abortion, and sexually-transmitted diseases. In 1991 the school curriculum was expanded to include information on the causes and transmission of AIDS.

WOMEN'S HEALTH

Health standards vary tremendously throughout Argentina. Although the average woman's life expectancy is 75.7 years, a woman living in Buenos Aires or another urban center has a life expectancy more than 9 years longer than one living in one of the rural provinces, such as Jujuy. For men, who have an average life expectancy of 68.9 years, this variation is not quite as dramatic, a difference of 7 years.

Argentina's maternal mortality rate, 100 deaths per 100,000 live births, is one of the lowest in South America. Yet complications of pregnancy, childbirth, and abortion are among the top five causes of death among women aged 15 to 49.

Leading Causes of Death

As in many other countries, the leading causes of death for Argentine women include cardiovascular diseases, chiefly heart attack and stroke, and various forms of cancer.

LEADING CAUSES OF DEATH Percentage of total deaths, 1991		
CAUSE	WOMEN	MEN
Cardiovascular diseases	47%	41%
Cancer	18%	19%
Breast	4%	—
Cervix	1%	—
Lung	1%	5%
Respiratory diseases	6%	6%
Infectious, parasitic diseases	4%	3%
Diabetes	3%	2%
Accidents	3%	5%
Suicide	<1%	1%
Homicide	<1%	1%

Smoking

About 23% of Argentine women are smokers, compared with 40% of men. Generally, smoking is more prevalent among the less educated, lower socioeconomic groups. In 1992 it was estimated that the use of tobacco caused about 13% of all male deaths but was not yet a major factor in female mortality.

AIDS

Argentina has the second highest incidence of AIDS in South America (after Brazil). In 1994 there were a total of 5,261 reported cases, but officials believe that there may be just as many or even more unreported cases; an additional 60,000 people are infected with HIV, the virus that causes AIDS. It is also estimated that women constitute about one-quarter of all those infected with the virus.

Although precise figures are not available, it is believed that as in the rest of Latin America, the major method of AIDS transmission is homosexual contact, with heterosexual contact accounting for about one-quarter of all cases. A major stumbling block in preventing the spread of the disease has been the church's prohibition of the use of condoms.

VIOLENCE AGAINST WOMEN

Violence against women is a national problem throughout Argentina. Even the government concedes that the country's ingrained patriarchal tradition has fostered a situation in which police, judges, and others turn a blind eye to the whole range of problems relating to violence against women. As a result, women are discouraged from reporting assaults, and because incidents are greatly underreported, the extent of the problem cannot be measured.

Domestic Violence

Although new family laws give women equal rights with their husbands, deeply entrenched traditional attitudes are extremely difficult to overcome, and in many Argentine homes the husband has complete authority over his wife and children. Spousal abuse is widespread, and there are few specific laws to protect battered wives from their abusive husbands. A law passed in 1995 enables the courts to keep an abusive husband out of the family home for up to 48 hours. Also on the federal level, the National Women's Council has launched special sensitivity training programs for police and other law enforcement personnel.

At the local level, more than 40 public and 80 private organizations have initiated programs to provide support and treatment for battered wives. In

Buenos Aires a 24-hour hotline has been installed to refer victims to appropriate medical, legal, and social services.

Rape

Rape is considered an "offense against decency" and is punishable by imprisonment for up to 25 years. However, most incidents are not reported, and those that are rarely come to trial. In addition, Argentine law exonerates a rapist if he marries the victim. Marital rape is generally considered a private matter and not prosecuted as a crime.

Prostitution

Prostitution itself is not illegal in Argentina, yet anyone who publicly offers sex for money may be punished by fines or detention of 5 to 21 days. It is the prostitute who is punished, not the client.

Procuring, keeping a brothel, or undertaking other activities related to prostitution are also against the law and punishable by lengthy prison sentences. However, these laws are not strictly enforced, and prostitution is a thriving industry in many urban centers.

FOR ADDITIONAL INFORMATION ON WOMEN

Argentine Embassy
1600 New Hampshire Avenue, NW
Washington, DC 20009, United States
Telephone: 202-939-6400

Association for the Work and Study of Women
Caribate de los Pozos 185
Buenos Aires, Argentina

Center for Women's Studies
Olleros 2554 P.B.
Buenos Aires 1426, Argentina

Conciencia
Florida 633-Piso 3
Buenos Aires 1055, Argentina

Consulate General of Argentina
Cultural Office
12 West 56th Street
New York, NY 10019, United States
Telephone: 212-603-0400

Foundation for Women's Research Studies
Parana 135 3 ro 13
Buenos Aires 1017, Argentina
Telephone: 1-476-2763
Fax: 1-476-2763

AUSTRALIA

Population: *18.3 million*
Women per 100 men: *100*
Women's voting rights: *1902*
Women in legislature: *18%*
Women's share of work force: *42%*
▲ Literacy rates: women—*99%;* men—*99%*
▲ Life expectancy: women—*80.9 years;* men—*75.0 years*
Average number of children: *1.9*
▲ Maternal mortality rate: *9*

Australia is an island continent in the Southern Hemisphere, located between the Indian and Pacific Oceans. Officially known as the Commonwealth of Australia, it is a federation of six states—New South Wales, Queensland, South Australia, Tasmania, Victoria, and Western Australia—and two territories: Northern Territory and Australian Capital Territory (ACT), the site of the nation's capital.

Australia is one of the most urbanized countries in the world. Approximately 85% of the population live in urban centers, with about a third of the population inhabiting the two largest cities, Sydney and Melbourne. About

26% of Australians are Roman Catholic, another 26% are Anglican, and about 24% belong to other Protestant denominations.

Australia is a relatively young country, settled in the late 1700s by the British who, after the American Revolution, sought a new colony to accept their convicts and other undesirables. Yet the country was already populated by an indigenous people, the Aborigines, who had arrived 40,000 years earlier, probably from Indonesia, and had scattered throughout the continent. As the British settlements grew, however, the Aborigines lost their land, fell prey to new diseases, and were often killed in conflicts with the settlers. Today, they make up about 1.6% of the total population. Living chiefly in remote areas, they suffer from malnutrition and receive inadequate education and medical care. Indigenous women are considered the most disadvantaged group in Australia.

Australia's immigration policy during the early 20th century continued to favor settlers from Britain and Ireland. Only after World War II was the policy eased to include groups from other European countries and more recently from the Middle East, Southeast Asia, and South America. In the past 50 years Australia's population has more than doubled, with immigration accounting for about half the increase. These new immigrants, constituting about 15% of the present population, are officially known as people of non-English-speaking background (NESB).

HISTORY OF THE WOMEN'S MOVEMENT

The 19th-century British settlers brought with them a strong desire for self-government and a number of democratic innovations, including compulsory education for girls as well as boys. Many young women started attending secondary school and even universities, and by the mid-1800s, they began organizing women's suffrage groups. In 1894 South Australia became the first colony to grant women the right to vote. In 1902, just one year after the Commonwealth was formed, Australia granted all women federal voting rights, becoming the second country in the world to do so. (New Zealand, in 1893, was the first.) In some states, however, it was not until 1908 that women could vote in local elections, and it was not until 1967 that all Aborigines, women as well as men, were allowed to vote.

Since the early 1900s, women's groups in Australia have lobbied for a wide range of reforms, including equal pay, child care, abortion law reform, prevention of violence against women, and the underrepresentation of women in government. Today a large number of highly effective private and public women's rights organizations function at federal, state, and local levels of government. Most recently, attention has focused on the needs of specific groups, particularly indigenous and NESB women, who have been especially hard hit during the current economic recession.

The government, in response to women's needs, has enacted a number of laws granting women equal status with men, including equal pay. An Office of the Status of Women monitors women's rights throughout the country, and a federal sex discrimination commissioner resolves complaints. However, in 1994 a federally-funded advisory body reported that Australian women still face discrimination throughout the legal system—in judicial interpretations, access to legal services, and the law itself.

WOMEN IN POLITICS

Despite the fact that Australia granted women the right to vote and stand for Parliament in 1902, it was not until 1943 that the first women were elected: Enid Lyons joined the House of Representatives and Dorothy Tangney was elected to represent Western Australia in the Senate. Gradually, more women joined their ranks, mostly in the Senate, but by the early 1970s the percentage of women in Parliament was still low: only 2% in 1972. Pressure from women's groups during the 1970s and 1980s brought more women into politics, and by 1983 the proportion of women in Parliament had increased to 8%. In 1986 the House of Representatives for the first time had a woman Speaker, Joan Child, who retained that post until 1990.

From 1983 to 1994 the percentage of women in Parliament nearly doubled to 15%, and after the 1996 elections, women made up a record 18% of the legislature: 20 in the 76-seat Senate (26%) and 21 in the 148-member House of Representatives (14%).

The first Australian woman to head a federal ministry was Annabelle Rankin, who was appointed minister of housing in 1966. By 1996, 2 of the 15 cabinet ministers (13%) were women: Jocelyn Newman (social security and minister assisting the prime minister for the Status of Women) and Amanda Vanstone (employment, education, training, and youth affairs). Other high-ranking women in the federal government included Judi Moylan, minister for family services, and Bronwyn Bishop, minister for defense industry, science, and personnel. In the Department of Foreign Affairs, out of a total of 82 heads of mission, only 6 were women.

The first woman to head a state or territory was Rosemary Follet, who became chief minister of ACT in 1989. The following year, two women became state premiers: Carmen Lawrence in Western Australia and Joan Kirner in Victoria. By 1995 there were two female state governors: Leneen Forde in Queensland and Roma Mitchell in South Australia. In addition, ACT was headed by Chief Minister Kate Carnell.

Australian women have generally fared better in state and local governments than on the national level. The number of women in state and territorial legislatures has doubled since the mid-1980s. By 1994 women occupied

16% of the seats in these chambers: 21% in upper houses, 14% in lower houses. South Australia had the largest representation of women members, 21%, while Victoria had the smallest, 12%.

At the local level, 20% of elected council members were women in 1992, up from 13% in 1986. The Northern Territory had the highest proportion, 30%, while Western Australia and Tasmania were tied for the lowest, each with 15%.

WOMEN'S EDUCATION

Education in Australia is compulsory through age 15 (16 in Tasmania) or year 10, after which two additional years of secondary school are optional. From 1980 to 1993 the number of girls remaining through year 12 jumped dramatically from 37% to 81%. For boys, who are somewhat more likely to enter vocational courses after year 10, the increase was from 32% to 72%. The literacy rates for Australian adults are among the highest in the world: 99% for both women and men.

As in most other developed countries, women in Australia make up more than half of all higher education students. At the undergraduate level, they are found chiefly in health, education, arts, and veterinary medicine courses.

At the postgraduate level, women make up 45% of all master's degree and

FEMALE ENROLLMENT Percentage of student body, 1992	
LEVEL	PERCENT
Primary school	49%
Secondary school	49%
Higher education	53%

WOMEN IN HIGHER EDUCATION Percentage of subject area		
SUBJECT	1983	1993
Health	54%	75%
Education	66%	73%
Arts	64%	68%
Veterinary science	44%	56%
Law	40%	48%
Business	30%	43%
Science	36%	40%
Agriculture	28%	35%
Architecture	21%	34%
Engineering	5%	13%

38% of all doctor's degree candidates. Again, the most popular fields of study among women students at these levels are health, education, and arts. Women make up 46% of medical students, 49% of law students.

Technical and Further Education (TAFE) colleges offer vocational and technical training. Not surprisingly, women predominate in hairdressing and office skills classes, while male students are more numerous in plumbing and engineering courses.

WOMEN'S EMPLOYMENT

By the mid-1990s approximately 63% of all Australian women of working age were in the labor force, up from 36% in 1966, representing a 42% share of the total. In comparison, the labor force participation rate of Australian men was 83%.

The percentage of married women in the work force has increased dramatically in the last thirty years, from 29% in 1966 to 53% in 1992. For unmarried women the rate remained relatively stable during this period, hovering around 50%. The labor force participation of NESB women, however, has declined slightly in recent years, from 47% in 1987 to 43% in 1994. In contrast, the participation rate of indigenous women has risen, especially among those aged 35 to 44, but this increase has been offset somewhat by high unemployment.

Discrimination in the Workplace

Although Australia has no bill of rights or other specific constitutional protection of equal rights, a number of laws, mostly passed during the last 30 years, prohibit discrimination on the basis of sex. In 1966 legislation lifted the ban

WOMEN'S LABOR FORCE PARTICIPATION Percentage of age group			
AGE	1986	1990	1994
15–19	62%	61%	58%
20–24	76%	80%	79%
25–34	60%	66%	67%
35–44	63%	72%	69%
45–54	52%	60%	65%
55–59	30%	31%	38%
60–64	12%	16%	16%

on hiring married women as permanent employees in the Commonwealth Public Service, and in 1969 the Commonwealth Conciliation and Arbitration Commission introduced the principle of equal pay for equal work.

In 1975 South Australia passed the first Sex Discrimination Act, and in 1984, Parliament passed a similar act prohibiting discrimination on the grounds of sex, marital status, or pregnancy. In 1986 Parliament passed the Affirmative Action (Equal Employment Opportunity for Women) Act, which required all private sector businesses, trade unions, community organizations, and large training programs to establish affirmative action programs for women. In 1992 revisions to the Sex Discrimination Act strengthened sexual harassment provisions and prohibited dismissal on grounds of family responsibilities.

Areas of Employment

Legally, women in Australia have the right to employment in all occupations, yet they tend to work mostly as clerks, salespersons, and personal service workers. The industries with the most women tend to be wholesale and retail trade, education, and health and community services. Across all occupations, whether in the public or private sector, women rarely occupy top-level positions; in private companies they make up only 1% of all executive directors. Only about 7% of working women hold administrative or managerial positions, against 15% of men. For every 100 men in such positions, there are 34 women in similar posts. In professional and technical occupations however, there are 74 women for every 100 men.

Women clearly dominate the field of education in Australia. In primary and secondary schools they account for 73% and 53% of teachers respectively. In higher education, however, they make up only 32% of the teaching staff and tend to concentrate in lower-level positions. Only 20% of senior lecturers and 11% of those above senior lecturer are women.

In the judicial system the proportion of women increased from 11% in 1981 to 25% in 1991. However, they are rarely seen in high-level positions; only 16% of all judges and magistrates are women, and only one sits on the seven-member High Court. Although 26% of lawyers are women, the proportion of female legal clerks is 63%. In the area of law enforcement, women's representation in the police force more than doubled, from 6% to 13%, during the decade from 1981 to 1991. In the field of medicine women constitute 21% of all physicians.

Like many other nations, Australia permits women to enlist in the armed forces, but it is one of the few countries where women are also allowed to serve on combat duty. Since 1992 some combat positions have been open to them, and women are now eligible for 99% of all navy and air force and 87% of army positions. By the mid-1990s women constituted from 10% to 15% of the total personnel in all three services.

One area where Australian women have significantly increased in number is self-employment. Approximately one-third of small and medium-sized businesses are owned by women, and an additional 28% are jointly owned by women and men.

Pay Differences

Overall, Australian women in nonagricultural industries earn about 91% of men's wages, one of the narrowest gender wage gaps in the world. Part of the difference in earnings is due to the fact that more women work in part-time and seasonal jobs, which tend to pay less. And those women who work full-time usually receive less overtime pay than men.

From 1988 to 1993 the ratio of women's earnings increased in several industries, including manufacturing, where women's wages rose from 75% to 80% of men's. Two areas where women's and men's wages are practically equal are public administration and defense.

Working Hours

Since 1980 there has been an increase in part-time employment for both women and men. However, about 43% of working women occupy part-time jobs, compared with only 11% of men. Full-time workers—both women and men—put in an average of 38 hours a week, but men usually spend four times as many hours as women working overtime.

Maternity Leave and Benefits

Under present federal and state laws, the majority of Australian women are eligible for a year of unpaid maternity leave. Only federal and some state employees are entitled to paid maternity leave. Federal employees receive full pay for 12 weeks. State benefits vary—in Victoria employees receive 12 weeks at full pay and in New South Wales, 6 weeks at full pay and 6 weeks at half pay.

Child Care

Child care is a major priority in Australia. As more women with young children have entered the work force, the demand for day care has soared. In response, the government increased the number of places more than fivefold between 1983 and 1994.

The government has also introduced Child Care Assistance, a form of fee relief available to low- and middle-income families. And in 1994 it introduced a Child Care Cash Rebate, which officially recognized child care as a legitimate expense in earning one's livelihood.

Unemployment

The economic recession that began in the 1980s greatly altered Australia's rates and patterns of unemployment. Both women and men suffered sharp increases in unemployment, but women tended to fare better than men, mostly due to a parallel growth of part-time jobs. By the mid-1990s the unemployment rate for women was lower than that for men, 8.8% as against 9.4%. Also, it took a woman an average of about 21 weeks to find a new job. For men this figure was 32 weeks.

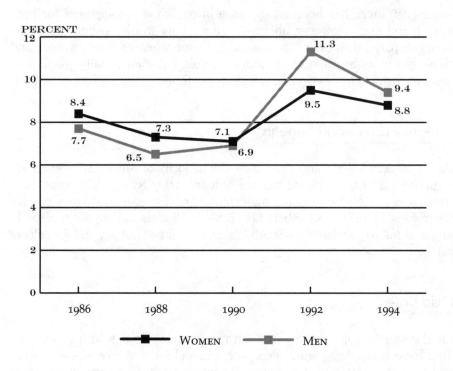

UNEMPLOYMENT RATES

Percentage of labor force

MARRIAGE AND DIVORCE

The past few decades have witnessed broad changes in attitudes toward marriage and divorce. In addition to a decrease in marriages and an increase in divorces, there has been a dramatic rise in cohabitation. There has also been a slight increase in the proportion of women living alone, from 10% in 1983 to 12% in 1993. In addition, recent years have seen a rise in one-parent families with dependent children, the vast majority of which are headed by women. In 1984 these female-headed families accounted for 5% of all households; in 1994 they made up 6% of the total.

Marriage

The minimum legal age for marriage is 18 for both women and men, or 16 with parental consent, but most couples marry much later. The average age of women at first marriage is 24.5 years; for men it is 26.7 years.

The annual marriage rate declined dramatically from the late 1960s to the early 1990s. One reason for the decline was the corresponding increase in cohabiting couples, who now account for about 8% of all couples. In the decade from 1983 to 1993, the proportion of couples who cohabited prior to marriage more than doubled, from 27% to 56%. Not surprisingly, this increase in cohabitation was accompanied by a rise in births to unmarried women, from about 15% of all births in 1983 to about 25% in 1993.

BIRTHS TO UNMARRIED WOMEN Percentage of total births		
AGE	1983	1993
Under 20	63%	87%
20–24	19%	45%
25–29	8%	18%
30–34	7%	13%
35–39	9%	15%
40 and over	13%	20%

Among Australia's indigenous population, traditional marriage customs are commonly observed, including arranged marriages, polygamy, and marriage for girls just after reaching puberty. The government recognizes these customs and considers the children of these marriages legitimate.

Divorce

One of the most important legal changes affecting Australian women was the Family Law Act, which took effect in 1976. This law enabled couples to

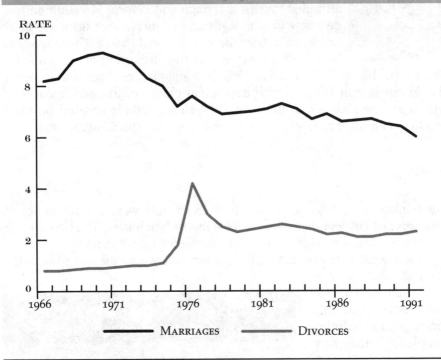

MARRIAGES AND DIVORCES
Per 1,000 population

RATE

— MARRIAGES   — DIVORCES

divorce on grounds of irretrievable breakdown of the marriage, established by one year's separation and no reasonable likelihood of reconciliation. Not unexpectedly, the implementation of this law resulted in a sharp increase in the number of divorces.

In 1993 there were over 43,000 divorces in Australia, representing an 11% increase from 1983. While 62% of divorces in 1983 involved couples with children, a decade later this proportion had declined to just over half. In cases where the divorcing parents cannot agree on terms of child custody, either spouse may submit the matter to the court. In the vast majority of cases custody is awarded to the mother.

FAMILY PLANNING

The Australian government's official policy toward family planning is to enable all women and men to make rational, informed decisions regarding their own fertility. The government promotes the effective use of contraceptives and contributes funds to two national family planning organizations: the Family Planning Associations in each state and territory and Women in Industry and Community Health (WICH).

Fertility Rate

The fertility rate in Australia is 1.9 children per woman, just under the 2.1 generally considered necessary for a population to replace itself. For indigenous women the fertility rate is considerably higher: 3.1 children.

BIRTHS BY AGE
Percentage of total births, 1993

AGE	PERCENT
Under 20	5%
20–24	20%
25–29	34%
30–34	30%
35–39	10%
40 and over	2%

Contraception

It is estimated that about 76% of Australian couples of childbearing age use some form of birth control, one of the highest rates of contraceptive use in the world.

CONTRACEPTIVE USE
Percentage of couples of childbearing age, 1986

METHOD	PERCENT
Female sterilization	28%
Birth control pill	24%
Male sterilization	10%
Intrauterine devices (IUDs)	5%
Condom	4%
Traditional methods	4%

Abortion

Abortion in Australia is legal, but only on certain grounds, which vary from one jurisdiction to the next. In some areas acceptable grounds include saving the woman's life or preserving her physical or mental health. In all states and territories, however, the consent of the woman is required and the procedure must be performed in a hospital or clinic by a registered medical practitioner.

Official information on abortion is available only through Medicare statistics, which show an increase in abortions from 57,800 in 1985–1986 to 76,900 in 1993–1994. However, it must be noted that these figures are only for fee-for-service procedures, not those performed in public hospitals.

Fertility Services

It is estimated that about 15% of Australian couples suffer some kind of fertility problem. A number of specialized clinics offer in vitro fertilization and gamete intrafallopian transfer (GIFT) techniques to help these couples. In 1990 in vitro fertilization resulted in 1,200 pregnancies, of which 73% resulted in live births. For GIFT procedures, the comparable figures were 780 pregnancies, with 72% resulting in live births.

Sex Education

Sex education is determined by each state or territory and is usually included in courses that also cover health education, personal and family relationships, and the roles of women and men in child care and family responsibility. In 1989 information on AIDS transmission and prevention was introduced into the curriculum.

WOMEN'S HEALTH

Australian women are among the healthiest in the world. Life expectancy rates for both women and men are among the highest: 80.9 years for women and 75.0 years for men. Correspondingly, maternal mortality rates have declined steadily over the past few decades and are among the world's lowest: 9 deaths for every 100,000 live births.

Health care in Australia is divided among federal, state, and local governments. Through Medicare, the federal government directly reimburses medical services performed by medical practitioners on a fee-for-service basis and indirectly funds hospitals and other services through grants to the states and territories, which have responsibility for public hospitals and community health services.

Leading Causes of Death

As in other highly industrialized countries, the leading causes of death among both women and men are cardiovascular diseases—primarily heart disease and stroke—and cancer. Breast cancer is the most common female cancer, affecting approximately 1 in every 15 women. Lung cancer, however, is second and rising, expected soon to surpass breast cancer.

LEADING CAUSES OF DEATH
Percentage of total deaths, 1992

CAUSE	WOMEN	MEN
Cardiovascular diseases	48%	41%
Cancer	24%	28%
Breast	4%	—
Lung	3%	7%
Cervix	<1%	—
Respiratory diseases	7%	9%
Accidents	3%	5%
Suicide	1%	3%
Homicide	<1%	<1%

Aboriginal and NESB Women

At 62 years, the life expectancy of indigenous women is considerably lower than that of other Australian women and does not appear to be increasing. Leading causes of death among these women include circulatory diseases, injuries, and poisoning. Their death rate from infectious and parasitic diseases is 13 times higher than that for other Australian women.

The health of NESB women, too, is below the national average. They tend to suffer high rates of work-related illnesses and injuries as well as emotional and mental disorders.

Smoking

Smoking is ranked as a major risk factor for premature death in Australia, and it is estimated to cause about 15% of all deaths. Yet it is still a common habit; about 30% of all women and 37% of all men smoke. Young women and men have the highest rates; nearly half of all women between 18 and 24 are smokers.

Over the past few decades the government has launched a number of campaigns aimed at reducing the incidence of smoking. In 1989 tobacco advertising was banned in all newspapers and magazines, and in 1990 the government launched its National Commission Against Tobacco Use in Young Women.

AIDS

Australian women have not been exempt from the AIDS epidemic, but the vast majority of cases occur among homosexual men. By 1993 the number of AIDS cases reported among women was 164, accounting for about 4% of all AIDS patients. An additional 790 women had been diagnosed as HIV positive, constituting nearly 5% of individuals infected with the virus that causes AIDS. The most common mode of transmission for women was sexual contact with an infected man.

VIOLENCE AGAINST WOMEN

Violence against women is recognized as a serious problem in Australia, even though very few statistics about it are available. What is known is that most cases, especially sexual assaults, are never reported. A 1993 National Crime and Safety Survey estimated that only about a quarter of sexual assaults are reported to the police.

Domestic Violence

Officials estimate that domestic violence may affect as many as one in three Australian families. The National Committee on Violence Against Women has formulated a national strategy to increase government support to victims and provide them with legal counseling. The government is also continuing its community education campaign, begun in 1991, and is considering a nationwide survey to determine the extent of domestic violence. Individual states and territories have their own community education programs, as well as special shelters for battered women and their children.

Rape

There are no reliable statistics on the incidence of rape. However, the Inquiry into Violence in Public Places, conducted in 1991, estimated that one-third of rapes are committed in the victims' homes and that in more than 60% of cases, the rapists are known to the victims; they are often current or former boyfriends, husbands, or other relatives. In all Australian states and territories, rape, even by a husband, is a criminal offense, punishable by imprisonment.

Prostitution

Prostitution itself is not illegal in Australia, although the activities associated with it, such as soliciting and keeping a brothel, are criminal offenses. However, since 1985 there has been a movement to decriminalize these activities and regulate prostitution. Victoria already has licensed brothels, and other states and territories are considering similar actions.

Female Genital Mutilation

Australia is a multicultural society with large numbers of immigrants from parts of the world where female genital mutilation is commonly practiced. Since 1991 the influx of women from Eritrea, Ethiopia, Somalia, and Sudan—four countries that practice infibulation, the most severe form of this custom—has risen nearly 150%, and the numbers are expected to grow as these immigrants sponsor others. Although Australian law does not specifically prohibit female genital mutilation, it is legally treated as assault.

FOR ADDITIONAL INFORMATION ON WOMEN

Australian Bureau of Statistics
National Office
Wing 5, Cameron Offices
Chandler Street
Belconnen, ACT 2617, Australia
Telephone: 06-252-6007
Fax: 06-253-1404

Office of the Status of Women
3–5 National Circuit
Barton, ACT 2601, Australia
Telephone: 06-271-5711
Fax: 06-271-5751

Australian Information Service
c/o Australian Consulate General
630 Fifth Avenue, 4th floor
New York, NY 10111, United States
Telephone: 212-408-8400

Embassy of Australia
1601 Massachusetts Avenue, NW
Washington, DC 20036, United States
Telephone: 202-797-3000

Research Center for Women's Studies
University of Adelaide
G.P.O. Box 498
Adelaide, SA 5001, Australia

Women's Research Unit
University of Sydney
127 Darlington Road
Sydney, NSW 2006, Australia

BANGLADESH

Population: *128.2 million*
▼ Women per 100 men: *94*
Women's voting rights: *1947*
Women in legislature: *11%*
Women's share of work force: 41%
Literacy rates: women—*24%;* men—*48%*
Life expectancy: women—*55.6 years;* men—*55.6 years*
Average number of children: *4.1*
Maternal mortality rate: *850*

The People's Republic of Bangladesh, located in southern Asia, ranks as one of the world's most populous countries and also one of the most crowded. Its 128.2 million people are squeezed into an area the size of Greece or the state of New York, producing a population density of about 2,200 people per square mile. India, in comparison, has a population density of 760, while the United States contains only about 74 people per square mile. The great majority of Bangladesh's population, about 83%, live in rural villages, and more than 50% of the working population are employed in agriculture.

Bangladesh is one of the world's least developed and most impoverished nations; nearly half its people live below the poverty level. And as in other underdeveloped countries, women account for a large majority of the poor and bear the major brunt of poverty. Islam is the state religion, and there are more Muslims in Bangladesh than in any other country except Indonesia. Muslims make up about 85% of the population; most of the remainder are Hindu, and there are tiny minorities of Buddhists and Christians.

Formerly part of Pakistan and known as East Pakistan, Bangladesh became a separate country in 1971, following a brief but bloody civil war with West Pakistan. Earlier, it had achieved independence from Britain in 1947, when India was partitioned into the mainly Hindu country of India and the mainly Muslim country of Pakistan, which comprised two wings, East and West Pakistan, located on either side of India. Since its separation from West Pakistan in 1971, Bangladesh has endured more than two decades of political instability marked by periods of autocracy and military rule. In 1991 a constitutional amendment established the parliamentary democracy that continues today.

The Bangladesh constitution guarantees equality for both sexes and even promotes women's political participation by reserving seats for them in Parliament. Yet Bangladeshi society is so permeated by deeply ingrained patriarchal traditions and values that in actuality women do not enjoy equal status and are considered subordinate to men. Centuries-old religious customs, especially the veiling and segregation of women, shape all social relationships and reinforce women's dependence on men. These customs play a critical role in depriving many women of education and employment.

In many families, particularly in rural villages, the birth of a daughter is met with disappointment. Sons, who will support their aged parents, are greatly favored over daughters, who are viewed as liabilities and are brought up to assume a subordinate position within the family as well as in society. Throughout Bangladesh, sons receive preferential treatment: more food, better health care, more education.

Despite these strong religious and cultural values, however, the government has been somewhat successful in helping improve women's access to education and employment, not only for the purpose of improving women's status but also as a means of curbing the country's population growth. The government has also enacted legislation aimed at protecting women's rights in such matters as child marriage, inheritance rights, child custody, and dowries. However, there is little funding to enforce these laws, and many women complain that they are not effective.

HISTORY OF THE WOMEN'S MOVEMENT

The early women's groups that appeared in the mid-1940s, just prior to the creation of Pakistan at the end of British rule, were concerned primarily with social reform. They focused on such issues as women's education and consisted mostly of upper-class, educated women from powerful political families who were following their male relatives into the political sphere.

Following Bangladesh's split with Pakistan in 1971, the emphasis of these groups gradually shifted to a demand for women's equality and the fight to eliminate discrimination. The problems surrounding the rebuilding of a war-torn nation also needed to be addressed. During the war Bangladeshi women suffered tremendously: Large numbers of women were left widows, many were tortured and raped, and millions fled to India. After the war, in 1972 the new government created the Bangladesh National Women's Rehabilitation and Welfare Foundation to assist in the relocation of these returning refugees. Four years later a Women's Affairs Cell was established in the President's Secretariat, and that same year the Jatiyo Mahila Sangstha (National Women's Organization) was founded. In 1978 the Ministry of Women's Affairs was established, and in 1984 an implementing agency, the Women's Affairs Directorate, was created.

Since the early 1980s, many private women's groups as well as nongovernmental organizations and government agencies have been concerned with a wide range of issues: opposing the practice of dowry, enforcing laws against rape and acid throwing, creating shelters for battered women, expanding educational and employment opportunities, promoting family planning, and affording women greater access to credit. Two of the best-known women's organizations, the Mahila Parishad (Women's Council) and Mahila Samiti (Women's Association), have actively mobilized women and involved them in pursuing a broad range of issues dealing with discrimination and equal rights. Other organizations are more concerned with specific activities or issues. Women for Women is primarily a research organization, while Naripokkho (For Women) emphasizes profeminist programs and policies. Among the most active governmental organizations have been the Jatiyo Mahila Sangstha and the Ministry of Women's Affairs.

One of the most volatile women's protest movements in the past several years was sparked by the government's passage of a constitutional amendment in 1988 establishing Islam as the state religion, a step many women viewed as repressive. A coalition of women's groups, called the Oikkyo Baddha Nari Samaj (United Women's Forum), mounted a vigorous campaign to defeat the amendment, and although protesters organized mass demonstrations and rallies, and even challenged the amendment in the Supreme Court, their efforts met with defeat.

More recently, Bangladeshi women's groups have become alarmed at the growing strength of a Muslim fundamentalist movement within the country. This upsurge, which first appeared in 1994, has been traced in part to a reaction against the feminist author Taslima Nasreen, whose writings and statements angered some Islamic groups. In retaliation, the fundamentalists called for her death and began a campaign of terrorism in which more than a thousand girls' schools were burned or vandalized and women were attacked for not strictly following Islamic laws calling for modest dress and behavior. The government has charged Nasreen with violating a section of the penal code that stipulates punishment for anyone convicted of insulting another person's religious beliefs, and although she fled to Sweden in mid-1994, she may eventually be tried in absentia. No charges, however, have ever been brought against those who threatened to kill her, even though such threats are also against the law.

WOMEN IN POLITICS

At first glance it seems paradoxical that Bangladesh, with its deeply ingrained patriarchal society, has had not one but two women prime ministers. Yet both Khaleda Zia, who served from 1991 to 1996, and Hasina Wazed, who defeated Zia in 1996 and is currently prime minister, rose to power through their close relationships with strong male leaders, both of whom were assassinated while serving as the country's president. Zia is the widow of army General Ziaur Rahman, who was killed by dissident army officers in 1981. Wazed is the daughter of Sheik Mujibur Rahman (no relation to Ziaur Rahman), considered by many to be the founder of modern Bangladesh. She and her sister Rahana were the only immediate family members who were not present when their father, mother, and the rest of their family were killed by right-wing army officers in 1975. In each instance, there was no suitable male heir to take their father's place, and the mantle of power was assumed by the widow or daughter. Although both Zia and Wazed achieved their political power through close kinships with slain male leaders, each woman has nevertheless emerged as an effective leader in her own right.

Few other women, however, have attained political power in Bangladesh. Because the country's constitution reserves 30 seats for women in the 330-seat Parliament, women are assured a minimum of 9% representation in the legislature. In 1996 the newly elected Parliament actually contained 35 women (5 elected in their own right and 30 in the seats reserved for them), accounting for 11% of the total, and by early 1997 three women had been named heads of ministries in the newly formed 31-member cabinet: Matia Chowdhury (agriculture and food); Syeda Sajeda Chowdhury (environment and forest); and Zinnatunnessa Talukder (primary and mass education).

Bangladeshi women are also seldom seen in other top-level government positions. There is only one woman ambassador, accounting for just 3% of the total. Women are also poorly represented in legislative bodies at the local level. In rural areas local government consists of 64 district councils and nearly 4,500 union councils, while urban areas are divided into 4 city corporations and 119 municipalities. In the union councils and municipalities, three seats are reserved for women in each body, while city corporations reserve 20% of their seats for women.

WOMEN'S EDUCATION

Primary education for girls and boys aged 6 to 10 is free throughout Bangladesh and has been compulsory since 1991. Yet the great majority of school-age children, especially girls, do not attend school, and the national literacy rates for adults are 24% for women and 48% for men. In urban areas about 70% of all primary school-age girls and 67% of boys do not attend school, and in rural communities, these percentages increase to 81% and 77% respectively. Dropout rates are also high. At the primary level, 55% of girls and 58% of boys do not complete school; at the secondary level, the dropout rate for girls jumps to 66%, while dropping slightly to 55% for boys.

Poverty is a principal reason families tend to keep their daughters out of school. Especially in rural areas, girls are needed for household chores and to care for younger siblings. Religious and social values also play a critical role in producing low female enrollment rates. Many families believe that educating a girl destroys her character and discourages her from assuming her subordinate position within the family as well as in society. Early marriage and the high value placed on preserving a girl's chastity cause many girls to drop out of school upon reaching adolescence, especially in areas with no separate schools for female students.

The Bangladesh government clearly established its commitment to improving wo-

FEMALE ENROLLMENT Percentage of student body, 1993	
LEVEL	PERCENT
Primary school	45%
Secondary school	33%
Higher education	16%

men's education with the launching of its First Five Year Plan (1973–1978), although its primary aim at that time was simply to enable women to better manage their households and care for their children.

Over the years, subsequent five-year plans have emphasized increasing female enrollment, reducing the literacy gender gap, providing job-related training and employment skills, and removing discriminatory references in textbooks and other materials. Among the government's most recent measures are the elimination of secondary school tuition for girls in rural areas, the payment of small stipends to families who keep their daughters in school, and the awarding of special scholarships for female students wishing to go on to higher education. Over the past decade, women's enrollment in higher education has grown from 20% to about 25% of the total student body. In medical colleges about 30% of the students are women and in dental schools the figure is about 40%. The subject areas with the lowest proportions of female students include agriculture and law.

FEMALE ENROLLMENT IN HIGHER EDUCATION
Number of women and percentage of student body, 1986

SUBJECT AREA	NUMBER	PERCENT
Humanities, religion	34,067	22%
Social, behavioral sciences	21,315	18%
Natural sciences	16,889	18%
Commercial, business administration	9,778	16%
Medical, health-related	2,334	26%
Math, computer science	2,067	22%
Education, teacher training	1,009	28%
Home economics	632	100%
Law	302	4%
Agriculture	289	6%
Architecture	40	11%

One of the country's most innovative educational concepts in recent years has been the establishment of nonformal community schools primarily for girls. Created in 1985 by the Bangladesh Rural Advancement Committee (BRAC), these schools now number more than 30,000 throughout Bangladesh, and of the million children enrolled, 70% are girls. One key to the success of the BRAC schools is their strong community involvement. Each school hires women teachers from the village and is run by a local committee that meets monthly with the students' parents. In addition, class hours are flexible and take into account the children's work demands. To make the curriculum more meaningful and helpful to the students, such subjects as health, hygiene, nutrition, and horticulture were added to the usual reading, arithmetic, and other academic subjects.

WOMEN'S EMPLOYMENT

Approximately 62% of all women in Bangladesh are in the labor force, making up a 41% share of the total. Most women work in rural agriculture and small-scale cottage industries. Because of the Islamic practice of *purdah* (keeping women secluded to guard their modesty and purity) working women are generally limited to tasks that can be done at home or out of the public eye, such as threshing, husking, or raising small livestock. Tasks that must be done in public—working in the fields or taking produce to market—are not considered suitable for women.

Discrimination in the Workplace

The Bangladesh constitution endorses the principle of equal rights for women and guarantees women equal protection under the law. But even though discrimination in employment is prohibited by law, enforcement is inadequate due to a lack of resources. In addition, most women are illiterate and unaware of their rights. And since so few female workers are employed in the formal work force, the vast majority of women are not even covered by these laws.

One area in which women workers are beginning to stand up for their rights is the country's thriving garment industry, which is the world's largest supplier of T-shirts to Europe and one of the major suppliers of clothing to the United States. Women hold the vast majority of jobs in these factories, often working 12 to 14 hours a day in abysmal conditions for less than the minimum wage and with no sick pay or other benefits. In the past, workers who complained were often forced to quit or physically abused, but in 1994 the Bangladesh Independent Garment Workers Union was organized—the country's first and only union founded and primarily run by women. Its formation was an important step in giving Bangladeshi women an official venue for complaining about working conditions without fear of losing their jobs.

Areas of Employment

A sizable majority of Bangladeshi women, 65%, work in rural agriculture; 27% work in the service sector; and 8% are employed in industry. Rarely are they seen in the highest-level positions; for every 100 men in administrative and managerial positions there are only 5 women in comparable posts. Women fare somewhat better in the professional and technical occupational groups, where for every 100 men there are 30 women.

In the early 1990s employment opportunities in the industrial sector grew more for women than for men, since most of the new jobs resulted from the tremendous expansion of the garment industry. Women filled 85% of the approximately half million new jobs created in these factories. Other industries that employ sizable numbers of women include pharmaceuticals and electronics.

Construction is another area that has provided some new opportunities for women; the government has established special building programs reserved exclusively for destitute women. Because these jobs require working in public, most women avoid them, and thus they tend to be filled by the very poor. The government has also attempted to increase women's participation in the public sector, reserving between 10% and 15% of government jobs for them. However, by 1995 only 4% of these positions were filled by women, a slight increase from 3% in the 1970s. The government has also set aside 60% of primary school teaching positions for women, but by 1990 only about 19% of such posts were actually filled by women.

In the judiciary women make up 8% of the total number of judges and magistrates, and they are concentrated mostly at the lower levels. Less than 1% of the police force are women, and

WOMEN IN EDUCATION Percentage of total		
LEVEL	1985	1990
Primary School	8%	19%
Secondary School	11%	10%
College	22%	14%
University	11%	14%

they are generally recruited to handle female criminal suspects. At the highest ranks in the police force, Class I and Class II, there are only 37 women, compared with 957 men. At the level of constable, there are 220 women, compared with over 79,000 men.

The Bangladesh armed forces offer limited opportunities for women. A small number of women are recruited to work in the medical corps or as switchboard operators, although in the civil war with Pakistan, women were active in transporting supplies and serving as informers. Some were even trained as soldiers.

Through the initiatives of nongovernmental organizations'

WOMEN IN THE JUDICIARY Number of judges and magistrates, 1994		
LEVEL	WOMEN	MEN
Supreme Court	0	13
Tribunals	2	8
Judge Court	40	521
Magistrates	192	2,000

credit programs, more and more Bangladeshi women are becoming self-employed. Many of these women entrepreneurs grow produce, prepare food, sew clothing, or make handicrafts for sale in village markets.

Access to Credit

Although a number of organizations, including the Bangladesh government, provide small loans for poor women, the first and best-known of these programs is the Grameen ("rural" in Bengali) Bank, founded by Muhammad Yunus in 1976. His revolutionary approach proved so successful that it has become a model for similar banks around the world.

Breaking with tradition, the Grameen Bank caters almost entirely to women, who make up 94% of its borrowers. It does not require collateral; instead, a potential borrower must enlist four friends to act as guarantors of her loan. This peer group approach has proved very successful, resulting in a 97% payback rate. The average loan is a little over $150 but can be as low as $10 or as high as $600, with an interest rate of 20%. The borrowed money is usually used for income-producing projects, such as the purchase of a cow, a sewing machine, or cloth.

Pay Differences

Although the government pays its female employees the same salaries as men, women civil service employees tend to be concentrated in the lowest-paying jobs. Women working in the private sector suffer tremendous wage discrimination, earning considerably less than men. It is estimated that in nonagricultural industries—the only areas where data are available—Bangladeshi women earn about 42% of men's salaries.

Maternity Leave and Benefits

By law a pregnant woman is entitled to paid maternity leave for 12 weeks: 6 weeks before and 6 weeks after the birth of her child. Whether in the public or private sector, this benefit is paid by her employer. Government employees receive this benefit after submitting certificates from their doctors. In the private sector, however, employers, especially the garment factory owners, tend to ignore this benefit and often fire employees who become pregnant.

Child Care

Between 1990 and 1994 the Bangladesh government provided day-care services for over 6,500 children of working mothers. Although factories of 50 or more employees are required to provide day-care facilities for children up to the age of seven, very few of these centers actually exist.

Working Hours

According to the Factory Act of 1965, female employees are not supposed to work more than nine hours a day. However, factory workers are often given production quotas so high that they cannot be filled within that time period, and as a consequence, they must work overtime, usually with no overtime pay.

MARRIAGE AND DIVORCE

Bangladesh's laws and customs relating to marriage and divorce are derived from traditional Islamic family law, the *shari'a,* which permits such practices as polygamy and unilateral divorce. Although the government has enacted legislation attempting to eliminate some of these discriminatory practices, enforcement is weak, and cases that are filed are seldom prosecuted.

Marriage

The minimum legal age for marriage in Bangladesh is 18 for women and 21 for men, raised from 16 and 18 respectively in 1984. According to official government records, the average age of first marriage is 18 years for women and 25.5 years for men. However, these figures probably do not reflect the many early marriages that occur in rural communities, where marriages are often not registered because most couples cannot afford the high registration fees. In these areas it is not unusual for a girl to be married upon reaching puberty.

Chastity is highly valued in Bangladesh, and a woman's virtue is considered a reflection on her family. However, strict observance of *purdah,* in which a woman is rarely allowed to leave the house and may do so only when her face and body are fully covered, is not widespread in Bangladesh. It is sometimes seen among middle- and lower-class families but rarely occurs among the very poor who cannot afford the luxury of keeping their wives and daughters confined to the house. But even when *purdah* is not strictly observed, women tend to be segregated from men and are expected to dress modestly and wear a head covering whenever in public.

Marriage in Bangladesh is often arranged by the bride's father, and although she may veto his choice of spouse, this seldom happens. Upon marriage, the bride is given by her father to the groom, who becomes her new guardian. Once she joins her husband's family, she becomes subordinate to all other household members, including the other women, and the way she achieves social standing is by having children, preferably sons.

Another common marriage custom is the giving of a dowry by the bride's family to the groom's. Although the Dowry Prohibition Act of 1980, amended in 1986, makes the giving or receiving of a dowry punishable by a fine and imprisonment, the practice is nevertheless widespread. The law is not strictly enforced, especially in rural communities, and the government seldom prosecutes cases that are filed. One of the most devastating consequences of the practice of dowry is the widespread problem of dowry deaths, that is, the torture and killing of brides whose husbands or in-laws were dissatisfied with their dowries.

Polygamy is legal in Bangladesh, and a man is entitled to take as many as four wives. Although the government has enacted legislation to protect a woman from her husband arbitrarily taking a second wife, the law applies only to registered marriages, and many marriages in rural villages are not registered.

The rules of inheritance set forth in Islamic law are notorious for discriminating against women. A female heir, for example, is entitled to only half the share of a male heir. In addition, if the couple have no children or only daughters, the widow receives a tiny portion of her husband's estate; most of it passes to the husband's male relatives leaving the widow virtually penniless. When there is a son to inherit his father's estate, he is expected to support his mother.

To protect a woman from destitution in the event of divorce or the death of her husband, she is entitled to claim a certain sum, called the *mohorana,* from her husband. It may be given to her when she marries or at the time of divorce. However, many wives do not claim their *mohorana* upon marriage for fear of angering their husbands, and women who demand it after divorce greatly reduce their chances of remarriage.

Divorce

Divorce, like other family matters, is under the jurisdiction of ancient Islamic law, which clearly discriminates against women. A husband can divorce his wife without a civil proceeding, simply by repeating, "I divorce thee" to his wife three times in the presence of witnesses. A wife, on the other hand, must go through a prolonged court procedure to divorce her husband. Although there are laws providing some protection against arbitrary divorce, these laws pertain only to registered marriages.

After divorce, the husband remains the guardian of his children, whom he must support. The wife is entrusted with caring for her sons until they are seven years old and for her daughters until they reach puberty. If a religious court deems that she leads an immoral life, or if she remarries, her children may be removed from her custody.

FAMILY PLANNING

As one of the world's most populous and most crowded countries, the newly independent Bangladesh launched a vigorous campaign aimed at curbing the country's burgeoning population growth. Due largely to the government's deep commitment to this goal combined with the cooperation and support of many donor and nongovernmental organizations, such as the World Bank and the Bangladesh Women's Health Coalition (BWHC), this campaign has been extraordinarily successful. It was responsible for a drastic jump in contraceptive use from less than 10% in the early 1970s to 40% in the mid-1990s, with a corresponding drop in the national fertility rate.

Fertility Rate

The average number of children born to each Bangladeshi woman is 4.1. Although this fertility rate is still far above the 2.1 generally recognized as the rate necessary for a population to maintain itself, it represents a tremendous decrease from the rate of 5.2 in 1982 and 7 in 1975.

FERTILITY RATES Average number of children per woman			
YEAR	TOTAL	URBAN	RURAL
1982	5.2	3.1	5.5
1992	4.1	2.8	4.3

As in many countries, fertility rates vary greatly between urban areas and rural communities. In many country villages large families are still favored, and the average woman has more than five children. Throughout much of the countryside it is also common for girls to marry and start their childbearing during adolescence, and about 14% of all births are to teenagers.

Contraception

Approximately 40% of all couples of childbearing age use some method of contraception, with about three-quarters relying on modern methods. The most popular is the birth control pill, followed by female sterilization and traditional methods.

Due to the government's massive campaign to reduce the country's soaring population growth, contraceptive use has increased dramatically since 1971. As part of its program, the government established a large number of health and family planning clinics throughout the country. It also sponsored mass media campaigns and trained more than 35,000 female workers to bring its message directly to people's doorsteps. In addition the government offered cash payments to women and men who agreed to undergo sterilization, as well as provided birth control pills and other contraceptive devices.

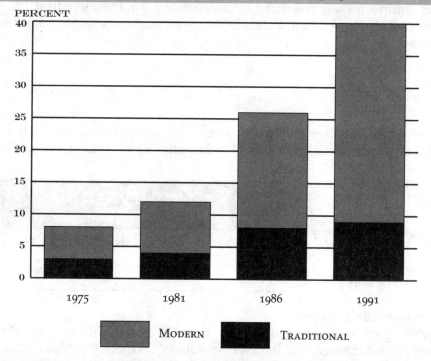

TRENDS IN CONTRACEPTIVE USE
Percentage of couples of childbearing age

PERCENT

MODERN   TRADITIONAL

CONTRACEPTIVE USE
Percentage of couples of childbearing age, 1991

METHOD	PERCENT
Birth control pills	15%
Female sterilization	9%
Traditional methods	9%
Condom	3%
Hormone injection	3%
Intrauterine devices (IUDs)	2%

Abortion

Although the government has instituted a massive campaign to check the country's soaring birthrate, it does not sanction the use of abortion as a means of family planning. As in many other overwhelmingly Islamic countries, abortion in Bangladesh is illegal in all circumstances except to save the life of the pregnant woman.

While it is likely that large numbers of women resort to illegal abortions, there are no available data on how many of these procedures are performed every year. It is known, however, that complications of these illicit procedures are responsible for a large percentage of female deaths.

WOMEN'S HEALTH

Poverty, poor nutrition, early marriage, and numerous, closely spaced pregnancies take an especially heavy toll on many Bangladeshi women, and it is not surprising that there are only 94 females for every 100 males. In general, women's health is poor, and their average life expectancy is 55.6 years, the same as that for men. In nearly every other country in the world, including some of the least developed nations, the average life expectancy for women is at least a year longer than men's. In Pakistan, for example, women's life expectancy is 58.1 years, while men's is only 56.8 years, and in neighboring India the life expectancy for women is 59.1 years, compared with 58.1 years for men.

The maternal mortality rate in Bangladesh is 850 deaths for every 100,000 live births, one of the highest rates in Asia, and considerably higher than the 340 of Pakistan or the 570 of India. The lifetime chances of a woman dying as a result of pregnancy or childbirth are one in 29, compared with one in 50 for Pakistani women and one in 49 for Indian women.

MEDICAL FACILITIES, EXPENDITURE

INSTITUTIONS, PERSONNEL	1985	1992
Hospitals	596	611
Government dispensaries	1,275	1,318
Medical colleges	9	14
Registered doctors	14,591	21,749
Registered nurses	6,418	10,607
Registered midwives	4,399	9,363
Expenditure on health*	**0.67%**	**1.25%**

*Percentage of gross domestic product.

Leading Causes of Death

Although there is little statistical information available about the leading causes of death in Bangladesh, it is known that a significant percentage of all female deaths—between 15% and 27%—are related to pregnancy. Approximately 28,000 women die every year as a result of illegal abortions, eclampsia, excessive bleeding, postpartum infections, and other complications; and an additional 375,000 are left with painful and debilitating conditions. Other major causes of death for both women and men include infectious and parasitic diseases, circulatory disorders, various forms of cancer, and injuries.

Chronic malnutrition is common throughout Bangladesh, affecting nearly 70% of all children under the age of five. It is most prevalent among women and girls due to the widespread preferential treatment given to males. In many families, the men and boys eat first and most, while the girls and women eat last and least. According to a 1995 government report, girls under the age of 5 consume about 16% fewer calories a day than boys in the same age range. For girls between 5 and 14, the caloric intake is 11% less, and for adult women it is 29% less. This reduced calorie intake brings with it a corresponding deficiency of vitamins and minerals. The resulting malnutrition is especially harmful to pregnant women, many of whom must bear the additional physical stress of having to maintain their heavy physical workload throughout their pregnancy.

Both the widespread malnutrition of girls in Bangladesh and their inadequate health care are clearly reflected in their relatively high death rates. Among infants under the age of one, the mortality rate for girls ranges from 105 to 125 deaths per 1,000 live births. The corresponding range for baby boys is from 90 to 115 deaths per 1,000 live births. Among children between the ages of one and four, the death rate is 16 in 1,000 for girls and 13 in 1,000 for boys. These figures are especially significant considering that in most parts of the world girls have a higher survival rate than boys. In the United States for example, among children between the ages of one and four the death rate is .5 per 1,000 for boys and .4 per 1,000 for girls.

Smoking

As in most other parts of the world, women smoke considerably less than men. In Bangladesh approximately 60% of men are smokers whereas only 15% of women smoke.

AIDS

There are few official statistics available about the prevalence of AIDS or HIV infection. According to government sources, only about six cases of AIDS and two dozen cases of HIV infection are reported each year, about 15% of them women. According to World Health Organization estimates, however, the actual number of HIV infections is considerably larger, closer to 15,000, and experts fear that it will continue to climb. Southeast Asia has the world's fastest-growing rate of HIV infection, and it is expected that by the year 2000, more Asians will be infected than the rest of the world combined.

As in many other developing countries, the primary mode of transmission in Bangladesh is through heterosexual contact. Contaminated blood is another source of HIV transmission, especially since most of the blood used for transfusions is not screened for the virus. Dirty needles used for vaccinations, acupuncture, or tattooing may also be a source of the virus.

VIOLENCE AGAINST WOMEN

In Bangladesh, as in most other patriarchal societies where women are considered subordinate to men, violence against women is endemic. Although there is little information on the prevalence of these acts of violence, it is known that the vast majority of incidents are not reported, and that wife beating, acid throwing (a common form of punishment inflicted by a rejected suitor or a man who disapproves of a woman's conduct), dowry death (killing of a bride for insufficient dowry), abduction, molestation, and rape are all on the rise. In 1993, 840 crimes against women were registered with the police; in 1994 this figure rose to 1,240. Although the government has attempted to address the situation by enacting legislation protecting women and punishing their abusers, even prescribing capital punishment, these laws are rarely enforced and are thus largely ignored. In addition, because women who file complaints are often ostracized, most victims prefer to remain silent.

Further compounding the problem are the many local religious courts that hold sway in rural communities throughout the country. Although the verdicts of these courts are not recognized in civil courts, they are accepted by the villagers, who generally approve of the clerics' punishments, which may include the flogging, caning, or stoning to death of women found guilty of adultery or other improper behavior. Sometimes, women who have been found guilty and punished by these courts later commit suicide because they are considered social outcasts and are no longer accepted by their families.

Domestic Violence

Wife battering is probably the most widespread form of violence against women in Bangladesh. It is also probably the most underreported, and there are no hard figures relating to its incidence.

The most drastic form of domestic violence in Bangladesh is the dowry death, when the bride is killed or driven to suicide by her husband and in-laws because they are dissatisfied with her dowry. In recent years dowries have become larger and more lavish, sometimes including expensive cars and trips abroad as well as large sums of money. In many families parents start saving for a daughter's dowry shortly after she is born. Sometimes, in order to find a suitable husband for their daughter, parents may promise a dowry they cannot afford. Other times, even when the promised dowry is delivered, the groom's family may demand additional gifts or money.

Although the government has prohibited the giving or receiving of dowries, the practice remains widespread, and it is estimated that hundreds, if not thousands, of women are killed or driven to suicide each year because their dowries were deemed too meager. In 1995 the government passed the Repression Against Women and Children Law, which provided the death penalty for persons convicted of involvement in dowry deaths as well as acid throwing and other acts of violence against women. However, this law is not widely enforced and is not considered much of a deterrent. The Repression Against Women and Children Law also created special courts in each of the country's 64 districts specifically to handle cases involving wife abuse and other forms of violence against women. The main purpose of these courts was to dispose of abuse cases more quickly by allowing them to bypass the greatly backlogged regular courts.

Rape

Rape is another serious, yet greatly underreported, problem in Bangladesh. One reason many young women never report having been raped is their fear of ostracization by friends and family and of the loss of any chance of marriage. And if they take the matter to a local religious court but cannot produce the three male witnesses required to corroborate their testimony, the women themselves may be found guilty of adultery and punished by public flogging, caning, or even stoning to death.

Because chastity is so highly valued in Bangladesh, victims of rape suffer tremendous social stigmatization and rejection by their families. During the civil war many women were subjected to mass rapes, and the new government, in an attempt to prevent such ostracization, declared the women *birangona,* or war heroines. The government also reserved 5% of government jobs for them, but most of these positions were never filled because so many of the victims never wanted to reveal that they had been raped.

Prostitution

Prostitution is legal for anyone over the age of 18, and Bangladesh has a thriving sex industry. One of the country's largest brothels is in Dhaka; it houses nearly 4,000 prostitutes in a 16-building complex. Many of Bangladesh's prostitutes are young girls from poverty-stricken families, 10 to 15 years old, who have been sold to brothels by their parents, kidnapped by criminal gangs, or lured to the big cities by unscrupulous con men who promise them legitimate jobs or marriage. Every year thousands of young Bangladeshi women are also transported to the Middle East, India, and Pakistan for the purposes of prostitution. Although there are federal laws prohibiting these activities, the police and local officials tend to look the other way.

One of the most effective organizations fighting prostitution is the Bangladesh National Women Lawyers Association (BNWLA), which conducts raids on brothels and rescues young girls who have been forced into prostitution. The BNWLA also provides shelters and job training for them. When a brothel is raided by the police, the rescued girls are often incarcerated, ostensibly for their own protection. Although some girls spend only a few days in jail, others may linger there for years. In addition to those rescued from brothels, girls who cannot return home because they have been raped, abducted, or subjected to domestic abuse are also kept in jail, and it has been estimated that over the past five years, the police have jailed more than 1,600 of these young girls.

FOR ADDITIONAL INFORMATION ON WOMEN

Bangladesh National Women Lawyers Association (BNWLA)
Chancery Chambers
Amin Court 7th Floor
Motijheel C/A
Dhaka, Bangladesh

Center for Analysis and Choice (CAC)
House 65, Road 6a
Dhanmondi
Dhaka 1209, Bangladesh
Telephone: 2-319-919
Fax: 2-817-969

Embassy of Bangladesh
2201 Wisconsin Avenue, NW
Washington, DC 20007, United States
Telephone: 202-342-8372

Jatiyo Mahila Sangstha
45 Baily Road
Dhaka, Bangladesh
Telephone: 2-401-390

Ministry of Women's Affairs
Women's Affairs Department
37/3 Eskaton Garden Road

Dhaka, Bangladesh
Telephone: 2-839-149

Permanent Mission of Bangladesh to the United Nations
821 United Nations Plaza, 8th floor
New York, NY 10017, United States
Telephone: 212-867-3434
Fax: 212-972-4038

UBINIG
5/3 Barabo Mahanpur Ring Road
Shamoli
Dhaka, Bangladesh
Telephone: 2-318428

Women for Women
63/2 Laboratory Road
Dhaka 1205, Bangladesh

Women Living Under Muslim Laws
55 Inner Circular Road
Dhaka, Bangladesh

BRAZIL

Population: *161.3 million*
Women per 100 men: *101*
Women's voting rights: *1932*
Women in legislature: *7%*
Women's share of work force: *36%*
Literacy rates: women—*77%;* men—*76%*
Life expectancy: women—*67.3 years;* men—*56.6 years*
Average number of children: *2.8*
Maternal mortality rate: *220*

Brazil is the most populous country in South America and also the largest in area, occupying nearly half the continent. It is the only South American country whose language and culture are derived from Portugal. The country remained under Portuguese rule from the early 16th century until 1822, when it became an independent empire.

The Brazilian population is mostly urban, with 77% living in cities. Nine out of 10 Brazilians are Roman Catholic, and the church has played a major role in shaping many of the country's laws and policies, especially those concerning women.

HISTORY OF THE WOMEN'S MOVEMENT

Brazil has endured much of the past century under the repressive rule of military dictatorships, and the early women's groups, which started forming in the 1920s, were largely devoted to opposing these regimes. Over the years their efforts greatly contributed to bringing about the reemergence of democracy.

More recently, especially since the installation of a civilian government in 1985, Brazilian women have focused on such concerns as domestic violence; child care; sex discrimination in employment; and reproductive issues, especially abortion reform. Health care reform is another important issue, primarily the need to improve services to reduce the high incidence of pregnancy-related deaths.

WOMEN IN POLITICS

Brazil's women won the right to vote in 1932 and voted for the first time the following year. Probably not coincidentally, that election placed the first woman in the national legislature: Carlota Pereira de Queiroz. Since then only a few others have joined her ranks, and by 1996 women made up only 7% of the National Congress. Five women sat in the 81-member Senate, accounting for 6% of that house, while 34 women served as deputies in the 513-member Chamber of Deputies, representing 7% of that body. Although greatly outnumbered by men as committee heads, female legislators have occasionally led such important committees as finance, labor, planning, and education.

While Brazil has never elected a woman head of state, in the 1994 elections two women were nominated as vice-presidential candidates of major parties. The first woman to head a cabinet ministry was appointed in 1982, and a decade later, there were three female ministers. However, their terms in office were very brief, and by 1996 there was only one female cabinet minister out of a total of 20: Dorothea Werneck of the Department of Industry, Trade, and Tourism. In the diplomatic service, in 1996, 3 out of 98 ambassadors were women, accounting for just 3%.

At the state level, there was only one female governor in 1996, and few women served in the legislative assemblies. At the municipal level women have fared somewhat better, serving as mayors of major cities, including São Paulo and Fortaleza. In 1992 nearly 200 women were elected mayors across the country. To improve women's representation in local government, a law was passed requiring political parties to make women 20% of their candidates in the 1996 municipal council elections.

WOMEN'S EDUCATION

Education is not compulsory in Brazil, and the educational system does not guarantee schooling for children over the age of six. On average, girls spend 4.7 years in school while boys spend 4.6 years. In 1970 the comparable figures were 2.4 years for girls and 2.5 for boys. The literacy rate for adults is 77% for women and 76% for men.

At both the undergraduate and graduate levels, psychology, literature, and arts classes are composed almost entirely of women, in contrast to agriculture and national defense courses, in which extremely low numbers of women are enrolled. At the graduate level, women account for about 32% of all candidates for master's and doctor's degrees.

FEMALE ENROLLMENT Percentage of student body, 1990	
LEVEL	PERCENT
Primary school	51%
Secondary school	57%
University (undergraduate)	52%

WOMEN IN HIGHER EDUCATION Percentage of subject area, 1980			
AREA OF STUDY	PERCENT	AREA OF STUDY	PERCENT
Undergraduate Level		**Graduate Level**	
Psychology	86%	Literature, arts	70%
Literature, arts	84%	Human, social sciences	38%
Human, social sciences	54%	Biological, health sciences	28%
Physical education	53%	Physical sciences, technology	18%
Biological, health sciences	41%	Agricultural sciences	11%
Medicine	24%		
Physical sciences, technology	18%		
Agricultural sciences	10%		
National defense	1%		

WOMEN'S EMPLOYMENT

Since the 1970s, growing numbers of women have entered the Brazilian labor market. By the early 1990s the proportion of all working-age women in the labor force was about 40%, the highest percentage in South America. Women constituted about 36% of the total work force, up from 31% in 1980. Brazilian men, in comparison, had a labor force participation rate of 82%.

Discrimination in the Workplace

Discrimination against women in the workplace was originally outlawed in the 1934 constitution, but the military regime that took over in 1937 suppressed both this right and other labor safeguards for women. The 1946 constitution reinstated the terms of the earlier constitution, but these were again rescinded by the regime that held power from 1964 to 1985. The 1988 constitution specifically forbids discrimination against women, especially with respect to wages, working conditions, and hiring practices.

WOMEN'S LABOR FORCE PARTICIPATION Percentage of age group, 1987	
AGE	PERCENT
10–14	11%
15–19	41%
20–24	52%
25–29	49%
30–39	52%
40–49	47%
50–59	33%
60 and over	11%

Areas of Employment

Women tend to be employed in a limited number of occupations, chiefly in the service sector. Those with the least education often work as household domestics, industrial workers, and farm laborers. Women with somewhat more education tend to become secretaries and sales clerks, while women with the highest levels of education often become teachers and nurses.

In all sectors of the economy, women are rarely found in managerial or administrative positions, and they are noticeably absent at the highest executive levels. For every 100 men in administrative or managerial posts there are only 21 women in similar positions. However, among professional and technical workers there are 133 women for every 100 men, one of the world's highest ratios in this occupational category.

Brazil's judiciary has very few female judges, and only 27% of public prosecutors are women. In the field of education 98% of preschool and 87% of primary school teachers are women. At the secondary level, this figure drops to 53%, and in institutions of higher learning women make up only 21% of the teaching staff.

With respect to the military services, Brazilian women are not allowed to serve in the armed forces. However, they may be employed in unarmed service divisions.

Pay Differences

Although the Brazilian constitution upholds the principle of equal pay for equal work, this policy is rarely enforced, and there is still a major gender gap in earnings. According to official sources, women's nonagricultural wages are about 76% of men's. Not only do women usually earn less for the same work, they tend to be employed in lower-paying jobs and to work fewer hours than men.

A recent study of women's and men's wages found that women start working at lower salaries than men and earn smaller raises. In comparing women and men in the same jobs, the study found that women's starting salaries were equivalent to twice the minimum wage, whereas those of men were 2.6 times the minimum wage. After 10 years on the job, the women were earning 7 times the minimum wage, while their male counterparts were earning nearly 11 times the minimum wage.

Maternity Leave and Benefits

The 1988 constitution provides maternity leave for 120 days, during which Social Security pays 100% of the mother's salary. The constitution also guarantees that she will not be dismissed from her job and offers fathers a five-day paternity leave.

While mandatory maternity benefits are helpful to many women, some employers try to avoid hiring women who are likely to become pregnant. Sometimes employers insist that job applicants produce sterilization certificates or simply hire women past childbearing age. In an attempt to discourage these practices, a 1995 law prohibited employers from requiring employees or applicants to take pregnancy tests or present certificates of sterilization. Employers who are found violating this law are subject to a one- to two-year jail sentence and a fine equal to 10 times the salary of the firm's highest-paid employee.

Child Care

Workers throughout Brazil are entitled to free assistance for child care in day nurseries and preschools. All children are entitled to this care up to the age of six.

Unemployment

Official government figures for unemployment in the early 1990s were 3.4% for women and 3.6% for men. These rates, however, excluded workers in some rural areas.

MARRIAGE AND DIVORCE

A sizable majority, nearly 60%, of all adult women in Brazil are married, and the pattern of a two-parent family predominates. However, the percentage of female-headed households has been steadily rising, from 13% of all households in 1970 to 22% in 1995.

Marriage

The legal minimum age for marriage is 21 for both women and men. With parental consent, it drops to 16 for girls and 18 for boys. However, most Brazilians tend to marry much later, and the average age at first marriage is 22.6 years for women and 25.3 years for men.

Under Brazil's civil code, the husband is the legal head of the family, with complete authority over the children and general family matters. A wife can control her own earnings and property, but her husband can legally dispose of any jointly owned property without her consent. Only since 1977 have married women had the option of keeping their own surname.

Divorce

Divorce did not become legal in Brazil until 1977, and even then the law permitted each person only one divorce in a lifetime and only after a three-year legal or five-year de facto separation. The once-in-a-lifetime condition was lifted in 1988.

By the mid-1990s about 4% of all Brazilian women were divorced, with most divorcees aged between 40 and 50. The divorce rate is significantly higher in urban areas than in rural regions. Generally a divorced woman is more likely to remain single than a divorced man.

Child custody is usually granted to the mother in contested divorces, and the father is expected to pay child support and education costs. However, payments are difficult to enforce.

FAMILY PLANNING

Over the past two decades Brazil has organized and maintained one of the world's most successful family planning programs. Yet contraception remains one of the nation's most contentious issues. On one side of the argument is the Roman Catholic Church, which forbids abortion and the use of modern contraceptives. On the other side are women's groups fighting for the decriminalization of abortion and increased access to family planning services.

Fertility Rate

The average number of children born to each woman in Brazil is 2.8, a substantial decrease from 4.4 in 1980, 5.8 in 1970, and 6.2 in 1960. However, there is considerable variation among different regions, with the highest fertility rates found among the rural poor of the north and northeast. Officially, births to teenagers account for nearly 10% of all births, although some estimates put this figure closer to 20%.

Contraception

Brazil has one of the world's highest rates of contraceptive use; it ranks among the top 10 countries worldwide and first in South America. Nearly 78% of couples of childbearing age use some form of contraception, and despite the church's ban, modern contraceptives are legal and used by approximately 71%. Thus, only about 7% of couples rely on traditional methods, such as rhythm or periodic abstinence.

CONTRACEPTIVE USE* Percentage of couples of childbearing age	
METHOD	PERCENT
Female sterilization	36%
Birth control pill	20%
Traditional methods	7%
Condom	6%
Intrauterine devices (IUDs)	4%
Injectable hormone	2%
Male sterilization	2%
Diaphragm	1%
*Estimated, 1996.	

Technically, sterilization is prohibited, but legislation to legalize it is likely to be passed during the late 1990s. The proposed law, supported by many women's groups but opposed by the church, authorizes voluntary sterilization in public hospitals for women and men over 25 who already have two children. It also mandates the government to provide a wide range of family planning services, including free contraceptive devices.

Abortion

Although the Brazilian penal code forbids abortion, it does not punish offenders in two circumstances: if there is no other way to save the woman's life or if the pregnancy resulted from rape. All other abortions are illegal and punishable by one to three years' imprisonment for the patient, the practitioner, and anyone who referred the woman to the practitioner.

The penal code is not strictly enforced, however, and it is estimated that as many as 3 million illegal abortions are performed every year, terminating approximately one out of every three pregnancies. Hospital records indicate that serious medical complications resulting from these unsafe abortions account for about 400,000 hospitalizations a year.

Sex Education

Sex education is not offered in the Brazillian school system but is sometimes available through the numerous private organizations that provide family planning services.

WOMEN'S HEALTH

Brazil's tremendous industrial growth since the 1950s has led to a rapid development of the country's urban centers and a resulting deterioration of services, especially in the area of health care. Programs aimed specifically at women were introduced in 1986, and the 1988 constitution created a Unified Health System to provide improved access to health care at all levels.

However, medical care is still poor, and average life expectancy is only 67.3 years for women and 56.6 years for men. This gap of 10.7 years between women and men is the second highest in the world after Russia's 13.7 years. Brazil's maternal mortality rate is high, about 220 deaths for every 100,000 live births. This rate, however, varies greatly by area; pregnancy-related deaths are much higher in the northern region than in southern areas.

Leading Causes of Death

Diseases of the cardiovascular system are the number one cause of death in all regions of Brazil among both women and men. Two-thirds of these deaths are due to stroke and heart disease.

Smoking

As in other South American nations, smoking is common in Brazil. About 33% of Brazilian women and 63% of men are smokers.

LEADING CAUSES OF DEATH*
Percentage of total deaths

CAUSE	WOMEN	MEN
Cardiovascular diseases	32%	25%
Cancer	11%	8%
Breast	1%	—
Cervix	1%	—
Lung	1%	2%
Pneumonia, other respiratory diseases	8%	8%
Infectious, parasitic diseases	6%	6%
Accidents	4%	9%
Homicide, other violence	1%	8%
Suicide	<1%	<1%

*Leading causes of death in 1989.

AIDS

Since 1982, when the first cases were reported, Brazil has been struggling to cope with its tremendous AIDS population. It has one of the world's highest number of recorded cases, more than 48,000, although it is estimated that only about half of all AIDS cases are actually reported. Another 700,000 individuals are believed to be infected with HIV, the virus that causes AIDS.

Women accounted for about 20% of all AIDS cases in 1994, as against 13% in 1992, and only about 10% in 1980. The most common method of transmission among women is heterosexual relations; next is intravenous drug use. In 1986 heterosexual transmission accounted for only 5% of all cases; by 1993 this proportion had jumped to 23%. For Brazilian men the primary mode of transmission is intravenous drug use, with homosexual relations next. One of the problems in reducing the spread of the disease is the scarcity and high cost of condoms, coupled with the reluctance of many men to use them.

MODES OF HIV TRANSMISSION
Percentage of total cases, 1992

METHOD	PERCENT
Sexual relations	66%
Intravenous drug use	27%
Contaminated blood products	5%
Perinatal (at birth)	1%

VIOLENCE AGAINST WOMEN

Violence against women is a major problem throughout Brazil. The law and criminal justice system tend to reflect the country's deeply ingrained cultural belief that women are inferior to men, and as a result they often protect the batterer, not the victim. Especially in rural areas, men who commit violent crimes against women, including sexual assault and even murder, are unlikely to be brought to trial. The vast majority of violent acts against women in Brazil are committed by people known to the victims, most often current or former spouses or companions. In only about 5% of cases are the assaults committed by strangers.

Domestic Violence

Domestic violence has long been a serious problem for Brazilian women. It is estimated that more than half of all women homicide victims are killed by current or former partners. For many years a husband who murdered his wife could be pardoned if he simply suspected that she had been unfaithful. Although the Supreme Court struck down this concept of "defense of honor" in 1991, the courts are still reluctant to prosecute and convict men who assault their wives.

Combating domestic violence is one of the main goals of today's women's movement in Brazil. In the late 1970s the slogan "Love does not kill" became the rallying cry for women's groups protesting the government's lax attitude toward this form of violence. In the early 1980s the government responded by creating special centers to assist the victims of spousal abuse, and several years later a shelter for battered women was established. By 1996 there were a total of six such shelters in the country.

Another governmental response to the problem has been the creation of hundreds of special police offices staffed with social workers, psychologists, and other trained personnel to assist battered women. First established in the late 1980s, they are now found in more than 125 cities. Since their inception, they have received more than 13,000 complaints of violence against women, 80% of which involved a present or former spouse. One Rio de Janeiro office receives about 300 complaints a month, while in São Paulo, there was an 18% increase in complaints in the first half of 1995 compared with the same period in 1994. Unfortunately, though, battered wives in rural areas have no access to special police offices, and abusive husbands in those parts of the country are unlikely to be brought to trial, even if they have raped or murdered their wives.

Rape

Despite the fact that rape is illegal and punishable by imprisonment, few rapists are brought to trial or convicted and the law even allows a convicted rapist to be exonerated if he marries the victim. Marital rape, though technically illegal, is not commonly viewed by the courts as a crime.

Prostitution

Prostitution is legal in Brazil, but the penal code does criminalize soliciting, procuring, and similar related activities.

The exploitation of child prostitutes has become a serious problem in recent years. The government estimates that there may be as many as half a million child prostitutes, working primarily in the thriving sex industry of the country's major tourist cities. Many others of these girls are imported by traffickers to remote mining communities and villages, where they are told that they will be employed as waitresses but are actually kept in brothels while trying to pay off their transportation costs and upkeep.

Female Genital Mutilation

While there have been reports of female genital mutilation being practiced as a puberty rite in some rural regions of Brazil, there are no official records or policies on this matter.

FOR ADDITIONAL INFORMATION ON WOMEN

Brazilian Embassy
3006 Massachusetts Avenue, NW
Washington, DC 20008, United States
Telephone: 202-745-2700
Fax: 202-745-2827

Brazilian Women's Federation
Rua São Domingos, 51
CEP 01326 São Paulo, Brazil
Telephone: 11-37-3251

**Permanent Mission of Brazil to the
United Nations**
747 Third Avenue
New York, NY 10017, United States
Telephone: 212-832-6868

Rio de Janeiro Women's Federation
Rua Ana Neri, 39/402
CEP 20910 Rio de Janeiro, Brazil

CANADA

Population: *28.5 million*
Women per 100 men: *103*
Women's voting rights: *1918*
Women in legislature: *19%*
Women's share of work force: *45%*
▲ Literacy rates: women—*99%;* men—*99%*
▲ Life expectancy: women—*81.0 years;* men—*74.6 years*
Average number of children: *1.9*
▲ Maternal mortality rate: *6*

Canada is a vast, diverse country occupying most of the northern portion of North America. It is a federation of 10 provinces—Alberta, British Columbia, Manitoba, New Brunswick, Newfoundland, Nova Scotia, Ontario, Prince Edward Island, Quebec, and Saskatchewan—and two territories: Northwest Territory and Yukon. In area, it is the second largest country in the world (after Russia), but its population is relatively small, less than half that of either France or Italy.

Most Canadians are descended from early European settlers, and English and French are both official languages. There are also large numbers of more recent immigrants from the Caribbean and Asia as well as a small indigenous population. Most Canadians, about 77%, are urban dwellers, and more than half the population live in two provinces: Ontario and Quebec. Approximately 46% of Canadians are Roman Catholic, 16% belong to the (Protestant) United Church, and 10% are Anglican.

HISTORY OF THE WOMEN'S MOVEMENT

Early women's groups in Canada began emerging in the mid-1800s, around the time the dominion was formed. They were concerned chiefly with educational opportunities for women and the right to vote, which was achieved piecemeal over more than a hundred years.

The first female voters were women landowners in Quebec, who were allowed to vote in 1809. Forty years later, however, their franchise ended when the word "male" was inserted into the colony's voting rights law. But in 1850 women landowners in Ontario were allowed to vote for school board members and by 1900 most Canadian women were voting in municipal elections. In 1916 Alberta, Manitoba, and Saskatchewan allowed women to vote in provincial elections, and other provinces soon followed.

At the national level, the Wartime Elections Act of 1917 granted voting rights to Canadian women serving in the armed forces and to close female relatives of military men serving overseas. The following year federal voting rights were extended to all women throughout Canada, even if some of them could not yet vote in provincial elections. Ironically, the last province to grant women voting rights was Quebec, in 1940. Finally, indigenous peoples, both women and men, were granted the right to vote in 1960.

The women's suffrage movement in Canada was relatively calm and peaceful, especially compared with its counterparts in the United States and Britain. One of the most important events was the so-called Persons Case. In 1929 five Canadian suffragettes persuaded the Privy Council to declare women "persons" and thus eligible for appointment to the Senate. This ruling reversed an earlier judicial interpretation of "persons," which had found that it did not include women.

More recently, particularly during the 1970s and 1980s, women's groups in Canada have concentrated on such issues as child care, equal pay, women's health, violence against women, and the decriminalization of abortion. In 1971 the Canadian government created the post of a minister responsible for the status of women and five years later established Status of Women Canada to advise the minister and coordinate and monitor government programs and policies. In 1973 the Women's Program was established as a funding source for over 500 national, regional, and local women's groups. The largest feminist organization in Canada today is the National Action Committee on the Status of Women; founded in the early 1970s, it is a coalition of 600 women's groups and represents about 3 million women.

The 1980s and 1990s witnessed a number of important firsts for Canadian women. In 1993 Kim Campbell became the country's first woman prime minister, although she held that office for only a few months. The first woman to sit on the Supreme Court, Bertha Wilson, was appointed in 1982; and two years later Jeanne Sauvé became the first woman to serve as the country's governor general. In 1989 Audrey McLaughlin became the first woman to lead a major federal political party, and two years later Rita Johnston became the first woman to head a province when she was elected premier of British Columbia. In 1992 Louise Frechette became Canada's first woman ambassador to the United Nations.

WOMEN IN POLITICS

The first woman in Parliament was elected to the House of Commons in 1921; the second joined the Senate in 1930. By 1996 women made up 19% of the Canadian Parliament. The 104-member Senate, whose members are appointed by the governor general, included 22 women, representing 21% of the total. The 295-seat House of Commons, whose members are elected by the people, included 54 women, 18% of that chamber. Three women have held the position of president of a parliamentary chamber: Muriel Fergusson, who headed the Senate from 1972 to 1974; Renaude La Pointe, who succeeded her and remained in the post until 1979; and Jeanne Sauvé, who led the House of Commons from 1980 to 1984.

In 1996 women headed 5 of the 22 cabinet departments (23%): Joyce Fairbairn, leader of the Senate as well as minister with special responsibility for literacy; Diane Marleau, minister of public works; Anne McLellan, minister of natural resources; Lucienne Robillard, minister for citizenship and immigration and acting heritage minister; and Jane Stewart, minister of national revenue. Other high-ranking women included three secretaries of state: Ethel Blondin-Andrew (training and youth); Hedy Fry (multiculturalism and status of women); and Christine Stewart (Latin America and Africa).

At the provincial level, in 1996 Catherine Callbeck was elected premier of Prince Edward Island and Nellie Cournoyer became the premier of Northwest Territories. At the local level, Canadian women have recently been elected mayors of several major cities, including Edmonton, Halifax, Ottawa, and St. John's.

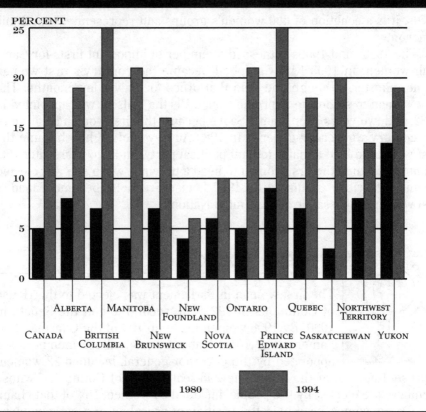

WOMEN IN PARLIAMENTARY ASSEMBLIES

PERCENT

Bars labeled (left to right): CANADA, ALBERTA, BRITISH COLUMBIA, MANITOBA, NEW BRUNSWICK, NEW FOUNDLAND, NOVA SCOTIA, ONTARIO, PRINCE EDWARD ISLAND, QUEBEC, SASKATCHEWAN, NORTHWEST TERRITORY, YUKON

■ 1980   ▮ 1994

WOMEN'S EDUCATION

The Canadian educational system requires a minimum of nine years of schooling for all girls and boys, and the literacy rate for adult women and men is among the world's highest: 99%. However, only 23% of all women have high school diplomas, and only 11% have university degrees. Among aboriginal women, only 3% hold university degrees. In higher education women make up 81% of students in health-related fields and 63% in commercial, management, and business departments. Yet women tend not to pursue the specific courses

FEMALE ENROLLMENT
Percentage of student body, 1993

LEVEL	PERCENT
Primary school	48%
Secondary school	49%
Higher education	54%

that lead to the highest-paid occupations in those fields; they make up only 29% of medical, 32% of law, and 37% of business administration students.

WOMEN'S UNIVERSITY DEGREES Percentage of student body		
LEVEL	1982	1992
Bachelor's degree	50%	55%
Master's degree	41%	48%
Doctor's degree	31%	36%

In recent years the Canadian government has offered special scholarships to indigenous individuals who wish to pursue full-time or part-time postsecondary education. Approximately two-thirds of the students who have accepted this offer have been women.

WOMEN'S EMPLOYMENT

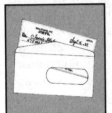

The proportion of working-age women in the Canadian labor force increased dramatically during the 1970s and 1980s, from 44% in 1974 to nearly 60% in 1991. Since then, however, this figure has dropped slightly to 58%, mainly as a result of the recent overall downturn in the economy. Still, women constitute a 45% share of the total labor force. Canadian men, in comparison, have a labor force participation rate of 87%.

Discrimination in the Workplace

Women's demands for equality in the workplace began surfacing following World War II, when large numbers of women started entering the labor

LABOR FORCE PARTICIPATION Percentage of total, 1993		
AGE/MARITAL STATUS	WOMEN	MEN
By Age		
15–24	65%	66%
25–44	77%	92%
45–54	72%	90%
55–64	36%	61%
65 and over	4%	10%
By Marital Status		
Married	61%	76%
Single	64%	70%
Separated, Divorced	62%	74%
Widowed	13%	23%

force. During the 1950s laws were enacted mandating equal pay for equal work, but the many working women segregated into occupations that had no male equivalents were not helped by this legislation.

By the 1970s women's groups began lobbying for the principle of equal pay for work of equal value. According to this criterion, every job category is evaluated on the basis of skill, effort, level of responsibility, and working conditions involved. A female-dominated category is then compared to a male-dominated category, and if the two are found to be comparable but the women's job receives less pay, the employer must make whatever adjustments are necessary to equalize them.

Federal equal-value legislation was enacted in 1977, but it applied only to the 10% of Canadian employees working for the federal government or in federally regulated industries. Most other workers are regulated by provincial laws, and during the 1980s some provinces—including British Columbia, Manitoba, Ontario, and Quebec—enacted similar legislation. Although the introduction of equal-value legislation marked a major advance for working women, many of these laws still have serious drawbacks, such as not covering businesses with fewer than 10 employees or jobs with no comparable male-dominated categories. Overall, only about one-third of the Canadian labor force are covered by equal-value legislation.

To help eliminate discrimination in hiring, in 1986 the federal government passed the Employment Equity Act, requiring employers to hire a larger proportion of women and other underrepresented groups. Some provinces—among them Manitoba, New Brunswick, Ontario, Quebec, and Saskatchewan—enacted similar laws. A Federal Contractors Program also took effect in 1986, requiring every company and organization with 100 or more employees to institute an employment equity program before applying for or receiving a federal contract.

Areas of Employment

Women are not legally excluded from any occupation in Canada but tend to work in traditionally female jobs. They represent 80% of clerical, 57% of service, and 45% of sales personnel. Women are also concentrated in teaching and health-related fields, such as nursing. Approximately 81% of all primary school teachers, 47% of secondary school teachers, and 34% of university teaching staff are women. Somewhat surprisingly, though, women account for 30% of all full professors.

Women's participation in traditionally male-dominated fields is slowly growing. In 1982 only 18% of all doctors, dentists, and other health care professionals were women. By 1993 they constituted 27%. And there has also been a sharp increase in women in administrative and managerial positions, from 27% in 1981 to 40% in 1993. Thus, for every 100 men in administrative or managerial positions, there are 68 women in comparable posts, a ratio that is one of the highest in the world in this occupational category. Similarly, among professional and technical workers, there are 127 women for every 100 men, also one of the highest ratios in this category.

WOMEN IN THE JUDICIARY Percentage of total judges			
COURT	1980	1985	1994
Supreme Court	0%	11%	22%
Appeals Court	0%	0%	7%
Trial Court	0%	7%	19%
Tax Court	0%	8%	12%

In recent years the Canadian government has launched a vigorous campaign to recruit and promote women in the foreign service. By 1995 14 women were heads of missions, accounting for 13% of all ambassadors, high commissioners, and consuls general. Women have also been entering the area of law enforcement. In Canadian police forces, including the Royal Canadian Mounted Police, the rate of women's participation in the mid-1990s ranged from 10% in British Columbia to 5% in New Brunswick. As in many other countries, women in Canada are allowed to enlist in the armed services, and they make up about 12% of the total military personnel. Canada is one of the few countries that also permits women to serve on combat duty.

Women entrepreneurs constitute one of the fastest-growing employment categories in Canada. By 1995 women represented 30% of the self-employed, up from 24% a decade earlier. Women have been starting their own businesses at three times the rate of men, and their success rate is twice that of men's. To facilitate access to credit, the Canadian Human Rights Act prohibits banks from discriminating against women in their lending policies, and several provinces have adopted equal credit opportunity guidelines.

Pay Differences

Despite the legislation requiring equal pay for work of equal value, many women are still not covered by these laws, and those who are covered tend to work in lower-paying jobs. As a result, women's average nonagricultural earnings are only about 63% of men's. A 1990 study found that women made up 20% of the workers in the 10 highest-paid occupations; they also accounted for 73% of those in the lowest-paid jobs.

Working Hours

Since the start of the recent economic recession, more women have been

PART-TIME EMPLOYMENT Percentage of total employment		
YEAR	WOMEN	MEN
1980	24%	6%
1985	26%	8%
1993	26%	10%

turning to part-time jobs, mostly because they are unable to find full-time positions. In 1993, 26% of working women were in part-time jobs, accounting for 69% of all part-time workers. Only about 10% of men had part-time employment.

Maternity Leave and Benefits

The federal government provides for 17 weeks of maternity leave for full-time workers. Nearly 60% of the mother's salary is paid by unemployment insurance for a period of 15 weeks. In recent years federal legislation has been expanded to include fathers and adoptive parents.

Child Care

Under the Canadian constitution, the delivery of child care is the responsibility of each province or territory; availability, cost, and quality thus vary from one area to the next. Throughout Canada, however, there are tremendous shortages of child-care spaces, especially for children under 18 months, and the federal government has launched a major initiative to create 150,000 new spaces by 1998.

Unemployment

The last several years have seen rising unemployment rates for both women and men. In 1980 the rate for women was 8.4%; by 1993 it had reached 10.6%. The comparable rates for men were 6.9% and 11.7% respectively. Interestingly, in 1980 women had a higher unemployment rate than men, whereas in 1993 this pattern was reversed, at least in part because more women accepted part-time positions.

MARRIAGE AND DIVORCE

As in many other countries in the developed world, the numbers of female-headed households and cohabiting couples are increasing. In addition, more and more Canadians, especially older women, are living alone.

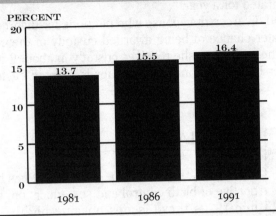

FEMALE-HEADED HOUSEHOLDS
Percentage of all families with children

PERCENT

1981: 13.7
1986: 15.5
1991: 16.4

Marriage

The minimum legal age for marriage in Canada is 18 or 19, depending on the province or territory. However, most couples marry much later. The women's average age at first marriage is one of the world's highest, 26.2 years. For men the corresponding age is 28.2, also among the world's highest.

A small but significant number of Canadians live together without being legally married, and the courts have started to acknowledge certain rights for these couples. For example, in the early 1990s a high court ruling held that a cohabiting spouse is covered by the insurance of the other partner. As the number of cohabiting couples has increased, so has the number of births to unmarried women; they accounted for 34% of all births in 1994, compared with 17% in 1986 and only 4% in 1960.

Canada is also beginning to acknowledge the rights of lesbian and gay couples. Discrimination on the basis of sexual orientation is prohibited by law, yet same-sex marriages are not allowed, and the courts have not extended the rights afforded to cohabiting heterosexual partners to gay and lesbian couples.

Divorce

The first comprehensive divorce legislation took effect in 1968, and since then Canada has seen a steady rise in the divorce rate. In 1993 there were nearly 80,000 divorces, a dramatic jump from 30,000 in 1970. By the mid-1990s it was estimated that the national divorce rate was 38, that is, for every 100 couples getting married in a single year, 38 couples were getting divorced.

The Divorce Act of 1985 revised the earlier legislation and introduced the no-fault divorce, in which a divorce is automatically granted if both spouses agree that the marriage has irretrievably broken down or if they have been separated for a year.

In contested divorces the spouse who petitions for divorce usually has a somewhat greater chance of being awarded custody of the children. When the mother is the petitioner, she receives custody in about 9 out of 10 cases; when the father is the petitioner, the mother is granted custody about half the time.

FAMILY PLANNING

Historically, the Canadian government has been very supportive of birth control and sex education, but during the mid-1970s these issues became highly politicized as women activists spoke out on both sides of these matters. Although the majority of feminist groups lobbied in favor of women's reproductive rights, others campaigned for a return to traditional values that promote the family and reject abortion.

Fertility Rate

The fertility rate in Canada is 1.9 children per woman, less than the 2.1 fertility rate generally considered necessary for a population to maintain itself. Most first-time mothers are between 24 and 29, and only about 7% of all births are to teenagers, well below the 13% of Canada's neighbor, the United States. In 1994 almost 40% of husband-and-wife families, and 60% of single-parent families had only one child.

Contraception

Contraceptive products are legal in Canada and are licensed and regulated by Health Canada and other governmental agencies. Although recent information about contraceptive use is not available, in the mid-1980s about 73% of couples of childbearing age relied on some form of family planning.

Abortion

Abortion was decriminalized in Canada in 1969, when a new section of the criminal code permitted the procedure in cases where the woman's life or

CONTRACEPTIVE USE
Percentage of couples of childbearing age, 1984

METHOD	PERCENT
Female sterilization	31%
Male sterilization	13%
Birth control pill	11%
Condom	8%
Intrauterine devices (IUDs)	6%
Traditional methods	4%
Diaphragm, other	2%

health was endangered. In 1988, however, that section was declared unconstitutional, and since then Canada has had no explicit abortion law. Pro-choice activists argue that no law is needed and that reproductive matters should be decided by each woman and her physician. Although the federal government, pressured by pro-life groups, has attempted to enact legislation setting limits on abortion, these efforts have failed.

The delivery and implementation of abortion services are the responsibility of each province and territory as part of its overall health care system. In rural areas access may be limited, and some hospitals have imposed their own restrictions. However, abortions are still widely performed. In 1993 there were nearly 105,000 abortions, representing 27 abortions for every 100 live births.

Sex Education

Sex education is not federally mandated in Canada. It is considered a provincial matter, determined by the religious and cultural attitudes of each region. However, there are federal guidelines, and many schools offer programs that deal with family planning. Information on AIDS transmission and prevention was introduced into the curriculum in 1987.

WOMEN'S HEALTH

Canadian women are among the world's healthiest. Their life expectancy is one of the highest, 81.0 years, an increase of 2 years since 1981. For men the average life expectancy is 74.6 years, a 2.5 year increase since 1981. The maternal mortality rate in Canada is among the world's lowest: 6 deaths for every 100,000 live births.

Recently, attention has focused on a number of women's health issues, including lung cancer, AIDS, and reproductive health. One recent development concerning reproductive health was Ontario's licensing of midwives in 1994, largely in response to women's groups campaigning for the use of midwifery services in prenatal and postnatal care.

Leading Causes of Death

As in other highly industrialized countries, the leading causes of death for both women and men are cardiovascular diseases, primarily heart disease and stroke, and cancer. Although breast cancer is now the leading cause of cancer deaths among women, it is expected soon to be surpassed by lung cancer.

Interestingly, Canada has one of the world's highest suicide rates: 15 per 100,000 population. In 1992 women accounted for about 21% of these deaths.

LEADING CAUSES OF DEATH
Percentage of total deaths, 1992

CAUSE	WOMEN	MEN
Cardiovascular diseases	41%	37%
Cancer	27%	28%
Breast	5%	—
Lung	5%	9%
Cervix	<1%	—
Respiratory diseases	7%	8%
Diabetes	3%	2%
Accidents	3%	5%
Suicide	<1%	3%
Homicide	<1%	<1%

Smoking

Smoking appears to be on the decline in Canada; yet 26% of women and 28% of men still smoke. In 1966 these percentages were 32% for women and 54% for men. Government concern about women's smoking habits has focused on teenagers and pregnant women and mothers of newborns. In 1993 the Women and Tobacco Working Group was created to address these concerns. As in many other countries, smoking is alarmingly widespread among youngsters. A recent survey indicated that among teenagers 15 to 19 years old, 24% of girls and 23% of boys are smokers. Among those aged 10 to 14, the rate of smoking, 7%, was the same for both girls and boys.

A major blow to the government's antismoking campaign occurred in

1995, when the Supreme Court struck down a law that had banned almost all tobacco advertising. Canada's tobacco industry had voluntarily removed all ads from radio and television during the 1970s, but a 1988 law prohibited print and billboard ads. It was this law that was found to be unconstitutional.

AIDS

As of March 1994, there were a total of 9,510 reported cases of AIDS in Canada, of which 6% were among women. Another 30,000 people were estimated to be infected with HIV, the virus that causes AIDS. As in other

INCIDENCE OF AIDS Number of cases, 1994		
AGE	WOMEN	MEN
Under 15	45	51
15–19	3	29
20–29	151	1,610
30–39	188	3,971
40–49	70	2,407
50 and over	91	894

industrialized countries, the main methods of transmission for women are sexual contact with infected men and intravenous drug use.

VIOLENCE AGAINST WOMEN

Violence against women has become recognized as a major social problem in Canada—a reflection of women's inequality in society as well as a contributing factor to that inequality. Over the past two decades it has become a matter of serious concern to the federal government, which has responded by creating a number of advisory and research councils as well as funding organizations. The government has also enacted legislation dealing with such issues as gun control and sexual offenders. One of the most important projects was Statistics Canada's Violence Against Women Survey, released in 1993, which found that of the 12,000 women interviewed, 51% reported having been victims of some act of violence by males since the age of 16.

Many nongovernmental organizations and women's groups have also made violence a priority. An important turning point in public consciousness occurred on December 6, 1989, when 14 young women at an engineering school in Montreal were murdered by a lone gunman. Shortly afterward, the Coalition on Violence Against Women was founded and launched a successful campaign to designate December 6 as National Day of Remembrance and Action on Violence Against Women.

Domestic Violence

Although spousal abuse is illegal in Canada, it is still widespread, and local, federal, and provincial governments have initiated a number of educational programs, surveys, shelters, and other projects to combat it. A recent study found that from 27% to 36% of women reported physical abuse by husbands or partners.

In 1993 Canada became the first country in the world to grant political refugee status to women facing domestic violence in their homelands. The first case to which the new guidelines were applied concerned an Ecuadoran woman who had suffered 10 years of severe abuse and whose husband threatened to kill her if she returned home.

However, antiviolence groups suffered a major setback in October 1994, when an Alberta judge acquitted a man of assaulting his wife on the grounds that the attack had been caused by his drunkenness. A month earlier the Supreme Court had overturned the conviction of a man accused of sexual assault on similar grounds. Women's advocates and prosecutors became alarmed that drunkenness could be used as a defense in trials against wife batterers, and in 1995 the federal government responded by passing an amendment to the criminal code eliminating extreme drunkenness as a valid defense.

Rape

Rape is a criminal offense in Canada, punishable by prison terms ranging from 10 years to life, but the vast majority of rapes are neither reported nor ever brought to trial. In 1982 legislation was passed to change the definition of rape to include marital rape.

Prostitution

Although prostitution itself is not illegal in Canada, the activities relating to it, such as soliciting and keeping a brothel, are against the law. However, enforcement is not a major priority, and prostitution is fairly widespread.

Female Genital Mutilation

Female genital mutilation (FGM) is not a practice indigenous to Canada, and there is no specific law prohibiting it. However, any mutilation of the body is banned under the present criminal code, which prohibits assault causing bodily harm.

In 1993 Canada became the first country to grant political asylum on the grounds that FGM is a form of abuse. Refugee status was granted to a Somali mother and her children because the woman's 10-year-old daughter would have been forced to undergo this ritual if she were returned to her homeland.

FOR ADDITIONAL INFORMATION ON WOMEN

Canadian Advisory Council on the Status of Women
110 O'Connor Street West, 9th floor
Ottawa, Ontario K1P 5M9, Canada
Telephone: 613-992-4975
Telex: 613-992-1715

Consulate General of Canada
Information Center, Consul Library
1251 Avenue of the Americas
New York, NY 10020, United States
Telephone: 212-596-1600

Embassy of Canada
501 Pennsylvania Avenue, NW
Washington, DC 20001, United States
Telephone: 202-682-1740

CHINA

Population: *1.2 billion*
▼ Women per 100 men: *95*
Women's voting rights: *1949*
▲ Women in legislature: *21%*
Women's share of work force: *43%*
Literacy rates: women—*68%;* men—*87%*
Life expectancy: women—*69.2 years;* men—*67.1 years*
Average number of children: *2.0*
Maternal mortality rate: *95*

The People's Republic of China is the most populous country on earth, containing 22% of the entire world's population. It occupies much of eastern Asia and is the world's third largest country in area (after Russia and Canada). Three-quarters of the population live in rural villages, each averaging 1,000 to 2,000 people grouped around a market town. Even though a relatively small proportion of the Chinese people live in urban areas, the actual number of city dwellers is larger than the total population of any country in the world except India.

China's government is controlled by the Communist Party, whose revolutionary forces took power in 1949. It is an authoritarian, repressive government that imposes strict censorship and metes out harsh penalties to dissidents. The state monitors and regulates all phases of its citizens' activities; a woman cannot marry or have a child without permission.

China's burgeoning population has long been a major concern to the government, which in 1979 instituted a mandatory family planning policy of one child per family. Although this policy has dramatically decreased the birthrate and slowed population growth, it has had an unintentional impact on the sex ratio of China's population and has led to an increase in violence against females, especially baby girls. Because sons are traditionally favored over daughters, many female fetuses are aborted; and baby girls are sometimes abandoned, allowed to die of neglect, or even killed by their parents.

HISTORY OF THE WOMEN'S MOVEMENT

Prior to the communist takeover, the Chinese lived in a feudal, patriarchal society in which women had few rights; they played a subordinate role in all spheres of life and focused primarily on the home and family. Living conditions were poor, food was scarce, health care was nearly nonexistent, and the mortality rate was very high. There were also extreme income inequalities. By means of a centralized economy, the communist regime redistributed income to provide every citizen with at least the minimum necessities. The state introduced a cradle-to-grave welfare system and raised living conditions to a basic level. However, the burgeoning population created such a drain on the country's resources that the standard of living was unable to rise above this minimum level until the 1980s, when economic reforms were introduced and the one-child policy began to take hold.

The 1949 constitution abolished the feudal system and officially gave women equality with men in all spheres of life: political, economic, cultural, social, and personal. This policy was reinforced in a 1982 constitution that guaranteed women equal pay for equal work, as well as access to education, inheritance rights, and equal ownership of property with their husbands. Because Chinese women did not have to struggle to obtain political rights, there was no need for a separate women's movement. But even under communism, equality was not truly achieved and traditional attitudes toward women persisted, especially in rural areas, where sons continued to be greatly favored over daughters.

It was not until periods of more radical change, such as Mao Zedong's Cultural Revolution (1966–1969), with its complete upheaval of Chinese society, that women started becoming more actively involved in politics. In the 1980s, with Deng Xiaoping's economic reforms, inequalities between women and men resurfaced; the jobs available to women often paid less and were less desirable than men's. This disparity provided the impetus for the modern-day women's movement, which gained momentum in the early 1990s as

Chinese women became more vocal. Today their priorities include improving women's employment opportunities and raising women's literacy rates, especially in rural villages where few girls are sent to school.

WOMEN IN POLITICS

The right of women to vote and stand for election was granted in the 1949 constitution and reaffirmed in subsequent constitutions. In 1996 women made up 21% of the National People's Congress (NPC), a percentage virtually unchanged from the mid-1970s.

In 1996 women constituted about 12% of the NPC's Standing Committee, the body that carries out the legislation of the Congress when it is not in session. Women were completely absent from the Communist Party's Politburo and made up only 6% of the Central Committee. In the cabinet, women headed 3 of the 40 ministries (8%): Peng Peiyun (family planning), Gu Xiulian (chemical industry), and Wu Yi (foreign economic relations and trade). Approximately 6% of the country's ambassadors were women, and at the county and township levels, women constituted about 22% of the deputies to local congresses.

WOMEN IN THE NATIONAL PEOPLE'S CONGRESS Percentage of total members	
YEAR	PERCENT
1955	12%
1975	23%
1985	21%
1996	21%

The largest nongovernmental organization for the improvement of women's status is the All-China Women's Federation (ACWF). It was established in 1949 for the purpose of educating women according to the Communist Party line and defending women's and children's rights. While it has no decision-making power, it can suggest courses of action; it was instrumental in advancing the 1992 Law Protecting Women's Rights and Interests. The ACWF also operates 2,100 legal consulting offices to help women redress violations of their rights.

WOMEN'S EDUCATION

Since 1949 the communists have instituted a vast and varied educational system that has repeatedly shifted its focus from ideological imperatives to practical efforts to train workers to compete in the modern world. During the Cultural Revolution all schools were closed for a year, and the universities for even longer, as Mao tried to rid them of "liberal" intellectuals. The resulting decline in Chinese education was profound. Since the mid-1980s, there has been a growing concern for academic quality and an emphasis on expanding scientific knowledge and providing vocational and technical skills, especially for women. Most of these reforms, however, have not yet reached the millions of children living in remote villages.

In 1986 nine years of education—six years of primary school and three years of junior middle school—became compulsory for both girls and boys. However, fewer girls than boys enter school and more drop out, especially in rural areas, where they are often kept out of school to help with farming and household chores. Another obstacle for many families is the tuition charged by the schools, and although some private and public assistance is available, many rural girls have no access to these funds. In addition, the typical farm family sees no advantage in educating a daughter who will soon be getting married and moving into her in-laws' household.

FEMALE ENROLLMENT
Percentage of student body

LEVEL	1980	1992
Primary school	45%	47%
Middle school	40%	43%
College and university	23%	34%
Postgraduate level	12%	25%

By 1990 slightly more than one-third of Chinese women had graduated from primary school, while nearly one-quarter had finished junior middle school. About 9% had completed senior middle school, and only 1% had graduated from college. Between 1982 and 1993, only 5% of all doctoral degrees were awarded to women.

The Chinese government has officially announced a serious commitment to eradicate illiteracy, and in the last four decades the literacy rate of women has soared from less than 10% to 68%. Yet in 1990, of the 22% of the country's population that were still illiterate, 70% were women.

LITERACY RATES
Percentage of total population, 1990

AGE	WOMEN	MEN	AREA	WOMEN	MEN
15–24	91%	97%	Urban	82%	94%
25–34	85%	96%	Rural	63%	84%
35–44	71%	91%			
45 and over	28%	66%	**Total population**	**68%**	**87%**

WOMEN'S EMPLOYMENT

Under the communist regime, Chinese society has been organized into work units—insular, closed, and all-embracing groups. A citizen is either born into a unit, such as a village, or is assigned the unit upon entering the labor force. The work unit controls all child-care and recreational facilities, as well as housing in the cities. It provides pensions and funerals, and if goods are rationed, the work unit is in charge. In other words, a work unit is a total community that oversees each member's whole life, including every woman's monthly fertility cycle.

This organization of society, with its guarantee to meet every member's needs, is referred to as the "iron rice bowl," and it is unique to China. Although they provide substantial benefits, the work units pay very low wages. During the 1950s and 1960s, when this system was being established, many families needed two incomes and many women were therefore propelled into the labor force. By 1995, the proportion of working-age Chinese women in the labor force was approximately 80%, one of the highest percentages in the world, and women made up about 43% of the country's total work force. Chinese men also had a very high labor force participation rate: 96%.

In 1978, in order to increase production and efficiency, the Chinese government started a movement toward a market economy. Remuneration is now linked to output. A family can contract with its work unit for a specific production quota and can keep whatever is left after taxes and quotas are paid. This system has particularly benefited women. Now that work units can recruit their employees instead of having them assigned, urban women have more job opportunities. And in rural areas, women are establishing small businesses or services. Two decades ago rural women contributed 25% of their family income; today they provide 40%.

WOMEN'S LABOR FORCE PARTICIPATION
Percentage of age group, 1990

AGE	WOMEN	MEN
15–19	68%	61%
20–24	90%	92%
25–29	90%	98%
30–34	91%	99%
35–39	91%	99%
40–44	88%	99%
45–49	81%	98%
50–54	62%	93%
55–59	45%	84%
60–64	27%	63%
65 and over	8%	33%

But the new economic system also has some major disadvantages for women. Since the state no longer pays for maternity leave, many employers are reluctant to hire women. Also, women continue to face widespread discrimination and sexual harassment.

Discrimination in the Workplace

The ACWF, responding to complaints from women, pressed for labor protection laws to curb gender-related discrimination. These laws, enacted in 1992, reaffirmed a woman's right to work and to receive equal pay for equal work. They also prohibited discrimination in promotion and hiring. In addition, work units could no longer refuse to recruit women or fire them or lower their wages during pregnancy and following childbirth.

Yet despite these laws, women still encounter widespread discrimination and disproportionately experience unfair demotions, wage cuts, and dismissals. A 1995 study reported that 70% of the employees who are fired or are likely to be fired during the restructuring of unprofitable state enterprises are women. Women under 35 and over 45 are the most affected and are the least likely to be retrained for other jobs. In situations where workers cannot be fired, they may be furloughed at 60% to 70% of their salaries. Most furloughed workers tend to be women.

The 1995 study also found that female employees are more likely than men to suffer salary cuts when a plant or company is in financial difficulty. Some employers reduce their female work force by lowering the retirement age for women to 40. The official retirement age is 55 for women and 60 for men.

Because a work unit has to absorb the cost of maternity, child care, and other employee benefits, it is often reluctant to hire women, and recruiting standards are sometimes raised for female job applicants. The problem of maternity benefits is one of the issues now facing the ACWF, which has suggested that the costs of these benefits be financed equally by both the husband's and wife's work units or provided through taxes.

Another form of discrimination is commonly seen in rural areas. As a village becomes wealthier and a woman's labor is no longer needed by the state, she may be eased out of the work force and "returned home" to care for her children, even though she might prefer to remain in the work force.

Areas of Employment

Women are employed in every occupational category but predominate in agriculture, where they work primarily as manual laborers. Since the introduction of economic reforms, the employment pattern in rural areas has changed, but mostly for men. While women have remained farmers, 70% of men have moved to higher-skilled, better-paying jobs in such areas as transportation or communications. And those women who do work in industry are usually found in the least-skilled, lowest-paying positions. For every 100 men in administrative or managerial positions, there are only 13 women in similar posts.

Although 33% of government officials are women, most are concentrated at the lower-paying county levels. At the national level, only 11% hold senior managerial positions. In the professions, however, women have increased their share to 37% of the total, up from 8% in 1949. Women constitute 55% of all medical personnel, about 35% of scientists and technicians, and nearly 30% of teachers. On average, there are 82 women in professional and technical positions for every 100 men in comparable posts.

WOMEN IN MAJOR OCCUPATIONAL GROUPS
Percentage of working women, 1990

AREA	PERCENT
Agriculture	75%
Industry	12%
Professional	5%
Business	3%
Service	3%

WOMEN IN EDUCATION
Percentage of total, 1991

LEVEL	PERCENT
Primary school	45%
Middle school	37%
Higher education	29%
Full professors	11%

Although women are allowed to enlist in the armed forces, they are not permitted to serve in combat roles. They work in such fields as medical services, telecommunications, and scientific research. By 1992 China had trained 290 female pilots and elevated 12 women to the rank of general.

The number of women entrepreneurs and small business owners in China is growing. In rural areas, where women account for one-third of the self-employed, they can receive preferential interest rates on loans for producing and processing agricultural products. In more developed areas, women make up half the self-employed.

Pay Differences

Women's jobs in China generally pay less than men's. Many of the industries staffed predominantly by women, such as textiles, tend to pay lower wages, and women working in higher-paying industries generally predominate at the lowest levels. As a result, Chinese women in nonagricultural jobs earn an average of 59% of men's wages.

Maternity Leave and Benefits

Employers are required to give women 90 days maternity leave with full pay. New mothers are also entitled to one hour of nursing time during the workday for one year. In accordance with China's population control policy, women who marry later in life and postpone childbirth may be rewarded with maternity leaves as long as seven months.

Child Care

Some work units provide child-care facilities for their workers. In urban areas about 70% of preschool children are enrolled in nurseries and kindergartens; in rural areas this figure is 32%.

Unemployment

By Western standards unemployment in China is extremely low: 1.1% for women and 0.8% for men. However, when employees are let go due to cutbacks and reorganizations, women constitute 70% of those who are laid off.

MARRIAGE AND DIVORCE

Over the past two decades the government's one-child-per-family policy to curtail the country's population growth has profoundly affected China's patterns of marriage and family structure. The majority of Chinese couples are marrying later, postponing childbearing, and limiting their families to one child. However, one serious—and unintended—consequence of this policy is the present imbalance in the country's sex ratio: 95 women for every 100 men. Because Chinese families traditionally place more value on sons than daughters, many couples use ultrasound techniques and selective abortion of female fetuses to guarantee that their one child will be a son. Thus, boys have started to outnumber girls, and the government has become alarmed that the scarcity of young women may result in a large number of permanent bachelors. Although some officials think that this scarcity may eventually make women more valuable in society, in some rural areas women are so scarce that there has been an upsurge in the abduction and selling of young women into marriage.

Marriage

The minimum legal age for marriage in China is 20 years for women and 22 for men. However, over the past four decades the average age at first marriage has been rising, partly due to the government's emphasis on postponing marriage and childbearing. In 1992 the average age at first marriage was 22.4 years for women and 25.1 years for men.

It is estimated that up to 30% of couples in China cohabit without being legally married. The many "early marriages," in which both the spouses are below the legal age limit, account for about two-thirds of all cohabiting couples, and the vast majority of these, about 90%, are found in rural communities.

The communist revolution overturned the centuries-old feudal marriage system in which a woman was relegated to a subordinate role in her mother-in-law's household. Obedience and submission were considered a woman's greatest virtues. The aim of marriage was to produce sons who would offer sacrifices to their father's ancestors and take care of their parents in old age. With the 1949 constitution came profound changes. Both partners were guaranteed equal status, property was to be jointly owned, a married woman could use her maiden name, and husbands and wives could inherit each other's property. The 1980 Marriage Law further reinforced monogamy and protected the legal rights of women. It specifically prohibited the feudal practices of arranged marriage, polygamy, concubinage (keeping a mistress), child daughters-in-law (taking a young girl into the family as a future bride), interference with a widow's remarriage, and requests for a bride price (selling of a bride). The 1992 Law Protecting Women's Rights and Interests further bolstered women's rights by protecting a woman's right to marry the partner of her choice and prohibiting interference with her freedom to marry or divorce.

Yet the ancient traditions are so deeply ingrained that they are difficult to overcome. Although arranged marriages have been outlawed, the custom still persists. In addition, it is not uncommon for a young woman's parents to demand money and gifts at the betrothal, a legal way to "sell" a bride. In rural communities it has long been customary for a newly married couple to move in with the husband's family. However, with the new legislation strengthening the rights of married women and the recent increase in per capita income, there has been a sharp decline in these three-generation households and a corresponding increase in nuclear families, which now account for more than 70% of Chinese families.

Divorce

One of the most profound changes in Chinese society has been the recent increase in divorce; though higher in urban areas, it is nevertheless rising throughout the country. In 1994 the divorce rate for the country as a whole was about 10, that is, for every 100 couples getting married there were 10 couples getting divorced. In Beijing this rate was about 24, exactly double the rate in 1990.

Approximately 70% of all divorces in China are initiated by wives, and one of the most common grounds for divorce is physical abuse. With respect to child custody, both parents have equal guardianship over their minor children.

FAMILY PLANNING

Since 1979 family planning in China has been dominated by the government's mandate of only one child per family. This policy was implemented to ensure that China's burgeoning population would not outstrip the country's resources and economic development.

One Child Per Family

Although this policy was established by the central government, it is administered at the local level by officials in the work units who disseminate family planning information, offer economic incentives, and mete out fines and other coercive measures. Couples who bear only one child receive a one-child certificate, which gives them preferential treatment in housing and job assignments, a monthly cash bonus while the child is growing up, and free medical care and education for the child. Retired couples are entitled to a 5% increase in their pensions.

The official penalty for having more than one child is a tax of up to 15% of the family's income; penalties grow harsher with each additional child. In some communities penalties for excess births may be levied against the mother's work unit as well, and a woman may feel intense pressure from her coworkers to limit the size of her family.

Disciplinary measures against families who violate the one-child policy may also include the withholding of social services, job demotions, and sometimes loss of employment. In some regions the fine for having an unauthorized child may be particularly harsh. In Guangzhou the standard fine is equivalent to 30% to 50% of seven years of the average resident's income. In cases where families have been unable to pay the fine, there have been reports of homes being knocked down and possessions confiscated or destroyed.

Although the one-child policy is compulsory, its enforcement varies widely from place to place. Generally, it has been more successful in cities than in rural areas. An urban family may not need the extra hands a child provides to contribute to a farm family's income. And the work unit provides a pension for retirees so that elderly parents are not financially dependent upon having a son.

In rural areas, where the majority of the people live, the one-child policy is particularly onerous. Rural couples desperately want a son who will support them in their old age, and they are likely to resort to aborting female fetuses to ensure that their one child will be a boy. An official in each work unit closely monitors every woman's menstrual cycle and contraceptive use. Women who become pregnant without authorization are pressured to have abortions, and those who already have more than one child may be ordered to undergo sterilization. Although the central government claims such tactics are not authorized, it admits that they may occur in some areas.

Fertility Rate

The average number of children born to each woman has declined dramatically, from 6.2 in 1950 to 2.0 in 1995, one of the lowest fertility rates in Asia. For urban women this decline started before the government began its one-child mandate in 1979, but among rural women it was a direct result of this policy. However, it should be noted that an estimated 6% of female births are never reported.

Approximately 64% of urban families and 41% of rural families have only one child. In the larger cities, such as Beijing and Shanghai, 98% of all couples have only one child. Generally, fertility rates are higher among illiterate women, rural women, and blue-collar workers.

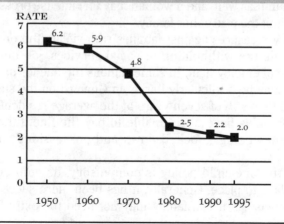

FERTILITY RATES
Average number of children per woman

Due largely to the government's programs to control population growth, more women are postponing childbearing until their middle or late 20s. Only about 4% of total births are to women under 20, one of the lowest rates of births to teenagers in Asia.

Contraception

All forms of contraceptive devices and drugs are legal in China, and as part of the policy of one child per family, their cost is partly subsidized by the government. In 1992 about 83% of couples of childbearing age used some form of contraception, the highest rate of contraceptive use in the world.

CONTRACEPTIVE USE Percentage of couples of childbearing age, 1992	
METHOD	PERCENT
Female sterilization	34%
Intrauterine devices (IUDs)	33%
Male sterilization	10%
Birth control pill	3%
Condoms, traditional methods	2%

Abortion

Abortion is legal throughout China and available upon request. It is commonly used to terminate a pregnancy resulting from failed birth control or for sex selection, even though the use of ultrasound and genetic testing to determine a fetus's sex for this purpose was specifically banned in the mid-1990s. Although accurate statistics on the abortion of female fetuses are not available, the government estimates that the overall male-to-female ratio of babies born in China in the early 1990s was 119 to 100, considerably higher than the normal 106 to 100.

In 1996 Fujian province—with a sex ratio of 115 males for every 100 females—attempted to curb the abortion of female fetuses by passing a law that denies a woman permission to give birth for five years if she aborts a fetus after a sex identification test. Further, a doctor who performs such tests more than twice is subject to having his or her medical license revoked. Other provinces have tried to reduce the desire for sons, and thus the abortion of female fetuses, by improving pensions for the elderly and providing retirement homes.

Abortions are also commonly performed in cases where a parent has a serious hereditary disease or the fetus has severe abnormalities. The National Maternal and Child Care Law, which came into effect in 1995, provides for mandatory abortion in cases where a child is likely to inherit a debilitating genetic defect or if either parent has a serious mental disorder or acute infectious disease.

About 10.5 million abortions were performed in 1992, an increase of 9.3% over 1980. Many Chinese women have repeated abortions, and it is not unheard of for a woman to have as many as eight during her lifetime. In rural areas, where health care tends to be poor, repeated abortions are a frequent cause of serious infections and other medical problems.

Sex Education

Sex education was introduced into Chinese middle schools in the mid-1980s in conjunction with the country's family planning program. In 1989 the curriculum was expanded to include information about the transmission and prevention of AIDS.

WOMEN'S HEALTH

Universal health care with an emphasis on preventive medicine has been the goal of the government's health program since 1949. The program's dramatic success has been evident in the remarkable increase in average life expectancy, from 32 years in 1950 to 69.2 years for women and 67.1 years for men in 1995. The primary aims of the health policy have been to improve sanitation, water quality, and human waste treatment as well as to eradicate cholera, plague, and typhoid—all major causes of death a few decades ago.

China's maternal mortality rate is 95 deaths for every 100,000 live births. In rural areas, where medical care is not as accessible, the rate of pregnancy-related deaths is considerably higher.

Leading Causes of Death

Today the leading causes of death for both women and men in China are similar to those in the industrialized world: heart disease, stroke, and other circulatory diseases; cancer; and respiratory diseases.

Smoking

Smoking has been a growing problem in China since the 1980s. China accounts for 30% of the world's cigarette consumption; 7% of women and 61% of men are smokers. Among women, smoking is more common among older, blue-collar workers and farmers and less prevalent among professionals.

LEADING CAUSES OF DEATH Percentage of total deaths, 1992				
	URBAN		RURAL	
CAUSE	WOMEN	MEN	WOMEN	MEN
Cardiovascular diseases	40%	36%	29%	26%
Cancer	18%	25%	13%	19%
Breast	1%	—	1%	—
Cervix	1%	—	1%	—
Lung	4%	7%	1%	3%
Respiratory diseases	18%	16%	28%	25%
Accidents	4%	6%	5%	8%
Suicide	2%	1%	5%	3%
Homicide	<1%	<1%	<1%	<1%

AIDS

When China opened its borders to trade in the 1980s, heroin use spread quickly, and the virus that causes AIDS soon began to appear among the population. The first HIV-positive case was identified in 1985. Eleven years later, 4,305 cases had been confirmed, though health officials estimated that as many as 100,000 Chinese were infected with the virus. The great majority of AIDS cases, over 70%, are transmitted through needles shared by drug users, and officials fear that the virus is spreading rapidly in the border areas where intravenous drug use is most common.

VIOLENCE AGAINST WOMEN

The Chinese government strongly condemns violence against women. A 1992 law specifically prohibits harming women, children, and elderly women, as well as abandoning infants and kidnapping and selling women.

"Missing" Girls

The one-child policy, coupled with the traditional Chinese preference for sons, has resulted in an increase in violence against baby girls. This situation, often called the "missing" girls problem, was addressed by the government in its 1992 Law to Protect Women's Rights and Interests. According to this law, Chinese citizens are "prohibited to drown, forsake, cruelly injure, or kill baby girls." The law also prohibits "discrimination against or the abuse of women who give birth to baby girls or bear no children."

However, although accurate statistics regarding female infanticide are unavailable, the problem does not seem to be abating. It should be noted, though, that some of these "missing" girls are not victims of infantcide but represent babies whose births were simply not reported, especially if they were the second or third child in the family.

Abduction for Sale into Marriage

Despite the government's efforts, China has a serious slavery problem. In 1993 the government reported 15,000 cases of women and girls who were abducted and sold into marriage or prostitution. Women's advocates, however, believe that many cases are unreported and that the actual total is much higher.

Throughout China's history, especially during times of famine, girls and young women were often sold into marriage by their parents. Although the communist government banned these marriages, a new form of involuntary marriage has recently appeared, especially in rural areas where the sex ratio imbalance has created a tremendous shortage of marriageable young women. In some villages there may be as few as 87 women for every 100 men.

Because of the great demand for young women, bands of criminals have started kidnapping young women or luring them away from their families with promises of legitimate jobs. The women are then transported to a distant part of the country, usually in Henan province, where they are sold to buyers. In an attempt to control this problem, in 1992 the government adopted the Decision on Severe Punishment of Criminals of Abducting and Trafficking Women and Children. This document states that any acts relating to the abduction, delivery, transfer, and sale of women and children, as well as bribery and shielding of the perpetrators, are considered criminal. It also imposes a penalty of a minimum of five years in prison. In 1994 however, one province sentenced 20 criminals to death for abducting and selling women and children. Yet despite these harsh sentences, the problem is still prevalent.

Domestic Violence

Although nationwide statistics on wife abuse are not available, surveys in various parts of China have indicated that 31% of rural and 21% of urban wives suffer some form of abuse. In Beijing 20% of all wives have reported being abused and in Shanghai, the rate is 29% to 33%. A recent report estimated that domestic violence is cited in about one-fourth of all divorces. Although physical abuse can be grounds for prosecution, penalties for killing a stranger are harsher than for killing a family member.

Little public attention had focused on domestic violence until 1993, when a nongovernmental organization established a Family Center in Beijing and installed a women's telephone hotline staffed by about 100 volunteers. In 1995

Beijing opened its first shelter for battered women, equipped with three beds. Shanghai's first shelter, with 20 beds, was established by a local businessman in 1996.

In Hunan province, the city of Changsha recently passed what may be the country's first regulation specifically aimed at preventing wife abuse. It instructs the local police to respond sympathetically and thoroughly when they receive complaints of wife beating.

Rape

Rape is illegal in China and carries a penalty of 7 to 10 years' imprisonment. If the rape results in serious injury or death, the penalty increases to a minimum of 10 years in prison or even a death sentence.

Prostitution

Prostitution has been illegal in China since the communist takeover, when the government took steps to close down brothels. Since the 1980s, however, prostitution has been growing rapidly throughout the country. In 1992 the Decision on Banning Prostitution tried to address this problem by prohibiting anyone from working as a prostitute or frequenting one. Although a procurer faces up to five years in prison, there is no penalty for the prostitute herself.

The increase in prostitution in recent years may be directly attributable to China's economic reforms, which led to a rise in urban unemployment, especially among women. Often, a young woman who moves to the city looking for work finds that prostitution is the only way she can earn a living.

FOR ADDITIONAL INFORMATION ON WOMEN

All China Women's Federation
15, Jian Guo Nei Street
100730 Beijing, China
Telephone: 1-513-41-26
Fax: 1-513-60-44

Chinese Information and Cultural Center
1230 Sixth Avenue
New York, NY 10020, United States
Telephone: 212-373-1800

Consulate General of the People's Republic of China
Culture Office
520 Twelfth Avenue
New York, NY 10036, United States
Telephone: 212-330-7425

Embassy of the People's Republic of China
2133 Wisconsin Avenue, NW
Washington, DC 20007, United States
Telephone: 202-328-2500

Women's Resource Center
127, Dianmen Don da Jie
Beijing, China

EGYPT

Population: *58.5 million*
Women per 100 men: *97*
Women's voting rights: *1956*
▼ Women in legislature: *2%*
Women's share of work force: *23%*
Literacy rates: women—*41%;* men—*65%*
Life expectancy: women—*62.8 years;* men—*58.9 years*
Average number of children: *3.7*
Maternal mortality rate: *170*

The Arab Republic of Egypt is located in northeastern Africa on the Mediterranean Sea and is the most populous African country after Nigeria. Egypt is one of the world's oldest civilizations, extending back to around 4000 B.C., when its ancient culture flourished and its empire was the political and commercial center of the world. Over the centuries, however, it came increasingly under foreign domination; in modern times the British were the last to rule Egypt when they declared it a protectorate in 1914.

Nine out of 10 Egyptians are Muslims; the remainder are Coptic Christians, the largest Christian minority in the Middle East. Islam is the state religion, and its legal code is the primary source of the country's civil law. Slightly more than half of Egyptians, 56%, live in rural regions.

With regard to women, Egypt is one of the Middle East's most liberal societies. However, although Egypt's constitution provides equal rights for women and men, various cultural and religious traditions, as well as some aspects of the country's laws, create great inequalities. Men control possessions and income alike, and particularly in rural Egypt and among the lower classes, women are viewed as morally inferior. An Egyptian woman is expected to defer to senior male relatives, avoid contact with all men who are not relatives, and wear the traditional head covering when in public. She cannot get a passport without permission from her husband or father. In addition, her sexual behavior and reputation are the most important component of her family's honor and are carefully guarded and monitored by her male relatives. An Egyptian woman can inherit only half the amount of a male heir, and a sole female heir receives only half of her parents' estate, the remainder going to more distant male relatives. A sole male heir, however, receives the entire estate.

HISTORY OF THE WOMEN'S MOVEMENT

The Egyptian feminist movement, the oldest of its kind in the Arab world, dates back to the early 1920s. Shortly after Britain declared Egypt independent in 1922, upper-class women joined forces and founded an organization called the Feminist Union. Its agenda was very broad, but its primary emphasis was on social and economic reforms, and not on political rights. Although the constitution of 1923 stipulated that all Egyptians were equal, very soon thereafter a law was passed granting men, but not women, the right to vote and run for public office.

It was not until after World War II that organizations composed of middle-class women began working for women's political rights. These activists were more militant than their earlier counterparts; in 1951 they stormed the Parliament protesting its exclusion of women, and in 1954 they staged a hunger strike calling attention to the fact that women had not been included in the assembly that was drafting the new constitution.

By 1956 it was clear to the government that the core of the feminist movement demanding suffrage had gained momentum and had mobilized a large following. Thus, the 1956 constitution granted women the right to vote and run for office. But there was an important condition: Unlike men, women had to petition the government to register to vote. (The women's movement, composed of upper- and middle-class women, did not object to these restrictions, which affected primarily the uneducated working class.

One of their arguments had been the absurdity of granting political rights to illiterate men while denying them to educated women.) As a result, not many women voted. In 1956 only 1% of registered voters were women. In 1972, 12% of voters were women, and by 1987 the proportion had increased to only 18%.

For many years Egypt's Islamic fundamentalists had remained somewhat neutral toward feminists, neither supporting nor attacking them. In the early 1950s, however, they began publicly proclaiming that a woman's place was in the home and that the most serious threat to society was women's refusal to obey men. At around the same time, the 1952 revolution, led by Gamal Abdel Nasser and his military officers, established an authoritarian regime throughout Egypt. The government minimized dissent by providing state welfare programs, and in the mid-1960s it banned political organizations, including both Islamic fundamentalist groups and women's organizations. Yet in Nasser's drive for economic development, his education and employment policies greatly benefited Egyptian women. In fact, his secular government became the country's strongest force for improving the status of women by bringing many middle- and lower-class women into the ranks of the educated and employed.

During the 1970s the social and economic climate changed drastically for women. In 1971 a new constitution reversed the earlier one by stating that gender equality would be applied only in cases that did not contradict Islamic law. At the same time, President Anwar Sadat instituted a major transition from socialism to a market economy, and because the government no longer guaranteed full employment, many working women lost their jobs. To make matters worse, the Islamic fundamentalist movement gathered strength during this period, and social pressure mounted for Egyptian women to return to the seclusion of their homes. Later, in 1977, when the government clashed with Islamic groups, it tried to distance itself from them and asserted a commitment to women's rights.

One of the most powerful women in Egypt at this time was President Sadat's wife, Jehan Sadat, who in 1979 persuaded her husband to sign a presidential decree reserving a certain number of seats for women in Parliament and on local councils. She was also influential in revising the personal status laws to benefit women, especially with respect to divorce. In 1985 these reforms were canceled by the government, but within two months pressure from women's groups forced passage of new legislation restoring many of the 1979 laws.

By the mid-1990s the status of women in Egypt was still being threatened by the resurgence of Islamic fundamentalism. By offering some of the basic education, health, and welfare services that the government had failed to provide, the fundamentalists had even gained the support of many women. These "Islamic feminists," in addition to calling for Egyptian women to stay at home and wear the traditional Muslim head covering, also advocated a complete segregation of the sexes throughout society.

Currently, many women's rights activists are concerned about the resurgence of Islamic fundamentalism, especially with respect to its condemnation of working women and its strong support for such customs as female genital mutilation and the traditional role of male relatives in enforcing a woman's chastity and appropriate sexual conduct. A growing number of women's organizations have been calling for a wide range of reforms, including changes to the personal status code, revisions to the marriage contract, the elimination of female genital mutilation, and support for the victims of domestic violence.

WOMEN IN POLITICS

Although Egyptian women have been able to vote and run for office for the past four decades, the number of women in elected positions has remained low. The constitution reserves 10 seats in the People's Assembly for presidential appointees, and generally a high proportion of these go to women and Coptic Christians to assure them some representation. After the 1995 elections, 9 women (5 elected, 4 appointed) held seats in the 454-member assembly, making up slightly less than 2% of the total. This representation of women in a national legislature remains one of the lowest in the world.

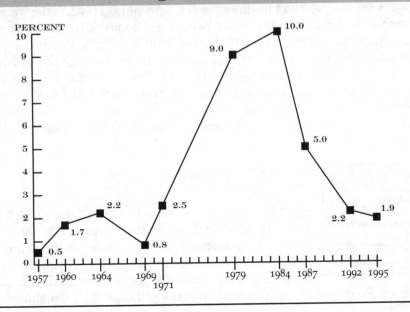

WOMEN IN THE PEOPLE'S ASSEMBLY
Percentage of total members

WOMEN IN LOCAL ASSEMBLIES Percentage of total members			
ASSEMBLIES	1983	1988	1992
Governates	15%	6%	4%
Centers	15%	2%	1%
Cities	11%	2%	1%
Neighborhoods	11%	4%	4%
Villages	6%	1%	1%
Total	**9%**	**2%**	**1%**

The first women were elected to the People's Assembly in 1957, and over the next two decades their representation remained low. However, after a 1979 law reserved 30 places in the People's Assembly and 20% of the seats in local assemblies for women, their numbers soared. But in 1984 this law was repealed, dramatically reducing the number of female legislators, from 36 in 1984 to 18 in 1987. Similarly, women's representation in local assemblies plummeted. The only body in which the proportion of women has been increasing, even if minimally, is the Shura, a legislative consultative council with limited powers. There the percentage of women rose from 3% in 1980 to just under 5% in 1995.

In 1996 women held 3 of the 32 seats (9%) in the Egyptian cabinet: Nawal al-Tatawi, the first woman to hold the position of minister of the economy and international cooperation; Amal Abd al-Rahim Osman, minister of insurance and social affairs; and Zenus Kamel Gouda, state minister for scientific research. The Egyptian judiciary has no female judges; and Islamic law considers a woman's testimony and judgment to carry half the weight of a man's. By 1996 there had never been a female president of the People's Assembly; and women were still barred from serving as provincial governors, city mayors, and in other high-ranking offices, although the legislature had made it legal in 1994 for women to run for the office of village mayor.

Egyptian women have been active in the country's diplomatic service since the 1960s, even reaching the rank of ambassador. In 1996, 10% of the nation's 1,042 diplomats were women, including 12 of the 150 ambassadors.

WOMEN'S EDUCATION

Egypt has free, compulsory education for girls and boys aged 6 to 12, though children generally enter the educational system at age 4. Employment or job training is prohibited for children under the age of 12, yet child labor remains widespread and keeps many children out of school. Furthermore, many Islamic parents withdraw their daughters from school when they reach puberty because Egyptian men, especially among the lower classes, prefer to marry women who have followed the custom of *purdah,* the keeping of girls and women secluded in their homes.

In recent years, as women have been playing an increasing role in Egypt's Muslim fundamentalist resurgence, the country's public schools have become a battleground between the religious fundamentalists and the more secular government. Some female high school students have been arrested for defying the government's 1994 ban on wearing the *niqab,* the traditional Muslim face-covering garment, in the public schools. Girls over the age of 12, however, are allowed to wear a head covering while in school, if they have their parents' consent. Efforts by fundamentalist parents to fight the ban were thwarted by a 1996 Supreme Court ruling that the ban did not violate the students' rights of religious freedom.

FEMALE ENROLLMENT
Percentage of student body, 1992

LEVEL	PERCENT
Preschool	49%
Primary school	45%
Secondary school	44%
Higher education	45%

LITERACY RATES
Percentage of total population

YEAR	TOTAL	WOMEN	MEN
1947	25%	16%	35%
1960	30%	16%	43%
1976	43%	28%	57%
1986	50%	38%	62%
1990	53%	41%	65%

The percentage of girls enrolled in primary school has been increasing gradually, from 58% of all girls in 1980 to 86% in 1990. However, girls are still outnumbered by boys at every level, but graduation rates are the same for both sexes.

In 1952 only 8% of the students enrolled in universities were women. By 1992 they made up 40% of the student body overall—specifically, 49% of

FEMALE UNIVERSITY DEGREE RECIPIENTS
Percentage of students by subject area, 1990

SUBJECT AREA	PERCENT	SUBJECT AREA	PERCENT
Pharmacy	49%	Agriculture	35%
Fine arts	47%	Architecture	25%
Medicine	44%	Engineering	16%
Dentistry	41%	Technology	16%
Science	37%	Electronics	7%

humanities students, 47% of education students, and 31% of law and social science students.

While adult literacy rates have been rising in Egypt over the past several decades, the literacy rate for women, 41%, is still one of the lowest in the Middle East. Although more than half of women under 45 can read and write, only 15% of women aged 45 to 64 are literate, and among women over 65, only 6%.

WOMEN'S EMPLOYMENT

In 1995 about 22% of working-age women had jobs outside the home, making up approximately 23% of Egypt's total work force. Although this represented a dramatic increase from 1966, when women accounted for only 4% of the labor force, it is still one of the lowest percentages in the world. Egyptian men, in comparison, had a labor force participation rate of 84%.

Egyptian women face strong social pressures from fundamentalist Islamic groups claiming not only that women belong in the home but that working women are a prime cause of men's unemployment. One economic opportunity that does exist for Egyptian women is participation in government relocation programs. Part of the national population policy includes moving people away from the Nile River valley to relieve the overpopulation and preserve agricultural land. One relocation program grants women five acres of desert land, a house, and a monthly income.

Discrimination in the Workplace

Although Egyptian law prohibits any discrimination based on sex, origin, religion, creed, or color, widespread inequalities remain in the area of employment. Some state-owned companies have discontinued hiring women so that they can remain in their "proper place" at home. In addition, certain fields—such as the judiciary, the army, and the police—are completely closed to women.

In the private sector women are barred from employment in occupations perceived as either dangerous or immoral, such as mining and working in bars or gambling clubs. Female employees cannot be scheduled to work between 8 P.M. and 7 A.M., except in hospitals and hotels, and then employers must provide security and transportation for them. However, many employers hire women only on a contractual basis to avoid meeting such legal requirements or providing benefits.

WOMEN IN MAJOR INDUSTRIES
Percentage of industry employees

INDUSTRY	1980	1990
Agriculture, hunting, fishing, forestry	2%	32%
Community, social, personal services	19%	27%
Finance, insurance, real estate	16%	27%
Trade, restaurants, hotels	5%	18%
Manufacturing	5%	14%
Transportation, storage, communications	6%	12%
Electricity, gas, water utilities	6%	11%
Construction	1%	8%
Mining, quarrying	11%	3%

Areas of Employment

Although women in Egypt are employed in a variety of industries, they are found primarily in the lowest-level positions. Since the early 1970s, an increasing number of working women have entered nonagricultural occupations, but approximately half of them are employed in low-paying, unskilled jobs, such as street cleaners, janitors, hotel workers, domestic servants, and hospital aides.

Egyptian women are noticeably absent in high-ranking positions. For every 100 men holding administrative or managerial jobs, there are only 12 women in comparable positions. In the category of professional and technological occupations, there are 39 women for every 100 men.

In the public sector women made up 30% of Egypt's government workers in 1992, more than double the proportion of 14% in 1980. In the teaching profession women dominate the early levels of education, making up 93% of preschool and 54% of primary school teachers. However, the proportion of women teachers drops to 40% in secondary schools and 29% in universities. With respect to the military, Egyptian women were once permitted to serve in support roles but are now barred completely.

One area where women's participation has grown dramatically is in business ownership. In 1976 Egyptian women owned only 2% of businesses; by 1988 this figure had jumped to 17%.

Pay Differences

In 1990 Egyptian women in nonagricultural industries earned an estimated 80% of men's wages, largely because they tended to be concentrated in lower-paying jobs; but even when they held positions comparable to men's, they were generally paid less. Another factor in the wage difference between women and men is that women are seldom promoted. When they are, they are most likely to be women over 50 and are usually not given a salary increase.

Working Hours

A special provision in the law grants women the right to part-time employment. In these positions they are paid half the salary and receive half the vacation benefits.

Maternity Leave and Benefits

Egyptian law grants a woman three months of maternity leave with pay up to three times during her lifetime. She is also entitled to a leave for up to two years to care for her child. During this time the government will pay either 25% of her salary or her benefits.

Child Care

Employers are encouraged, and in some cases required, to establish day-care centers for their employees. However, while the number of these facilities increased by 187% from 1982 to 1991, the quality of child care remains poor and only 4% of Egyptian children use these services.

Unemployment

Since the transition from socialist policies to a market economy during the 1970s, women's unemployment rates have been much higher—sometimes three times higher—than men's.

UNEMPLOYMENT RATES Percentage of total labor force			
YEAR	TOTAL	WOMEN	MEN
1984	8.4%	17.7%	6.2%
1986	13.7%	22.7%	11.6%
1988	13.0%	25.8%	8.7%
1990	8.6%	17.9%	5.2%
1991	9.6%	21.3%	5.9%

MARRIAGE AND DIVORCE

For the Muslim majority, laws and practices concerning marriage, divorce, and personal status generally follow the traditional Islamic law, or *shari'a*. Common law applies to the Christian minority.

Most women in Egypt are married and live with a husband and children. Of the 16% of households headed by women, widows account for 78% of these; divorced or separated women constitute 9%. Married women whose husbands have emigrated overseas head 10% and never-married women account for the remaining 3%.

Marriage

The minimum legal marriage age in Egypt is 16 for women and 18 for men. However, the average age of women at first marriage has risen from 19.9 years in 1960 to 22.4 years in 1992, with the corresponding ages for men showing similar increases and remaining three to four years higher than for women. A 1993 government study found that women who have had more schooling tend to get married later than those with little or no education.

Egyptian couples tend to start their families shortly after marriage. Pregnancy outside marriage is strongly discouraged; only 1% of total births are to unmarried women, one of the world's lowest rates of out-of-wedlock births. Because a woman's virtue is often considered a reflection on her male relatives, the penalties for unwed motherhood are extremely harsh; in some regions an unmarried mother may be abandoned by her family or even killed.

Traditionally, in Islamic families a man's ideal bride is the daughter of his father's brother. While this practice, called endogamy, has declined among the urban middle and upper classes since the 1950s, more than half of all lower-class marriages—rural and urban—are still endogamous. Islam also permits polygamy; a man may marry up to four wives, but a woman may have only one husband. In 1979 a revised family status law was passed, but because it conflicted with Islamic family law it was repealed in 1985. In 1995 the religious community accepted a proposed marriage contract law that allows a husband and wife to negotiate the terms of their marriage, including the wife's right to work, study, and travel abroad and the husband's right to take another wife.

WOMEN'S AGE AT MARRIAGE
Percentage of educational level attained, 1993

| | MARRIAGE AGE | | |
EDUCATIONAL LEVEL	UNDER 16	16–19	20 AND OVER
None	47%	44%	9%
Primary school	37%	54%	9%
Secondary school	0%	31%	69%
University	0%	0%	100%

Religious intermarriage, particularly by women, is strongly discouraged by Islamic law. Non-Muslim men must convert to Islam in order to marry Muslim women, while non-Muslim women need not convert to marry Muslim men.

Divorce

Divorce in Egypt is mostly seen among the urban lower classes, and remarriage is common for both women and men. Prior to 1979 a Muslim husband could divorce his wife by publicly declaring to her "I divorce thee" three times in front of witnesses. A woman, however, could divorce her husband only by going to court and legally proving that he had failed to support her or had a harmful moral effect on the family, a lengthy process that could take up to seven years. Custody of the children was automatically granted to the husband, though he was required to support his ex-wife for a year.

The Women's Rights Law of 1979 strengthened a woman's right to divorce and child custody but it was repealed in 1985. According to a proposed 1995 law, which allows a husband and wife to negotiate whether or not he can take another wife, a woman can divorce her husband on the grounds of polygamy if her marriage contract specifies that it is prohibited. The new marriage law also proposes agreement on the division of property and a financial settlement following divorce.

FAMILY PLANNING

Egypt's growing population, along with its increasingly limited water resources, has forced family planning and population control to become a national issue. The government's program, administered in part by the minister of state for population and family welfare, involves promoting the use of contraception, improving the status of women, increasing women's participation in the labor force, expanding available agricultural lands, and moving the population away from the crowded Nile River valley.

Not surprisingly, there is strong Islamic resistance to family planning programs that include contraception, abortion, and sex education. Such plans are sometimes seen as a form of genocide against Muslims and as a defense for extramarital sex. Many Egyptians, particularly in rural areas, value large families, and women are often reluctant to practice any form of birth control.

Fertility Rate

Despite Islamic leaders' strong opposition to the use of contraception, Egypt is one of the few countries in the Middle East with recent substantial declines in its fertility rate. In 1995 the fertility rate was 3.7 children per woman, one of the lowest in Africa, and a dramatic decrease from 7.0 in 1960. The fertility rate in urban areas is even lower than the national average: fewer than 3 children per woman. Births to teenagers account for 9% of the total.

Contraception

Contraception is legal in Egypt, and its use, which is actively promoted by the government, has been rising steadily in recent years. In 1992 approximately 47% of couples of childbearing age used some form of birth control, nearly double the 24% in 1980.

CONTRACEPTIVE USE
Percentage of couples of childbearing age, 1992

METHOD	PERCENT	AVERAGE AGE OF WOMAN
Intrauterine devices (IUDs)	28%	33.3 years
Birth control pill	13%	34.0 years
Traditional methods	2%	36.1 years
Condom	2%	38.4 years
Female sterilization	1%	41.3 years
Diaphragm, other	1%	N/A

Abortion

Under Islamic law, abortion is illegal except to save the woman's life. Under Egypt's civil law, however, abortion is legal and widely and quietly available throughout the country. A doctor need only certify that the abortion is necessary for the woman's mental health.

Sex Education

Due largely to strong Islamic opposition, sex education is unavailable in the Egyptian school system. However, family planning clinics throughout the country provide information on birth control and reproductive health.

WOMEN'S HEALTH

The Egyptian National Charter of 1962 states that "the right of health welfare is foremost among the rights of every citizen." Accordingly, the Ministry of Health provides free basic health care at public medical facilities. Most of these facilities, however, are concentrated in the cities; only 30% of doctors and 10% of nurses serve in rural areas.

Despite an overall shortage of doctors and modern equipment throughout the country, longevity has climbed steadily over the past few decades, and the average Egyptian woman's life expectancy, 62.8 years, is one of the highest in Africa. Correspondingly, the maternal mortality rate, 170 deaths per 100,000 live births, is one of the lowest in Africa.

LIFE EXPECTANCY At birth, in years		
YEAR	WOMEN	MEN
1952	39.0	39.0
1960	53.8	51.6
1976	55.3	52.9
1986	60.3	57.8
1991	64.4	61.9
1992	65.9	62.5
1994	62.8	58.9

Leading Causes of Death

Cardiovascular diseases, primarily heart attack and stroke, have overtaken infectious and parasitic diseases as the leading cause of death among both sexes.

LEADING CAUSES OF DEATH Percentage of total deaths, 1987		
CAUSE	WOMEN	MEN
Cardiovascular diseases	33%	34%
Infectious, parasitic diseases	21%	18%
Senility	18%	14%
Bronchitis, pneumonia	12%	9%
Cancer	2%	3%
Breast	<1%	—
Cervix	<1%	—
Lung	<1%	<1%
Homicide, other violence	2%	3%
Accidents	1%	3%

Smoking

Nearly a third of Egyptian men are smokers, but only 2% of women smoke. This is one of the lowest female smoking rates in the world.

AIDS

By 1993 there were 48 reported cases of AIDS among Egyptian women, accounting for 20% of the total of 236 recorded cases. However, according to the World Health Organization, by 1994 an estimated 7,500 Egyptians were believed to be infected with HIV, the virus that causes AIDS.

VIOLENCE AGAINST WOMEN

The incidence of violent acts against women in Egypt is largely unknown, but it is believed to be high. The vast majority of cases are never reported or even discussed. In recent years there have been reports of women being attacked on the streets for not wearing the traditional Muslim head covering.

Domestic Violence

Matters of domestic violence are seldom discussed in Egyptian society, which has a strong tradition of privacy within the family. However, spousal abuse is believed to be quite common, and several nongovernmental agencies have launched programs offering counseling, legal advice, and other services to battered wives.

Rape

Rape is illegal in Egypt and punishable by a maximum sentence of 15 to 25 years or by death if the victim is killed. However, the woman's family or the local police will often allow a rapist to avoid a jail sentence if he marries the victim. Marital rape is not considered a crime.

Prostitution

Since 1951 prostitution has been illegal in Egypt and punishable by imprisonment. Yet although no statistics are available, it is thought to be prevalent, especially in urban centers.

Female Genital Mutilation

Female genital mutilation (FGM), ranging from excision of the clitoris to the more drastic infibulation, is a common ritual in Egypt. Although reliable statistics are scarce, approximately half of all Egyptian females undergo this procedure, with the proportion climbing as high as 80% among rural women and the urban poor. The practice is not historically Islamic; it is an African ritual predating the introduction of Islam, and some Coptic Christians practice it as well.

Proponents of FGM maintain that it prevents homosexuality, sexual promiscuity, and prostitution. It is considered a means of safeguarding a woman's honor, and in some communities a woman is not considered marriageable unless she has undergone the procedure.

In 1995, responding to pressure from human rights and women's organizations, the government issued a decree allowing the procedure to be carried out only one day a week in government hospitals and prohibiting barbers and other nonmedical practitioners from performing it. The following year, the Ministry of Health banned it completely, although many Egyptians were expected to defy this ruling.

FOR ADDITIONAL INFORMATION ON WOMEN

Alliance for Arab Women
28 Adly Street, Apartment 7
Cairo, Egypt
Telephone: 2-393-9899
Fax: 2-393-6820

Arab Women Solidarity Association
25 Murad Street
Giza, Egypt
Telephone: 2-272-3976

Association for Development and Enhancement of Women
P.O. Box 1065, Ataba
Cairo, Egypt
Telephone: 2-350-2267/2021;
or 2-921-144

Embassy of Egypt
1666 Connecticut Avenue, NW
Washington, D.C. 20009, United States
Telephone: 202-667-3402

New Women Center for Research & Training
2 Al Amir Qadadar Street
2nd floor, Apartment 62
Cairo, Egypt
Telephone: 2-354-3553

Permanent Mission of the Arab Republic of Egypt to the United Nations
36 East 67th Street
New York, NY 10021, United States
Telephone: 212-879-6300

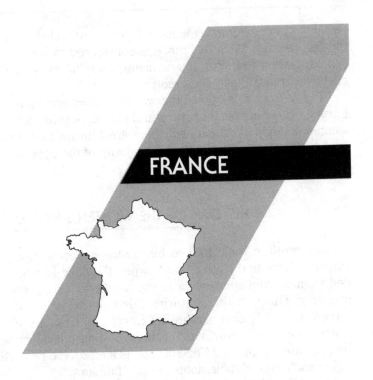

FRANCE

Population: *57.7 million*
Women per 100 men: *105*
Women's voting rights: *1944*
Women in legislature: *5%*
Women's share of work force: *42%*
▲ Literacy rates: women—*99%;* men—*99%*
▲ Life expectancy: women—*82.0 years;* men—*73.5 years*
Average number of children: *1.7*
Maternal mortality rate: *15*

WOMEN NOBEL PRIZE WINNERS		
Marie Curie	Physics	1903
	Chemistry	1911
Irène Joliet-Curie	Chemistry	1935

France, located in western Europe, ranks third in area among European countries (after Russia and the Ukraine). The country's history extends back to before the Christian era; it was conquered by Julius Caesar and remained under Roman rule for 500 years until taken over by the Franks in the 5th century. Modern France is considered to have been established in 843 A.D., when Emperor Charlemagne's territories were divided up among his three grandsons by the Treaty of Verdun.

Today France is one of the world's major economic powers as well as Europe's most important agricultural nation. Approximately 81% of the population are Roman Catholic, but there are Muslim (5%), Protestant (2%), and Jewish (1%) minorities. The great majority of the population, 74%, are urban dwellers.

HISTORY OF THE WOMEN'S MOVEMENT

French women have had to overcome a patriarchal domination that extended back to the 5th century, when the Salic Law of the Franks prohibited women from succeeding to the throne and from owning or inheriting property. Through the centuries this subordination of women was reinforced by the Roman Catholic Church. During the French Revolution women were politically active alongside men but never achieved equality. Instead, the Napoleonic Code of 1804 placed severe restrictions on women's rights and reduced their status to that of minors.

Until World War I there were few improvements in women's status and little support for women's suffrage, even after voting rights were granted to men in 1848. After the war, when women started entering the work force, a series of women's suffrage bills were introduced—and defeated—in 1919, 1929, 1932, and 1935. Finally, in 1944 French women won the right to vote, almost a century after men. In 1946, the constitution of the Fourth Republic guaranteed equal rights for women, a provision that was incorporated into the Fifth Republic's constitution of 1958.

In the 20 years following World War II, the French population rose, economic production increased fivefold, and the country's wealth grew rapidly. Since 1965 women have been entering the labor force in unprecedented numbers. However, at the same time unemployment has been high, primarily because the service sector, which provides more part-time and temporary employment, has overtaken the industrial sector in terms of job growth.

The modern French feminist movement derived its inspiration from the May Events of 1968, when students and unions staged massive antigovernment protests. At first the women's movement was greatly influenced by the far left and tended to emphasize theoretical issues rather than try to change government policies. However, during the 1970s women's groups mounted a major campaign for reproductive rights, and in 1974 abortion became legal. But following that victory, the women's movement lost strength and momentum, undermined by internal conflicts. Efforts to improve women's employment status in the 1980s were not successful. More recently, feminist groups have been focusing on such issues as increasing women's participation in electoral politics and eliminating sexual harassment in the workplace.

WOMEN IN POLITICS

France is one of the few countries in the world ever to have had a woman head of government: Edith Cresson became prime minister in 1991. Her term in office, however, was relatively short, lasting slightly less than a year. The first women were elected to the French Parliament in 1945, when 33, 6% of the total, were elected to the National Assembly. The following year 21 women joined the Senate, making up 7% of that chamber. Although French women today make up 53% of the electorate and vote in equal numbers with men, they are still greatly underrepresented in the national legislature. In the 1995 election, women won only 5% of the total seats in Parliament: 29 of the 577 deputies in the National Assembly (5%) and 18 of the 321 senators (6%) were women. And as yet, no woman has served as president of either chamber.

French women have been more successful in achieving high position through appointment. In the 32-member cabinet named by prime minister Alain Juppé in 1995, 4 of the seats (13%) were held by women: Anne-Marie Couderc, minister delegate for employment; Anne-Marie Idrac, minister of state for transportation; Corinne Lepage, minister of the environment; and Margie Sudre, minister of state for Francophone affairs. In the previous cabinet women had occupied 12 of the 41 seats (29%). In the foreign service the first woman ambassador was appointed in 1972, and by 1995 women served in 4% of those positions.

WOMEN IN THE NATIONAL ASSEMBLY Percentage of total members	
YEAR	PERCENT
1945	6%
1951	4%
1973	2%
1983	6%
1995	5%

The French delegation to the European Parliament, where women occupy 26 of the 87 seats (30%), is the only nationally elected body in which women have achieved a sizable representation. In addition, from 1979 to 1982 Simone Veil, one of these delegates, held the office of the president of the European Parliament.

French women have fared somewhat better at the local level than in national politics, winning 17% of municipal council seats in 1995. However, only 4% of mayors were women.

WOMEN'S EDUCATION

Education in France is free beginning at age 2, and compulsory for both girls and boys between the ages of 6 and 16. All children average 12 years of schooling, and the country's overall literacy rate—99% for both sexes—is among the highest in the world. Girls tend to do better in school than boys: more of them graduate and go on to higher levels of education. Of those students passing the *baccalauréat* exam when they complete high school, 57% are women.

Women's studies programs were introduced into French secondary schools in 1987. The courses include such topics as women's roles in modern society as well as throughout history.

In the universities women constitute a large majority, 70%, of students in humanities and pharmacy courses; they account for 58% of law students, 49% of medical students, 47% of commerce and business students, but only 36% of students in the sciences and 21% of those in engineering. Competing with the universities is a parallel network of prestigious institutions, called *grandes écoles,* which were founded by Napoleon and train many of the future leaders in French business and government. Female students are entering these institutions in the same proportion as the universities: 70% in the humanities schools, 56% in the business schools, and 23% in the science and technology schools.

FEMALE ENROLLMENT Percentage of student body, 1993	
LEVEL	PERCENT
Primary school	48%
Secondary school	50%
Higher education	52%

Over the past decade the French government has launched campaigns to encourage female students to enter technology and other fields in which they are underrepresented. The secretary of state for the rights of women established programs in 1984 and 1989 informing girls of the many options open to them, stressing technical subjects for girls, training teachers, and encouraging employers to hire more female technical graduates. In 1992 and again in 1993, advertising campaigns aimed at teenage girls told them, "It's technical, it's for you."

WOMEN'S EMPLOYMENT

Since the mid-1960s, there has been a steady increase in the number of French women working outside the home. In 1995, 57% of working-age women were in the labor force, making up 42% of the total work force.

WOMEN'S LABOR FORCE PARTICIPATION, AGES 25–49

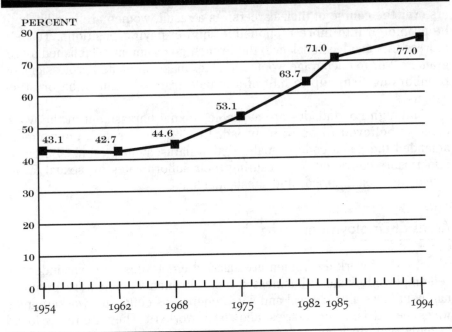

PERCENT

43.1 42.7 44.6 53.1 63.7 71.0 77.0

1954   1962   1968   1975   1982 1985   1994

French men, in comparison, had an 83% participation rate. Among women, those aged between 25 and 49 had the highest participation rate.

Many French women work out of economic necessity, with their wages contributing 46% of the average family income. They stop working only temporarily for childbearing, and almost immediately return to their jobs. In 1993, 78% of mothers with one child and 71% of mothers with two children were in the labor force. With three or more children, a woman is more likely to stay home: Only 42% of such mothers worked.

Discrimination in the Workplace

The French government has passed several laws granting specific rights and protective measures for working women: equal pay for equal work (1972), a ban on sex discrimination (1975), equal employment opportunities (1983), and protection against sexual harassment (1992). Nevertheless, there is still widespread inequality in the workplace. It takes young French women longer than men to find their first job, and even with the same level of education, women are generally hired at lower levels. It is also harder for women to obtain permanent contracts: They fill 52% of limited-term jobs.

Once they have a job, fewer working women (24%) than men (30%) have access to continuing education or training provided by their employers over the course of their careers. As a result, women are less likely to be promoted into more responsible, higher-paying positions. To help redress this gender imbalance, the French government established a program in 1987 to encourage women to enter male-dominated professions by reimbursing firms up to half of a female trainee's education or other expenses.

Although no statistics are available, sexual harassment in the workplace is believed to be widespread. In 1991 the French government amended the penal code to make sexual harassment a criminal offense. Supervisors convicted of pressuring their subordinates for sexual favors face up to a year in prison and substantial fines.

Areas of Employment

About 88% of working women are salaried employees; the remainder are self-employed or small business owners. French women work predominantly in low-status clerical and service jobs—as child-care workers, midwives, beauticians, secretaries, and social workers. They are rarely found in high-level, decision-making positions and constitute only 6% of industry executives. In general, for every 100 men in administrative or managerial posts, there are only 10 women in similar positions.

The French judicial system is somewhat more open to women, who account for 43% of all judges. Teaching also attracts many women; they make up 77% of primary and 58% of secondary school teachers. However, at the university level, women account for only 28% of professors. Overall, in the category of professional and technical occupations, there are 71 women for every 100 men.

WOMEN IN MAJOR OCCUPATIONAL GROUPS Percentage of group, 1990	
OCCUPATIONAL GROUP	PERCENT
Services	69%
Clerical	64%
Sales	48%
Professional, technical	42%
Agricultural	32%
Production, transport	15%
Administrative, managerial	9%

French women are eligible to serve in the armed forces and make up approximately 5% of military personnel. Unlike most other countries, France permits women to serve on combat duty. In 1976 Valerie Andrée became France's first woman general of the air force.

Pay Differences

The difference between women's and men's wages has continued to narrow in recent years, especially among white-collar workers. French women in nonagricultural industries now earn an average of about 81% of men's wages, one of the world's narrowest gender wage gaps.

Although French law mandates equal pay for equal work, women still tend to be paid less than their male counterparts. A 1994 study found a 20% gap between women and men in the private sector and an 18% gap in the public sector.

WOMEN'S EARNINGS Percentage of men's		
OCCUPATIONAL GROUP	1986	1993
Professional, managerial	69%	71%
White-collar employees	82%	89%
Skilled blue-collar employees	76%	83%

Working Hours

About 25% of French female employees work part time, compared with 4% of men; women make up 85% of all part-time workers. This imbalance contributes to women's lower average earnings and often prevents them from qualifying for such benefits as paid holidays, sick leave, or pension rights.

Maternity Leave and Benefits

During pregnancy all medical fees and medications are paid for by the French social security system, which also pays 84% of a woman's wages for 6 weeks of maternity leave before the birth and 10 weeks afterward. Each mother also receives monthly payments equivalent to about $300 until her child reaches 18.

Child Care

France maintains one of the world's most extensive systems of high-quality child-care facilities. In 1993, 99% of all children aged three to five were enrolled in all-day preschools, at minimal cost in parochial schools or at no cost in public schools. For children under three, there are a large number of day-care centers, called *crèches*, which are partly subsidized by the local government and charge tuition on a sliding scale. Also available for infants and toddlers are many day-care homes run by government-licensed babysitters.

Unemployment

Unemployment has been high in France for the last decade, and since 1985 women's unemployment rates have consistently ranged from 3.7 to 5.3 percentage points higher than men's. Women account for 56% of the jobless, and their length of unemployment lasts an average of 50 days longer than men's. The main reason women become unemployed is that they are released at the end of a fixed-term contract.

In 1993, 13.7% of working women were unemployed, compared with 10.0% of men. In addition, 28.4% of young women aged 15 to 24 were unemployed in 1994, compared with 21.5% of men in the same age bracket. This disparity reflects the fact that it is more difficult for female workers to find entry-level jobs.

MARRIAGE AND DIVORCE

The Napoleonic Code of 1804 decreed that a husband was the legal head of the household, with total authority over his children and all financial matters. Legislation abolishing this concept was not passed for more than 160 years, and it was introduced in two stages. In 1970 women were made equal partners in parental authority, but it was not until the mid-1980s that they were officially granted autonomy in fiscal matters. A 1985 law allowed each spouse to work freely and collect his or her own income and enabled either partner to manage the joint assets of the marriage. It also permitted a child to be given the name of both parents.

The number of single-parent families in France has been increasing steadily, with women heading about 86% of such families. About 15% of children under the age of 19 live with only one parent. Divorced women account for 38% of single mothers, widows for 33%.

Marriage

The minimum legal age for marriage is 18 for both women and men, 15 for women with parental consent. But French couples tend to marry much later. On average, women first marry at 27.3 years—one of the world's highest average marriage ages—and men at 29.8 years. Over the last decade the number of women marrying before age 20 has dropped by 75%.

As in other developed countries, more and more French couples are choosing to cohabit either before or instead of marrying. Correspondingly, births to single women have increased dramatically over the past few decades, from 6% of all births in 1960 to 32% in 1992. Approximately 85% of babies born to cohabiting couples are legally recognized by their fathers within a year of birth.

In recent years France has had to deal with the practice of polygamy, which is widespread among many of its African immigrants. It is estimated that in the Paris metropolitan region alone, as many as 200,000 people live in polygamous families: usually a husband, two to four wives, and each wife's many children. In 1995 the government decreed that it would legally recognize only one wife and that all other marriages would be officially annulled.

Divorce

France's divorce law was revised in 1975 to allow divorce by mutual consent, and since then the divorce rate has tripled. For every 100 couples getting married in one year, approximately 33 couples get divorced. Of those divorces not jointly pursued, 60% are initiated by women.

When a couple divorce, spouses continue to share parental authority, although wives are granted custody nearly 90% of the time. Children have the right to support from both parents, but about 35% of fathers default on their payments, and the government has begun to pursue these delinquent fathers. Following divorce, few women remarry.

FAMILY PLANNING

France is overwhelmingly Roman Catholic, but despite the church's prohibition against modern contraceptives and abortion, both are legal and widely available. Their use is actively supported and promoted by the government.

Fertility Rate

The fertility rate in France is 1.7 children per woman, a rate that has been slowly decreasing since the mid-1980s. As women have been marrying later and delaying childbearing in order to complete their education and start their careers, the average age of mothers at the birth of their first child has been increasing, from 25 in 1965 to 28.4 in 1991. Teenage births account for only 3% of total births, one of the lowest teenage birthrates in Europe. Approximately two-thirds of all teenage pregnancies end in abortion.

Contraception

Modern contraceptives have been legal in France since 1967 and the proportion of all French couples of childbearing age using some form of birth control is approximately 81%, the second highest rate of contraception in the world after China. This high rate is due to some extent to the government's partial reimbursement of the cost of birth control pills and intrauterine devices (IUDs). Also, in 1993 the French government, concerned about the spread of AIDS and other sexually transmitted diseases, slashed the cost of condoms by two-thirds to encourage greater use by teenagers.

AVERAGE AGE OF WOMEN AT BIRTH OF FIRST CHILD	
YEAR	AGE
1960	25.0
1975	26.7
1985	27.5
1991	28.4

CONTRACEPTIVE USE Percentage of couples of childbearing age, 1988	
METHOD	PERCENT
Birth control pill	30%
Intrauterine devices (IUDs)	26%
Traditional methods	15%
Female sterilization	7%
Condom	4%

Abortion

The legalization of abortion is considered the single most significant accomplishment of the women's movement in France. Despite tremendous opposition, a temporary law was enacted in 1975, making France the first predominantly Roman Catholic country to legalize abortion. In 1979, after a five-year trial period, the law became permanent. According to this law, abortions during the first 10 weeks of pregnancy are available to women who believe themselves to be in a state of distress as a result of their pregnancy. One major restriction is a mandatory one-week waiting period between the initial consultation and the actual procedure.

Approximately 200,000 abortions are performed annually in France, a rate that has held steady since the mid-1980s. About one-quarter of all abor-

ABORTION RATES
Percentage of total, 1991

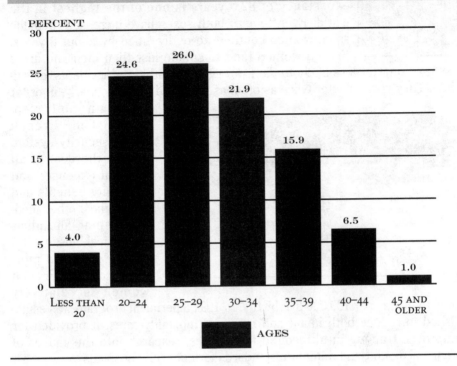

PERCENT

4.0	24.6	26.0	21.9	15.9	6.5	1.0
LESS THAN 20	20–24	25–29	30–34	35–39	40–44	45 AND OLDER

AGES

tions are accomplished with RU 486 (mifepristone), a drug developed by a French pharmaceutical company in 1980.

Government support for abortion seems to have become firmly established in France. In 1983 the government began reimbursing women 70% of the cost of abortions. In 1988 the minister of health pressured the manufacturer of RU 486 to continue distributing the drug when, threatened by an international boycott, the company considered discontinuing it. In 1993, to curb antiabortion protests, impeding access to an abortion facility was ruled a misdemeanor. In 1995, however, in a case where pro-life demonstrators blocked access to a Paris hospital abortion ward, they were acquitted on the grounds that a fetus is a future human being.

Sex Education

Sex education is included in the school curriculum throughout France. In 1987 specific information about the transmission and prevention of AIDS was added to the course of study.

WOMEN'S HEALTH

French women are among the healthiest; their life expectancy of 82.0 years is one of the highest in the world. Even though both sexes have increased their life span, women continue to outlive men by about 8 years. French women tend to smoke less than men and are a half to a quarter less likely to die from violent deaths, car accidents, or suicide. They visit a doctor twice as often as men, and more regularly, in order to obtain contraceptives. The French social security system covers the cost of all hospital expenses and maternity benefits and 80% of most other medical, dental, and pharmaceutical bills.

LIFE EXPECTANCY At birth, in years		
YEAR	WOMEN	MEN
1980	77.0	69.0
1982	78.9	70.7
1985	79.4	71.3
1988	80.5	72.3
1991	81.1	73.0
1992	82.0	73.5

The maternal mortality rate for French women is relatively low, 15 deaths per 100,000 live births. In 1994 a perinatal program was established to reduce both infant and maternal mortality rates. It provided for improved training in ultrasound techniques, research into the causes of neonatal deaths, and minimum standards for maternity hospitals.

Leading Causes of Death

The two major causes of death among French women are cardiovascular diseases, primarily heart attack and stroke, and cancer.

Recently, a trial breast cancer screening program was launched in a limited area of the country, offering mammograms to all women between the ages of 50 and 69 every three years.

Smoking

About 33% of French women smoke, compared with 49% of men. An alarming trend, however, appeared in a recent study: More teenage girls than boys are starting to smoke. In an effort to reduce the incidence of smoking among both women and men, the government passed a law in 1991, the strictest in Europe, requiring cigarette packaging to carry health warnings.

LEADING CAUSES OF DEATH Percentage of total deaths, 1992		
CAUSE	WOMEN	MEN
Cardiovascular diseases	37%	29%
Cancer	22%	32%
Breast	4%	—
Lung	1%	7%
Cervix	<1%	—
Accidents	6%	6%
Pneumonia	3%	3%
Mental disorders	3%	2%
Suicide	1%	3%
Homicide	<1%	<1%

AIDS

The proportion of women with AIDS has grown from 10% of reported cases in 1986 to 20% in 1994, when it was estimated that a total of 90,000 people were infected with HIV, the virus that causes AIDS. Men in France are most likely to contract the disease through sexual contact with a male partner. Women, on the other hand, are likely to become infected through intravenous drug use (37%), sexual contact with a male partner (36%) and blood transfusions (14%). AIDS screening is not required for pregnant women, but since 1994, mothers planning to nurse their babies must be tested for HIV.

VIOLENCE AGAINST WOMEN

Although the French government strongly condemns violent acts against women, they nonetheless continue to be widespread. Estimates indicate that the great majority of cases, perhaps 90%, are never reported.

Domestic Violence

Although the French penal code classifies wife beating as a felony, it is still commonplace. In 1993 nearly 16,000 incidents were reported, up from 13,000 in 1990. Included in the 1993 figures were 98 assaults that resulted in death.

In addition to about 60 different private organizations that assist battered women, the government provides shelters, counseling, financial assistance, and a telephone hotline. In 1995 about 500 staff members were added to these facilities.

Rape

The penalty for rape ranges from 5 to 20 years in prison, and since 1990 the courts have not distinguished between rape and marital rape. In 1995 there were over 6,500 reported incidents of rape or other sexual assault, up from 4,500 in 1990. Family members or acquaintances account for about 68% of rapes of women aged 18 or older; among girls 17 and under this figure jumps to 81%. France is one of the few countries where victims of sexual assault are entitled to financial compensation by the government.

Prostitution

According to the French penal code, aiding, abetting, or living off the earnings of a prostitute is an offense punishable by a fine and imprisonment. Although the government has attempted to curtail prostitution by offering counseling and job training to the women and prosecuting traffickers and pimps, it is still a thriving industry in many French cities.

Female Genital Mutilation

The French government estimates that 20,000 adult women and 7,000 girls living in France, chiefly immigrants from sub-Saharan Africa, have been subjected to this ritual. Nothing was done to curtail this practice for many years, until pressure from doctors and social workers began to mount. Under a law that prohibits harming children, the practitioner, as well as both parents, may be sentenced to prison, and in 1983 France became the first nation to bring criminal charges for female genital mutilation. In 1993 the government launched an advertising campaign to inform immigrants that the practice is illegal and that violators are subject to prosecution.

FOR ADDITIONAL INFORMATION ON WOMEN

Association de Femmes Responsables
8/11 Residence Dampierre
59800 Lille St. Maur, France

Conseil National de Femmes Françaises
11 Rue Viarmes
75001 Paris, France

Embassy of France
4101 Reservoir Road, NW
Washington, DC 20007, United States
Telephone: 202-944-6000

French Cultural Service
Information Service
972 Fifth Avenue
New York, NY 10021, United States
Telephone: 212-439-1400

International Council of Women
13, rue Caumartin
75009 Paris, France
Telephone: 14-742-1940
Fax: 14-266-2623

Population: *81.2 million*
▲ Women per 100 men: *106*
Women's voting rights: *1919*
▲ Women in legislature: *26%*
Women's share of work force: *40%*
▲ Literacy rates: women—*99%;* men—*99%*
Life expectancy: women—*79.1 years;* men—*72.7 years*
▲ Average number of children: *1.3*
Maternal mortality rate: *22*

WOMAN NOBEL PRIZE WINNER		
Christiane Nüsslein-Volhard	Physiology or Medicine	1995

The Federal Republic of Germany is the most populous country in Western Europe and one of the world's leading economic powers. Following World War II, Germany was divided into two separate countries, but the nation was reunified in October 1990. This merger of the highly industrialized, democratic Federal Republic of Germany (West Germany) and the communist-ruled

German Democratic Republic (East Germany) led to a wide range of social, political, and economic changes for women in both sectors.

Present-day Germany is made up of 16 *Länder,* or states. The former East Germany comprised 5 of them, now called the new Länder. The remaining 11 from the former West Germany, now referred to as the old Länder, contain about 80% of the country's total population. In both the new and old Länder the great majority of people, about 76%, live in urban centers. Protestants make up nearly half (49%) of the population, and they tend to live mostly in the northern regions. About 45% are Roman Catholics, concentrated in the south.

HISTORY OF THE WOMEN'S MOVEMENT

Women's groups in Germany started emerging in the mid-1800s, shortly before the country was first unified in 1871. These early groups campaigned for educational and employment opportunities as well as for increased political representation. Following World War I, women were granted the right to vote, and in the first elections of the new democratic republic they captured 8% of the seats in the German parliament.

By the early 1930s, chronic political instability and worsening economic conditions enabled Adolf Hitler, the leader of Germany's National Socialist Party, to seize power and create one of the most repressive, brutal, and destructive regimes in the history of the world. Based on an ideology of nationalism, anti-Semitism, and anticommunism, his Third Reich embarked on an aggressive expansionism that led to World War II. During Hitler's rule many of the goals that German women had attained were suddenly lost: Abortion was banned, birth control clinics were closed, women were barred from the legislature, university enrollment of female students was severely limited, and many women were forced out of their jobs. Producing the next generation of Germans became paramount, and women were expected to stay home and fulfill their roles as wives and mothers, living up to the ideal expressed in the slogan *"Kinder, Küche, Kirche"* (children, kitchen, church).

In the aftermath of World War II, Germany was divided into two separate countries: East Germany and West Germany. Women's lives took very different turns depending on whether they lived in communist East Germany or democratic West Germany. In the east, one of the government's primary objectives was to move more women into the work force, while in the west the government provided no special incentives or protections for working women. Women's political representation in the East German legislature was practically double that of West Germany, largely because a certain number of seats were allotted to them.

In East Germany abortion became legal, unrestricted, and financed by the government in 1973. West Germany in contrast, had a restrictive abortion law. From 1976 abortion was legal only if the fetus had severe abnormalities, was a danger to the woman's life, was the result of rape, or was causing stress to the woman (social grounds). In some communities, especially those with large Catholic populations, abortions were practically impossible to obtain.

With the reunification of the two Germanys in 1990, two very different sets of laws and policies had to be merged. With respect to abortion, a two-year interim period was created during which each territory continued to abide by its original law. In 1992 the Bundestag (federal parliament) passed a compromise bill that permitted unrestricted first-trimester abortions after mandatory counseling. But this law never went into effect. It was invalidated in 1993 by the Federal Constitutional Court because it violated the constitution's protection of the rights of the unborn. Furthermore, the court's ruling was in some ways more restrictive than West Germany's original abortion law. It decreed, for example, that national health insurance would no longer pay for abortions performed for social grounds, which had previously accounted for 90% of all legal abortions. Only abortions performed for medical reasons would be covered by the state insurance system.

Before reunification, East Germany had only one recognized women's organization, which propagated the official line of the ruling Communist party. West Germany supported a wide range of women's groups, and after reunification many similar organizations appeared in the eastern region. One of the most influential associations today is the German Women's Council, a nationwide lobbying group representing more than 100 different women's organizations. Among the major issues concerning German women today are abortion reform, employment opportunities for women, and domestic violence.

The new German government has officially pledged its commitment to the advancement of women. In 1991 it established a federal Ministry for Women and Youth, incorporating the 1987 Ministry for Women. Working with other ministries and federal agencies, its goal is to advance the status of women in all spheres of life. In 1994 the Bundestag passed the Second Equal Rights Act, which dealt primarily with equality in employment, especially in the federal administration.

At the state level, all Länder have established special equal rights offices, and 12 have created ministries for women. At the local level, there are more than 1,250 equal rights and women's offices throughout the country; the first established by a city was in Cologne in 1982.

WOMEN IN POLITICS

The proportion of women in the 672-member Bundestag rose from 8% in 1980 to 26% in 1994, one of the highest proportions of female legislators in the world. The Bundestag's president was Rita Süssmuth, who had been serving since 1988 and was the second woman to hold that office. The first, Annemarie Renger, occupied that position from 1972 to 1976. In the Bundesrat (federal council), women occupied 13 (19%) of the 68 appointed seats.

In 1996 just 2 of the 17 German ministerial posts (12%) in the federal cabinet were held by women: Claudia Nolte (families, senior citizens, women, and youth); and Angela Merkel (nature conservation and nuclear safety). Six out of 140 (4%) ambassadors were women, and women made up 35% of the 99 members of the German delegation to the European Parliament, up from 20% in 1984. Another high-ranking woman in the German government was Jutta Limbach, the president of the Federal Constitutional Court.

At the state level, the proportion of women in the 16 legislatures ranged from a low of 11% to a high of 36%. Four state parliaments had female Speakers, and one state, Schleswig-Holstein, was led by Minister-President Heide Simonis. At the local level, women made up 27% of the local councils in the towns and cities with a population of more than 100,000. In some of the larger cities they accounted for 40%.

WOMEN'S EDUCATION

Education is compulsory for all German children when they reach the age of six. It generally extends for 10 years, and for those students in vocational or apprenticeship programs, it is obligatory until age 18. Adult literacy rates are among the world's highest: 99% for both women and men.

Coeducation was introduced into German schools in the 1950s. In recent years, there has been a concerted effort to make the curriculum less gender-biased and to interest girls in traditionally male subjects and careers. However, in universities and polytechnics, women are still found mostly in the language, humanities, social science, and other departments traditionally regarded as women's fields.

FEMALE ENROLLMENT
Percentage of student body, 1992

LEVEL	PERCENT
Primary/secondary	54%
Higher education	43%

WOMEN IN HIGHER EDUCATION
Percentage of subject area, 1993

SUBJECT AREA	PERCENT
Languages, humanities, sport	63%
Art, art history	56%
Agriculture, forestry, food science	49%
Medicine	47%
Law, economics, social science	41%
Mathematics, natural science	33%
Engineering	14%

Women make up 42% of students in the vocational training system, where their most popular vocations are store clerk, medical and dental assistant, clerical worker, and hairdresser. Only 31% of students in polytechnic programs are women.

WOMEN'S EMPLOYMENT

Before reunification, women in East Germany were expected to work outside the home, and by 1989 approximately 85% of all working-age women were in the labor force. Even mothers of small children were expected to work. In West Germany only 57% of working age women worked; and their employment was often interrupted for marriage, child raising, or caring for a sick family member.

By the mid-1990s approximately 62% of all working-age women in Germany were in the labor force, nearly 75% in the new Länder and 60% in the old Länder. Altogether they had a 40% share of the country's total labor market. Men, in comparison, had a participation rate of about 87%. About 35% of all working women had children under the age of 18. Among mothers aged 25 to 34, about 42% were employed, while 52% of those aged 35 to 45 worked.

Discrimination in the Workplace

The German constitution prohibits discrimination on the basis of gender. Yet the Labor Ministry has acknowledged that women do not always receive equal pay for equal work. Several recent decisions by the National Labor Court have ruled in favor of women who sued their employers for equal pay.

The Second Equal Rights Act of 1994 was designed to help redress inequalities in the area of employment, especially in the civil service. It specifically increased the penalties for sexual harassment, whether in the public or private sector, and mandated that government agencies appoint commissioners for women's affairs and establish promotion plans for women. The law also required public agencies to give preference to women candidates with the same qualifications as men wherever women were underrepresented. Many individual states have enacted similar legislation.

In 1995, however, a landmark ruling by the European Court of Justice stated that Germany's Second Equal Rights Act gave women priority over men and thus violated the European Union's equal opportunities law. Although the court's ruling is not binding on its member nations, women's groups in Germany expressed dismay and planned to wage a campaign to amend the European Union law rather than revise the German law.

Areas of Employment

In both the old and new Länder, the great majority of working women, about 75%, are employed in service occupations. One difference between the two regions though, is the proportion of women at different levels of responsibility. In the old Länder only 11% of working women occupy managerial positions, while nearly 40% are employed at the lowest levels. In the new Länder 20% hold managerial posts, and only 22% are in the lowest-level jobs.

Throughout Germany women are sorely underrepresented in top-level decision-making government positions. In the federal ministries they make up 7% of heads of divisions, 5% of heads of directorates, and 3% of heads of directorates general. In the foreign service women occupy 12% of senior positions but less than 5% of all heads of missions abroad. In the judiciary 4 of the 16 judges on the Federal Constitutional Court are women, including the president. In general, the proportion of women judges is about 20%; of prosecutors, about 19%.

In education women account for 62% of primary and secondary school teachers; but in colleges and universities men predominate. Only 6% of professors are women. Before reunification, this figure was 5% in West Germany, 4% in East Germany.

In the German armed services women are generally limited to serving in civilian positions, usually in administration. Since 1975 women have been allowed to enlist as officers in the medical service corps, and by 1993 women accounted for 0.4% of all military personnel. The first woman general was appointed in 1994.

Approximately one-quarter of all businesses in Germany are run by women; in the new Länder the proportion is closer to one-third. Most of these businesses are in trade and service industries, though some are in manufacturing and crafts. In recent years increasing numbers of women have been starting their own businesses; by the mid-1990s almost one in three new enterprises was started by a woman.

WOMEN IN MAJOR OCCUPATIONAL GROUPS
Percentage of group, 1991

OCCUPATIONAL GROUP	OLD LÄNDER (WEST GERMANY)	NEW LÄNDER (EAST GERMANY)
Domestic work	97%	89%
Textiles	90%	94%
Personal care	85%	93%
Health care	85%	91%
Social work	81%	95%
Office work	67%	88%
Food preparation	64%	83%

Pay Differences

Women throughout Germany tend to be concentrated in lower-paying occupations and at lower levels than their male counterparts. In addition, many more women than men work part-time, and they take time off for childbearing and child raising. As a result, women generally earn less than men; in all nonagricultural industries their wages average about 76% of men's. Even among the self-employed, women tend to earn less than men. About 25% of all self-employed men are in the highest income bracket, compared with only 8% of women in this category.

Working Hours

About 33% of all working women have part-time jobs, compared with 3% of men. In the old Länder 35% of women work part-time, while in the new Länder this proportion is closer to 15%.

Women make up 93% of all part-time workers, even more in the old Länder, where the women who choose part-time work are mostly mothers of young children. In the new Länder female part-time workers tend to be mostly older women.

Maternity Leave and Benefits

Working women in Germany are entitled to maternity leave starting 6 weeks before the baby's due date and extending for 8 weeks following the birth (12 weeks in cases of premature or multiple births). During this period, the woman receives 100% of her salary and is protected from dismissal.

The government's child-raising allowance provides monthly payments, called *Kindergeld,* over a period of two years. The amount of the payment is determined by the family's income, and it can be claimed by whichever parent looks after the child.

Parental leave is designed to enable working mothers and fathers to stay at home or reduce their working hours to less than 19 hours a week. Such leave may extend up to three years, during which time the employee's job is guaranteed.

Child Care

Child-care facilities are surprisingly inadequate in Germany. As increasing numbers of women entered the labor force, the country was unable to meet the growing demand for child care. By the mid-1990s only a tiny percentage of toddlers were in nursery school, and 60% of children three to five years old were enrolled in preschool. The scarcity of day-care facilities, combined with the half-day schedule of the public schools, makes it difficult for German women to pursue a career while raising young children.

To help alleviate the child-care shortage, the German government recently mandated all state governments to provide child-care places for all children starting at age three. This policy, scheduled to be implemented by 1996, was especially onerous for the old Länder, where child-care facilities were far from adequate before reunification.

Unemployment

The overall unemployment rate for women in Germany in 1994 was 11.2%, compared with 8.3% for men. Reunification took an especially heavy toll on working women in the former East Germany. The industries in which women predominated—social work, teaching, health care, and retailing—all suffered tremendously in the transition from communism to a market economy, and large numbers of women lost their jobs. In 1994 more than two-thirds of the unemployed in the new Länder were women. The women's unemployment rate was 21.3%, compared with 9.5% for men.

Jobless rates have remained considerably lower in the old Länder, though there too women's rates have long been slightly higher than men's. The unemployment rate for women in 1994 was 8.4%, and women accounted for about 48% of the total unemployed. The jobless rate for men was 8.1%.

MARRIAGE AND DIVORCE

Although the marriage rate in Germany has been declining since reunification, and women and men are marrying later, traditional attitudes toward marriage and family still predominate. Among people aged 30 to 65, more than three-quarters are married and living with their spouse. Single-parent families have been increasing, though, and households headed by women account for 30% of all households in the new Länder, 12% in the old Länder.

Marriage

The legal minimum age for marriage is 18 for both women and men, 16 with parental consent. However, German couples tend to marry much later. The average age at first marriage for women is 26.1 years, for men, 28.5 years.

These are among the highest marriage ages in the world. Births to unmarried women account for 15% of all births.

Traditionally, German men have had authority over their wives and children. In West Germany, until 1958 a husband could legally terminate his wife's employment without notifying her. He also had the authority to make the final decision in all family matters. Although a 1958 law eliminated these patriarchal rights, it nevertheless stated that if the parents could not agree in matters concerning the children, the father had the final say. A 1977 reform of the Marriage and Family Law finally granted equal rights to women within the family. In 1994 a civil law gave each spouse the right to keep her or his surname.

Divorce

The divorce law was reformed in 1977 to replace the principle of guilt with the concept of irretrievable breakdown. A revised law, which took effect in 1987, provided support payments to the divorced spouse who could not obtain gainful employment because of child-raising obligations, ill health, or other reasons. The divorce rate in Germany is about 30, that is, for every 100 couples getting married each year, about 30 couples get divorced.

Children's Names

An unusual law affecting German families is the Law of Names, which was written into the civil code in 1900 and is still in effect. According to this law, a child's name must reflect its gender. Thus, there are boy's names, like Alexander and Daniel, and girl's names, such as Maria and Julia, but no "unisex" or ambiguous names, like Hemingway, which was declared unlawful in 1984.

FAMILY PLANNING

Contraception has long been legal and widely available in both the old and new Länder. However, many German women consider the recent changes in abortion legislation a major setback.

Fertility Rate

The fertility rate in Germany is 1.3 children per woman, one of the lowest in the world. The steepest decline in the birthrate has occurred in the new Länder, especially in the state of Brandenburg, where births have decreased by more than two-thirds since 1989. In the other new Länder births have dropped by more than half. The country's proportion of births to teenagers, about 3% of total births, is one of the lowest in the world.

BIRTHS BY AGE Percentage of total births, 1991	
AGE	PERCENT
Under 15	<1%
15–19	3%
20–24	22%
25–29	39%
30–34	29%
35–39	8%
40–44	1%
45–49	<1%

High unemployment and economic uncertainty are suggested as the primary reasons for the declining birthrate, a phenomenon also seen in other formerly communist countries. In an attempt to reverse this trend, the government of Brandenburg started offering payments equivalent to about $650 to couples for every baby they have. Birthrates in the old Länder have also dropped in recent years but not nearly as precipitously as in the new Länder.

Contraception

Throughout Germany, about 75% of all couples of childbearing age use some form of contraception, one of the world's highest rates of contraceptive use. By far the most popular method is the birth control pill.

CONTRACEPTIVE USE Percentage of couples of childbearing age*	
METHOD	PERCENT
Birth control pill	59%
Intrauterine devices (IUDs)	6%
Condom	4%
Traditional methods	3%
Diaphragm, other	2%
Sterilization, female and male	1%
*Estimated, 1992.	

Sterilization, which was never widely used for contraception, has started to gain popularity in the last few years, especially in the new Länder. In Brandenburg alone, the number of sterilizations climbed from about 400 to over 6,000 annually.

Abortion

Since 1993 Germany has had one of Europe's most restrictive abortion laws. Technically, all abortions are illegal; however, neither the woman nor

ABORTION RATES
Percentage of total abortions, 1993

AGE	PERCENT	MARITAL STATUS	PERCENT
Under 15	<1%	Single	39%
15–18	2%	Married	53%
19–25	23%	Widowed	<1%
26–30	27%	Divorced	6%
31–35	24%		
36–40	15%		
41–45	7%		
Over 45	<1%		

the physician is punishable if the woman has undergone mandatory counseling followed by a three-day "reflection period." There are about 1,700 recognized counseling centers throughout the country, and in addition to providing counseling on abortion, they offer information on family planning and other personal matters.

In 1989, before reunification, 80,000 abortions were performed in East Germany, where they were available on request. About the same number of registered, legal abortions were performed in West Germany, which had a more restrictive abortion law. In 1993, following the court's new abortion ruling, the total number of abortions in both the old and new Länder dropped to just over 110,000. One of the main reasons for this decrease was that abortions performed for social reasons, the category that had previously accounted for 90% of all abortions in West Germany, were no longer paid for by the state insurance system.

Sex Education

The 1992 abortion ruling also included a section mandating the Federal Central Office for Health Education to develop sex education materials for schools, vocational training institutes, and other educational facilities. These materials cover such topics as pregnancy and contraception. Information on the transmission and prevention of AIDS was introduced into the curriculum in 1989.

WOMEN'S HEALTH

The German people enjoy a high standard of health care. The average life expectancy for German women is about 79.1 years, up from 77.8 years a decade ago. For men the comparable figures are 72.7 years and 71.2 years. The overall

LEADING CAUSES OF DEATH
Percentage of total deaths, 1993

CAUSE	WOMEN	MEN
Cardiovascular diseases	53%	44%
Cancer	22%	26%
Breast	4%	—
Lung	2%	7%
Cervix	1%	—
Respiratory diseases	4%	5%
Accidents	2%	4%
Suicide	<1%	2%
Homicide	<1%	<1%

maternal mortality rate in Germany is 22 deaths for every 100,000 live births, although the rate is somewhat higher in the new Länder.

About 90% of the population belong to the public health insurance system, which provides basic medical care, including maternity services. Most of the remaining 10% of the population are privately insured or covered under a pension fund or similar program.

Leading Causes of Death

As in other highly industrialized countries, the leading causes of death for both women and men are heart disease, stroke, and various forms of cancer.

Smoking

Smoking is fairly common in Germany. About 27% of all women smoke, compared with 42% of men. Women make up about one-third of the country's approximately 17 million smokers.

AIDS

Of the 11,500 cases of AIDS reported by mid-1994, 9.5% were among women. Of the 64,100 recorded cases of HIV infection women accounted for 16%. Most of the affected women were between the ages of 20 and 30; for men the highest rate occurred among those aged 30 to 40.

The most prevalent mode of HIV transmission among women is intravenous drug use. Sexual contact with a male partner is responsible for about 27% of cases, and contaminated blood transfusions account for about 12%.

Eating Disorders

A growing number of German women and girls are afflicted with eating disorders. It is estimated that 60,000 women in the old Länder are anorexic, 400,000 are compulsive eaters, and 500,000 suffer from bulimia. Comparable figures for the new Länder are not available.

VIOLENCE AGAINST WOMEN

Violence against women is a major concern throughout the country. In 1992 the federal government issued a comprehensive report on violent acts against women, and in 1994 it launched a major public education campaign through church groups and schools.

Domestic Violence

It is estimated that about 4 million German women a year are abused by their husbands or partners. Officially, neither the authorities nor the law condone domestic violence; yet the police and prosecutors tend to regard wife battering as a private matter, and abusers are rarely brought to trial. Recently, the federal Ministry on Women and Youth embarked on a major research project to obtain information on the incidence of wife abuse and other acts of violence against women. A special report was issued in 1995.

Before reunification, there were no shelters for battered wives in East Germany, where domestic violence was rarely discussed and largely ignored. West Germany had about 120 refuges before reunification. By 1995 there were more than 330 shelters throughout the country, more than 100 of them in the new Länder.

Rape

In 1994 there were 6,095 reported cases of rape, down slightly from 6,376 the previous year. Rape has long been a criminal act in both the new and old Länder, punishable by from six months to 10 years in prison. Marital rape, however, is not considered a crime, and it is believed that one in five wives has experienced at least one incident. Germany is one of the few countries where sexual assault victims are entitled to financial compensation by the government.

Prostitution

Prostitution is legal in Germany, though there are laws prohibiting trafficking in women. In the former West Germany brothels were limited to certain areas and hours, and prostitutes were required to have regular medical checkups. In the former East Germany prostitution was illegal, punishable by imprisonment.

FOR ADDITIONAL INFORMATION ON WOMEN

Deutscher Frauenrat
(German Women's Council)
Simrockstrasse 5
53113 Bonn, Germany
Telephone: 228-223-008
Fax: 228-218-819

Embassy of Germany
4645 Reservoir Road, NW
Washington, DC 20007, United States
Telephone: 202-298-4000

German Information Center
950 Third Avenue, 24th floor
New York, NY 10022, United States
Telephone: 212-888-9840

Women's International Studies Europe
Zaehringerstrasse 14
6900 Heidelberg 1, Germany
Telephone: 6221–23253

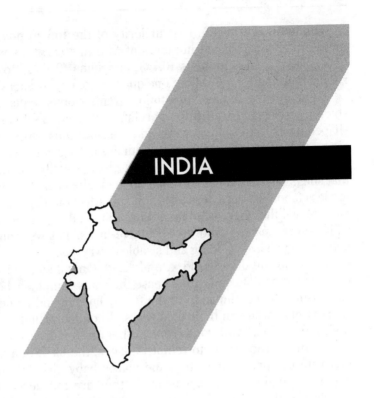

INDIA

Population: *931.0 million*
▼ Women per 100 men: *93*
Women's voting rights: *1950*
Women in legislature: *9%*
Women's share of work force: *25%*
Literacy rates: women—*39%;* men—*64%*
Life expectancy: women—*59.1 years;* men—*58.1 years*
Average number of children: *3.6*
Maternal mortality rate: *570*

WOMAN NOBEL PRIZE WINNER		
Mother Teresa	Peace	1979

India, in the heart of Asia, is the world's second most populous country (after China) and has one of the oldest civilizations. Colonized by Britain in the 1700s, India's struggle for independence began toward the end of the 19th century. It intensified after World War I, and in 1947 the new nation was created.

Hindus make up the vast majority of the Indian population, 83%, but there are also significant numbers of Muslims (11%), as well as Christians (2%), Sikhs (2%), Buddhists (0.7%), and Jains (0.4%). Most Indians live in rural communities; only about one-quarter are city dwellers.

Although the Indian constitution grants women equal rights with men, strong patriarchal traditions persist, and women's lives continue to be shaped by centuries-old customs and classifications: caste, class, region, ethnicity, and religion. In most Indian families a daughter is viewed as a liability, a burden, and from early childhood a girl is usually conditioned to believe that she is inferior and subordinate to men. She is the "lesser" child—receiving less food, less care, less attention and affection. Especially in rural areas, parents feel that there is no point in sending a daughter to school, since she will soon be married and go off to live in her in-laws' home. And she will need an expensive wedding and sizable dowry.

Sons, on the other hand, are idolized. Only a son can light the funeral pyres of his parents and thus release the souls from their bodies; only a son can ensure the continuation of the family lineage and name; only a son will support his parents in their final years. A common Hindu wedding blessing wishes the bride, "May you be the mother of a hundred sons."

From crowded cities to remote villages, the birth of a daughter is often met with disappointment. In some places baby girls are allowed to die of neglect or malnutrition; occasionally they are murdered. Of the approximately 15 million baby girls born in India every year, nearly one-quarter will not live to see their 15th birthday.

HISTORY OF THE WOMEN'S MOVEMENT

Women's groups in India started emerging in the early 1900s, and at first focused on social reform, particularly such issues as *sati* (the burning alive of a widow on her husband's funeral pyre), child marriage, access to education, and working conditions. With the rise of nationalism, more and more women joined the struggle for independence. Bolstered by this increased activism, women's groups campaigned vigorously—and successfully—for social and political equality with men. The 1950 constitution gave them this equality, granting voting rights to all women and men over the age of 21.

The 1960s and 1970s witnessed the rise of many grassroots women's movements protesting local problems, such as rising prices, the sale of alcohol, and unfair housing practices. Since the 1980s, attention has focused more on discrimination and sexual harassment in employment, inadequate health care, and the increasing violence against women—specifically, the abortion of female fetuses, the killing of baby girls, dowry deaths, the revival of *sati*, and wife battering.

The government's response has been a concerted effort to overcome these problems. As early as 1971, it appointed the Committee on the Status of Women in India, and the country's sixth Five Year Plan, covering 1980 to 1985, was the first to include a chapter on women. In 1985 the Department of Women and Child Development was created, and in 1992 the National Commission for Women was established to study and monitor all constitutional and legal safeguards for women, review existing legislation, suggest revisions, and investigate complaints involving women's rights.

WOMEN IN POLITICS

Despite the country's deeply ingrained patriarchal attitudes, India is one of the few countries ever to have elected a woman as prime minister: Indira Gandhi served from 1966 until 1977 and again from 1980 until her assassination in 1984. (Although not related to Mohandas Gandhi, the nonviolent activist who led the country's struggle against British rule, she was the daughter of Jawaharlal Nehru, the nation's first prime minister, who served from 1947 until his death in 1964.)

With the exception of Indira Gandhi, Indian women have been noticeably absent in elected political office, especially at the highest levels. Women were first elected to Parliament in 1952, when they accounted for about 5% of the total members. By 1996 this proportion had risen to only 9%, and only 1 woman sat in the 25-member cabinet: Kanti Singh, minister of human resources. However, there were 5 women in the 52-member Council of Ministers, and 5 women ambassadors out of 120. In the entire foreign service, including ambassadors, women made up nearly 9% of the total personnel. At the state level, only one out of 25 governors was a woman.

At the local level, a 1993 constitutional amendment required every state to guarantee that all local elected bodies, urban as well as rural, reserve one-third of their seats for women. The aim of this amendment was to involve large numbers of women throughout the country in the political decision-making process.

WOMEN'S EDUCATION

The Indian constitution calls for eight years of compulsory education for girls and boys aged 6 to 14. However, enrollment rates vary tremendously. In some states primary school enrollment for girls is 100%, while in others it barely reaches 60%.

Dropout rates are higher for girls than for boys. Girls are often kept at home to perform household chores and care for younger siblings. Half the girls who start primary school drop out before completing it, most during the first year. Of those who go on to middle school, another 20% do not finish, and of the remaining girls who enter secondary school, 10% leave before graduation. To help boost school attendance, some regions have opened local courtyard schools just for girls and have started using elderly women to escort the girls to and from school and also to take care of their younger siblings.

Despite high dropout rates, girls' school enrollments have increased considerably over the past several decades. Correspondingly, literacy rates for women have also risen. Yet women still lag far behind men, and rural women are twice as likely to be illiterate as their urban counterparts. There are also tremendous regional differences. Women in the state of Kerala have the highest literacy rate, 86%, while those in Rajasthan have the lowest, 20%.

In higher education female students tend to study psychology, social anthropology, and education—all traditionally regarded as women's subjects.

FEMALE ENROLLMENT Percentage of student body			
LEVEL	1951	1971	1993
Primary school	28%	37%	43%
Middle school	16%	29%	39%
Secondary school	14%	26%	34%
Higher education	10%	20%	33%

LITERACY RATES Percentage of total population		
YEAR	WOMEN	MEN
1951	9%	27%
1961	15%	40%
1971	22%	46%
1981	28%	53%
1991	39%	64%

They are found less frequently in natural and applied science courses. Women make up 31% of students in medical and health-related programs, 20% in commercial and business administration classes, and 9% of those in law school.

WOMEN'S EMPLOYMENT

Women in India make up about one-quarter of the work force. Over the past few decades, the percentage of working-age women entering the labor force has been rising steadily, reaching 31% in 1995. The participation rate of men aged 15 to 64, in comparison, has remained fairly steady, at about 90%. Rural women are more than twice as likely to work as their urban counterparts.

Employment and Poverty

One of the most serious problems facing India is widespread poverty. According to government estimates, three-quarters of India's poor live in extreme poverty, a figure that translates to 8% to 10% of all adults and 20% to 25% of all children.

In poor households the woman's ability to work is often the family's only means of survival, and working women are the critical factor in moving their families out of poverty. Compared with men, women contribute larger shares of their earnings to support their families. Raising a woman's income translates directly into better nutrition and health care for herself, her husband, and her children.

Government programs to combat poverty have concentrated on moving more women into the work force through massive adult literacy and training projects, increasing health and child-care facilities, and improving access to credit. One of the most successful nongovernmental programs is the women's bank that was founded two decades ago in the city of Ahmedabad (the capital of Gujarat) by the Self-Employed Women's Association (SEWA). Run entirely by women for women, the SEWA Cooperative Bank enables its customers to achieve economic independence by opening savings accounts for them and providing low-interest loans. Many of the bank's customers are illiterate, using only a thumbprint to sign papers, and they request only small sums of money, sometimes as little as 500 rupees (about $15) to start or expand their businesses. Because few women in the community own land or other property, the bank allows them to use their jewelry as collateral. Since its inception, the SEWA bank has helped thousands of poor women, and similar banks have begun to appear in other communities.

Discrimination in the Workplace

The Indian constitution, supported by legislation, prohibits discrimination against women and endorses the principle of equal pay for equal work. Despite these provisions, however, discrimination and sexual harassment are widespread, though rarely mentioned, problems. In addition, the vast numbers of women who work outside the formal sector are not covered by these or other labor laws and thus have no job security or benefits.

Areas of Employment

The great majority of working women, about 80%, are employed in agriculture and related fields. The remaining female workers are employed chiefly in various service industries. Many work in sales and clerical jobs; rarely do they occupy high-level positions. For every 100 male managers and administrators there are just 2 women in similar positions, one of the world's lowest ratios in this occupational category. Indian women fare somewhat better in the occupational group composed of professional and technical workers; 26 women for every 100 men. Yet this ratio too places India among the world's lowest-ranked countries in this category.

One reason is that Indian women are poorly represented in the field of education. In most other countries women predominate in teaching, especially at the lower levels, but in India only 29% of primary and 33% of secondary school teachers are women. The proportion of female teachers in all institutions of higher education is 21%, 19% in universities. One traditionally male-dominated field into which women have just started to make inroads is the military. Since 1992 women have been allowed to enlist, although only in nonmilitary jobs. By 1995 women made up a tiny fraction of total military personnel: 1 woman to every 6,000 men. In the national police service nearly 2% of all personnel were women.

Pay Differences

The Indian constitution mandates equal pay for equal work, and this principle was reinforced by the 1975 Equal Remuneration Act. However, this law does not apply to agriculture, the area where most women are employed and where the government has even legislated gender-based pay scales with lower wages for female workers. Although official statistics are not available, it is estimated that women in India probably earn an average of about 50% of men's wages.

Maternity Leave and Benefits

Working women in India are entitled to maternity benefits under the Employees' State Insurance Plan, which provides a 90-day leave with pay equivalent to the woman's normal salary or daily wage. Women working in industries not covered by this plan, such as manufacturing and mining, are eligible for similar benefits under a different law. In practice, however, it is not unusual for a woman to be fired when she becomes pregnant.

Child Care

Under the Factories Act of 1976, workplaces that employ 30 women or more, including casual and contract laborers, must provide a child-care facility. But this law is not strictly enforced and does not cover the many women working outside the formal sector.

Unemployment

In the mid-1990s the official overall unemployment rate for Indian women was 1.5%, compared with 2.1% for men. Urban workers had much higher jobless rates than those in rural regions. In urban areas the rates were 4.7% for women and 4.5% for men, while in rural regions the comparable rates were 0.3% and 1.1% respectively.

MARRIAGE AND DIVORCE

India has a number of different laws concerning marriage and divorce. In the mid-1950s the Hindu personal laws, which apply to all Hindus, Buddhists, Sikhs, and Jains, were completely overhauled, banning polygamy and giving women rights to inheritance, adoption, and divorce. The Muslim population has its own code of personal laws, which differs considerably from that of the Hindus. Polygamy, for example, is permitted, and a Muslim husband is entitled to as many as four wives. A Muslim wife, on the other hand, may have only one husband.

But despite the various official laws protecting women's rights, traditional patriarchal attitudes still prevail and are strengthened and perpetuated within the home. In most Indian families a husband has complete authority over his wife and children.

Marriage

Marriage in India is considered essential for every girl, no matter what her class, caste, religion, or ethnicity. Most marriages, even among the wealthy upper class, are arranged by the parents of the bride and groom. However, many marriages are said to be "semi-arranged," that is, although the young woman's parents may conduct the search for likely candidates—sometimes through professional matchmakers or matrimonial advertisements in newspapers—she has the option of vetoing her parents' choices.

According to official records, the average age at first marriage for women is 19.5 years; for men, 23.4 years. By the age of 25, 9 out of 10 Indian women are married. It is interesting to note that since the beginning of the 20th century, the average age of Indian brides has increased 6.4 years, while that of grooms has risen only 3.4 years.

A 1976 amendment to the Child Marriage Restraint Act raised the minimum legal age for marriage from 15 to 18 for women and from 18 to 21 for men. However, in many communities illegal child marriages are still common and in some rural areas nearly half the girls between 10 and 14 are

AVERAGE AGE AT MARRIAGE
In years

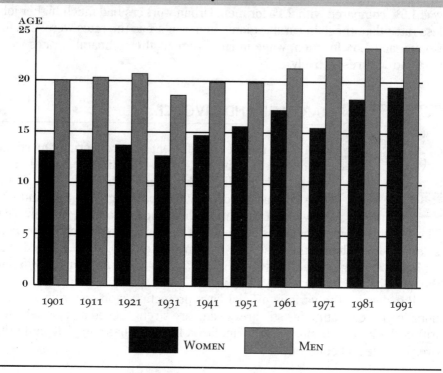

married. Usually, the young brides continue living at home until they reach 16 or 17, at which time there may be a second marriage ceremony when they move into their in-laws' home.

Dowries

Another Indian tradition that persists even though it is banned by law is the dowry. Years ago, a dowry consisted of gold jewelry, fine silk saris, and other gifts given to the bride by her family. It was considered a form of compensation because a daughter could not inherit a share of her parents' property. Today lavish gifts are still given, often along with large sums of money, and parents may start saving for a daughter's dowry soon after she is born. It is estimated that the average dowry today is equivalent to five times the family's annual income and that the high cost of weddings and dowries is a major cause of indebtedness among India's poor.

The Dowry Prohibition Act of 1961 imposed stiff fines and a minimum sentence of five years in prison for anyone giving or requesting a dowry.

Recent amendments to the law expanded the definition of a dowry to include gifts and requests for gifts after the marriage, not just at the time of betrothal. However, the law is rarely enforced and the practice remains widespread.

Divorce

Divorce is rare in India and is considered a shameful admission of a woman's failure as a wife and daughter-in-law. In 1990 divorced women made up a miniscule 0.08% of the total female population.

A 1976 amendment to the Special Marriage Act added mutual consent as a cause for divorce. Other grounds for divorce include cruelty, adultery, and desertion. Under Islamic law a Muslim husband may divorce his wife unilaterally, a privilege not afforded his wife.

FAMILY PLANNING

India's population has been growing rapidly for decades, nearly doubling over the past 30 years. In 1951 a family planning program was launched in an attempt to curtail population growth, but acceptance has been slow, and the birthrate has declined only slightly.

Fertility Rate

The fertility rate in India is 3.6 children per woman, down from 4.5 children in 1981 and 5.9 in 1960. Most births are to women in their 20s, though births to teenagers are also high, accounting for 11% of all births. There are also wide variations among different regions; urban birthrates are considerably lower than those of rural areas. In 1992 the urban birthrate was 24.0 births per 1,000 women, compared with 31.1 in rural regions.

Contraception

From 1970 to 1990 the percentage of couples of childbearing age using contraception rose from 10% to about 45%.

A recent innovation in the area of contraception research in India has been the development of an antipregnancy vaccine. It prevents a fertilized egg from implanting in the uterus by temporarily stimulating the body to produce antibodies against chorionic gonadotropin, a hormone essential for

CONTRACEPTIVE USE
Percentage of couples
of childbearing age, 1990

METHOD	PERCENT
Sterilization, female and male	30%
Condom	6%
Traditional methods	5%
Intrauterine devices (IUDs)	2%
Birth control pill	1%

pregnancy. Currently, the vaccine is being tested among a small number of Indian women.

Because many Indian couples are reluctant to use contraceptives or have no access to them, local governments are devising other incentives to induce them to limit the size of their families. In the state of Tamil Nadu, for example, officials are offering a special benefit to families that have one or two daughters and no sons. If one parent agrees to undergo sterilization, the family will receive regular payments for each daughter as long as she remains in school. When she reaches her 20th birthday, she will receive a lump sum that she can use for her dowry or as tuition for higher education. In its first year 4,000 families enrolled in the program.

Abortion

Prior to the passage of the Medical Termination of Pregnancy Act of 1971, abortions were legal only to save the woman's life. This legislation expanded the grounds for terminating pregnancy to include preservation of the woman's physical or mental health, cases resulting from rape or incest, or when the fetus suffers severe abnormalities. Abortions performed in public hospitals are free, and all documents are kept confidential. Since the law went into effect, it is estimated that 250,000 legal abortions have been performed annually.

Illegal abortions, however, are thought to far outnumber the legal procedures; some estimates put the number as high as 6 million a year. One reason is that the legal procedures are limited to certain approved medical institutions, and in the countryside, where most Indian people live, these facilities are few and far between. Many rural women are compelled to seek the help of local midwives and other untrained practitioners, who perform these abortions with crude instruments under insanitary conditions.

Another reason for the high number of illegal procedures is that Indian law specifically prohibits abortions for the purpose of sex selection. Yet since the mid-1970s, when parents found that modern medical techniques could determine the sex of a fetus and thus enable them to identify and abort female fetuses, the practice has become commonplace. To help curb this trend, the government enacted legislation in 1994 prohibiting anyone from conducting or requesting a test to determine the sex of a fetus. Violators are subject to a stiff fine and imprisonment of up to three years. However, enforcement is difficult, and the practice is still widespread.

Government officials even suspect that the dispproportionate abortion of female fetuses may be a major underlying cause of the recent decline in the nation's sex ratio. In 1971 there were 930 females for every 1,000 males. A decade later this figure had increased to 934, but by 1991, instead of continuing to rise, the ratio dropped to 927, lower than the 1971 figure. This sex ratio is one of the lowest in the world.

WOMEN'S HEALTH

Although health care in India has improved somewhat in recent decades, it is still poor, as indicated by low life expectancy and high maternal mortality rates. Poor nutrition, inadequate health facilities, and excessive childbearing exact a heavy toll on Indian women.

The average life expectancy for women in India is 59.1 years; for men, 58.1 years. Although these figures are not very high, they represent a tremendous increase from just two decades ago, when life expectancy was 44.7 years for females and 46.4 years for males. And at the beginning of the 20th century, life expectancy was only 23.3 years for women and 22.6 years for men.

During the 1970s the Indian government launched a number of health care programs aimed specifically at girls and women. The Family Welfare Program included medical care for pregnant women and their babies, and the expansion of a network of clinics to provide greater access to health care. By 1994 there were 21,000 primary health centers, 131,000 subcenters, and 2,000 community centers. Yet maternal mortality in India is still high: 570 deaths for every 100,000 live births. It is estimated that pregnancy-related deaths account for about one-quarter of all fatalities among women aged 15 to 29 and are related to the large number of unsafe illegal abortions.

Leading Causes of Death

The use of vaccines and other drugs over the past several decades has greatly reduced mortality rates from smallpox, cholera, malaria, and similar diseases. Yet infectious diseases remain the major cause of death among both women and men.

BIRTH AND DEATH RATES
Births per 1,000 women; deaths per 1,000 population

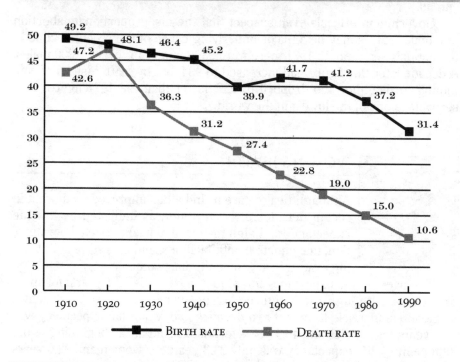

BIRTH RATE ■   DEATH RATE ■

Smoking

Smoking is a serious health problem in India, but not among women; only 3% of women smoke, compared with 40% of men.

AIDS

By 1996 India had the world's largest number of people infected with the AIDS virus. As many as 1.75 million people were infected, with women accounting for an estimated 23%. Officials fear that by the end of the century, 1 million Indians will be sick with AIDS and from 20 to 50 million will be infected. Heterosexual relations are the main mode of HIV transmission in India, though infection through intravenous drug use is becoming more common. Contaminated blood products account for about 12% of infections, and homosexual relations for less than 1%.

With the rising incidence of HIV infection, an unusual social phenome-

LEADING CAUSES OF DEATH Percentage of total deaths, 1985		
CAUSE	WOMEN	MEN
Infectious diseases	41%	41%
Circulatory disorders	11%	13%
Injury	6%	7%
Cancer	4%	4%
Pregnancy-related	2%	—

non has been noticed in some health clinics: matchmaking for HIV-positive women and men. Marriage is very important in Indian society, and this sort of matrimonial brokerage service allows infected young women and men to meet each other, marry, and even have children, though there is a 30% to 40% chance that a child would be infected with the virus.

VIOLENCE AGAINST WOMEN

The past decade has witnessed a growing pattern of violence against women, especially domestic violence. Government agencies, along with nongovernmental organizations and women's groups, are actively confronting the problem, seeking changes in legislation and law enforcement policies as well as bringing the issue into the open.

One recent innovation was the creation of special women's courts, with female judges and prosecutors, just to handle cases of violence against women, from sexual harassment to murder. One goal of the courts is to shorten the judicial process from the usual 10 years to one or two. The courts were first established in New Delhi, and after a highly successful one-year trial period during which they handled about 1,000 cases, they were expanded to other cities.

Female Infanticide

Because of the tremendous preference for sons over daughters, the killing of baby girls is not uncommon in some parts of India. It is estimated that as many as 10,000 infant girls are killed every year. Sometimes the baby is abandoned or allowed to die of starvation. In other cases she may be poisoned with the milky sap of a local shrub or fertilizer chemicals. Occasionally, the baby is fed dry unhulled grains of rice that penetrate her windpipe, and in some cases, she may be strangled or smothered.

Indian law bans infanticide and imposes penalties of life imprisonment or death. However, few cases are brought to trial, especially in rural areas, and those that do reach the courts seldom result in conviction.

Domestic Violence

The most dramatic form of domestic violence in India is the physical abuse, torture, and even murder of young brides whose husbands or in-laws are dissatisfied with their dowries. In a typical dowry dispute, the groom's family physically harasses the young woman and may even kill her or provoke her to commit suicide. Sometimes, especially if the wife is burned to death, it is passed off as a kitchen accident. Most dowry deaths occur among lower- and middle-class families, but the practice is found in all castes and religious groups.

Government concern about dowry deaths led to a 1986 amendment to the penal code, which stated that in every unnatural death of a woman during the first seven years of marriage, if cruelty or harassment could be proven, the court must presume that her husband or in-laws were responsible. Despite this amendment, convictions are rare. Yet in 1994 the government reported a decline in dowry deaths, to 4,300 from nearly 5,400 the previous year. However, other estimates put the 1994 figure closer to 6,200 incidents, and for the first nine months of 1995 the government reported 7,300 dowry deaths.

Rape

About 10,000 cases of rape are reported every year, and approximately one-quarter of them involve girls under the age of 16. But the great majority of sexual assaults are never reported. The victims are ashamed, the police are notoriously insensitive, and the criminal justice system is slow to act. Although the penalty for rape is severe—seven years in prison—convictions are rare.

Sati

Sati is the centuries-old custom in which a widow is burned alive on her husband's funeral pyre. It has been illegal since 1829, but incidents continue to occur, and in the 1980s, with a resurgence of Hindu fundamentalism in parts of the country, some religious leaders—and even some women—have pressed for the legalization of this practice.

The turning point came in 1987, when an 18-year-old widow in the village of Deorala in Rajasthan chose to have herself burned alive on her husband's funeral pyre. The site soon attracted thousands of religious pilgrims, who worshipped the young woman as a goddess. Women's groups, mobilized by this event, mounted a tremendous anti-*sati* campaign, and later that year the government passed the Commission of Sati Prevention Act to prevent the practice and curb its glorification. Under this law anyone who abets the commission of *sati* may be sentenced to life imprisonment or death.

Prostitution

Prostitution itself is not illegal in India, but the Suppression of Immoral Traffic Act of 1956 prohibited trafficking in women and girls for the purposes of prostitution. In 1986 the law was revised to cover all persons who are sexually exploited for commercial purposes and to increase the penalties. The new law also mandated that prostitutes be interrogated by women police officers or social workers.

But despite the government's attempts to curtail prostitution, it remains a thriving industry in many large cities where there are enormous numbers of impoverished young women. Estimates put the number of prostitutes in India at about 2 million, with 400,000 thought to be under the age of 18.

FOR ADDITIONAL INFORMATION ON WOMEN

Center for Women's Development Studies
25, Bhai Virsingh Marg
New Delhi 110 001, Delhi, India
Telephone: 11-374-5530
Fax: 11-374-6705

Consulate General of India
Information Section
3 East 64th Street
New York, NY 10021, United States
Telephone: 212-879-8048

Embassy of India
2107 Massachusetts Avenue, NW
Washington, DC 20008, United States
Telephone: 202-939-7000

Research Center for Women's Studies
SNDT Women's University
Santa Cruz, (West)
Juhu Road
Bombay 400 049, India
Telephone: 22-612-8462

Tata Institute of Social Sciences
Women's Studies Unit
P.O. Box 8313, Sion-Trombay Road
Deonar, Bombay 400 088, India
Telephone: 22-551-0400

ISRAEL

Population: *5.8 million*
Women per 100 men: *102*
Women's voting rights: *1948*
Women in legislature: *8%*
Women's share of work force: *42%*
Literacy rates: women—*89%;* men—*95%*
Life expectancy: women—*78.5 years;* men—*75.1 years*
Average number of children: *2.8*
▲ Maternal mortality rate: *7*

Israel is a small Middle Eastern country located at the eastern end of the Mediterranean Sea. It was established in 1948 after a decades-long campaign by Jews around the world to create a national homeland. The new nation was formed from part of Palestine, which had been under British control since the end of World War I. As soon as its independence was declared, however, Israel's Arab neighbors rejected the existence of the new state and immediately attacked its settlements. The continued contest over territory, fueled by religious differences with the Muslim Middle East, compelled Israel to spend much of the next four decades at war. However, by the mid-1990s several historic peace agreements had been signed, including one giving limited self-rule to Palestinians in Gaza and the West Bank, two territories that Israel captured during war with Egypt and Jordan in 1967.

The great majority of Israel's population, 82%, are Jewish; 14% are Muslim; and there are also small Christian and Druze minorities. Among the Jewish population, approximately one-third are Orthodox (strictly observant of religious laws and customs). Because Israel was founded as a Jewish homeland, and religious parties have always been a political force in coalition governments, religion plays a major role in all spheres of life, and many issues concerning women—marriage, divorce, family matters—are largely determined by religious law.

HISTORY OF THE WOMEN'S MOVEMENT

The women's movement in Israel dates back to before 1900, when large numbers of Jews from Russia and other eastern European countries began settling in Palestine. These immigrants called themselves Zionists, after Mount Zion in Jerusalem. The Jewish women who immigrated at this time were less concerned with women's rights than with building the new Jewish community.

The first formal women's groups started appearing in the early 1900s, during the second wave of immigration. These settlers created a type of communal living system, called a *kibbutz,* in which everyone labored equally. Initially, however, women were assigned traditional female roles, in the kitchen and laundry, and were excluded from decisions about communal affairs. Resentful of their subordinate position and unequal participation, a group of women activists met in 1911 to articulate the problems of women workers. They believed that equality with men could be achieved by training women to perform the same jobs as men. To free them from the daily tasks of child care so that they could spend more time working, these women instituted a system of collective child care in which the women of the *kibbutz* rotated the responsibility of caring for the children.

The 1950s and 1960s saw a massive influx of new immigrants to Israel, largely from North Africa, and many of these new women became factory workers, clerks, and other low-skilled laborers. Through the mid-1970s the women's movement focused on improving working conditions as well as women's status and political representation.

The participation of many women in the 1973 Yom Kippur War resulted in dramatic changes in attitudes toward women. By the late 1970s, the feminist movement gained considerable momentum and political influence. The first national feminist conference was held in 1978.

From the mid-1980s through the early 1990s, women's groups turned their attention to the assimilation of new immigrant groups, specifically, the large influx of Jews from the Soviet Union and the two airlifts of Ethiopian Jews in 1984–1985 and 1991. Today Israeli women's groups continue to lobby for a wide range of issues, from eliminating discrimination to increasing employment opportunities and focusing attention on domestic violence.

Although Israel has no ministry dealing exclusively with women's affairs, a Knesset (parliament) Committee for the Advancement of the Status of Women was recently created to deal with women's rights and representation, marital laws, economic opportunities for women, violence against women, and similar issues. In addition, an adviser to the prime minister on the status of women recommends legislative, administrative, and other measures as well as coordinating the government's policies and activities concerning the issue of women's status.

WOMEN IN POLITICS

With the notable exception of Golda Meir, Israel's only woman prime minister, who served from 1969 to 1974, Israeli women have been consistently underrepresented in both elected and appointed office. Although women have held the right to vote since Israel became a nation in 1948, the Knesset has never consisted of more than 10% women, and that percentage was reached only once, in 1955. In the election of 1996 only 9 women were elected to the 120-seat legislature, accounting for slightly less than 8% of the total membership.

In the cabinet appointed by Prime Minister Netanyahu following his election in 1996, only 1 out of 18 ministerial positions (6%) was held by a woman: Limor Livnat, communications minister. In the foreign service, only four women served as ambassadors. At the local level, no municipality or local council was headed by a woman, and although women had been elected to 68% of these governing units, only 11% of all elected local officials were women. Nevertheless, this was an increase from 4% in 1950.

WOMEN'S EDUCATION

Education in Israel is compulsory for all children aged 5 to 16 and is free for all children up to age 18. Preschool is available for children aged three to six. At the primary school level, 72% of Jewish students attend secular schools, with the balance attending religious schools. Arab education is administered separately; Israeli Arabs follow the same basic curriculum, but it is taught in Arabic and includes Arab and Druze lit-

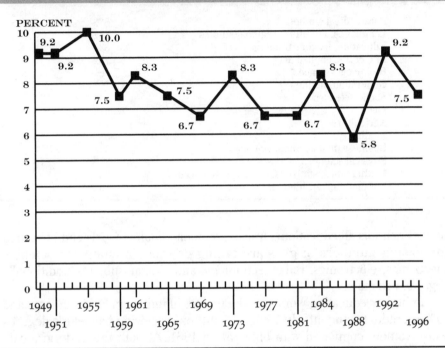

WOMEN IN THE KNESSET
Percentage of total members.

erature and history. In 1947 less than one-third of Arab and Druze children attended school, and only about 22% of them were girls. Today virtually all girls between the ages of 5 and 16 are in school.

Overall, the literacy rate for Israeli women is 89%; for men, 95%. On average, women attend school for 11.7 years and men for 11.9 years. Among the Jewish population, female students spend an average of 12.0 years in school, while males spend 12.1 years. Among the Arab and Druze populations, the comparable figures are 9.0 and 10.2 years.

At all levels of education, the participation rates of boys and girls are very similar, with female students predominating slightly in academic secondary schools, and nearly equaling male students in technical-vocational secondary schools. In intermediate and sec-

FEMALE ENROLLMENT
Percentage of student body, 1992

LEVEL	PERCENT
Primary school	49%
Secondary school	51%
Higher education	53%

WOMEN UNIVERSITY DEGREE RECIPIENTS
Percentage of subject area, 1992

SUBJECT AREA	PERCENT
Paramedical studies	87%
Languages, literature, regional studies	84%
Education, teacher training	83%
Art, crafts, applied arts	79%
Biological sciences	66%
General humanities	56%
Social sciences	54%
Law	41%
Agriculture	40%
Medicine	38%
Business, management science	33%
Physical sciences	33%
Mathematics, statistics, computer sciences	32%
Engineering, architecture	16%

ondary schools all educational tracks are open equally to girls and boys, and increasing numbers of girls are taking courses in computer science, mechanics, electronics, radar technology, and similar subjects traditionally regarded as male.

In higher education women make up 56% of undergraduate students and 51% of graduate students. In 1992, 52% of those receiving bachelor's degrees were women, compared with only 25% in 1961. At both the undergraduate and graduate levels, education, humanities and paramedical courses were overwhelmingly composed of women, while few women were enrolled in engineering and other technological fields. At the postgraduate level, women received 46% of master's degrees but only 3.5% of doctoral degrees.

Since 1995, a special curriculum addressing gender equality has been included in the Israeli school system, from preschool through college. Its primary aim is to prevent the use of stereotypes and male-dominated language by teachers as well as in textbooks and other educational materials.

WOMEN'S EMPLOYMENT

In 1993, 43% of working-age Israeli women were in the labor force, up from 21% in 1954, and by far the highest percentage of female participation in the Middle East. Israeli men, in comparison, had a labor force participation rate of 84%.

Although 48% of Jewish women worked outside the home, for Arab and Druze women this proportion dropped to 16%. Altogether, Israeli women constituted a 42% share of the total labor force, again by far the highest proportion in the Middle East.

The past few decades have seen a steady increase in the number of working mothers with children under the age of 15. In 1986, 57% of mothers were working; by 1993 this figure had jumped to 68%.

WOMEN'S LABOR FORCE PARTICIPATION Percentage of age group, 1993			
AGE	PERCENT	AGE	PERCENT
18–24	42%	55–59	41%
25–34	60%	60–64	20%
35–44	66%	65+	6%
45–54	61%		

Discrimination in the Workplace

In the early days of the nation, laws were enacted to protect female workers. For instance, the Women's Work Law of 1954 prohibited women from working in jobs that might be injurious to their health and set forth the rights of pregnant women. Over the years legislation focused more on promoting women's equal participation in the work force. In 1959 the Employment Service Act prohibited employment discrimination against women, and in 1964 the Male and Female Workers (Equal Pay) Act established the principle of equal pay for equal work. However, it did not provide the means to enforce it.

The 1988 Equal Employment Opportunity Law made discrimination on the basis of gender or family status illegal in job advertising, hiring, training, promotion, and firing. It also made sexual harassment a criminal offense, punishable by a substantial fine and imprisonment for up to two years. However, the number of harassment complaints has been relatively small, and many of them have lacked the required proof.

An important development in recent years, has been the introduction of affirmative action measures. In 1993 the Government Corporations Law stipulated that government corporations must appoint to their boards new directors "of the gender not appropriately represented." This policy of affirmative action was upheld by the Israeli Supreme Court in November 1994, and approximately 40% of the directors appointed in the four months following this decision were women, compared with the 2% of women on these boards prior to that date. In 1995 legislation was passed requiring the civil service to give preference to women whenever male and female candidates for similar positions had similar qualifications.

Areas of Employment

Israeli women are still concentrated in a small number of female-dominated occupations, such as teaching and health services. However, very few women reach the highest levels, even in these fields. For every 100 men in

WOMEN IN MAJOR OCCUPATIONAL GROUPS
Percentage of group, 1993

OCCUPATIONAL GROUP	PERCENT
Clerical	69%
Service	60%
Professional, technical	54%
Sales	37%
Administrative, managerial	18%

administrative or managerial positions, there are only 22 women in similar posts. In the civil service, where women constitute over 60% of employees, there are no female directors general of a ministry; and only 1% of those in the highest rank, 10% in the second rank, and 16% in the third rank are women. It is expected that the affirmative action law passed in 1995 will rectify this situation.

In the occupational group consisting of professional and technical workers, women outnumber men 117 to 100. One profession where women have risen to prominence is in the judicial branch of government; in the mid-1990s, women held about one-third of all judgeships and occupied 2 of the 12 seats on the Supreme Court. Women made up 24% of judges in the District Courts and 39% of those in the Magistrates Courts. (Because of religious laws, women are not allowed to serve on the Jewish rabbinical courts or the Islamic Kadi courts.)

In the field of education women make up about 74% of all employees. They account for 85% of primary and 63% of secondary school teachers; but less than a third of the faculty in higher education. About 25% of all university lecturers, and only 9% of full professors, are women. In the Arab schools Arab women constitute 53% of primary school teachers but only 27% of secondary school teachers.

Women's participation in defense has long been a tradition in Israel, even predating the formation of the state. As far back as the early 1900s, women helped guard and defend the young Jewish settlements, and during the British Mandate, from 1922 to 1948, they continued to defend the community against Arab attacks. During the War of Independence, women fought side by side with men in the newly formed Israel Defense Forces (IDF).

Today, the IDF is the only army in the world that has compulsory military service for women. But it is not equal service. Only Jewish women are eligible, and despite the fact that the law requires women aged 18 to 26 to perform military service, there are many exemptions. For example, married women, pregnant women, and mothers are exempt, and religious women often perform alternative service, such as volunteering in schools, hospitals, or old age homes. As a result, while the IDF drafts about 90% of all men between 18 and 21, only about 60% of women are inducted. Another difference is that women serve for only 20 months whereas men serve 36 months, and while men must report for one month of training in the reserves each year until age 51, few women past the age of 25 are ever called for reserve duty. Women are also noticeably absent in high-ranking positions. In 1995 there were only two women officers with the rank of major general, the third highest rank in the service.

Although women were barred from combat duty for many years, in 1995 this restriction was successfully challenged when the Supreme Court ruled in favor of a woman officer who had been rejected for pilot training, which would qualify her to serve in a combat aviation position. This ruling was particularly significant, since in Israel a successful military career plays a pivotal role in achieving high office in government or a high rank in civilian employment. Service in combat positions has generally been the fastest route to promotion, and until 1995 women's inability to serve in these positions hindered them from achieving equality with men in both public service and private employment.

Israeli women are also active in the police force, making up 18% of the total personnel. Although many of these women are lawyers and serve as legal advisers and prosecutors, others are involved in a wide range of police activities, from traffic control to criminal investigation and administration.

In recent years one growing employment area for women has been small business ownership. A number of public and private groups have been established to help women entrepreneurs with financial assistance through grants and loans. In 1993 women applicants made up 22% of those requesting assistance from the Small Businesses Foundation.

Pay Differences

On average, Israeli women in nonagricultural industries earn about 75% of men's wages. This discrepancy between women and men occurs largely because women tend to be employed at lower-paying levels and in part-time jobs. Even when women and men earn the same salaries, men tend to receive more fringe benefits, such as overtime pay and car and telephone allowances, which can account for up to 40% of an employee's take-home pay. Legislation has recently been introduced into the Knesset that would expand the definition of "salary" to include all such fringe benefits.

Working Hours

In 1993, 53% of working women were employed in full-time jobs, compared with 82% of men. On average, women worked 30 hours a week and men 42 hours. One of the reasons many women choose part-time work is that the public elementary school day ends at noon or one o'clock.

Maternity Leave and Benefits

The Women's Work Law of 1954 prohibited the firing of pregnant women and mandated a 12-week maternity leave at 75% of the woman's salary (increased to 100% in 1994). It also provided either parent up to a full year's leave without pay and shorter working hours for the mother until the child reaches the age of one.

Child Care

Nurseries and day-care centers are available for children up to the age of three. They are run by women's organizations but supervised and subsidized by the Ministry of Labor and Welfare. Tuition is on a sliding scale, determined by the mother's income. In 1993 more than 61,000 children were enrolled in these centers.

Unemployment

In recent years unemployment rates in Israel have been consistently higher for women than for men. In 1993 the unemployment rate for women was 50% higher than for men. Women

UNEMPLOYMENT RATES Percentage of labor force		
CATEGORY	1980	1993
Total	4.8%	10.0%
Women	6.0%	12.1%
Men	4.1%	8.5%

accounted for more than half of the unemployed and received an average of 25% less unemployment pay.

MARRIAGE AND DIVORCE

At the time the Law for the Equal Rights of Women was passed in 1951, the government, under pressure from the religious parties, decided that most matters relating to marriage and divorce would be excluded from the civil courts and placed under the jurisdiction of the religious courts. This decision was implemented by the Jurisdiction (Marriage and Divorce) Law of 1953, and thus the Orthodox rabbinical courts gained control over marriage, divorce, and other matters of personal status in all sectors of the Jewish community—whether or not those involved were Orthodox. Non-Jewish citizens are covered by their own religious courts, either Islamic or Christian.

Roughly one in 10 Israeli families is headed by a single parent, usually a woman, and one-third of these families live below the poverty line. Most of these single mothers are divorcees, abandoned wives whose husbands refuse to divorce them, or widows. In 1992 the Single Parent Law increased benefits and awarded education grants to low-income, single-parent families. This legislation was enacted in response to the large influx of single-parent families from the Soviet Union and Ethiopia in the late 1980s. Only about 2% of all births are to unmarried women, one of the lowest percentages of out-of-wedlock births in the world.

Marriage

Although most matters concerning marriage are under the jurisdiction of religious courts, the government has enacted certain civil laws that take precedence over religious statutes. One such law prohibits polygamy, which is allowed under Muslim law; another concerns the inheritance rights of widows. Civil law also sets the legal minimum marriage age at 17 for both women and men. Most Israelis, however, marry much later; for women the average age at first marriage is 23.9 years, for men, 26.7 years.

Orthodox Jewish marital practices include a *mikvah,* or ritual bath, in which a bride immerses herself before her marriage and, once married, after each menstrual period. Also according to religious law, a childless widow may not remarry until her husband's brother has had an opportunity to claim her, and he must perform certain rituals set down in ancient texts to free him from his obligation.

Both Jewish and Israeli civil law recognize the rights of a woman living with a man out of wedlock, as long as neither party is married to another person. The children of such couples have the same status as children born to married couples. However, according to Jewish law, if a married woman bears children by a man other than her husband, these children are considered illegitimate, and neither they nor their progeny can marry another Jew for seven generations. This situation sometimes arises because a woman who is abandoned by her husband or is unable to obtain a divorce from the religious court cannot legally marry. The children of a married man and an unmarried woman do not bear the same stigma.

Divorce

In 1992 over 6,500 divorces were granted. Under Jewish law only the husband can grant his wife a divorce, although both parties must consent. It is estimated that as many as 10,000 women, known as *agunot,* or "anchored" women, have been denied a divorce by their husbands, some for as long as 20 years.

Under the 1973 Spouse (Property Relations) Law, an Israeli couple may enter into a financial agreement before or after they have married. If there is no such agreement, the property acquired during the marriage is divided equally upon divorce. With respect to child custody, both parents are legal guardians for their children, although in practice most children remain with their mothers. In cases where a husband refuses to pay the alimony awarded to his wife by the court, she receives payment from the National Insurance Institute. In 1993 over 15,000 women received these monthly child support payments.

FAMILY PLANNING

Although contraception is legal in Israel, the government has followed a policy favoring large families, and family planning is not a priority.

Fertility Rate

The fertility rate in Israel is 2.8 children per woman, down from 3.8 in 1970, and the lowest fertility rate in the Middle East. Among Muslim women, the fertility rate is considerably higher than the national average: 4.7 children. Births to teenagagers are among the lowest in the world; in 1990, they accounted for only 3% of all births.

Contraception

Family planning information and guidance are available to women of all ethnic and religious groups. Although the use of birth control is frowned upon by religious authorities, it is estimated that 65% of Israeli couples of childbearing age use some form of birth control. However, official statistics on the specific kinds of contraceptives used are not available.

Abortion

In 1992 nearly 16,400 legal abortions were performed in Israel, a ratio of one abortion for every seven live births. Since 1976, abortions have been legal in four circumstances: if the pregnancy endangers the woman's physical or mental health; if the pregnancy is the result of rape or incest; if the woman is under 17 or over 40; or if there is evidence of a serious fetal defect. In addition, applications for abortions must be approved by a three-member committee.

The 1976 law also included socioeconomic reasons as legal grounds for abortion, and this category accounted for the majority of procedures. Three years later, under pressure from Orthodox religious leaders, this section of the law was repealed.

Sex Education

Sex education in Israeli schools has been mandated since 1987, but implementation of programs has been slow. However, several advisory centers for adolescents offer information on family planning; sexual relations; and sexually transmitted diseases, including AIDS.

WOMEN'S HEALTH

Israelis enjoy high-quality health care, and their life expectancy is the highest in the Middle East, although for non-Jews it lags behind that of the Jewish population. On average, the life expectancy for women is 78.5 years, while for men it is 75.1 years. Not surprisingly, Israel's maternal mortality rate is one of the lowest in the world: 7 deaths for every 100,000 live births. Only Canada, Norway, and Switzerland have a lower maternal mortality rate.

Health services are provided through the National Health Insurance Law, which covers the entire Israeli population. In addition to basic services provided to both women and men, women are covered for obstetric and gynecological expenses, including fertility tests, as well as routine screenings for breast and uterine cancer.

LIFE EXPECTANCY
At birth, in years

| | JEWISH | | NON-JEWISH | |
YEAR	WOMEN	MEN	WOMEN	MEN
1980	76.2	72.5	73.4	70.0
1985	77.3	73.9	75.8	72.0
1991	79.0	75.4	75.7	74.2

LEADING CAUSES OF DEATH
Percentage of total deaths, 1992

CAUSE	WOMEN	MEN
Cardiovascular diseases	41%	40%
Cancer	21%	19%
Breast	4%	—
Lung	2%	4%
Cervix	<1%	—
Accidents	3%	4%
Diabetes	3%	2%
Mental disorders	3%	2%
Pneumonia	2%	2%
Suicide	1%	2%
Homicide	<1%	<1%

Leading Causes of Death

In 1991 the leading causes of death for both women and men were cardio-vascular disorders, primarily heart disease and stroke, and cancer.

Smoking

Smoking in Israel is a fairly common habit. It is estimated that 25% of all women and 38% of all men are smokers.

AIDS

By 1994, of the 281 AIDS patients in Israel, 26 of these cases (9%) were women. According to the World Health Organization, by the end of 1994 approximately 2,000 Israelis were infected with HIV, the virus that causes AIDS.

VIOLENCE AGAINST WOMEN

Violence against women is widespread throughout Israel and growing. It has been a major concern of the government since the late 1980s, when a special committee issued a report on the problem. The turning point in the nation's approach to the issue came in 1991, with the passage of a law aimed specifically at combating violence in the family. The following year the Knesset created a Committee for the Advancement of Women, which dealt directly with the issue of violence.

Domestic Violence

Domestic violence is a serious problem for Israeli women; in 1995 an estimated 200,000 women were beaten or abused by their husbands; 16 were murdered by male relatives. Under secular law, personal assault is punishable by 15 years' imprisonment, but victims receive no protection during the filing process and thus seldom register complaints. In addition, if a Jewish woman flees her home without permission from the rabbinical court, she can be deemed a "rebellious wife" and lose such rights as custody of her children and financial support.

In 1991 the government enacted the Law for the Prevention of Violence in the Family, which allowed legal authorities to act expeditiously against a violent family member. It also created seven centers for the prevention of family violence, with another eight planned for the future. These centers provide a variety of services, including legal counseling and workshops for abusive husbands. The Ministry of Labor and Welfare, which helps finance the centers, has also established the National Council for Battered Women, an umbrella organization for all services to victims of abuse.

Six shelters for battered women, one exclusively for Arab women, have been established by various nongovernmental women's organizations, which have also installed a network of seven emergency telephone hotlines. Approximately 420 women and 600 children use these facilities every year. The Ministry of Labor and Welfare covers about half the cost of the shelters for Jewish women and the entire cost of Arab women's shelters. Since 1993, medical treatment for victims of domestic violence has been covered by national health insurance.

Rape

Rape is punishable by 4 to 14 years in prison; if a gun or knife is used to threaten the victim, the penalty increases to 20 years. A 1988 amendment to the penal code erased any differentiation between rape and marital rape, and in a 1990 amendment all sexual crimes were deemed to be more serious if committed within the family. The law of evidence was amended in 1991 to allow a woman to appear in court as a witness against her husband in cases of domestic violence and rape.

By the mid-1990s there were seven rape crisis centers throughout Israel, one of them specifically for Arab women. The number of women using these centers reached nearly 4,000 in 1993, more than triple the 1,160 women who used them in 1990. However, the number of rapes actually reported in 1993 was only 2,266.

Prostitution

Prostitution is illegal in Israel, and solicitation is punishable by three months' imprisonment. Living off the earnings of a prostitute carries a penalty of five years in prison.

FOR ADDITIONAL INFORMATION ON WOMEN

Consulate General of Israel
Information Office
800 Second Avenue
New York, NY 10017, United States
Telephone: 212-499-5300

Council of Women's Organizations in Israel
26 Sh. Ben Maimon
Jerusalem 92261, Israel
Telephone: 2-631-303
Fax: 2-662-811

Embassy of Israel
3514 International Drive, NW
Washington, DC 20008, United States
Telephone: 202-364-5500

Israeli Feminist Movement
82 Ben-Yehuda Street
Tel Aviv 63435, Israel
Telephone: 3-523-4917
Fax: 3-544-9191

Women's Studies Program
University of Haifa
Mt. Carmel
Haifa 31999, Israel
Telephone: 4-240-111

ITALY

Population: *57.9 million*
▲ Women per 100 men: *106*
Women's voting rights: *1945*
Women in legislature: *9%*
Women's share of work force: *32%*
▲ Literacy rates: women—*99%;* men—*99%*
Life expectancy: women—*80.5 years;* men—*73.7 years*
▲ Average number of children: *1.3*
Maternal mortality rate: *12*

WOMEN NOBEL PRIZE WINNERS		
Grazia Deledda	Literature	1926
Rita Levi-Montalcini*	Physiology or Medicine	1986

*Dual citizenship with the United States.

The Republic of Italy, in southern Europe, is a long peninsula extending into the Mediterranean Sea. The country also includes two large islands, Sardinia and Sicily, and several smaller ones. Italy has had an illustrious past as the seat of the Roman Empire and, later, as the birthplace of the Renaissance. Today, it ranks among the leading commercial nations of the Western world.

Italy's population is homogeneous, and about two-thirds of Italians live in cities. The seat of Roman Catholicism, the independent enclave of Vatican City, is located in Rome, and 84% of Italians are Catholic. Although Roman Catholicism is no longer the formal state religion, the church remains a political force. Yet over the years, its influence on Italian laws and policies has diminished, especially in such matters as divorce, birth control, and abortion.

HISTORY OF THE WOMEN'S MOVEMENT

Italy was united into one kingdom in 1861 and became a republic following its defeat by the Allied powers in World War II. In 1945, amid little controversy, women were granted the right to vote and run for office. Both leading political parties supported it: the Communist Party on ideological grounds and the Christian Democrats for the practical reason that they expected the majority of women to join their ranks.

Although women had been active in the resistance movement during the war and in political parties following the war, the modern Italian women's movement dates back only to 1970, when an organization called the *Movimento della Liberazione delle Donne* (Women's Liberation Movement) was formed in Rome. During the early 1970s a number of other mostly small groups of middle-class women emerged based on the consciousness-raising groups that were popular in the United States at that time. By the mid-1970s the Italian women's movement had a base on which to develop; fueled by the economic stagflation of that period, it grew rapidly into a national movement. Lower-class women began emerging from their homes on an unprecedented scale to participate in collective action, fighting for better housing and improved social services. When a referendum was called in 1974 to repeal the divorce rights law that had been passed in 1970, women's groups had a strong foundation from which to work, and they successfully defeated the motion with a sizable majority, 60%, of the vote.

The battle to reform the abortion laws further united the various strands of the women's movement. In 1975 feminists opened clandestine abortion clinics in Florence and staged mass demonstrations in Rome. They collected 800,000 signatures calling for a referendum, many more than the 500,000 that were needed. Although the referendum never took place, in 1978 Parliament passed a law legalizing abortion. When a referendum was called in 1981 to overturn this legislation, women successfully defeated the proposal with more than two-thirds (68%) of the vote. In recent years Italian women's organizations have been focusing their attention on violence against women, especially rape. By the mid-1990s, they had collected more than 300,000 signatures to pressure Parliament into passing stricter legislation.

In 1984, in response to the growing women's movement, the prime minister's office established the National Commission for Equal Opportunities, composed of 29 women representing Italy's political parties, associations, unions, and cultural organizations. Its tasks include reporting existing discrimination and proposing legislative changes to eliminate it. In addition, the commission conducts and publicizes research on discrimination and encourages women to run for elected office.

WOMEN IN POLITICS

Although Italian women have been voting for more than 50 years, their representation in Parliament has been meager, never higher than 7% between the years 1948 and 1983. In 1987 the National Commission for Equal Opportunities pressured the political parties to nominate more female candidates, resulting in an increase to 11%. In 1992 the same commission launched a "Vote for Women" campaign, and although it was challenged on the grounds that it discriminated against men, the courts ruled in its favor. But the campaign was not effective, and women's participation in Parliament that year dropped by two percentage points. Before the 1994 parliamentary elections, a new rule required political parties to change the ways in which they nominated female and male candidates. As a result, women were elected to 13% of seats—the highest representation ever. In the 1996 election the percentage of women dropped again, to 9%. Sixty-three women were elected to the 630-seat Chamber of Deputies (10%), while 25 women were elected to the 315-member Senate (8%).

The highest political position ever attained by an Italian woman is the presidency of the Chamber of Deputies, which is second in line to the national presidency, after the head of the Senate. Only two women have held

		CHAMBER OF	BOTH
	WOMEN IN PARLIAMENT		
	Percentage of chamber		
YEAR	SENATE	DEPUTIES	CHAMBERS
1979	4%	9%	7%
1983	5%	8%	7%
1987	7%	13%	11%
1992	10%	8%	9%
1994	9%	15%	13%
1996	8%	10%	9%

this position: Nilde Iotti, who served from 1979 to 1992, and Irene Pivetti, who took office in 1994.

Very few women have served in the Italian cabinet. Since 1980, there have never been more than 3 female ministers appointed by the prime minister, once in 1993 and again in 1996. The three women in the 20-member 1996 cabinet were Rosi Bindi (health), Anna Finocchiaro (equal opportunities), and Livia Turco (social solidarity). Out of a total of 49 vice ministers, 9 were women.

Women are also poorly represented in the foreign service. Italy has a total of 205 ambassadorial posts, and one person may hold more than one post. In the mid-1990s five of these posts (2%) were held by two women—one holding three, the other holding two. In Italy's delegation to the European Parliament, women's participation has been one of the lowest of all member countries. After the 1994 election, women made up only 13% of Italy's 87-member delegation. Only one other country, Portugal, had a lower percentage of women in its delegation.

At the regional level, Italian women are again poorly represented in elected office, the proportion of councilors and aldermen varying between 6% and 9%. This situation is expected to improve in future elections, however, since a new law requires no more than two-thirds of the candidates in large towns, and three-quarters in smaller towns, to be of one sex.

WOMEN'S EDUCATION

Education in Italy is compulsory for girls and boys for eight years (five years of primary school and three years of middle school). Upon successful completion, students are awarded a general certificate of education, which is considered indispensable for any type of employment, although the level of education affects the salaries of men much more than those of women. The average starting salary for a woman with a college degree is only one and a half times that of a woman with an elementary education; a male college graduate earns almost four times the salary of a man with only an elementary education.

FEMALE ENROLLMENT Percentage of student body, 1992	
LEVEL	PERCENT
Primary school	49%
Secondary school	49%
University	51%

Since 1962, when the required number of years of education was raised from five to eight, more students have been continuing to secondary school and higher education, and as many women as men are

WOMEN UNIVERSITY DEGREE RECIPIENTS
Percentage of subject area, 1993

SUBJECT AREA	PERCENT
Humanities	81%
Business	58%
Law	58%
Engineering	23%
Medicine	23%
Pharmacology	13%
Biological sciences	9%
Mathematics	9%

doing so. Adult literacy rates in Italy are the same for both women and men: 99%.

Although girls attend school in the same proportion as boys, they tend to study different subjects. Some courses—such as secretarial, primary school teaching, health care, languages, and tourism—are studied almost exclusively by girls, while construction, agriculture, fishing, and transport are studied almost entirely by boys. The existence of some single-sex schools tends to encourage this disparity, which in turn leads students into separate occupations when they enter the labor market.

AVERAGE STARTING SALARY BY YEARS OF SCHOOLING
Monthly, in thousands of lire

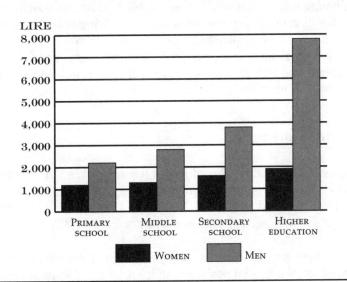

WOMEN'S EMPLOYMENT

Since 1980, increasing numbers of women have entered the Italian work force, largely as a result of increased compulsory education levels and the simultaneous growth of the service sector. Approximately 37% of working-age women work outside the home, and they make up about 32% of the total labor force, one of the lowest percentages of female work force representation in Europe. Italian men, in comparison, have a work force participation rate of 79%.

Discrimination in the Workplace

The Italian government has passed legislation to promote equal opportunities for women in the area of employment. However, not all laws have been fully implemented, and men are still favored over women for many jobs, especially those leading to higher management positions. In addition, women tend to receive lower pay for comparable work.

As early as 1963, a law was passed guaranteeing women access to all public sector jobs. A 1977 law barred discrimination with regard to hiring, training, job titles, responsibilities, wages, and promotion. As a consequence, some laws that had been enacted to protect women—such as barring them from working in quarries, mines, or tunnels—were found to be discriminatory and thus illegal.

In 1991 the Italian government passed a bill promoting affirmative action and imposing a system of financial penalties for employers convicted of discriminating against women. It also established equal opportunity advisers to monitor discriminatory practices as well as bring lawsuits on behalf of women victims, but their implementation has been delayed.

Although sexual harassment is prohibited by some labor contracts in both the private and public sectors, it is not illegal in Italy. As a result, victims of harassment have no legal recourse through the courts.

Areas of Employment

Italian women tend to be employed in low-paying jobs, such as teaching or clerical work. About 71% of the 1.7 million service sector jobs that were created since 1980 are filled by women. During this same period the proportion of female factory and agricultural workers declined to 23% and 7% respectively.

Italian women are rarely seen in high-level jobs; for every 100 men in administrative or managerial positions, there are only 4 women in comparable posts, one of the world's lowest female ratios in this occupational category. However, Italian women fare much better in professional and technical jobs; for every 100 men in these positions, there are 86 women.

Women were first admitted as judges in 1965, and by 1994 they made up 24% of the total. Since women made up half the applicants for starting-level judgeships in the mid-1990s, the government expects the number of female judges to equal that of men by the end of the decade. Italian women have also been making gains in farm management. Although the total number of farms decreased by 8% from 1980 to 1990, the number of farms managed by women increased by 10%, making up 26% of the total.

In an attempt to encourage women entrepreneurs, a law was passed in 1992 to facilitate women's access to credit. This legislation also established training courses for women interested in starting their own businesses. The percentage of self-employed women rose from 13% in 1980 to 17% in 1994.

Pay Differences

The wage gap between women and men has continued to narrow since 1980, when all women working in nonagricultural industries received an average of 70% of men's wages. By the end of the decade women's wages had increased to 80% of men's, one of the world's narrowest gender wage gaps.

Working Hours

Part-time work in Italy is defined as work that is carried out in fewer than the normal working hours and has a fixed-term contract. This kind of work did not exist in Italy before 1984, and by 1990 only 5% of the total labor force was employed part time, the lowest rate in Europe. This part-time work force comprised approximately 10% of working women and 4% of men The government is actively encouraging the creation of additional part-time jobs so that more mothers can work outside the home.

Maternity Leave and Benefits

By law, an employed woman is obligated to take a maternity leave for two months before and three months after the birth of a child. During this period she receives her full salary, with the government paying 80% and her employer 20%. Sometimes, however, this benefit actually works against women, since employers having to bear these costs are more apt to hire men. At the end of this period a working mother can choose to remain home with her child for an additional six months at 30% of her salary, which is covered by the government. Maternity leave is also available to self-employed women and women managing farms. In these cases benefits are paid by the social insurance system.

Child Care

In 1971 the Italian government established a network of public day-care facilities partially financed by employers and the federal and local governments, which accept children up to age three based on need, with the fees set according to each family's income. However, only about 5% of children under three are accommodated by these facilities, and many more spaces are needed. Between the ages of three and six, children may attend kindergarten, which is free, and 90% of all children in this age group do so.

Unemployment

The unemployment rate for women has remained high throughout the 1980s and 1990s. In 1982, 12.9% of working women were unemployed, and by 1994 the proportion had risen to 15.8%. The comparable rates for men were 5.0% and 9.0% respectively. Many of the jobs lost in this period were low-skilled positions filled by women with only primary school education. The number of jobs for women who had completed middle school or higher actually increased.

MARRIAGE AND DIVORCE

In 1990, 9 out of 10 Italian families were headed by two parents. Of the more than 220,000 single-parent households, nearly 83% were headed by women, and more than two-thirds of these households fell below the poverty line. Widows headed about 68% of these families, separated and divorced women 26%, and single women 6%. In recent years the marriage rate has decreased, while the divorce rate has increased.

Marriage

The minimum legal age for marriage is 16 for women and 18 for men. Most couples, however, marry much later. On average, women first marry at 23.2

years and men at 27.1 years. In 1994 over 285,000 couples got married, a decrease of almost 3% from the previous year.

Italian family law was reformed in 1975 to guarantee equality between husband and wife. Previously, the husband was the legal head of the household and had the right to control his wife's activities and behavior. The 1975 law also gave children born out of wedlock the same legal rights as legitimate children, including inheritance rights. However, births to unmarried women are relatively uncommon, accounting for only about 7% of all births.

Divorce

Divorce was legalized in 1970, and when family law was reformed in 1975, legal separation became possible on the grounds of irreconcilable differences. The same legislation decriminalized adultery. In 1994 over 27,500 couples were divorced, a dramatic 15% increase in divorces over 1993. The Italian annual divorce rate of almost 10 divorces for every 100 couples getting married has doubled since 1970.

A divorced woman is entitled to a share of her ex-husband's pension, and all property acquired during the marriage is considered community property, to be shared equally. Child custody is determined by the court but is generally granted to the mother.

 ## FAMILY PLANNING

Although the Roman Catholic Church has battled hard against contraception and abortion, both are legal in Italy. Family health clinics, established in 1975, provide information and advice on contraception, as well as other aspects of health care. In 1991 the government instituted a Women's Welfare project to disseminate information on such topics as contraception, pregnancy, cancer prevention, and menopause.

Fertility Rate

Italian women have one of the lowest fertility rates in the world, and the lowest in Italy's history. From the mid-1960s to the mid-1990s, the fertility rate dropped by half, from an average of 2.6 children per woman to 1.3. Only 4% of births are to teenagers.

Italy's low birthrate, which is well below the replacement level of 2.1 births per woman, has become a major government concern. The Ministry of Family is considering a number of measures to encourage larger families, such as making more part-time work available to women, expanding child-care facilities, and cutting taxes for families with children.

Contraception

Approximately 78% of Italian couples of childbearing age use some form of birth control, one of the world's highest rates of contraception. It is estimated that nearly half use traditional methods, such as rhythm and periodic abstinence. Condoms and birth control pills are the most popular modern contraceptives, while the use of spermicides and intrauterine devices, never very widespread, has been decreasing. Sterilization procedures—both tubal ligations and vasectomies—are the least popular methods of birth control.

Abortion

Until 1978 abortion was illegal and punishable by up to five years' imprisonment. Yet tens of thousands of women underwent illegal abortions each year, and officials estimate that approximately 20,000 deaths occurred annually as a result of these unsafe procedures. Following legalization the highest number of abortions, 234,801 was recorded in 1982. Since then the number has decreased each year, dropping to 155,172 in 1992.

Abortion is now permitted during the first trimester for economic, medical, psychological, or social reasons. After the first trimester, an abortion can be performed only if the woman's health is in danger or there is evidence of fetal abnormality.

Fertility Services

In recent years Italy has become a center for infertility treatments, especially in vitro fertilization. There are more than 100 private fertility clinics throughout the country, and about 2,000 fertility procedures are performed each year. Because Italy has no laws regulating these private clinics, they have become a mecca for women who, because of their age or marital status, are not eligible for fertilization procedures in their own country.

Sex Education

Sex education courses are not offered in Italian schools. However, information can be obtained through family health clinics and a government booklet that includes information on reproductive health. Information on the transmission and prevention of AIDS was added to the school curriculum in 1993.

WOMEN'S HEALTH

Health standards have been rising steadily in Italy, and life expectancy for both women and men is among the highest in the world. At the same time, maternal mortality rates have declined to 12 deaths per 100,000 live births. The legalization of abortion is believed to have contributed considerably to this drop in pregnancy-related deaths.

LIFE EXPECTANCY At birth, in years		
YEAR	WOMEN	MEN
1980	77.4	70.6
1985	78.8	72.2
1990	80.5	73.7

Leading Causes of Death

As in other industrialized nations, the leading causes of death for both women and men in Italy are cardiovascular diseases and cancer. Recently, the government has become alarmed by a rise in obesity among children, especially since this is considered a risk factor for cardiovascular disease later in life.

Smoking

Italians have a high rate of smoking. About 26% of women and 46% of men are smokers.

LEADING CAUSES OF DEATH Percentage of total deaths, 1991		
CAUSE	WOMEN	MEN
Cardiovascular diseases	49%	39%
Cancer	23%	30%
Breast	4%	—
Lung	2%	9%
Cervix	<1%	—
Respiratory diseases	5%	7%
Diabetes	5%	2%
Accidents	4%	5%
Chronic liver disease	2%	3%
Suicide	<1%	1%
Homicide	<1%	<1%

AIDS

By the mid-1990s an estimated 90,000 Italians were infected with HIV, the virus that causes AIDS. Although women accounted for a small percentage of these cases, government studies have found that the incidence of AIDS among women is rising. In 1985 they accounted for 195 cases, or 19% of the reported total; by 1993 the number of women's AIDS cases had grown to 945, or 22% of the total.

VIOLENCE AGAINST WOMEN

Since the 1970s, women's groups in Italy have been focusing on the problem of violence against women, and although specific antiviolence legislation has been proposed several times, it has never been enacted. In the summer of 1995, after media attention focused on a series of gang rapes of young women and child sexual abuse cases, the prime minister committed his government to strengthening the law against rape.

Domestic Violence

No firm data are available on domestic violence in Italy, although it is believed to be fairly widespread. In 1994 the official number of cases filed with the courts was 869, up very slightly from 866 in 1993. According to officials, battered wives rarely press charges against their abusers on account of fear, shame, or ignorance of the law. A government telephone hotline offers legal and medical help to abused women, and since 1994, volunteer groups have been working with regional governments to establish shelters for battered women.

Rape

The current law on rape, dating back to 1936, classifies rape as a moral offense (a misdemeanor), not as a crime against a person. The penalty is three years in prison, but with plea bargaining and suspended sentences, many convicted rapists serve no time at all. The law does not distinguish between spousal and other rape.

Legislation proposed in 1995 would make rape a felony and increase the sentence to five years, with even harsher sentences for gang rape and cases involving minors. Another major change would mandate automatic prosecution, without the victim having to initiate it.

Prostitution

Prostitution is legal in Italy, although living off the earnings of a prostitute is illegal and punishable by imprisonment. Prostitutes are required to undergo periodic health checks.

Although the extent of the problem is not known, in recent years media reports have focused public attention on the trafficking of women and forced prostitution, usually involving illegal immigrants who are fearful of contacting the authorities.

FOR ADDITIONAL INFORMATION ON WOMEN

Centro Italiano Femminile
Via Carlo Zucchi, 25
00165 Rome, Italy
Telephone: 6-622-1507
Fax: 6-622-1167

Embassy of Italy
1601 Fuller Street, NW
Washington, DC 20009, United States
Telephone: 202-328-5500

Fronte Italiano di Liberazione Femminile
Plaza SS. Apostoli 49
00187 Rome, Italy
Telephone: 6-678-0504

Permanent Mission of Italy to the United Nations
2 United Nations Plaza, 24th floor
New York, NY 10017, United States
Telephone: 212-486-9191

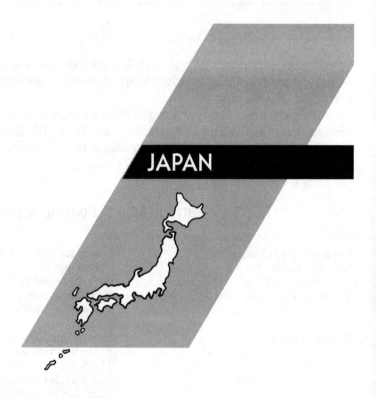

JAPAN

Population: *125.8 million*
Women per 100 men: *103*
Women's voting rights: *1945*
Women in legislature: *8%*
Women's share of work force: *40%*
▲ Literacy rates: women—*99%;* men—*99%*
▲ Life expectancy: women—*83.0 years;* men—*76.6 years*
▲ Average number of children: *1.5*
Maternal mortality rate: *18*

Japan is an island nation located off the northeastern coast of Asia. It consists of four densely populated main islands and more than 30,000 smaller, scattered ones. Despite its small size and few natural resources, Japan is highly industrialized and a major world economic power.

The Japanese people form a very homogeneous ethnic group, and a sizable proportion of the population, about 77%, live in urban centers. The great majority practice both Buddhism and Shintoism. There is also a very small (1%) Christian minority.

HISTORY OF THE WOMEN'S MOVEMENT

Japan's emergence as a modern nation dates back to 1868, when a representative government replaced nearly 700 years of feudal military rule. The new government instituted sweeping changes, including compulsory education for both girls and boys, but traditional Confucian values persisted and women were still expected to fulfill their roles as wives and mothers. Although women did enjoy some new rights and freedoms under the new government, they were not allowed to vote or join political groups and still needed parental consent for marriage.

It was not until Japan surrendered to the Allies in 1945, ending World War II, that Japanese women again encountered major social and economic changes. After 60 years of campaigning for women's suffrage, they were finally granted the right to vote. The new constitution, which took effect in 1947 included equal rights for women and men and revised earlier laws that had discriminated against women in property ownership, inheritance, education, and employment.

In 1950, however, before the impact of these changes could be fully felt, war in Korea and Japan's alliance with the West created a new political climate. Former Japanese leaders who had been purged during the period of Allied occupation after the war were again allowed to gain political control, and with them they brought their traditional attitudes toward women. The Korean War, however, also produced a positive development for women: It stimulated the Japanese economy and opened vast opportunities for employment. As large numbers of women started working outside the home, they also began forming political groups, which during the 1960s and 1970s campaigned actively—and largely successfully—for a variety of reforms, ranging from improved working conditions to the removal of discriminatory provisions in the nationality law.

During the early 1990s, however, Japan suffered a severe economic crisis that continues to depress the labor market. Women are no longer as welcome in the labor force and are once more facing widespread discrimination in hiring, promotion, and training. Other issues currently targeted by women's groups include environmental issues, the educational system, and the meager representation of women in high-level positions in business as well as in government.

WOMEN IN POLITICS

While Japanese women have made tremendous strides in many areas, they are seldom seen in leadership and decision-making roles, especially in the area of politics. Women were first elected to the Diet, the national legislature, in 1946, gaining 8% of the seats in the House of Representatives. The following year, 10 women were elected to the House of Councillors, making up 4% of that body.

Fifty years later, after the 1996 elections,

WOMEN IN THE DIET Percentage of total members			
CHAMBER	1980	1986	1996
Total Diet	3%	4%	8%
House of Representatives	2%	2%	5%
House of Councillors	7%	8%	14%

women's representation in the entire Diet was still only 8%. They occupied 23 of the 500 seats in the House of Representatives (5%) and 35 of the 252 seats in the House of Councilors (14%). In 1993 Takako Doi became the first woman in Japan's history to be named Speaker of the House of Representatives. Seven years earlier, she had attained the distinction of becoming the first woman leader of a major political party.

The first woman cabinet member was appointed in 1960, and in 1993 a record three cabinet posts were filled by women. After the 1996 elections, however, the newly formed cabinet included no women at all.

While women make up nearly 15% of Japan's Foreign Ministry employees, rarely has one ever been appointed an ambassador. The first was named in 1980, and by 1996 there were only 2 women ambassadors out of a total of 113. Elsewhere in the government, three women served in high-ranking positions: justice of the Supreme Court, the commissioner of cultural affairs, and the commissioner of the Social Insurance Agency.

Japan is divided into 47 prefectures. In 1996 not a single one was headed by a woman governor. Similarly, women's participation in prefectural advisory councils has been meager, though slowly increasing. In 1994 the prime minister initiated a plan to increase female representation on these panels, setting a target of 30% by mid-1995. However, compliance was so poor that the target had to be cut to 15%, and by the end of 1995 only about a third had even met the reduced quota.

In local government women made up about 6% of city and 2% of town and village assemblies during the mid-1990s. The first woman to serve as a city mayor was elected in 1991, and by 1994 a total of four women mayors headed two cities, one town, and one village.

WOMEN'S EDUCATION

Nine years of education is compulsory for both girls and boys, and Japan's adult literacy rates are among the highest in the world: 99% for both women and men.

Japanese elementary schools provide general education for children aged 6 to 12. Lower secondary schools continue the general curriculum, while upper secondary schools offer additional specialized courses. The curriculum of the lower secondary schools

FEMALE ENROLLMENT
Percentage of student body, 1993

LEVEL	PERCENT
Primary school	49%
Secondary school	49%
University	40%

became a rallying point for women's groups following World War II, when they succeeded in tearing down age-old gender stereotypes by making home economics classes compulsory for boys as well as girls. In the 1950s, with the return of traditional attitudes, the curriculum was revised: Boys were required to take industrial arts, while only girls took home economics. Again women's groups mobilized, and in 1993 home economics was once more made compulsory for both boys and girls. The following year it also became mandatory for all students in upper secondary schools.

Women constitute 40% of higher education students—only 29% in the universities but 92% in the junior colleges. In postgraduate studies Japanese women make up 19% of master's degree and 17% of doctoral degree candidates. The most popular areas of study for women are humanities, social science, education, and health.

Other kinds of educational opportunities available in Japan include vocational and technology colleges and a popular University of the Air, which uses radio, television, and other media. Enrollment began in 1985, and by 1993 the university student body numbered 48,000, half of whom were women.

With respect to the military academies, restrictions on women taking the entrance examinations for the National Defense Academy and the National Defense Medical College were lifted in 1992. The following year women were also allowed to take examinations to become student pilots for the Maritime Self-Defense Forces and the Air Self-Defense Forces.

WOMEN'S EMPLOYMENT

In 1993 about half of all working-age Japanese women worked outside the home, up from 47% in 1980. They accounted for about 40% of the total labor force, up slightly from 39% a decade earlier. Japanese men, in comparison, had a labor force participation rate of 84%.

The average age of all women workers in 1993 was 36 years, and almost 70% of them were married. Approximately one in four had graduated from a junior college or other institution of higher education.

Discrimination in the Workplace

The Japanese constitution prohibits discrimination against women in the workplace, and the 1986 Equal Employment Opportunity Law specifically targeted discrimination in such areas as recruitment, pay, and working hours. However, the law does not actually prohibit discrimination; it simply advises employers to "endeavor" to avoid it. Compliance is encouraged by offering subsidies and similar rewards rather than issuing fines and other punitive measures for violations. Many companies, however, blatantly flaunt the law. In 1995 some of the country's largest employers publicly announced plans to greatly reduce or even totally freeze the hiring of women.

Another way in which Japanese women encounter discrimination in employment is the two-track hiring system common in many companies. The career track is generally reserved for men, while the clerical track, which tends to pay less and offer fewer promotions, is chiefly for women. Although the Labor Standards Law bans discrimination with respect to wages, it does not address the inequitable hiring and promotion practices fostered by the tracking system. However, in late 1996, in a landmark decision, a Tokyo court ruled that 12 female employees of a credit association were owed nearly $900,000 in back wages to make up for raises they would have received had they been promoted at the same rate as their male counterparts.

Discrimination against Japanese women is also sometimes promoted by the very laws that were originally designed to protect them. For example, legislation that prohibits women from working late at night often prevents them from working on automobile plant assembly lines.

Sexual harassment is not clearly defined in Japanese law and has not yet been fully examined by the government. Only about 5 to 10 sexual harassment cases are filed each year, and although some women employees have won their cases, in each instance the court cited an unlawful act under the civil code without directly mentioning sexual harassment. As public attention has focused on discrimination and harassment in recent years, growing numbers of government agencies have installed telephone hotlines and designated special ombudsmen to handle complaints.

Areas of Employment

Nearly 85% of Japan's working women are employed in three areas: services (32%), retail businesses and restaurants (27%), and manufacturing (25%). About 45% of women are clerical workers, and large numbers are also employed as nurses, teachers, and domestic help. Whether in private industry or the public sector, women rarely reach high-level positions. For every 100 men in administrative or managerial posts, there are only 9 women in comparable jobs, one of the lowest representations of women in this occupational category among the world's developed nations.

In 1995, of all women public employees on the national level, only 0.5% had reached the rank of bureau director general, and 0.7% had attained the level of divisional director. At the prefecture level, women constituted 2.2% of department managers. In the private sector, in companies with more than 100 employees, the proportion of women managers was 1.7% at the division level, 2.9% at the section level, and 6.6% at the subsection level. In a recent survey of more than 2,000 Japanese companies, women accounted for only 0.1% of the total members of boards of directors.

In the occupational category consisting of professional and technical workers, Japanese women fare considerably better. For every 100 men in these positions, 72 women occupy similar posts. One reason is that many women become teachers, but even in this profession they are concentrated at the lowest levels.

WOMEN IN EDUCATION
Percentage of total, 1992

LEVEL	PERCENT
Elementary	60%
Lower secondary	39%
Upper secondary	22%
Junior college	39%
University	10%

About 6% of all lawyers registered with the Japanese Bar Association in 1995 were women, up from 4% in 1980. Nearly 3% of prosecutors were women, up from 1% in 1980, and the proportion of female judges was nearly 4%, up from 2% in 1980. In law enforcement women made up nearly 3% of all police officers; however, they tended to work in traffic control, public relations, crime investigation, and the guarding and escorting of VIPs. Although Japanese women may enlist in the armed forces, they are barred from positions where they might be involved in combat.

One category where women have been increasing in significant numbers is the area of self-employment. Of all self-employed workers with employees, women accounted for 19% by the mid-1990s, a substantial jump from only 3% in 1980.

Pay Differences

On average, full-time women employees in nonagricultural industries in Japan earn about 51% of men's wages. Government officials point out that women take time off for childbirth and child care and thus work fewer years than men. However, the two-track hiring system is an important factor in keeping women in lower-paying positions.

Working Hours

In recent years many women, especially those caring for a family, have resorted to part-time employment. By 1995 there were 6 million women part-time workers, accounting for 32% of the entire part-time work force, up from only 19% in 1980.

Of the total Japanese work force, a greater percentage of women than men work in part-time jobs. About 35% of all working women are employed part time, compared with only 12% of working men.

Maternity Leave and Benefits

Japanese women are entitled to a maternity leave starting 6 weeks before their due date (10 weeks in cases of multiple births) and 8 weeks following delivery. During this period the mother receives 60% of her salary.

After maternity leave, mothers or fathers who stay home to take care of their infants are entitled to monthly payments of 25% of their salaries. These payments end when the child reaches the age of one.

Child Care

The vast majority of working parents rely on public day-care centers, private facilities at company offices, and babysitters. In 1992 there were over 22,000 public day-care centers accommodating nearly 2 million children. However, many additional places were needed, and in 1993 the government launched a campaign to increase the number of child-care centers by offering subsidies to companies that provided them for their employees.

Unemployment

The official number of unemployed women reached over 700,000 in 1993, constituting an unemployment rate of 2.6%, one of the lowest in the world. The comparable figure for men was 2.4%. However, rates for both women and men are expected to rise during the late 1990s as the economy worsens.

MARRIAGE AND DIVORCE

As in many other industrialized countries, marriages in Japan are declining, while divorces are rising. Of the nearly 41 million households, about 23% consist of a single person, usually a woman. Although many of these women are widows living alone, there has been a recent rise in the number of unmarried young women in their 20s. The number of single-parent families in Japan has also been climbing, due chiefly to the rising divorce rate.

Only about 1% of all births are to unmarried women, one of the world's lowest rates of out-of-wedlock births. Not only is there tremendous social discrimination against single mothers, but they also face great economic pressures. Their taxes are higher than those of married women, and they pay higher day-care fees.

Marriage

The minimum legal age for marriage is 20 for both women and men, and 16 and 18 respectively with parental consent. Most couples marry much later, though, after many years of schooling and establishing a career. For women the average age at first marriage is 26.9 years; for men, 30.3 years. These are among the highest marriage ages in the world.

Although Japan is one of the most modern and highly industrialized countries in the world, the Japanese marriage has been shaped by centuries of traditional attitudes. While the typical modern Japanese husband is "wedded" to his job, his wife, even if she works full time, is still expected to take responsibility for managing the home and caring for the family. In an attempt to get men more involved with their families, the Ministry of Education has sponsored special parent education classes aimed specifically at fathers. In 1994 the government provided subsidies to companies establishing these parenting classes at their workplace.

Also in recent years, women's groups have been attacking Japan's marriage laws. Under the present legislation, when a couple marry, they must register the surname they will use. Both husband and wife must have the same surname, and it is usually the husband's that is chosen. Attempts to revise the law have been under way since the mid-1990s. One revision would allow wives and husbands each to keep their own surname. Another would remove the ban on a woman remarrying within six months after the end of her marriage.

The nationality law that women's groups fought to revise in the 1970s and 1980s stipulated that children of a Japanese father could always claim Japanese nationality, but children of a Japanese mother could do so only if the father's nationality was unknown or if he had none. Under the 1985 revision of the law, children can claim Japanese nationality if either parent is a Japanese national.

Divorce

Divorce rates in Japan are among the lowest in the developed world but are rising even so. In 1992, 179,000 divorces were granted, up from 142,000 in 1980. On average for every 100 couples who get married every year, approximately 24 get divorced.

Divorce by mutual consent has been legal for nearly a century and is by far the most common type of divorce today. If a couple cannot agree on terms, a family court determines child custody, support, and alimony. Contested divorces are granted on the following grounds: infidelity, severe mental illness, malicious abandonment, maltreatment or cruelty, severe insult or contempt, incompatibility, and loss of love between the spouses.

In about three-quarters of all divorces, child custody is granted to the mother. Child support is paid by fathers in only about 25% of cases, even when it is ordered by the court.

FAMILY PLANNING

Historically, the concept of limiting births for economic reasons dates back several centuries, when birth control methods included abortion and infanticide. Just prior to World War II, population growth became a national policy and a popular slogan advised, "Bear children, swell the population." In the aftermath of the war, the birthrate started dropping. In 1947 the fertility rate was an average of 4.5 children for each woman, but by 1985 it had dropped to 1.8. In the late 1980s the government attempted to reverse this trend by increasing child-care allowances, leave time, and similar measures. But by 1996 the birthrate had declined even further, prompting some villages to grant cash rewards to couples having babies.

Fertility Rate

The fertility rate in Japan is 1.5 children per woman, one of the lowest in the world. Since many women are marrying later, they are having children later, and the average age of first-time mothers is 27. Conversely, births to teenage mothers account for only 1% of all births, the lowest rate of births to teenagers in the world.

Contraception

Approximately 64% of Japanese couples of childbearing age use some form of birth control, and it is not unusual for couples to use more than one method. The great majority of couples rely on condoms; but traditional methods, such as rhythm, are also popular. Oral contraceptives are not legal for birth control purposes in Japan, and intrauterine devices (IUDs) and diaphragms are in short supply. Sterilization, though legal, is seldom used for birth control.

CONTRACEPTIVE USE
Percentage of couples of childbearing age, 1992

METHOD	PERCENT
Condom	48%
Traditional methods	17%
Intrauterine devices (IUDs)	3%
Female sterilization	3%
Male sterilization	1%
Birth control pill	1%
Diaphragm, other methods	1%

Abortion

The 1948 Eugenic Protection Law permitted abortion in cases where a parent has a hereditary disease, where the pregnancy endangers the woman's health or economic status, where the pregnancy resulted from rape, or where the fetus has severe abnormalities and would not be able to survive outside the womb. The law also stipulated that a married woman could not have an abortion without her husband's consent.

ABORTION RATES BY AGE
Percentage of total, 1992

AGE	PERCENT
Under 20	8%
20–24	21%
25–29	17%
30–34	20%
35–39	20%
40–44	12%
45 and over	1%

All other abortions, including those for sex selection, are illegal and punishable by a maximum of one year in prison for the woman and from three months to seven years for the practitioner. In actuality, however, the law is interpreted liberally, and abortion is practically available on request.

For many years abortion was widely used as a form of birth control, and during the mid-1960s more than a million were performed annually. In recent years, with the rising use of condoms, abortion rates have declined to between 300,000 and 400,000 a year.

Sex Education

Sex education for both girls and boys is included in all educational activities and focuses on health, home life, and personal relations. Family planning is taught in health and physical education classes as well as in home economics. In secondary schools information on the transmission and prevention of AIDS was added to the curriculum in 1987.

WOMEN'S HEALTH

Japanese women and men are probably the healthiest in the world; their life expectancy far exceeds that of people in any other country. For women the average life expectancy is 83.0 years; for men, 76.6 years. Similarly, the maternal mortality rate, 18 deaths per 100,000 live births, is among the lowest in Asia.

Leading Causes of Death

As in other highly industrialized countries, the leading causes of death for both women and men are cardiovascular diseases, primarily heart disease and stroke, and cancer.

Historically, Japanese women have had a very low rate of breast cancer, but in the 1970s, it started climbing. Doctors attributed this trend to a "westernization" of the Japanese diet and a tremendous increase in fat consumption. In 1955 only 9% of the average person's daily calories came from fat; by the late 1980s, it had reached 25%.

LEADING CAUSES OF DEATH
Percentage of total deaths, 1993

CAUSE	WOMEN	MEN
Cardiovascular diseases	41%	32%
Cancer	23%	30%
Lung	3%	6%
Breast	2%	—
Cervix	<1%	—
Pneumonia	9%	10%
Accidents	3%	5%
Kidney disease	2%	2%
Suicide	2%	3%
Liver disease	1%	2%
Infectious, parasitic diseases	1%	2%
Homicide	<1%	<1%

Smoking

Smoking, long popular among men, is considered to be unfeminine. Recently however, it has become somewhat more popular among

SMOKING RATES Percentage of total		
YEAR	WOMEN	MEN
1970	13%	78%
1990	14%	59%
1994	13%	60%

young Japanese women. Although the legal age for purchasing cigarettes is 20, minors have no difficulty buying them, especially from the many vending machines.

Japan is one of the few industrialized countries where cigarette advertising is still allowed on television, and tobacco companies have recently started targeting women. The Ministry of Finance, which regulates the tobacco industry, acknowledges a "risk factor" associated with smoking but denies that smoking has been proved to be harmful.

AIDS

By 1993 the total number of reported AIDS cases in Japan was 592, with women accounting for only 4%. The number of people infected with HIV, the virus that causes AIDS, was 2,765,

AIDS AND HIV INCIDENCE Percentage of reported cases, 1993			
AGE	TOTAL	WOMEN	MEN
Under 20	7%	12%	1%
20–29	51%	75%	28%
30–39	22%	9%	33%
40–49	14%	2%	24%
50 and over	7%	1%	14%

and 21% of these were women. By 1995 an estimated 6,200 Japanese were infected with HIV. Although a 1989 law required doctors to report the names of infected patients to the prefectural governor within a week of diagnosis, it is likely that many cases go unreported.

MODES OF HIV TRANSMISSION Total number of cases; percentage of women, 1993				
	AIDS		HIV-POSITIVE	
MODE OF TRANSMISSION	TOTAL CASES	PERCENT WOMEN	TOTAL CASES	PERCENT WOMEN
Blood products	375	<1%	1,728	<1%
Homosexual contact	75	—	177	—
Heterosexual contact	69	19%	523	64%
Intravenous drug use	2	—	8	—
Other/unknown	71	1%	329	70%
Total	**592**	**4%**	**2,765**	**21%**

According to recent government statistics, the AIDS virus in Japan has been spread chiefly through contaminated blood products, and it is estimated that hemophiliacs account for about half of all those infected. Although methods of killing the virus in blood products had been devised and used in other countries in the early 1980s, Japan did not approve these techniques until mid-1985.

Since sexual contact is another common mode of HIV transmission, one reason the Japanese government is reluctant to legalize birth control pills is that it would most likely result in a decrease in condom use and an increase in the spread of the virus.

VIOLENCE AGAINST WOMEN

Violence against women in Japan remains largely unreported. Victims are often fearful of bringing shame on their families and are reluctant to press charges. In recent years feminist groups have conducted surveys to determine the actual prevalence of violent crimes against women, and by publicizing their results, they hope to focus attention on this problem.

Domestic Violence

Although domestic violence is prohibited by law, it is largely condoned, and in a recent study 59% of Japanese women reported physical abuse by a male partner. A battered wife often prefers to return to her parents' home than to file charges against an abusive husband. In recent years local governments have become somewhat more sensitive to this problem, and many police and prefectural offices have established special women's consultation departments to handle cases of spousal abuse.

Rape

Like domestic violence, rape is seldom reported, and the number of recorded cases has been dropping steadily.

Only about 65% of reported rape cases are prosecuted, and the penalty is imprisonment with labor for not less than two years. Cases of indecent assault are prosecuted less frequently, usually only half come to trial, and the penalty is imprisonment with labor for not less than six months and not more than seven years.

RAPE AND INDECENT ASSAULT Number of cases and percentage prosecuted				
	RAPE		INDECENT ASSAULT	
YEAR	NUMBER	PROSECUTIONS	NUMBER	PROSECUTIONS
1985	2,120	63%	1,604	46%
1988	1,786	64%	1,398	50%
1990	1,540	50%	1,417	50%
1992	1,431	65%	1,566	50%

Prostitution

Prostitution was a thriving industry in Japan until 1956, when the Antiprostitution Law imposed penalties on prostitutes' clients as well as the prostitutes themselves. As a result, prostitution decreased as many Japanese men started joining sex tours to other Asian countries, notably Korea, the Philippines, and Thailand. More recently, since the 1980s, increasing numbers of young women from these countries have been entering Japan to work in the country's sex industry. Today, the Antiprostitution Law is still strictly enforced, and the government has been actively shutting down brothels, dating clubs, and other enterprises involved in prostitution. About 2,000 arrests are made each year, and nearly three-quarters are prosecuted.

Japan's Comfort Women

One of Japan's most shameful episodes involving prostitution occurred during World War II, when huge numbers of young women, known as "comfort women," were held captive and forced to provide sex for Japanese soldiers. From 80,000 to 200,000 young women—mostly from Korea but also from the Philippines, Indonesia, and China as well as Japan—were kidnapped and enslaved in Imperial Army brothels throughout the vast Japanese empire as a means of reducing the large number of rapes committed by Japanese servicemen. Immediately following the war, an estimated 55,000 young Japanese women were recruited by the government to work in brothels servicing the American occupation forces. Government officials were afraid that the U.S. soldiers would behave the same way in Japan that Japanese forces had when they occupied overseas territories.

Many of Japan's comfort women did not survive the war. Large numbers of them succumbed to venereal disease and maltreatment. Those who survived tended to keep their ordeal a secret, but after nearly three decades of silence, some of them began demanding an apology and reparation from the

Japanese government. In 1995 the government established an organization, the Asian Women's Fund, to collect voluntary private donations to provide compensation payments to the women who had been victimized. The following year Japan's prime minister offered a formal written apology and started making the first payments. However, many of the women refused to accept the money, objecting to the use of private contributions instead of government funds.

FOR ADDITIONAL INFORMATION ON WOMEN

Embassy of Japan
2520 Massachusetts Avenue, NW
Washington, DC 20008, United States
Telephone: 202-939-6700

Institute for Women's Studies
Ochanomizu University
Otsuk 2-1-1, Bunyo-ku
Tokyo 112, Japan

Consulate General of Japan
Japan Information Center
299 Park Avenue, 16th floor
New York, NY 10171–0025, United States
Telephone: 212-371-8222

National Women's Education Center
728 Sugaya, Ranzan-machi
Hiki-gun
Saiutama-ken 355–02, Japan

**Women's League for Protection of
Human Rights**
2-32-25, Kownji Min
Suginami-ku
Tokyo 166, Japan

MEXICO

Population: *93.6 million*
Women per 100 men: *101*
Women's voting rights: *1947*
Women in legislature: *14%*
Women's share of work force: *30%*
Literacy rates: women—*86%;* men—*91%*
Life expectancy: women—*75.2 years;* men—*69.3 years*
Average number of children: *3.0*
Maternal mortality rate: *110*

Mexico, officially called the United Mexican States, is a federal republic with 31 states and a Federal District (Mexico City). It occupies southern North America and is the third most populous country in the Americas (after the United States and Brazil). Before the arrival of the Spanish in the early 16th century, a number of advanced native Indian civilizations flourished, including the Maya, Toltec, and Aztec. After 300 years of Spanish rule, Mexicans won their independence in 1821.

Today's Mexican population comprises 60% Mestizos (people of mixed American Indian and European ancestry), 30% American Indians, 9% Europeans, and 1% Others. About 71% of the population are urban, and Mexico

City and its environs—with a population of 20 million—contain the largest concentration of people in the world.

Mexico is overwhelmingly Roman Catholic (89%), and although the church was officially separated from the state in 1859, it remains a powerful political force. In general, the culture is strongly influenced by deeply ingrained gender roles and stereotypes: For women the traditional role is one of submissiveness; for men it is *machismo,* an aggressive, dominating manliness.

HISTORY OF THE WOMEN'S MOVEMENT

Since independence, Mexican women have generally been excluded from the political process. When the 1917 constitution was drafted, it was argued that not all women were capable of exercising their political rights, and so women were not granted suffrage. It was not until 1947 that women were finally successful in obtaining the right to vote and run for office, but only in municipal elections. They could not vote or stand for office in national elections until 1953. Despite a 1974 equal rights amendment aimed at eliminating discrimination in Mexican law, enforcement has lagged; women's rights have not been fully respected, and women are still generally considered subordinate to men.

During the 1970s a new wave of feminism emerged among middle-class urban women, beginning with the creation of *Mujeres en Acción Solidaria* (Woman Acting in Solidarity), an association that mobilized women through consciousness-raising groups. In 1974 the *Movimiento de Liberación de la Mujer* (National Women's Liberation Movement) was formed and focused on the legalization of abortion. A number of other women's groups followed, but this decade was marked by the consolidation and subsequent splitting apart of these organizations.

In the 1980s lower-class women also became active in the feminist movement, forming associations to combat violence against women, especially rape and spousal assault. In 1989 they met with some success when the Mexican penal code was modified to increase the punishment for rape, but the issues of abortion rights and domestic violence have not yet been addressed, and these three issues remain the focus of Mexico's women's movement today.

WOMEN IN POLITICS

Despite the fact that Mexican women make up 52% of the registered voters, their representation in politics has been meager. From 1953 to 1970, women activists generally limited themselves to participating in political parties rather than running for national elected office. However, women have never made up more than 20% of the leadership positions in the three main parties, and usually not even that much. The first woman to enter presidential politics was Rosario Ibarra de Piedra who became a candidate for the post in 1982. In 1994 two more women ran for president, although all went down to defeat.

After the elections in 1994, women made up 14% of the General Congress: 17 members of the 128-seat Senate (13%) and 70 members of the 500-seat Chamber of Deputies (14%). Prior to these elections, women constituted 6% of the Senate and 8% of the Chamber of Deputies. Only one woman has ever served as head of the Chamber of Deputies: María Moreno Uriegas, who took office in 1994.

In 1996 two women (12%) served as cabinet ministers: Julia Caravias Lillo (environment, natural resources, fisheries) and Silvia Hernández Enríquez (tourism). Other women in high-level positions included Antonia Lozana (attorney general) and Norma Samaniego Breach (comptroller general). Eleven women served as ambassadors, making up 8% of the total. In the judicial branch of the government women have a somewhat greater presence, accounting for 11% of the Supreme Court of Justice of the Nation. At the state level, only three women have ever been state governors; two were elected, one was appointed by the state congress. In 1996 there were none.

Mexican women are more active in nongovernmental organizations (NGOs), heading 38% of these groups. Of the NGOs dealing with women's and children's issues, women head 97% and 65% respectively.

WOMEN'S EDUCATION

In Mexico education is compulsory for both girls and boys aged 6 to 18. Yet only about 40% of women in Mexico have more than a primary school education, and 15% have no education at all. The indigenous population lags behind; 46% of Indian women lack an education, compared with 37% of men.

The country's overall adult literacy rate is 86% for women and 91% for men. Women make up 62% of the illiterate population, but the gap between men and women is slowly narrowing.

At the university level, 45% of students in literature and fine arts

FEMALE ENROLLMENT Percentage of student body, 1992	
LEVEL	PERCENT
Primary school	48%
Secondary school	49%
Pre-university high school	48%
Professional/technical high school	57%
Higher education	45%

classes and 42% of history majors are women. In technical fields, such as engineering, computing, and chemistry, women make up only 14% of the student body.

WOMEN'S EMPLOYMENT

In 1995 approximately one-third of working-age Mexican women were in the labor force. They made up 30% of the total work force, up from 25% in 1979. Mexican men, in comparison, had a participation rate of 83%.

Toward the end of 1994, Mexico suffered a severe financial crisis. The devaluation of the Mexican peso and subsequent financial difficulties translated into an inflation rate of 50% a year. While prices of essential items climbed, unemployment reached its highest level in 12 years, since the previous currency devaluation. By the middle of 1995, 2 million people had lost their jobs, the manufacturing sector was operating at only 30% capacity, and 20% of the 1.5 million registered small businesses were expected to fail. The middle class was especially hard hit, and many women with children were forced into the labor market to supplement family incomes that had been eroded by inflation.

WOMEN'S LABOR FORCE PARTICIPATION Percentage of age group, 1992	
AGE	PERCENT
25–34	42%
35–44	41%
45–54	37%
55–64	25%

Discrimination in the Workplace

The right to work, the rights of working mothers, and the principle of equal pay for equal work are all protected under the Mexican constitution, but they are not enforced. Many employers, even the Mexico City police force, hire only women who can certify that they are not pregnant. And those women who later become pregnant are likely to be fired.

In 1990 sexual harassment was defined as a crime in legislation passed by the Chamber of Deputies. As a result, women workers have recently begun to press harassment charges against their employers.

Areas of Employment

Over half of all working Mexican women are employed in six fields: commerce (19%), domestic service (11%), secretarial services (11%), financial services (4%), nursing (3%), and education (3%). A large number of women work in the informal sector of the economy, which is estimated to account for a third of the total nonagricultural work force. Many of these women are pieceworkers, street vendors, and other marginal laborers.

No matter what industry they work in, Mexican women are rarely seen in high-level positions. For every 100 men in administrative or managerial jobs, there are only 24 women in comparable posts. Among professional and technical workers, women fare considerably better: 76 women for every 100 men in these positions.

About 3% of Mexico's working women are business entrepreneurs. Most of them are owners of small- and medium-sized enterprises. About 39% are in the restaurant or hotel business, another 34% are in commerce, and 26% are in services.

Pay Differences

Although the 1970 Labor Code provided that "equal pay shall be given for equal work performed in equal posts, hours of work and conditions of efficiency," there is a wide gap between women's and men's earnings. On average, women's wages in nonagricultural industries in Mexico are about 75% of men's.

Maternity Leave and Benefits

By law, women receive 12 weeks of maternity leave at full pay, financed by the Mexican Institute of Social Security (IMSS). Their jobs are also guaranteed for one year. However, this law is rarely enforced.

Child Care

The IMSS runs over 450 day-care centers for children of working families, but these facilities are far from adequate and have long waiting lists. Some large companies provide day-care centers for their employees or help pay for private child-care arrangements. In 1993 about 19% of children under age six were placed in day-care centers.

Unemployment

In 1993 the official unemployment rate for Mexican women was 3.1%, compared with 2.1% for men. This low rate, however, did not reflect the many unstable, marginal jobs of the informal sector, such as street vending or domestic service.

There is no national unemployment insurance in Mexico. However, labor law requires employers to pay dismissed workers a lump sum equal to three months' pay. Also, workers are entitled to an additional 20 days' pay for each year of service.

MARRIAGE AND DIVORCE

In the decade from 1980 to 1990, the number of Mexican families increased from 13.5 million to 16.2 million. The proportion of these families headed by women varied by region, from 16% in rural areas to 19% in urban centers.

Marriage

The minimum legal age for marriage is 18 years for both sexes; with parental consent it drops to 14 for women and 16 for men. However, most couples marry later. The average age of first marriage is 20.6 years for women and 24.1 years for men. About 16% of couples cohabit, and in 1985 about 28% of births were to unmarried women.

The Federal District (Mexico City) civil code gives wives and husbands equal authority over their children and financial resources. However, the civil codes of some other states designate the husband as the head of the household, with total authority over his wife and children.

Divorce

Divorce has been legal in Mexico since 1931, and in 1974 the law was reformed to give women equal rights with men in filing for separation and divorce. In cases where divorce is by mutual consent, the wife can receive payments for food for a period based on the length of the marriage if her income is deemed insufficient and she does not remarry. In contested divorces the court may award alimony and determine child custody.

FAMILY PLANNING

Although Mexico is overwhelmingly Roman Catholic, contraceptive devices are legal and widely available. Slowing the country's population growth has been a primary concern of the government, which has launched nationwide campaigns promoting birth control and distributing contraceptives.

Fertility Rate

The average number of children born to Mexican women is 3.0, a dramatic decline from a fertility rate of 6.8 in 1960. Births to teenagers make up 11% of total births.

Contraception

Recent data on contraceptive use are not available, but it is known that the use of birth control measures among Mexican couples of childbearing age increased dramatically from nearly 30% in 1976 to 53% in 1987. This increase was attributed to the government's large-scale distribution of birth control devices that started during the 1970s. Although birth control pills were the most popular form of contraception during that period, the favored method now is female sterilization. The use of traditional methods, such as rhythm, has remained fairly constant since the 1970s.

In 1987 a National Commission for Human Rights study brought to light complaints that some public hospitals were practicing forced sterilization on poor and illiterate women who had entered the facilities to give birth. Despite the fact that a 1984 General Health Law allows criminal action against anyone pressuring a woman to undergo sterilization or performing it without her consent, the number of such complaints has continued to rise.

CONTRACEPTIVE USE Percentage of couples of childbearing age, 1987	
METHOD	PERCENT
Female sterilization	19%
Birth control pill	10%
Intrauterine devices (IUDs)	10%
Traditional methods	8%
Diaphragm, other methods	3%
Condom	2%
Male sterilization	1%

Although many Mexican women use contraceptives, they do not always use them properly. For example, 60% to 75% of women taking birth control pills purchase them directly from a pharmacy without a doctor's prescription and therefore may not receive proper instructions for their use. In a recent study about 21% of women under the age of 20 reported using a form of birth control when they became pregnant with their first child.

Abortion

According to the 1931 penal code, abortion is legal only when the woman's life is in danger or if the pregnancy resulted from rape or incest. The punishment for performing or undergoing an abortion in any other circumstances is a jail sentence, usually from one to three years. This penalty, however, has had little effect on the number of women seeking illegal abortions each year. In 1990 an estimated 533,100 illegal abortions were performed; these procedures terminated about 17% of all pregnancies. The great majority of illegal abortions are performed in insanitary conditions, and about one-fifth result in complications severe enough to require medical attention. Although there are no official statistics available, it is generally believed that most of the women undergoing illegal abortions already have three or more children.

Sex Education

Sex education is taught in secondary schools in keeping with the government's objective of slowing the population growth and reducing the number of abortions. Along with promoting sex education in the schools, the government distributes contraceptives through hospitals and clinics.

WOMEN'S HEALTH

The life expectancy of Mexican women is 75.2 years, an increase of about 10 years since 1970. For men, life expectancy is 69.3 years. The maternal mortality rate is 110 deaths per 100,000 live births, and a majority of these pregnancy-related deaths, about 65%, occur in rural areas.

In 1984 the General Health Law established the right to health care, including reproductive health. More recently, the government has implemented health care policies specifically aimed at women, such as "Child- and Mother-Friendly Hospitals" and "Health Begins at Home," which encourages women to receive and share health information with their family. The government has also affirmed its commitment to reduce maternal mortality and to make the health of girls, pregnant women, and nursing mothers a priority.

LEADING CAUSES OF DEATH Percentage of total deaths, 1992		
CAUSE	WOMEN	MEN
Cardiovascular diseases	25%	19%
Cancer	13%	8%
Cervix	2%	—
Breast	1%	—
Lung	1%	2%
Diabetes	9%	5%
Infectious, parasitic diseases	6%	6%
Pneumonia	5%	4%
Accidents	5%	13%
Homicide	1%	6%
Suicide	<1%	1%

Leading Causes of Death

The leading causes of death in Mexico for both women and men are cardio-vascular diseases, chiefly heart disease and stroke, and cancer.

Smoking

The smoking rate among Mexican women is one of the highest in the world: 44%. Mexico is also one of the few countries where smoking rates are similar for women and men. Approximately 47% of men are smokers.

AIDS

In 1994 an estimated 200,000 Mexicans were infected with HIV, the virus that causes AIDS. Nearly 3,500 cases of AIDS were reported in 1995, with women accounting for nearly a third, a dramatic increase from 12% in 1982. Most women with AIDS are aged 15 to 29.

VIOLENCE AGAINST WOMEN

Violence against women is a serious problem in Mexico, one that is widely underreported and often covered up. In 1991 a group of women professionals established the Pro Victims Committee to analyze the problem and propose steps to eliminate it.

Domestic Violence

Domestic assault is a misdemeanor in Mexico, but in 10 states, "correcting" a wife and children is not a crime unless it involves cruelty or unnecessary frequency. Often, an abusive husband is pardoned or given a very light prison sentence if his victim's wounds heal within 15 days. Women are generally reluctant to file charges against abusive husbands, and the police are often unwilling to intervene in what they consider to be a private family matter. Although the extent of wife abuse is not known, one government study found that one-third of the women surveyed had been victims of domestic violence. Mexico has no shelters for battered women.

Rape

With the 1989 penal code reforms, rape became punishable by 8 to 14 years in prison—21 years in the case of gang rape. In addition, a rapist was no longer allowed to avoid prison by paying a fine.

In Mexico City and 13 states, special agencies have been established to deal with rape and other forms of sexual assault. In addition, many nongovernmental organizations and women's groups have pressured the government to provide aid for rape victims. Although the attorney general's office in the Federal District operates rape crisis centers throughout Mexico City, these centers are seldom used. Some of the women who have gone to these facilities have reported being subjected to humiliating and abusive treatment by the centers' police and medical examiners. Although the female population of the city is more than 10 million, only 627 women used these centers in 1995.

Prostitution

Prostitution is illegal in Mexico, and the penalty is a fine and six months to five years in prison. The penalty for procuring is a fine and six months to eight years in prison.

FOR ADDITIONAL INFORMATION ON WOMEN

Consulate General of Mexico
8 East 41st Street
New York, NY 10017, United States
Telephone: 212-689-0456

**Interdisciplinary Program on
   Women's Studies**
El Colegio de Mexico

Camino al Ajusco No. 20
C.P. 01000 Mexico D.F., Mexico

Mexican Embassy
1911 Pennsylvania Avenue, NW
Washington, DC 20006, United States
Telephone: 202-269-3972

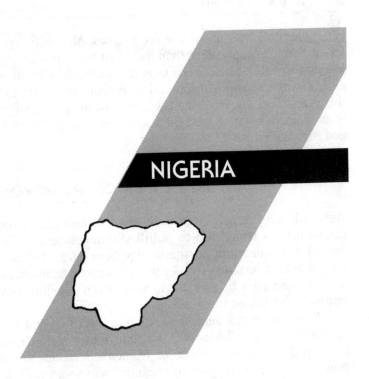

NIGERIA

Population: *98.1 million*
Women per 100 men: *102*
Women's voting rights: *1957 in south, 1978 in north*
Women in legislature: *N/A (no elected legislature)*
Women's share of work force: *34%*
Literacy rates: women—*42%;* men—*63%*
Life expectancy: women—*56.6 years;* men—*54.1 years*
Average number of children: *6.2*
Maternal mortality rate: *1,000*

Nigeria, located in west Africa, is the most populous country on the continent and the 10th most populous in the world. A British colony for nearly two centuries, Nigeria obtained its independence in 1960. Since then the country has endured more than two decades of military rule and a costly civil war. In 1967 the Eastern Region seceded as the Republic of Biafra. Three years and more than a million casualties later, the secessionists surrendered.

About 50% of the Nigerian population are Muslim, 40% are Christian, and the remainder practice various indigenous African religions. The population is largely rural; only about 15% live in cities. Although there are over 250 different ethnic groups, more than half of all Nigerians belong to one of the following three: the Muslim Hausa in the north, the Christian Ibo in the southeast, and the mixed Muslim and Christian Yoruba in the southwest. With this great diversity, Nigerian laws and customs, especially those concerning women, have been shaped by a wide range of traditional religious, ethnic, and regional values.

HISTORY OF THE WOMEN'S MOVEMENT

Women in southern Nigeria were granted the right to vote in 1957 during the country's transition to political independence. The franchise was extended to women in northern Nigeria in 1978, and the elections in 1979 proved to be a turning point for women's participation in government: More women than men turned out to vote. Even Muslim women, fully veiled, waited in line to cast their ballots.

Women's groups began emerging in the 1980s and became much more visible and vocal in the early 1990s. One of the most influential organizations today is the National Council of Women's Societies, an umbrella organization of more than 40 women's groups, whose primary aim is to improve women's education and training. Other issues that currently concern Nigerian women's groups include employment opportunities, legal rights, and political representation.

WOMEN IN POLITICS

Since Nigeria's independence, no matter what type of government has been in power—military or civilian—women have been sorely underrepresented. In 1996 the country was ruled by the military Provisional Ruling Council (PRC). There was no elected national legislature and women made up 9% of the PRC's 32-member Federal Executive Council, a body similar to a cabinet. Although the PRC announced plans to return the country to democratic rule in 1998, progress on this front has been slow.

WOMEN'S EDUCATION

In 1976 Nigeria implemented universal primary education, giving every child the right to free elementary schooling. During the next decade the number of primary schools nearly doubled, while the number of students

FEMALE ENROLLMENT Percentage of student body, 1993	
LEVEL	PERCENT
Primary school	44%
Secondary school	55%
Higher education	24%

more than doubled, reaching 14.5 million. However, it is estimated that slightly more than half of all girls of primary school age are not in school, and of those who do enroll, many soon drop out. Some localities have tried to reduce the female dropout rate by prohibiting parents from taking their daughters out of school.

Among adults the literacy rate is 42% for women and 63% for men. To combat this widespread illiteracy, a government commission was established in 1992 to find ways of encouraging women to enroll in special literacy classes. With the help of various United Nations agencies, Nigeria expects to teach 3 million people to read and write by the end of the decade.

WOMEN'S EMPLOYMENT

During colonial times Victorian attitudes toward women were widely accepted throughout Nigeria: Few women worked and most participated only in activities that involved the home. After independence this pattern continued, and only in recent years, as more women have been completing secondary and higher education, have they started entering the work force in large numbers. By the mid-1990s about 43% of all working-age Nigerian women had jobs outside the home, and they constituted about 34% of the total labor force. Nigerian men, in comparison, had a participation rate of 85%.

Discrimination in the Workplace

The Nigerian constitution guarantees equal rights to all citizens and expressly forbids all forms of discrimination. However, these provisions are not always implemented, and laws specifically protecting women are not regularly enforced. For example, while Nigerian women are not specifically barred from any area of employment, the government does allow employers to follow certain religious and customary practices that discriminate against women. And although more and more women are entering the formal sector every year, they do not receive equal wages for equal work.

Areas of Employment

Nigerian women are predominantly employed in agriculture and are responsible for producing over 70% of the nation's food supply. Outside agriculture women tend to be employed in low-paying occupations such as sales, clerical, and factory work. They rarely occupy high-level, decision-making positions. For every 100 men in administrative or managerial positions, there are only 6 women in similar posts, one of Africa's poorest representations of women in this occupational category. Among professional and technical workers, Nigerian women fare somewhat better. For every 100 men in these positions, 35 women hold comparable jobs.

In the federal government women make up nearly a quarter of the total staff, up from 13% in 1986. However, the grade level in which they have the highest representation, 33%, is the lowest, whereas the highest level has the smallest proportion of female employees, 11%. The federal ministries and departments with the highest concentrations of women employees are justice (44%), health and human services (42%), the civil service commission (39%), defense (35%), and education/youth development (34%).

Generally, Nigerian women with the highest levels of education are found in health care: They account for 70% of nurses, 30% of dentists, 25% of pharmacists, and 18% of doctors. Many women are also employed in education. About 42% of all primary and 33% of secondary school teachers are women. At the university level, however, women make up only about 12% of the teaching staff.

The number of women engineers has grown significantly in recent years, from fewer than 20 in 1979 to more than 200 by the mid-1990s. Another area where women have made noticeable inroads is the legal profession. By 1995 as many women as men were lawyers, and more than 60 women judges sat on the High Court, up from only 10 in 1985.

In recent years the government has attempted to encourage women to develop small business enterprises. In 1989 the People's Bank was established to grant loans to low-income earners, primarily women, to develop or expand small-scale farming, food processing, trading, or other business ventures. By 1994 women had received about 70% of the bank's total loans.

Pay Differences

Although the principle of equal pay for equal work is supposed to apply to all government employees, it is generally not enforced, and women who work in the private sector have no protection at all. It is estimated that on average, Nigerian women earn about two-thirds of men's wages.

Maternity Leave and Benefits

A 12-week, fully paid maternity leave is guaranteed to all women government workers as well as many in the private sector. In addition, new mothers are often allowed shorter working hours so that they can care for their children.

Child Care

The Nigerian government has no official policy regarding child care, and there are very few public facilities for young children. Most day-care centers are privately owned, and they vary greatly in quality. In many communities there is a tremendous need for additional centers, and many women cannot work because of a shortage of child-care facilities.

Unemployment

For many years Nigeria was a predominantly agricultural country. With the discovery of oil in 1958, the nation's economic fortunes improved dramatically, but the slump in the global oil market in the early 1980s created serious financial difficulties and high unemployment.

Generally, unemployment is higher in urban centers than in rural areas, and those hardest hit are the young. By the mid-1990s, urban women aged 15 to 19 had the highest women's unemployment rate, 38%, compared with 40% for their male counterparts. The next highest rate was among women aged 20 to 24, who had a jobless rate of 33%, compared with 40% for men in the same age range. The lowest unemployment rate was among urban women aged 50 to 59, only 2.2%; compared with 3.9% for urban men in the same age range.

MARRIAGE AND DIVORCE

Most Nigerian women marry at an early age, usually in their teens, and have large families. Only about 18% of urban households and 13% of rural ones are headed by women.

Marriage

The average age of Nigerian women at first marriage is 18.7 years, but there are tremendous variations among religious, ethnic, and regional groups.

AVERAGE AGE AT MARRIAGE By ethnic group and region		
ETHNIC GROUP	REGION	AGE
Hausa	North	By 15
Ibo	Southeast	Over 19
Yoruba	Southwest	Over 20

Arranged marriages are common among the Muslim Hausa, who usually marry off their young daughters before they reach puberty. In some regions poor families have been known to sell their young daughters into marriage.

Nigerian marriage laws tend to uphold traditional patriarchal values and acknowledge the husband as the head of the family, with complete authority over his wife and children. In many places a wife cannot obtain a passport without her husband's consent, and in some states she may not be able to own property or even inherit her husband's property unless she can prove that she helped acquire it. As a consequence, a widow is often left penniless as her husband's property is taken by her in-laws. In some regions the widow herself is considered part of the husband's property and may be inherited by his oldest male relative.

Polygamy

Polygamy is legal in Nigeria and widely practiced in all regions and among all ethnic groups, both in Muslim and Christian communities. In 1990 41% of all married women were in a polygamous marriage; in the northwest this figure reached 50%.

In a polygamous marriage the husband is required to treat each wife equally and provide her with separate living quarters. In some communities a man is allowed to have as many as four wives. A woman, on the other hand, is permitted only one husband.

Purdah

Purdah is the Islamic practice of keeping women and girls secluded from any men who are not their husbands or family members. This custom is most prevalent among the Hausa in the far north, and in its strictest form women are confined to the house and cannot work, travel, or even be seen in public.

Divorce

According to Nigerian law, a divorce may be granted if both parties agree and have been separated for two years. In cases without mutual consent, grounds for divorce include adultery, desertion, and a three-year separation.

Although divorce is relatively rare, it is more common in cities than in the countryside.

FAMILY PLANNING

The first family planning clinic in Nigeria opened in 1958, and in 1964 the National Council of Women's Societies helped establish a network of centers offering reproductive counseling. Since 1988, the Nigerian government has actively supported birth control programs, but despite these efforts, family planning services are considered woefully inadequate.

Fertility Rate

The fertility rate in Nigeria is 6.2 children per woman, down from 6.8 in 1960. Among women who have completed at least secondary schooling, the average is only 4.2 children. The Muslim Hausa have the highest fertility rate: 6.6 children.

Most young women in Nigeria are mothers by the age of 20, and births to teenagers account for 14% of the total number of births. Although large families are common, about 12% of families have only one child.

Contraception

The proportion of Nigerian couples of childbearing age who use some form of birth control is only about 6%, one of the world's lowest rates of contraception. About 3.5% use birth control pills or other modern methods, a dramatic increase from less than 1% in 1980. Traditional methods are used by 2.5%, a significant decrease from 5.5% in 1980. One reason for this change in the pattern of contraceptive use is the government's policy, dating back to 1988, of actively encouraging the sale of modern contraceptives in pharmacies. It was found that many Nigerian women were too embarrassed to ask for them in public clinics.

CONTRACEPTIVE USE Percentage of couples of childbearing age, 1990	
METHOD	PERCENT
Traditional methods	2.5%
Birth control pill	1.2%
Intrauterine devices (IUDs)	0.8%
Hormone injection	0.7%
Condom	0.4%
Female sterilization	0.3%

Abortion

Under the 1958 criminal code, abortion is permitted only when two physicians certify the woman's life is endangered by the pregnancy. Because of this highly restrictive law, many Nigerian women, especially teenagers, resort to illegal abortions. Young women between the ages of 11 and 20 account for approximately two-thirds of the patients hospitalized with medical complications resulting from these unsafe illegal abortions. One study found that nearly 80% of pregnant secondary school students had undergone previous abortions. Among pregnant university students, this proportion rose to 95%.

The punishment for illegal abortion is severe: 7 to 14 years in prison for the woman, up to 14 years in prison for the practitioner, and up to 3 years for anyone supplying abortion devices. This law, however, is not strictly enforced, and prosecution is rare. Past attempts to liberalize the abortion law have been defeated by vigorous opposition from religious groups.

WOMEN'S HEALTH

Since the 1960s, the Nigerian government has sought to improve health standards, and in 1986 the Primary Health Care Program succeeded in more than doubling the proportion of Nigerian women with access to medical care, from 30% to 66%. However, health care is still poor, and parts of Nigeria are among the most disease-ridden in the world. Although average life expectancy is low—56.6 years for women and 54.1 years for men—it has increased by more than 10 years for both women and men over the past two decades.

Religious and ethnic customs, such as early marriage and large family size, exact an especially heavy toll on the health of Nigerian women. The country's maternal mortality rate is 1,000 deaths per 100,000 live births, with illegal teenage abortions believed to account for about 15% of these fatalities. The chances of a Nigerian woman dying as a result of pregnancy or childbirth are 1 in 16.

Leading Causes of Death

As in many other sub-Saharan African countries, the leading causes of death for both women and men include infectious and parasitic diseases— such as dysentery, malaria, pneumonia, tetanus, tuberculosis, and AIDS—

as well as cancer, heart disease, and injuries. Among young women, especially teenagers, complications of childbirth and illegal abortion are major causes of death.

In 1996 an outbreak of bacterial meningitis in northern Nigeria struck a reported 50,000 people, and killed about 10% of them, mostly women, children, and the elderly. One of the difficulties in treating diseases like bacterial meningitis is that many of the victims hide their illness. According to local folklore, these diseases are plagues sent to punish those who have committed moral offenses.

Smoking

Nigeria has one of the world's lowest proportions of women smokers. While 53% of men smoke, only about 3% of all women smoke, one of the lowest female smoking rates in the world. In rural areas, however, it is not uncommon for women to sniff tobacco.

AIDS

Although precise information on the prevalence of AIDS in Nigeria is not available, the World Health Organization estimated that in 1994 more than a million Nigerians were infected with HIV, the virus that causes AIDS. As in other African countries, the AIDS virus is spread almost entirely through heterosexual relations, and a 1990 study of commercial sex workers in certain urban areas found nearly 15% to be HIV-positive. Transmission through homosexual relations or intravenous drug use is believed to be minimal.

Vesico-Vaginal Fistula

Vesico-vaginal fistula, a serious medical condition related to pregnancy, affects an estimated 100,000 Nigerian women. It is a tearing of the tissue between the bladder and vagina, and most often occurs in young women undergoing prolonged obstructed labor. Among the Hausa it is often caused when an incision, called the "gishiri cut," is made through the vagina in a frantic attempt to release the fetus.

Because of this fistula, urine continually leaks out through the woman's birth canal; in cases where the rectum has also been torn, fecal matter also oozes out. Unless corrected by surgery, this condition remains a lifelong affliction.

VIOLENCE AGAINST WOMEN

Violence against women is widespread throughout Nigeria, cutting across all religious, ethnic, and regional boundaries. It is seldom reported, however, and even when cases are brought to trial, convictions are rare.

Domestic Violence

According to the Nigerian penal code, a man can "correct" his wife as long as the "correction" does not leave a scar or require a stay of more than 21 days in a hospital. The police rarely intervene in cases of domestic violence, and victims are discouraged from filing charges.

The Nigerian government offers no specific social services or shelters for abused women. It is a common belief among women, especially those in polygamous marriages, that some form of physical abuse is a normal condition of marriage. Women are also sometimes beaten for alleged inappropriate or immodest behavior.

Rape

Although rape is illegal and punishable by life imprisonment, it is rarely reported. Victims, fearing humiliation and discrimination, prefer to remain silent rather than to press charges against their attackers. In cases that are brought to trial, a witness's corroboration is required for conviction.

With respect to marital rape, Nigerian law prohibits a husband from forcing his wife to submit to sex, but he cannot be prosecuted for rape. If a wife wishes to press charges, her husband can be prosecuted for assault.

Prostitution

Prostitution itself is not illegal in Nigeria, but the law does criminalize acts associated with prostitution, such as soliciting or operating a brothel. In some areas prostitution is fairly widespread, and government measures have been somewhat successful in closing a large number of brothels.

Female Genital Mutilation

Female genital mutilation is a ritual practiced throughout Nigeria, primarily in the Christian south but also among Muslims in the north. It is estimated that about half of all women have undergone some form of genital mutilation, ranging from removal of the clitoral hood to the complete removal of the clitoris and infibulation, a procedure in which the clitoris and labia are removed and the edges are stitched together, leaving only a small opening for the passage of urine.

The procedure is usually performed before puberty but may be done anytime from the first week of life to just after marriage or the birth of the woman's first child. Often, it is performed without anesthesia by a female elder using a knife, razor blade, or even a shard of glass. Infections, severe bleeding, and other serious health problems often result, sometimes leading to permanent, crippling injury and even death.

The government officially opposes female genital mutilation, and the Ministry of Health has sponsored public education projects aimed at warning communities about its dangers. However, little else has been done to abolish this widespread custom.

FOR ADDITIONAL INFORMATION ON WOMEN

Consulate General of Nigeria
Nigerian Information Services
828 Second Avenue
New York, NY 10017
United States
Telephone: 212-808-0301

Embassy of Nigeria
1333 16th Street, NW
Washington, DC 20036
United States
Telephone: 202-986-8400

**Ministry of Social Development,
 Youth and Sport**
National Committee on Women and
 Development
5 Kofo Abayomi Street
Victoria Island, Lagos, Nigeria

**National Council of Women's
 Societies Nigeria**
Plot Pc 14, Ahmed Onibudo Street
Off Idowu Taylor Street
Victoria Island, Lagos, Nigeria

PHILIPPINES

Population: *69.2 million*
Women per 100 men: *97*
Women's voting rights: *1937*
Women in legislature: *13%*
Women's share of work force: *31%*
Literacy rates: women—*93%;* men—*94%*
Life expectancy: women—*70.2;* men—*64.9*
Average number of children: *3.8*
Maternal mortality rate: *280*

The Philippines is a string of more than 7,000 tropical islands off the south-east coast of Asia. About 95% of the people live in the largest 11 islands; most of the remaining islands are tiny, less than a square mile in area.

The great majority of Filipinos, 83%, are Roman Catholic. Protestants make up 9% of the population, Muslims account for 5%, and Buddhists and others the remaining 3%. Approximately half of all Filipinos are urban dwellers.

HISTORY OF THE WOMEN'S MOVEMENT

The Philippines was a Spanish colony for nearly 400 years before it was ceded to the United States at the end of the Spanish-American war in 1898. Under American influence, Filipinos enjoyed increased political freedom as well as improvements in health care and education. For the first time, Philippine women were permitted to enroll in colleges and universities and allowed to pursue professional careers.

By the 1920s and 30s, therefore, a core of educated, economically independent women had emerged. Encouraged by visiting American suffragettes, they campaigned for the right to vote, and the 1935 constitution included a provision stating that voting rights would be extended to women if more than 300,000 of them would support the measure in a national plebiscite. When the votes were counted, more than 450,000 ballots had been cast in favor of the amendment, and in 1937 women were granted the right to vote.

Philippine independence, which had been slated for 1945, was delayed by World War II and the Japanese occupation of the islands from 1942 to 1945. Following the war, the country was reoccupied by the United States until 1946, when independence was granted.

In the 50 years since independence, Philippine women have played an active role in the political developments that have shaped the nation. Their efforts helped to topple the devastating 14-year dictatorship of Ferdinand Marcos and usher in the subsequent democratic government headed by the country's first woman president, Corazon Aquino.

Today the Philippines is still under democratic rule and struggling to recover from the tremendous economic deterioration that resulted largely from the corruption of the Marcos regime. Women's groups have turned their attention to the pressing matters at hand: widespread poverty and malnutrition, child care, violence against women, health care, and family planning services.

WOMEN IN POLITICS

Corazon Aquino, the first woman head of state in Southeast Asia, rose to power following the assassination of her husband, a popular political leader opposed to the Marcos regime. She was installed as president in 1986 after Marcos fled into exile and was elected to the post the following year. Although Aquino's victory was largely attributed to her wide support by Philippine women, many of whom called themselves "Cory's Crusaders," she was later criticized for not being especially helpful in furthering the rise of other women to high government posts—she appointed women to only 2 out of 20 cabinet positions. By mid-1996 her successor, Fidel Ramos, had named 3 women ministers to his 22-member cabinet (14%): Mina Gabor (tourism), Corazon de Leon (social welfare and development), and Carmencita Reodica (health).

After the 1992 elections, women made up 13% of the Philippine national legislature. Twenty-three were elected and 2 appointed to the 204-member House of Representatives (12%), up from 17 in 1987. In the 24-member Senate 4 women were elected (17%), exactly double the 1987 figure.

Philippine women have had some success in reaching high-level positions in the diplomatic service. In 1993 13 women served as ambassadors and 10 held the rank of assistant secretary in the foreign service home office. At the municipal level, in 1992, 8% of mayors were women, up from 5% in 1980

WOMEN'S EDUCATION

The Philippine constitution guarantees free primary education to all children, and although schooling is not compulsory, attendance is high, especially among female students. In fact, the Philippines is one of the few Asian countries where women outnumber men in higher education. Approximately 10% of all women are college graduates, compared with 7% of men. The literacy rates for women and men are virtually the same: 93% for women and 94% for men.

At the undergraduate level, the fields of study with the highest concentrations of female students are the social sciences, education, nutrition, and dietetics. The areas with the lowest female enrollments are architecture, engineering, fine arts, humanities, and law. Only recently were women's studies courses introduced.

Women were not admitted to Philippine military academies or similar institutions until 1992, when the Women in Development and Nation-Building Act ensured equal opportunities for the appointment, admission, training, graduation, and commission of women in all military schools. That year, 16 female students became the first to enroll in the Philippine Military Academy.

FEMALE ENROLLMENT Percentage of student body, 1992	
LEVEL	PERCENT
Primary school	49%
Secondary school	50%
Higher education	59%

WOMEN'S EMPLOYMENT

Philippine women have been entering the labor force in increasing numbers. By the mid-1990s about 38% of working-age women were in the labor force, and they constituted 31% of the total work force. Philippine men, in comparison, had a labor force participation rate of 85%.

Over the past decade the nation's struggling economy has caused high unemployment, especially among women, and large numbers of Filipinas have had to find work overseas. By 1995 the Philippines was providing more women for the overseas labor market than any other country.

Discrimination in the Workplace

Philippine law specifically prohibits discrimination against women in the workplace in hiring, promotion, and training. The law also outlines criminal penalties for discrimination, but enforcement is lax, and violations do occur. Except for those Filipinas employed by the federal government or by government-owned or -controlled companies, women workers face widespread discrimination, especially with respect to wages and opportunities for promotion.

A 1993 survey by the Institute of Labor Studies found that sexual harassment in the workplace was widespread, though greatly underreported due to victims' fears of losing their jobs. A Supreme Court ruling that year upheld a decision that sexual harassment was valid cause for firing an employee.

Areas of Employment

Officially, the Women in Development and Nation-Building Act assures Philippine women equal access to employment in all occupations and economic opportunities, including the armed forces. Yet women predominate in two major areas of employment: wholesale and retail trade (about 64%) and community social and personal services (about 55%). One industry where the sexes are almost evenly balanced is manufacturing, where women make up about 46% of all workers. In real estate, finance, and business services women make up about 40% of all workers; in agriculture, about 25%.

In all industries women tend to predominate in lower-ranking, lower-paying positions. For every 100 men in administrative or managerial jobs, there are only 38 women in comparable posts. However, Filipinas fare substantially better in professional and technical positions, where they outnumber

WOMEN IN MAJOR OCCUPATIONAL GROUPS
Percentage of group

OCCUPATIONAL GROUP	1980	1990
Sales	65%	66%
Professional, technical	61%	65%
Service	58%	58%
Clerical	46%	54%
Administrative, managerial	25%	27%
Agriculture	24%	26%

men 172 to 100, one of the world's highest ratios of women to men in this occupational category.

The number of women in the judicial system has risen significantly, from 6% in 1981 to 13% in 1992. Women judges are found in most courts; they make up 26% of trial court judges and 21% of appeals court judges. In education women constitute 93% of primary school and 85% of secondary school teachers. They make up 58% of the teaching staff in colleges and universities, and 63% in technical and vocational schools. The participation of women in the civil service has traditionally been high among Philippine women, usually about 52%. However, at the highest levels, women are outnumbered by men more than two to one.

The number of self-employed women is increasing steadily at an annual rate of 4%, compared with 3% for men. The government has been actively assisting women entrepreneurs by offering them seed capital and low-interest loans that require no collateral and are repayable in five years.

Overseas Workers

High unemployment rates since the mid-1980s have forced many Filipinos to find work overseas. More than half of these 2 million workers are women, and even though many of them have college degrees, nearly 60% of them work as maids or other domestic helpers. About 35% are officially said to work in the entertainment industry, mostly as dancers and choreographers, but it is believed that they are actually employed as sex workers.

More than 175 different countries employ Philippine workers. In all of Asia, female migrant workers from the Philippines outnumber their male counterparts by 12 to 1. Saudi Arabia receives the largest share of Philippine workers, but few are women. Japan is next, with about equal numbers of women and men, while women predominate in Hong Kong and Singapore. In Singapore alone, more than 75,000 Filipinas work as maids. The European countries with the highest proportions of Filipinas include Belgium,

Germany, Greece, Italy, and Spain. Canada and the United States also have significant numbers.

In addition to enduring poor working conditions, Filipinas employed overseas often suffer sexual harassment and physical abuse, ranging from physical assault and rape to murder. In 1995 worldwide media attention focused on the plight of these overseas workers when a Philippine maid in Singapore was hanged for killing another maid and a four-year-old boy, despite testimony that the boy had died accidentally and the maid had been killed by the child's irate father. In a second incident the same year, a 16-year-old maid in the United Arab Emirates was sentenced to death for killing her employer after he raped her. Eventually, her sentence was reduced to a year in prison.

Pay Differences

On average, Philippine women working in nonagricultural industries earn about 61% of men's wages. Only in two occupational areas do they earn more than men: professional and clerical. In sales they earn about the same as men, and in all other areas—including administrative, service, and agricultural—they earn less. Women at the highest levels of management—administrators, managers, and executives—earn only about one-third the salary of their male colleagues.

Maternity Leave and Benefits

Maternity benefits are available to many Philippine women. In the public sector, though, only married women are eligible for these benefits. In general, maternity leave begins 10 weeks before the woman's due date and extends 4 weeks after delivery. She receives 100% of her salary for 60 days, paid by social security.

Child Care

Child care has long been a serious problem for working mothers in the Philippines. Between 1985 and 1990 the number of day-care centers nearly doubled, reaching more than 14,000. However, more than half of all villages were still left with no public child-care facilities. And despite a 1990 law mandating a day-care center in every village, funding for the project has not been forthcoming, and the law has not been implemented.

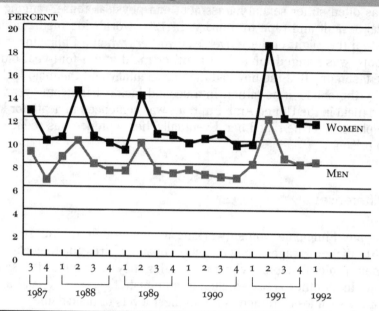

UNEMPLOYMENT RATES
Percentage of labor force

PERCENT

1987 1988 1989 1990 1991 1992

WOMEN

MEN

Unemployment

Since the start of the economic crisis in late 1983, unemployment has been widespread throughout the Philippines. Women have been especially hard hit, since they tend to be the last ones hired and the first ones fired. At the start of 1992, the unemployment rate for women was 11.5%, compared with 8.2% for men, with urban rates far exceeding those in rural areas.

Interestingly, unemployment in the Philippines has not shifted gradually but rather has fluctuated markedly. The lowest rate for women, 9.2%, was recorded in early 1989, while the highest rate, 18.3%, occurred in mid-1991. The comparable rates for men during those same periods were 7.5% and 11.9% respectively.

MARRIAGE AND DIVORCE

Religious laws and policies have played a major role in shaping Philippine attitudes toward marriage and divorce. Since Filipinos are overwhelmingly Roman Catholic, the country's laws largely reinforce the Church's teachings. A separate Code of Muslim Personal Laws applies to the Muslim minority.

The typical nuclear family—two parents and their children—is the predominant family structure in the Philippines. Only about 14% of all families are headed by women.

Marriage

The minimum legal age for marriage in the Philippines is 18 for both women and men. On average, though, women marry at 23.8 years and men at 26.3 years. About 60% of all Philippine women aged 15 to 49 are married or living with a partner; 37% have never been married; and only 3% are widowed, divorced, or separated. Births to unmarried women make up only 6% of the total number of births.

For more than 35 years the law governing most family matters was the civil code, which gave a husband tremendous authority over his wife and children. In 1987 a new Family Code removed most of the civil code's discriminatory provisions, giving women legal equality with their husbands in many areas. For example, a wife now has the right to practice her profession or career without her husband's consent. In addition, a widow has the right to remarry before the expiration of the traditional 300 days of mourning, and she can maintain authority over her children after remarriage. A few inequities still remain, however. If a wife attempts to conceal that her pregnancy was caused by another man, her husband can have the marriage annulled; but no similar provision exists for a wife whose husband fathers a child by another woman.

The Code of Muslim Personal Laws follows traditional customs and allows polygamy, permitting a man to have more than one wife but a wife to have only one husband.

Divorce

The 1987 Family Code does not provide for divorce but does allow annulment ("Declaration of Nullity of Marriage") on psychological grounds. Since divorce is not an option, anyone wishing to dissolve a marriage and remarry must get an annulment.

The 1987 code also extends the grounds for legal separation. Earlier, the only two available grounds for separation were attempts on the life of the spouse and either adultery by the wife or concubinage by the husband. A wife was guilty of adultery if she ever engaged in sexual relations with another man, whereas concubinage was defined as keeping a mistress, having sex under scandalous circumstances, or cohabiting with another woman. The new grounds for legal separation include repeated physical violence or abusive conduct, pressure to change religious or political affiliation, drug addiction, alcoholism, homosexuality, or abandonment for more than one year. The new code also allows either partner to claim sexual infidelity instead of having to specify adultery or concubinage.

As a result of this change in the law, permanent legal separation ("unofficial divorce") has become a popular option for many Filipinos, especially the poor, who cannot afford the legal fees for an annulment. In most of these cases, the mother retains the children but the husband provides little or no support for them.

The Muslim code permits divorce but restricts the divorced woman from remarrying within three months. A widow is prohibited from remarrying within four months and 10 days after her husband's death.

FAMILY PLANNING

The Roman Catholic Church has had a profound influence on the country's family planning policies. In recent years women's groups, encouraged by support from President Ramos, have actively lobbied for increased family planning services as well as for liberalization of the country's abortion law.

Fertility Rate

The fertility rate in the Philippines is 3.8 children per woman, down from 5.0 in 1980 and 6.0 in 1970. Approximately 6% of all births are to teenagers.

Contraception

Despite the country's meager family planning services, about 40% of couples of childbearing age use some form of birth control, up from 32% in 1980.

CONTRACEPTIVE USE Percentage of couples of childbearing age, 1993	
METHOD	PERCENT
Traditional methods	15%
Female sterilization	12%
Birth control pill	9%
Intrauterine devices (IUDs)	3%
Condom	1%
Male sterilization	<1%

Abortion

Abortion in the Philippines is allowed only to save the woman's life, and many women resort to illegal abortions. While there are no official statistics on the incidence of these clandestine procedures, it is estimated that complications from unsafe, illegal abortions account for about 10% of all pregnancy-related deaths.

Sex Education

Sex education is neither mandated nor widely available in the Philippines. In the late 1960s and 1970s, population education programs were introduced in the secondary schools, but they focused primarily on the dangers of population growth and premarital sex.

WOMEN'S HEALTH

The average life expectancy in the Philippines is 70.2 years for women and 64.9 years for men. These numbers represent an increase of nearly 10 years for both women and men since 1970. The maternal mortality rate is 280 deaths per 100,000 live births.

In recent years the government has launched several health care programs, including an immunization program targeting tuberculosis, diphtheria, pertussis (whooping cough), polio, measles, hepatitis B, and tetanus. Malnutrition, another major health problem, is the focus of a government nutrition service that screens women for iron deficiency and provides vitamin supplements.

Leading Causes of Death

The leading causes of death among Philippine women are heart disease, cancer, tuberculosis, and pregnancy-related disorders. Specific data on causes of death are not available, though it is known that among women aged 40 to 59, the incidence of breast cancer is rising steadily.

Smoking

Philippine men have one of the highest rates of smoking in the world: 84%. Women smoke considerably less; only about 16% of them are smokers.

AIDS

The actual extent of AIDS and HIV infection in the Philippines is not known, but the World Health Organization has estimated that by 1994 about 18,000 people were infected with the virus, and that the rate of infection was climbing rapidly. By mid-1993 there were 171 reported cases of AIDS among women, more than three-quarters of them among women aged 15 to 29. Of the 175 cases reported among men, about half were among those aged 30 to 44.

Heterosexual contact is the most common mode of HIV transmission among women, and it has been suggested that one reason the reported incidence among women is so high is that female sex workers have been tested much more extensively than members of other high-risk groups, such as homosexual men and blood recipients. It is also thought that many of the young Filipinas working in sex industries overseas return home infected with the virus.

Although the government has attempted to organize a national anti-AIDS campaign, it has been thwarted by strong opposition from church leaders, who condemn the use of condoms.

VIOLENCE AGAINST WOMEN

Violence against women is a serious problem in the Philippines, but one that goes largely unreported. The country's laws, courts, and police tend to protect men, and female victims rarely press charges.

Domestic Violence

Although assault is a crime according to the Philippine penal code, domestic violence is largely ignored and considered a private family matter in which others, especially the police, should not interfere. When cases are brought to trial, penalties are mild; a husband who kills his wife when he discovers her in the act of adultery may be imprisoned for as long as six years or as little as six months plus one day.

While the actual extent of domestic violence is unknown, it is estimated that 6 out of 10 Philippine wives experience some form of physical abuse. A women's crisis center in Manila has reported receiving more than 100 calls a week from battered women.

In recent years, largely as a result of pressure from women's groups, the government has proposed legislation to impose harsher penalties for wife beating and to provide greater protection for battered wives. In addition, a 1993 order from the president created special women's desks in police stations in areas with the highest rates of domestic abuse. These desks are run by trained officers, usually women, who assist and provide support for the victims. By 1995 a program was under way to train enough officers to provide women's desks throughout the country. Government-run shelters for battered women were established in 1991 by the Department of Social Welfare and Development, but the first year they were in operation, they housed fewer than 200 women.

Nongovernmental women's organizations have continued to make domestic violence a top priority. In addition to lobbying for increased law enforcement, they provide a variety of services, including crisis hotlines, shelters, training centers, and legal counseling.

Rape

According to a 1989 government report, cases of rape were reported at a rate of one every five hours, but officials estimated that even these incidents represented only about 5% of the actual number of cases. More recently, the frequency of rape has been estimated to be as high as one every six minutes. A 1990 report suggested that marital rape, which is not considered a crime, accounted for about 90% of reported cases.

Women's groups maintain that penalties for rape are too lenient and that because Phillipine society is so dominated by men, women accept rape as part of the culture. In addition, many rape victims are minors who are willing to accept an incestuous relationship rather than subject the family to shame and embarrassment.

In 1994 legislation was proposed to change the definition of rape, making it a crime against a person (a public offense) and not a crime against chastity (a private offense). This legislation would also make marital rape a crime and allow the wife's family or the state to file a complaint on her behalf.

Prostitution

Prostitution is illegal in the Philippines, but penalties are light and its incidence is widespread. Women's groups are campaigning for harsher penalties for procurers as well as education, training, and rehabilitation programs for prostitutes. They are also lobbying for shelters and support services for the estimated 60,000 sexually abused and exploited child prostitutes.

Prostitution and sex slavery have long plagued the Philippines. During the Japanese occupation of the islands in World War II, large numbers of Filipinas were enslaved as "comfort women" to provide sex for Japanese soldiers. For decades after the war, many of these women remained silent about their ordeal, too embarrassed to tell anyone—especially their husbands and children. Nearly three decades after the close of the war, the plight of these women was brought to light, and a number of them instituted lawsuits seeking an official apology and compensation from the Japanese government. In 1995 Japan announced the creation of a private fund to aid the thousands of women, not just Filipinas, who had been victimized during the war. The following year the Japanese government issued a formal apology to the women and started distributing the funds. Many of the women, however, refused to accept the money because it had come from private donations, not government funds.

During the American occupation of the islands two large military bases—the Clark Air Base and Subic Bay Naval Station—became centers for a thriving prostitution industry. Although the American occupation ended in 1946, the bases remained until the 1990s and prostitution continued to flourish, especially during the Vietnam war, when the number of military personnel on the islands mushroomed.

In the 1980s, under President Marcos, the Ministry of Tourism actively promoted sex tourism, officially called a "hospitality industry," thereby attracting huge numbers of male tourists, mostly from Japan. With the change of administration in 1986, the sex tours were banned, and travel guides and agencies found operating such tours lost their licenses. Today the government's sex tours are gone, as are the American military bases, but prostitution is still widespread.

FOR ADDITIONAL INFORMATION ON WOMEN

Center for Women's Resources
No. 116 Maginhawa Street
Teachers' Village
Quezon City, Metro Manila, Philippines
Telephone: 2-921-6810
Fax: 2-921-6810

Consulate General of the Republic of the Philippines
Cultural Office
556 Fifth Avenue
New York, NY 10036, United States
Telephone: 212-764-1330

Development Institute for Women in Asia-Pacific
The Philippine Women's University
Taft Avenue
Manila, Philippines
Telephone: 2-521-3383
Fax: 2-522-4002

Embassy of the Philippines
1600 Massachusetts Avenue, NW
Washington, DC 20036, United States
Telephone: 202-467-9300
Fax: 202-467-9417

National Commission of Women of the Philippines
1743 Taft Avenue
Manila, Philippines
Telephone: 2-588-201
Fax: 2-521-8985

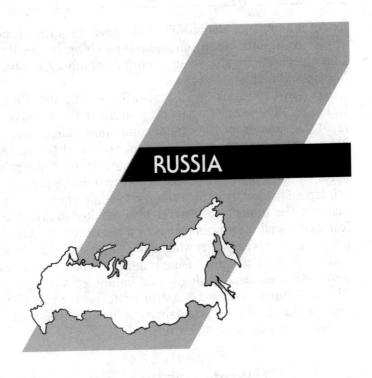

RUSSIA

Population: *148.4 million*
▲ Women per 100 men: *113*
Women's voting rights: *1918*
Women in legislature: *7%*
▲ Women's share of work force: *48%*
▲ Literacy rates: women—*99%;* men—*99%*
Life expectancy: women—*71.0 years;* men—*57.3 years*
▲ Average number of children: *1.5*
Maternal mortality rate: *75*

Russia, also known as the Russian Federation, is the largest and most popu-lous of the 15 republics that the Soviet Union comprised until its dissolution in 1991. In area it is the largest country in the world, stretching from eastern Europe across northern Asia to the Pacific. Its population, though, is unevenly distributed; the highest concentrations are found in European Rus-sia, but large numbers of people also live in southern Siberia and the far eastern region. Nearly three-quarters of all Russians are urban dwellers.

Russia has one of the world's widest ranges of nationalities and ethnic groups—over 120—but the single largest group, Russians, constitute about

82% of the total population. While the great majority of the Russian people are nonreligious, about one-quarter belong to the Russian Orthodox Church. There are also small minorities of other Christian denominations, Muslims, Buddhists, and Jews.

The sweeping changes that followed the dissolution of the Soviet Union in 1991 wreaked havoc throughout the Russian Federation. The rapid transition from 70 years of communist rule to democracy and a market economy brought an end to censorship and an expansion of individual rights and freedoms. Under the new government, the principle of equality between women and men was established in the Russian constitution and reinforced in various laws dealing with employment, civil rights, and family matters. The transition, however, also resulted in dramatic economic, political, and social upheavals that took a heavy toll on Russian society: rising prices, falling wages, growing unemployment, deteriorating health care and public services, increasing crime and corruption, and—perhaps most devastating—a soaring death rate combined with a declining birthrate. Although measures were instituted to revive the ailing economy and reverse the decline in population, by the mid-1990s, the outlook for the immediate future was still bleak.

HISTORY OF THE WOMEN'S MOVEMENT

The evolution of the women's movement in Russia was unlike that in most other countries. The right to vote, which women fought so bitterly for in the United States, Britain, and elsewhere, was handed to Russian women at the close of the Russian Revolution in 1918. By the time the Soviet Union was founded in 1922, two other major rights for women—divorce and abortion—had also been granted.

Probably the earliest women's organizations were the *zhenotdels*, or women's sections, established by the ruling Communist Party in 1918. These groups were not concerned with women's rights but focused on spreading the party ideology and encouraging women to join the work force and participate in the labor movement. However, women lost many of their rights and their lives changed radically under the totalitarian rule of Joseph Stalin, which began in 1922. Political, civil, and personal rights were abolished, including divorce (1930) and abortion (1936). As the country embarked on a period of massive industrialization, large numbers of jobs were created; and although Soviet women were extolled as the country's "great army of labor," most women were employed in the lowest-paying, most strenuous jobs, usually in factories.

Following Stalin's death in 1953, his successor, Nikita Khrushchev, initiated a policy of de-Stalinization that included lifting the bans on divorce and abortion. Khrushchev also created the Soviet Women's Committee, a nongovernmental organization whose announced purpose was to promote women's participation in the labor force but actually seemed more concerned with spreading worldwide propaganda about women's equality in the Soviet Union.

Over the years Soviet women continued to swell the ranks of the work force, and by the mid-1960s they accounted for slightly more than half of the total labor force. Yet they were still expected to fulfill their traditional roles as wives and mothers. In the late 1970s an independent feminist group, called Maria, appeared in Leningrad (now St. Petersburg), openly protesting the exploitation and degradation of women and directing public attention to specific issues such as the substandard conditions in the hospitals where abortions were performed. But Maria was short-lived; its members were soon arrested and either deported or sent to prison.

The Soviet leadership passed to Mikhail Gorbachev in 1985, and under his direction the women's councils of the 1920s were reborn. Within two years, more than 240,000 of them were established throughout the country. But like the earlier *zhenotdels,* they were largely controlled by the Communist Party, and because they lacked political influence, their members soon lost interest and the councils disappeared.

The current women's movement in Russia dates back to the process of democratization in the late 1980s and early 1990s. Many Russian women started becoming politically active during that period; new groups began emerging, and by the mid-1990s they numbered over 300. Some of these groups focused on environmental and social matters, but others addressed feminist issues such as equal rights for women, especially in employment, and increased representation of women in government.

WOMEN IN POLITICS

Under Soviet rule, although women were encouraged to join the Communist Party, they rarely rose to high office and were generally excluded from decision-making positions. In 1920 women made up only 7% of the total party membership, and none served on the Central Committee. Four decades later, women constituted 20% of the party membership but only 3% of the Central Committee.

Since the founding of the Russian Federation, women have continued to be underrepresented in politics. After the elections in 1995, they constituted only 7% of the two-chamber Federal Assembly. Only 1 woman was elected to the 178-member (<1%) Council of the Federation (upper house); 44 of the 451 members (10%) of the State Duma (lower house) were women. By early 1997, only one woman had been named to the new 29-member cabinet: Tatiana Dmitriyeva (health). No women served as ambassadors.

WOMEN'S EDUCATION

The Russian educational system is compulsory for both girls and boys through secondary school, and the literacy rate for both women and men is among the highest in the world: 99%.

As a rule, female students take the same courses and study the same subjects as their male counterparts. Women make up a large percentage of students studying law and medicine. In 1993 female students accounted for about 15% of those receiving doctoral degrees.

FEMALE ENROLLMENT Percentage of student body, 1992	
LEVEL	PERCENT
Primary school	50%
Secondary school	61%
Primary technical school	37%
Secondary technical school	64%
University	52%

WOMEN'S EMPLOYMENT

For the seven decades of Soviet rule, women were actively encouraged to work outside the home, and after the transition to democracy, they remained a major presence in the work force. In 1995 women accounted for a 48% share of the total work force, one of the world's highest representations of women in any labor force. Approximately 72% of all working-age women were working outside the home, compared with 82% of Russian men.

Discrimination in the Workplace

The Labor Code of the Russian Federation prohibits discrimination on the basis of sex in the area of employment. In practice, however, violations do occur, and an estimated 3 million women are thought to work under adverse conditions. The Labor Code prohibits women from performing heavy labor or working in an unhealthy environment. It also mandates that pregnant women be assigned shorter working hours and transferred to less strenuous work, while women with children under the age of three should not work overtime or at night. These rules, however, are largely ignored.

Despite various employment laws protecting women, widespread discrimination occurs in hiring and firing. Employers prefer to save on maternity and child-care costs by hiring men rather than women, and female employees tend to be the first ones fired when a company suffers cutbacks. It is estimated that 90% of all workers who are laid off are women.

Areas of Employment

The industries employing the highest percentages of women are health and social services (84%), education (84%), trade and food retailing (82%), and state lending and insurance bodies (81%).

In the legal profession women constitute 40% of all lawyers and more than half of all city and district court judges but in other occupational areas they are rarely seen in high-level positions. In medicine nearly 70% of all physicians are women, but most are either general practitioners or pediatricians, only 6% are surgeons. Women hold 11% of senior executive positions in industry, 10% in communications, 8% in agriculture, and 1% in construction.

Russia is one of the few countries where women have traditionally undertaken military service, even serving on combat duty during wartime. In the mid-1990s, women made up 9% of the armed forces.

Pay Differences

Despite the fact that Russian women are guaranteed equal pay for equal work, they are often paid less than their male colleagues. In addition, they tend to be employed in lower-paying jobs in lower-paying industries. As a result, in 1995 women's average earnings in all industries except agriculture were only about 40% of men's, a dramatic drop from 75% in 1991 and one of the largest gender wage gaps in the world.

Maternity Leave and Benefits

Russian law mandates that working women are entitled to maternity leave from 70 days prior to childbirth to 70 days after delivery. If medical complications arise, the leave is extended an additional 16 days. Working mothers are also guaranteed a monthly allowance for child care until their children reach the age of 18 months.

Child Care

Child-care facilities in Russia, like other services, have recently suffered drastic cutbacks. In 1990 there were 88,000 centers throughout the country; two years later 6,000 of them had closed.

Unemployment

In 1993 the official unemployment rate for women was 1.1%, compared with 0.4% for men. Women constituted approximately 75% of the unemployed, and nearly 60% of these women were college or technical school graduates. More than half of all jobless women had children under the age of 16.

Unemployed women find it more difficult than men to find new jobs. In 1993 it took an average of more than five months for an unemployed woman to find work, while it took a man less than two months.

MARRIAGE AND DIVORCE

Russian couples are marrying less and divorcing more. Out-of-wedlock births are increasing, especially among teenagers, and the number of single mothers, either divorced or never married, continues to grow. In 1994 it was estimated that between 15% and 20% of all families were headed by a single parent, with women accounting for 94% of those households. Nearly half of all female-headed households with children under 16 had incomes below the official poverty level.

Marriage

Although the minimum legal age for marriage is 18 for both women and men, the average age at first marriage is 21.7 years for women and 24.4 years for men. The total number of marriages registered in 1993 was 1,107,000. Three years earlier, 1,320,000 marriages were recorded.

The recent decline in the marriage rate has been attributed in part to the current economic uncertainty. Yet many women still want to have children, and there is a growing trend of births to unmarried women. In 1990 births to single mothers accounted for 15% of all births; by 1993, this proportion had climbed to 18%. About a third of these unmarried mothers do not live with a partner but with their parents or other relatives.

Divorce

The number of divorces granted in 1993 was 663,000, compared with 560,000 in 1990. In the same year the divorce rate was 60, that is, for every 100 couples getting married, 60 were getting divorced. In 1990 the comparable divorce rate was 42.

According to the Marriage and Family Code, each partner is allowed an equal share of joint property. The court decides the terms of child custody if

MARRIAGES AND DIVORCES
In thousands

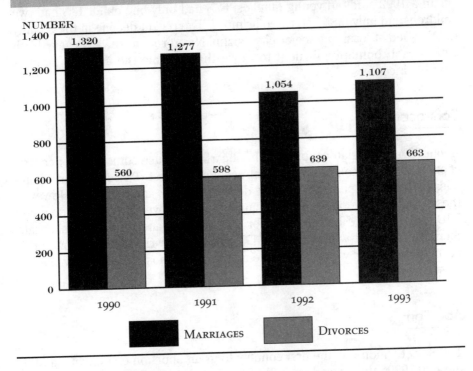

NUMBER

1990: Marriages 1,320, Divorces 560
1991: Marriages 1,277, Divorces 598
1992: Marriages 1,054, Divorces 639
1993: Marriages 1,107, Divorces 663

■ MARRIAGES ▪ DIVORCES

the couple cannot agree; joint custody is not an option in Russia. The court can also order the husband to pay child support, but these payments are difficult to collect, and the new economic system makes it easier for men to hide their incomes from tax collectors and ex-wives. To reduce this problem, the government is preparing legislation offering more flexible payment terms.

FAMILY PLANNING

The Russian government has no official policy concerning family planning. In 1992 a nongovernmental organization established 25 family planning centers, and a federal program was slated for the mid-1990s.

Fertility Rate

The fertility rate in Russia is 1.5 children per woman, which is down significantly from 2.2 in 1990 and represents one of the lowest fertility rates in the world. About 15% of all births are to teenagers, one of the highest rates of teen births among the world's developed nations.

In a 1992 study of young families, 67% had only one child, 13% had two children, and only 0.8% had three or more. The recent decline in the fertility rate has led at least one major city, Nizhni-Novgorod, to reward every birth with a cash bonus equivalent to more than double the average family's monthly income.

Contraception

About 32% of Russian couples of childbearing age use some form of contraception. Of those couples using contraception, almost 70% use modern methods: birth control pills, intrauterine devices (IUDs), and condoms. However, these products are often in short supply; in recent years many condom and IUD factories have had to close for lack of latex and other raw materials. Sterilization is not widely practiced. It requires a written application and is permitted only for women over the age of 35 or those who already have at least two children.

Abortion

The Soviet Union was the first country to grant abortion on demand, and by the mid-1990s the procedure had become the most widely used method of birth control. In 1993 there were nearly 3.5 million abortions in Russia, more than twice the number of births. In some regions it is not unusual for a woman to undergo as many as nine abortions during her lifetime. Ironically, the scarring that sometimes results from repeated abortions can become a major cause of infertility later on.

Fertility Services

Rising infertility among Russian women has prompted the recent growth of a new industry: fertility clinics. Most women who use the clinics are married, but more and more mature single women are coming to the clinics for artificial insemination and in vitro fertilization. There are about a dozen such centers throughout the country, and the demand for fertility services is rising rapidly.

The country's largest private clinic, located in Moscow, sees more than 2,500 patients a year, and although its fees are substantial, it provides free services to widows, mothers of sons killed in combat, and women who have lost a child under the age of 16. When treating a married woman whose

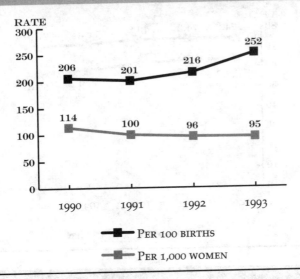

ABORTION RATES
Per 100 births; per 1,000 women aged 15 to 49

RATE

- ■ PER 100 BIRTHS
- ■ PER 1,000 WOMEN

husband has insufficient or nonviable sperm, it is not uncommon for the husband to have a brother or cousin provide the needed sperm cells.

Sex Education

Since the Russian government has no official policy relating to sex education, it is not mandatory in the schools. However, information on the transmission and prevention of AIDS was added to the school curriculum in 1989.

WOMEN'S HEALTH

The most devastating problem facing the Russian Federation is the rapidly declining health of its people. Unlike most of the world, Russia's average life expectancy has been decreasing, slowly but steadily, over the past decade. In 1994 the average life expectancy for Russian women was 71.0 years; for men, it was only 57.3 years, by far the lowest male life expectancy in the developed world.

Heart disease, cancer, and infectious diseases are all on the rise in Russia. Even suicide and homicide rates are climbing. This alarming medical and social crisis has been attributed to a number of factors: shortages of antibiotics, vaccines, and other medical supplies; an antiquated, overbur-

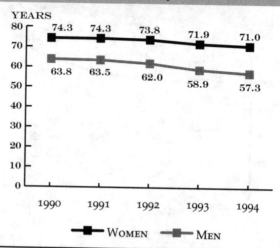

LIFE EXPECTANCY
At birth, in years

YEARS

WOMEN: 74.3 (1990), 74.3 (1991), 73.8 (1992), 71.9 (1993), 71.0 (1994)

MEN: 63.8 (1990), 63.5 (1991), 62.0 (1992), 58.9 (1993), 57.3 (1994)

■ WOMEN   ■ MEN

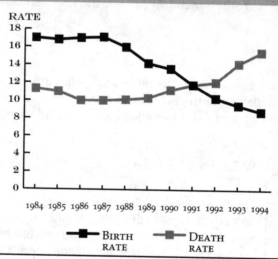

BIRTH AND DEATH RATES
Per 1,000 population

RATE

1984 1985 1986 1987 1988 1989 1990 1991 1992 1993 1994

■ BIRTH RATE   ■ DEATH RATE

dened health care system; and long-term environmental pollution, including radiation from nuclear power plants, test sites, and waste dumps. It is estimated that the nuclear accident at the Chernobyl power plant in 1986 alone exposed more than 5 million people to dangerous levels of radiation.

Rampant alcoholism, especially among men, is another major contributor to the rising death rate, not only from the diseases caused by habitual drinking, but also from the high rate of industrial accidents caused by workers drinking on the job. Alcohol consumption in Russia is among the world's highest and is climbing rapidly; it is estimated that one-fifth of the average family's income is spent on alcohol. In addition, many drinkers have resorted to homemade spirits, kerosene, and other deadly chemicals; alcohol poisoning from these substances has more than doubled since 1992.

Deaths in Russia now occur at nearly twice the rate of births and the average life expectancy, especially for men, has been dropping steadily. In 1994 there were 15.6 deaths per 1,000 people, but only 9 births. Another sign of deteriorating health is the rising maternal mortality rate: 75 pregnancy-related deaths for every 100,000 live births, one of the highest rates of any developed nation.

Leading Causes of Death

The major causes of death for both women and men in Russia are cardiovascular diseases, such as heart attack and stroke, and various forms of cancer.

Smoking

Smoking is one of the few health hazards affecting many more Russian men than women. About 9% of all women smoke, compared with 60% of men. Government antismoking campaigns have not proved successful, and Russian doctors, instead of admonishing their patients to stop smoking, have been known simply to advise them to switch to American cigarettes, which are lower in tar and nicotine than Russian brands.

LEADING CAUSES OF DEATH
Percentage of total deaths, 1993

CAUSE	WOMEN	MEN
Cardiovascular diseases	64%	43%
Cancer 13%	15%	
Breast	3%	—
Lung 1%	5%	
Cervix	<1%	
Atherosclerosis, embolism thrombosis	6%	3%
Accidents	4%	13%
Bronchitis, emphysema, asthma	2%	3%
Homicide, other violence	2%	6%
Suicide	<1%	4%

AIDS

According to the World Health Organization, in 1994 about 3,000 Russians were infected with HIV, the virus that causes AIDS. Official government records showed that by the start of 1994 there were only 264 reported cases of HIV infection among Russian girls and women.

VIOLENCE AGAINST WOMEN

As in many other countries, violence against women in Russia is seldom reported; consequently, its extent is largely unknown. Every year thousands of women are killed or permanently injured as a result of acts of violence.

Domestic Violence

Spousal abuse is a serious problem for many Russian women. It is estimated that as many as 15,000 women are killed each year by their husband or partner, and many more are beaten and raped. In 1994 the Ministry of Internal Affairs reported 54,000 cases of domestic violence, a figure considered conservative by various nongovernmental organizations. As living conditions continue to deteriorate throughout the country, this kind of abuse is expected to get even worse.

Most spousal abuse goes unreported because the victims are embarrassed and feel it is pointless to go to the authorities. In fact, there is little the authorities can do, since there are no laws against domestic violence in Russia. A husband can be charged only with hooliganism, and his wife must provide a written statement and a witness to corroborate her testimony.

The government's response to domestic violence has been the creation of special crisis centers that provide victims with medical care and psychological counseling. These centers have been established in Moscow, St. Petersburg, and several other major cities.

Rape

Although 14,400 cases of rape were recorded in 1993, the actual number is probably much higher, since in this area, too, the great majority of incidents go unreported. Police are reluctant to investigate such cases, and many victims never press charges. To prove rape, the victim must present a mass of evidence, including medical records and proof of resistance. Many doctors are unwilling to get involved, fearing lengthy court appearances. In an effort to provide some assistance to rape victims, the government established a rape victims' center and hotline in Moscow in 1993.

Prostitution

While prostitution itself is not illegal in Russia, the keeping of brothels, corruption of minors, and procuring of prostitutes for monetary gain are against the law.

FOR ADDITIONAL INFORMATION ON WOMEN

Center For Gender Studies
Institute for Socioeconomic Studies of
  Population
Krasikova Street 27
Moscow 117218, Russia
Telephone: 095-125-7302/129-0400

**Permanent Mission of the Russian
  Federation to the United Nations**
Public Relations Office
136 East 67th Street
New York, NY 10021, United States
Telephone: 212-861-4900/01/02

Embassy of the Russian Federation
2650 Wisconsin Avenue, NW
Washington, DC 20036, United States
Telephone: 202-298-5700

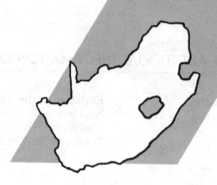

SOUTH AFRICA

Population: *42.7 million*
Women per 100 men: *101*
Women's voting rights: *1930—whites; 1983—Indians, coloreds;*
1994—Africans
▲ Women in legislature: *25%*
Women's share of work force: *36%*
Literacy rates: women—*70%;* men—*70%*
Life expectancy: women—*67.9 years;* men—*62.4 years*
Average number of children: *4.0*
Maternal mortality rate: *230*

WOMAN NOBEL PRIZE WINNER		
Nadine Gordimer	Literature	1991

South Africa, occupying the southernmost portion of the African continent, is a large, diverse, highly industrialized country with a wealth of natural resources. The population is officially classified into four racial groups: African, 75%; white, 14%; colored (people of mixed racial origin), 9%; and

Indian, 3%. The great majority of South Africans are Christian; there are also small minorities of Hindus (2%) and Muslims (2%). About 63% of the population live in cities.

The earliest white settlers were the Boers, or Afrikaners, who arrived at the Cape of Good Hope from Holland in 1652 and attempted to establish an independent republic in the late 1700s. However, the British seized and colonized the Cape in the early 1800s, and thousands of settlers arrived soon after. A system of white supremacy slowly evolved so that in 1930, when a law was passed granting women the right to vote, it applied only to white women. A strict separation of the races, called apartheid, was firmly established by the late 1940s, and with it came major upheavals throughout the nation. Although the country's population was overwhelmingly black, the government was controlled by a small white minority. Strict rules were imposed for each of the four racial groups, and nearly 4 million nonwhites were removed from white cities and relocated to segregated townships and homelands.

Over the past several years South Africa has witnessed sweeping changes as four decades of white-ruled apartheid gave way to a new era of nonracial democracy. The constitution of 1996, building upon the base of the Interim Constitution and Charter of Fundamental Rights adopted in 1993, provides some of the broadest guarantees of rights in the world for both women and men. It specifically prohibits discrimination on the basis of gender as well as race, age, pregnancy, marital status, and sexual orientation. All of its provisions are slated to take effect by 1999.

HISTORY OF THE WOMEN'S MOVEMENT

Modern day women's groups became active during the 1950s, when even the all-white Black Sash focused its energies on opposing apartheid. One of the most famous protests occurred on August 9, 1956, when thousands of women staged a rally and march to protest the infamous Pass Law, which required all Africans over the age of 16 to carry a pass when venturing into white cities. Nearly four decades later, August 9 was declared National Women's Day, a public holiday commemorating South African women's struggle for equality.

During the mid-1980s, as apartheid started to crumble, women's groups began focusing on other issues, including equal employment rights, marriage and divorce reforms, reproductive rights, and the need to increase women's representation in government. Indian and colored women and men had been granted the right to vote in 1983, and the franchise was extended to all Africans—women and men—in 1994.

Today local women's groups, nongovernmental organizations and government agencies are concentrating on translating the constitution's promise of equal rights into concrete laws and mechanisms for implementation and enforcement. One of the most active of these organizations is the Women's National Coalition (WNC), which was launched in 1992 to ensure that women's rights were incorporated into the new constitution. The WNC's membership includes a wide range of national and regional groups, ranging from community organizations to professional associations, political parties, and religious groups. A number of groups are also focusing on specific issues, such as health care, education, violence against women, and women's legal rights.

WOMEN IN POLITICS

Winnie Mandela was thrust onto the political stage in 1972, when the government arrested and imprisoned her husband, Nelson Mandela, a leading activist against apartheid. Replacing him as spokesperson for the African National Congress (ANC), she soon became a worldwide symbol of the fight against apartheid. During much of her husband's 27 years in prison, she was subjected to police harassment and even banishment. When Nelson Mandela was released from prison in 1990, he resumed his political activities and was elected president of South Africa in 1994. Winnie Mandela won a seat in Parliament in those same elections and was named a deputy minister in the new government. However, she lost that position in 1995, largely as a result of political opposition within the ANC.

Winnie Mandela was not the only woman elected to the new legislature; 25% percent of the members of the two-chamber Constitutional Assembly were women, a dramatic increase from only 3% in 1985. The main reason for this upsurge, which gave South Africa one of the highest proportions of female legislators in the world, was the ANC's decision to allot one-third of its slate to women. Of the 400 members of the National Assembly, 106 (27%) were women, including Frene Ginwala, the first woman ever to hold the position of Speaker. In the 90-seat Senate, 16 women (18%) were elected.

Within the federal government 25 select committees deal with various aspects of government, and each committee consists of 19 to 25 members. Women are well represented in the committees on welfare (18); health (14); arts, culture, and language (12); and science and technology (12). But they are poorly represented in those on foreign affairs (5); justice (5); trade and industry (5); labor (4); sport and recreation (4); safety and security (4); mineral and energy affairs (4); and transport (2).

At the cabinet level, in 1996 only 3 of the 28 posts (11%) were held by women: Nkosazana Dlamini-Zuma (health), Sankie Mthembi-Nkondo (housing), and Stella Sigcau (public enterprises). South Africa had no women ambassadors.

WOMEN IN PROVINCIAL GOVERNMENT
Number of women members; percentage of legislative body, 1994

PROVINCE	EXECUTIVE COUNCIL		LEGISLATURE	
	NUMBER	PERCENT	NUMBER	PERCENT
Eastern Cape	3	30%	11	23%
Eastern Transvaal	1	10%	5	26%
Gauteng	2	20%	21	28%
KwaZulu-Natal	0	0%	14	20%
Northern Cape	2	20%	6	30%
Northern Transvaal	2	20%	7	23%
North-West	1	10%	5	25%
Orange Free State	2	20%	4	20%
Western Cape	1	10%	10	31%

At the provincial level, not one of the country's nine provinces was headed by a woman. Women also tended to be poorly represented in provincial legislatures (30 to 100 members) and executive councils (maximum 10 members). At the local level, women were elected to 8% of town clerkships in the 1995 elections, the same percentage elected in 1991.

WOMEN'S EDUCATION

South Africa mandates 10 years of compulsory education for girls and boys, starting with a year of preschool and extending up to the age of 16. However because schooling was compulsory only for whites and Indians until 1994 tremendous disparities in education developed, especially since children of different races had to attend separate schools.

The overall literacy rate for both women and men is roughly 70% but drops to 50% in some rural areas. Generally, literacy is highest among whites in metropolitan centers and lowest among coloreds in rural areas.

Boys tend to have a higher dropout rate than girls: 53% compared with 44% at the primary level, and 51% and 46% respectively at the secondary level. Among female university students, nearly 50% are white, 38% African, 7% colored, and 6% Indian. The single largest concentration of African women university students—nearly 40,000—

FEMALE ENROLLMENT
Percentage of student body, 1993

LEVEL	PERCENT
Preschool	51%
Primary school	47%
Secondary school	53%
Higher education	48%

is enrolled in the University of South Africa (Unisa), a correspondence school. Across all racial lines and in all schools, however, South African women tend to study the traditionally female subjects.

In technikons, or technical colleges, women make up only

WOMEN IN HIGHER EDUCATION Percentage of subject area, 1993	
SUBJECT AREA	PERCENT
Home economics	99%
Legal studies	37%
Health	37%
Mathematics	31%
Commerce	31%
Computer science	30%
Architecture	28%
Agriculture	17%
Engineering	7%

about 29% of the total student body. As in universities, women seldom take engineering, architecture, agriculture, and computer science courses but predominate in secretarial and home economics classes. In postgraduate programs women constitute 46% of honors students, 32% of master's students, and 24% of doctoral candidates.

WOMEN'S EMPLOYMENT

In the mid-1990s, according to official records, about 42% of South African women aged 15 to 64 worked outside the home, making up about 36% of the total labor force. However, these figures excluded many subsistence agricultural workers and other laborers, so that the actual percentage of women in the work force was believed to be much higher, perhaps as much as 50%. South African men, in comparison, had an official participation rate of 75%.

Discrimination in the Workplace

In a 1993 report prepared by the WNC, women were found to constitute a disproportionate number of those who were unemployed, underemployed, impoverished, and subject to oppressive working conditions. Throughout the work force, women receive lower wages and fewer benefits than men, pay higher taxes, and have no job security.

Although the Labor Relations Act of 1966 deals with unemployment and maternity benefits, it does not cover domestic workers, public service employees, casual workers, or the self-employed. Thus, vast numbers of women are excluded from its protection. Over the next few years, the government, in conjunction with various women's groups and agencies, will undertake the enormous task of revising the Labor Relations Act and writing new legislation to guarantee equality for women and protect them from sexual harassment and other forms of discrimination.

Areas of Employment

South African women in the formal labor force tend to be employed in service occupations, ranging from domestic work to nursing. In every sector of the economy, however, they are concentrated at the lowest levels and rarely seen at the highest. A 1994 study of public sector employees revealed that women constituted 2% of the highest-ranking employees, 30% of mid-level workers, and 61% of those at the lowest levels. Overall, for every 100 men in administrative or managerial positions, 24 women hold similar posts. However, among professional and technical workers women outnumber men by 103 to 100.

In the area of education, in 1991 women made up 76% of all primary and 43% of all secondary school teachers. In higher education women accounted for 29% of all teaching staff, including 15% of all assistant professors and 6% of full professors. The professions in which women are poorly represented include architecture (7%), law (6%), medicine (3%), and engineering (2%).

WOMEN IN MAJOR OCCUPATIONAL GROUPS
Percentage of group, 1991

OCCUPATIONAL GROUP	PERCENT
Services	68%
Clerical, sales	57%
Professional, technical	51%
Agriculture	25%
Production, supervisory	20%
Executive, administrative	19%

WOMEN IN THE JUDICIARY
Number of women; percentage of total, 1994

LEVEL	NUMBER	PERCENT
Regional magistrate	8	5%
Senior magistrate	1	1%
Magistrate	220	24%
Attorney general	0	0%
Deputy attorney general	3	7%
Senior state advocate	33	26%
State advocate	39	44%
Senior public prosecutor	6	17%
Public prosecutor	528	43%

In the judiciary women make up about 48% of the total personnel at the Department of Justice, but here again they are concentrated at the lower levels. In 1995 only 1 of the 20 Appeals Court judges and only 1 of the 138 provincial Supreme Court judges were women.

The first women law enforcement officers in South Africa were hired in 1972, and until 1981 all of them were white. Colored, Indian, and African women were admitted to police forces in 1981, 1982, and 1983 respectively. Although the number of women in law enforcement has increased over the past decade, they are found mostly in the lower ranks.

South African women are allowed to enlist in the armed forces, but they are not drafted and cannot serve on combat duty. They make up approximately 18% of uniformed personnel and 29% of the civilian force. Of the female uniformed personnel, 93% are white. In the civilian force this proportion drops to 56%.

About 28% of all self-employed workers and employers are women, but large numbers of them are street vendors and other low-skilled laborers, not business entrepreneurs. It is very difficult for women to start businesses in South Africa. Banks are reluctant to lend a woman capital and often require her husband's signature. Of the 40,000 entrepreneurs who have received loans from the state-funded Small Business Development Corporation since its founding in 1981, only about 25% have been women, most of them white.

Pay Differences

As in many other countries, women in South Africa earn significantly less than men, partly because they work mainly in low-paying job categories in low-paying industries. Even when they do the same jobs as men, they are almost always paid less. In a study of managerial, professional, and supervisory positions in some of the country's largest and most prestigious companies, it was found that white women earned 98% to 100% of white men's salaries, Indian women earned 84%, colored women earned 73%, and African women earned 70%.

Working Hours

Throughout the South African labor force, women predominate in temporary, casual, and part-time work. In many industries—such as agriculture, wholesale and retail trade, restaurants and hotels, and domestic services—there are more part-time than full-time women employees.

Maternity Leave and Benefits

The vast majority of South African women have no guaranteed maternity leave or other benefits. Only in specific industries where trade unions have negotiated labor contracts are pregnant women assured of not losing their jobs while taking time off for childbirth. Sometimes women are compelled by their employers to have regular contraceptive injections so that they will not become pregnant and have to take time off from work.

Child Care

There are very few public day-care facilities for South Africans. Overall, only about 2% of all children under three and 14% of children aged three to six are in some sort of preschool program.

Unemployment

Because so many South Africans work in the informal sector of the economy, it is very difficult to measure unemployment accurately. The government's official estimate puts the country's overall jobless rate at about 18%, with women making up 53% of the unemployed.

A 1993 survey provided two sets of unemployment figures. Using a strict definition, women were found to have an unemployment rate of 21%, compared with 16% for men. With the definition expanded to include jobless people who had given up hope of finding work, the unemployment rate rose to 36% for women and 24% for men.

MARRIAGE AND DIVORCE

South Africa's transition to democracy brought with it major changes in the laws governing marriage and divorce. Marriages between people of different races are no longer prohibited, as they were under apartheid, and husbands are no longer considered to have complete authority over their wives and children. But many South Africans, especially Muslims and some Africans, are not subject to these new laws; they are allowed to live under their own religious or tribal customary laws, which permit polygamy, arranged marriages, and dowries.

The traditional nuclear family predominates in South Africa, but more and more households are headed by a single parent, usually a woman. In 1993 approximately 35% of all South African households were headed by women; only about half of these were single-person households.

FEMALE-HEADED HOUSEHOLDS
Percentage of households that are headed by women, 1993

GROUP	RURAL	URBAN	METRO	ALL
African	44%	35%	36%	41%
Colored	8%	38%	23%	28%
Indian	—	17%	11%	14%
White	9%	10%	15%	15%
Total	42%	29%	30%	35%

Marriage

While the minimum legal age for marriage is 21 for both women and men, most South Africans marry much later. According to official statistics, women's average age at first marriage is 25.7 years, the oldest in all of Africa. For men the average age is 27.8 years. In customary marriages, however, the brides and grooms tend to be younger, but these marriages are not registered and are not included in official figures.

Among the first measures enacted by President Mandela's government were laws giving wives and husbands equal authority over children and other family matters. The Promotion of Equality Between Men and Women Act eliminated all remaining vestiges of a husband's control over his wife's property and financial affairs. These laws did not apply to customary marriages, however, although some recent reforms in customary law have recognized wives for the purpose of obtaining pensions, workmen's compensation, and inheritance. In some regions customary laws are being revised to eliminate certain discriminatory policies, such as regarding a wife as a minor.

Divorce

South Africa has a no-fault divorce system in which both parties may agree to dissolve the marriage on grounds of irreconcilable differences or irretrievable breakdown of the relationship. Divorce in a customary marriage is subject to a complex system of special laws and frequently involves the return of a dowry.

Child support continues to be a serious problem, even though the law clearly states that both parents are responsible for supporting their children in proportion to their respective means. Failure to provide support is a criminal offense, but sanctions are rarely imposed. In some regions the default rate is as high as 85%.

FAMILY PLANNING

The government's support for family planning has been a contentious issue in South Africa. Under apartheid, the white-ruled government promoted the use of contraception. However, this was often interpreted by nonwhites as a form of population control.

Fertility Rate

The fertility rate in South Africa is 4.0 children per woman, down from 4.9 in 1980 and 5.7 in 1970. Fertility rates vary greatly among different racial groups, as well as within each group. For example, among African women living in rural areas the fertility rate is about 5.7, while among those in urban centers it is 2.8.

FERTILITY RATES Average number of children per woman		
GROUP	1984	1994
African	4.7	4.3
Colored	3.1	2.3
Indian	2.8	2.2
White	2.1	1.6

In 1991 teenage pregnancies accounted for about 15% of all live births. About 4% of these births were to girls under the age of 15. To address the concern about the high rate of teenage pregnancies, the government has enacted legislation allowing teenagers to obtain contraceptives without parental consent.

Contraception

About 50% of South African couples of childbearing age use some form of birth control. Diaphragms and other barrier methods are the most widely used methods, followed by birth control pills, female sterilization, and intrauterine devices.

CONTRACEPTIVE USE Percentage of couples of childbearing age, 1988	
METHOD	PERCENT
Diaphragm, other	20%
Birth control pill	13%
Female sterilization	8%
Intrauterine devices (IUDs)	5%
Condom	1%
Male sterilization	1%
Traditional methods	1%

Availability of contraception and family planning services varies widely. In some remote regions women have no access to contraceptive devices or information, and even when contraceptives are available, a wife sometimes cannot obtain them without her husband's written consent. At the other extreme, contraceptives are sometimes administered to women without their knowledge or consent. In some areas new mothers are automatically given a contraceptive hormonal injection immediately following childbirth, a procedure commonly referred to as the "fourth stage of labor."

Abortion

Abortion became legal in 1975 with the passage of the Abortion and Sterilization Act. However it was a fairly restrictive law, allowing abortion only if the woman's physical or mental health was endangered; if there was a substantial risk that the child would have a serious physical or mental defect; if the pregnancy resulted from rape or incest; or if the woman was mentally impaired or unable to understand the responsibilities of parenthood. Because legal abortions were so difficult to obtain, as many as 300,000 women turned to illegal abortions every year and many of them died as a result.

In 1996 the South African Parliament replaced the 1975 law with one of the world's most liberal abortion laws. The new law permits abortion on demand during the first 12 weeks of pregnancy, financed by the state if the woman is not covered by private medical insurance. In addition, although a minor must be advised to consult her parents, she is still entitled to an abortion even if they disapprove.

Sex Education

Since reducing the number of teenage pregnancies is one of its major priorities, the government recently added sex education to the national school curriculum. The government is also investigating ways to provide family planning services specifically to adolescents.

WOMEN'S HEALTH

One of the greatest obstacles to the development of new government health programs is the scarcity of accurate statistical data. There is very little reliable information on such basic indicators as life expectancy or maternal mortality. And information gathered before the 1990s often excludes Africans.

Estimates for life expectancy are 67.9 years for women and 62.4 years for men, with whites outliving nonwhites by about 9 years. Maternal mortality is estimated at 230 deaths per 100,000 live births. In 1994 the government initiated a program to help reduce pregnancy-related deaths by providing pregnant women with free medical care in state-subsidized hospitals or other facilities. After birth, this care is extended for 42 days, longer in cases where complications have arisen.

Leading Causes of Death

Major causes of death among South African women include diseases of the circulatory system, respiratory disorders, cancer, infectious diseases, and complications of childbirth. Among the most common infectious diseases are tuberculosis, measles, malaria, and hepatitis. However, the single largest official category of causes of death is simply called "ill-defined causes," probably because so many women have no access to formal health care and their diseases are never diagnosed, let alone treated.

AIDS

By 1994 the World Health Organization estimated that as many as 650,000 South Africans were infected with HIV, the virus that causes AIDS, and that one out of every five people is expected to be infected by the year 2020. Heterosexual relations are responsible for transmitting the virus in about 80% of all cases.

During the 1980s, in the first few years of the epidemic, AIDS affected far fewer women than men. Recently, however, the pattern has reversed. In 1995 a total of 1,120 cases of AIDS were reported, and women accounted for slightly more than half.

VIOLENCE AGAINST WOMEN

South Africa is a violent country. Even though there are no accurate statistics on violence against women, government officials agree that it is both widespread and growing. It cuts across all racial, regional, religious, and socioeconomic groups.

Domestic Violence

Domestic violence is rampant throughout South Africa. Over half of all female murder victims are killed at the hands of their husband or partner. Yet spousal abuse is rarely reported, largely due to ingrained cultural attitudes and the reluctance of the police to intervene in domestic issues. Even so, physical abuse is cited as a cause of marital breakdown in half of all divorce actions brought by women.

A recent government survey estimated that over 40% of all South African women have been raped or assaulted by their husband or partner. For many years marital rape was not considered a punishable offense, but since 1993, the Prevention of Family Violence Act has made it possible for a man to be convicted of raping his wife. This legislation also simplifies injunction and arrest procedures. For example, it empowers a judge or magistrate to issue an order automatically arresting a spouse who violates a restraining order. The abusive spouse can then be sentenced to as long as a year in prison. About 10,000 of these injunctions are ordered every year.

Although some shelters for battered women have been established by local women's groups and nongovernmental organizations, there are no state-funded shelters or counseling services for victims.

Rape

Police officials believe that only about 5% of all rapes are actually reported. Even so, from January 1 through October 31, 1994, over 25,000 cases of rape involving women over 18 were recorded. This represented a 17% increase over the same period of the previous year.

One of the world's first full-time courts for sexual offenses was opened in Cape Town in 1993. Its goal was to deal with rape cases as swiftly and effectively as possible and to alleviate the trauma associated with such cases. For example, in this court a woman under the age of 18 does not have to face her accused rapist.

Sentences for convicted rapists in South Africa can be quite severe; if the rape is accompanied by extreme violence, the sentence can be life imprisonment. However, only about one-quarter of accused rapists are convicted.

Prostitution

Prostitution has long been furtive but commonplace in South Africa. Following the recent liberalization of many laws, some government officials have suggested that prostitution be regulated and restricted to designated "red light" districts.

Female Genital Mutilation

Female genital mutilation is a custom practiced by some African tribes inhabiting remote regions of the country. It is not considered to be widespread and is largely condoned by the South African government.

FOR ADDITIONAL INFORMATION ON WOMEN

Center For Women's Studies
University of South Africa
P.O. Box 392
Pretoria 0001, Republic of South Africa

Consulate General of South Africa
333 East 38th Street, 9th floor
New York, NY 10016, United States
Telephone: 212-213-4880

**Embassy of the Republic of
  South Africa**
3051 Massachusetts Avenue, NW
Washington, DC 20008, United States
Telephone: 202-232-4400

**National Council of Women of
  South Africa**
P.O. Box 1242
Johannesburg 2000
Republic of South Africa
Telephone: 11-834-1366
Fax: 11-461-26172

SWEDEN

Population: *8.8 million*
Women per 100 men: *103*
Women's voting rights: *1919*
▲ Women in legislature: *41%*
▲ Women's share of work force: *48%*
▲ Literacy rates: women—*99%;* men—*99%*
▲ Life expectancy: women—*80.8 years;* men—*75.3 years*
Average number of children: *2.1*
▲ Maternal mortality rate: *7*

WOMEN NOBEL PRIZE WINNERS		
Selma Lagerlöf	Literature	1909
Nellie Sachs	Literature	1966
Alva Myrdal	Peace	1982

The Kingdom of Sweden, located on the Scandinavian peninsula in northern Europe, is a highly industrialized nation that provides its people with one of the most bountiful social welfare systems in the world, and one of the heaviest tax burdens. The great majority of Swedes, 83%, are urban dwellers, and 87% are members of the Evangelical Lutheran Church. Ethnically, the population is overwhelmingly Swedish, with small minorities of Lapps, Finns, and immigrants from Africa, the Middle East, and the countries of the former Yugoslavia.

HISTORY OF THE WOMEN'S MOVEMENT

Women's groups began emerging in Sweden during the late 19th century. One of the earliest, established in 1873, was the Society for Married Women's Rights, which was successful in obtaining for wives the right to dispose of their own property and wages. Although women in some areas voted in local elections as early as 1862, the right to vote and stand for office in national elections was granted to all Swedish women in 1919, although it did not come into force for another two years.

During World War I large numbers of Swedish women started entering the work force, and by the early 1920s, women had been granted greater access to education as well as a number of civil rights. In 1921 a married woman was finally no longer considered a permanent minor under her husband's guardianship but was declared to be of legal age when she reached 21—a right single women had been granted in 1884.

Today, women's organizations abound in Sweden. The oldest and best known is the Fredrika Bremer Organization, named for the feminist writer. It was founded in 1884 to fight for women's rights and now is largely devoted to expanding women's influence and representation in government. Other feminist groups are affiliated with political parties or focus on particular issues, such as aiding immigrant women or victims of violence. Some women's groups concentrate on nongender-related issues, such as world peace or environmental concerns. One of the newest organizations, founded in 1984, is the National Organization of Emergency Shelters for Battered Women, which not only aids victims of violence but also provides information and educational programs on a wide range of issues related to equality. In 1982 all organizations promoting women's and men's equality were given a boost by the government, which started allowing them to receive federal grants.

WOMEN IN POLITICS

With the 1994 elections, Swedish women attained the highest legislative profile in the world, capturing a record 41% of the seats in the Riksdag (parliament). In addition, Birgitta Dahl became Speaker of the Riksdag, succeeding another woman, Ingegerd Troedsson. Also in 1994, women held 43% of the seats in the Riksdag's standing committees, where the most important political work is accomplished.

Women were first elected to the Riksdag in 1921, and although a few others joined their ranks during the 1920s and 1930s, their numbers did not start growing until after World War II. In the elections of 1991, however, the proportion of women actually dropped five percentage points—the first decline since 1928—and many newly created women's networks began pressuring the political parties to nominate more women. In response, the parties introduced a policy of "every other candidate a woman," which brought about the stunning results of 1994. On the local level, the results were similar: women made up 41% of municipal councillors and 48% of county councillors.

In the Cabinet, by 1996 11 women held 52% of all ministerial posts: Annika Ähnberg (agriculture, food, fishery); Laila Freivalds (justice); Lena Hjelm-Wallén (foreign affairs); Yiva Johansson (education and science); Maj-Inger Klingvall (health, social affairs); Anna Lindh (environment); Ulrica Messing (labor); Marita Ulvskog (cultural affairs); Ines Uusmann (transportation, communications); Margot Wallström (health, social affairs); and Margareta Winberg (labor). This representation of women in a federal cabinet was by far the highest in the world.

But of the other high-level government positions, including 31 under secretaryships of state, only 29% were held by women. Swedish women were also underrepresented at the top levels in the Ministry of Foreign Affairs, with only 20 women at the executive level (11%), and 11 serving as ambassadors (9%). There were 10 women in the 22-member Swedish delegation to the European Parliament, the second highest proportion (45%) of women in any delegation; Finland was first, with 63%.

WOMEN'S EDUCATION

Nine years of education are compulsory for Swedish girls and boys aged 7 to 16, and the great majority of students (97%) continue to secondary school for three years. The adult literacy rate is 99% for both sexes, one of the highest in the world.

About one in five students advances to higher education within three years of graduating from secondary school, and women make up about 60% of first-year university students. In graduate degree programs about 36% of the student body are women. In 1992 women accounted for 28% of those receiving doctoral degrees, more than double the 13% in 1975.

FEMALE ENROLLMENT Percentage of student body, 1993	
LEVEL	PERCENT
Primary school	49%
Secondary school	49%
Undergraduate	56%

WOMEN COLLEGE GRADUATES
Percentage of subject area

SUBJECT	1980	1992
Nursing	83%	86%
Teaching	74%	83%
Culture, information, communication	48%	60%
Administrative, economic, social work	47%	59%
Technology	9%	22%

Although all Swedish primary school children study the same subjects for the same length of time, including domestic science and technology, when girls and boys have a choice of electives in grade 7, they tend to choose different courses, with girls favoring languages and nursing and boys choosing engineering and the natural sciences. This trend continues throughout secondary school; girls outnumber boys in the humanities, social work, and nursing programs, and boys predominate in technical programs.

The Swedish government is concerned about this academic gender imbalance and is working toward a more even distribution of girls and boys in the different courses of study. In 1992 the Higher Education Act was passed with the aim of increasing the proportion of women in postgraduate studies, and in 1994 a new nationwide curriculum emphasized equality between women and men. Also, the government has recently established a number of special gender-targeted programs and projects, such as summer technology courses for girls and nursing for boys. In addition, the government has proposed a long-term goal: that neither sex should constitute less than 40% of students in any educational program.

WOMEN'S EMPLOYMENT

Since the 1960s, women have entered the labor force in increasing numbers, and by 1994 Sweden had one of the world's highest proportions of working women, 80%, though this was down from a high of 85% in 1990. Because working-age men in 1994 also had a very high rate of labor force participation, 89%, the female share of the total work force was only 48%. Still, this share of the work force was one of the largest in the world.

The Swedish government has been committed to promoting equality for its citizens by encouraging women to achieve economic independence through employment. With the expansion of social services in the 1960s and 1970s, large numbers of women entered the labor force, but mostly in the traditional women's fields such as nursing and child care.

An important step toward economic independence for Swedish women was the introduction of separate taxation for married couples in 1971. Previously, couples had been assessed jointly, and because of Sweden's progressive tax policy women had little to gain by entering the labor force. The government credits the new policy with helping to change the perception of women from dependent wives and mothers to independent wage earners.

WOMEN'S LABOR FORCE PARTICIPATION Percentage of age group, 1993	
AGE	PERCENT
25–34	81%
35–44	88%
45–54	89%
55–64	63%

Discrimination in the Workplace

Sweden's equal opportunity policy was formally introduced in 1972 with the establishment of an Equal Opportunities Advisory Committee attached to the office of the prime minister. The Equal Opportunities Act of 1980 was the first law promoting equal rights. It included a ban on sex discrimination, stipulated the active promotion of equal opportunities, and established the office of the equal opportunities ombudsman, whose responsibilities included disseminating information and hearing cases of alleged discrimination. Women may also file complaints with the courts, but the most popular option entails mediating claims through the employee's labor union.

A new Equal Opportunities Act, passed in 1992 and amended in 1994, required employers to promote a balanced distribution of women and men and make a special effort to recruit the underrepresented sex. The act also strengthened the ban on discrimination except in cases where it was part of a conscious effort to promote equality. In addition, it expanded the definition of work of equal worth and called for inequalities in pay to be corrected. In recent years, however, with the downturn in the economy, labor unions have become reluctant to mediate wage discrimination cases and women have begun turning to the courts with test cases concerning equal pay for comparable work.

Sexual harassment in Sweden is prohibited by the penal code, and women may file complaints with their union or the equal opportunity ombudsman. A 1987 survey conducted by the ombudsman found that 17% of the women responding reported incidents of harassment in the workplace. The Equal Opportunities Act of 1992 required employers to actively prevent sexual harassment, and in 1993 the government allocated funds to develop effective safeguards against this problem. As with other forms of employment discrimination, women may file harassment complaints with the ombudsman, the courts, or their unions.

WOMEN IN MAJOR OCCUPATIONAL GROUPS
Percentage of group, 1990

OCCUPATIONAL GROUP	PERCENT
Clerical	77%
Service	77%
Professional, technical	56%
Sales	48%
Administrative, managerial	39%

Areas of Employment

Despite the Swedish government's laws and policies encouraging women to work in all industries and at all levels of responsibility, women workers tend to be concentrated in health care (87%) and social services (72%). And within any industry, they tend to be employed in jobs with lower status and salaries. In the area of health care, women make up 95% of all nurses, assistant nurses, and paramedics, and 65% of mental health nurses, but only about 33% of physicians.

Although women have not reached parity with men in administrative and managerial posts, Sweden has the world's highest proportion of women in this occupational category. For every 100 men in administrative or managerial positions, there are 64 women in comparable jobs. In the public sector women hold about 30% of all managerial posts, while in the private sector the proportion is just under 10%.

Among professional and technical workers, Swedish women outnumber men, again enjoying one of the world's highest ratios:

WOMEN IN EDUCATION
Percentage of total, 1990

LEVEL	PERCENT
Grades 1–3	99%
Grades 4–6	65%
Secondary school	46%
Higher education	28%
Full professors	7%

127 women for every 100 men. One of the reasons there is such a high proportion of women in this occupational group is that many become teachers.

The judiciary in Sweden is composed of permanent and nonpermanent judges, with women accounting for only 17% of permanent and 54% of nonpermanent positions. These percentages mark an increase from 12% and 40% respectively a decade ago.

Although a quarter of military personnel in Sweden are female, nearly all are employed in support areas, such as clerical and health care, and only 2% are officers. In July 1989, women were admitted into all combat positions, the last job category to be opened to them.

The area of female entrepreneurship has been growing steadily in Sweden, with women starting 19% of all new businesses in 1993, up from 15% in 1989. Most of these companies are in the service sector. Recognizing that women entrepreneurs make an important contribution to the Swedish economy, the government has begun promoting and supporting companies run by women. A new organization provides them with information, advisory services, training, and some financing.

Pay Differences

In 1995 women's nonagricultural wages were about 89% of men's, one of the smallest gender wage gaps in the world. Most of the difference in wages, according to a 1993 government study, is attributable to different job distributions of women and men according to their age, occupation, and education. However, in 1% to 8% of cases the pay difference is due solely to gender. These findings resulted in an amendment to the Equal Opportunities Act stipulating that organizations with 10 or more employees must submit to the equal opportunities ombudsman the results of an annual survey comparing the pay of their female and male employees.

The 1993 study also found that in the public sector, when employees' education levels are the same, women are paid less, and that the higher the education level, the larger the wage gap. For example, a woman with only a secondary school education working for the federal government earned 93% of the wages of a man with the same education, whereas the salary of a woman with a postgraduate degree amounted to only 87% of that of a man with the same credentials.

Working Hours

A sizable proportion of Swedish women in the labor force, 40%, work part time, compared with 9% of men. On average, in 1993 women worked 33 hours a week and men worked 41 hours. Both "short" part-time hours (maximum of 19 hours a week) and "long" part-time hours (20 to 34 hours a week) enable many mothers with young children to work outside the home.

Maternity Leave and Benefits

An important part of Sweden's social welfare policy gives both women and men the opportunity to work and raise a family at the same time, and maternity benefits are very generous. Nearly all Swedish women work until their first child is born and return to work within a year. Both parents are entitled to 30 days of childbirth leave at 90% of their salary. An additional 300 days can be split between the parents as long as the father takes at least one month's leave. This "father's month," however, can be taken at any time before the child's eighth birthday. In 1990, 39% of fathers used at least a portion of their childbirth leave, up from 22% in 1980.

Another benefit for parents is a cash payment for women who are unable to work during the last two months of pregnancy. In addition, a child-care allowance is given to parents with children between the ages of one and three to ease the financial burden if one parent remains home to care for the children.

Child Care

The Child Care Act of 1985 guarantees a place in a day-care center for every preschooler between the ages of 1 and 6, and in a leisure time center for every child between 7 and 12. In 1993, 58% of preschool children were placed in day care, and 29% of school-age children were enrolled in leisure time centers. The fees for these centers are minimal, about 15% of the total cost.

Unemployment

The early 1990s saw the worst recession in Sweden since the 1930s, in which unemployment rose from 1.5% for both sexes in 1991 to 6.6% for women and 10.4% for men in 1993. By 1994, however, the rates had dropped somewhat, to 5.1% for women and 7.5% for men.

MARRIAGE AND DIVORCE

Attitudes toward family structure have changed considerably over the last few decades, and as the marriage rate has decreased, the divorce rate has increased. At the same time, cohabitation has become widespread.

About a quarter of all households in Sweden are headed by women. Of these households, only about one in five consists of a single woman living alone.

Marriage

The minimum legal age for marriage is 18 for both women and men, but couples usually marry much later, often after several years of cohabiting.

The average age of women at first marriage is 30.4 years, the highest in the world. For men the corresponding age is 32.9 years. In the early 1990s there were an average of 40,000 marriages a year.

Most Swedish couples live together before marriage, and Sweden has one of the world's highest rates of cohabitation. In 1992 about a quarter of all couples were cohabiting. About 42% of the women in these partnerships were between the ages of 25 and 44, with another 35% aged from 45 to 64. Of the men in these relationships, 39% were between the ages of 25 and 44, while 38% were between 45 and 64.

Although Sweden has not legalized same-sex marriages, in 1994 the government passed partnership laws extending tax, inheritance, and next of kin rights to gay and lesbian couples. However, partners in these relationships are not allowed to be married in a church or adopt children. Within the first year these partnerships were permitted, they were granted to 330 couples.

Directly related to the high incidence of cohabitation is Sweden's high rate of out-of-wedlock births. Approximately half of all babies are born to unmarried women, a tremendous jump from 1960, when only about 11% of births were to single mothers.

BIRTHS TO UNMARRIED WOMEN Percentage of total births	
YEAR	PERCENT
1960	11%
1970	19%
1980	40%
1990	47%
1992	50%

Divorce

After a rapid climb in the 1960s and 1970s, the number of divorces leveled off in the 1980s to about 18,000 per year. By 1992 the annual rate had increased to about 19,000, twice that of 1960. Sweden has one of the world's highest divorce rates: For every 100 couples getting married each year, approximately 48 couples get divorced.

A complete revision of Sweden's divorce laws in 1973 resulted in the availability of no-fault divorce at the request of either or both spouses, with no required separation period. The only impediment to immediate divorce occurs in cases where only one parent petitions for divorce or where there are children under 16. In those cases there is a mandatory six-month deliberation period during which both partners are encouraged to enroll in a free program of marriage counseling.

Further modifications to the divorce laws in 1983 emphasized joint custody as the responsibility of both parents, regardless of the relationship between them. Joint custody is automatic, though it is still most common for children to live with their mother. Both parents are expected to contribute toward their children's support, but if a parent fails to pay, the social security system makes the payment.

FAMILY PLANNING

To improve maternal health and assist parents in planning their families, the Swedish government instituted a Family Planning Program in the 1970s. It provides education about sexuality and personal relations, contraceptive services, and access to safe abortion.

Fertility Rate

The average number of children born to Swedish women during their lifetime is 2.1, an increase from a fertility rate of only 1.6 in the early 1980s. The government attributes this rise to the massive development of day-care centers and the introduction of parental insurance, both of which have enabled more women to work outside the home while raising a family. The average age of first-time mothers in 1990 was 26.2 years, a substantial increase from 24.4 years in 1974. In 1991 only 1% of all births were to teenagers, one of the lowest such rates in the world.

Contraception

In 1981, the latest year for which information is available, approximately 78% of couples of childbearing age used some form of contraception. Condoms, birth control pills, and intrauterine devices were the most widely used methods. In a 1988–1989 study of all Swedish women aged 16 through 49, not just those in monogamous relationships, it was found that about 66% were using some form of contraception.

CONTRACEPTIVE USE
Percentage of couples of childbearing age, 1981

METHOD	PERCENT
Condom	25%
Birth control pill	23%
Intrauterine devices (IUDs)	20%
Traditional methods	7%
Sterilization, female, male	3%

Abortion

Sweden's policy on abortion evolved gradually over the course of the 20th century. In 1910 abortion was totally banned and punishable by imprisonment, but in 1938 legislation was passed to allow abortions on medical, humanitarian, and eugenics grounds. In the 1950s abortion was also made available to women who were ill and those with large families, sometimes on condition that they undergo sterilization at the same time. In 1963 the grounds for abortion were expanded to include possible fetal damage.

In the period from 1930 to 1960, only 3,000 to 6,000 legal abortions were approved each year, but an estimated 15,000 to 20,000 illegal abortions were also performed. In the 1960s women's groups began lobbying for a more liberal abortion law, and in 1974 the Riksdag approved the Abortion Act, which defined abortion as a woman's right and provided it on demand. By 1980 about 35,000 abortions were performed annually, and within 10 years this figure rose to nearly 40,000. However, since then the abortion rate has declined, with only about 34,000 abortions performed in 1994.

Under the present law, a woman has the right to an abortion up to the 18th week of pregnancy, and from the 18th to the 22nd week with permission of the National Board of Health and Welfare. However, the great majority of abortions, more than 90%, take place before the 12th week. Legislation also stipulates that the procedure be performed in a hospital.

Sex Education

Sex education was introduced into the school curriculum in 1942, initially focusing on anatomy, physiology, and birth control; it became compulsory in 1955. In the 1970s the curriculum was restructured to include sexuality, ethics, feelings, and gender roles; in the mid-1980s Sweden's school system became one of the first in the world to include information on AIDS and other sexually-transmitted diseases. Sex education normally begins in the first grade, with approximately 15 hours devoted to it each school year.

WOMEN'S HEALTH

The Swedish people are among the world's healthiest, with an exceedingly long life span. In 1992 the life expectancy was 80.8 years for women and 75.3 years for men, among the highest in the world. Not surprisingly, the maternal mortality rate is among the lowest in the world: 7 deaths per 100,000 live births. One reason maternal deaths are so low is that all pregnant women are entitled to free regular checkups at maternal health centers.

The health care system is administered at the local level and financed primarily through taxes, with patients paying a small copayment. In 1992 the government established the Institute for Public Health; one of its priorities was to promote increased research into women's health problems.

Leading Causes of Death

The leading causes of death are the same for both women and men, with cardiovascular diseases, primarily heart attack and stroke, accounting for about half of all deaths.

LEADING CAUSES OF DEATH
Percentage of total deaths, 1992

CAUSE	WOMEN	MEN
Cardiovascular diseases	51%	50%
Cancer	21%	22%
Breast	3%	—
Lung	2%	4%
Cervix	<1%	—
Pneumonia	5%	4%
Diabetes	2%	2%
Accidents	2%	3%
Suicide	<1%	2%
Homicide	<1%	<1%

Smoking

The proportion of smokers in Sweden decreased during the 1980s, except among older women. Men reduced their use of tobacco more than women, so that by 1991 Sweden was one of the very few countries where smoking was more prevalent among women than men—about 30% of women and 26% of men smoke. A 1994 government study noted an alarming trend: that among ninth graders, 29% of girls and 16% of boys were regular smokers.

AIDS

According to the World Health Organization, in 1994 an estimated 3,000 Swedes were infected with HIV, the virus that causes AIDS. During 1995 only 116 new cases of AIDS were reported. As in other European countries, the most common method of transmission is homosexual contact, and many more men than women are infected.

VIOLENCE AGAINST WOMEN

Preventing violence against women has become a high priority in Sweden, and the government has implemented a number of measures, including stiffer penalties for abusers, better support for victims, and a variety of policies and programs aimed at prevention. Despite these measures, however, the number of reported violent crimes against women has increased, and research indicates that many acts of violence go unreported. In 1993 the government created a Commission on Violence Against Women to review these issues and make further recommendations.

Domestic Violence

In 1994 nearly 18,600 cases of assault against women were reported to the police. In three-quarters of these cases, the assailant was known to the victim, usually a spouse. When convicted, abusers are usually sentenced to jail or psychiatric treatment.

In 1988 the government passed a Restraining Orders Act enabling the courts to prohibit an abusive spouse from having any contact with his victim. In the same year an Injured Party's Counsel Act was passed to pay for victims' legal costs. Women in extreme danger of being assaulted may receive a bodyguard, a trained police dog, or an electronic alarm to summon the police. Shelters and telephone hotlines are operated by various voluntary organizations subsidized by the national and local governments.

Rape

In 1994 about 1,800 rapes were reported to the police, fewer than the 2,100 reported in 1993, but an increase from the 1992 figure of 1,400. There is no legal distinction in Sweden between rape and marital rape, and it is also illegal for a man to have sexual relations with someone who is in a state of helplessness due to alcohol or drug use. The punishment is 2 to 6 years in prison, with 4 to 10 years for aggravated rape.

In the early 1980s a number of changes were made to the law concerning the prosecution of assault and rape cases. Prosecution no longer depends on the victim making an accusation; anyone with information of such a crime can report it. In addition, it is no longer permissible for the court to take into consideration any testimony regarding the morals and previous sexual behavior of the victim.

Prostitution

Prostitution is legal in Sweden, unless a minor is involved. Procuring, however, is prohibited. Although the estimated number of women engaged in street prostitution has decreased from 1,000 in 1980 to 700 in 1993, the number of women working in massage parlors and similar establishments is thought to be increasing.

Female Genital Mutilation

Because of the growing number of immigrants from countries where female genital mutilation is a common practice, Sweden has passed legislation specifically forbidding this custom.

FOR ADDITIONAL INFORMATION ON WOMEN

Association of Swedish Women
Bergsgatan 7 B
S-112 23 Stockholm, Sweden
Telephone: 8-52-09-55

Embassy of Sweden
1501 M Street, NW
Washington, DC 20005, United States
Telephone: 202-467-2600

Fredrika Bremer Association
Hornsgatan 52
S-117 21 Stockholm, Sweden
Telephone: 8-44-32-61

Swedish Information Service
885 Second Avenue, 45th floor
New York, NY 10017, United States
Telephone: 212-583-2550

Swedish Institute
Box 7434
S-103 91 Stockholm, Sweden
Telephone: 8-789-20-00
Fax: 8-20-72-48

Population: *58.0 million*
Women per 100 men: *104*
Women's voting rights: *1928*
Women in legislature: *10%*
Women's share of work force: *44%*
▲ Literacy rates: women—*99%;* men—*99%*
Life expectancy: women—*79.0 years;* men—*73.6 years*
Average number of children: *1.8*
▲ Maternal mortality rate: *9*

WOMAN NOBEL PRIZE WINNER		
Dorothy Hodgkin	Chemistry	1964

The United Kingdom is an island nation located in the Atlantic Ocean off the mainland of Europe. It is made up of England, Scotland, Wales (often collectively known as Great Britain), and Northern Ireland, the six Irish counties that remained in the union after the Irish Free State gained autonomy from Britain in 1922. Despite its tiny size, the United Kingdom has long been a major world power. During the 19th century it flourished as the hub of the vast British Empire that encircled the globe, and even though its political strength and economic power have greatly diminished, it remains one of the most highly industrialized and influential nations in the world.

Although it is one of Europe's smallest countries, the United Kingdom is one of the continent's most densely populated and highly urbanized; about 92% of the people live in cities. Approximately 55% of the population are Protestant (mostly Church of England, Church of Scotland, or Church of Wales), 10% are Roman Catholic, and the remainder are made up of small minorities of Muslims, Hindus, Sikhs, Jews, and others.

HISTORY OF THE WOMEN'S MOVEMENT

The women's movement in the United Kingdom can be traced back to the 1700s, when individual women started campaigning for equality with men, chiefly focusing on education and family matters. In 1792, Mary Wollstonecraft published *A Vindication of the Rights of Woman,* now considered to be the first major feminist work. In it she argued for increased educational opportunities for women as well as political equality with men.

Large and extremely militant feminist groups emerged in the mid-1800s, concerned mostly with winning the right to vote. The first women's suffrage committees started forming around 1865, and although Parliament defeated John Stuart Mill's attempt to include women in a voting rights amendment, some progress was made: In 1869 unmarried female taxpayers were allowed to vote in local elections.

With the turn of the century, the campaign for universal women's suffrage moved into high gear. Led by Emmeline Pankhurst, Lydia Baker, and others, mobs of suffragettes disrupted Parliament, destroyed property, staged hunger strikes, and used other militant tactics to draw attention to their demands. Following the outbreak of World War I, however, large numbers of these women turned their energies to the war effort—driving ambulances, working in munitions plants, and performing many other traditionally male duties. When the war ended in 1918, somewhat in recognition of their tremendous contribution to the war effort, Parliament granted voting rights to women over the age of 30. That year also marked the first time a woman was elected to Parliament. However, as a protest against British policy in her homeland, Irish nationalist Constance Markiewicz refused to swear allegiance to the Crown and thus could not take her seat in the House of Commons. The following year, American-born Nancy Astor was elected to the House of Commons and became the first woman to sit as a member of Parliament. In 1928 suffrage was extended to all women over 21, giving them complete political equality with men.

During the mid-1960s the women's movement in the United Kingdom regained momentum, focusing on such issues as equal pay, violence against women, abortion reform, and increasing women's representation at all levels of government. In 1969 the Women's National Commission was established as an independent advisory body representing women's views on a wide range of issues to various governmental departments and agencies. In 1987 the government created a ministerial group on women's issues, which was upgraded to a cabinet subcommittee in 1992. Its responsibilities include reviewing and developing government policies on women's issues and overseeing their implementation.

WOMEN IN POLITICS

Although Britain's reigning monarch, Queen Elizabeth II, bears the official title of head of state, her position is largely ceremonial and she wields no political power. The most prominent woman in recent British politics is Margaret Thatcher, who became the country's first woman prime minister in 1979 and held that office until 1990.

Despite the fact that the United Kingdom is one of the few countries where a woman has served as prime minister, women are sorely underrepresented throughout high levels of government. Only 63 (10%) of the 650 members of the House of Commons were women in 1996, up from 4% in 1983. The highest-ranking woman was Betty Boothroyd, who in 1992 became the first woman elected Speaker of the House. In the House of Lords, whose members are not elected, women made up about 7% of the total membership.

Women are rarely appointed to cabinet posts; only 2 of the 25 departments (8%) were headed by women in 1996: Virginia Bottomley (national heritage) and Gillian Shephard (education and employment). In the European Parliament, the U.K. delegation included only 16 female members, 18% of the country's total representatives, a slight increase from 15% in 1984.

Women make up about 27% of the diplomatic service in the United Kingdom but are rarely appointed to senior positions. They constitute nearly 40% of entry-level employees but only 2% of the 150 or so ambassadors and heads of overseas missions. Of the top 24 positions at the Foreign and Commonwealth Office in London, women occupy only 2.

In local government, British women have fared slightly better. In 1985 the proportion of women in county, district, and municipal councils was 19%. By 1993 it had risen to 25%.

WOMEN'S EDUCATION

All children from age 5 (4 in Northern Ireland) to 16 are entitled to free, full-time education. The literacy rate for both women and men is 99%, although according to a recent government study, about 16% of the adult population still have difficulty with basic reading, writing, or math skills.

In 1989 the national curriculum was redesigned to offer a more balanced, less sexually stereotyped range of subjects. The number of girls taking courses in science, computing, and technology increased markedly, though they are still outnumbered by boys. Other recent government programs have focused on encouraging more girls to consider careers in science and engineering. These include Women into Science and Engineering, which provides hands-on experience for girls aged 13 and 14, and the Technical and Vocational Education Initiative, which promotes girls' interest in technological subjects.

The enrollment of women in higher education continues to increase. While fewer than 10% of engineering and technology students are female, there are nearly as many women as men in computer science and mathematics courses. Women are also well represented in medicine and science departments. At the postgraduate level, women constitute about 28% of all full-time students; and they account for nearly one in five students in mathematics, engineering, and physical science courses.

FEMALE ENROLLMENT Percentage of student body, 1993	
LEVEL	PERCENT
Primary school	49%
Secondary school	50%
Higher education	49%

A recent trend in the United Kingdom has been an increase in the number of women returning to school after years of working or raising a family. Special "access" or "returners" courses train them to reenter the work force or prepare them for higher education. Nearly 40% of all women entering higher education programs are over 21.

WOMEN IN HIGHER EDUCATION Number of women's degrees, percentage of total		
YEAR	NUMBER	PERCENT
1980–1981	78,000	35%
1985–1986	103,000	39%
1990–1991	152,000	45%

WOMEN'S EMPLOYMENT

Women are an active and vital part of the British work force. In 1995 approximately 71% of all working-age women were in the labor force, one of the highest percentages in the world, and a significant increase from 63% in 1979. Overall, they constituted a 44% share of the total labor force. British men, in comparison, had a work force participation rate of 91%.

Discrimination in the Workplace

The Equal Pay Act of 1970 came into effect in 1975 and established the right to equal pay for women and men employed in the same or similar work. It also covered bonuses, overtime pay, holidays, sick leave, and other terms of employment. A 1983 amendment to the Equal Pay Act allowed workers to claim equal pay for work of equal value.

The Sex Discrimination Act of 1975 made discrimination on the grounds of sex unlawful in employment and training as well as in housing and other areas. The Sex Discrimination Act of 1986 lifted restrictions on the number of hours women could work, established common retirement ages for women and men, and extended antidiscrimination provisions to household employees and businesses with fewer than five employees. In 1995 the government adopted regulations ensuring that part-time workers, the vast majority of whom are women, would be entitled to the same employment protection rights as full-time workers.

Complaints about sex discrimination or pay inequities are filed with special industrial tribunals, which handle about 1,500 claims a year. In recent years amendments to equality legislation have increased maternity leave and benefits and removed the compensation cap in sex discrimination cases, allowing an industrial tribunal to award whatever amount it considers appropriate.

In 1986 a court ruling established that certain instances of sexual harassment can be interpreted as acts of sex discrimination and therefore are subject to the Sex Discrimination Act. In 1992 the government prepared a series of guidelines on sexual harassment for employers and employees and distributed them to every employer with 10 or more workers, about 100,000 companies in all. Two years later the Criminal Justice and Public Order Act of 1994 made sexual harassment a criminal offense.

Areas of Employment

Although women have the legal right to employment in all occupations, they work predominantly in service industries. They lag behind men in the fields of science and technology as well as in the upper echelons of industry, where they account for only 3% of all senior executives. Overall, for every 100 men in administrative or managerial positions, there are 49 women in comparable posts. In the category of professional and technical workers, women fare somewhat better: 78 women for every 100 men in these positions.

Women have made some progress at all levels of the civil service. The proportion of women in the topmost positions has more than doubled, from 4% in 1984 to over 9% in 1993, while the number of women in senior and middle management has increased correspondingly. In the field of education 65% of teachers are women—more than 80% in nursery and primary schools and nearly 50% in secondary schools. In higher education women make up 21% of the teaching staff.

British women have a long history of serving in the armed forces and currently constitute about 7% of the total personnel. In the past they worked primarily in support services—such as nursing, administration, and law—but in recent years many more opportunities have opened to them, and they can now serve on combat duty on ships or as air crew. Law enforcement is another area where increasing numbers of women are entering a male-dominated profession. By the mid-1990s they made up more than 13% of police personnel, a slight increase from 12% in 1990.

WOMEN'S EMPLOYMENT
Percentage of area, 1992

AREA	PERCENT
Nursing	92%
Pharmacy	43%
Medicine	31%
Dentistry	25%
Veterinary medicine	25%
Law	21%
Accounting	10%
Surveying	9%
Architecture	6%

Most recently, women have made substantial inroads into another previously all-male vocation: the clergy. In 1994 the Church of England ordained its first woman, and there are now nearly 1,400 women priests throughout Britain, constituting about 10% of the total Anglican clergy.

Although it is usually more difficult for women to start new businesses, the number of self-employed women in the United Kingdom has grown steadily over the past decade, and they now make up a quarter of all self-employed workers. To encourage women to become entrepreneurs, the government has been guaranteeing loans made by banks or other institutions to businesses unable to get conventional loans because they lack security. Other government programs provide training, counseling, and similar services to women starting their own businesses.

Pay Differences

Women's average earnings in Great Britain have increased steadily in recent years. In all nonagricultural industries, women earn about 70% of men's wages. Because so many women work part time, they tend to be concentrated in lower-paying jobs, and even when they work full time, they tend to earn less overtime pay and receive fewer bonuses.

Working Hours

One of the most distinctive features of the British labor market is the large number of women choosing jobs that offer part-time hours, job sharing, or "flexi-time" arrangements; 90% of part-time workers are women.

About 45% of working women work less than 30 hours a week, and studies have indicated that the vast majority of these women, 92%, do so as a matter of choice, not because they cannot find full-time employment. Of all men in the labor force, only 6% work part time.

Maternity Leave and Benefits

All working women, no matter how long or what hours they have worked, are entitled to 14-week maternity leaves during which all their nonwage benefits must be continued. In addition, women with two years of continuous full-time service or five years working 8 to 16 hours a week are entitled to extend their maternity leave to 40 weeks.

Maternity pay, mandated by the 1975 Employment Protection Act, consists of 90% of a woman's average earnings for 6 weeks followed by a flat rate for 12 weeks. To qualify, women must be earning enough to pay contributions to national insurance and must have worked at least 26 weeks. Self-employed women and those who do not meet the eligibility requirements receive flat-rate payments from the government.

Child Care

Nearly 65% of all families with children under five use some form of child care—usually a nursery school, playgroup (part-time nursery), unpaid family member, or paid child minder. In the last decade the number of registered child minders and private nursery schools more than doubled. However, there is still a need for affordable child care, especially for single parents, and the government has launched a major initiative to create 50,000 new after-school and holiday programs for children over five.

OCCUPATIONAL GROUPS
Part-time vs full-time work, numbers, in thousands

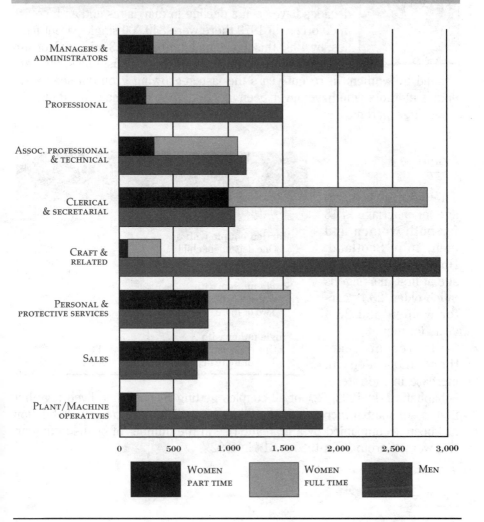

MANAGERS & ADMINISTRATORS

PROFESSIONAL

ASSOC. PROFESSIONAL & TECHNICAL

CLERICAL & SECRETARIAL

CRAFT & RELATED

PERSONAL & PROTECTIVE SERVICES

SALES

PLANT/MACHINE OPERATIVES

| WOMEN PART TIME | WOMEN FULL TIME | MEN |

Unemployment

The United Kingdom is one of the few countries in the world where the unemployment rate for women tends to be considerably lower than that for men. In 1993 the unemployment rate for women was 7.5%, compared with 12.4% for men. In addition, unemployed women tend to find jobs sooner than men. However, mothers with young children are more likely to be unemployed than those without dependent children.

MARRIAGE AND DIVORCE

As in many other industrialized countries, the past few decades have seen a decline in marriages and an increase in divorces. In 1979 there were 840,000 single-parent families; by 1991 this figure had jumped to 1.3 million. Not surprisingly, the vast majority of these households, 90%, are headed by women. In recent years the fastest-growing group of single parents is mothers who have never been married; they now make up about 35% of all single parents.

Marriage

The minimum legal age for marriage is 18 for both women and men, 16 in Scotland. However, the average age at first marriage is much older: 23.1 years for women and 25.4 years for men.

In recent years there has been an increase in the rate of cohabitation. In 1992, 62% of all couples getting married had lived together first, a substantial increase from 16% in 1972. This upsurge in cohabitation has been accompanied by a dramatic rise in the number of births to unmarried women, from 5% in 1960 to 31% in 1992.

TYPES OF HOUSEHOLDS
Percentage of total

HOUSEHOLD	1985	1992
Married couple with		
One dependent child	19%	17%
Two or more dependent children	69%	64%
Single mother with		
One dependent child	4%	5%
Two or more dependent children	7%	12%
Single father with		
One dependent child	1%	1%
Two or more dependent children	1%	1%

Divorce

The divorce rate in the United Kingdom is fairly high; for every 100 couples who get married each year, 42 couples get divorced. In 1969 the Divorce Reform Act made irreconcilable differences the sole grounds for divorce, and over the years the law was amended to include adultery, desertion for a two-year period, and mutual separation for two years. The Family Law Bill, which was passed in 1996 to take effect in 1998, requires a waiting period of 12 months, 18 months for couples with children or in contested cases. No divorce will be granted until the couple has agreed on the division of assets, child custody, and other matters. The new law also requires the government to pay for marriage counseling for any couples who desire it.

With respect to child support, a special agency was created in 1993 to trace delinquent parents, whether divorced or never married, for the purpose of collecting support payments from them.

FAMILY PLANNING

The United Kingdom considers family planning a vital health care service that contributes to better maternal and child health as well as the stability of the family. Under the National Health Service, all family planning services are free.

Fertility Rate

The average number of children born to British women is 1.8, down slightly from 1.9 in 1980. Births to teenagers account for nearly 9% of the total. Concern for the large number of teenage pregnancies has prompted the government's Health of the Nation program to focus its efforts on girls under 16 in an attempt to cut the present rate in half.

Most British women tend to have their children between the ages of 25 and 29, though a growing number are postponing childbearing until their 30s and 40s, after they have become established in a career. The government estimates that about 20% of women born in the 1960s will remain childless.

Contraception

Overall, about 81% of British couples of childbearing age use some form of contraception, a percentage that has remained fairly constant over the past decade. The most commonly used methods are birth control pills, sterilization, and condoms; and many couples rely on more than one method.

CONTRACEPTIVE USE
Percentage of couples
of childbearing age, 1986

METHOD	PERCENT
Birth control pill	19%
Condom	16%
Sterilization, male	16%
Sterilization, female	15%
Intrauterine devices (IUDs)	8%
Traditional methods	8%
Diaphragm, other	4%

Abortion

Abortion has been legal in Great Britain since 1967. To obtain an abortion, two medical practitioners must agree that the woman is not more than 24 weeks pregnant and that continuing the pregnancy would involve greater mental or physical risk to her or her other children than terminating it. There is no time limit on performing abortions to save the woman's life, prevent permanent physical injury, or in cases where the child is likely to be born with serious abnormalities.

In Northern Ireland abortion is legal only to save the woman's life or when the pregnancy might seriously damage her mental or physical health.

Fertility Services

Louise Brown, born in the United Kingdom in 1978, was the world's first "test-tube baby," conceived through an in vitro fertilization method developed by two British researchers. Today British couples can choose from a wide range of fertility services.

In 1990 the Human Fertility and Embryo Act created a licensing authority to regulate fertility treatments and human embryo research. Although it permits artificial insemination from a donor and in vitro fertilization, it bans commercial surrogacy agencies.

Sex Education

Since 1993, sex education has been compulsory in secondary schools throughout England and Wales. The curriculum includes information about AIDS and other sexually-transmitted diseases but also stresses moral considerations and the responsibilities of parenthood. In Scotland sex education is covered in a program on social and personal relationships, and in Northern Ireland each school is allowed to determine the level and type of sex education offered according to the moral and religious attitudes of the region and the maturity of its students.

WOMEN'S HEALTH

British women are living longer, healthier lives than ever before. Life expectancy for both women and men has been steadily climbing: In 1992 it was 79.0 years for women and 73.6 years for men, up from 77.4 for women and 71.7 for men in 1985. The maternal mortality rate of 9 deaths per 100,000 live births is one of the lowest pregnancy-related death rates in the world.

A comprehensive range of medical services, mostly free and available to all, is provided by the National Health Service. The only exceptions are dental care and drugs, for which most patients make partial payments. However, pregnant women, children, and the elderly are exempt from these payments. About 5% of the population belong to private health insurance programs, for which they pay an annual fee. But these programs rarely cover pregnancy and other conditions affecting women.

Leading Causes of Death

As in many other highly industrialized countries, the leading causes of death for both women and men are heart disease, stroke, and cancer.

In recent years two unusual medical trends have come to light: women born in the Asian subcontinent have a 46% higher rate of heart disease than the national average, and women from the Caribbean have double the mortality rate from stroke. The Department of Health is focusing on these trends and introducing programs targeted at improving the diet and lifestyles of women in both groups.

LEADING CAUSES OF DEATH
Percentage of total deaths, 1992

CAUSE	WOMEN	MEN
Cardiovascular diseases	46%	45%
Cancer	24%	28%
Breast	5%	—
Lung	4%	8%
Cervix	1%	—
Pneumonia	6%	3%
Diabetes	2%	1%
Accidents	1%	2%
Suicide	<1%	1%
Homicide	<1%	<1%

Smoking

Smoking rates for women and men in the United Kingdom are 27% and 37% respectively. Both figures represent a major drop in smoking since 1974, when the rates were 40% for women and 51% for men. Smoking among children, however, is a major concern: 10% of girls and 9% of boys aged 11 to 15 smoke regularly. To help reduce tobacco use and the many serious disorders related to it, the government has launched a number of antismoking campaigns, some aimed primarily at women. A voluntary agreement with the tobacco industry bans advertising in magazines if a third or more of their readers are young women.

AIDS

The incidence of AIDS and HIV infection has grown dramatically since the early 1980s, when reporting first began. By the end of 1994 the World Health Organization estimated that about 25,000 people in the United Kingdom were infected with HIV, the virus that causes AIDS. About 2,500 cases had been reported among women, and nearly one-quarter of the more than 500 babies born to infected women developed AIDS before the age of one.

As the incidence of HIV infection has grown, the proportion of infected women has also increased. In 1988 women accounted for about 12% of all new cases; by 1992 this figure had risen to 18%.

VIOLENCE AGAINST WOMEN

Violence against women is a major concern in the United Kingdom, and the government has created a ministerial interdepartmental working group on domestic violence to promote a coordinated response to the problem. Many government programs are aimed at strengthening law enforcement and increasing the number and kinds of services for victims.

Domestic Violence

Domestic violence is largely underreported and thus difficult to measure, but it accounts for one-third of all recorded crimes against women and one-quarter of all violent crimes against women. Homicide statistics show that nearly half of all murdered women are killed by a current or former husband or partner.

Government responses to domestic violence have included programs to raise the public's awareness of the problem, efforts to make the judicial system more sensitive to the needs of victims, and an emphasis on the need for police intervention and active prosecution of abusers. The first shelter for battered women in the United Kingdom was opened in 1972, and today there are hundreds throughout the country. Battered wives can also apply for personal protection orders and receive free legal aid if they are economically dependent on their abusers.

Rape

More than 4,000 cases of rape are recorded each year, and it is estimated that many more go unreported. In about two-thirds of all cases, the rapist is someone the victim knows, often a spouse. Under British law, marital rape is a criminal offense.

In 1994 a new law made it easier to convict rapists by abolishing a previously required judge's warning to the jury that a victim's testimony alone should not be considered adequate for a rape conviction. Throughout most of the United Kingdom life imprisonment is the maximum sentence for rape, attempted rape, and buggery (sodomy). In Scotland, which has a separate legal system, penalties vary according to the kind of court involved. A sheriff sitting with a jury may impose a sentence of up to three years in prison, while a judge in the High Court may impose a sentence of life imprisonment. Most rape and sexual assault cases are tried in the High Court.

A variety of governmental and nongovernmental organizations offer a wide range of services for rape victims. Rape crisis centers have been established in many areas, and some police stations have special facilities where rape victims are interviewed by female officers and examined by female doctors. The United Kingdom is one of the few countries to offer sexual assault victims financial compensation.

Rape victims are afforded anonymity by the 1976 Sexual Offences Act, which was expanded in 1992 to include victims of other forms of sexual assault. The Crown Court Witness Service provides advice and support to witnesses, and proposed witness protection laws would make it an offense to intimidate a witness, juror, or anyone assisting the police.

Prostitution

Prostitution itself is legal, but prostitutes may not solicit on the street; and people who encourage, control, or exploit the prostitution of others are prosecuted. In England and Wales a 1985 law made it an offense for male customers to "kerbcrawl" (cruise) looking for prostitutes or persistently to solicit a woman in a public place. A proposal to liberalize the prostitution laws and legalize brothels was rejected by the government in 1985, and there have been no plans to reconsider that decision.

Female Genital Mutilation

Significant numbers of immigrants from African and Asian areas where female genital mutilation is a traditional ritual are now living in the United Kingdom, and the government has enacted legislation prohibiting this practice.

FOR ADDITIONAL INFORMATION ON WOMEN

British Information Services
845 Third Avenue
New York, NY 10022, United States
Telephone: 212-752-5747

Embassy of Great Britain
3100 Massachusetts Avenue, NW
Washington, DC 20008, United States
Telephone: 202-462-1340

Equal Opportunities Commission
Overseas House
Quay Street
Manchester M3 3HN, United Kingdom
Telephone: 61-833-9244

National Alliance of Women's
  Organizations
279–281 Whitechapel Road
London E1 1BY, United Kingdom
Telephone: 71-247-7052
Fax: 71-247-4490

National Council of Women of
  Great Britain
36 Danbury Street
London N1 8JU, United Kingdom
Telephone: 71-354-2395
Fax: 71-247-4490

Office of Population Censuses
  and Surveys
St. Catherine's House
10 Kingsway
London WC2B 6JP, United Kingdom
Telephone: 71-242-0262

United Kingdom Department of
  Education and Employment
Sex Equality Branch
Caxton House
6–12 Tothill Street
London SW1H 9NF, United Kingdom
Telephone: 71-273-3000
Fax: 71-273-5124

Women's National Commission
Caxton House
6–12 Tothill Street
London SW1H 9NF, United Kingdom
Telephone: 71-273-5486
Fax: 71-273-4906

UNITED STATES

Population: *263.4 million*
Women per 100 men: *105*
Women's voting rights: *1920*
Women in legislature: *11%*
Women's share of work force: *46%*
▲ Literacy rates: women—*99%;* men—*99%*
▲ Life expectancy: women—*79.7 years;* men—*72.8 years*
Average number of children: *2.1*
Maternal mortality rate: *12*

WOMEN NOBEL PRIZE WINNERS		
Jane Addams	Peace	1931
Pearl Buck	Literature	1938
Emily Balch	Peace	1946
Gerti Cori	Physiology or Medicine	1947
Maria Goeppert-Mayer	Physics	1963
Rosalyn Yallow	Physiology or Medicine	1977
Barbara McClintock	Physiology or Medicine	1983
Rita Levi-Montalcini*	Physiology or Medicine	1986
Gertrude Elion	Physiology or Medicine	1988
Toni Morrison	Literature	1993

*Dual citizenship with the United States.

The United States of America is a vast, diverse country stretching across the North American continent between Mexico and Canada, and also including Hawaii in the Pacific Ocean and Alaska on the northwestern border of Canada. In population it is the third largest nation in the world (behind China and India), and in area it is the fourth largest (after Russia, Canada, and China). With its wealth of natural resources, pioneering spirit, and multicultural population, the United States is a major economic and political world power.

After more than 150 years of European rule, the United States declared its independence from Great Britain on July 4, 1776, and after seven more years of war, the signing of the Treaty of Paris in 1783 sealed the new nation's independence. The young country at that time consisted of 13 states, from Massachusetts (which included Maine) in the north to Georgia in the south.

Today the United States comprises 50 states and the District of Columbia, containing the city of Washington, the seat of the nation's capital. Three-quarters of the population are urban, and more than 40 metropolitan areas have populations of over a million. Approximately 83% of Americans are white, 12.5% are black, 4% are Asian or Pacific Islander, and 0.8% are American Indian, Eskimo, or Aleut. Hispanic Americans, who may be of any race, make up 10% of the population. With respect to religion, 56% of Americans are Protestant, 26% are Roman Catholic, and 2% are Jewish. There are also smaller minorities of Muslims, Hindus, Buddhists, and many others.

HISTORY OF THE WOMEN'S MOVEMENT

During the early 1800s the proliferation of common (public) schools throughout the expanding country, along with the founding of numerous

AGE DISTRIBUTION OF WOMEN Number in thousands, percent change 1970–1995			
	NUMBER		%
AGE	1970	1995	CHANGE
Under 5	8,413	9,837	+17%
5–13	17,987	16,607	-8%
14–17	7,782	7,087	-9%
18–24	12,131	12,507	+3%
25–34	12,697	20,835	+64%
35–44	11,863	21,238	+79%
45–54	12,028	15,447	+28%
55–64	9,803	11,140	+14%
65–74	7,002	10,544	+51%
75–84	3,684	6,814	+85%
85 and over	919	2,593	+182%

women's academies and seminaries, produced substantial numbers of educated young women. With this increased education came a growing involvement in social issues and the gradual emergence of women's groups devoted to achieving equal rights with men.

The specific event generally considered to mark the beginning of the American feminist movement was the Women's Rights Convention in Seneca Falls, New York, in 1848. Organized by Elizabeth Cady Stanton and Lucretia Mott and attended by 300 women, the convention adopted Stanton's Declaration of Sentiments, which asserted that all men and women were equal. This manifesto also listed a number of grievances and called for full legal, social, and political equality with men, along with increased educational and professional opportunities. Most important, though, was its demand for the right to vote, formally launching the American campaign for women's suffrage.

Over the next several years women activists, known as suffragettes, sponsored a number of similar conventions and undertook extensive speaking tours in an attempt to foster support for their cause. With the close of the Civil War in 1865, however, the suffrage movement suffered a major setback. During the war the campaign had been set aside while the suffragettes devoted their energies to supporting the movement to abolish slavery. They fully expected that when the Constitution was amended to grant the newly freed slaves the right to vote, the franchise would also be extended to women. Much to their dismay, when the 15th Amendment to the Constitution was drafted, it granted voting rights to the freed male slaves, but not to women, white or black.

Following this defeat, the suffragettes moved into high gear and grew more militant—holding massive rallies and demonstrations in Washington, D.C. and other cities, staging boycotts and hunger strikes, destroying property, chaining themselves to public buildings, and carrying out other acts of civil disobedience. Many of them were arrested and jailed, and although they succeeded in drawing attention to their cause, an 1869 proposed constitutional amendment specifically granting women the right to vote was defeated in Congress. Over the next several decades, a series of similar bills met the same fate.

At the state level, however, pressure to incorporate voting rights into state constitutions proved more successful. Wyoming granted women the right to vote when it became a territory in 1869 and continued this policy when it attained statehood in 1890. Other states soon followed: Colorado in 1893; Idaho and Utah in 1896; California in 1911; Kansas, Oregon, and Arizona in 1912; Nevada and Montana in 1914; and New York in 1917.

With the outbreak of World War I, the suffragettes turned their energies to the war effort, and in 1920 after the war, Congress approved the 19th Amendment granting American women the right to vote. Having attained its primary goal, the feminist movement began dwindling in size and energy.

Some activists, however, continued to fight for such issues as equal rights with men and legislation protecting women in the workplace.

During World War II American women again became a vital part of the war effort; more than 6 million went to work for the first time, mostly in factory or clerical jobs in war-related industries. By 1945, 37% of women were working outside the home, a substantial jump from the 28% who were working in 1940. In the aftermath of the war, however, a surge of antifeminism throughout the country resulted in many women leaving their jobs to stay home and care for their families; by 1950 34% of women were working outside the home. Over the next few years, though, as the postwar economy boomed and new jobs were created, once again many women started entering the work force, and by 1960 women's participation was up to 38%. Feminist groups during that period focused on such issues as equal pay, employment opportunities, and child care.

The modern women's movement in the United States dates back to the early 1960s, when large numbers of women, led by author Betty Friedan and others, created a new brand of militant feminism. As more and more women entered the work force, they were encountering widespread discrimination in hiring, promotion, and working conditions. Fueled by this blatant discrimination, the new wave of feminism attracted a wide following throughout the country. In 1960 President Kennedy created a Commission on the Status of Women, and its report, released in 1963, documented widespread sex-based discrimination. That same year the Equal Pay Act was passed, and in 1964 Congress approved the Civil Rights Act, which prohibited discrimination on the basis of sex as well as race, religion, and national origin.

When the National Organization for Women (NOW) was founded two years later, it further mobilized women to fight for increased political representation, equal rights in employment and education, and women's reproductive rights. Many similar groups followed, including the Women's Equity Action League (WEAL) and the National Women's Political Caucus, (NWPC) the first national women's organization founded specifically to promote women's participation in positions of political leadership.

One of the most hotly debated issues during the 1970s was the Equal Rights Amendment (ERA), passed by Congress in 1972 but never adopted because it failed to win ratification by the required three-quarters of the states. This amendment would have added to the Constitution this simple statement: "Equality of rights under the law shall not be denied or abridged by the United States or by any State on account of sex." Although it was widely supported by women's groups throughout the country, it was also staunchly opposed by many organizations, the most vocal of which was Stop ERA, headed by antifeminist activist Phyllis Schlafly. By 1978 only 35 states had ratified the amendment, and even though Congress passed a resolution the next year extending the original seven-year dead-

STATES RATIFYING THE EQUAL RIGHTS AMENDMENT (1972–1978)

Alaska	Kansas	New Hampshire	South Dakota
California	Kentucky	New Jersey	Tennessee*
Colorado	Maine	New Mexico	Texas
Connecticut	Maryland	New York	Vermont
Delaware	Massachusetts	North Dakota	Washington
Hawaii	Michigan	Ohio	West Virginia
Idaho*	Minnesota	Oregon	Wisconsin
Indiana	Montana	Pennsylvania	Wyoming
Iowa	Nebraska*	Rhode Island	

*Ratification later rescinded.

line to 1982, ERA supporters could not mobilize enough strength to win the three necessary additional states. The ERA therefore expired, and although identical amendments were introduced in later Congresses, they were never approved.

Despite the failure of the ERA to win ratification, the growing feminist movement of the 1970s provided the impetus for many successful campaigns and firsts for American women: In 1972 the Education Amendments prohibited sex-based discrimination in colleges and universities; in 1973 the landmark Supreme Court ruling *Roe v. Wade* legalized abortion; in 1974 Ella Grasso of Connecticut became the first woman governor to be elected entirely in her own right, not as her husband's successor; in 1975 Congress ordered U.S. military academies to accept female students; in 1978 NASA accepted women for astronaut training; in 1981 Sandra Day O'Connor became the first woman to sit on the Supreme Court (she was joined in 1993 by Ruth Bader Ginsburg); also in 1981, Jeane Kirkpatrick became the first woman to represent the United States as ambassador to the United Nations; in 1983 Sally Ride became the first American woman in space; in 1984 Geraldine Ferraro became the first female vice-presidential candidate of a major political party; in 1990 Antonia Novello became the first woman surgeon general; in 1993 Janet Reno became the nation's first woman attorney general; and in 1997 Madeleine Albright became the country's first woman secretary of state.

Today thousands of formal and informal women's groups are flourishing throughout the United States. Many focus on specific issues, such as abortion rights or discrimination against black or immigrant women. Others, such as the Feminist Majority Foundation, continue to campaign for a wide range of issues, including eliminating sex-based discrimination in employment and education, fighting efforts to roll back affirmative action programs, increasing government support for child-care facilities, reforming the health care system, and enacting and enforcing stricter laws against domestic violence.

WOMEN IN POLITICS

Although American women have been voting for more than 70 years and more women than men tend to vote, the U.S. has never elected a female president or vice president. The only woman who came close was Geraldine Ferraro, who in 1984, became the Democratic candidate for vice president, the first—and only—woman ever nominated for this position by a major political party.

The first woman in the U.S. Congress was Jeanette Rankin, who was elected to the House of Representatives from the state of Montana in 1916. From 1920 to 1970 only 10 women served in the Senate and 65 in the House, and most of them were there because their husbands had died while in office and they had been appointed to serve the remainder of their husbands' terms. No woman has yet become Speaker of the House of Representatives or majority leader of the Senate.

With the elections of 1996, the percentage of women in Congress reached just over 11%; 9 women in the 100-seat Senate (9%) and 51 in the 435-member House (12%). These figures represented a slight increase from the previous Congress, in which women made up nearly 11% of the total membership—9 members of the Senate and 48 members of the House of Representatives.

In early 1997 women constituted 29% of the 14 members of the U.S. Cabinet: Madeleine Albright (state); Alexis Herman (labor); Janet Reno (justice); and Donna Shalala (health and human services). Other women in high-level federal positions included Carol Browner, administrator of the Environmental Protection Agency; Shirley Chater, commissioner of the Social Security Administration; Charlene Barshefsky, U.S. trade representative; Kathleen McGinty, chair of the Council on Environmental Quality; Audrey Manley, acting Surgeon General; Martha Riche, director of the Bureau of the Census; Alice Rivlin, vice chair of the Federal Reserve System; and Sheila Widnall, secretary of the Air Force. In the Foreign Service, 28 women out of a total of 165, served as ambassadors.

Only 14 women have ever been elected governor. By 1997 there were only two: Christine Todd Whitman of New Jersey and Jeanne Shaheen of New Hampshire. However, there were 18 women serving as lieutenant governors, up from 11 in 1994.

Women have fared somewhat better in state legislatures than they have in Congress. The first female state legislators were elected in 1894,

WOMEN IN THE UNITED STATES CONGRESS

1917
1919
1921
1923
1925
1927
1929
1931
1933
1935
1937
1939
1941
1943
1945
1947
1949
1951
1953
1955
1957
1959
1961
1963
1965
1967
1969
1971
1973
1975
1977
1979
1981
1983
1985
1987
1989
1991
1993
1995
1997

0   10   20   30   40   50   60

WOMEN IN THE HOUSE

WOMEN IN THE SENATE

WOMEN IN THE UNITED STATES CABINET

YEAR APPOINTED	NAME	DEPARTMENT	PRESIDENT
1933	Frances Perkins	Labor	F. D. Roosevelt
1953	Oveta Culp Hobby	HEW*	Eisenhower
1975	Carla Anderson Hills	HUD*	Ford
1977	Juanita Kreps	Commerce	Carter
1977	Patricia Roberts Harris	HUD*	Carter
1979	Patricia Roberts Harris	HEW*	Carter
1979	Shirley Hufstedler	Education	Carter
1983	Elizabeth Dole	Transportation	Reagan
1983	Margaret Heckler	HHS*	Reagan
1987	Ann D. McLaughlin	Labor	Reagan
1989	Elizabeth Dole	Labor	Bush
1991	Lynn Martin	Labor	Bush
1992	Barbara Franklin	Commerce	Bush
1993	Hazel O'Leary	Energy	Clinton
1993	Donna Shalala	HHS*	Clinton
1993	Janet Reno	Justice	Clinton
1997	Madeleine Albright	State	Clinton
1997	Alexis Herman	Labor	Clinton

* HEW = Health, Education, and Welfare; HUD = Housing and Urban Development; HHS = Health and Human Services (known as HEW prior to 1980).

WOMEN GOVERNORS

NAME	STATE	YEARS IN OFFICE
Nellie Tayloe Ross	Wyoming	1925–1927
Miriam "Ma" Ferguson	Texas	1925–1927
		1933–1935
Lurleen Wallace	Alabama	1967–1968
Ella Grasso	Connecticut	1975–1980
Dixy Lee Ray	Washington	1977–1981
Martha Collins	Kentucky	1983–1987
Madeleine Kunin	Vermont	1985–1991
Kay Orr	Nebraska	1987–1991
Rose Mofford	Arizona	1988–1991
Barbara Roberts	Oregon	1991–1995
Ann Richards	Texas	1991–1995
Joan Finney	Kansas	1991–1995
Christine Todd Whitman	New Jersey	1994–
Jeanne Shaheen	New Hampshire	1997–

WOMEN IN STATE LEGISLATURES

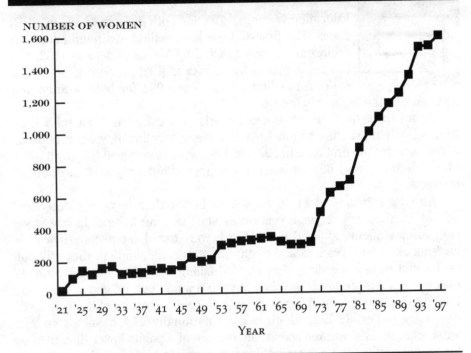

NUMBER OF WOMEN

YEAR

when three women were elected to the Colorado House of Representatives. Two years later, Utah became the first state with a female state senator. Between 1920 and the early 1970s, the number of women in state legislatures rose slowly. However, with the founding of the National Women's Political Caucus in 1971, scores of women began entering the political arena, and the percentage of female state legislators soared, from 8% in 1975 to 22% in 1997. The states with the highest proportion of women were Washington (38%); Arizona (37%); Colorado (35%); Nevada (33%); and Vermont (32%). Those with the lowest women's representation were Alabama (4%); Kentucky (9%); Oklahoma (10%); Louisiana (11%); and Mississippi (12%). Throughout the country women held 24 top legislative posts in 1997: senate presidents in 3 states, senate minority leaders in 8 states, house Speakers in 4 states, and house majority leaders in 9 states.

At the municipal level, 9 of the country's 50 largest cities had women mayors in 1997: Cincinnati, Ohio; Las Vegas, Nevada; Long Beach, California; Minneapolis, Minnesota; Portland, Oregon; San Diego, California; San Jose, California; Tulsa, Oklahoma; and Virginia Beach, Virginia.

WOMEN'S EDUCATION

Education is compulsory for both girls and boys in all 50 states. The first of these laws setting minimum education requirements was enacted by Massachusetts in 1852, and the most recent by Alaska in 1929, before it became a state. Adult literacy rates are 99% for both women and men, among the highest in the world.

About three-quarters of American girls now complete high school, up from slightly more than half in 1970. In college enrollment, women outnumbered men for the first time in 1979; in 1995 women received 53% of all bachelor's degrees and 52% of master's degrees, but only 40% of doctoral degrees.

Although girls tend to do as well or better than boys in elementary school, by the early teenage years they start lagging behind. In one study comparing students' skills, 9-year-old girls were found to outscore their male classmates in both reading and math; but at age 13, although they still outperformed boys in reading, they started falling behind in math. By age 17 they were still more proficient than boys in reading but the gap in math continued to widen. Similar findings have been seen in results of the Scholastic Assessment Test (SAT), which is used nationally as a basis for college admission. In 1996 women scored an average of 4 points lower than men on the verbal section of the exam but lagged 35 points behind on the mathematics section. However, this total gap of 39 points represented an improvement over the 57-point gap seen in 1987.

In 1994, 18 of the nation's 126 medical schools reported a majority of women in their first-year classes. Overall, women constituted 39% of medical, 43% of law, and 34% of business school students.

For many years female students were barred from United States military academies, but through an order of Congress they were admitted for the first time in 1976. By the mid-1990s, women made up about 13% of the total student body, and in June 1995, for the first time in its 193-year history, the vale-

FEMALE ENROLLMENT
Percentage of student body, 1992

LEVEL	PERCENT
Primary school	48%
Secondary school	49%
Higher education	56%

WOMEN'S COLLEGE ENROLLMENT
Percentage of total female students

RACE	1975	1985	1993
White	86%	86%	82%
Black	12%	11%	12%
Hispanic	4%	5%	7%

WOMEN'S DEGREES IN HIGHER EDUCATION
Percentage of subject area

SUBJECT	BACHELOR'S 1971	BACHELOR'S 1992	MASTER'S 1971	MASTER'S 1992	DOCTOR'S 1971	DOCTOR'S 1992
Home economics	97%	89%	94%	83%	61%	76%
Library science	92%	92%	81%	80%	28%	68%
Education	75%	79%	56%	77%	21%	60%
Health sciences	77%	84%	55%	80%	17%	58%
English	66%	66%	61%	66%	29%	58%
Foreign languages	74%	71%	64%	67%	35%	56%
Psychology	44%	73%	41%	71%	24%	60%
Public administration	68%	78%	50%	70%	24%	53%
Communications	35%	35%	61%	62%	13%	48%
Visual, performing arts	60%	62%	47%	56%	22%	44%
Biological science	30%	52%	34%	52%	16%	38%
Social science	37%	46%	29%	43%	14%	34%
Law	5%	67%	5%	33%	<1%	27%
Business	9%	47%	4%	35%	3%	23%
Physical science	14%	33%	13%	27%	6%	22%
Mathematics	38%	47%	27%	39%	8%	21%
Computer science	14%	29%	10%	28%	2%	13%
Engineering	1%	14%	1%	15%	1%	10%

dictorian of the West Point graduating class was a woman. In 1996, in a case involving the Virginia Military Institute, the Supreme Court ruled that state-supported military colleges could not exclude women, even if they offered a similar alternative program for women at a nearby college.

Sex discrimination in colleges and universities is specifically prohibited by a federal law known as Title IX of the Education Amendments of 1972. It applies to all educational institutions receiving federal financial assistance; any school violating the law may lose its funding. Suits may be brought with the particular federal agency that funds the institution or by private lawsuit.

Title IX prohibits discrimination in a number of areas, including student admissions and employee hiring and promotion. In the area of athletics, it specifically states that sports opportunities for both sexes must be substantially proportionate to the school's full-time undergraduate enrollment. Thus, if 53% of the student body are women, about 53% of the school's varsity athletes should also be women. By the mid-1990s, despite a number of successful lawsuits against several major colleges and universities, compliance in this area was still somewhat spotty. However, many colleges and universities around the country have started building up their women's athletics departments and are offering more scholarships to female athletes. As a result, the number of women participating in collegiate sports has soared, from about 30,000 in 1972 to more than 110,500 in the mid-1990s.

In recent years the Supreme Court extended coverage of Title IX to sexual harassment. Under federal guidelines issued in 1996, a school that does not take adequate steps to stop such harassment by faculty members and other school employees would be in violation of the law. Court rulings have been divided, however, over whether Title IX also covers the harassment of one student by another. In 1994 the Gender Equity in Education Act called for teachers to treat all students equally and also for the removal of gender bias in textbooks. However, no funds were appropriated to implement this law.

WOMEN'S EMPLOYMENT

Over the last four decades, American women have been entering the work force in increasing numbers, and by the mid-1990s they made up 46% of the total labor force. According to the U.S. Bureau of the Census, approximately 59% of all women over the age of 16 were working outside the home, compared with 75% of men in the same age range. When comparing U.S. labor force participation rates with those of women and men in other countries, a different calculation is necessary, since many other countries and international organizations use a slightly different age bracket—15 through 64—when computing participation rates. When this "working age" range is used to calculate U.S. labor force participation rates, they rise to 68% for women and 81% for men.

Over the past two decades, rising costs and decreasing wages have brought many married women into the labor market. By 1994 about 47% of all families with children derived their income from both parents, up from 36% in 1975. Further, three out of four working women in 1994 had school-age children, and 42% had children under the age of six. Another recent trend has been an increase in the number of women in their 50s entering or reentering the work force; about 65% of women in this age group are now working, up from 54% in the mid-1980s.

Women's participation in the labor force also varies from state to state. By 1994 West Virginia was the only state where fewer than half the women over 16 worked (46%). States with more than 65% of women in the work force were Minnesota (70%); Alaska (68%); Nebraska and Wisconsin (67%); Colorado, Iowa, New Hampshire, North Dakota, South Dakota, and Utah (66%); and Vermont (65%). The most populous states were found in the middle range: California (57%); Texas (60%); New York (53%); Florida (55%); Pennsylvania (55%); and Illinois (60%).

Discrimination in the Workplace

Equal employment opportunities for women are guaranteed by the Equal Pay

WOMEN IN THE LABOR FORCE

Percentage of women aged 16 and over, share of total labor force

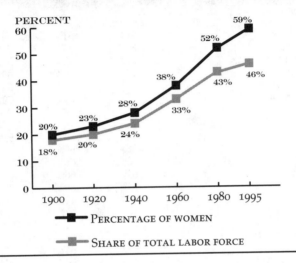

PERCENT

PERCENTAGE OF WOMEN

SHARE OF TOTAL LABOR FORCE

Act of 1963, the Civil Rights Act of 1964, and the Civil Rights Act of 1991. Women are also protected by state and local laws, some of which provide even more extensive coverage than federal laws. Since the 1960s, many states have also adopted affirmative action programs and policies in which women and minorities receive preferential treatment in employment, education, and state contracts. In recent years, however, some states—including California, Colorado, Florida, Illinois, and Oregon—have started modifying or even eliminating these programs altogether on the grounds that they constitute reverse discrimination.

Although the principle of equal pay for equal work was achieved as early as 1923 for women employed in the federal civil service, it was not mandated for private sector employees until the Equal Pay Act of 1963. In 1994 the Fair Pay bill was proposed to expand the coverage of the earlier law to include the principle of equal pay for work of equal value. This legislation, applying to both the public and private sectors, would prohibit discrimination among employees in jobs that may be dissimilar in some respects but equivalent in terms of required skills, effort, working conditions, and responsibility.

Title VII of the Civil Rights Act of 1964 made it unlawful for an employer to discriminate on the basis of sex (or race, color, religion, or national origin) in any aspect of employment, including hiring, training, promotion, firing, pay, benefits, or other working conditions. In 1978 Title VII was extended to prohibit discrimination because of pregnancy or childbirth. The Civil Rights Act of 1991 further increased protection against sex discrimination by adding significant financial penalties: punitive damages up to

WOMEN'S PARTICIPATION IN LABOR FORCE
Percentage of category, women aged 16 and over

CATEGORY	1970	1980	1994
By Race			
White women	43%	51%	59%
White men	80%	78%	76%
Black women	50%	53%	59%
Black men	77%	70%	69%
Hispanic women	—	47%	53%
Hispanic men	—	81%	79%
By Age			
16–19	44%	53%	51%
20–24	58%	69%	71%
25–34	45%	66%	74%
35–44	51%	66%	77%
45–54	54%	60%	75%
55–64	43%	41%	49%
65 and over	10%	8%	9%
By Marital Status			
Single	57%	64%	67%
Married	40%	50%	61%
Divorced, separated, widowed	40%	44%	48%
With Children Under 6			
Single	—	44%	52%
Married	30%	45%	62%
Divorced, separated, widowed	52%	60%	62%
With Children Aged 6 to 17			
Single	—	68%	68%
Married	49%	62%	76%
Divorced, separated, widowed	67%	75%	78%

$300,000 per claimant and compensatory damages for back pay, medical bills, and other costs.

Both civil rights laws are enforced by the Equal Employment Opportunity Commission (EEOC), which issues guidelines for compliance and investigates complaints. If a complaint cannot be resolved through arbitration, the EEOC may file suit in court or authorize the complainant to do so. In 1992 the EEOC received more than 41,000 complaints of sex discrimination, up from 31,000 in 1985.

Sexual harassment is generally defined as unwelcome sexual advances or requests for sexual favors that are either imposed as a condition of a person's employment or promotion or create an intimidating, hostile, or offensive work environment. In 1986 the Supreme Court ruled sexual harassment a form of sex discrimination prohibited under Title VII of the 1964 act. Workers wishing to file charges may do so through their state's Human Rights

Commission or the EEOC, which by the mid-1990s, was handling more than 15,000 complaints of sexual harassment a year.

Areas of Employment

While women in the United States have made some inroads into traditionally male-dominated areas, the overall pattern shows a labor force sharply segregated by sex. The great majority of American women are still concentrated in low-paying clerical, sales, and technical occupations. For every 100 men in administrative or managerial positions, there are 67 women in comparable positions, a ratio that falls far short of equality with men yet is one of the world's highest.

Not surprisingly, American women are least represented at the highest levels of leadership and responsibility. In the mid-1990s women made up 31% of all managers in private industry but only 6% of corporate executives and officers. In the federal government, where women accounted for 44% of the total work force, they occupied only 13% of the top-level posts. Among Wall Street's major investment and brokerage houses, women accounted for fewer than 10% of all partners and managing directors, and in the country's 250 largest law firms, only 14% of all partners were women. However, in 1996 for the first time women held more than 10% of directors' seats at the country's 500 largest companies; 83% had at least one woman on their board of directors, 35% had at least two.

In 1986 the term "glass ceiling" was first used to describe the invisible barrier preventing women from reaching the uppermost levels of management. In 1991 Title II of the Civil Rights Act created a special Glass Ceiling Commission to study this problem. That same year the Department of Labor's Report on the Glass Ceiling Initiative found that U.S. companies were not adequately monitoring the recruitment, hiring, and promotion of women. It also discovered that women were more likely to be placed in staff positions such as public relations and human resources than in line positions such as sales and production—and that employees promoted to executive posts were more likely to come from line positions.

In the occupational category consisting of professional and technical workers, American women outnumber men 103 to 100, but they are generally found in the lower-level positions. In the legal profession, women make up about 25% of the nation's lawyers; 35% of the 25,000 employed by the executive branch of the federal government; and 12% of all federal judges—2 of the 9 Supreme Court judges (22%), 24 of the 179 Circuit Court judges (13%), and 75 of the 649 District judges (12%). At the state level, about 10% of all judges are women.

Education has traditionally been a female-dominated profession, and in 1993 women made up 98% of nursery and kindergarten teachers, 86% of

WOMEN'S SHARE OF OCCUPATIONS
Percentage of category

OCCUPATION	1983	1994
Secretary	99%	99%
Private child care worker	97%	97%
Registered nurse	96%	94%
Bank teller	91%	90%
Librarian	87%	84%
Office clerk	81%	80%
Psychologist	57%	59%
Physician's assistant	36%	54%
Sales clerk	48%	49%
Postal clerk	37%	44%
Pharmacist	27%	38%
Mail carrier	17%	34%
Lawyer	15%	25%
Physician	16%	22%
Architect	13%	17%
Dentist	7%	13%
Police officer, detective	6%	11%
Engineer	6%	8%
Firefighter	1%	2%
Auto mechanic	<1%	2%

elementary school teachers, and 58% of secondary school teachers. However, in colleges and universities they accounted for only 43% of the teaching staff. In science and engineering departments, only about 9% of professors were women, more than double the 4% in 1973.

Women make up only about 20% of the total number of U.S. doctors. The specialties with the largest female concentrations are internal medicine (15%); pediatrics (14%); family practice (9%); obstetrics and gynecology (7%); psychiatry (7%); and anesthesiology (5%).

Another traditionally male-dominated area where American women have started to make significant inroads is the military. Following the creation of the Army Nurse Corps in 1901, most women in the military were nurses, but during World War I women were assigned to clerical and administrative jobs as well. During World War II women became part of the regular armed forces, but until the mid-1970s they made up only 1% of all uniformed military personnel.

The repeal of limits on the percentages of enlisted women and female officers, together with changes in Department of Defense policy and the admission of female students to U.S. military academies, prompted growing numbers of women to enter the service. In 1993, 12% of all enlisted personnel and 12% of officers were women. Although most women in the military still serve in health care, administration, and other traditional female jobs, increasing numbers are becoming pilots, navigators, mechanics, technicians, and even military police. And although women are now permitted to fly combat missions and serve on combat ships, they are still excluded from ground combat units.

One of the fastest-growing areas for working women is self-employment. In 1970 women owned fewer than 5% of the nation's businesses. By the mid-1990s more than a third of entrepreneurs were women, and women were opening new businesses at twice the rate of men. Loans to women approved by the Small Business Administration doubled from nearly 2,000 in 1984 to nearly 4,000 in 1993, and the dollar amounts involved tripled. By 1996 women owned nearly 8 million companies in the United States, up from nearly 4.5 million in 1987. About 3.5 million of these companies were home-based enterprises, a popular option for mothers of young children and other women who wish to remain at home while operating a small business.

Pay Differences

The 1980s and early 1990s saw a significant narrowing in the wage gap between American women and men. Excluding workers in agricultural occupations, American women in 1995 earned an average of 75% of men's wages, up from 71% in 1992 and 62% in 1982. Furthermore, when women's salaries were compared with those of men in similar jobs, the gap narrowed even more, with women earning 85% to 95% of men's salaries. According to a 1995 survey, those areas with the narrowest gender wage gaps were college and university administration, engineering, and library science. The largest gaps were in veterinary medicine, hospital administration, and financial services.

The difference in overall earnings between women and men is attributable to a number of factors. Women are not only sometimes paid less than men for similar work but also tend to be concentrated in lower-level jobs and in lower-paying industries. In addition, women tend to work more in seasonal and part-time jobs, and their careers are often interrupted for child raising.

Working Hours

Traditionally, more women than men have worked in part-time jobs. Overall, about 25% of all working women work part time, that is, less than 35 hours a week. For men this figure is 11%.

While women make up 41% of the full-time labor force, they account for 67% of part-time workers. Many women, especially those with preschool children, prefer part-time work, as do many older women who are returning to the work force after divorce, the death of a spouse, or child rearing.

Maternity Leave and Benefits

The Family and Medical Leave Act, signed into law in 1993, applies to about 45 million Americans: all government workers and people in firms with more than 50 employees. It permits any employee, male or female, who has worked at least one year to take up to 12 weeks of unpaid leave a year to recover from childbirth or care for a newborn or adopted child, other children, or another family member. During this period the employer must continue to provide health care benefits and guarantee the worker's job. Most states also guarantee some sort of maternity and other forms of medical leave, mostly without pay or as a combination of paid and unpaid leave.

Child Care

Finding adequate, affordable care for preschool children is a major concern of many working mothers in the United States. The government does not provide child-care facilities, and each family must make its own arrangements. In 1994 child care was the second largest monthly expense for most families, after rent or mortgage payments. Households earning less than $14,400 a year spent about a quarter of their income on child care. Those with annual incomes over $54,000 spent 6% of their earnings on child care.

During 1994 about 41% of American preschoolers were cared for by relatives, while 30% were enrolled in nursery schools or other child-care centers. Another 17% were cared for in informal day-care facilities. About 6% of preschool children went to work with their mothers, and about 5% were cared for by baby-sitters or other household employees.

In recent years a growing trend has been for private companies to help meet the child-care needs of their employees. Some companies offer on-site facilities for preschoolers; others provide care for mildly sick children; some offer partial reimbursement for child care; and others simply provide referral services.

Unemployment

In 1994 the unemployment rate for American women was 6.0%, compared with 6.2% for men. Not surprisingly, women without high school diplomas were much more likely to be jobless than college graduates: 12.4% compared with 2.9%.

UNEMPLOYMENT RATES
Percentage of labor force

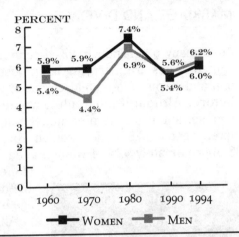

PERCENT

- 1960: Women 5.9%, Men 5.4%
- 1970: Women 5.9%, Men 4.4%
- 1980: Women 7.4%, Men 6.9%
- 1990: Women 5.6%, Men 5.4%
- 1994: Women 6.2%, Men 6.0%

■ WOMEN   ■ MEN

WOMEN'S UNEMPLOYMENT RATES
Percentage of age group, 1994

AGE	WHITE	BLACK	HISPANIC
16–19	13.8%	32.6%	22.2%
20–24	7.4%	19.6%	13.5%
25–34	5.1%	11.7%	10.1%
35–44	4.2%	8.0%	9.2%
45–54	3.7%	4.9%	8.0%
55–64	3.7%	4.9%	7.1%
65 and over	3.9%	4.4%	3.6%

Unemployment also varied by state. Those with the highest jobless rates for women were Louisiana, at 9.0% (7.3% for men); California, at 8.4% (8.7% for men); the District of Columbia, at 8.0% (8.3% for men); Alaska, at 7.5% (4.7% for men); and West Virginia, at 7.5% (10.1% for men). Those with the lowest rates were Nebraska, at 3.3% (2.5% for men); North Dakota, at 3.3% (4.4% for men); Iowa, at 3.4% (3.9% for men); Minnesota, at 3.4% (4.6% for men); and South Dakota, at 3.6% (3.1% for men).

Unemployment rates also varied by race and age. Overall, white women had an unemployment rate of 5.2% in 1994, compared with 11.0% for black women and 10.7% for Hispanic women. The comparable unemployment rates for men were 5.4% for whites, 12.0% for blacks, and 9.4% for Hispanic Americans.

Unemployment insurance in the United States is provided by a combined federal-state program that covers the great majority of American workers. The amount and duration of the weekly payments are determined by each state.

MARRIAGE AND DIVORCE

As in many other industrialized countries, women in the United States are marrying later, postponing childbearing, and having more children out of wedlock than ever before. Although most adult women live with their spouse, about one in nine households is headed by a woman, and an unprecedented 13.5 million women, roughly one in seven, live alone. In 1992 approximately 42% of women aged 65 and over lived alone, compared with 16% of men in the same age bracket.

Although the actual number of two-parent families has been increasing, its rate of growth has been outpaced by the increase in single-parent families. In 1994 almost one-third of families with children were headed by single parents, and in more than 85% of those families, those parents were women.

FEMALE-HEADED HOUSEHOLDS Percentage of total female-headed households, 1994	
MARITAL STATUS	PERCENT
Divorced	36%
Never married	26%
Widowed	20%
Married, husband absent	18%

While most American women do marry, it is estimated that increasing numbers of young women will remain single throughout their lives. In 1970, 11% of women 25 to 29 years old and 6% of women aged 30 to 34, were unmarried. By 1992 both these percentages had tripled, to 33% and 19% respectively.

Marriage

The legal minimum age for marriage varies by state, with most states setting 18 as the age for both women and men. In many states the age requirement drops to 16 or even lower with parental consent. However, most American women are marrying much later. In 1993 the average age at first marriage was 25.8 years for women and 28.1 years for men.

A blood test for syphilis is required by most states, and a waiting period of one to five days is often imposed between the issuing of the marriage license and wedding ceremony. Many states bar marriages between first

MARRIAGE RATES 1940–1993
Marriages per 1,000 population

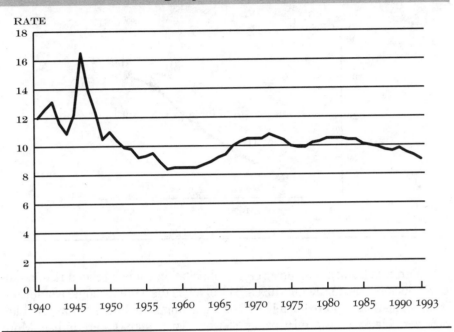

cousins, and ceremonies must generally be performed by qualified religious or public officials. In all states marriage certificates must be registered with the local civil authorities.

In 1993 there were approximately 2,334,000 marriages, 9.0 marriages per 1,000 population, the lowest rate in 30 years. After peaking at 16.4 in 1946, just after World War II, the marriage rate started declining. It started leveling off in the late 1950s and slowly started rising again after 1962. It then climbed to a high of 10.9 in 1972 before entering its current decline.

In 1993 the states with the highest marriage rates were Nevada (88.7), Arkansas (15.0), Hawaii (14.9), South Carolina (14.4), Tennessee (14.3), Idaho (12.7), Kentucky (12.0), and Utah (11.1). (The unusually high rate for Nevada is due largely to the large numbers of couples who travel there from other states to get married in its many hotels and resorts.) The states with the lowest marriage rates were the District of Columbia (5.2), Massachusetts (6.2), Pennsylvania (6.4), California (6.5), New Jersey (6.8), and North Carolina (6.8).

The number of American couples choosing to cohabit has grown approximately 600% in the last few decades. In 1960 roughly half a million couples were cohabiting; by 1994 this figure had reached 3.6 million. Most of these couples (60%) were aged between 25 and 44.

BIRTHS TO UNMARRIED WOMEN
Percentage of total births

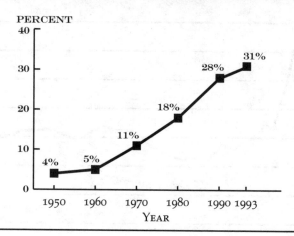

PERCENT

40

31%

30   28%

20   18%

11%

10
4%   5%

0

1950 1960 1970 1980 1990 1993
YEAR

With this tremendous upsurge in cohabitation came a related rise in out-of-wedlock births. In the mid-1990s, 31% of all births were to single women, up from 4% in 1950. Approximately 40% of these unmarried mothers were white, 36% were black, 21% were Hispanic, 2% were Asian, and 2% were Indian. More than half were in their 20s; less than a third were in their teens.

Although same-sex marriage is not yet legal anywhere in the United States, it has recently become a hotly debated issue. In 1991 San Francisco instituted a procedure by which gay and lesbian couples could register as domestic partners and thus be entitled to certain health, retirement, and other benefits. By 1995 Massachusetts, New York, and Vermont had granted same-sex couples the right of adoption. In these states such an adopted child is now legally entitled to inheritance and other benefits from both parents. Previously, only one parent could adopt the child, and the other partner could not be legally recognized as the second parent. Also in recent years, some states, municipalities, other governmental entities, and private corporations have started extending medical coverage and other benefits to the partners of gay and lesbian employees.

But the issue of same-sex marriage became the focus of a widespread debate in 1993, when the Supreme Court of the state of Hawaii paved the way for legalizing such relationships. After ruling that denying marriage licenses to same-sex couples was presumed unconstitutional, it sent the issue back to a lower court for a further hearing. That hearing was held in late 1996, and although it resulted in the court ordering the state to stop denying marriage licenses to same-sex couples, the order was immediately suspended pending an appeal to the State Supreme Court. In the meantime, a number of other states, fearing that Hawaii would legalize same-sex marriages, started drafting legislation specifically aimed at preventing the recognition of gay and lesbian marriages, since any licensed marriage in one state must be recognized in other states. By the end of 1996 16 states had passed such laws and 20 states had defeated them. At the federal level, the Defense of Marriage Act was passed by Congress and signed into law by the President in late 1996. It declared that states are not obliged to recognize same-sex marriages registered in other states and also denied federal recognition and benefits to partners in these marriages.

Divorce

In 1993, the number of divorces in the United States was about 1,187,000, translating into 51 couples getting divorced for every 100 couples who married that year. In another way of expressing the divorce rate, there were 4.6 divorces per 1,000 population, down from a high of 5.4 in 1979. The states with the highest divorce rates were Oklahoma (7.1), Arkansas (6.9), Alabama (6.5), Tennessee (6.5), Wyoming (6.5), Arizona (6.2), New Mexico (6.2), and Florida (6.1). States with the lowest divorce rates were Massachusetts (2.7), Connecticut (3.1), New York (3.1), New Jersey (3.1), Pennsylvania (3.3), Maryland (3.4), District of Columbia (3.4), Rhode Island (3.4), and North Dakota (3.5).

In 1969 California became the first state to introduce no-fault, or unilateral, divorce, and within a few years every other state had passed similar legislation. The no-fault divorce removes the concept of blame and allows one partner to dissolve a marriage at any time and for any reason. In fault-based divorces, that is, cases where one spouse sues the other, acceptable grounds vary by state but usually include adultery, abandonment, cruelty, and imprisonment.

In recent years many states have started reevaluating their no-fault divorce laws with the intention of modifying them or eliminating them altogether. Georgia, Hawaii, Idaho, Illinois, Iowa, Michigan, and Pennsylvania are among the states considering such changes as limiting no-fault divorce to couples without children, requiring marriage counseling or a mandatory waiting period, or denying no-fault decrees in cases where one spouse opposes the divorce.

Individual states also have different residency requirements for divorce, ranging from none to a year, as well as varying policies governing child custody and support, visitation rights, and property distribution. Most states have a policy of equitable distribution of marital property, which is generally defined as property acquired during the marriage. Nine states—Arizona, California, Idaho, Louisiana, Nevada, New Mexico, Texas, Washington, and Wisconsin—have community property laws, requiring the equal distribution of property acquired by each spouse prior to marriage as well as during the marriage.

One of the most serious problems facing many divorced mothers is the nonpayment of child support. In 1992 it was estimated that less than half of all parents who were supposed to receive child support actually received full payments. Traditionally, state governments have been responsible for collecting child support and have used such methods as suspending the driver's licenses of chronic nonpayers, distributing "wanted" posters, and searching computerized databases to locate delinquent parents. However, since nonpaying parents often move to other states, in 1992 Congress passed the Child Support Recovery Act, making nonpayment of child support a federal crime. Thus, for the first time federal attorneys were allowed to pursue those parents who willfully failed to pay at least $5,000 or fell more than a year behind in their payments. The law also set the maximum punishment for a first offense at six months' imprisonment with a fine of $5,000. Another tactic recently introduced for collecting child support payments entails garnisheeing the federal tax refunds of delinquent parents. In 1995 a record $828 million in child support payments was collected by this method.

FAMILY PLANNING

Contraceptives have been legal throughout the United States since 1965, when the Supreme Court ruled that states could no longer ban the use of contraceptives by married couples. Today the government approves and supports family planning services. The cornerstone of the federal program is Title X of the Public Health Service Act of 1970, which provides basic reproductive health care services to low-income women through public and private family planning centers throughout the country. The only major stipulation is that the funds may not be used for abortion.

Fertility Rate

The average number of children born to American women is 2.1, one of the highest fertility rates among the world's developed nations. For white women this figure drops to 2.0 children and for black women it rises to 2.4. For women of all races, about 63% of all pregnancies result in a live birth, 24% are terminated through abortion, and another 14% end in miscarriage.

In 1993 there were just over 4 million births in the United States: 79% to white women, 17% to black women, and 4% to Asian or Pacific Islanders. The number of births has been declining steadily over the past several years; one reason is that there are fewer women aged 15 to 29, the major childbearing years; all the baby boomers are now over 30.

The United States ranks first in births to teenagers among all industrialized nations, even though the percentage of births to teenage mothers has

BIRTHS BY AGE Percentage of total births			
AGE	1970	1980	1992
Under 20	18%	16%	13%
20–24	38%	34%	26%
25–29	27%	31%	29%
30–34	11%	15%	22%
35–39	5%	4%	8%
40 and over	1%	1%	1%

been declining in recent years, most likely due to an increased use of condoms.

Since the introduction of hormone treatments and other modern techniques to overcome fertility problems, the number of multiple births has been rising. In 1993 more than 100,000 babies were born in multiple births, the highest number ever reported. The number of women who gave birth to three or more babies was 95.5 per 100,000 live births, up from 40.3 in 1982 and 27.8 in 1972. Another factor in this increase was the larger proportion of women having children at a later age.

Contraception

Approximately 74% of all married or other monogamous couples of childbearing age use some form of contraception. Sterilization, both tubal ligations for women and vasectomies for men, is the most commonly used method.

CONTRACEPTIVE USE Percentage of couples of childbearing age, 1988	
METHOD	PERCENT
Female sterilization	23%
Birth control pill	15%
Male sterilization	13%
Condom	11%
Diaphragm, similar devices	6%
Traditional methods	5%
Intrauterine devices (IUDs)	2%

In 1995 the Food and Drug Administration declared a new contraceptive device, Norplant, safe for use. Consisting of six small hormone-filled capsules that are implanted under the skin of a woman's upper arm, it provides five years of continuous birth control and has a failure rate of only 1%. Since testing of Norplant began in 1991, it has been used by about a million American women.

Abortion

One of the most controversial and divisive issues in recent decades has been that of abortion. On one side of the argument are those who believe that the decision to terminate a pregnancy should be left entirely to each woman and her physician. On the opposite side are those who believe that

METHODS OF CONTRACEPTION
Percentage of age group, 1990

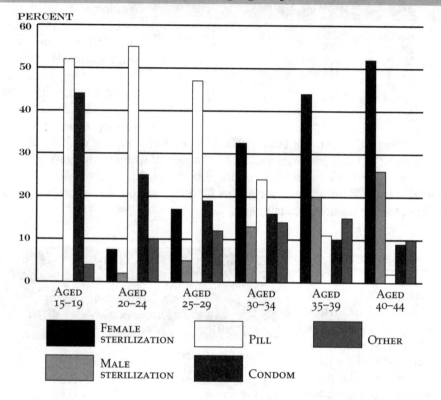

any form of abortion is murder. Between these two extremes are a wide range of viewpoints concerning such aspects as the time limit during which abortion should be allowed, whether parental consent should be required for teenagers, and whether government funds or facilities should be used.

Abortion has been legal throughout the United States since the Supreme Court's 1973 landmark decision in *Roe v. Wade*. In that case the Court ruled that state laws prohibiting first-trimester abortions or limiting them to certain circumstances were unconstitutional. Over the following decades, subsequent decisions modified this ruling somewhat. In its latest ruling concerning abortion, the Supreme Court in 1992 again reaffirmed the legality of abortion but allowed states to impose certain restrictions. By 1996 about 35 states had enacted parental consent laws, and some had imposed mandatory 24-hour waiting periods. In addition, 10 states had passed informed consent laws requiring abortion providers to give their patients detailed information about abortion risks and alternatives.

ABORTION RATES
Per 100 live births

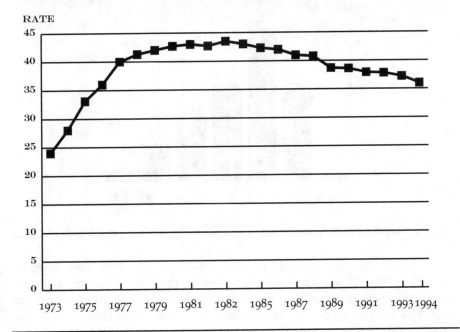

RATE

1973 1975 1977 1979 1981 1982 1985 1987 1989 1991 1993 1994	

Although public opinion surveys indicate that the majority of Americans favor abortion rights, it is the antiabortion, or pro-life, groups who have been the most vocal and whose protests outside abortion clinics attracted nationwide attention during the 1980s and early 1990s. In some instances abortion opponents became violent; clinics were bombed, and physicians and other employees were threatened, harassed, and even killed. By mid-1994 a total of 600 such incidents had been reported. During 1995, however, the number of incidents started declining, due in some part to the enforcement of a 1994 law permitting civil and criminal actions to be taken against protesters obstructing access to abortion clinics.

In 1994 just over 1.4 million abortions were performed in the United States, down from the 1990 high of 1.6 million. Approximately one-third of the women having abortions were aged 20 to 24. Women in the age groups from 15 to 19 and 25 to 29 each accounted for about 21% of the total.

Approximately 89% of abortions are performed during the first trimester of pregnancy, and another 10% during the second trimester. Although third-trimester abortions are legal in some states, very few are performed each year. In 1996, despite strong opposition from antiabortion groups, President Clinton vetoed a measure that would have completely banned all late-term (third-trimester) abortions.

ABORTIONS BY AGE
Percentage of total abortions, 1993

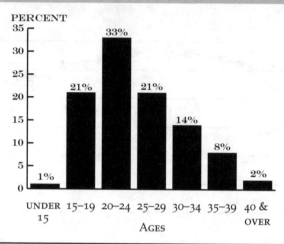

PERCENT

Ages	Percent
UNDER 15	1%
15–19	21%
20–24	33%
25–29	21%
30–34	14%
35–39	8%
40 & OVER	2%

Although the abortion pill RU 486 (mifepristone) had been used by more than 200,000 women in France, Sweden, the United Kingdom, China, and about 20 other countries since it was developed in 1980, it was not approved for use in the United States until 1996. Also that year, it was reported that the anticancer drug methotrexate had been found to be effective in inducing abortion, even though the drug had not been officially approved by the Food and Drug Administration for this purpose. It is expected that as the use of these abortion drugs increases, there are likely to be dramatic changes in the tactics of antiabortion groups. Since the drugs can be obtained from a doctor's office, women can avoid going to special abortion clinics where they can be targeted by protesters. In addition, many doctors who may have stopped performing surgical abortions because they were being harassed by abortion opponents may now prescribe abortion drugs for their patients.

Fertility Services

A wide variety of fertility services are available to the estimated 5 million American couples who are unable to conceive a baby or carry it to term. Modern scientific techniques—such as in vitro fertilization; gamete intrafallopian tube transfer (GIFT); and, most recently, intracytoplasmic sperm injection—are offered at about 300 fertility centers throughout the country. Approximately 50,000 of these procedures are performed annually, and an estimated 40,000 babies conceived through these methods were born in the United States between 1981 and 1995.

During the 1980s, the increasing use of in vitro fertilization and similar techniques created a number of complex legal and ethical issues, especially in cases involving sperm or egg cells provided by donors. One of the most problematic situations was surrogate motherhood, an arrangement in which a woman agrees, usually by contract and for a fee, to bear a child for a couple because the wife is infertile or cannot sustain a pregnancy. The surrogate mother's egg cell (or sometimes the wife's) is fertilized in the laboratory by the husband's sperm and implanted in the surrogate's uterus. When the baby is born, the surrogate gives up all parental rights, and the child is adopted by the wife.

One of the most highly publicized cases involving surrogacy took place in New Jersey in the late 1980s. When the infant, later known as Baby M, was born, the surrogate mother refused to give her up. After a lengthy lawsuit, the court declared the surrogacy contract invalid and treated the case as a custody dispute. The baby's father was given custody, and the surrogate mother was granted visitation rights.

By 1990 there were about 4,000 births to surrogate mothers in the United States, but because of the many legal and ethical issues involved, a number of states have passed laws curtailing the practice. Arizona, Indiana, Louisiana, Nebraska, New York, Vermont, and Washington have made surrogacy contracts void and unenforceable. In New Hampshire and Virginia, surrogacy contracts are legal but unenforceable and may be revoked by either party. In Michigan, any party to a surrogacy contract may be found guilty of a misdemeanor punishable by a fine of up to $10,000 and imprisonment of up to a year.

Sex Education

Sex education is available in schools throughout the United States. Individual states, communities, and school boards determine the curriculum; but in general, children in lower grades learn about families and personal relationships, while older students study reproductive health and sexually-transmitted diseases, including AIDS. In some communities, high schools provide free condoms to students.

WOMEN'S HEALTH

Despite the fact that the United States is the only industrialized country without a national health service or universal health insurance, its people are among the healthiest in the world. The average life expectancy in 1995 was 79.7 years for women and 72.8 years for men. Among whites

LIFE EXPECTANCY At birth, in years		
YEAR	WOMEN	MEN
1970	74.7	67.1
1975	76.6	68.8
1980	77.4	70.0
1985	78.2	71.1
1990	78.8	71.8
1995	79.7	72.8

these figures were 80.3 years for women, 73.7 years for men; among blacks the corresponding figures were 74.8 years for women and 65.8 years for men. Contributing to the high life expectancy rate for women is a fairly low incidence of maternal mortality: 12 pregnancy-related deaths for every 100,000 live births. However, when compared with other industrialized nations, the United States has one of the highest rates of maternal mortality.

Health care financing in the United States is provided by a mixed public-private system. About 85% of the total population are covered by employer-supported health plans, individually purchased plans, or by one of the government's two major programs: Medicare, which provides insurance for everyone 65 and over and the disabled; and Medicaid, which covers about half of the low-income population under 65. Women constitute about 57% of all Medicare patients and 59% of Medicaid recipients. About 15% of all Americans have no health insurance at all; women make up 46% of the uninsured.

Leading Causes of Death

Heart disease is the leading cause of death among American women as well as men; it accounts for about 34% of women's deaths. The next most common cause of death among women is cancer, with lung cancer leading the list.

Although the number of lung cancer cases in women has doubled since the early 1970s, making it the most common cause of cancer deaths among women, breast cancer is the most common cancer; one in every nine American women may expect to develop it during her lifetime. Fortunately, the last few decades have seen tremendous advances in the diagnosis and treatment of this form of cancer. As a result, although the increase in incidence rose 50% between 1950 and 1990, the death rate increased by only 4%.

Breast cancer incidence and death rates vary by age and race. In general, there is a higher incidence of the disease among white women but a higher death rate among black women. During the past two decades, white women under 65 experienced a 7% decline in deaths from breast cancer, while black women in the same age bracket experienced an increase of 19%.

LEADING CAUSES OF DEATH Percentage of total deaths, 1991		
CAUSE	WOMEN	MEN
Cardiovascular diseases	46%	40%
Cancer	23%	24%
Lung	5%	8%
Breast	4%	—
Cervix	<1%	—
Pneumonia	4%	3%
Accidents	3%	5%
Diabetes	3%	2%
Suicide	<1%	2%
Homicide	<1%	2%

Smoking

Since the mid-1960s, when the government launched its antismoking campaign, smoking has declined steadily among both women and men. By the mid-1990s approximately 24% of women and 28% of men were smokers, down from 34% and 52% respectively in 1965. However, smoking is still popular among adolescents and young women constitute the fastest-growing group of smokers.

In 1996 American medical researchers found evidence that cigarette smoking causes more damage to women's lungs than to men's, and that black women are more seriously affected than white women. Women's lungs have narrower air passages than men's, and because blacks' air passages tend to be narrower than those of whites, they are thus damaged more by the effects of smoking. In addition, women do not recover as much lung capacity as men do after they have stopped smoking.

SMOKING RATES Percentage of age group, 1993		
AGE	WOMEN	MEN
12–17	10%	9%
18–25	27%	31%
26–34	29%	31%
35 and over	21%	27%

SMOKING AMONG TEENAGERS Percentage of group, 1995		
RACE	FEMALE	MALE
White	40%	37%
Black	12%	28%
Hispanic	33%	35%

DEATH RATES AMONG WOMEN AGED 25–44
Per 100,000 population

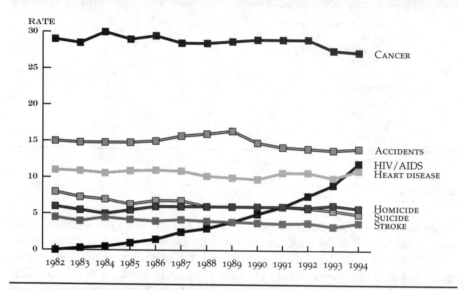

DEATH RATES AMONG MEN AGED 25–44
Per 100,000 population

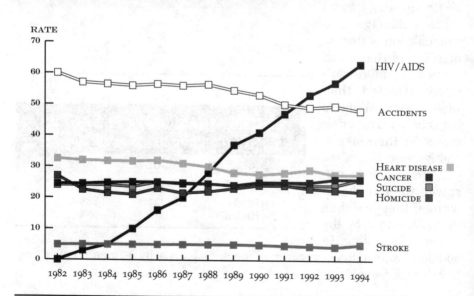

AIDS

Between 1981, when the disease was first identified, and the mid-1990s more than 500,000 cases of AIDS were reported in the United States. Women accounted for about 14%. The people most affected by HIV infection were those aged 25 to 44. In this group AIDS constituted the leading cause of death for men and the third leading cause of death for women (after cancer and accidents). It was responsible for 11% of all deaths among women and 23% of all deaths among men.

In 1992, for the first time, sexual contact with a male partner became the leading mode of HIV transmission among women, exceeding intravenous drug use. For men, sexual contact with a male partner was the most common method of transmission, followed by intravenous drug use.

Eating Disorders

Eating disorders are about 10 times more common in women than men and are most prevalent among adolescent and young women. Those suffering

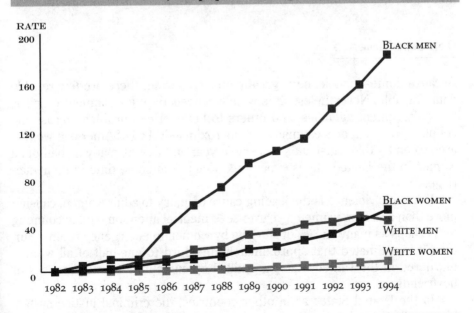

DEATH RATES FROM AIDS
Per 100,000 population, aged 25–44

from anorexia starve themselves so drastically that they become severely emaciated and debilitated. From 5% to 8% of anorexic girls die within 10 years of diagnosis, mostly from suicide or severe malnutrition.

Bulimia is a slightly more common eating disorder in which the young woman goes on periodic eating binges but keeps her weight down by inducing vomiting or taking laxatives, diuretics, or enemas. Generally, bulimia is more responsive to treatment than is anorexia. Most recently, a third condition, called binge eating, has become recognized as a common eating disorder. In this condition the woman periodically gorges herself, without purging afterwards, and usually becomes obese.

 ## VIOLENCE AGAINST WOMEN

It is estimated that 2.5 million women in the United States are victims of violent crime every year. More than two-thirds of these women are attacked by people they know, usually a current or former husband or boyfriend. Although black women are twice as likely as white women to be robbery victims, there is little difference between the races in rates of rape or assault.

There is a tremendous disparity in the national homicide rates for white and black women. In 1992 the murder rate for white women was 2.8 per 100,000; the rate for black women was 13.1 per 100,000. The corresponding homicide rates for white and black men were 9.1 and 67.5 respectively.

Domestic Violence

Because domestic violence is greatly underreported, there are few reliable data available. Nevertheless, it is widely conceded by government officials, law enforcement agencies, and others to be a serious problem across the country. Some experts estimate that approximately 11% of American women are beaten by their husbands in a single year and that as many as half of all women in the United States experience violence at some time in their marriage.

Domestic violence is the leading cause of injury to adult women, causing more than a million women a year to seek medical attention, and accounting for perhaps as many as 30% of all visits by women to emergency rooms. Further, it is estimated that approximately one-third to one-half of all women murdered in the United States are killed by current or former spouses or boyfriends.

In the United States as in other countries, the criminal justice system historically treated domestic violence as a private matter between a husband

IN A RECENT STUDY OF SPOUSAL MURDER CASES

OF THE MALE DEFENDANTS	OF THE FEMALE DEFENDANTS
▲ 46% pleaded guilty	▲ 39% pleaded guilty
▲ 41% were convicted	▲ 31% were convicted
▲ 11% were not prosecuted	▲ 16% were not prosecuted
▲ 2% were acquitted	▲ 14% were acquitted
▲ 81% of those found guilty went to jail for an average of 16.5 years	▲ 57% of those found guilty went to jail for an average of 6 years

and wife. The emphasis was on mediating the dispute rather than arresting the offender. In 1984, however, the attorney general's Task Force on Family Violence shifted that emphasis and advocated mandatory arrest policies. By the mid-1990s one-third of all states had instituted such policies, and in virtually all states arrest was officially considered the preferred response to an incident of spousal abuse. Many states also had laws specifically defining domestic violence as a crime. In 1994 the Violence Against Women Act declared domestic violence a federal crime, recognizing violent crimes against women as violations of their civil rights, and entitling them to sue for damages in a federal court. In 1996, however, in the first civil suit brought under the new law, a Virginia judge ruled it unconstitutional. A Connecticut judge, on the other hand, upheld the law, and both cases are likely to be heard by the Supreme Court. The 1994 law also provided states with funds for education, training, and other programs to protect battered women.

Shelters for victims of domestic violence have sprung up across the country over the past few decades. The earliest facilities, many of them in private homes, were opened in the early 1970s by women's groups and other organizations. A decade later there were hundreds of shelters across the country, many of them at least partially supported by federal funds.

Another measure to aid battered wives is the civil protection order, a legal means of barring an abusive spouse or partner from the home. In 1983 only 17 states provided such protection, but 10 years later virtually every state had some form of civil protection. Nearly every state also had antistalking legislation to prevent offenders from repeatedly and maliciously following and harassing their victims. However, because enforcement of these laws is difficult, they are not always effective.

Another recent legal development regarding domestic violence concerns the traditional privilege of spousal immunity, the principle that one spouse should never be forced to testify against the other. Over the past several years, many states have enacted laws removing this privilege in cases of domestic violence. Previously, many abusive husbands were never brought to trial because their wives were afraid to press charges or testify. Under the new laws prosecutors can force abused wives to testify against their husbands.

Rape

Rape is thought to be the most underreported of all violent crimes in the United States. Although there is little available information on the incidence of rape, estimates range from 310,000 to 680,000 rapes and other sexual assaults on women every year. What is known is that a great many victims, probably close to 50%, are under 18; about 15% are under age 12. It is also known that most often the offender is someone known to the victim—a husband, lover, friend, or relative—and that because the victim is so overcome by feelings of shame and fear she usually tells no one about it. As a result, it is believed that fewer than half of all rapes are reported; and only a small fraction of those reported are ever brought to trial.

Penalties for convicted rapists vary according to the age of the victim, whether a weapon was used, whether the victim became pregnant or contracted a sexually-transmitted disease as a result of the assault, and other factors. Over the past decade the average sentence—10 years—has remained stable although the actual time served in prison increased from 3.5 years in 1985 to 5 years in 1993.

In 1974 Michigan became the first state to pass a law breaking with the traditional view that a rape victim had to provide proof of resistance, that her attire might have provoked the assault, and that the court had a right to examine her character and previous sexual conduct before determining whether a crime had been committed. The new law, which has served as a model for other states, eliminated both the requirement of proof of resistance and the need for corroborating testimony. It also contained a rape shield measure, protecting the victim's privacy by not allowing testimony about her lifestyle, conduct, or sexual history.

In 1977 Oregon became the first state to make marital rape illegal, and since then every state has eliminated the marital rape exception that prevented men from being prosecuted for raping their wives. At the federal level, in 1986 Congress passed the Sexual Abuse Act, which reformed federal rape laws and extended their coverage to other sexual offenses. In 1995 Congress enacted new rules for federal courts, allowing the introduction of evidence relating to the offender's previous history of sexual assaults.

Acquaintance rape, also commonly called date rape, has drawn nationwide attention in recent years as a serious problem at colleges and universities across the country. In a 1985 survey of over 6,000 students on 32 campuses, researchers found that one in every six female students had been a victim of rape or attempted rape during the previous year and that more than 80% of these victims knew their rapist. In the same study, 1 in 15 male students admitted raping or trying to rape a female student during the preceding year. Similar studies have indicated that alcohol is frequently involved and that most victims never tell anyone about their experience—neither their families, school officials, nor the local authorities. Some

RAPE: RELATIONSHIP OF OFFENDER TO VICTIM Percentage of total reported rapes, 1992–1993	
RELATIONSHIP	PERCENT
Acquaintance	53%
Stranger	18%
Current or former boyfriend	16%
Current or former spouse	10%
Other relative	3%

experts believe that date rape may be a common but unspoken reason for many female students dropping out of college or transferring to other schools.

By the early 1990s rape had become acknowledged as the most common violent crime on U.S. college and university campuses. Schools responded in a variety of ways: implementing more effective reporting and judicial procedures; improving campus security; providing counseling and other assistance for victims; and creating special student-run workshops, theatrical performances, and other educational programs to increase students' awareness of sexual assault and dating violence. The government underscored the need for such programs in the Higher Education Amendments of 1992, which required colleges and universities receiving federal student financial aid to develop programs promoting an awareness of rape and other sexual offenses.

Prostitution

Except for parts of Nevada, prostitution is illegal throughout the United States and is punishable by a fine and/or imprisonment. However, enforcement is generally not strict, and although there may be as many as a million female prostitutes, annual arrests number around 57,000.

It is estimated that only about 20% of prostitutes are "street walkers"; the rest work in brothels, massage parlors, escort services, and similar enterprises. In some major cities there are reports of hundreds of young women from Thailand, Japan, and other Asian countries forced into prostitution and held captive in brothels in order to repay their airfare and other costs.

Proponents of legalized prostitution argue that each state should be able to license prostitutes, require them to have periodic medical checkups that include tests for AIDS, and restrict brothels to specific areas. In 1973 Nevada legalized prostitution in all counties with fewer than 50,000 people, and by the mid-1990s there were about 40 brothels throughout the state. They are strictly regulated by local health departments and other agencies and the prostitutes have weekly medical checkups and monthly AIDS tests. The brothels are also subject to a number of strict regulations. For example, they cannot be located on a main street or within 300 yards of a church or school.

Female Genital Mutilation

This ritual is not indigenous to the United States but is practiced among certain African and Asian immigrants. It is estimated that as many as 150,000 girls and women in the United States have undergone this procedure or are at risk of being forced to do so. A law making the procedure a federal crime was passed by Congress in late 1996. Earlier that year, the issue of female genital mutilation drew nationwide attention when United States immigration officials granted political asylum to a young woman from Togo who fled her country to escape this procedure. This was the first case in which the United States officially recognized female genital mutilation as a form of persecution and thus grounds for asylum.

FOR ADDITIONAL INFORMATION ON WOMEN

Center for the American Woman and Politics (CAWP)
Eagleton Institute of Politics
Rutgers University
New Brunswick, NJ 08901, United States
Telephone: 908-828-2210
Fax: 908-932-6778
Web site: http://www.rci.rutgers.edu
/~cawp

League of Women Voters
1730 M Street, NW
Washington, DC 20036, United States
Telephone: 202-429-1965

National Council For Research on Women
Sara Delano Roosevelt Memorial House
47–49 East 65th Street
New York, NY 10021, United States
Telephone: 212-570-5001

National Organization for Women (NOW)
National Headquarters
1000 16th Street, NW
Washington, DC 20005, United States
Telephone: 202-331-0066
Fax: 202-785-8576
Web site: http://www.now.org

National Women's Studies Association
University of Maryland
College Park, MD 20742, United States
Telephone: 301-405-5573

United States Bureau of the Census
Population Division
Washington, DC 20233, United States
Telephone: 301-457-2422
Fax: 301-457-2643

COUNTRY
TABLES

The following tables present statistics from 140 different countries according to six major categories concerning the status of women. Altogether, the countries included in these tables represent more than 99% of the world's population. The only countries that have been excluded are those with populations of less than 1 million. Countries highlighted in **boldface** are covered in much greater detail in the preceding section containing individual country profiles.

All of the data in these tables represent the most recent available information for each country. A number that appears with a ▲ symbol indicates that the country ranks in the world's top 10% of that category; a ▼ symbol indicates that the country ranks in the bottom 10%. The symbol "—" means that the missing information is either not available or not applicable.

POPULATION

COUNTRY	CONTINENT	TOTAL POPULATION (Millions)	FEMALES PER 100 MALES
Afghanistan	Asia	23.1	▼ 95
Albania	Europe	3.4	▼ 95
Algeria	Africa	28.5	100
Angola	Africa	11.0	103
Argentina	S. America	34.2	102
Armenia	Asia	3.3	104
Australia	Oceania	18.3	100
Austria	Europe	7.8	▲107
Azerbaijan	Asia	7.0	105
Bangladesh	Asia	128.2	▼ 94
Belarus	Europe	10.1	▲114
Belgium	Europe	10.0	104
Benin	Africa	5.3	102
Bolivia	S. America	8.0	102
Bosnia-Herzegovina	Europe	4.3	101
Brazil	S. America	161.3	101
Bulgaria	Europe	8.8	104
Burkina Faso	Africa	10.3	102
Burundi	Africa	6.3	104
Cambodia	Asia	9.4	▲108
Cameroon	Africa	13.2	101
Canada	N. America	28.5	103
Central African Rep.	Africa	3.4	▲106
Chad	Africa	6.3	103
Chile	S. America	14.2	102
China	Asia	1,238.3	▼ 95
Colombia	S. America	35.1	102
Congo	Africa	2.5	104
Costa Rica	N. America	3.4	98
Croatia	Europe	4.7	▲106
Cuba	N. America	11.0	99
Czech Republic	Europe	10.3	▲106
Denmark	Europe	5.1	102
Dominican Republic	N. America	7.9	97
Ecuador	S. America	11.8	99
Egypt	Africa	58.5	97
El Salvador	N. America	5.7	104
Eritrea	Africa	2.6	99
Estonia	Europe	1.5	▲112
Ethiopia	Africa	58.0	100
Finland	Europe	5.0	▲106
France	Europe	57.7	105
Georgia	Asia	5.4	▲111
Germany	Europe	81.2	▲106
Ghana	Africa	17.4	101
Greece	Europe	10.2	103
Guatemala	N. America	10.6	98

(continued)

POPULATION *(cont.)*

COUNTRY	CONTINENT	TOTAL POPULATION (Millions)	FEMALES PER 100 MALES
Guinea	Africa	6.7	99
Haiti	N. America	7.1	104
Honduras	N. America	5.9	98
Hungary	Europe	10.4	▲107
India	Asia	931.0	▼ 93
Indonesia	Asia	201.4	101
Iran	Asia	66.7	97
Iraq	Asia	21.2	▼ 96
Ireland	Europe	3.4	100
Israel	Asia	5.8	102
Italy	Europe	57.9	▲106
Ivory Coast	Africa	14.4	97
Jamaica	N. America	2.5	100
Japan	Asia	125.8	103
Jordan	Asia	4.7	▼ 95
Kazakhstan	Asia	16.4	▲106
Kenya	Africa	27.8	100
Korea, North	Asia	23.9	103
Korea, South	Asia	45.1	98
Kuwait	Asia	1.6	97
Kyrgyzstan	Asia	4.2	105
Laos	Asia	4.8	103
Latvia	Europe	2.6	▲114
Lebanon	Asia	3.0	105
Liberia	Africa	3.0	98
Libya	Africa	5.4	▼ 92
Lithuania	Europe	3.7	▲111
Macedonia	Europe	2.0	98
Madagascar	Africa	14.1	102
Malawi	Africa	11.3	102
Malaysia	Asia	20.1	98
Mali	Africa	10.7	103
Mauritania	Africa	2.3	102
Mexico	N. America	93.6	101
Moldova	Europe	4.3	▲110
Morocco	Africa	28.2	100
Mozambique	Africa	16.3	102
Myanmar	Asia	46.5	101
Nepal	Asia	22.1	▼ 95
Netherlands	Europe	15.4	102
New Zealand	Oceania	3.5	102
Nicaragua	N. America	4.4	105
Niger	Africa	9.1	102
Nigeria	Africa	98.1	102
Norway	Europe	4.3	102
Pakistan	Asia	134.9	▼ 92
Panama	N. America	2.6	97

(continued)

POPULATION *(cont.)*

COUNTRY	CONTINENT	TOTAL POPULATION (Millions)	FEMALES PER 100 MALES
Paraguay	S. America	4.8	98
Peru	S. America	23.8	99
Philippines	Asia	69.2	97
Poland	Europe	38.7	105
Portugal	Europe	9.8	▲107
Puerto Rico	N. America	3.6	105
Romania	Europe	23.5	102
Russia	Europe	148.4	▲113
Rwanda	Africa	8.3	102
Saudi Arabia	Asia	17.6	▼ 81
Senegal	Africa	8.3	100
Sierra Leone	Africa	4.7	103
Singapore	Asia	2.8	97
Slovakia	Europe	5.3	104
Slovenia	Europe	1.9	▲106
Somalia	Africa	10.1	102
South Africa	Africa	42.7	101
Spain	Europe	39.2	103
Sri Lanka	Asia	18.3	101
Sudan	Africa	28.9	99
Sweden	Europe	8.8	103
Switzerland	Europe	6.9	104
Syria	Asia	14.7	98
Taiwan	Asia	20.9	▼ 94
Tajikistan	Asia	5.0	101
Tanzania	Africa	30.7	102
Thailand	Asia	58.2	102
Togo	Africa	4.1	102
Trinidad and Tobago	N. America	1.3	102
Tunisia	Africa	8.9	98
Turkey	Asia	62.0	▼ 96
Turkmenistan	Asia	3.5	103
Uganda	Africa	20.4	101
Ukraine	Europe	51.4	▲117
United Arab Emirates	Asia	1.7	▼ 52
United Kingdom	Europe	58.0	104
United States	N. America	263.4	105
Uruguay	S. America	3.1	105
Uzbekistan	Asia	19.8	102
Venezuela	S. America	21.4	99
Vietnam	Asia	73.8	103
Yemen	Asia	13.8	102
Yugoslavia	Europe	10.4	102
Zaire	Africa	43.8	102
Zambia	Africa	9.3	102
Zimbabwe	Africa	11.5	101

WOMEN IN POLITICS

COUNTRY	WOMEN IN LEGISLATURE	WOMEN IN CABINET	YEAR OF WOMEN'S VOTING RIGHTS*
Afghanistan	—	▼ 0%	1964
Albania	6%	7%	1920
Algeria	7%	▼ 0%	1962
Angola	15%	7%	1975
Argentina	▲22%	▼ 0%	1947
Armenia	6%	▼ 0%	1921
Australia	18%	13%	1902
Austria	▲23%	▲30%	1918
Azerbaijan	▼ 2%	15%	1921
Bangladesh	11%	10%	1947
Belarus	5%	8%	1919
Belgium	15%	13%	1948
Benin	7%	▲20%	1956
Bolivia	6%	▼ 0%	1952
Bosnia-Herzegovina	5%	▼ 0%	1949
Brazil	7%	5%	1932
Bulgaria	14%	6%	1944
Burkina Faso	6%	13%	1958
Burundi	11%	9%	1961
Cambodia	6%	▼ 0%	1955
Cameroon	12%	5%	1946
Canada	19%	▲23%	1918
Central African Rep.	4%	8%	1986
Chad	8%	10%	1958
Chile	7%	14%	1931
China	▲21%	8%	1949
Colombia	10%	18%	1957
Congo	▼ 1%	14%	1963
Costa Rica	16%	8%	1949
Croatia	7%	4%	1945
Cuba	▲23%	12%	1934
Czech Republic	10%	▼ 0%	1920
Denmark	▲33%	▲35%	1915
Dominican Republic	10%	▲38%	1942
Ecuador	5%	6%	1928
Egypt	▼ 2%	9%	1956
El Salvador	11%	8%	1939
Eritrea	▲21%	4%	1955
Estonia	11%	▼ 0%	1918
Ethiopia	10%	13%	1955
Finland	▲34%	▲39%	1906
France	5%	13%	1944
Georgia	7%	6%	1918
Germany	▲26%	12%	1919

(continued)

WOMEN IN POLITICS *(cont.)*

COUNTRY	WOMEN IN LEGISLATURE	WOMEN IN CABINET	YEAR OF WOMEN'S VOTING RIGHTS*
Ghana	8%	12%	1954
Greece	6%	7%	1949
Guatemala	14%	13%	1946
Guinea	▼ 0%	15%	1958
Haiti	3%	15%	1950
Honduras	11%	7%	1957
Hungary	11%	7%	1945
India	9%	4%	1950
Indonesia	11%	5%	1945
Iran	4%	▼ 0%	1963
Iraq	11%	▼ 0%	1980
Ireland	13%	13%	1928 (1918)
Israel	8%	6%	1948
Italy	9%	15%	1945
Ivory Coast	8%	10%	1956
Jamaica	12%	13%	1944
Japan	8%	▼ 0%	1945
Jordan	3%	7%	1974
Kazakhstan	11%	3%	1924
Kenya	4%	5%	1963 (1956)
Korea, North	▲20%	4%	1946
Korea, South	3%	5%	1948
Kuwait	▼ 0%	▼ 0%	—
Kyrgyzstan	6%	12%	1918
Laos	9%	▼ 0%	1958
Latvia	15%	▼ 0%	1918
Lebanon	▼ 2%	▼ 0%	1952
Liberia	6%	17%	1946
Libya	—	6%	1964
Lithuania	7%	▼ 0%	1921
Macedonia	3%	10%	1946
Madagascar	6%	5%	1959
Malawi	6%	4%	1961
Malaysia	11%	8%	1957
Mali	3%	▲25%	1956
Mauritania	▼ 0%	4%	1961
Mexico	14%	12%	1947
Moldova	5%	▼ 0%	1978
Morocco	▼ 1%	▼ 0%	1959
Mozambique	▲25%	5%	1975
Myanmar	—	▼ 0%	1935
Nepal	3%	▼ 0%	1951
Netherlands	▲30%	▲31%	1919
New Zealand	▲29%	4%	1893

(continued)

WOMEN IN POLITICS *(cont.)*

COUNTRY	WOMEN IN LEGISLATURE	WOMEN IN CABINET	YEAR OF WOMEN'S VOTING RIGHTS*
Nicaragua	16%	6%	1955
Niger	4%	13%	1948
Nigeria	—	9%	1957/1978
Norway	▲39%	▲39%	1913
Pakistan	▼ 2%	7%	1947
Panama	7%	▲27%	1946 (1941)
Paraguay	4%	9%	1962
Peru	9%	14%	1955
Philippines	13%	14%	1937
Poland	13%	6%	1918
Portugal	9%	13%	1976 (1931)
Puerto Rico	—	—	1935 (1929)
Romania	5%	▼ 0%	1946 (1929)
Russia	7%	3%	1918
Rwanda	17%	5%	1961
Saudi Arabia	—	▼ 0%	—
Senegal	12%	9%	1945
Sierra Leone	8%	5%	1961
Singapore	5%	▼ 0%	1947
Slovakia	15%	13%	1920
Slovenia	14%	13%	1945
Somalia	▼ 0%	▼ 0%	1956
South Africa	▲25%	11%	1994 (1930, 1983)
Spain	18%	▲27%	1931
Sri Lanka	5%	▲21%	1931
Sudan	4%	4%	1965 (1953)
Sweden	▲41%	▲52%	1919
Switzerland	17%	14%	1971
Syria	10%	6%	1953 (1949)
Taiwan	11%	3%	1946
Tajikistan	3%	13%	1924
Tanzania	17%	13%	1959
Thailand	6%	5%	1932
Togo	▼ 1%	5%	1956
Trinidad and Tobago	18%	14%	1946
Tunisia	7%	4%	1956
Turkey	▼ 2%	5%	1930
Turkmenistan	5%	▼ 0%	1927
Uganda	17%	13%	1962
Ukraine	4%	4%	1919
United Arab Emirates	—	▼ 0%	—
United Kingdom	10%	8%	1928 (1918)
United States	11%	▲29%	1920

(continued)

WOMEN IN POLITICS *(cont.)*

COUNTRY	WOMEN IN LEGISLATURE	WOMEN IN CABINET	YEAR OF WOMEN'S VOTING RIGHTS*
Uruguay	6%	8%	1932
Uzbekistan	5%	5%	1938
Venezuela	6%	7%	1946
Vietnam	19%	6%	1946
Yemen	▼ 1%	▼ 0%	1967/1970
Yugoslavia	3%	7%	1943
Zaire	6%	4%	1960
Zambia	7%	9%	1962
Zimbabwe	11%	12%	1957

* The date indicates when all adult women won the right to vote in any major election, local or national. Date in parentheses indicates when the vote was first granted to a large group of women, but not all.

WOMEN'S EDUCATION

COUNTRY	LITERACY RATE*		FEMALE ENROLLMENT**		
	WOMEN	MEN	PRIM.	SECOND.	HIGHER ED.
Afghanistan	▼13%	44%	▼33%	—	33%
Albania	63%	80%	48%	45%	52%
Algeria	44%	71%	45%	45%	31%
Angola	28%	56%	48%	—	▼17%
Argentina	96%	96%	▲50%	52%	53%
Armenia	98%	99%	—	—	—
Australia	▲99%	99%	49%	49%	53%
Austria	▲99%	99%	49%	47%	47%
Azerbaijan	96%	99%	—	—	49%
Bangladesh	24%	48%	45%	33%	▼16%
Belarus	97%	99%	—	—	51%
Belgium	▲99%	99%	49%	49%	48%
Benin	▼16%	32%	▼34%	▼29%	29%
Bolivia	73%	89%	47%	46%	▲74%
Bosnia-Herzegovina	88%	97%	—	▲53%	50%
Brazil	77%	76%	▲51%	▲57%	52%
Bulgaria	97%	99%	48%	50%	▲57%
Burkina Faso	▼ 8%	27%	▼39%	35%	23%
Burundi	▼20%	47%	45%	39%	26%
Cambodia	▼22%	48%	—	—	—
Cameroon	48%	72%	46%	41%	—

(continued)

WOMEN'S EDUCATION *(cont.)*

COUNTRY	LITERACY RATE* WOMEN	MEN	FEMALE ENROLLMENT** PRIM.	SECOND.	HIGHER ED.
Canada	▲99%	99%	48%	49%	54%
Central African Rep.	46%	63%	▼39%	▼29%	▼16%
Chad	31%	60%	▼32%	▼18%	▼ 9%
Chile	94%	95%	49%	51%	44%
China	68%	87%	47%	43%	34%
Colombia	90%	90%	▲50%	▲54%	51%
Congo	59%	78%	46%	42%	19%
Costa Rica	94%	94%	49%	51%	—
Croatia	95%	99%	49%	51%	48%
Cuba	94%	96%	48%	52%	▲58%
Czech Republic	▲99%	99%	49%	50%	44%
Denmark	▲99%	99%	49%	49%	53%
Dominican Republic	81%	81%	49%	—	▲55%
Ecuador	87%	91%	49%	50%	39%
Egypt	41%	65%	45%	44%	45%
El Salvador	68%	72%	▲50%	▲53%	33%
Eritrea	▼10%	20%	45%	▼29%	24%
Estonia	▲99%	99%	49%	51%	51%
Ethiopia	26%	43%	40%	45%	▼ 8%
Finland	▲99%	99%	49%	▲54%	53%
France	▲99%	99%	48%	50%	52%
Georgia	98%	99%	—	—	—
Germany	▲99%	99%	▲54%	▲54%	43%
Ghana	49%	73%	45%	39%	▲17%
Greece	89%	97%	48%	48%	50%
Guatemala	47%	61%	46%	45%	47%
Guinea	▼19%	47%	▼32%	▼25%	▼12%
Haiti	40%	46%	48%	—	49%
Honduras	70%	71%	▲50%	▲55%	39%
Hungary	▲99%	99%	49%	49%	51%
India	39%	64%	43%	34%	33%
Indonesia	79%	89%	48%	45%	▼14%
Iran	55%	75%	47%	43%	30%
Iraq	41%	68%	44%	38%	38%
Ireland	▲99%	99%	49%	51%	47%
Israel	89%	95%	49%	51%	53%
Italy	▲99%	99%	49%	49%	51%
Ivory Coast	26%	47%	42%	▼30%	30%
Jamaica	88%	79%	▲50%	52%	▲57%
Japan	▲99%	99%	49%	49%	40%
Jordan	73%	91%	49%	50%	49%
Kazakhstan	96%	99%	49%	—	51%
Kenya	65%	84%	49%	41%	28%
Korea, North	▲99%	99%	49%	—	48%

(continued)

WOMEN'S EDUCATION *(cont.)*

COUNTRY	LITERACY RATE*		FEMALE ENROLLMENT**		
	WOMEN	MEN	PRIM.	SECOND.	HIGHER ED.
Korea, South	96%	99%	48%	48%	34%
Kuwait	73%	80%	49%	49%	▲61%
Kyrgyzstan	96%	99%	—	—	—
Laos	41%	67%	44%	39%	32%
Latvia	▲99%	99%	49%	51%	53%
Lebanon	89%	94%	48%	—	53%
Liberia	▼18%	49%	▼35%	▼28%	28%
Libya	57%	86%	48%	▲56%	46%
Lithuania	98%	98%	48%	50%	—
Macedonia	88%	97%	48%	49%	52%
Madagascar	73%	87%	49%	49%	45%
Malawi	39%	70%	45%	34%	28%
Malaysia	75%	88%	49%	51%	50%
Mali	▼20%	35%	▼37%	32%	▼14%
Mauritania	25%	48%	43%	33%	▼15%
Mexico	86%	91%	48%	49%	45%
Moldova	94%	99%	49%	—	51%
Morocco	▼22%	49%	40%	41%	36%
Mozambique	▼20%	54%	42%	38%	26%
Myanmar	76%	88%	48%	39%	47%
Nepal	▼13%	39%	▼32%	32%	24%
Netherlands	▲99%	99%	▲50%	48%	45%
New Zealand	▲99%	99%	49%	49%	54%
Nicaragua	66%	64%	▲51%	▲58%	49%
Niger	▼7%	18%	▼36%	▼29%	▼15%
Nigeria	42%	63%	44%	▲55%	24%
Norway	▲99%	99%	49%	48%	54%
Pakistan	▼22%	48%	▼34%	▼29%	28%
Panama	89%	90%	48%	51%	▲58%
Paraguay	90%	93%	48%	46%	—
Peru	81%	94%	48%	47%	47%
Philippines	93%	94%	49%	50%	47%
Poland	▲99%	99%	49%	50%	▲59%
Portugal	81%	89%	48%	▲53%	▲56%
Puerto Rico	88%	90%	—	▲59%	▲60%
Romania	95%	99%	49%	49%	—
Russia	▲99%	99%	▲50%	▲61%	47%
Rwanda	44%	65%	▲50%	44%	52%
Saudi Arabia	46%	70%	46%	44%	19%
Senegal	▼19%	37%	40%	35%	40%
Sierra Leone	▼16%	42%	41%	▼17%	24%
Singapore	84%	95%	47%	50%	—
Slovakia	▲99%	99%	49%	50%	42%
Slovenia	88%	97%	49%	49%	48%
					54%

(continued)

WOMEN'S EDUCATION *(cont.)*

COUNTRY	LITERACY RATE*		FEMALE ENROLLMENT**		
	WOMEN	MEN	PRIM.	SECOND.	HIGHER ED.
Somalia	▼14%	36%	▼34%	35%	20%
South Africa	70%	70%	47%	▲53%	48%
Spain	98%	98%	48%	51%	51%
Sri Lanka	86%	93%	48%	51%	41%
Sudan	31%	55%	43%	44%	40%
Sweden	▲99%	99%	49%	49%	▲56%
Switzerland	▲99%	99%	49%	47%	36%
Syria	52%	84%	47%	44%	38%
Taiwan	79%	93%	—	—	—
Tajikistan	97%	99%	49%	47%	—
Tanzania	52%	77%	49%	44%	▼13%
Thailand	91%	96%	49%	48%	53%
Togo	33%	64%	▼39%	▼25%	▼13%
Trinidad and Tobago	96%	99%	49%	50%	38%
Tunisia	50%	75%	46%	45%	41%
Turkey	69%	90%	47%	38%	35%
Turkmenistan	97%	99%	—	—	—
Uganda	46%	71%	43%	34%	33%
Ukraine	97%	99%	49%	—	52%
United Arab Emirates	77%	78%	48%	51%	▲75%
United Kingdom	▲99%	99%	49%	50%	49%
United States	▲99%	99%	48%	49%	▲56%
Uruguay	97%	97%	49%	▲53%	53%
Uzbekistan	96%	98%	—	—	—
Venezuela	90%	91%	▲50%	▲57%	47%
Vietnam	89%	96%	48%	50%	50%
Yemen	▼20%	65%	▼24%	▼12%	▼16%
Yugoslavia	88%	97%	49%	50%	53%
Zaire	64%	84%	42%	32%	—
Zambia	67%	84%	47%	37%	28%
Zimbabwe	78%	89%	▲50%	44%	27%

* Percent of population aged 15 and over who can read and write a simple sentence about their everyday life.
** Prim. = Primary level; Second. = secondary level; Higher ed. = Higher education.

WOMEN'S EMPLOYMENT

COUNTRY	WOMEN'S SHARE OF THE WORK FORCE*	LABOR FORCE PARTICIPATION RATE WOMEN**	MEN**
Afghanistan	▼ 9%	▼ 9%	85%
Albania	41%	63%	86%
Algeria	▼10%	▼ 8%	76%
Angola	38%	54%	91%
Argentina	29%	32%	80%
Armenia	▲48%	69%	79%
Australia	42%	63%	83%
Austria	40%	55%	80%
Azerbaijan	43%	56%	78%
Bangladesh	41%	62%	84%
Belarus	▲47%	▲73%	82%
Belgium	34%	42%	82%
Benin	▲47%	▲77%	88%
Bolivia	26%	25%	78%
Bosnia-Herzegovina	38%	47%	79%
Brazil	36%	40%	82%
Bulgaria	▲47%	68%	76%
Burkina Faso	46%	▲77%	94%
Burundi	▲47%	▲79%	96%
Cambodia	41%	50%	95%
Cameroon	33%	41%	87%
Canada	45%	58%	87%
Central African Rep.	45%	70%	92%
Chad	21%	23%	90%
Chile	29%	33%	83%
China	43%	▲80%	96%
Colombia	22%	23%	81%
Congo	39%	53%	88%
Costa Rica	22%	26%	87%
Croatia	44%	56%	77%
Cuba	33%	42%	84%
Czech Republic	45%	▲74%	82%
Denmark	45%	▲75%	89%
Dominican Republic	▼16%	▼18%	87%
Ecuador	19%	▼20%	79%
Egypt	23%	22%	84%
El Salvador	25%	29%	87%
Eritrea	37%	53%	38%
Estonia	46%	71%	78%
Ethiopia	37%	53%	91%
Finland	▲47%	▲73%	80%
France	42%	57%	83%
Georgia	45%	64%	80%
Germany	40%	62%	87%

(continued)

WOMEN'S EMPLOYMENT *(cont.)*

COUNTRY	WOMEN'S SHARE OF THE WORK FORCE*	LABOR FORCE PARTICIPATION RATE WOMEN**	MEN**
Ghana	39%	49%	78%
Greece	27%	30%	79%
Guatemala	▼17%	▼19%	85%
Guinea	39%	59%	96%
Haiti	41%	51%	79%
Honduras	20%	24%	87%
Hungary	46%	67%	82%
India	25%	31%	90%
Indonesia	39%	46%	85%
Iran	19%	23%	93%
Iraq	22%	24%	78%
Ireland	30%	36%	82%
Israel	42%	43%	84%
Italy	32%	37%	79%
Ivory Coast	34%	51%	93%
Jamaica	46%	▲75%	86%
Japan	40%	50%	84%
Jordan	▼11%	▼10%	72%
Kazakhstan	43%	68%	82%
Kenya	39%	51%	82%
Korea, North	46%	65%	75%
Korea, South	40%	47%	76%
Kuwait	▼16%	25%	94%
Kyrgyzstan	44%	65%	78%
Laos	44%	▲76%	98%
Latvia	▲47%	71%	79%
Lebanon	27%	27%	77%
Liberia	29%	36%	85%
Libya	▼10%	▼10%	79%
Lithuania	45%	70%	79%
Macedonia	41%	53%	78%
Madagascar	39%	55%	90%
Malawi	40%	57%	94%
Malaysia	35%	52%	91%
Mali	▼16%	▼16%	92%
Mauritania	23%	26%	85%
Mexico	30%	33%	83%
Moldova	▲48%	70%	81%
Morocco	21%	23%	88%
Mozambique	▲47%	▲78%	93%
Myanmar	36%	51%	93%
Nepal	33%	43%	91%
Netherlands	38%	47%	83%
New Zealand	36%	49%	89%

(continued)

	WOMEN'S SHARE OF THE	LABOR FORCE PARTICIPATION RATE	
COUNTRY	WORK FORCE*	WOMEN**	MEN**
Nicaragua	26%	32%	88%
Niger	46%	▲80%	95%
Nigeria	34%	43%	85%
Norway	41%	68%	90%
Pakistan	▼13%	▼16%	90%
Panama	28%	34%	83%
Paraguay	21%	24%	89%
Peru	24%	26%	78%
Philippines	31%	38%	85%
Poland	46%	71%	84%
Portugal	37%	48%	84%
Puerto Rico	29%	29%	75%
Romania	▲47%	69%	78%
Russia	▲48%	72%	82%
Rwanda	▲47%	▲80%	96%
Saudi Arabia	▼ 8%	▼10%	81%
Senegal	39%	52%	87%
Sierra Leone	32%	40%	89%
Singapore	31%	53%	84%
Slovakia	46%	71%	82%
Slovenia	▲50%	65%	77%
Somalia	38%	55%	92%
South Africa	36%	42%	75%
Spain	25%	26%	80%
Sri Lanka	27%	30%	82%
Sudan	23%	27%	87%
Sweden	▲48%	▲80%	89%
Switzerland	36%	53%	91%
Syria	▼18%	▼17%	79%
Taiwan	33%	45%	73%
Tajikistan	43%	56%	78%
Tanzania	▲47%	▲73%	86%
Thailand	44%	67%	86%
Togo	36%	46%	88%
Trinidad and Tobago	30%	39%	92%
Tunisia	25%	28%	83%
Turkey	34%	48%	87%
Turkmenistan	44%	64%	81%
Uganda	40%	60%	92%
Ukraine	46%	70%	80%
United Arab Emirates	▼ 9%	▼19%	90%
United Kingdom	44%	71%	91%
United States	46%	68%	81%
Uruguay	32%	39%	83%

(continued)

WOMEN'S EMPLOYMENT (cont.)

COUNTRY	WOMEN'S SHARE OF THE WORK FORCE*	LABOR FORCE PARTICIPATION RATE WOMEN**	MEN**
Uzbekistan	45%	64%	76%
Venezuela	28%	33%	81%
Vietnam	▲47%	▲77%	92%
Yemen	▼14%	▼12%	90%
Yugoslavia	42%	55%	77%
Zaire	35%	47%	90%
Zambia	30%	36%	89%
Zimbabwe	34%	41%	82%

* Percentage of total work force.
** Percentage of women and men aged 15–64.

EMPLOYMENT: OCCUPATIONAL GROUPS
Women per 100 men

COUNTRY	A&M*	P&T**	CLERICAL	SALES	SERVICE
Afghanistan	▼ 1	▼ 16	▼ 9	▼ 2	▼ 4
Albania	—	—	—	—	—
Algeria	6	38	22	▼ 2	23
Angola	7	▼ 7	—	—	—
Argentina	7	121	—	—	—
Armenia	—	—	—	—	—
Australia	34	74	79	11	▲339
Austria	20	92	198	149	243
Azerbaijan	—	—	—	—	—
Bangladesh	5	30	▼ 8	▼ 3	87
Belarus	—	—	—	—	—
Belgium	15	89	85	88	173
Benin	7	43	32	▲1,303	33
Bolivia	20	72	81	▲ 250	▲263
Bosnia-Herzegovina	—	—	—	—	—
Brazil	21	▲133	57	39	237
Bulgaria	▲ 44	▲127	▲696	180	220
Burkina Faso	16	35	48	194	28
Burundi	16	44	57	25	—
Cambodia	—	—	—	—	—
Cameroon	11	32	45	66	46
Canada	▲ 68	▲127	▲399	86	133
Central African Rep.	10	▼ 23	31	172	▼ 13

(continued)

EMPLOYMENT: OCCUPATIONAL GROUPS *(cont.)*
Women per 100 men

COUNTRY	A&M*	P&T**	CLERICAL	SALES	SERVICE
Chad	—	—	—	—	—
Chile	24	108	84	89	▲263
China	13	82	35	88	107
Colombia	37	72	121	66	229
Congo	6	40	38	195	46
Costa Rica	30	81	102	49	146
Croatia	31	123	208	98	125
Cuba	23	91	181	129	84
Czech Republic	—	—	—	—	—
Denmark	17	▲170	192	97	▲263
Dominican Rep.	27	98	83	37	▲267
Ecuador	35	79	96	59	174
Egypt	12	39	54	26	▼ 9
El Salvador	22	76	104	174	261
Eritrea	14	—	31	47	47
Estonia	—	—	—	—	—
Ethiopia	13	31	62	185	158
Finland	31	▲159	298	130	250
France	10	71	180	94	219
Georgia	—	—	—	—	—
Germany	—	—	—	—	—
Ghana	10	55	42	▲807	53
Greece	11	76	103	61	77
Guatemala	▲ 48	82	89	129	261
Guinea	—	—	—	—	—
Haiti	▲ 48	65	146	▲ 846	188
Honduras	38	100	124	155	▲ 263
Hungary	▲139	96	▲ 380	▲ 223	▲ 306
India	▼ 2	▼ 26	▼ 7	7	22
Indonesia	7	69	21	105	135
Iran	4	48	▼ 15	▼ 2	▼ 8
Iraq	15	78	▼ 7	10	19
Ireland	18	88	171	54	106
Israel	22	117	223	59	150
Italy	4	86	—	—	—
Ivory Coast	—	▼ 18	23	109	30
Jamaica	—	▲147	192	—	255
Japan	9	72	150	62	118
Jordan	6	51	28	▼ 1	▼ 15
Kazakhstan	▲ 91	▲194	▲2,567	▲1,227	▲1,223
Kenya	—	—	—	—	—
Korea, North	4	33	30	76	141
Korea, South	4	74	67	91	156
Kuwait	5	58	35	▼ 3	85
Kyrgyzstan	—	—	—	—	—

(continued)

EMPLOYMENT: OCCUPATIONAL GROUPS *(cont.)*
Women per 100 men

COUNTRY	A&M*	P&T**	CLERICAL	SALES	SERVICE
Laos	—	—	—	—	—
Latvia	—	—	—	—	—
Lebanon	▼ 2	61	—	—	—
Liberia	12	33	44	116	▼ 15
Libya	—	—	—	—	—
Lithuania	—	—	—	—	—
Macedonia	—	—	—	—	—
Madagascar	—	—	—	—	—
Malawi	9	39	29	24	26
Malaysia	▼ 1	87	106	51	77
Mali	25	▼ 23	63	141	71
Mauritania	8	▼ 26	43	31	81
Mexico	24	76	115	47	82
Moldova	—	—	—	—	—
Morocco	34	32	—	4	61
Mozambique	13	▼ 26	18	—	—
Myanmar	13	72	33	142	24
Nepal	30	57	▼ 5	23	23
Netherlands	16	74	138	75	238
New Zealand	▲48	92	▲457	163	207
Nicaragua	14	75	—	—	—
Niger	—	—	—	—	—
Nigeria	6	35	23	177	▼ 13
Norway	34	▲130	▲372	112	▲301
Pakistan	▼ 3	▼ 22	▼ 3	▼3	16
Panama	▼ 1	103	275	74	126
Paraguay	19	105	80	89	255
Peru	28	69	99	113	60
Philippines	38	▲172	119	189	138
Poland	18	▲152	334	▲506	—
Portugal	23	119	105	74	190
Puerto Rico	40	115	226	56	72
Romania	36	111	237	▲295	—
Russia	—	—	—	—	—
Rwanda	9	47	48	47	35
Saudi Arabia	▼ 0	▼ 11	▼ 1	▼ 1	▼ 4
Senegal	4	▼ 20	26	30	156
Sierra Leone	9	47	70	▲222	18
Singapore	19	68	293	69	—
Slovakia	30	▲137	▲540	219	—
Slovenia	29	124	▲348	152	▲355
Somalia	—	—	—	—	—
South Africa	24	103	183	78	216
Spain	10	89	97	83	141
Sri Lanka	33	82	69	25	—

(continued)

EMPLOYMENT: OCCUPATIONAL GROUPS *(cont.)*
Women per 100 men

COUNTRY	A&M*	P&T**	CLERICAL	SALES	SERVICE
Sudan	▼ 2	40	23	9	18
Sweden	▲64	▲127	▲336	91	▲332
Switzerland	6	61	112	128	203
Syria	▼ 3	59	19	▼ 1	▼ 6
Taiwan	—	—	—	—	—
Tajikistan	—	—	—	—	—
Tanzania	—	—	—	—	—
Thailand	29	111	94	150	128
Togo	9	27	31	▲586	59
Trinidad and Tobago	29	121	222	92	112
Tunisia	10	44	41	7	28
Turkey	4	47	48	7	▼ 11
Turkmenistan	—	—	—	—	—
Uganda	—	—	—	—	—
Ukraine	—	—	—	—	—
United Arab Emirates	▼ 2	34	▼ 13	▼ 2	32
United Kingdom	▲49	78	318	181	195
United States	▲67	103	▲392	100	150
Uruguay	26	▲157	101	67	210
Uzbekistan	—	—	—	—	—
Venezuela	23	123	158	53	136
Vietnam	—	—	—	—	—
Yemen	▼ 2	▼ 13	▼ 5	4	▼ 3
Yugoslavia	—	—	—	—	—
Zaire	10	▼ 20	▼ 15	133	19
Zambia	6	47	45	188	29
Zimbabwe	18	67	37	78	42

*A&M = Administrative and mangerial positions.
** P&T = Professional and technical positions.

(continued)

MARRIAGE AND DIVORCE			
COUNTRY	AVERAGE AGE AT FIRST MARRIAGE WOMEN	MEN	BIRTHS TO UNMARRIED WOMEN*
Afghanistan	▼17.8	25.3	23%
Albania	20.4	25.1	—
Algeria	23.7	27.7	—
Angola	▼17.9	23.8	—
Argentina	22.9	25.3	30%
Armenia	21.7	24.7	5%
Australia	24.5	26.7	25%
Austria	23.5	27.0	25%
Azerbaijan	21.7	24.4	▲ 4%
Bangladesh	▼18.0	25.5	—
Belarus	21.8	24.5	9%
Belgium	22.4	24.8	12%
Benin	▼18.3	24.9	—
Bolivia	22.1	24.5	—
Bosnia-Herzegovina	22.2	26.1	7%
Brazil	22.6	25.3	—
Bulgaria	21.1	24.9	19%
Burkina Faso	▼17.4	27.0	—
Burundi	21.9	25.2	—
Cambodia	21.3	24.3	—
Cameroon	19.7	26.2	—
Canada	▲26.2	28.2	34%
Central African Rep.	18.9	24.1	—
Chad	▼16.5	23.0	—
Chile	23.6	25.7	34%
China	22.4	25.1	—
Colombia	22.6	25.9	—
Congo	21.9	27.0	—
Costa Rica	22.2	25.1	41%
Croatia	23.6	26.6	8%
Cuba	19.9	23.5	—
Czech Republic	21.7	24.7	10%
Denmark	▲25.6	28.4	▼47%
Dominican Republic	20.5	26.1	—
Ecuador	21.1	24.3	—
Egypt	22.4	26.7	▲ 1%
El Salvador	19.4	24.7	▼67%
Eritrea	—	—	—
Estonia	21.7	24.4	31%
Ethiopia	▼17.1	23.3	—
Finland	▲26.1	28.5	27%
France	▲27.3	29.8	32%
Georgia	21.7	24.2	19%
Germany	▲26.1	28.5	15%

(continued)

MARRIAGE AND DIVORCE *(cont.)*

COUNTRY	AVERAGE AGE AT FIRST MARRIAGE WOMEN	MEN	BIRTHS TO UNMARRIED WOMEN*
Ghana	21.1	26.9	—
Greece	22.5	27.6	▲ 3%
Guatemala	20.5	23.5	—
Guinea	▼16.0	26.8	—
Haiti	23.8	27.3	—
Honduras	20.0	24.4	—
Hungary	21.0	24.8	16%
India	19.5	23.4	—
Indonesia	21.1	24.8	—
Iran	19.7	24.2	—
Iraq	22.3	26.3	—
Ireland	23.4	24.4	18%
Israel	23.9	26.7	▲ 2%
Italy	23.2	27.1	7%
Ivory Coast	18.9	27.1	—
Jamaica	▲29.7	30.8	▼84%
Japan	▲26.9	30.3	▲ 1%
Jordan	24.7	27.8	—
Kazakhstan	21.7	24.4	13%
Kenya	21.1	25.5	—
Korea, North	—	—	—
Korea, South	24.7	27.8	▲ 1%
Kuwait	22.4	25.2	—
Kyrgyzstan	21.7	24.4	12%
Laos	—	—	—
Latvia	22.4	24.0	20%
Lebanon	23.2	—	—
Liberia	19.7	26.6	—
Libya	18.7	24.6	—
Lithuania	21.7	24.4	8%
Macedonia	22.2	26.1	7%
Madagascar	20.3	23.5	—
Malawi	▼17.8	22.9	—
Malaysia	23.5	26.6	—
Mali	▼16.4	—	—
Mauritania	23.1	29.8	—
Mexico	20.6	24.1	28%
Moldova	21.7	24.4	11%
Morocco	22.3	27.2	—
Mozambique	22.2	—	—
Myanmar	22.4	24.6	—
Nepal	▼17.9	21.5	—
Netherlands	23.2	26.2	13%
New Zealand	▲26.7	28.8	36%

(continued)

	AVERAGE AGE AT FIRST MARRIAGE		BIRTHS TO UNMARRIED
COUNTRY	WOMEN	MEN	WOMEN*
Nicaragua	20.2	24.6	—
Niger	▼16.3	23.7	—
Nigeria	18.7	—	—
Norway	24.0	26.3	▼43%
Pakistan	21.7	26.5	—
Panama	21.9	25.4	▼75%
Paraguay	21.8	26.0	31%
Peru	22.7	25.7	—
Philippines	23.8	26.3	6%
Poland	23.0	26.2	7%
Portugal	22.1	24.7	16%
Puerto Rico	22.3	24.1	27%
Romania	21.1	24.9	▲ 4%
Russia	21.7	24.4	18%
Rwanda	21.2	—	—
Saudi Arabia	21.7	25.6	—
Senegal	23.7	30.4	—
Sierra Leone	▼18.0	27.4	—
Singapore	▲27.0	29.8	—
Slovakia	22.2	25.4	8%
Slovenia	24.1	28.4	28%
Somalia	20.1	26.5	—
South Africa	▲25.7	27.8	—
Spain	23.1	26.0	10%
Sri Lanka	24.4	27.9	6%
Sudan	24.1	—	—
Sweden	▲30.4	32.9	▼50%
Switzerland	▲25.0	27.9	6%
Syria	21.5	25.7	—
Taiwan	▲25.8	29.0	—
Tajikistan	21.7	24.4	8%
Tanzania	20.6	24.9	—
Thailand	22.7	24.7	—
Togo	20.3	26.5	—
Trinidad and Tobago	22.3	27.9	—
Tunisia	▲25.0	28.1	—
Turkey	21.5	24.6	—
Turkmenistan	21.7	24.4	▲ 4%
Uganda	19.0	23.9	—
Ukraine	21.7	24.4	12%
United Arab Emirates	23.1	25.6	—
United Kingdom	23.1	25.4	31%
United States	▲25.8	28.1	31%
Uruguay	22.9	25.2	26%

(continued)

MARRIAGE AND DIVORCE *(cont.)*

COUNTRY	AVERAGE AGE AT FIRST MARRIAGE		BIRTHS TO UNMARRIED WOMEN*
	WOMEN	MEN	
Uzbekistan	21.7	24.4	▲ 4%
Venezuela	21.2	24.8	—
Vietnam	23.2	24.5	—
Yemen	▼15.0	22.9	—
Yugoslavia	22.2	26.1	—
Zaire	20.0	24.9	—
Zambia	20.0	25.1	—
Zimbabwe	20.7	25.4	—

*Percentage of total births.

FAMILY PLANNING

COUNTRY	FERTILITY RATE****	CONTRACEP-TIVE USE***	BIRTHS TO TEENS**	ABORTION POLICIES*
Afghanistan	▼6.6	▼ 2%	8%	M
Albania	2.8	10%	▲3%	L
Algeria	3.6	47%	6%	C
Angola	▼6.9	▼ 2%	9%	C
Argentina	2.7	74%	13%	C
Armenia	2.5	22%	14%	L
Australia	1.9	▲76%	5%	C
Austria	▲1.6	71%	8%	L
Azerbaijan	2.4	17%	5%	L
Bangladesh	4.1	40%	14%	M
Belarus	1.7	23%	12%	L
Belgium	1.7	▲79%	4%	C
Benin	▼6.9	9%	11%	M
Bolivia	4.6	30%	9%	C
Bosnia-Herzegovina	▲1.6	—	11%	L
Brazil	2.8	▲78%	10%	C
Bulgaria	▲1.5	▲76%	▼20%	L
Burkina Faso	6.3	8%	11%	C
Burundi	▼6.5	9%	4%	C
Cambodia	5.1	44%	6%	M
Cameroon	5.5	16%	11%	C
Canada	1.9	73%	7%	L
Central African Rep.	5.5	16%	14%	M
Chad	5.7	20%	▼18%	M
Chile	2.5	43%	12%	M

(continued)

COUNTRY	FAMILY PLANNING			
	FERTILITY RATE****	CONTRACEP- TIVE USE***	BIRTHS TO TEENS**	ABORTION POLICIES*
China	2.0	▲83%	4%	L
Colombia	2.6	66%	11%	M
Congo	6.1	15%	11%	C
Costa Rica	3.0	▲75%	14%	C
Croatia	1.7	—	9%	L
Cuba	1.8	70%	▼25%	L
Czech Republic	1.8	69%	12%	L
Denmark	1.7	▲78%	▲ 3%	L
Dominican Republic	2.9	56%	14%	M
Ecuador	3.3	53%	11%	C
Egypt	3.7	47%	9%	C
El Salvador	3.8	53%	▼15%	C
Eritrea	5.6	▼ 3%	—	C
Estonia	▲1.6	—	13%	L
Ethiopia	▼6.8	▼ 4%	8%	C
Finland	1.9	▲80%	4%	C
France	1.7	▲81%	▲3%	C
Georgia	2.1	17%	14%	L
Germany	▲1.3	▲75%	▲ 3%	C
Ghana	5.7	13%	10%	C
Greece	▲1.4	—	8%	L
Guatemala	5.1	23%	11%	M
Guinea	▼6.8	▼ 5%	▼16%	C
Haiti	4.7	10%	7%	C
Honduras	4.6	47%	11%	M
Hungary	1.7	73%	12%	C
India	3.6	45%	11%	C
Indonesia	2.8	50%	11%	M
Iran	4.8	65%	9%	M
Iraq	5.5	14%	8%	C
Ireland	2.1	60%	4%	M
Israel	2.8	65%	▲ 3%	C
Italy	▲1.3	▲78%	4%	C
Ivory Coast	▼7.1	▼ 3%	▼17%	M
Jamaica	2.2	67%	14%	C
Japan	▲1.5	64%	▲ 1%	C
Jordan	5.4	35%	5%	C
Kazakhstan	2.4	30%	10%	L
Kenya	6.0	33%	11%	C
Korea, North	2.3	67%	▲ 2%	L
Korea, South	1.8	▲79%	▲ 2%	C
Kuwait	3.0	35%	7%	C
Kyrgyzstan	3.5	31%	6%	L
Laos	6.4	18%	9%	M
Latvia	▲1.6	19%	12%	L

(continued)

FAMILY PLANNING

COUNTRY	FERTILITY RATE****	CONTRACEP- TIVE USE***	BIRTHS TO TEENS**	ABORTION POLICIES*
Lebanon	2.9	55%	7%	M
Liberia	▼6.6	6%	14%	C
Libya	6.2	14%	11%	M
Lithuania	1.8	12%	10%	L
Macedonia	2.0	—	11%	L
Madagascar	5.9	17%	10%	M
Malawi	▼6.9	13%	11%	C
Malaysia	3.4	48%	4%	C
Mali	▼6.9	▼ 5%	▼17%	M
Mauritania	5.2	▼ 3%	12%	M
Mexico	3.0	53%	11%	C
Moldova	2.1	22%	12%	L
Morocco	3.4	42%	6%	C
Mozambique	6.3	▼ 4%	10%	L
Myanmar	4.0	13%	7%	M
Nepal	5.2	23%	10%	C
Netherlands	▲1.6	▲76%	▲ 2%	L
New Zealand	2.1	70%	8%	C
Nicaragua	4.8	49%	14%	M
Niger	▼7.3	▼ 4%	▼18%	M
Nigeria	6.2	6%	14%	M
Norway	2.0	▲76%	5%	L
Pakistan	5.9	12%	5%	C
Panama	2.8	58%	▼15%	C
Paraguay	4.1	48%	10%	M
Peru	3.3	59%	9%	C
Philippines	3.8	40%	6%	M
Poland	1.9	▲75%	7%	C
Portugal	▲1.6	66%	9%	C
Puerto Rico	2.2	70%	11%	L
Romania	▲1.5	57%	14%	L
Russia	▲1.5	32%	▼15%	L
Rwanda	6.3	21%	5%	C
Saudi Arabia	6.2	14%	8%	C
Senegal	5.8	7%	12%	M
Sierra Leone	6.3	▼ 4%	▼19%	C
Singapore	1.7	74%	▲ 2%	L
Slovakia	1.9	74%	11%	L
Slovenia	▲1.5	—	9%	L
Somalia	▼6.8	▼ 1%	4%	M
South Africa	4.0	50%	▼15%	L
Spain	▲1.2	59%	5%	C
Sri Lanka	2.4	62%	8%	M
Sudan	5.6	9%	9%	C
Sweden	2.1	▲78%	▲ 1%	L

(continued)

	FAMILY PLANNING			
COUNTRY	FERTILITY RATE****	CONTRACEP- TIVE USE***	BIRTHS TO TEENS**	ABORTION POLICIES*
Switzerland	▲1.6	71%	▲ 2%	C
Syria	5.6	20%	8%	M
Taiwan	1.7	▲75%	5%	C
Tajikistan	4.7	21%	4%	L
Tanzania	5.7	10%	13%	M
Thailand	2.1	66%	11%	C
Togo	6.3	12%	11%	C
Trinidad and Tobago	2.3	53%	11%	C
Tunisia	3.0	50%	6%	L
Turkey	3.2	63%	9%	L
Turkmenistan	3.8	20%	▲ 3%	L
Uganda	▼7.0	▼ 5%	13%	C
Ukraine	▲1.6	23%	▼16%	L
United Arab Emirates	4.1	41%	9%	M
United Kingdom	1.8	▲81%	9%	C
United States	2.1	74%	13%	L
Uruguay	2.3	72%	11%	C
Uzbekistan	3.7	28%	5%	L
Venezuela	3.1	49%	10%	M
Vietnam	3.7	53%	▲ 3%	L
Yemen	▼7.4	7%	10%	M
Yugoslavia	1.9	55%	10%	L
Zaire	▼6.5	9%	13%	C
Zambia	5.7	15%	12%	C
Zimbabwe	4.8	43%	9%	C

****Average number of children per woman.
*** By percentage of couples of childbearing age.
** Percentage of total births.
* M = most restrictive; L = least restrictive; C = with conditions. (See definitions under *Abortion* in glossary)

	WOMEN'S HEALTH			
COUNTRY	LIFE EXPECTANCY* WOMEN	MEN	MATERNAL MORTALITY**	LIFETIME CHANCES OF DYING FROM PREGNANCY RELATED CAUSES (ONE IN...)
Afghanistan	▼42.0	41.0	▼1,700	▼ 9
Albania	75.5	69.6	65	549
Algeria	65.0	63.0	160	174
Angola	▼46.1	42.9	▼1,500	▼ 10
Argentina	75.7	68.9	100	370
Armenia	74.7	69.0	50	800
Australia	▲80.9	75.0	▲ 9	▲5,848
Austria	▲79.5	72.9	▲10	▲6,250
Azerbaijan	74.2	66.6	22	1,894
Bangladesh	55.6	55.6	850	29
Belarus	76.4	66.8	37	1,590
Belgium	79.1	72.3	▲10	▲5,882
Benin	53.7	49.9	990	15
Bolivia	65.4	59.0	650	33
Bosnia-Herzegovina	78.9	72.4	—	—
Brazil	67.3	56.6	220	162
Bulgaria	74.8	67.8	27	2,469
Burkina Faso	48.9	45.6	930	17
Burundi	49.2	45.9	▼1,300	▼ 12
Cambodia	49.9	47.0	900	22
Cameroon	54.0	51.0	550	33
Canada	▲81.0	74.6	▲6	▲8,772
Central African Rep.	▼44.1	41.0	700	26
Chad	▼47.1	43.9	▼1,500	▼ 12
Chile	76.5	69.4	65	615
China	69.2	67.1	95	526
Colombia	74.9	69.3	100	385
Congo	55.3	50.1	890	18
Costa Rica	77.0	72.4	55	606
Croatia	77.3	70.1	—	—
Cuba	76.3	72.7	95	585
Czech Republic	76.3	68.5	15	3,704
Denmark	78.1	72.7	▲ 9	▲6,536
Dominican Republic	68.1	63.9	110	313
Ecuador	67.6	63.4	150	202
Egypt	62.8	58.9	170	159
El Salvador	66.5	58.0	300	88
Eritrea	51.8	48.3	▼1,400	13
Estonia	74.9	64.7	41	1525
Ethiopia	▼45.6	42.4	▼1,400	▼ 11
Finland	▲79.6	71.7	11	4,785

(continued)

WOMEN'S HEALTH *(cont.)*

COUNTRY	LIFE EXPECTANCY* WOMEN	MEN	MATERNAL MORTALITY**	LIFETIME CHANCES OF DYING FROM PREGNANCY RELATED CAUSES (ONE IN...)
France	▲82.0	73.5	15	3,922
Georgia	75.7	68.1	33	1,443
Germany	79.1	72.7	22	3,497
Ghana	55.8	52.2	740	24
Greece	▲80.1	74.7	▲ 10	▲7,143
Guatemala	64.4	59.7	200	98
Guinea	▼43.0	42.0	▼1,600	▼ 9
Haiti	56.4	53.1	▼1,000	21
Honduras	66.1	61.9	220	99
Hungary	73.8	64.5	30	1,961
India	59.1	58.1	570	49
Indonesia	64.0	60.0	650	55
Iran	65.5	65.0	120	174
Iraq	64.8	63.0	310	59
Ireland	77.9	72.2	▲ 10	4,762
Israel	78.5	75.1	▲ 7	5,102
Italy	▲80.5	73.7	12	▲6,410
Ivory Coast	54.2	50.8	810	17
Jamaica	74.8	70.4	120	379
Japan	▲83.0	76.6	18	3,704
Jordan	67.8	64.2	150	123
Kazakhstan	73.1	63.9	80	521
Kenya	60.5	56.5	650	26
Korea, North	73.0	66.7	70	621
Korea, South	74.0	67.4	130	427
Kuwait	75.4	71.2	29	1,149
Kyrgyzstan	72.4	64.3	110	260
Laos	50.0	47.0	650	24
Latvia	75.2	65.3	40	1,563
Lebanon	67.0	63.1	300	115
Liberia	54.0	52.0	560	27
Libya	62.5	59.1	220	73
Lithuania	76.2	66.5	36	1,543
Macedonia	75.9	71.5	—	—
Madagascar	55.0	52.0	490	35
Malawi	▼47.7	46.3	560	26
Malaysia	71.6	67.5	80	368
Mali	▼45.6	42.4	1,200	▼ 12
Mauritania	▼47.6	44.4	930	21
Mexico	75.2	69.3	110	303
Moldova	72.3	65.5	60	794

(continued)

	WOMEN'S HEALTH *(cont.)*			
COUNTRY	LIFE EXPECTANCY* WOMEN	MEN	MATERNAL MORTALITY**	LIFETIME CHANCES OF DYING FROM PREGNANCY RELATED CAUSES (ONE IN...)
Morocco	62.5	59.1	610	48
Mozambique	▼48.1	44.9	▼1,500	▼ 11
Myanmar	62.2	57.9	580	43
Nepal	50.3	51.5	▼1,500	13
Netherlands	▲80.4	74.1	12	5,208
New Zealand	78.0	71.9	25	1,905
Nicaragua	64.6	62.0	160	130
Niger	▼46.1	42.9	1,200	▼ 11
Nigeria	56.6	54.1	1,000	16
Norway	▲80.3	74.1	▲ 6	▲8,333
Pakistan	58.1	56.8	340	50
Panama	74.1	70.1	55	649
Paraguay	69.1	64.8	160	152
Peru	67.9	63.4	280	108
Philippines	70.2	64.9	280	94
Poland	75.8	66.7	19	2,770
Portugal	78.2	70.7	15	4,167
Puerto Rico	77.9	68.8	—	—
Romania	73.3	66.0	130	51
Russia	71.0	57.3	75	889
Rwanda	50.2	46.9	▼1,300	▼ 12
Saudi Arabia	65.2	61.7	130	124
Senegal	▼48.3	46.3	1,200	14
Sierra Leone	▼42.6	39.4	▼1,800	▼ 9
Singapore	76.4	70.8	▲ 10	▲ 5,882
Slovakia	77.2	68.7	—	—
Slovenia	78.4	70.5	13	5,128
Somalia	▼46.6	43.4	▼1,600	▼ 9
South Africa	67.9	62.4	230	109
Spain	▲80.5	73.4	▲ 7	▲11,904
Sri Lanka	72.5	68.3	140	298
Sudan	51.0	48.6	660	27
Sweden	▲80.8	75.3	▲ 7	▲ 6,803
Switzerland	▲81.7	74.6	▲ 6	▲10,417
Syria	66.9	63.2	180	99
Taiwan	78.6	72.0	—	—
Tajikistan	71.7	66.8	130	164
Tanzania	50.0	47.0	770	23
Thailand	71.9	65.0	200	238
Togo	54.8	51.3	640	25

(continued)

WOMEN'S HEALTH *(cont.)*

COUNTRY	LIFE EXPECTANCY* WOMEN	MEN	MATERNAL MORTALITY**	LIFETIME CHANCES OF DYING FROM PREGNANCY RELATED CAUSES (ONE IN...)
Trinidad and Tobago	73.5	68.5	90	483
Tunisia	70.2	67.4	170	196
Turkey	73.4	68.6	180	174
Turkmenistan	68.4	61.8	55	478
Uganda	52.7	49.4	1,200	▼ 12
Ukraine	74.8	65.5	50	1,250
United Arab Emir.ates	72.9	68.6	26	938
United Kingdom	79.0	73.6	▲ 9	▲6,173
United States	▲79.7	72.8	12	3,968
Uruguay	75.3	68.9	85	512
Uzbekistan	72.1	66.0	55	491
Venezuela	75.2	69.4	120	269
Vietnam	67.6	63.4	160	169
Yemen	52.4	49.4	▼1,400	▼ 10
Yugoslavia	76.0	71.0	—	—
Zaire	53.7	50.3	870	18
Zambia	54.5	52.4	940	19
Zimbabwe	60.1	56.5	570	37

*At birth, in years.
**Deaths per 100,000 live births.

Significant Signposts on the Road to Equality

The modern women's movement dates back to 18th-century Europe, when a number of individual women, including Mary Wollstonecraft, started publicly defying the widely held view that women were innately inferior to men and should be subject to men's control. They argued for a wide range of women's rights, including educational opportunities and political, social, and economic equality with men.

1792 United Kingdom
Mary Wollstonecraft publishes *A Vindication of the Rights of Woman,* now considered the first major feminist work and a keystone of the modern women's rights movement.

1803 United Kingdom
Britain passes its first abortion law, banning the procedure at any time after the quickening of the fetus; 1837 revision includes period before the quickening as well.

1804 France
The Napoleonic Code imposes severe restrictions on women's rights, granting absolute authority to husbands and fathers.

1822 United Kingdom
Francis Place, a labor reformer, promotes birth control in his pamphlet, "To the Married of Both Sexes of the Working People."

1824 United States
Weavers in Pawtucket, Rhode Island, conduct the first labor strike involving both women and men workers.

1825 United Kingdom
Richard Carlile publishes the first book on birth control, *Every Woman's Book: Or, What Is Love?*

1826 United States
The first public high schools for girls open in Boston and New York.

1829 India
Legislation officially outlaws *sati,* the Hindu custom of burning a widow alive on her husband's funeral pyre.

1830 United States
Congress makes abortion a statutory crime.

1833 Germany
Friedrich Wilde invents the diaphragm, forming it from ivory, silver, gold, or latex. Fifty years later, it is made of rubber.

United States
Oberlin College opens its doors as the first coeducational college.

1838 France
Flora Tristan publishes *Pérégrinations d'une paria,* describing her lengthy battle with her estranged husband over child custody and support.

1839 United Kingdom
Parliament passes the Infant Custody Act, the first legislation in favor of women's rights ever proposed in the House of Commons; among other things, it permits a mother to receive custody of her children under age seven as long as it cannot be proven that she committed adultery.

United States
Mississippi is the first state to permit a married woman to hold property, including earned income, in her own name.

1842 United Kingdom
Women, girls, and boys under age 10 are forbidden from working in mines. Five years later, legislation limits women's and children's working hours in factories.

1845 Sweden
Daughters are given equal inheritance rights with sons.

1848 United States
The first women's rights convention, organized by Lucretia Mott and Elizabeth Cady Stanton, is held in Seneca Falls, New York; it formally launches the fight for women's voting rights.

1851 United States
Female Medical College of Pennsylvania, later renamed Woman's Medical College, becomes the first women's medical college in the world.

1854 Norway
Equal inheritance rights are granted to daughters and sons.

1856 India
Hindu widows are granted the right to remarry.

1857 Denmark
Women are granted occupational freedom, now allowed to work in trades, crafts, and professions formerly closed to them.

Russia
The first high school for girls is founded.

1863 Norway
Unmarried women are no longer legally considered minors.

Finland
Women in rural areas can vote in local elections.

1865 Germany
The Allgemeiner Deutscher Frauenverein (General German Women's Association) is founded in Leipzig, promoting education and employment opportunities for women.

1867 New Zealand
Women taxpayers are allowed to vote in local elections.

Switzerland
The first female medical student is admitted to the University of Zurich.

United Kingdom
John Stuart Mill introduces into Parliament the first debate on women's suffrage, attempting to substitute "persons" for "men" in an amendment to the Representation of the People Bill.

1869 France
A new weekly periodical, *Les droits des femmes (Women's Rights)*, is founded by a man, Léon Richer, to promote women's rights.

Russia
The first female physician receives her medical degree.

United States
The National Woman Suffrage Association is founded, becoming the moving force behind the women's suffrage movement. Wyoming, a new territory, becomes the first American political entity to grant women the right to vote; it continues this policy after attaining statehood in 1890.

1870 Vatican City
Pope Pius IX declares that any Roman Catholic woman undergoing an abortion is subject to excommunication.

1884 United Kingdom
Oxford University admits women students but will not award them degrees until 1920.

1885 Australia
The Women's Suffrage League is founded.

1886 India
Grant Medical College in Bombay admits women.

1893 New Zealand
New Zealand becomes the first nation in the world to grant women's suffrage.

1900 Brazil
The Federation for the Advancement of Women is founded.

Germany
A new civil code grants women equality with men except in areas concerning marriage and family matters; a wife is given parental authority only in exceptional circumstances.

Japan
The first medical school for women is founded in Tokyo.

1902 Australia
Following New Zealand, Australia becomes the world's second country to grant women voting rights.

1902 United States
Ten countries are represented at the International Woman Suffrage Conference held in Washington, D.C.; Susan B. Anthony presides.

1903 France
Marie Curie becomes the first woman to be awarded a Nobel Prize; together with her husband, Pierre, she shares the prize in physics.

1905 Germany
Heidelberg and Freiberg Universities are the first to allow women students to matriculate.

1906 Russia
Universities first open to women students.

1908 United States
New York City passes the Sullivan Ordinance, prohibiting women from smoking in public places.

1916 United States
Having introduced the term "birth control" in 1914, Margaret Sanger, a public health nurse in New York City, opens the first family planning clinic in Brooklyn.

1920 France
Abortion is made illegal and the sale of contraceptives is banned.

Russia
Russian women become the first to get abortion on request.

United States
The 19th Amendment to the Constitution grants women the right to vote.

1921 **Canada**
Agnes MacPhail becomes the first woman elected to Parliament.

United Kingdom
Marie Stopes opens the first Mother's Clinic for Birth Control in London; initially, only married women are admitted.

1923 **Italy**
Mussolini restricts women's access to work and education.

Turkey
President Mustafa Kemal bans the custom requiring women to veil their faces.

1928 **United Kingdom**
Great Britain grants voting rights to women over 21. Women over 30 had the right to vote since 1918.

1929 **India**
The Child Marriage Restraint Act is passed, with the aim of ending the practice of forced marriages of young girls.

1930 **Italy**
The criminal code makes it a crime to disseminate birth control information, increases penalties for abortion, and defines women's adultery as more serious than men's.

Vatican City
Pope Pius XI issues the encyclical *Casti connubii,* declaring the rhythm method as the only acceptable form of birth control.

1931 **United States**
Jane Addams is the first woman to win the Nobel Prize for peace.

1934 **China**
The ancient practice of binding women's feet is banned.

1936 **Ireland**
Selling, importing, or advertising any form of birth control is made illegal.

1939 **Haiti**
Women are first admitted to universities.

1953 **United Nations**
Vijaya Lakshmi Pandit becomes the first woman elected president of the U.N. General Assembly.

1954 **India**
Polygamy is outlawed.

1960 **United States**
The first birth control pill, Enovid, is approved for use and goes on the market.

Ceylon (now Sri Lanka)
Sirimavo Bandaranaike becomes prime minister—the world's first woman to hold this office.

1961 Bahamas
Women gain the right to vote—in the last North American country to grant suffrage.

1962 Paraguay
Women gain the right to vote—in the last South American country to grant suffrage.

1963 Russia
Soviet cosmonaut Valentina Tereshkiva is the first woman in space.

United States
Betty Friedan's *The Feminine Mystique* is published; this best-selling book challenges the idealization of the traditional feminine role of wife and mother.

1964 United States
The Civil Rights Act prohibits discrimination on the basis of race, sex, religion, or national origin.

1966 Australia
Married women are no longer barred from working as permanent employees in public service jobs.

India
Indira Gandhi becomes the nation's first woman prime minister.

1967 France
Contraception is legalized.

United Kingdom
The new Abortion Act overturns the 1861 law outlawing abortion under all circumstances. Abortion is now legal if two doctors find that pregnancy would imperil the physical or mental health of the woman.

1968 Vatican City
Pope Paul VI issues the encyclical *Humanae vitae*, reiterating the church's ban on all artificial means of contraception.

1969 Israel
Golda Meir becomes prime minister of Israel, the first woman to hold this office.

1970 Italy
Divorce is permitted for the first time.

1971 India
Women win the right to abortion.

1972 United Kingdom
The first shelter for battered women is founded.

United States
Title IX of the Education Amendments prohibits sex discrimination in several areas, including student admissions, employee hiring, and student athletics.

1973 United States
A landmark Supreme Court decision, *Roe v. Wade,* overturns state laws forbidding abortion during the first trimester.

1974 France
Ligue du Droit des Femmes (Women's Rights League) is founded; its first head is Simone de Beauvoir.

1975 United Nations
The United Nations observes International Women's Year and proclaims 1976–1985 the Decade for Women "to promote equality between men and women." The First World Conference on Women meets in Mexico City. Future conferences are held in 1980 in Copenhagen, in 1985 in Nairobi, and in 1995 in Beijing.

1976 West Germany
The first shelter for battered women is established in West Berlin.

United States
Military academies admit women under a 1975 order of Congress.

1977 Brazil
Divorce is legalized—but with a limit of one in a lifetime, a condition rescinded in 1988.

Canada
The federal government passes a law establishing the principle of equal pay for work of equal value.

1978 Italy
Abortion is legalized during the first 90 days of pregnancy for women aged 18 and over.

United Kingdom
Lesley Brown gives birth to the world's first test-tube baby (conceived in vitro).

United States
NASA accepts women for astronaut training.

1979 China
The government institutes a mandatory family planning policy of one child per family.

Egypt
Family law is codified—giving women the right to seek divorce, gain custody of their children, and retain the family residence.

1979 Iran
The edict of 1975 ordering all women to wear the *chador* (Muslim head covering) in public is repealed.

Spain
Parliament decriminalizes the use of contraceptives.

United Kingdom
Margaret Thatcher becomes the first woman elected prime minister of a European country.

1980 China
Revisions in the Marriage Law prohibit arranged marriages, polygamy, and requests for bride price; and the minimum age for marriage for women is raised from 18 to 20.

France
Novelist Marguerite Yourcenar is elected to the Académie Française —the first woman member since its founding in 1635.

Iraq
Women gain the right to vote—in the most recent Asian country to grant women's suffrage.

1981 United States
Sandra Day O'Connor becomes the first woman to sit on the Supreme Court.

1983 Bangladesh
A new law institutes the death penalty for anyone found guilty of committing a dowry death (the killing of a bride for insufficient dowry).

1984 Egypt
The government repeals a 1979 law reserving 30 seats in Parliament for women; the number of female legislators quickly drops from 36 to 18.

Liechtenstein
Women gain the right to vote—in the last European country to grant women's suffrage.

1986 Argentina
The ban on public distribution of contraceptives is lifted.

1987 India
The High Court of Rajasthan upholds the law banning *sati,* the burning alive of a widow on her husband's funeral pyre.

Philippines
The Family Code allows annulment of marriage for psychological reasons and extends grounds for legal separation; divorce is still banned.

1989 Denmark
Denmark is the first country to legalize same-sex marriages, which are officially called registered partnerships.

Romania
Among the new government's first acts are a repeal of the ban on abortion and an easing of access to contraception.

1992 China
Laws prohibit the killing of baby girls and the kidnapping and selling of girls and women.

Ireland
Voters approve constitutional amendments allowing women to travel out of the country to obtain abortions and also to receive information on overseas abortion clinics. Abortions are still banned except to save the woman's life.

1992 Japan
Female students are now allowed to take entrance exams for military academies.

1993 Canada
Canada is the first country to grant political asylum to women facing domestic violence if forced to return to their homelands.

Russia
The first registered rape victims' center opens in Moscow.

1994 Middle East
Rising Islamic fundamentalism gains strength in many areas; groups of vigilantes attack women on the streets for not wearing the traditional head covering.

South Africa
By granting voting rights to all Africans—women and men—South Africa becomes the last country on the continent to grant women's suffrage.

1995 China
The first shelter for battered women opens in Beijing.

Egypt
A new law allows women and men to negotiate the terms of their marriage contract, including the wife's right to work and the husband's right to take another wife.

Iran
For the first time, women are allowed to attain the rank of judge; however, they cannot preside over legal hearings.

Ireland
Ireland becomes the last major European nation to lift its ban on divorce.

1996 Egypt
The Ministry of Health officially bans female genital mutilation; however, this measure is expected to have little effect on curbing the practice.

Japan
The government issues an official apology and offers compensation to the hundreds of surviving "comfort" women—girls and young women who were forced into prostitution for the benefit of Japanese soldiers during World War II.

United States
The Food and Drug Administration conditionally approves RU 486, the French abortion pill, for use in the United States. It is expected to be available to American women by 1998.

GLOSSARY

Abortion policies: Divided into three categories—Least restrictive: abortion on request; Most restrictive: abortion allowed only to save the woman's life; With conditions: abortion granted on various grounds, including fetal abnormalities, to preserve the woman's physical or mental health, to terminate pregnancy caused by rape or incest.

Affirmative action: The policy of granting preferential treatment to women (or any group) deemed to have suffered discrimination in the past. It is applied mostly to hiring, training, and promotion practices.

Annulment: A formal declaration that invalidates a marriage. An annulment differs from a divorce in that a divorce terminates a legal status while an annulment establishes that a marriage never existed.

Arab countries: Algeria, Egypt, Iraq, Jordan, Kuwait, Lebanon, Libya, Morocco, Saudi Arabia, Sudan, Syria, Tunisia, United Arab Emirates, Yemen.

Childbearing age: Women between the ages of 15 and 44, occasionally including women up to the age of 49.

Cohabitation: The state of living together as a couple in a long-term relationship, but without the legal sanction of marriage.

Contraceptive use rate: The percentage of married or other monogamous couples of childbearing age who use any form of contraception, whether modern or traditional.

Couples (using contraceptives): Married, cohabiting, or other monogamous couples.

Developed countries: A designation established by the United Nations for statistical purposes, not necessarily a reflection of any country's stage of development. The countries in this category are Albania, Armenia, Azerbaijan, Australia, Austria, Belarus, Belgium, Bosnia-Herzegovenia, Bulgaria, Canada, Croatia, Czech Republic, Denmark, Estonia, Finland, France, Georgia, Germany, Greece, Hungary, Ireland, Italy, Japan, Kazakhstan, Kyrgyzstan, Latvia, Lithuania, Macedonia, Moldova, Netherlands, New Zealand, Norway, Poland, Portugal, Romania, Russia, Slovakia, Slovenia, Spain, Sweden, Switzerland, Tajikistan, Turkmenistan, Ukraine, United Kingdom, United States, Uzbekistan, and Yugoslavia.

Developing countries: A designation established by the United Nations for statistical purposes, not necessarily a reflection of any country's stage of development. The countries in this category are Afghanistan, Algeria, Angola, Argentina, Bangladesh, Benin, Bolivia, Brazil, Burkina Faso, Burundi, Cambodia, Cameroon, Central African Republic, Chad, Chile, China, Colombia, Congo, Costa Rica, Cuba, Dominican Republic, Ecuador, Egypt, El Salvador, Eritrea, Ethiopia, Ghana, Guatemala, Guinea, Haiti, Honduras, India, Indonesia, Iran, Iraq, Israel, Ivory Coast, Jamaica, Jordan, Kenya, Kuwait, Laos, Lebanon, Liberia, Libya, Madagascar, Malawi, Malaysia, Mali, Mauritania, Mexico, Morocco, Mozambique, Myanmar, Nepal, Nicaragua, Niger, Nigeria, North Korea, Pakistan, Panama, Paraguay, Peru, Philippines, Rwanda, Saudi Arabia, Senegal, Sierra Leone, Singapore, Somalia, South Africa, South Korea, Sri Lanka, Sudan, Syria, Taiwan, Tanzania, Thailand, Togo, Trinidad and Tobago, Tunisia, Turkey, Uganda, United Arab Emirates, Uruguay, Venezuela, Vietnam, Yemen, Zaire, Zambia, and Zimbabwe.

Divorce rate: Unless otherwise specified, the number of couples who get divorced each year compared with the number of couples who get married.

Fertility rate: The average number of children born to each woman during her lifetime. A fertility rate of 2.1 is considered necessary for a population to maintain itself.

Infant mortality rate: The annual number of deaths of infants under age one per 1,000 live births.

Informal sector of the economy: Generally refers to such workers as street vendors, household domestics, cottage industry workers, and others who do not receive regular wages and in many cases are not eligible for medical insurance, pensions, or other benefits. All other workers, including farmers, make up the *formal sector* of the economy.

Islamic countries: Nations with a Muslim population of over 50%: Afghanistan, Albania, Algeria, Azerbaijan, Bangladesh, Burkina Faso, Chad, Egypt, Guinea, Indonesia, Iran, Iraq, Ivory Coast, Jordan, Kuwait, Kyrgyzstan,

Lebanon, Libya, Mali, Mauritania, Morocco, Niger, Nigeria, Pakistan, Saudi Arabia, Senegal, Sierra Leone, Somalia, Sudan, Syria, Tajikistan, Tunisia, Turkey, Turkmenistan, United Arab Emirates, Uzbekistan, and Yemen.

Labor force: All persons in employment—salaried employees, employers, wage earners, and unpaid family members—as well as all the unemployed, including those seeking work for the first time and those with previous work experience.

Latin America and the Caribbean countries: Argentina, Bolivia, Brazil, Chile, Colombia, Costa Rica, Cuba, Dominican Republic, Ecuador, El Salvador, Guatemala, Haiti, Honduras, Jamaica, Mexico, Nicaragua, Panama, Paraguay, Peru, Puerto Rico, Trinidad and Tobago, Uruguay, and Venezuela.

Life expectancy: The number of years a person born today would live if today's patterns of mortality remained unchanged throughout his or her life.

Literacy rate: The percentage of people aged 15 and over who are capable of reading and writing a simple statement about their everyday life.

Marital rape: The rape of a woman by her husband.

Maternal mortality rate: The number of pregnancy-related deaths for every 100,000 live births.

Roman Catholic countries: Nations with a Roman Catholic population of over 50%: Argentina, Austria, Belgium, Bolivia, Brazil, Burundi, Chile, Colombia, Costa Rica, Croatia, Cuba, Dominican Republic, Ecuador, El Salvador, France, Guatemala, Haiti, Honduras, Hungary, Ireland, Italy, Lithuania, Mexico, Nicaragua, Panama, Paraguay, Peru, Philippines, Poland, Portugal, Rwanda, Slovakia, Slovenia, Spain, Uruguay, and Venezuela.

Spousal rape: *See* Marital rape.

Work force: *See* Labor force.

Working-age women: Women between the ages of 15 and 64.

BIBLIOGRAPHY

Acero, Lillian, et al. (1991): Textile Workers in Brazil and Argentina: A Study of the Inter-relationships Between Work and Household. Tokyo: United Nations University Press.

Adler, Leonore Loeb (1993): International Handbook of Gender Roles. Westport, CT: Greenwood.

Afkhami, Mahnaz, and Haleh Vaziri (1996): Claiming Our Rights: A Manual for Women's Human Rights Education in Muslim Societies. Bethesda, MD: Sisterhood Is Global Institute.

Agonito, Rosemary (1977): History of Ideas on Woman. New York: Perigee Books.

Alan Guttmacher Institute (1994): Clandestine Abortion: A Latin American Reality. New York: Alan Guttmacher Institute.

Australia (1994): Australian Women's Year Book 1994. Canberra, ACT: Australian Bureau of Statistics, Office of the Status of Women.

Azarcon, Carin C. (1994): Education: course content of sex education. Pacific Law Journal 25:635.

Baby M, (1988): 109 N.J. 396, 537 A. 2d 1227.

Ballara, Marcella, comp. (1992): Women and Literacy. London: Zed Books Ltd.

Banks, Arthur, Alan J. Day, and Thomas Muller (eds.) (1996): Political Handbook of the World 1995–96. Binghamton, NY: CSA Publications.

Basu, Amrita (ed.) (1995): The Challenge of Local Feminisms: Women's Movements in Global Perspective. Boulder, CO: Westview Press.

Belran, Ruby Palma, and Aurora Javate DePias (eds.) (1992): Filipino Women Overseas Contract Workers . . . At What Cost? Manila: Goodwill Trading Co.

Belsito v. Clark (1994): 67 Ohio Misc. 2d 54, 644 N.E. 2d 760.

Berdan, Frances (1984): The Aztecs of Central Mexico. New York: Holt.

Berer, Marge, with Sunanda Ray (1993): Women and HIV/AIDS: An International Resource Book. New York: Harper.

Blum, Andrea, et al. (1993): WAC Stats: The Facts About Women. New York: Women's Action Coalition.

Boulding, Elise, et al. (1976): Handbook of International Data on Women. Beverly Hills, CA: Sage Publications.

Brandel, Abby (1995): Legislating surrogacy: a partial answer to feminist criticism. *In:* Maryland Law Review 54:488.

Brooks, Geraldine (1996): Nine Parts of Desire: The Hidden World of Islamic Women. New York: Doubleday.

Brown, Emily R. (1995): Changing the marital rape exemption: I am chattel (?!); hear me roar. American Journal of Trial Advocacy 18:657.

Bruce, J., C.B. Lloyd, and A. Leonard (1995): Families in Focus: New Perspectives on Mothers, Fathers, and Children. New York: The Population Council.

Buchwald, Emilie, Pamela Fletcher, and Martha Roth (eds.) (1993): Transforming a Rape Culture. Minneapolis: Milkweed Editions.

Bullock, Susan (1994): Women and Work. London: Zed Books Ltd.

Canada (1994): Annual Demographic Statistics (government publication). Ottawa.

Canada (1994): Canadian Guidelines for Sexual Health Education (government publication). Ottawa: Ministry of National Health and Welfare.

Canada (1995): Women in Canada: A Statistical Report, 3rd Edition. Ottawa: Statistics Canada.

Carr, Dana, and Ann Way (1994): Women's Lives and Experiences. Washington, DC: U.S. Agency for International Development.

Castles, Ian (1993): Women in Australia. Canberra, ACT: Australian Bureau of Statistics.

Chollat-Traquet, Claire (1992): Women and Tobacco. Geneva: World Health Organization.

Commonwealth Expert Group Staff (1991): Beyond Apartheid: Human Resources for a New South Africa. Portsmouth, NH: Heinemann.

Cook, Rebecca J. (ed.) (1994): Human Rights of Women. Philadelphia: University of Pennsylvania Press.

De La O, Maria (1994): Profile: Evan Wolfson; the fight for same-sex marriage. *In:* Sum. Human Rights 21:22.

Di Lisa, Mona, and Constance Herndon (eds.) (1994): The 1995 Information Please Women's Sourcebook. Boston: Houghton Mifflin Co.

Doe v. Attorney General (1992): 194 Mich. App. 432, 487 N.W. 2d 484.

Dolling, Yolanda, and Polly Cooper (eds.) (1991): Who's Who of Women in World Politics: Biographies of Women Currently in Government or Legislatures. New Providence, NJ: Bowker-Saur.

Dorgan, Charity A. (ed.) (1995): Gale Country and World Rankings Reporter. Detroit: Gale.

Duff, Johnette, and George G. Truitt (1994): The Marriage Handbook. New York: Plume.

Emmott, Bill (1993): Japanophobia: The Myth of the Invincible Japanese. New York: Times Books.

Engineer, Asghar Ali (1992): The Rights of Women in Islam. New York: St. Martin's Press.

Faulkner v. Jones (1995): 51 F. 3d 440.

Faulkner v. Jones (1995): WL 468727 (4th Cir.).

Fleck, Susan, and Constance Sorrentino (1994): Employment and unemployment in Mexico's labor force. In: Monthly Labor Review 117.

Franck, Irene M., and David M. Brownstone (1995): Women's World. New York: Harper-Collins.

Freeman, Jo (ed.) (1995): Women, A Feminist Perspective. Mountain View, CA: Mayfield Publishing Company.

Galb, Joyce, and Marian L. Palley (eds.) (1994): Women of Japan and Korea: Continuity and Change. Philadelphia: Temple University Press.

Gelles, Richard J. (1997): Intimate Violence in Families, 3rd Edition. Thousand Oaks, CA: Sage.

Genovese, Michael (1993): Women as National Leaders. Thousand Oaks, CA: Sage.

Goldfarb, Herbert (1995): Overcoming Infertility. New York: John Wiley & Sons.

Goldstein, Debra H. (1995): Sex-based wage discrimination: recovery under the Equal Pay Act, Title VII, or both. In: Alabama Lawyer 56(Sept.):294.

Gómez, E. Gómez (ed.) (1993): Gender, Women, and Health in the Americas. Washington, DC: Pan American Health Organization.

Greenspan, Karen (1994): The Timetables of Women's History. New York: Simon & Schuster.

Guy, Donna J. (1991): Sex and Danger in Buenos Aires: Prostitution, Family, and Nation in Argentina. Lincoln, NE: University of Nebraska Press.

Hawaii State Bar Association (1995): Same-sex marriage. Hawaii Bar Journal, February, 1995:48.

Healey, Kaye (ed.) (1995): The Australian Women's Directory: A Comprehensive National Guide to Women's Organizations and Services. Balmain, NSW: Pearlfisher Publications.

Heise, Lori (1993): Violence against women: the hidden health burden. In: World Health Statistics Quarterly 46(1):78–84.

Henshaw, Stanley K., and Evelyn Morrow (1990): Induced Abortion: A World Review 1990 Supplement. New York: Alan Guttmacher Institute.

Hicks, George (1995): The Comfort Women: Japan's Brutal Regime of Enforced Prostitution in the Second World War. New York: W.W. Norton & Co.

Human Rights Watch (1991): Criminal Injustice: Violence Against Women in Brazil. New York: Human Rights Watch.

Human Rights Watch (1995): Human Rights Watch Global Report on Women's Human Rights. New York: Human Rights Watch.

Humana, Charles (1992): World Human Rights Guide. New York: Oxford University Press.

Hunter, Brian (ed.) (1995): The Statesman's Year Book 1995–1996. New York: St. Martin's Press.

India (1993): India Economic Information Yearbook, 1992–1993. New Delhi: National.

India (1994): India, 1993 (government publication). New Delhi: Indian Ministry of Information and Broadcasting.

International Institute for Strategic Studies Staff (1995): The Military Balance, 1995–1996. New York: Oxford University Press.

International Labor Office (1994): 1994 Yearbook of Labor Statistics. 53rd Issue. Geneva: International Labor Organization.

Inter-Parliamentary Union (1995). Women in Parliaments, 1945–1995: A World Statistical Survey. Geneva: Inter-Parliamentary Union.

Israel (1993): Statistical Abstract of Israel (government publication). Jerusalem: Israeli Central Bureau of Statistics.

Italy (1994): Ruolo e prospettive delle donne nell' economia (government publication). Rome.

Italy (1995): The National Commission for Equal Opportunities for Men and Women. Laws for Women (government publication). Rome: Italian Prime Minister's Office.

Iwao, Sumiko (1994): The Japanese Woman: Traditional Image and Changing Reality. Cambridge, MA: Harvard University Press.

Jacobson, Jodi (ed.) (1994): Family, Gender, and Population Policy: Views from the Middle East. New York: The Population Council.

Jacobsson, Ranveig, and Karin Alfredsson (1993): Equal Worth: The Status of Men and Women in Sweden. Stockholm: Swedish Institute.

Jaffe, Maureen, and Sonia Rosen (eds.) (1996): Forced Labor: The Prostitution of Children. Washington, DC: U.S. Department of Labor, Bureau of International Labor Affairs.

Japan (1992): Tenth Japanese National Fertility Survey (government publication). Tokyo: Japanese Ministry of Health and Welfare.

Japan (1993): The Labor Conditions of Women, 1992 (government publication). Tokyo: Japanese Ministry of Labor.

Japan (1993): Statistical Abstract of Education, Science and Culture (government publication). Tokyo: Japanese Ministry of Education.

Japan (1994): Japanese Women in the World Today (government publication). Tokyo: Prime Minister's Office, Office for Gender Equality.

Japan (1994): Summary of the White Paper on Crime (government publication). Tokyo: Japanese Ministry of Justice.

Japan (1995): Japan Statistical Yearbook (government publication). Tokyo.

Jayawardena, Kumari (1986): Feminism and Nationalism in the Third World. London: Zed Books Ltd.

Jeffreys-Jones, Rhodri (1995): Changing Differences: Women and the Shaping of American Foreign Policy, 1917–1994. New Brunswick, NJ: Rutgers University Press.

Kandiyoti, Deniz (ed.) (1991): Women, Islam and the State. Philadelphia: Temple University Press.

Kane, Joseph Nathan (1981): Famous First Facts. New York: H.W. Wilson.

Karl, Marilee (1995): Women and Empowerment: Participation and Decision-Making. London: Zed Books Ltd.

Kelber, Mim (ed.) (1994): Women and Government: New Ways to Political Power. Westport, CT: Praeger Publications.

Kindersley, Dorling (1996): Chronicle of the Olympics, 1896–1996. New York: D.K. Publishing.

King, Alexa E. (1995): Solomon revisited: assigning parenthood in the context of collaborative reproduction. In: UCLA Women's Law Journal 329:5.

King, Elizabeth M., and M. Anne Hill (eds.) (1993): Women's Education in Developing Countries: Barriers, Benefits, and Policies. Baltimore, MD: Johns Hopkins University Press.

Kristof, Nicholas D., and Sheryl WuDunn (1995): China Wakes: The Struggle for the Soul of a Rising Power. New York: Random House.

Kublin, Michael, and Hyman Kublin (1991): China, 3rd Edition. Boston: Houghton, Mifflin.

Lee, Shin-wa (comp.) (1995): International Directory of Women Political Leadership. College Park, MD: Center for Political Leadership and Participation.

Liswood, Laura A. (1995): Woman World Leaders. London: HarperCollins.

Lucas, Ann M. (1995): Race, class, gender and deviancy: The criminalization of prostitution. In: Berkeley Women's Law Journal 10:47.

Mann, Jonathan M., Daniel J.M. Tarantola, and Thomas W. Netter (1992): AIDS in the World. Cambridge, MA: Harvard University Press.

Martin, Jorge (1994): English polygamy law and the Danish Registered Partnership Act: a case for the consistent treatment of foreign polygamous marriages and Danish same-sex marriages in England. In: Cornell International Law Journal 27:419.

Mencher, Joan P., and Anne Okongwu (eds.) (1993): Where Did All the Men Go?: Female-Headed/Female-Supported Households in Cross-Cultural Perspective. Boulder, CO: Westview Press.

Metz, Helen Chapin (ed.) (1992): Nigeria: A Country Study, 5th Edition. Washington, DC: Library of Congress, Federal Research Division.

Mexico (1992): Estados Unidos Mexicanos: Resumen General, XI Censo General de Poblacion y Vivienda, 1990 (government publication). Mexico City: Instituto Nacional de Estadistica Geografia e Informatica.

Morgan, Robin (ed.) (1997): Sisterhood is Global. New York: Doubleday.

Morin, Ann Miller (1995): Her Excellency: An Oral History of American Women Ambassadors. New York: Twayne Publishers.

Mosher, Steven W. (1993): A Mother's Ordeal. San Diego: Harcourt Brace and Company.

Naral Foundation (1992): Who Decides? A State-by-State Review of Abortion Rights, 3rd Edition. Washington DC: Naral Foundation.

Nelson, Barbara J., and Najma Chowdhury (eds.) (1994): Women and Politics Worldwide. New Haven: Yale University Press.

Nelson, Vednita (1993): Prostitution: where racism and sexism intersect. Michigan Journal of Gender and Law 1:81.

Nigeria (1990): Nigeria: Demographic and Health Survey (government publication). Lagos: Nigeria Federal Office of Statistics.

O'Connell, Helen (ed.) (1994): Women and the Family. London: Zed Books Ltd.

Organization for Economic Co-Operation and Development (1995): Education at a Glance: OECD Indicators. Paris: Organization for Economic Co-Operation and Development (OECD).

Pahl, R.E. (1988): On Work. Oxford, England: Basil Blackwell Ltd.

Pan-American Health Organization (1994): Health Conditions in the Americas (2 vols.). Washington, DC: Pan-American Health Organization (PAHO).

Philippines (Gabriela Commission on Women's Political Rights) (1992): Because We Dare to Struggle: A Documentation Report on State Violence Against Women in the Philippines, 1990–1992. Manila.

Psacharopoulos, George, and Zafiris Izannatos (1992): World Bank Case Studies on Women's Employment and Pay in Latin America. Washington, DC: The World Bank.

Population Action International (1993): Closing the Gender Gap: Educating Girls (wall chart). Washington, DC: Population Action International (PAI).

Population Action International (1995): Reproductive Risk: A Worldwide Assessment of Women's Sexual and Maternal Health (wall chart). Washington, DC: Population Action International (PAI).

Population Action International (1995): Women's Well-Being: Key Indicators on Women's Reproductive Health and Educational Status (wall chart). Washington, DC: Population Action International (PAI).

Population Reference Bureau (1995): PRB Media Guide to Women's Issues, 1995. Washington, DC: Population Reference Bureau (PRB).

Population Reference Bureau (1995): The World's Women (wall chart). Washington, DC: Population Reference Bureau (PRB).

Rao, Aruna (1991): Women's Studies International. New York: Feminist Press.

Read, Phyllis J., and Bernard L. Witlieb (1992): The Book of Women's Firsts. New York: Random House.

Robey, Bryant, Shea O. Rutstein, and Leo Morris (1993): The fertility decline in developing countries. *In:* Scientific American, December:60–67.

Rushwan, Hamid (1990): Female circumcision. *In:* World Health, April-May:16–17.

Schmittroth, Linda (ed.) (1991): Statistical Record of Women Worldwide. Detroit: Gale Research, Inc.

Schuler, Margaret (ed.) (1986): Empowerment and the Law: Strategies of Third World Women. New York: United Nations, UNIFEM.

Schuler, Margaret (1992): Freedom From Violence: Women's Strategies from Around the World. New York: OEF International.

Sen, Gita, Adrienne Germain, and Lincoln C. Chen (eds.) (1994): Population Policies Reconsidered: Health, Empowerment, and Rights. Harvard Series on Population and International Health. Boston: Harvard School of Public Health.

Shah, Iqbal H. (1994): The advance of the contraceptive revolution. *In:* World Health Statistics Quarterly 47:9–15.

Sharma, Arvind (ed.) (1987): Women in World Religions. Albany: State University of New York Press.

Sharpe, Sydney (1994): The Gilded Ghetto: Women and Political Power in Canada. Toronto: HarperCollins.

Shreir, Sally (ed.) (1988): Women's Movements of the World: An International Directory and Reference Guide. Harlow, Essex, UK: Longman.

Simon, Toby, and Cathy Harris (1993): Sex Without Consent, Volume I: A Peer Education Training Manual for Secondary Schools. Holmes Beach, FL: Learning Publications.

Simon, Toby, and Cathy Harris (1993): Sex Without Consent Volume II: A Peer Education Training Manual for Colleges and Universities. Holmes Beach, FL: Learning Publications.

Sivard, Ruth (1995): Women . . . A World Survey. Washington DC: World Priorities.

Smyre, Patricia (1993): Women and Health. London: Zed Books Ltd.

Snyder, Margaret C., and Mary Tadesse (1995): African Women and Development. London: Zed Books Ltd.

Snyder, Paula (ed.) (1992): The European Women's Almanac. New York: Columbia University Press.

Stromquist, Nelly P. (ed.) (1991): Women and Education in Latin America: Knowledge, Power, and Change. Boulder, CO: Lynne Rienner Publications.

Swart, Jeffrey J. (1994): The wedding luau: who is invited? Hawaii, same-sex marriage, and emerging realities. *In:* Emory Law Journal 43:1577.

Sweden (1995): Women and Men in Sweden, 1995. Stockholm: Statistics Sweden, Gender Statistics Unit.

Taeuber, Cynthia M (1996): Statistical Handbook on Women in America. Phoenix: Oryx Press.

Tilly, Louise A., and Joan W. Scott (1987): Women, Work, and Family. New York: Routledge.

Toubia, Nahid (1993): Female Genital Mutilation: A Call for Global Action. New York: Women, Ink.

Toubia, Nahid. (ed.) (1994): Arab Women: A Profile of Diversity and Change. New York: The Population Council.

Trager, James (1994): The Women's Chronology. New York: Holt.

United Kingdom (1993): Women in Britain. London: Foreign and Commonwealth Office.

United Nations (1989): Violence Against Women in the Family. New York: United Nations.

United Nations (1990): The Situation of Women (wall chart). New York: United Nations.

United Nations (1990/1991): Directory of Projects on the Prevention of Prostitution in Asia and the Pacific. New York: United Nations Economic and Social Commission for Asia and the Pacific.

United Nations (1991): Inventory of Population Projects in Developing Countries Around the World, 1991. New York: United Nations Fund for Population Activities.

United Nations (1991): United Nations Nuptiality Chart (wall chart). New York: United Nations.

United Nations (1991): The World's Women, 1970–1990. New York: United Nations.

United Nations (1992): Demographic Yearbook—Special Issue: Population Aging and the Situation of Elderly Persons. New York: United Nations.

United Nations (1993): African Statistical Yearbook 1990–1991 (4 volumes). New York: United Nations Economic Commission for Africa.

United Nations (1994): Abortion Policies: A Global Review (3 volumes). Population Studies No. 129.

United Nations (1994): Statistical Compendium on Women in Asia and the Pacific. New York: United Nations.

United Nations (1994): Statistical Yearbook, 39th Edition. New York: United Nations.

United Nations (1994): United Nations Educational, Scientific, and Cultural Organization Statistical Yearbook, 1994. Paris: United Nations Educational, Scientific, and Cultural Organization (UNESCO).

United Nations (1994): Women in Asia and the Pacific, 1985–1993. New York: United Nations.

United Nations (1994): World Contraceptive Use (wall chart). New York: United Nations.

United Nations (1995): Preparations for the Fourth World Conference on Women: Action for Equality, Development and Peace: Review and Appraisal of the Implementation of the Nairobi Forward-Looking Strategies for the Advancement of Women. New York: United Nations, Commission on the Status of Women.

United Nations (1995): The State of the World Population. New York: United Nations Population Fund.

United Nations (1995): Women in a Changing Global Economy: 1994 World Survey on the Role of Women in Development. New York: United Nations Department for Policy Coordination and Sustainable Development.

United Nations (1995): World Abortion Policies (wall chart). New York: United Nations.

United Nations (1995): The World's Women, 1995. New York: United Nations.

United Nations (1996): Concise Report on World Population Monitoring, 1996: Reproductive Rights and Reproductive Health. New York: United Nations, Commission on Population and Development.

United Nations (1996): The Progress of Nations, 1996. New York: United Nations Children's Fund (UNICEF).

United Nations Center for Social Development and Humanitarian Affairs (1991): Women in Politics and Decision-Making in the Late 20th Century. Dordrecht, the Netherlands: Martinus Nijhoff.

United Nations Department for Economic and Social Information and Policy Analysis (1995): Demographic Yearbook, Vol. 45. New York: United Nations.

United Nations Development Programme (1995): Human Development Report, 1995. New York: Oxford University Press.

United Nations Development Programme (1996): Human Development Report, 1996. New York: Oxford University Press.

United States (1990): Gender and Generation in the World's Labor Force (U.S. government publication/wall chart). Washington, DC: U.S. Bureau of the Census.

United States (1992): Population Trends: Egypt (U.S. government publication). Washington, DC: U.S. Department of Commerce.

United States (1995): Statistical Abstract of the United States, 115th Edition. Washington, DC: U.S. Bureau of the Census.

United States (1995): World Population Profile, 1994 (U.S. government publication). Washington, DC: U.S. Bureau of the Census.

United States (1996): Country Human Rights Practices, 1995 (U.S. government publication). Washington, DC: U.S. Department of State.

United States v. Commonwealth of Virginia (1995): 44 F. 3d 1229.

U.S. Bureau of the Census (1993): Educational attainment in the United States: March 1993 and 1992. *In:* Current Population Reports, Series P20–476.

Wijeyaratne, P., et al. (eds.) (1994): Gender Health and Sustainable Development: A Latin American Perspective. Lanham, MD: Bernan Associates.

Wolchik, Sharon L. (1995): Democratization in Central and Eastern Europe: Progress or Regression for Women? Washington, DC: The Atlantic Council of the United States, 1995.

Wolfson, Evan (1994–1995): Crossing the threshold: equal marriage rights for lesbians and gay men and the intra-community critique. New York University Review of Law and Social Change 21:567.

World Bank (1991): Gender and Poverty in India. Washington, DC: World Bank.

World Bank (1995): World Development Report, 1995: Workers in an Integrating World. New York: Oxford University Press.

World Bank (1995): Women in a Changing Global Economy: 1994 World Survey on the Role of Women in Development. New York: United Nations, Department for Policy Coordination and Sustainable Development.

World Health Organization (1989–1994): World Health Statistics Annual(s). Geneva:WHO.

World Health Organization (1993): The Health of Young People. Geneva: WHO.

World Health Organization (1993): Women and Substance Abuse. Geneva: WHO.

Yach, Derek (1996): Tobacco in Africa. World Health Forum 17(1):29–36.

Abbott, Margaret, 77
Abortion, 121–27, 502–05
  for sex selection, 127, 152
  grounds, 123
  illegal, 126
Abortion pill, 122, 124–25, 470, 518
Addams, Jane, 46
Affirmative action, 60
Afghanistan, 482–506
  CEDAW, 19
  Islamic fundamentalism , 16
  school enrollment, 36, 38
African National Congress, 402
Åhnberg, Annika, 416
AIDS, 128, 143–45, 161
Albania, 77, 482–506
Albright, Madeleine, 447, 448, 450
Algeria, 482–506
  abortion, 125
  contraceptive use, 115, 121
  Islamic fundamentalism, 16
  literacy increase, 30
All-China Women's Federation
    (ACWF), 238, 241
Allgemeiner Deutscher Frauen-
    verein (Germany), 512
Al-Tatawi, Nawal, 256
Andorra, 125
Andrée, Valerie, 272
Angola, 76, 482–506
Anthony, Susan B., 513
Aquino, Corazon, 20, 375
Argentina, 166–76
  abortion, 173, 502
  AIDS, 175
  births to unmarried, 172, 499
  contraception, 173, 502, 517
  death, leading causes, 174
  divorce, 172
  domestic violence, 175–76
  education, 168–69, 488
  employment, 169–71, 492, 495
  fertility rate, 173, 502
  life expectancy, 174, 506
  literacy, 168, 488
  marriage, 171–72, 499
  maternal mortality, 174, 506
  politics, 168, 485
  prostitution, 176
  rape, 158, 176
  sex education, 173–74
  sex ratio, 166, 482
  sexual harassment, 61
  smoking, 174–75
  teenage births, 173, 502
  voting rights, 167, 485
  women's movement, 167–68
Armenia, 482–506
Arranged marriage, 96–97
Arystanbekova, A. Kh., 18
Asia Foundation, 17
Asian Women's Fund, 161, 352
Asia-Pacific Women in Politics, 17
Astor, Nancy, 429
Ataeve, Aksoltan, 18
Aung San Suu Kyi, Daw, 46
Australia, 177–91
  abortion, 187, 502
  affirmative action, 182
  AIDS, 189–90
  births to unmarried, 185, 499
  contraception, 187, 502
  death, leading causes,188–89
  divorce, 185–86
  domestic violence, 190
  education, 180–81, 488
  employment, 181–84, 492, 495,
    515
  FGM, 191
  fertility rate, 187, 502
  life expectancy, 188, 506
  literacy, 180, 488
  marriage, 185–86, 499
  maternal mortality, 188, 506
  Olympics, 77
  politics, 179–80, 485
  prostitution, 190–91
  rape, 190
  sex education, 188
  sex ratio, 177, 482

sexual harassment, 182
smoking, 189
teenage births, 187, 502
voting rights, 178, 485
women's movement, 178–79,
  513
Austria, 482–506
  cohabitation, 91
  divorce rate, 99
  domestic violence, 156
  employment, part-time, 72
  European Parliament, 25
  legislature quota system, 20
  Nobel prize winner, 45
  pay differences, 71
  unemployment, 76
Azerbaijan, 482–506

Baby M, 471
Bahamas, 515
Bahrain, 13
Baker, Lydia, 429
Balch, Emily, 46
Banco Solidario (Bolivia), 73
Bandaranaike, S., 19, 20, 514
Bangladesh, 192–209
  abortion, 204–05, 502
  AIDS, 206–07
  contraception, 118, 203–04, 502
  death, leading causes, 205–06
  divorce, 202
  domestic violence, 152, 207–08
  education, 34, 196–97, 488
  employment, 197–200, 492, 495
  fertility rate, 203, 502
  Islamic fundamentalism, 194
  life expectancy, 205, 506
  literacy, 196, 488
  marriage, 201–02, 499
  maternal mortality, 205, 506
  politics, 195, 485
  prostitution, 208–09
  rape, 208
  sex ratio, 8, 192, 482
  smoking, 206
  teenage births, 203, 502
  voting rights, 192, 485
  women's movement, 193–95
Bangladesh Independent Garment Workers Union, 198
Bangladesh National Women
  Lay005rs Association, 209
Bangladesh National Women's
  Rehabilitation and Welfare
  Foundation, 194
Bangladesh Rural Advancement
  Committee (BRAC), 47, 197
Bangladesh Women's Health
  Coalition (BWHC), 203
Barbara, Agatha, 20
Beauvoir, Simone de, 516
Barshefsky, Charlene, 448
Belarus, 482–506
  divorce rate, 99
  unemployment, 76
Belgium, 482–506
  abortion, 121, 125
  armed forces, 70
  divorce rate, 99
  domestic violence, 154
  employment, part-time, 72
  European Parliament, 25
  legislature quota system, 20
  pay differences, 71
  rape, 157
  unemployment, 76
  voting rights, 13
Bellamy, Carol, 18
Benin, 482–506
  FGM, 163
  school enrollment, 36, 38
  tro-kosi, 153
Bernardino, Minerva, 18
Bertini, Catherine, 18
Bhutto, Benazir, 19, 20
Bindi, Rosi, 328
Birth control. See Contraception
Births to unmarried, 86 91–94,
  499,–502
Bishop, Bronwyn, 179

Black Sash (South Africa), 401
Blair, Bonnie, 79
Blankers–Koen, Fanny, 79
Blondin–Andrew, Ethel, 223
Bolivia, 482–506
  abortion, 125
  credit, access to, 73
  domestic violence, 152, 156
  education, higher, 37
  fertility rate changes, 108
  pay differences, 71
  president, 20
  sexual harassment, 61
  unemployment, 76
Boothroyd, Betty, 430
Bosnia–Herzegovina,482–506
  rape, mass, 158
  war fatalities, 17
Botswana, 108
Bottomley, Virginia, 430
Brazil, 210–20
  abortion, 216–17, 502
  AIDS, 218
  contraception, 216, 502
  death, leading causes, 217–18
  divorce, 215, 516
  domestic violence, 219
  education, 212, 488
  employment, 212–14, 492, 495
  FGM, 220
  fertility rate, 216, 502
  life expectancy, 217, 506
  literacy, 212, 488
  marriage, 215, 499
  maternal mortality, 217, 506
  politics, 211, 485
  prostitution, 220
  rape, 220
  sex education, 217
  sex ratio, 210, 482
  smoking, 217
  teenage births, 216, 502
  voting rights, 211, 485
  women's movement, 211, 513
Breach, N. Samaniego, 355
Bride price, 96
Brisco–Hooks, Valerie, 79
Brooks, Angie, 18
Brown, Lesley, 516
Browner, Carol, 448
Brunei, 13
Brundtland, Gro, 20
Buck, Pearl, 46
Bulgaria, 482–506
  unemployment, 76
Burkina Faso, 38, 163, 482–506
Burma. See Myanmar
Burnell, Jocelyn Bell, 45
Burundi, 482–506
  abortion, 125
  fertility rate changes, 108
  inheritance rights, 97
  rape, mass, 158
  school enrollment, 38

Callbeck, Catherine, 223
Camara, M. Bangoura, 18
Cambodia, 482–506
  prostitution, 160
  rape, mass, 158
  war fatalities, 17
Cameroon, 482–506
  adultery, 100
  contraceptive use, 118
  FGM, 163
  fertility rate changes, 108
  polygamy, 95
  voting rights, 13
Campbell, Kim, 20, 223
Canada, 221–35
  abortion, 230–31, 502
  AIDS, 233
  births to unmarried, 86, 229, 499
  contraception, 230, 231, 502
  death, leading causes, 232
  divorce, 229–30
  domestic violence, 154 234, 518
  education, 224–25, 489
  employment, 15, 225–28, 492,
    495, 516

FGM, 234–35
  fertility rate, 230, 502
  life expectancy, 231, 506
  literacy, 224, 489
  marriage, 228–29, 499
  maternal mortality, 231, 506
  Olympics, 77
  politics, 223–24, 485, 514
  prostitution, 234
  rape, 234
  sex education, 231
  sex ratio, 221, 482
  sexual harassment, 61
  smoking, 232–33
  teenage births, 230, 502
  violence, 233–35
  voting rights, 222, 485
  women's movement, 222–23
Cancer deaths, 143
Carlile, Richard, 511
Carnell, Kate, 179
Cáslavská, Vera, 79
Central African Republic, 482–506
  bride price, 96
  FGM, 163
  pay differences, 71
  polygamy, 95
  prime minister, 20
  school enrollment, 34, 36, 38
Central American Parliament
  (Parlacen), 26
Chad, 482–506
  bride price, 96
  education, nonformal, 43
  FGM, 163
  school enrollment, 36, 38
Chamorro, Violeta, 20
Charles, Mary Eugenia, 20
Chater, Shirley, 448
Child, Joan, 179
Child care, 74–75
Child custody/support, 100–01
Chile, 482–506
  abortion, 125
  divorce, 98
  domestic violence 152, 154
  credit, access to, 73
  marriage age, 87
  Nobel prize winner, 46
  pay differences, 71
  rape, 159
  unemployment, 76
  voting rights, 13
China, 236–51
  abortion, 247–48, 503
  AIDS, 249
  contraception, 247, 503
  death, leading causes, 248, 249
  divorce, 244–45
  domestic violence, 250–51, 518
  education, 238–39, 489
  employment, 240–43, 492, 496
  fertility rate, 246–47, 503
  foot binding, 11, 514
  life expectancy, 248, 506
  literacy, 239, 489
  marriage, 243–44, 499, 517
  maternal mortality, 248, 506
  Olympics, 77
  one child policy, 245–46
  politics, 238, 485
  prostitution, 160, 251
  rape, 251
  sex education, 248
  sex ratio, 243, 482
  smoking, 248–49
  teenage births, 247, 503
  voting rights, 238, 485
  women's movement, 237–38
Chowdhury, Matia, 195
Chowdhury, Syeda Sajeda, 195
Ciller, Tansu, 20
Cohabitation, 84, 91–94
Collins, Martha, 450
Colombia, 482–506
  contraceptive use, 118
  education, higher, 39
  fertility rate changes, 108
  pay differences, 71
  rape, marital, 158

Comaneci, Nadia, 79
Congo, 95, 97, 482–506
Contraception, 109–21, 502–05
   methods, 115, 119–20
Cooper, Charlotte, 77
Cori, Gerty, 44–45, 46
Corrigan, Mairead, 46
Costa Rica, 482–506
   abortion, 125
   contraceptive use, 118
   domestic violence, 156
   pay differences, 71
   unemployment, 76
Coubertin, Pierre de, 77
Couderc, Anne–Marie, 269
Cournoyer, Nellie, 223
Credit, access to, 73
Cresson, Edith, 20, 269
Croatia, 17, 76, 482–506
Cuba, 482–506
   cohabitation, 92
   contraceptive use, 115
   education, higher, 37
   marriage age, 87
Curie, Marie, 45, 513
Cuthbert, Betty, 79
Czech Republic, 76, 99, 482–506

Dahl, Birgitta, 415
Death, leading causes, 142–43
Decade for Women, 17
Deledda, Grazia, 45
Deng Xiaoping, 237
Denmark, 482–506
   abortion, 121
   births to unmarried, 86
   child care, 75
   divorce rate, 99
   employment, part-time, 72
   European Parliament, 25
   labor force, 15
   legislators, 25
   legislature quota system, 20
   occupational freedom, 58, 512
   Olympics, 77
   pay differences, 71
   rape, 159
   same-sex marriage, 94, 517
   unemployment, 76
   voting rights, 13
Didrikson, Midred "Babe," 79
Discrimination in the workplace,
   54–61. See also Sexual
   harassment
Divorce, 83–85, 98–101
Djibouti, 125
Dlamini–Zuma, Nkosazana, 402
Dmitriyeva, Tatiana, 389
Doi, Takako, 340
Dole, Elizabeth, 450
Domestic violence, 153–56
Dominica, 20
Dominican Rep., 482–506
   ambassador to U.N., 18
   birth control in work, 74
   cohabitation, 92
   contraceptive use, 118
   credit, access to, 73
   education, 39, 43
   fertility rate changes, 108
   sterilization, female, 115
Domitien, Elizabeth, 20
Dowdeswell, Elizabeth, 18
Dowry, 96
Dowry death, 155
Durrant, Patricia, 18

Ecuador, 482–506
   abortion, 125
   cohabitation, 92
   contraceptive use, 118
   domestic violence, 154 155, 156
   fertility rate changes, 108
   pay differences, 71
   unemployment, 76
   voting rights, 13
Education, 28–47, 488–91
Egypt, 252–66
   abortion, 263, 503
   AIDS, 265
   births to unmarried, 261, 499

contraception, 118, 263, 503
   death, leading causes, 264
   divorce, 262, 516
   domestic violence, 265
   education, 256–58, 489
   employment, 258–60, 492 496
   FGM, 266, 518
   fertility rate, 263, 503
   Islamic fundamentalism,
      254–55, 257
   life expectancy, 264, 506
   literacy, 258, 489
   marriage, 10, 260–62, 499 518
   maternal mortality, 264, 506
   politics, 255–56, 485
   prostitution, 265–66
   rape, 265
   sex education, 263
   sex ratio, 8, 252, 482
   smoking, 265
   teenage births, 263, 503
   voting rights, 253, 485
   women's movement, 253–55
Elion, Gertrude, 45, 46
Elizabeth II (U.K.), 430
El Salvador, 482–506
   births to unmarried, 93
   contraceptive use, 118
   fertility rate changes, 108
   marriage age, 87
   unemployment, 76
Employment, 48–82, 492–98
Enríquez, Silvia Hernández, 355
Equal Rights Amendment (ERA)
   (U.S.), 446–47
Eritrea, 482–506
   armed forces, 70
   domestic violence, 154
   FGM, 163
   school enrollment, 38
Estonia, 482–506
   divorce rate, 158
   unemployment, 76
Ethiopia, 482–506
   abortion, 125
   armed forces, 70
   contraceptive use, 111
   FGM, 163
   marriage, 86, 96–97
   school enrollment, 38
European Parliament, 25–26, 94
European Union, 42
Every Woman's Book, or What Is
   Love? 511

Fairbairn, Joyce, 223
Family planning, 102–27 502–05
Federation for the Advancement
   of Women (Brazil), 513
Female genital mutilation (FGM),
   162–64
Feminine Mystique, The, 515
Feminist Majority Foundation, 447
Feminist Union (Egypt), 253
Ferguson, Miriam "Ma," 450
Fergusson, Muriel, 223
Ferraro, Geraldine, 447, 448
Fertility rate, 102–09, 502–05
Finland, 482–506
   abortion, 125
   divorce rate, 99
   employment, part-time, 72
   European Parliament, 25
   IUDs, 115
   legislators, 25
   pay differences, 71
   unemployment, 76
   voting rights, 13, 512
Finnbogadottir, Vigdis, 20
Finney, Joan, 450
Finocchiaro, Anna, 328
Follet, Rosemary, 179
Foot binding, 11, 514
Forde, Leneen, 179
France, 267–80
   abortion, 121, 276–77, 503
   AIDS, 279
   births to unmarried, 86, 275, 499
   contraception, 118, 276, 503, 515
   death, leading causes, 278, 279
   divorce, 275, 511

domestic violence, 279
   education, 270, 489
   employment, 15, 270–74, 492,
      496
   European Parliament, 269
   FGM, 280
   fertility rate, 275, 503
   life expectancy, 278, 506
   literacy, 270, 489
   marriage, 274–75, 499
   maternal mortality, 278, 506
   Nobel prize winners, 267, 513
   politics, 269, 485
   prostitution, 280
   rape, 280
   sex education, 277
   sex ratio, 267, 482
   sexual harassment, 271
   smoking, 278
   teenage births, 275, 503
   voting rights, 268, 485
   women's movement, 268–69,
      510, 512, 516, 517
Franklin, Barbara, 450
Franklin, Rosalind, 45
Fraser, Dawn, 79
Frechette, Louise, 223
Fredrika Bremer Association, 415
Friedan, Betty, 446, 515
Freivalds, Laila, 416
Fritsche, Claudia, 18
Fry, Hedy, 223

Gabor, Mina, 376
Gandhi, Indira, 20, 297, 515
Georgia, 482–507
German Women's Council, 283
Germany, 281–94
   abortion, 121, 290–91, 503, 513
   affirmative action, 60
   AIDS, 292
   births to unmarried, 289, 499
   contraception, 290, 503, 511, 513
   death, leading causes, 292
   divorce, 289
   domestic violence, 293, 516
   education, 284–85, 489, 513
   employment, 285–88, 492
   European Parliament, 284
   fertility rate, 289–90, 503
   life expectancy, 291, 506
   literacy, 284, 489
   marriage, 288–89, 499, 513
   maternal mortality, 292, 506
   Nobel prize winner, 281
   Olympics, 77
   politics, 283–84, 485
   prostitution, 294
   rape, 293
   sex education, 291
   sex ratio, 281, 482
   sexual harassment, 285
   smoking, 292
   teenage births, 290, 503
   violence, 293–94
   voting rights, 281, 282, 485
   women's movement, 282–83,
      512
Ghana, 482–507
   abortion, 125
   contraceptive use, 118
   credit, access to, 73
   FGM, 162, 163
   fertility rate changes, 108
   inheritance rights, 97
   literacy increase, 30
   school enrollment, 33
   tro-kosi, 153
   unemployment, 76
Ginsburg, Ruth Bader, 447
Ginwala, Frene, 402
Goeppert–Mayer, Maria, 46
Gorbachev, Mikhail, 389
Gordimer, Nadine, 46
Gouda, Zenus Kamel, 256
Graf, Steffi, 79
Grameen Bank, 73
Grasso, Ella, 447, 450
Greece, 482–506
   births to unmarried, 93
   employment, part-time, 72

European Parliament, 25
   legislature quota system, 20
   pay differences, 71
   unemployment, 76
Green, Rosario, 18
Griffith–Joyner, Florence, 79
Gu Xiulian, 238
Guatemala, 482–507
   domestic violence, 154
   fertility rate changes, 108
   marriage age, 87
   Nobel prize winner, 46
   rape, 159
Gueiler, Lidia, 20
Guinea, 483–507
   ambassador to U.N., 18
   FGM, 163

Haiti, 483–507
   contraceptive use, 118
   Olympics, 77
   president, 20
   prime minister, 20
   school enrollment, 38
   universities, women in, 514
Hammurabi, Code of, 10
Harris, Patricia Roberts, 450
Health, 128–50, 506–09
Heckler, Margaret, 450
Henie, Sonja, 79
Herman, Alexis, 448, 450
Heyzer, Noeleen, 18
Hills, Carla Anderson, 450
Hjelm–Wallén, Lena, 416
Hobby, Oveta Culp, 450
Hodgkin, Dorothy, 46
Honduras, 483–507
   domestic violence, 154, 156
   Housewives Union, 170
Hufstedler, Shirley, 450
Human Rights Watch, 17
Hungary, 483–507
   abortion, 125
   contraceptive use, 118
   divorce rate, 99
   pay differences, 71
   unemployment, 76

Iceland, 20
Idrac, Anne–Marie, 269
Iles, Annette Des, 18
Illiteracy. See Literacy
India, 295–309
   abortion, 304–05, 503, 515
   AIDS, 306–07
   contraception, 118, 303–04, 503
   death, leading causes, 305, 307
   divorce, 303
   domestic violence, 308
   education, 33, 297–98, 489, 513
   employment, 298–301, 493, 496
   female infanticide, 307
   fertility rate, 303, 503
   life expectancy, 305, 507
   literacy, 31, 298, 489
   marriage, 95, 301, 500, 512, 514
   maternal mortality, 305, 507
   Nobel prize winner, 295
   politics, 18, 297, 486
   prostitution, 309
   rape, 308
   sati, 308–09, 511, 517
   sex ratio, 295, 305, 483
   smoking, 306
   teenage births, 303, 503
   voting rights, 296, 486
   women's movement, 296–97
Indonesia, 483–507
   comfort women, 161
   contraceptive use, 118
   credit, access to, 73
   fertility rate changes, 108
   HIV, 144
   literacy increase, 30
   Inheritance laws, 97
   International Center for
      Research on Women, 17
   International Labor Organization
      (ILO), 59
   International Olympic Commit-
      tee (IOC), 77, 79

International organizations, 17
International Women's Health
  Coalition, 17
Iotti, Nilde, 328
Iran, 483–507
  contraceptive use, 115, 121
  dress code, 516
  family planning, 121
  Islamic fundamentalism, 16
  women judges, 518
Iraq, 483–507
  contraceptive use, 118
  voting rights, 517
Ireland, 483–507
  abortion, 126, 517
  birth control, 514
  divorce, 98, 518
  domestic violence, 156
  employment, part-time, 72
  European Parliament, 25
  Nobel prize winners, 46
  pay differences, 71
  president, 20
  unemployment, 76
Islam (Muslim)
  divorce, 101
  fundamentalism, 16, 518
  shari'a (family law), 86–87
Israel, 310–24
  abortion, 320–21, 503
  affirmative action, 315
  AIDS, 322
  births to unmarried, 319, 500
  contraception, 320, 503
  death, leading causes, 322
  divorce, 319–20
  domestic violence, 323
  education, 312–14, 489
  employment, 314–18, 493, 496
  fertility rate, 320, 503
  life expectancy, 321, 507
  literacy, 313, 489
  marriage, 318–19, 500, 514
  maternal mortality, 321, 507
  politics, 312, 486
  prostitution, 324
  rape, 323
  sex education, 321
  sex ratio, 310, 483
  sexual harassment, 315
  smoking, 322
  teenage births, 320, 503
  voting rights, 312, 486
  women's movement, 311–12
Italy, 325–37
  abortion, 121, 334, 503, 514, 516
  affirmative action, 330
  AIDS, 336
  births to unmarried, 86, 333,
    500
  contraception, 334, 503, 514
  death, leading causes, 335
  divorce, 333, 515
  domestic violence, 336
  education, 328–29, 489
  employment, 330–32, 493, 496
  European Parliament, 328
  fertility rate, 333, 503
  life expectancy, 335, 507
  literacy, 329, 489
  marriage, 332–33, 500
  maternal mortality, 335, 507
  Nobel prize winners, 325
  politics, 327–28, 486
  prostitution, 337
  rape, 336
  sex education, 334
  sex ratio, 325, 483
  sexual harassment, 330
  smoking, 335
  teenage births, 333, 503
  voting rights, 326, 486
  women's movement, 326–27,
    514
Ivory Coast, 483–507
  adultery, 100
  credit, access to, 73
  domestic violence, 153
  FGM, 163

Jamaica, 483–507

abortion, 125
  ambassador to U.N., 18
  births to unmarried, 93
  contraceptive use, 115, 118
  domestic violence, 155
  education, higher, 39
  marriage age, 93
  unemployment, 76
Japan, 338–52
  abortion, 121, 347, 503
  AIDS, 349–50
  births to unmarried, 86 345, 500
  contraception, 118, 346–47, 503
  comfort women, 161, 351–52,
    518
  death, leading causes, 348
  divorce, 345–46
  domestic violence, 154, 350
  education, 340–41, 489, 513, 518
  employment, 341–44, 493 496
  fertility rate, 346, 503
  life expectancy, 348, 507
  literacy, 340, 489
  marriage, 344–45, 500
  maternal mortality, 348, 507
  Olympics, 77
  politics, 339–40, 486
  prostitution, 351
  rape, 350–51
  sex education, 347–48
  sex ratio, 338, 483
  sexual harassment, 342
  smoking, 349
  teenage births, 346, 503
  voting rights, 339
  women's movement, 339
Jatiyo Mahila Sangstha, 194
Johansson, Iva, 416
Johnston, Rita, 223
Joliet-Curie, Irène, 46
Jordan, 483–507
  contraceptive use, 118
  fertility rate changes, 108
  literacy rate, 29, 30
  pay differences, 74
Joyner–Kersee, Jackie, 79

Kazakhstan, 18, 483–507
Kennedy, John F., 446
Kenya, 483–507
  contraceptive use, 118
  credit, access to, 73
  domestic violence, 152, 154
  dowry, 96
  FGM, 163
  fertility rate changes, 108
  inheritance rights, 97
  literacy increase, 30
  pay differences, 71
Khrushchev, Nikita, 388
Kinigi, Sylvie, 20
Kirkpatrick, Jeane, 447
Kirner, Joan, 179
Klingvall, Maj–Inger, 416
Korbut, Olga, 79
Korea, North, 483–507
Korea, South, 483–507
  abortion, 123
  births to unmarried, 93
  comfort women, 161
  contraceptive use, 115, 118
  domestic violence, 156
  infanticide, 152
  marriage, 95, 97
  "missing" girls, 8
  pay differences, 70, 71
  prostitution, 160
  unemployment, 76
Kreps, Juanita, 450
Kumaratunga, C., 19, 20
Kunin, Madeleine, 450
Kuwait, 483–507
  birth control pills, 115
  dowry, 96
  literacy rate, 29
  marriage, 86
  Olympics, 77
  prostitution, 160
  voting rights, 13
Kyrgyzstan, 483–507

Labor force, 3, 50–58, 492–95
Lagerlöf, Selma, 45
Laos, 483–507
  domestic violence, 153
LaPointe, Renaude, 223
Latvia, 483–507
  unemployment, 76
Latynina, Larissa, 80
Lawrence, Carmen, 179
Lebanon, 29, 96, 483–507
Leon, Corazon de, 376
Lepage, Corinne, 269
Les droits des femmes, 512
Levi-Montalcini, Rita, 46
Liberia, 483–507
  abortion, 125
  FGM, 163
  fertility rate changes, 108
  president, 20
  rape, mass, 158
  U.N. General Assembly, 18
  voting rights, 13
  war fatalities, 17
Liberia-Peters, Maria, 20
Libya, 483–507
  literacy increase, 30
Liechtenstein, 18, 517
Life expectancy, 2, 129–36 506–09
Ligue du Droit des Femmes, 516
Lillo, Julia Caravias, 355
Limbach, Jutta, 284
Lindh, Anna, 416
Literacy, 29–32, 33, 34, 35, 488–91
  and fertility, 32, 36, 37
Lithuania, 483–507
  divorce rate, 99
  prime minister, 20
  unemployment, 76
Livnat, Limor, 312
Lozana, Antonia, 355
Luther, Martin, 12
Luxembourg, 25
Lyons, Enid, 179

Macedonia, 483–507
MacPhail, Agnes, 514
Madagascar, 153, 483–507
Madres de Plaza de Mayo, 167
Mahila Parishad, 194
Mahila Samiti, 194
Malawi, 118, 143, 483–507
Malta, 20, 125
Malaysia, 483–507
  child support, 100
  domestic violence, 154, 155, 156
  polygamy, 95
Mali, 483–507
  FGM, 163
  fertility rate changes, 108
  polygamy, 94
  school enrollment, 38
Mandela, Winnie, 402
Manley, Audrey, 448
Mao Zedong, 237
Maria (Russia), 389
Marital rape, 157–58
Markiewicz, Constance, 429
Marleau, Diane, 223
Marriage, 83–97, 499–502
Martin, Lynn, 450
Maternal mortality, 136–41,
  506–09
Maternity leave/benefits, 74
Mauritania, 483–507
  contraceptive use, 118
  FGM, 163
  polygamy, 95
McGinty, Kathleen, 448
McLaughlin, Ann, 450
McLaughlin, Audrey, 223
McClintock, Barbara, 46
McLellan, Anne, 223
Meir, Golda, 20, 312, 515
Menchu, Roberta, 46
Merkel, Angela, 284
Messing, Ulrica, 416
Mexico, 353–62
  abortion, 360, 504
  AIDS, 361
  births to unmarried, 358, 500
  contraception, 118, 359–60, 504

death, leading causes, 361
  divorce, 358
  domestic violence, 362
  education, 355–56, 490
  employment, 356–58, 493, 497
  fertility rate, 359, 504
  life expectancy, 360, 507
  literacy, 355, 490
  marriage, 358, 500
  maternal mortality, 360, 507
  politics, 354–55, 486
  prostitution, 362
  rape, 362
  sex education, 360
  sex ratio, 353, 483
  sexual harassment, 61
  smoking, 361
  teenage births, 359, 504
  voting rights, 354, 486
  women's movement, 354
Meyer, Debbie, 80
Meyfarth, Ulrike, 80
Micro banks, 73
Miller, Shannon, 80
"Missing" girls, 8
Mistral, Gabriela, 46
Mitchell, Roma, 179
Mofford, Rose, 450
Moldova, 483–507
  divorce rate, 99
"Morning after" pill, 119, 159
Morocco, 483–508
  contraceptive use, 115, 118
  domestic violence, 154
  fertility rate changes, 108
  literacy rate, 29
  rape, 159
  school enrollment, 38
Morrison, Toni, 46
Mott, Lucretia, 445, 511
Moutawakel, Nawal El, 79
Movimento della Liberazione delle
  Donne (Italy), 326
Movimiento de Liberación de la
  Mujer (Mexico) 354
Moylan, Judi, 179
Mozambique, 483–508
  marriage, 86
  school enrollment, 38
Mthembi-Nkondo, S., 402
Mujeres en Acción Solidaria
  (Mexico), 354
Muslim. See Islam
Myanmar, 483–508
  domestic violence, 153
  Nobel prize winner, 46
  prostitution, 152, 160
Myrdal, Alva, 46

Napoleonic Code, 268, 510
Naripokkho (Bangladesh), 194
Nasreen, Taslima, 194
Nasser, Gamal Abdul, 254
National Action Committee on the
  Status of Women (Canada),
  223
National Council of Women's
  Societies (Nigeria), 364
National Organization for
  Women (NOW) (U.S.), 446
National Organization of Emer-
  gency Shelters for Battered
  Women (Sweden), 415
National Program for the Promo-
  tion of Equal Opportunities
  for Women in the Educa-
  tional Area (Argentina), 169
National Woman Suffrage
  Association (U.S.), 512
National Women's Political
  Caucus (U.S.), 446, 451
Nepal, 483–508
  credit, access to, 73
  education, nonformal, 43, 47
  life expectancy, 133
  marriage, 86
  "missing" girls, 8
  school enrollment, 36
Netherlands, 483–508
  affirmative action, 60
  armed forces, 70

births to unmarried, 86
cohabitation, 92
contraceptive use, 118
divorce rate, 99
domestic violence, 153, 154, 156
employment, part–time, 72
European Parliament, 25
FGM, 162
legislators, 25
legislature quota system, 20
pay differences, 71
prostitution, 162
rape, 158, 160
same-sex marriage, 94
sexual abuse, 152
sexual harassment, 61
unemployment, 76
Netherlands Antilles, 20
Newman, Jocelyn, 179
New Zealand, 483–508
  birth control pills, 115
  domestic violence, 155, 156
  employment, part-time, 72
  maternity leave, 74
  pay differences, 71
  rape, marital, 158
  sexual abuse, 152
  unemployment, 76
  voting rights, 13, 512, 513
Nicaragua, 483–508
  domestic violence, 156
  president, 20
  unemployment, 76
Niger, 483–508
  credit, access to, 73
  FGM, 163
  fertility rate changes, 108
  school enrollment, 38
Nigeria, 363–73
  abortion, 370, 504
  AIDS, 371
  contraception, 118, 369, 504
  death, leading causes, 370–71
  divorce, 368–69
  domestic violence, 372
  education, 38, 364–65, 490
  employment, 365–67, 494, 497
  FGM, 164, 372–73
  fertility rate, 369, 504
  life expectancy, 370, 508
  literacy, 365, 490
  marriage, 367–68, 501
  maternal mortality, 370, 508
  politics, 364, 487
  prostitution, 372
  rape, 372
  sex ratio, 363, 483
  smoking, 371
  teenage births, 369, 504
  tro-kosi, 153
  voting rights, 364, 487
  women's movement, 364
Nobel prize, 44–46, 513, 514
Nolte, Claudia, 284
Nonformal educational
  programs, 43–47
Norway, 483–508
  affirmative action, 60
  armed forces, 70
  contraceptive use, 115, 118
  divorce rate, 99
  domestic violence, 154
  employment, part-time, 72
  FGM, 162
  inheritance rights, 512
  legislators, 25
  legislature quota system, 20
  Nobel prize winner, 46
  occupational freedom, 58
  Olympics, 77
  pay differences, 71
  prime minister, 20
  same-sex marriage, 94
  sexual abuse, 152
  unemployment, 76
  unmarried women, 512
  voting rights, 13
Novello, Antonia, 447
Nüsslein–Volhard, C., 46

O'Connor, Sandra Day, 447, 517

Ogata, Sadako, 18
Oikkyo Baddha Nari Samaj
  (Bangladesh), 194
O'Leary, Hazel, 450
Olympics, women in, 77–81
Oman, 13
Orr, Kay, 450
Osman, A. Abdal–Rahim, 256
Pakistan, 483–508
  abortion, 125
  contraceptive use, 118
  domestic violence, 152, 156
  dowry, 96
  education, 34, 38, 43
  fertility rate changes, 108
  marriage, arranged, 97
  "missing" girls, 8
  prime minister, 19, 20
  rape, 157
  unemployment, 76
Panama, 483–508
  births to unmarried, 93
  cohabitation, 92
  education, higher, 39
  sterilization, female, 115
  unemployment, 76
Pandit, V. Lakshmi, 18, 514
Pankhurst, Emmeline, 429
Paraguay, 484–508
  contraceptive use, 118
  fertility rate changes, 108
  marriage, 86, 87
  pay differences, 71
  unemployment, 76
  voting rights, 515
Pascal-Trouillot, Ertha, 20
Pay differences, 70–71
Peng Peiyun, 238
Perec, Marie-José, 80
Peregrinations d'une paria, 511
Perkins, Frances, 450
Perón, Eva (Evita), 167
Perón, Isabel, 20, 167
Perón, Juan, 167
Perry, Ruth, 20
Peru, 484–508
  contraceptive use, 118
  domestic violence, 156
  fertility rate, 104, 108
  marriage age, 87
  Olympics, 77
  rape, 157, 158
  school enrollment, 34
  unemployment, 76
  war fatalities, 17
Philippines, 374–86
  abortion, 382–83, 504
  AIDS, 383–84
  births to unmarried, 381, 501
  contraception, 118, 382, 504
  death, leading causes, 383
  divorce, 381–82, 517
  domestic violence, 384–85
  education, 376, 490
  employment, 377–80, 494, 497
  fertility rate, 382, 504
  life expectancy, 383, 508
  literacy, 376, 490
  marriage, 380–81, 501
  maternal mortality, 383, 508
  politics, 375–76, 487
  prostitution, 385–86
  rape, 385
  sex education, 383
  sex ratio, 374, 484
  sexual harassment, 377
  smoking, 383
  teenage births, 382, 504
  voting rights, 375, 487
  women's movement, 375
Piedra, Rosario Ibarra de, 355
Pintassilgo, M. de Lourdes, 20
Pivetti, Irene, 238
Place, Francis, 510
Planinc, Milka, 20
Poland, 484–508
  abortion, 16, 125, 126
  child care, 75
  Nobel prize winner, 46
  pay differences, 71
  prime minister, 20

unemployment, 76
Politics, women in, 19–26
  Central American Parliament,
    26
  European Parliament, 25–26
  national cabinets, 21–23
  national legislatures, 19–25
  world leaders, 19, 20
Polygamy, 94–95
Pope Paul VI, 515
Pope Pius IX, 512
Pope Pius XI, 514
Portugal, 484–508
  employment, part–time, 72
  European Parliament, 25
  pay differences, 71
  prime minister, 20
  unemployment, 76
  voting rights, 13
Press, Irena, 81
Press, Tamara, 81
Prostitution, 160–62
Prunskiene, Kazimiera, 20
Puerto Rico, 484–508
  unemployment, 76

Qatar, 13
Queiroz, C. Pereira de, 211

Rahman, Mujibur, 195
Rahman, Ziaur, 195
Rankin, Annabelle, 179
Rankin, Jeanette, 448
Rape, 156–60
Ray, Dixy Lee, 450
Religion and
  abortion, 122–25, 126
  contraception, 117–21
  marriage & divorce, 83–84, 101
Religious fundamentalism, 16
Renger, Annemarie, 284
Reno, Janet, 447, 448, 450
Reodica, Carmencita, 376
Retton, Mary Lou, 81
Richards, Ann, 450
Riche, Martha, 448
Richer, LÉon, 512
Ride, Sally, 447
Rivlin, Alice, 448
Roberts, Barbara, 450
Robillard, Lucienne, 223
Robinson, Mary, 20
Roe v. Wade, 121, 446, 468, 516
Romania, 484–508
  abortion, 517
  rape, 159
  unemployment, 76
Ross, Nellie Tayloe, 450
RU 486, 122, 124–25, 470, 518
Rudolph, Wilma, 81
Russia, 387–99
  abortion, 394, 395, 504, 513
  AIDS, 398
  births to unmarried, 392, 501
  contraception, 394, 504
  death, leading causes, 397
  divorce, 392–93
  domestic violence, 398
  education, 390, 490, 512, 513
  employment, 59, 390–92, 494
  fertility rate, 393, 504
  life expectancy, 395–97, 508
  literacy, 390, 490
  marriage, 392, 393, 501
  maternal mortality, 397, 508
  Olympics, 77
  politics, 389, 487
  prostitution, 399
  rape, 398–99, 518
  sex education, 395
  sex ratio, 387, 484
  smoking, 397
  teenage births, 394, 504
  voting rights, 388, 487
  women's movement, 388–89
Rwanda, 484–508
  contraceptive use, 118
  prime minister, 20
  rape, mass, 158
  war fatalities, 17

Sachs, Nellie, 46
Sadat, Jehan, 254
Sadik, Nafis, 18
Same-sex marriage, 94
Sanger, Margaret, 513
Saudi Arabia, 484–508
  abortion, 200
  discrimination, economic, 61
  literacy increase, 30
  Olympics, 77
  prostitution, 160
  voting rights, 13
Sauvé, Jeanne, 223
Schlafly, Phyllis, 484
School enrollment, 4, 34–43,
    488–91
  higher education, 37–41, 42–43
  primary, 34–36, 38–39
  secondary, 36–37, 40–41
Self-Employed Women's Associa-
    tion (SEWA) (India), 73, 299
Senegal, 484–508
  contraceptive use, 118
  dowry, 96
  FGM, 163
  fertility rate, 104, 108
  polygamy, 94
  school enrollment, 38
  voting rights, 13
Sexual harassment, 60–61
Sex ratios, 6–8
Shaheen, Jeanne, 448, 450
Shalala, Donna, 448, 450
Shari'a. See Islam
Shephard, Gillian, 430
Sierra Leone, 484–508
  abortion, 125
  FGM, 163
Sigcau, Stella, 402
Simonis, Heide, 284
Singapore, 484–508
  domestic violence, 153
  pay differences, 71
  polygamy, 95
  sterilization, female, 115
  unemployment, 76
Singh, Kanti, 297
Slovakia, 484–508
  smoking, 148
  unemployment, 76
Slovenia, 76, 484–508
Smith, Michelle, 81
Smoking, 146–49
Society for Married Women's
    Rights (Sweden), 415
Somalia, 484–508
  domestic violence, 154
  FGM, 163
  Islamic fundamentalism, 16
  rape, mass, 158
  school enrollment, 38
  war fatalities, 17
Soule, Aileen, 81
South Africa, 400–13
  abortion, 410, 504
  AIDS, 411
  contraception, 118, 409–10, 504
  death, leading causes, 411
  divorce, 408
  domestic violence, 152, 411–12
  education, 403–04, 491
  employment, 404–07, 494, 497
  FGM, 412
  fertility rate, 409, 504
  life expectancy, 410, 508
  literacy, 403, 491
  marriage, 407–08, 501
  maternal mortality, 410, 508
  Nobel prize winner, 400
  politics, 402–03, 487
  prostitution, 412
  rape, 412
  sex education, 410
  sex ratio, 400, 484
  teenage births, 409, 504
  voting rights, 401, 487
  women's movement, 401
Soviet Women's Committee, 388
Spain, 484–508
  birth control, 115
  contraception, 516

divorce, 98
domestic violence, 156
employment, part–time, 72
European Parliament, 25
legislature quota system, 20
pay differences, 71
unemployment, 76
Sri Lanka, 484–508
births to unmarried, 93
contraceptive use, 115, 118
domestic violence, 154, 156
dowry, 96
fertility rate changes, 108
pay differences, 70, 71
president, 19, 20
prime minister, 19, 20, 514
prostitution, 160
unemployment, 76
voting rights, 13
Stalin, Joseph, 388
Stanton, E. Cady, 445, 511
Stewart, Christine, 223
Stewart, Jane, 223
Stop ERA (U.S.), 446
Stopes, Marie, 514
Suchocka, Hanna, 20
Sudan, 484–508
contraceptive use, 118
FGM, 163
fertility rate changes, 108
marriage, 86, 97
rape, 159
Sudre, Margie, 269
Suffrage. See Voting rights
Süssmuth, Rita, 283
Suttner, Bertha von, 45
Sweden, 414–27
abortion, 424, 504
AIDS, 425
births to unmarried, 86, 422,
501
contraception, 423, 504
death, leading causes, 425
divorce, 422–23
domestic violence, 426
education, 416–17, 491
employment, 58, 417–21, 494,
498
European Parliament, 416
FGM, 427
fertility rate, 423, 504
life expectancy, 424, 508
literacy, 416, 491
marriage, 421–22, 501
maternal mortality, 424, 508
Nobel prize winners, 414
politics, 415–16, 487
prostitution, 427
rape, 158, 426
sex education, 424
sex ratio, 414, 484
sexual harassment, 418
smoking, 425
teenage births, 423, 504
voting rights, 415, 487
women's movement, 415, 511
Switzerland, 484–508
births to unmarried, 93
CEDAW, 19
divorce rate, 99
education, higher, 37, 512
FGM, 162
pay differences, 71
rape, marital, 158
unemployment, 76
Syria, 484–508
literacy increase, 30
pay differences, 71
unemployment, 76
Szabó, Ecaterina, 81
Szymborska, Wislawa, 46

Taiwan, 484–508
prostitution, 160
Tajikistan, 484–508
Taliban, 16
Talukder, Zinnatunnessa, 195
Tangney, Dorothy, 179

Tanzania, 484–508
domestic violence, 154
education, nonformal, 43
FGM, 163
fertility rate changes, 108
legislature quota system, 20
pay differences, 70, 71
Teenage births, 108–09, 110–13,
141, 502–05
Teresa, Mother, 46
Tereshkiva, Valentina, 515
Thailand, 484–508
adultery, 100
contraceptive use, 118
credit, access to, 73
domestic violence, 152, 156
education, nonformal, 43
fertility rate changes, 108
pay differences, 71
prostitution, 152, 160
rape, marital, 158
unemployment, 76
voting rights, 13
Thatcher, M., 20, 430, 516
Togo, 484–508
FGM, 163
fertility rate changes, 108
inheritance rights, 97
polygamy, 94
school enrollment, 36
tro-kosi, 153
Trinidad and Tobago, 484–509
abortion, 125
ambassador to U.N., 18
contraceptive use, 118
domestic violence, 155, 156
fertility rate changes, 108
unemployment, 76
Tristan, Flora, 511
Troedsson, Ingegerd, 415
Tro-kosi, 153
Tunisia, 484–509
contraceptive use, 115, 118
fertility rate changes, 108
literacy increase, 50
polygamy, 95
unemployment, 76
Turco, Livia, 328
Turkey, 484–509
contraceptive use, 121
domestic violence, 154, 156
Islamic fundamentalism, 16
literacy increase, 30
"missing" girls, 8
pay differences, 71
polygamy, 95
prime minister, 16
unemployment, 76
veils, outlawing of, 514
Turkmenistan, 484–509
ambassador to U.N., 18
Uganda, 484–509
AIDS, 143
domestic violence, 154
FGM, 163
fertility rate changes, 108
inheritance rights, 97
life expectancy, 129
rape, mass, 158
school enrollment, 33
war fatalities, 17
Ukraine, 99, 484–509
Ulvskog, Marita, 416
Undset, Ingrid, 45
Unemployment, 75–76
United Arab Emirates, 484–509
marriage, 86
voting rights, 13
United Kingdom, 428–42
abortion, 121, 438, 505, 510, 515
AIDS, 440
births to unmarried, 86, 436,
501
contraception, 118, 437, 505,
510, 511, 514
death, leading causes, 439
divorce, 436
domestic violence, 440, 515

education, 431, 491, 512
employment, 15, 59, 432–35,
494, 498, 511
European Parliament, 430
FGM, 441
fertility rate, 437, 505
life expectancy, 438, 509
literacy, 431, 491
marriage, 436, 501
maternal mortality, 438, 509
Nobel prize winner, 428
politics, 430, 487
prostitution, 441
rape, 157–58, 441
sex education, 438
sex ratio, 428, 484
sexual harassment, 432
smoking, 439–40
teenage births, 437, 505
voting rights, 429, 487, 514
women's movement, 429–30,
511, 512
United Nations, 17, 516
Children's Fund (UNICEF), 18
Commission on the Status of
Women, 17, 25
Committee for the Elimination
of Discrimination
Against Women
(CEDAW), 17–19
Decade for Women, 17, 516
Development Fund for
Women (UNIFEM), 17
Division for the Advancement
of Women (DAW), 17
Environment Program
(UNED), 18
International Research and
Training Institute for the
Advancement of Women
(INSTRAW), 17
Population Fund (UNFPA), 18
World Food Program, 18
United Nations, women in, 18, 514
United States, 443–80
abortion, 122, 467–70, 505,
511, 516, 518
affirmative action, 455
AIDS, 145, 475
births to unmarried, 86, 464,
501
CEDAW, 19
contraception, 118, 467, 468,
505, 513, 514
death, leading causes, 472–73,
474
divorce, 465–66
domestic violence, 151, 152,
153, 154, 476–77
education, 452–54, 491, 511,
515, 516
employment, 15, 59, 454–62,
494, 498
FGM, 480
fertility rate, 466, 505
life expectancy, 471–72, 509
literacy, 452, 491
marriage, 462–65, 501, 511
maternal mortality, 472, 509
Nobel prize winners, 44–45,
443, 514
Olympics, 77
politics, 448–51, 487
prostitution, 479–80
rape, 478–79
sex education, 471
sex ratio, 443, 484
sexual harassment, 454, 456–57
smoking, 473
teenage births, 467, 505
voting rights, 445, 487, 512, 513
women's movement, 444–48,
511, 513, 515
Uriegas, Maria Moreno, 355
Uruguay, 484–509
education, higher, 39
pay differences, 71
unemployment, 76

Uusmann, Ines, 416
Uwilingiyimana, Agathe, 20
Uzbekistan, 97, 484–509

Van Dyken, Amy, 81
Vanstone, Amanda, 179
Veil, Simone, 26, 269
Venezuela, 484–509
armed forces, 70
cohabitation, 92
legislature quota system, 20
Olympics, 77
unemployment, 76
Vesico-vaginal fistula, 371
Vietnam, 484–509
IUDs, 115
pay differences, 70, 71
prostitution, 160
Vindication of the Rights of
Woman, A, 12, 429, 510
Violence, 151–64
Voting rights, history of, 12–15

Wage gap. See Pay differences
Wallace, Lurleen, 450
Wallström, Margot, 416
Wazed, Hasina, 20, 195
Werleigh, Claudette, 20
Werneck, Dorothea, 211
Whitman, Christine, 448, 450
Widnall, Sheila, 448
Wilde, Friedrich, 511
Williams, Betty, 46
Wilson, Bertha, 223
Winberg, Margareta, 416
Witt, Katerina, 81
Wollstonecraft, M., 12, 429, 510
Women's Equity Action League
(WEAL) (U.S.), 446
Women's National Coalition
(South Africa), 402
Women's rights, history of, 8–19,
518–28
Women's Rights Convention,
Seneca Falls, NY, 445, 511
Women's Studies International, 17
Women's studies programs,
41–43
Women's suffrage. See Voting
rights, history of
Women's Suffrage League
(Australia), 513
Work force. See Labor force
Wu Yi, 238

Yallow, Rosalyn, 46
Yemen, 484–509
contraceptive use, 118
domestic violence, 153
literacy, 29
marriage, 86
school enrollment, 36, 38
Yourcenar, Marguerite, 517
Yugoslavia, 20, 484–509
Yunus, Mohammad, 199

Zaire, 484–509
FGM, 163
inheritance rights, 97
literacy increase, 30
marriage, 86
Olympics, 77
school enrollment, 38
Zambia, 484–509
AIDS, 143
armed forces, 70
domestic violence, 154
fertility rate changes, 108
inheritance rights, 97
life expectancy, 129
pay differences, 71
Zelaya, Ilsa Diaz, 26
Zia, Khaleda, 20, 195
Zimbabwe, 484–509
abortion, 125
contraceptive use, 115, 118
fertility rate changes, 108
inheritance rights, 97